ESSENTIAL SECRETARIAL STUDIES

SHEILA T. STANWELL

JOSEPHINE SHAW
M.Inst.A.M. F.B.S.C.
ILO Vocational Training Expert

The text has been produced solely by the authors and does not commit the International Labour Organisation in any way

First published 1974
by Edward Arnold (Publishers) Ltd
41 Bedford Square, London WC1B 3DQ
Reprinted 1978, 1979, 1981

ISBN: 0 7131 1788 5

Printed in Great Britain by Butler and
Tanner Ltd, Frome and London

Preface

The aim of ESSENTIAL SECRETARIAL STUDIES is to provide a textbook for secretarial students by presenting information on the skills and knowledge required by most secretaries in most offices.

In compiling the contents the authors have borne in mind four considerations: firstly, their own experience of secretarial work in industry, commerce and government, and their professional experience in secretarial and teacher training both in this country and overseas; secondly, the opinions of leading businessmen and women concerning secretarial training requirements; thirdly, the syllabuses of the Royal Society of Arts examinations—*Secretarial Duties, Stage II, Personal Secretarial Practice, Stage III*, and the recently introduced *Diploma for Personal Assistants*; and the London Chamber of Commerce and Industry *Private Secretary's Certificate* and *Private Secretary's Diploma* examinations; and fourthly, and perhaps most important, the personal qualities, professional knowledge and *savoir faire* which distinguish the secretary from the shorthand-typist.

The authors have assumed that all students who are preparing for secretarial careers are either learning or have already learnt typewriting and shorthand-typewriting or audio-typewriting—the tools of the trade—but auxiliary information on these subjects has been included to teach their application to the work of a secretary, for example taking and typing minutes of meetings and composing letters.

In addition to the stenographic skills, there is a hardcore of general knowledge which all secretaries should possess. ESSENTIAL SECRETARIAL STUDIES endeavours to indicate the range of this knowledge. The depth to which each topic should be studied depends very much on the sphere of the secretary's work. For example, whilst all secretaries should understand the structure of the business world, the elements of company organisation and the basic principles of keeping financial records, the secretary to the chairman of a large commercial or industrial company will need to study these subjects more thoroughly than, say, a medical secretary, a school secretary or a publisher's secretary.

ESSENTIAL SECRETARIAL STUDIES has been designed to appeal to students taking secretarial courses in colleges of commerce, colleges of further education and private secretarial colleges; but it should also be suitable for the higher forms of secondary and comprehensive schools, and for shorthand-typists who would like to prepare themselves for secretarial positions either by private study or by attending in-service upgrading courses or part-time day or evening courses.

A book of this size and scope has clearly required a considerable amount of fact-finding and collection of data. At each stage of its preparation, from the original research to the final proof-reading and checking, the authors have been grateful for the assistance and valuable suggestions offered by friends and colleagues in the professions and in industry and commerce. The authors would particularly like to mention the help given by: George W. Ashton, Olive G. Cutbush, Roy E. Guyver, Rosemary M. Harris, Gillian Morton, Robert Shepherd, Marguerite R. Silverman, Moira K. Swift, Roger P. Warson and Ronald Warson.

CONTENTS

Part I
The Secretarial Function

1

What is a Secretary?

"Secretaries are tending to drop their title in favour of that of 'Personal Assistant' . . . So few employers nowadays make an adequate distinction between 'shorthand-typist' and 'secretary' that it would seem a natural line of defence for people with superior skills and experience to change the name which describes their work."

"Constant role in a changing world" by Joyce Barker, *Times Educational Supplement.*

THE SECRETARIAL FUNCTION*

For many years there has been some confusion about the usage of the words *shorthand-typist* and *secretary*. Although colleges have been producing well-trained and qualified secretaries, many secretarial posts have been filled by typists with

*The term **The Secretarial Function** is used in this book to describe the work that secretaries do—and which is implied by various titles such as *Secretarial Studies, Secretarial Duties, Secretarial Practice*; it is not used in the meaning assigned to it in Management Studies.

less than adequate shorthand and more than adequate ambition and self-confidence. In short, one answer to the question "What is a secretary?" could be said to be, "Any girl who can persuade an employer that she is a secretary."

SHORTHAND-TYPIST OR SECRETARY?

One reason for this is mentioned in the quotation at the head of the chapter: few employers nowadays make an adequate distinction between 'shorthand-typist' and 'secretary', so those secretaries who really do carry out what we shall shortly describe as 'The Secretarial Function' have changed their job titles and we now hear of "personal secretaries", "private secretaries", "personal assistants", "top secretaries", "senior secretaries", "executive secretaries" and "management-aides".

Another reason is that some words carry with them a sense of respect and others are considered less noble; undertakers are now called "funeral directors" or "morticians", dustmen may be called "sanitation engineers". In trying to make a clear distinction between "shorthand-typist" and "secretary" we are fighting a battle against human nature on both sides of the desk. Most "bosses"* like to refer to 'my secretary' and to pass remarks such as, "I'll tell my secretary to post it to you immediately", even though the secretary may be shared by two or three officials and her actual duties comprise little more than taking dictation, transcribing, typing letters and delivering and collecting mail. From the other side of the desk, it is the ambition of every shorthand-typist to work as a secretary and so the sooner she is referred to as 'my secretary' the more she is encouraged to refer to herself as 'Mr. So-and-so's secretary'.

What then is the intrinsic difference between a shorthand-typist and a secretary? What work does a secretary do and what sort of training does she require? In other words: What should be the contents of a book entitled ESSENTIAL SECRETARIAL STUDIES, a book whose stated aim is to 'provide a textbook for secretarial students by presenting information on the skills and knowledge required by most secretaries in most offices'?

COMPILING THE CONTENTS

In compiling the contents the authors considered four sources of information: firstly, they wrote to several leading businessmen and women and asked them to

* There are several words—such as *manager*, *chief*, *employer*, *boss*, *official*, *officer*, *executive*, *principal*—which may be used to name the person for whom a secretary works. *Boss* is classified as slang by the Concise Oxford Dictionary (5th edition), but the authors feel that usage should occasionally give way to style. In this instance they have chosen *boss* because it is the word which most naturally comes to mind. In other contexts, the words *chief* and *employer* have been used. The chief may be a man or a woman but "the boss" has been referred to in the masculine gender throughout the book because male chiefs and employers are undoubtedly in the majority. Similarly, secretaries have been referred to as female although in many cultures, particularly those which differ radically from the western way of life, there are no women secretaries and all secretarial and clerical posts are held by men.

write a short answer to the question 'What do you expect of your secretary?'; secondly, the syllabuses and examination papers provided by leading examining bodies, the syllabuses for full-time secretarial courses and the programmes for short secretarial upgrading and improvement courses were analysed and classified; thirdly, the authors drew on their own experience as specialists in secretarial and teacher training; and fourthly, by consulting relevant books, periodicals and the published results of analyses of secretarial training requirements, the authors tried to list the personal qualities, professional knowledge and savoir-faire which distinguish the secretary from the shorthand-typist.

The following extracts from some of the replies received from leading businessmen and women show the diversity of secretarial work; they also indicate that really good secretaries possess something which is more instinctive than learnt.

"What are the basic essentials? Accurate shorthand and spelling, and ability to set out work neatly and clearly. But a good typist should have these qualifications and so, in addition, other attributes are required to make the perfect secretary.

"Common-sense is pretty important and if this is present in good measure, a secretary will be able to cope with most situations, but a few of the required qualifications are worth mentioning. She should show initiative and be adaptable and unruffled at times of stress and strain. She should be discreet and be tactful not only in person but, also, on the telephone, in dealing with customers, clients and members of the staff of the organisation with which she works. Loyalty is important and the perfect secretary should be able to keep her boss right without appearing to be too bossy!

"Finally, she should be neat in appearance, and good humour at all times will carry her a long way. She will probably have to take in her stride a hundred and one things which crop up from time to time. It can be an exacting job but her boss too can help to make it interesting and rewarding."

The Chairman of a regional electricity board.

"One takes for granted that a secretary who has reached a top-level appointment will have the education and experience to make her technically competent in handling correspondence, dictation, typing, filing and all the work of a Chairman's office. Over and above a purely technical competence, I think there are five personal qualities I look for:

"1. To be consistently helpful to all—including my fellow directors, all the staff, the office junior and the man with the wrong telephone number.

"2. To be completely loyal to the Company—not discussing confidential matters or passing on spicy secrets.

"3. To have confidence and initiative to act in my absence, but without such an excess of initiative that a brick wall is built round me and I become inaccessible, except to the few.

"4. To have understanding of the Company, of me, my job, and my philosophy. To be able to accurately anticipate how I will react to a situation and what I will want to know next.

"5. To have a sense of humour, and humanity—including the ability to be wrong occasionally!"

The Chairman and Managing Director of a very large electrical component manufacturing company.

"Taking for granted basic secretarial skills, I would look for the following qualities:

Literacy—an editor's letters must be impeccably spelt and punctuated. When I dictate, I can look after my own grammar and syntax, but I like to be able to give a girl just the gist of a letter and leave her to compose it on her own.

Common-sense—without which the most brilliant talents are not much use.

Reliability—ditto.

Good health—not just a gift of God, it can be cultivated.

Tact, imagination, initiative—for dealing with authors, a sensitive race. Tact implies a good memory for who-wrote-what and so on."

A woman director and editor of a large publishers; she is frequently absent on business or tied up in conferences, leaving her secretary to work unsupervised.

"Good-tempered, unruffled and willing to do everything from keeping at bay awkward citizens to dashing off at lunch-time buying my cosmetics for me.

"Essential requirement—ability to make a good cup of tea and a strong cup of coffee, several in fact.

"She mustn't be a clockwatcher or groan if I give her an urgent letter at five to six. She must be ready to interrupt one urgent job to start another even more urgent one.

"She must be able to answer at least three telephones at once and sound equally charming to the caller at the other end of the telephone however harassed she might be.

"I have said nothing about efficiency in shorthand and typewriting, which I suppose all bosses take for granted anyway.

Woman columnist on national newspapers.

"On a radio station routine is frequently interrupted with programme emergencies, so my secretary has to be not necessarily calm, but *controlled*. She should be artistic, even a little theatrical, so that she can have a genuine interest in programmes, and even have occasional ideas for their improvement. However, I do *not* want her to take an active part in studio work as this will turn her into a split personality with split loyalties.

"In emergencies she will be expected to act quickly with the minimum of advice, and in her daily encounter with visitors have a good 'bedside manner', soothing down nervous broadcasters, tactfully keeping unwanted artists at bay, and keeping an eye on clock and schedules so that she is aware of what is (or should be!) on the air at any given time.

"To set an example her spoken and written English must be of a high standard, and it is preferable that she has a good general musical knowledge. Most of all, perhaps, she must have an acute consciousness of time, as programme schedules and operation charts work down to seconds, and everything must dovetail smoothly.

"I expect her to be accurate in shorthand rather than fast, with a flair for setting out letters elegantly, and able to use her own imagination in constructing routine correspondence and in filing.

"I like her to dress gay, but talk quietly, yet be a colourful and enthusiastic addition to what is, after all, a glamorous occupation."

Controller of Programmes of a national broadcasting service.

The two following analyses of "Topics listed in examination and course syllabuses" and "Subjects included in secretarial course curricula in private and LEA colleges and schools" indicate the weighting given to the various topics by the examining bodies and this, of course, has an influence on those responsible for drawing-up syllabuses in schools and colleges. The words used in the analyses (*All*, *Most*, *Some*, *Few*) indicate the following percentages:

All	100%
Most	60%–99%
Some	36%–59%
Few	10%–35%

The following extracts are taken from newspapers, books and journals. They indicate that people who write about secretaries and their work are more or less in agreement that the basic skills of shorthand-typewriting are taken for granted. These skills are 'the tools of the trade' and in addition to them there are certain personal qualities (such as tact and loyalty), certain other skills (like using the telephone and handling people) and a large amount of other knowledge (such as how to arrange travel, how to take minutes and prepare agenda) which the competent secretary is expected to possess.

"An employer usually expects an experienced secretary not only to be a competent shorthand-typist, but to be able to relieve him of some of his less important work. While the scope of a secretary's duties depends not only on her capability but on the extent to which her employer is inclined to delegate work, there are certain duties which all secretaries may expect

TOPICS LISTED IN EXAMINATION AND COURSE SYLLABUSES

Topic	Listed in examination and course syllabuses
Giving and receiving information, correspondence, communications	All
Appointments and reception duties	All
Filing, indexing, storage and retrieval of information, reminder and follow-up systems	All
Reference books and sources of information	Most
Travel arrangements	Most
Meetings and committee procedure	Most
Reprography	Most
Banking and post office transactions	Most
Telephone	Most
Mail-handling, including messenger services	Some
Statistics, charts, visual material	Some
Styles of address	Some
Structure of Business, including types of ownership and organisation, methods of control, basic management techniques	Some
Office appliances, equipment, machinery	Some
Receipts and payments, including petty cash	Few
Human relations, including development of good relations with immediate superior, colleagues, other employees and the public; tact, loyalty and other desirable personal qualities	Few
Abbreviations	Few
Control and design of forms	Few
Public relations, press releases, conferences	Few
The background of the office worker in large and small organisations	Few
Reading and correction of proofs	Few
Deductions from pay, inc. PAYE	Few
Personnel including induction of junior staff, training, records, labour relations	Few
Office stationery and stores	Few
Simple advertisements	Few
Appearance	Few
Office furniture and layouts	Few

SUBJECTS INCLUDED IN SECRETARIAL COURSE CURRICULA IN PRIVATE AND LEA COLLEGES AND SCHOOLS

Subject	Included in the curriculum
Typewriting	All
Shorthand and/or audio-typing	All
English	Most
Commerce or Structure of Business	Most
Secretarial Duties/Practice/Studies	Most
Optional extras, e.g. Foreign Shorthand, Languages, Computer Appreciation, Politics, Advertising	Some
Correspondence	Some
Accounts	Few
Law	Few

to do. These include typing her employer's correspondence from dictation or from notes, filing his letters and other documents, keeping a record of his engagements and seeing that he has all the necessary documents and information for meetings and conferences. . . . In addition, she will probably have to open and read correspondence . . . take his telephone calls . . . deal with some enquiries herself and make arrangements for his business journeys. . . . A good secretary must have all the attributes of a good shorthand typist and much more besides. She should have a pleasant manner and common sense, thoughtfulness, adaptability, sense of humour, initiative and above all, discretion, loyalty and absolute integrity."

Careers, HMSO.

"A good secretary can think for you, act for you, anticipate your every whim, and increase your output phenomenally. By her charm and the reverence with which she speaks your name, she can spread a favourable image of you throughout your company. By the tactful way she conveys your peremptory messages she will please your friends and soothe your enemies. By the information she unobtrusively feeds to you and the filing system that she miraculously keeps up to date she will give the most featherbrained and forgetful employer an image of omniscience that is nothing less than awe-inspiring. . . . Most of us would have preferred to be born Eastern Potentates waited on by willing slaves. This fading hope can be revived and realised by the acquisition of a good secretary. The breath of paradise enters the office, routine becomes rhapsody, mountains of work are smoothed by her gentle touch, your temper is soothed and your ego inflated. You return home relaxed and invigorated, confident that in this tiresome world there is one haven where your wisdom is not only apparent but unquestioned!

How to win the business battle, Eric Webster, John Murray, 1964.

"Why does the secretary play such an important role in office life? A successful business depends on the effectiveness of its executives; in turn, their efficiency depends on the quality of the support of their secretaries. As executives and managers themselves are expected to be far less deskbound than ever before, their secretaries become key figures in the office. . . .

"The personal qualities a secretary must show can be defined as loyalty to her chief and the art of anticipating his needs. She should feel a sense of identification with her employer company, its policies and practices. She should be able to act independently, using her initiative and authority, and yet appreciate that she is part of a team with which she must co-operate. Her well-balanced relations with the other members of the staff at all levels are vitally important. Ideally she should have an above average command of English, spell well, and be a good communicator.

> "However, a secretary is not merely a pale shadow of her chief, and personal qualities must be reinforced technically by good accurate typing, shorthand and/or audio skills and a sound knowledge of general office procedure."
>
> "All Sorts of Secretary," Stella Fisher, *The Daily Telegraph*, September 1971.

The last extract in this section is a little longer than the others because it is the only one written by a secretary; it covers the past twelve years from the time she left school until the present day.

> "When I left school at the age of 17—12 years ago—I regarded everyone I met in the office where I went to work as sophisticated and knowledgeable . . . I called all the men, including the liftboy 'Sir'.
>
> "I was teetering on the lowest rung of the commercial ladder, a junior shorthand typist (a now extinct breed). . . . I never saw the dowager who acted as right arm to the chairman; she communed with the world via a harassed little girl who was forever running about the building with files or cheques just like me. . . .
>
> "There was nothing greater to expect from life than elevation to the secretarial ranks, but you had to work you way up through an endless spiral of lesser jobs and it was highly unlikely you'd get to the top before you were 40. . . .
>
> "I wanted to hire a junior shorthand typist a little while ago.
>
> 'You mean a secretary,' said the agency.
>
> 'No, I only want a girl straight out of school. Of course she could become a secretary later.'
>
> 'Um, well for our purposes you'd better call the vacancy secretarial.'
>
> "I was worried that we'd have girls applying who were older and more experienced than we needed; I shouldn't have bothered. The oldest we had was 18, and none of them could type. Of those who said they could take shorthand, only two could read it back, but neither of them could read it back correctly. I rang the agency.
>
> "Well, what do you expect for £1,000 a year?" they said.
>
> "Like dustmen being called refuse operatives, the humble junior is called a secretary. Her pay has been quadrupled since I landed in the in-tray and she isn't nervous any more. . . .
>
> "But what has happened at the other end of the ladder, now I've reached it? . . . And what does my "top" job actually entail?
>
> "I write my boss's letters, add up his petty cash slips for him, correct his grammar and his spelling, translate his foreign mail, book his travel, arrange his hotel accommodation, remind him of his family's birthdays, call in plumbers, have his pool cleaned, have his car serviced, have his pets spayed, watch his diet (but not too strictly), keep his cupboard stocked with whisky, remember not to let him feel unwanted by always ensuring

that there are a few messages for him to attend to, and by far the most important, make tea and coffee all day long.

"The wheel has come full circle. The other "secretaries" can get drinks from an automatic dispensing machine, but my boss likes his china tea and his freshly percolated coffee . . ."

"The Secretary Circus", Ann White, *The Sunday Times*, 16 April 1972.

PRIMARY AND SECONDARY FUNCTIONS

From these sources of information a fairly clear picture begins to emerge and a distinction can be made between *primary* and *secondary* secretarial functions.

The words *primary* and *secondary* are not meant to imply 'more important' and 'less important'. They have been chosen to indicate that the *primary functions* are those that almost all secretaries in all offices in all parts of the world are expected to perform; they are in fact the basic skills—typewriting, taking dictation, answering the telephone, dealing with mail, receiving visitors and keeping a desk diary, filing, duplicating.

The *secondary functions* require knowledge rather than skill, and the more knowledge a secretary has, the better she will do her work and the more interesting she should find it. A secretary certainly needs to have a knowledge of the business world, the divisions of industry and commerce and particularly the branch of industry or commerce with which her employer is concerned. She also needs to know about her own organisation, its structure and objects, and the procedures of the company, corporation or institute. Some of this background knowledge varies with the type of work her organisation is concerned in, and her boss's profession; the legal secretary, the medical secretary, the school secretary, the technical secretary, the expatriate secretary (the secretary working overseas), the secretary in the theatrical or film world, in broadcasting or television—each of these requires a certain amount of specialised knowledge.

Nowadays managers, executives, officials and employers frequently travel on business—and they expect their secretaries to make all the travel arrangements for them.

A knowledge of correspondence and communications is needed in almost all secretarial work and the ability to compose letters from outline notes or draft replies without instruction is one important feature which distinguishes the secretary from the shorthand-typist; this ability is greatly valued by employers because it means that a considerable amount of simple correspondence can be handed over to the secretary thus freeing the boss from routine letters and leaving him more time to compose and draft those technical or difficult letters in which the correct wording is so important.

Other attributes which a secretary is expected to possess include the ability to use reference books and sources of information, a knowledge of committee procedures and taking minutes, and how to handle money and keep simple accounts of receipts and payments.

The information included in the chapter on Human Relations is important but difficult to examine. This may explain why such points as appearance and demeanour, loyalty, relationships within the organisation, establishing a satisfactory rapport with the boss (becoming his *alter ego*) are more frequently mentioned in articles on secretarial work than in examination syllabuses.

The final chapter deals with Personnel matters. A well-qualified secretary should clearly have an understanding of current legislation affecting office workers, and the rights and obligations of employees. Also included in this chapter is the training and induction function which the experienced secretary is frequently called upon to perform; this includes introducing newcomers to co-workers and helping to familiarise them with their new surroundings. The experienced secretary should also be able to act as adviser and teacher to junior staff on any aspect of their work; for example, although the experienced secretary is no longer concerned with typing schedules and large tabulations, she should be able to show junior typists how to plan their work, which size and weight of paper to use, and so on, if they come to her for advice.

A plan of the primary and secondary secretarial functions is shown in the chart opposite on page 13, and the chapters which follow cover all the topics mentioned.

The authors hope that students who have worked through the book will be able to tackle most secretarial jobs with confidence, and will also be successful in secretarial examinations. There is no doubt that some secretarial posts demand specialised knowledge, and the secretary who wishes to prepare herself for a particular type of post should be aware that she needs more than a basic secretarial training.

One further remark should be addressed to trainee-secretaries: even with first-class speeds, education, training and examination results, the really good secretary possesses a sixth sense which enables her to tune in to her boss's mood, to anticipate his wishes, to assess the demands of a situation and react accordingly; for example, she needs to be able to judge instinctively whether the occasion demands that she should withdraw or take over the reins. Her overall responsibility is to contribute to her boss's output and efficiency by being reliable and good-humoured; she must avoid any habits of speech and bearing which could become grating or discordant.

The aspiring successful secretary would be well advised to remember Ecclesiastes III from time to time, the passage which starts, "Everything has its appointed hour" and includes "there is a time for silence and a time for speech". She might sometimes feel like showing it to her boss—bosses are human-beings too.

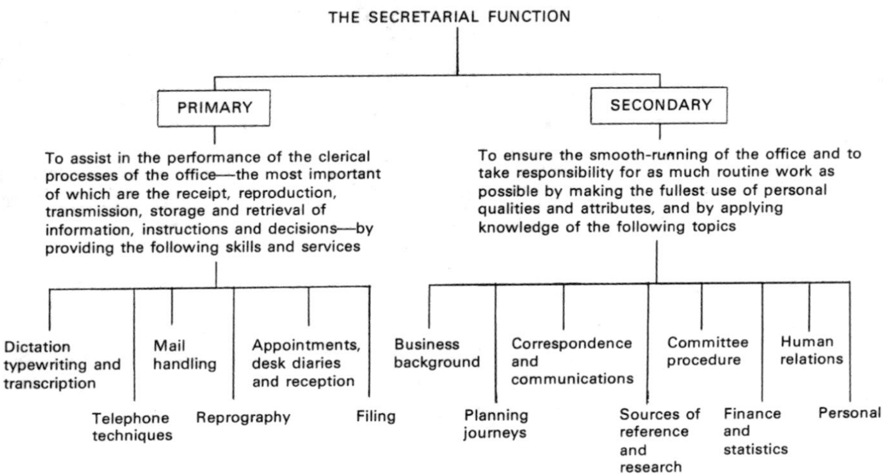

JOB TITLES

We started this chapter by mentioning the difference between a shorthand-typist and a secretary; we also listed other titles which secretaries use. Here are some suggested definitions which you may like to use as a basis for your Group Discussion topic at the end of this chapter.

Shorthand-typist A shorthand-typist spends the larger part of her time taking dictation, transcribing her shorthand and presenting her work for signature. She may also be expected to answer the telephone, deal with mail, receive callers, and assist with filing and duplicating—particularly in a small organisation.

Audio-typist An audio-typist's duties are much the same as a shorthand-typist's, but an audio-typist transcribes recorded dictation whereas a shorthand-typist transcribes shorthand.

Audio-typists and shorthand-typists are usually expected to be able to perform any of the duties listed under PRIMARY FUNCTIONS on THE SECRETARIAL FUNCTION chart. If, in addition to these duties, they need to know how to carry out work covered by two or more of the headings listed under

SECONDARY FUNCTIONS their work may fairly be described as secretarial and they may call themselves *secretaries*. Under this broad title we may distinguish:

Junior Secretary A girl who has successfully completed a secretarial course at school or college and is in her first job or has less than three years' experience.

Senior Secretary A secretary of considerable experience (more than eight years, for example) whose value to her employer is not solely due to her excellent skills but also to her wide knowledge of the firm, the industry and her boss's profession.

Personal or Private Secretary Secretaries who work for only one official are frequently called *Personal* or *Private* secretaries to distinguish them from secretaries who work for several junior executives or who perform the secretarial duties for several people (e.g. the draughtsmen in a drawing office) none of whom has sufficient work to occupy a full-time secretary.

Executive Secretary or Personal Assistant* A secretary who has sufficient knowledge of her chief's specialisation and the branch of commerce, industry or the profession and the organisation in which he is working, will be able to have a considerable amount of work delegated to her. Such a secretary will perform fewer and fewer primary functions (and may in fact have a junior secretary or shorthand-typist working for her) and more and more secondary functions. She will be able to take decisions, give instructions and even represent her boss on business occasions. She will really become the chief's *alter ego* and may well be promoted to the executive ranks of the organisation. Many successful professional women have reached their positions by being promoted from the secretarial into the executive ranks—this is especially true if admission to their chief's profession is not by examination. For example, it is necessary to acquire certain qualifications before entering the legal or medical professions, but some positions in advertising and public relations, publishing, journalism, the travel industry and commerce, can be attained by taking advantage of the learning situation in which the executive secretary or personal assistant finds herself. As Margery Hurst, the well-known owner of the Brook Street Bureaux writes in her book *No Glass Slipper*, "Times have changed and some firms today are prepared to train a handful of women executives. But in my opinion, ninety per cent of women in industry who reach management levels still enter the firm as secretaries."

* The term *personal assistant* is also applied to young men and women who are understudying senior managers as part of a management training programme.

SECRETARIAL EXAMINATIONS AND QUALIFICATIONS

Whilst the status of the secretary has always been determined by her personal qualities, her expertise in office skills, her invaluable 'aide' qualities and at times her real shortage on the market, a further factor has now been suggested—namely, that she should possess a recognised academic and/or professional qualification. In addition to examinations in secretarial skills and functions, the aspiring secretary is now encouraged to make a special study in one or other of the subjects related to the sphere in which she hopes to work, and to obtain additional qualifications in Economics, Commerce, Management Studies, Industrial Relations and similar fields.

This is undoubtedly an important factor in the preparation of mature secretaries and the development is to be commended; however, behind these new areas of interest remains the wide range of topics which the secretary needs to study if she is to carry out her duties efficiently and intelligently. These topics, which are included in most of the secretarial examination syllabuses of well-known examining bodies, are covered in the various chapters of this book.

Most schools and colleges encourage their students to sit for these public examinations. Privately-owned colleges also issue their own diplomas to successful students.

The examinations of the London Chamber of Commerce and the Royal Society of Arts in secretarial subjects are accepted both nationally and internationally. The Royal Society of Arts offers a *Secretarial Duties, Stage II (Intermediate)* examination and a *Personal Secretarial Practice, Stage III (Advanced)* examination.

The *Diploma for Personal Assistants* is an examination conducted by the Royal Society of Arts for students following post 'A' level secretarial courses. The first examination was held in June 1973. The subjects of the scheme are:

Communication
Office Administration
  (a) Techniques of the Office
  (b) Office Management
Practical Correspondence
  (Shorthand or Audio)
together with EITHER
Economic Aspects of Business OR
Law and Procedure of Meetings OR *both*

Candidates will also have to take an oral test. In the Practical Correspondence section the examination will be presented mainly in the form of office-style dictation, and it is recommended that candidates should be able to take dictation at 100 words per minute.

The London Chamber of Commerce provide three secretarial examinations: the *Secretarial Studies Certificate*, the *Private Secretary's Certificate* and the *Private Secretary's Diploma*.

The *Secretarial Studies Certificate* is suitable for students who are taking full-time courses prior to first employment. The examination comprises four sections:

Communications
Background to Business
Office Practice
Shorthand Typewriting OR Audio Typewriting Duties

(The average dictation speed will be 80 words per minute and the recording will last approximately 13 minutes. A minimum typewriting speed of 35 words per minute is needed.)

Candidates must be at least 18 years of age in the year in which they take the *Private Secretary's Certificate* examination. The examination comprises six sections:

Communications
Office Organisation and Secretarial Procedures
Structure of Business
Shorthand Typewriting Duties (100 words per minute shorthand, 45 words per minute typewriting) OR Audio Typewriting Duties (45 words per minute typewriting)
Interview

The object of the interview is to satisfy the examiners that candidates have the personality and aptitude of mind considered necessary in a secretary to Middle-Management.

The London Chamber of Commerce also awards the most widely accepted top qualification obtainable by an experienced senior secretary—the *Private Secretary's Diploma*, holders of which qualify for full membership of the Institute of Qualified Private Secretaries. The diploma examination comprises six sections:

Private Secretarial Practice, Part 1—Communications
Private Secretarial Practice, Part 2—Private Secretarial Duties
Management Appreciation
Meetings
Shorthand Typewriting Duties—office-style dictation at a variety of speeds
Interview

In the Meetings section candidates have to produce a report or minutes of a meeting which is shown on a sound film of some 20 minutes' duration.

FURTHER READING

An Analytical Approach to BEA's Secretarial Training, W. S. Barry, Pergamon Press.
Top Secretary, Mary Bosticco, Business Books Ltd.
Almost a Marriage, Vera Sugg, Frederick Muller Ltd.
No Glass Slipper, Margery Hurst, Sphere Books Ltd.
Office Work, HMSO.
Top Secretary, Margaret Baker and Sheila Creasey, Lutterworth Press.
How to be an Effective Secretary, L. Secreton, Pan Books.
Secretary, M. K. Benét, Sidgwick & Jackson.
The Secretary's Role, The Industrial Society.
Personal Assistants and Senior Secretaries, The Industrial Society.
Stenographic and Secretarial Curricula Guide, United States Government Printing Office, Washington, 1967.

GROUP DISCUSSION

The terms 'private secretary', 'personal secretary', 'senior secretary', 'top secretary', 'executive secretary' are frequently heard. Decide by discussion:

a What is the specific meaning, if any, of each term and what distinguishes them from each other.
b Which terms, if any, could usefully be adopted in the terminology of secretarial training and grading.
c If any of the terms should be dropped from usage.
d How you think secretarial work could be classified.
e Whether the terms 'personal assistant' and 'management aide' carry any additional meaning.
f Which terms you think should be retained. Arrange these terms in a column in order of importance; alongside each term, complete a second column headed 'Age range'. Complete columns three and four headed 'Qualifications' and 'Duties' respectively. When you have completed the table, type it as a display exercise.

EXERCISES

1 Some employers complain that every young shorthand-typist who works for one man calls herself a private secretary. What training, experience and knowledge do you consider a private secretary should possess?
2 Consider the type of secretarial work you might like to do when you leave school. Is there any specialised knowledge which you should acquire? How do you think you should prepare yourself for the kind of work you wish to do?

3 Explain the following words and expressions:

a gist
b instinctive
c inaccessible
d *savoir-faire*
e intrinsic
f peremptory
g expatriate
h rapport
i *alter ego*
j demeanour

4 Your brother has recently qualified as a dentist. He wishes to employ a receptionist/secretary and asks your advice as to what he should ask for in the way of education, training, qualifications and experience. What advice would you give him?

5 The London Chamber of Commerce *Private Secretary's Certificate* examination includes an interview, the aim of which is "to satisfy the Board that candidates have the personality and aptitude of mind considered necessary in a Secretary to Middle Management". What do you understand by 'Middle Management'? For what personal traits do you think the Board will (a) award and (b) deduct marks?

6 What would you consider to be the advantages and disadvantages of working as secretary to:

a an executive in a large advertising agency
b An individual who is not a member of a large business organisation (e.g. a member of Parliament or the owner of a small factory)?

Part II
Primary Secretarial Functions

2

Dictation, Typewriting and Transcription

"A good secretary must be a wizard at shorthand, an above-average typist and a good grammarian."

A leading personnel officer

DICTATION

There are various ways in which the contents of letters and documents to be typed can be conveyed to the secretary. We have called these different ways *Transmission Methods* and they are listed for comparison on the chart on pages 22 and 23.

If an organisation provides facilities for all the methods listed, the dictator can choose the one which he finds most suitable for the work he is doing at any particular time.

For communications of particular difficulty, significance or importance, such as policy, technical or prestige letters, the dictator may prefer to draft in long-hand so that he can revise, amend and polish the wording until it expresses

COMPARISON OF TRANSMISSION METHODS

Method	Advantages	Disadvantages
1 MANUSCRIPT DRAFT	1 If well written, easy to copy. 2 Typist can work in any language in which she is literate. 3 Gives dictator time to amend his draft and polish the wording. 4 Assists a dictator who is working in a second language.	1 Time-consuming for the boss, but despite this one of the commonest methods in some offices and in some parts of the world, mainly owing to lack of trained stenographers. 2 Time-consuming for the typist, if the draft is difficult to read. 3 Further time is wasted if the draft is badly prepared—queries and re-types.
2 SHORTHAND* a *Symbol systems*	1 Mobility and editing ability of verbatim reporter. 2 Given a good shorthand writer, an efficient, accurate and speedy method. 3 High-speed writers can take dictation at over 180 w.p.m. 4 Most writers can cope with short spurts at 120+ w.p.m.	1 Shorthand-writer's time wasted by interruptions during dictation. 2 Language restriction in some cases. 3 Comparatively long learning period. 4 Some shorthand writers never take the trouble to become completely proficient.
b *Alphabetic systems* (using a few symbols but mainly standard English letters)	1 Comparatively easy and quick to learn. 2 Speed of 80 w.p.m. can be attained after approximately 50 hours instruction.	1 Language restriction, although some systems have versions in other languages. 2 Ceiling of 80/100 w.p.m. depending upon length of "take"
c *Machine shorthand*	1 Easy to learn up to commercial speeds of 100/120 w.p.m., and comparatively easy up to verbatim speeds of 200/220 w.p.m. 2 Results in a clear and unambiguous note which is easy to read not only for the operator but possibly for typists who cannot use the stenotyping machine. 3 Can be used in any European language in which the operator is proficient. 4 Ability to watch speaker aids intelligent anticipation and, in verbatim field, assists accurate identification of speakers.	1 The weight and bulk of the machine make it cumbersome in office use. 2 The cost of the machine and its paper. 3 The virtual impossibility of finding a college that teaches it.

3 RECORDED DICTATION a *Individual machines*	1 Typist available for other clerical tasks when boss is dictating. 2 Boss can dictate away from office and outside office hours. 3 Media can be mailed. 4 Typist can transcribe any language in which she is literate.	1 Sometimes dictator and/or typist resistance. 2 Necessity to train dictators. 3 Transcriber needs excellent linguistic ability.
b *Centralised systems*	1–4 as above. 5 Work can be evenly spread. 6 After initial installations costs and teething troubles, probably the most efficient and economical method.	1 Loss of personal contact. 2 Needs an efficient supervisor to organise work, control flow and deal with technical faults.
4 OUTLINE NOTES AND/OR BRIEF VERBAL INSTRUCTIONS	1 Quick and efficient if the secretary has the necessary linguistic skills. 2 Typist can work in any language in which she is literate (it is usually easier to compose a short letter than to take dictation in a second language).	1 Demands a typist with i Excellent linguistic ability. ii A good knowledge of both her organisation and her boss's expertise.
5 NRD (NON-RECORDED DICTATION) or DIRECT MACHINE DICTATION.	1 Immediate production; in an ideal situation as the dictator speaks the last word, the typist has only to type that word and the complimentary close and take the work out of the machine—the letter is ready for immediate signature and despatch. 2 The typist can work in any language in which she is proficient.	1 Inevitable delays owing to paper-handling may irritate a fast dictator. 2 Time-consuming for a good dictator; impossible for a bad one. 3 Fast and accurate typing required.

* The efficiency of shorthand dictation as a transmission method also depends upon the boss being "a good dictator", i.e. able to dictate reasonably fluently without too many pauses, hesitations or alterations. A person's ability to dictate can be improved by practice, and dictator training courses usually result in improved performance.

PRODUCING A PERFECT LETTER

1. DICTATION

The dictator must 1. Know what he wants to say. 2. Have a good command of language. 3. Dictate to a shorthand writer or a recording machine.

2. TRANSCRIPTION

The transcriber must 1. Select paper and carbons. 2. Understand sense. 3. Spell and punctuate correctly. 4. Type quickly and accurately. 5. Display attractively. 6. Proof read, type envelope, assemble enclosures. 7. Present for signature.

3. PRESENTATION

The letters are presented for signature in a special Signature Book—the pages are made of heavy blotting paper.

4. DESPATCH

The top copies are put in envelopes together with any enclosures ready for mailing; the carbon copies are sorted for filing and distribution.

precisely what he wants to say in a style which he hopes will impress the receiver of the letter and cause him to react as the writer of the letter wants him to.

An executive may wish to dictate to his secretary 'face to face'—she will probably have learnt one of the many written shorthand systems or she may use machine shorthand—or he may dictate into a dictating machine.

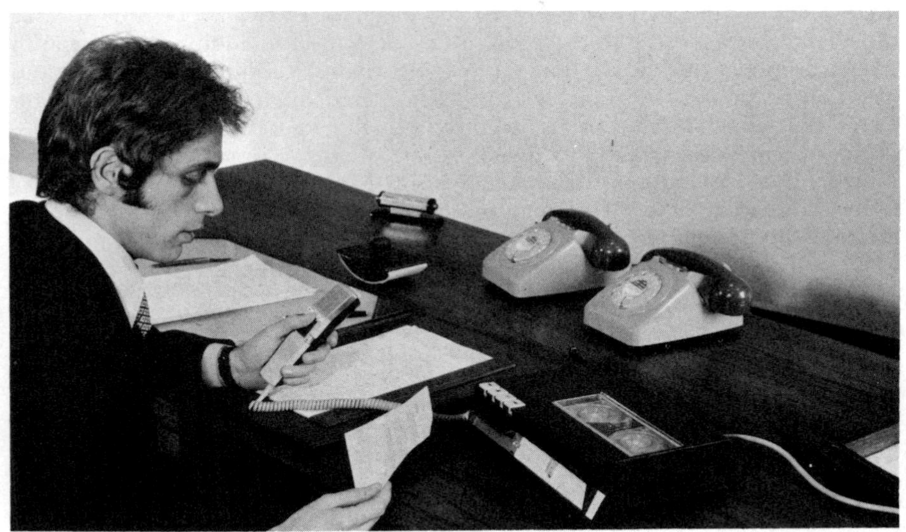

An executive using a Philips dictation machine. The dictation is recorded on tape which is enclosed in a cassette.

One of the most efficient transmission methods is for the executive to give his secretary brief outline notes or verbal instructions so that she can compose and type the letters herself or dictate them to a junior typist or typing centre. It cannot be emphasized too strongly that the ability to write a good letter from brief instructions is one of the most highly prized secretarial skills and the subject will be discussed at greater length in Chapter 9, *Correspondence and Communications*.

Occasionally, mainly in emergencies, bosses dictate 'direct on to the machine'. This has become known as **NRD—non-recorded dictation.*** Of course the dictation is not really given 'direct to the machine'—the secretary is the vital intermediary; she hears the dictation, processes it through her brain and fingers and immediately turns the spoken words into correctly spelt and punctuated English so that the typed letter is ready for signature within seconds of the last word being dictated. This is the fastest way of producing a typed version of person-to-person dictation but there are provisos which prevent it being

* *The Reduction of Correspondence Costs*, H. P. Cemach, Anbar Publications Ltd.

universally recommended: for example, the dictator must know exactly what he wants to say and never change his mind in the middle of the dictation.

Shorthand Although many secretarial advertisements nowadays stipulate "good shorthand- and/or audio-typist" and although well-qualified audio-typists are sometimes appointed to secretarial posts, a large number of executives—perhaps the majority—still prefer their secretaries to be able to take shorthand dictation. Audio-typing is a most useful additional secretarial accomplishment but the day has yet to come when the ability to take shorthand dictation accurately and quickly is not considered one of the most important secretarial skills. If you are at present studying to be a secretary, you are probably learning to write shorthand as part of your training. There are many shorthand systems and you should have some idea of the ways in which they differ from each other. You may at some time be asked to assist with the recruitment of junior staff and you should be prepared for applicants who write systems other than the one you yourself write.

The SYMBOL SYSTEMS are widely used in all parts of the English-speaking world. The two best known are *Gregg* and *Pitman*. In Pitmans shorthand the outlines are based on forms derived from a cartwheel, and vowels are indicated by writing the outlines in one of three positions—above, on or through the line. In Gregg shorthand the forms are derived from an ellipse, there is no position writing and there is no need to make a distinction between thick and thin strokes. Several new symbol systems have been invented during the past few years. One of them—*Teeline*—is reputed to be very successful and is increasing in use and acceptability. Another new system is called *Simplex*; this was published in America in 1969.

and finally Turkish coffee. After
dinner, we reclined in the living
room on couches covered with
Oriental rugs and cushions.

Simplex shorthand.

ALPHABETIC SYSTEMS are so-called because they use the standard letters of the English alphabet and writers use their normal handwriting, but for additional speed individual letters are written without tails and flourishes, i's are not dotted and t's are not crossed.

i may be written ı not i
u may be written υ not u
t may be written ı not t and
l may be written ℓ to distinguish it from ı (t)

Some alphabetic systems use signs and characters for very frequently occurring words like 'and' and 'the' and for frequently occurring syllables like '-tion', '-ter' and '-ed'. One of the most widely used alphabetic systems is *Speedwriting*. *Stenoscript*, *Speedhand* and *Notehand* are the names of three other systems. One of the newest alphabetic systems is *PitmanScript* invented by the owners of Pitman shorthand.

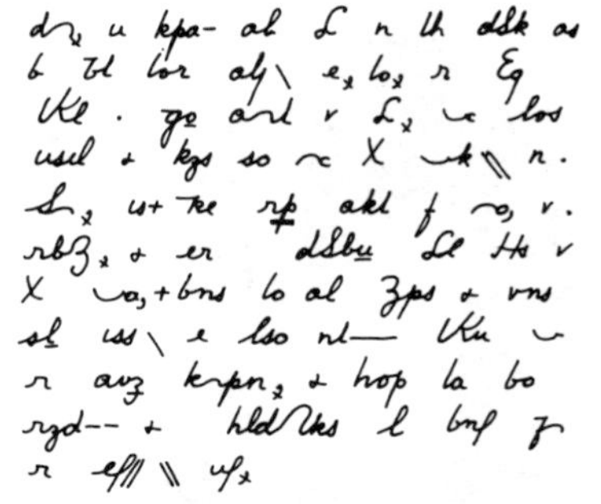

Most alphabetic shorthand systems have fewer rules and special signs to be memorised than the symbol systems; because of this they can be learnt fairly quickly. It is claimed that the average student should reach a speed of 80 words per minute after about 50 hours' tuition, that is a 13-week term with three lessons a week, or six weeks of daily tuition. The writer's hand and fingers have to make more movements more quickly when writing alphabetic systems than when writing symbol systems. Because of this, alphabetic systems seem to have an in-built speed limit of about 80 words per minute and only the most talented writers can sustain speeds of over 100 words per minute. However, it is claimed that a speed of 80 words per minute is sufficient for most office-type dictation because, although dictators do speak faster from time to time, these speed spurts are usually short and a sustained high-speed writing ability is not needed. Nevertheless, leading national and international organisations still require top grade secretaries to hold high-speed shorthand certificates. The memory load imposed by the many special forms for common words and the abbreviating and phrasing principles found in the conventional symbol shorthand systems certainly lengthen the learning time, but they enable conscientious students to reach speeds of over 120 words per minute. Many symbol-system writers attain sustained speeds of over 150 words per minute and those who wish to train for verbatim reporting can reach speeds of 200 words per minute and over.

Speedwriting shorthand.

Leading national and regional examination bodies accept candidates for shorthand examinations without regard to the system of shorthand used, although, as a proportion of the total marks is allotted to the candidate's own shorthand notes at the lower speed examinations, candidates are asked to notify the examining bodies in advance of the system of shorthand they will be writing.

MACHINE SHORTHAND is an alternative to handwritten shorthand and the operator uses a machine instead of a notebook and pen. The notes, though printed, still have to be transcribed just as shorthand notes have to be transcribed. The correct name for machine shorthand is **stenotyping** and it is to be preferred because in fact no shorthand symbols are used. Instead, ordinary letters of the alphabet are printed in type on a band or roll of paper which moves on automatically as the keys of the machine are struck. Unlike a typewriter, the keys of a stenotyping machine can be struck with both hands simultaneously, just as a chord is played on a piano. Stenotyping systems are based on phonetics and each time the keys are struck the operator prints a syllable or word.

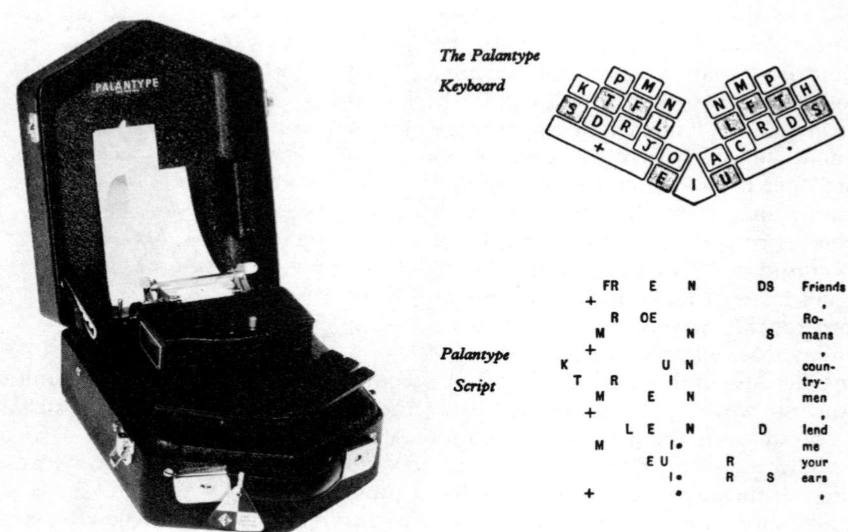

The *Palantype* machine (left), keyboard (upper right) and script (lower right).

The British method of stenotyping, which is called *Palantype*, uses a keyboard which has 29 keys arranged so that the initial consonants can be struck with the left hand, the vowels by the thumbs, and the final consonants by the right hand. The keys are very largely repeated in either hand, so that for the word 'nun', for example, there is both an initial and a final 'N'. Longer words are simply broken down into their component syllables.

```
                          T  H
 P         A
       L   A   N
   T       A I        P
SK    R      I        PT
      R  E
 K       O         R DS
         O   • L
    +      E U
    M          N
SP           I• C       H
      F  O
        N  E
   T         I
 K     L     I
```

The PALANTYPE script records all human speech phonetically

Here is part of a band produced by a stenotypist on a Palantype machine. As you can see, the band is not very difficult to read. In fact, after some training, many typists can transcribe the bands even though they are not stenotypists. This feature of the method is a great asset in verbatim reporting in conferences and courses, for the printed bands can be taken from the stenotypists and given to teams of typists to transcribe, whilst the stenotypists take a few minutes' break before returning to the conference to continue reporting.

Other advantages of stenotyping are its legibility, and the possibility it affords of recording technical matter, or a foreign language so long as the operator has a good knowledge of it. Look at the examples and see how many of them you can read without referring to the transcription.

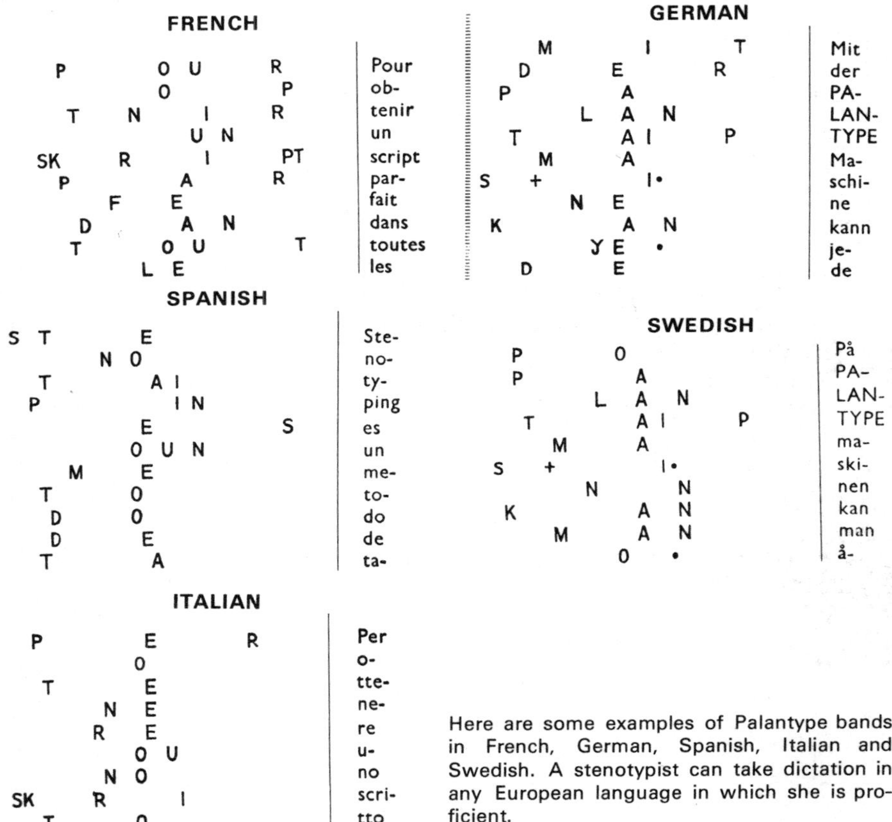

Here are some examples of Palantype bands in French, German, Spanish, Italian and Swedish. A stenotypist can take dictation in any European language in which she is proficient.

Taking dictation The amount of the secretary's time which is spent in taking dictation varies from office to office. It depends to some extent on the following factors:

a A large organisation may provide alternative transmission methods and the boss may like to dictate some of his work into the centralised audio-typing service, thus freeing his secretary for other duties.

b The work may mainly consist of technical reports which the boss may like to draft himself in longhand.
c The secretary may compose some of the routine letters herself.
d The secretary may have an assistant to whom either she or her boss may dictate some of the less important work.

Some bosses establish a regular time each day for giving dictation especially if their work allows them to keep to such a routine. Others have to fit in their dictation time between meetings and other work. Sometimes the delivery and collection times of the local postal services demand that correspondence is dealt with between certain hours.

No matter when the employer plans to deal with his correspondence, the secretary should be prepared to take dictation at any time and must always have her notebook and pens or pencils ready.

Efficient secretaries usually keep two notebooks—one, in which messages and reminders are noted, acts as a memo pad; the second notebook is kept solely for dictation. Here are some hints about shorthand notebooks:

a A spiral-bound notebook is recommended. Choose a notebook with hard covers if you can—you may not always take dictation seated at a table and it is difficult to write good shorthand in a soft covered notebook if you are writing on your knee.
b As far as possible, keep your notebook ready for dictation by ruling margins and dating the next few pages; keep a rubber band round the used portions so that whenever you open the book, it opens at the next fresh page.
c Always date the pages at the bottom so that you can easily find old dictation.
d Always rule a fairly wide margin so that you can fit in additions or alterations. You will also find the margins useful for noting odd reminders, such as checking a reference or an amount or an address or a name.
e Make a clear note about the number of copies needed and to whom they are to be distributed. Note carefully instructions about 'blind' copies (that is, copies which have part of the top copy screened off by placing a slip of plain scrap paper between the carbon paper and the copy) and NOO or "Not on original" copies (that is, copies which have an additional message typed on them, meant to be seen only by the recipients of those copies and not by the person to whom the letter is actually addressed).
f If your notebook is nearly full, take a second one with you when you are called for dictation.
g Use an asterisk or a coloured pencil to indicate or flag important items which must be given priority.
h At the end of each item of dictation rule a clear line and number each piece of dictation with a reference number. If each page is dated and each item of dictation is numbered, you should be able to find a certain letter amongst your old notes fairly easily. Remember that occasions may arise

when your shorthand notes provide the only record of a communication that has been sent from your office; these occasions do occur from time to time and are caused by such events as a lost or missing file, or if the original was so confidential that no copies were kept. (Remember that it is also possible to "read" the impression of a letter left on a new sheet of carbon paper—in some espionage or counter-espionage films you may have seen carbon paper being burnt as a security measure.) Sorting through old notebooks is a very good test of your shorthand because you will probably not be helped at all by your memory. Shorthand writers call their notes "cold notes" if some time elapses between the time the notes were written and the time they are transcribed.

i As you finish each piece of transcription, draw a light diagonal line through the shorthand notes.

j If your boss hands you letters and other papers as he is dictating, number the letters to correspond with the number of the notes and take in a manilla folder with you to keep all the reference material neat and tidy. You may find it useful to clip a sheet of paper to the front of the manilla folder, so that you have a note of any new items for your boss's information such as phone messages, additional appointments or points which you wish to discuss with him.

k When your notebook is full, number it and write the starting and finishing dates clearly on the front cover. Store your notebooks in consecutive order and keep them for at least a year.

l As ink notes are easier to read and more permanent, many secretaries prefer to use a fountain pen or a good ball-point pen. Fountain pens must be kept filled; pencils—several of them—should be kept ready sharpened. It is always wise to have several sharpened pencils ready in case the pen goes dry or the ball-point pen will not write on some parts of the paper.

m If you are told to sign the letters yourself, you should type "Dictated by . . ., signed in his absence" at the foot of the letter.

You should be comfortably seated, facing the dictator, when you are taking dictation and, if possible, your notebook should be resting on a desk or table. Practice "flipping" over the pages so that you can turn over to a new page quickly and quietly. One way of doing this is to turn up slightly the bottom left-hand corner of the page and gradually, using your left hand, slide the whole page up as you are writing with your right hand. By the time you are writing on the bottom line of the page, your left hand will have guided the page so that the bottom line is almost level with the second or third line of the next new page. As you finish writing on the bottom line of the full page, a quick flip with the left hand will turn over the page and your right hand will be in position to write on the top line of the next fresh page.

A secretary should be quiet and composed whilst she is taking dictation. Some dictators pause during dictation to think how they are going to word

Right-handed shorthand writers find it easier to work with their margins on the left. The illustration shows the method usually adopted by left-handed writers.

the next part of the letter; then they dictate fairly quickly once they have organised their thoughts. Use these pauses (and other pauses in dictation such as those caused by telephone calls and interruptions) to read over your notes, insert punctuation, clarify any badly written outlines and note any other points which may need special attention, such as enclosures.

If you do not know or understand a word or expression which is dictated, do not interrupt the dictation. Wait until the end of the letter and then ask any questions you need to about words, phrases, meanings or the spelling of proper names.

Sometimes the dictator asks for the dictation to be read back. If the secretary has written good notes and polished them during any pauses or interruptions, reading back should not present any problems. If you cannot keep up with the dictation, ask the dictator to slow down—he would rather do this than be bothered with queries afterwards. If you are worried about the construction of any sentence, ask if you can read it back and make any corrections.

If your boss has had several interruptions during a dictating session, ask him if he would like you to change any inadvertent repetitions when you are transcribing. For example, phrases like "very much", "very glad", "very pleased", may be repeated over and over again if the dictator's train of thought or flow of words has been interrupted. You may find yourself transcribing "I was very glad to hear that you will be in town next week and shall be very glad to see you at 10.30 a.m. next Friday . . .". It is easy to find a substitute for one of the "very glad" phrases.

It is small points like this that build up a working partnership between a boss and his secretary; most bosses are happy to know that they can rely upon their secretaries to tidy up their dictation if necessary.

Recorded dictation. Instead of dictating their letters to a shorthand writer, some executives prefer to dictate into a recording machine. The material on to which the dictation is recorded is known as the medium. Various makes of machine use different media. Some use plastic belts, some use plastic sheets which look like a heavy type of carbon paper, some use plastic discs (similar to gramophone records), and some use tape or wire which can be on spools or in cassettes.

Media are either magnetic or non-magnetic. Magnetic media, usually wire or tape, may be used over and over again as new dictation automatically erases the previous dictation; if the dictator wants to change or correct what he has dictated he can do so by re-recording over the original dictation.

Non-magnetic media can be used only once. As the dictation cannot be erased, corrections and alterations have to be made at the end of the dictation so the transcriber must listen to the corrections before she starts to type the letter. As the recording is permanent, once it has been transcribed the medium can be stored for record purposes or thrown away.

Some machines both record and play back what has been dictated. These are known as *dual purpose machines.** Some manufacturers make two machines—one for recording and one for transcribing.

You can see that there is a frame holding an oblong slip of paper at the front right-hand side of each machine; this is called the *index slip* or *indicator slip* or *time strip*. As dictation proceeds a small cursor or moving indicator moves across the index slip and indicates the amount of time taken by the dictation.

* One disadvantage of dual-purpose machines (if there is only one machine in the office) is, of course, that the boss cannot use it for dictating whilst the typist is transcribing.

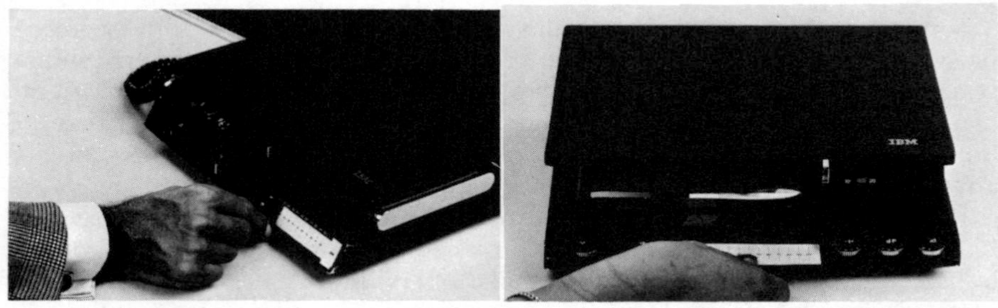

The IBM Executary Dictating Unit and Transcribing Unit.

When the dictator comes to the end of a letter he presses an "end-of-letter" button on his microphone; this causes a mark to be made on the index slip and enables the transcriber to judge the length of the letter.

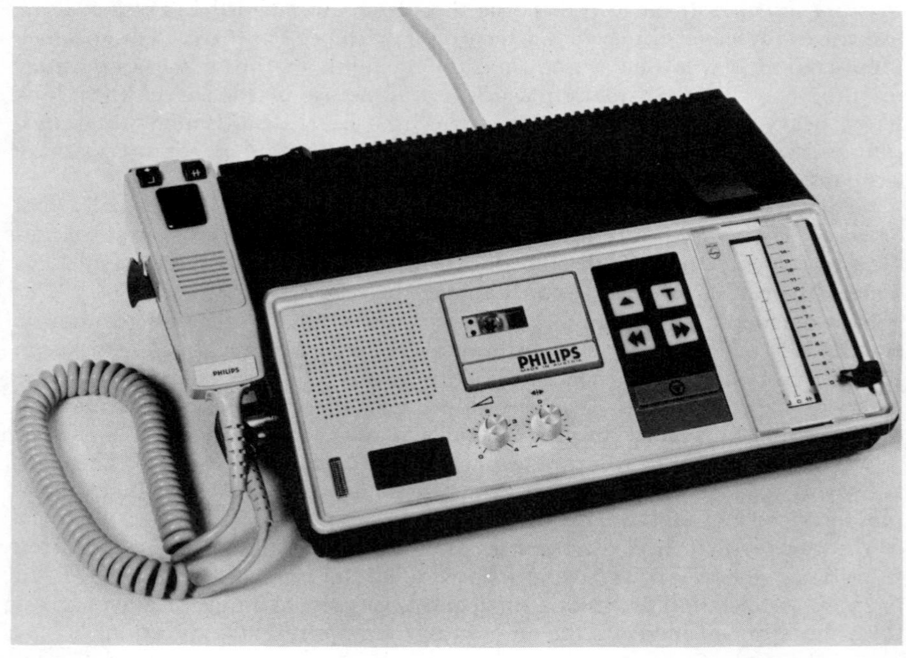

The Philips 98 Electronic Dictating Machine—a dual-purpose dictation/transcription machine. It is 248 mm × 260 mm × 89 mm and weighs 3·7 kg.

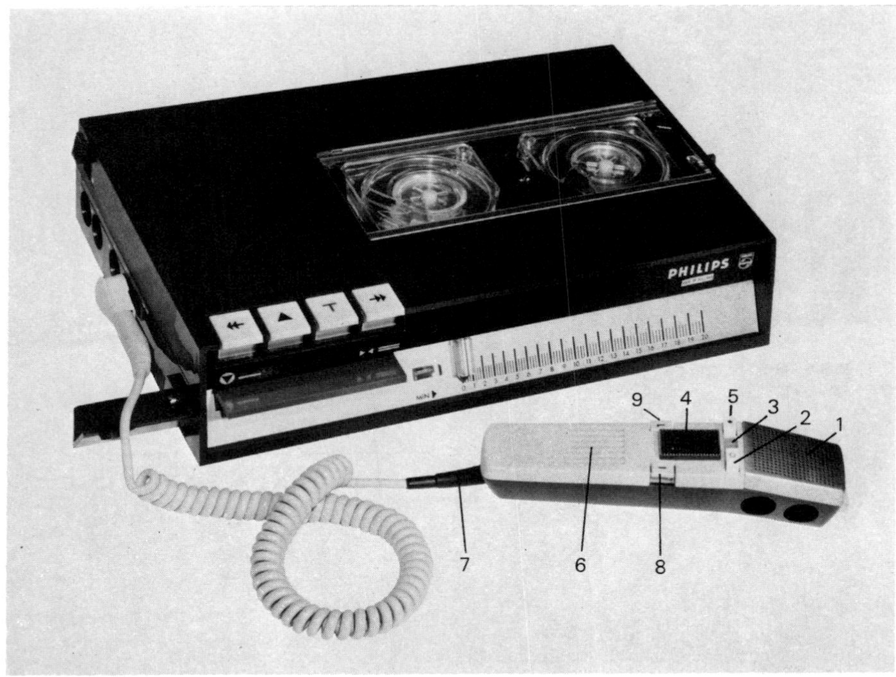

The Philips 84 Dictating Machine showing the parts of microphone.

1 The microphone. 2 The "record" button. 3 The warning light. 4 The "speech" switch—it slides downwards to start dictating and upwards to stop. 5 The "rewind" button—this enables the dictator to play back part of the dictation. 6 The loudspeaker. 7 The cord which attaches the microphone to the dictating machine. 8 The "instruction" button. 9 The "end-of-letter" button.

Another button on the microphone makes an "instruction" mark and indicates the place on the belt or band or tape where the dictator has given instructions about the matter to be transcribed, such as whether it is a letter or a memorandum and how many carbon copies are needed.
The advantages of recording machines are

a Whilst the dictation is being given the secretary can be doing other work.

b Dictation can be given at any time convenient to the employer, for example after office hours. Small portable machines are made which an executive can take home or take with him on business trips.

c Some media can be sent through the post—an employer who is away on a long business trip can record his reports on his pocket recorder and mail the media back to his secretary so that she can transcribe them ready

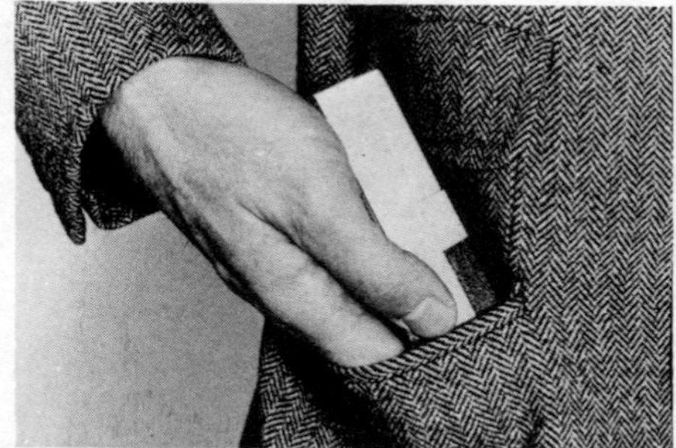

The Philips 85 Pocket Memo is a battery-operated recorder which uses a micro-cassette. The Pocket Memo weighs only 0·4 kg. The micro-cassette can be mailed in an ordinary post box.

for him when he returns to the office.

d In a large office work can be evenly distributed among the typists.

Many large companies consider that the overall effect of these advantages is a great saving in time and money and they have, therefore, established centralised dictating systems as part of their office services. In a centralised dictating system all the transcribers, known as audio-typists, work in a central audio-transcription centre under the general guidance of a supervisor whose job it is to arrange an even distribution of work amongst the audio-typists; the supervisor also makes sure that all dictation is quickly and accurately transcribed and checked, and that the final typed copies are taken to the originator of the dictation as soon as possible.

A Peter Williams Tel-e-sec 3-bank system incorporating Philips 84 dictation machines.

Centralised dictating systems can operate in three ways:

1 Each executive has a dictating machine in his office and the recorded bands or belts or cassettes are taken to the central transcribing unit by messengers.

2 The "bank" system of *remote control* dictation. A number or "bank" of machines are installed in the audio-typing centre. The executive does not have a machine in his office; all he has is a microphone fitted with the necessary operating controls and all the microphones in all the offices are wired to the dictating machines in the central audio-typing unit. These microphones may look like a telephone receiver and some remote control dictation systems are so designed that the installation is incorporated into the private internal telephone circuit or into the GPO internal/external system. When an executive wants to dictate a letter he lifts his receiver, dials the appropriate code, waits to hear the signal that tells him a machine is free and waiting to take his dictation—and then he starts to dictate. When the recording is finished, the supervisor of the audio-typing centre takes the band, belt or tape and it is put into one of the transcribing machines for the audio-typist to type.

3 The *tandem* system. With this system each typist has a unit comprising two dual-purpose machines, one on the lower part and the other on the upper part. Whilst the typist is transcribing from one machine, the other is available to record dictation. If the typist has any queries, she can contact the

A typist operating a Tel-e-sec Tandem System.

dictator by internal telephone, speak directly to him or play back to him any part of his recording so that he can confirm, explain or correct. The tandem system is favoured by some companies because there is direct contact between the dictator and the audio-typist which makes the audio-typist's work less impersonal.

Whenever a centralised dictating system is introduced it is advisable to mount a short training programme for the executives because the success of the system will depend upon the dictators being trained to use it properly.* A well-trained dictator:

1 starts by identifying himself by stating his name, department and telephone extension;
2 tells the typist how many copies he wants taken before he begins to dictate;
3 tells the typist of any special layout or paper to be used;
4 mentions the length of the dictation and size of paper to be used;
5 tells the typist if the correspondence carries enclosures;
6 precedes any instructions by saying "Typist, please . . ."
7 speaks clearly and steadily, holding the microphone near his mouth;
8 dictates punctuation and indicates new paragraphs;
9 spells out any unusual names and words, foreign names and names which can be confused, e.g. Thomson/Thompson, Pattison/Paterson;
10 dictates numbers, amounts of money and addresses slowly and clearly;
11 stops the machine while he is answering the telephone or speaking to someone else;
12 sends any necessary supporting papers or files to the typist.

Despite the advantages of recorded dictation which are listed on pages 35 and 36, not every specialist in office procedures and routines is convinced of its efficiency. Critics of the system make the point that routine correspondence need not be dictated—it should be written by the secretary herself; and more complicated material may be revised so much during dictation that the secretary has to play back all the dictation before she can start to type. In cases such as this some secretaries actually take down the recorded dictation in shorthand and edit it into a straightforward draft before starting to transcribe. And as we noted on page 21, if the wording of a document has to be particularly precise and the style singularly appropriate to an important issue, the executive may prefer to draft the document in longhand; furthermore, it is easier to assess the overall impression your communication is going to give the receiver if you can review and check the whole draft in a visual form than if you have to rely upon an audio playback.

Another criticism of recorded dictation was made by a Mr A. R. Jackson who wrote to *The Daily Telegraph*† suggesting an addendum to Parkinson's

* *The Art of Dictation*, Eva Roman, Gower Press.
† *The Reduction of Correspondence Costs*, H. P. Cemach, Anbar Publications.

Law.* Mr Jackson's Law states **that work expands as the facilities for creating it expand.**

Mr Jackson explains:

> "Theoretically (dictating machines) enable the typist to do the work in half the time . . . but (in practice) . . . Give the executive a dictating machine and what does he do? What, indeed, is he encouraged to do? Why, of

* Parkinson's Law states that work expands in order to fill the time available for its completion. *Parkinson's Law or the Pursuit of Progress*, C. Northcote Parkinson, J. Murray.

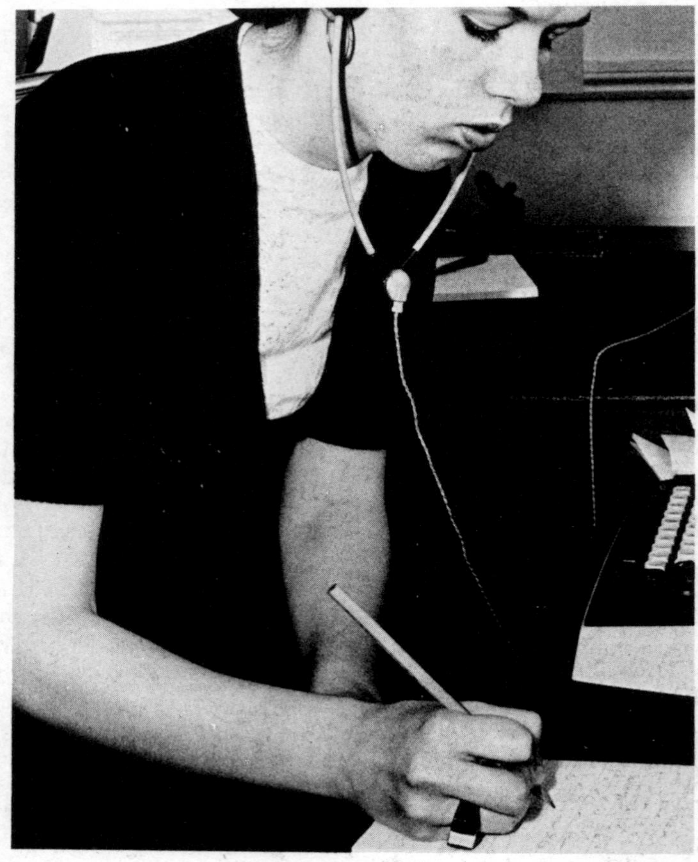

The first thing this secretary does when she arrives at the office in the morning is to see if her chief has left any messages for her on the recording machine. If there are any messages, she will write them down in her notebook; she will probably write the messages in shorthand.

course, to dictate more and more and more. . . . So, whereas he needed only one secretary when he dictated to *her*, now he needs two typists to keep pace with the increasing outgoings of verbiage. . . ."

The criticism regarding the use of recorded dictation and routine and complicated correspondence could, of course, also be made about shorthand dictation although many executives find it more agreeable to dictate to a person than to a machine; however, just as the ability to write shorthand has more applications than the taking-down of correspondence—for example, for taking messages and minutes of meetings—so can the dictating machine be used for other purposes such as recording telephone conversations and conference proceedings.

The dictating machine also provides a convenient means by which the chief can give his secretary instructions after normal office hours or when she is temporarily out of her office, perhaps at lunch or on an errand in another part of the building.

When the dictating machine is used in this way, the first thing the secretary should do when she arrives at her office in the morning should be to check if there are any messages recorded on the machine. She should note any special instructions or messages containing phone numbers or figures; she may turn on the machine and hear something like this:

> "Good morning, Angela. A couple of things cropped up after you'd left last night. My dentist's receptionist rang through to say they had had a cancellation so they could give me an early appointment after all, and a message came through that the trouble at the Works about the threatened strike had got a lot worse in the last 24 hours so I want to have a short informal meeting with the Labour Relations people at half past ten to see what we can do. So . . . if anyone asks for me early on tell them I hope to be in by ten and tell John, Mike and Steve that I want them up here for a meeting at half past. Please prepare the papers I'll need—and don't forget the Press Cutting file—try to get it up to date by including any interesting bits from today's papers. Thank you."

". . . many companies now are keenly aware of the need to present a first-class 'image'—the first impact of any such image generally comes through a letter. . . ."

The Financial Times, 8 May 1972

You may have heard expressions such as 'the company's image' and 'creating a favourable image'. 'Image' in this sense means the impression a company gives to its clients or customers, the public and other firms in the same industry—in fact, to the whole of the outside world.

Few firms or individuals work for altruistic reasons. They are in business to make money and the profits they make largely depend upon the annual volume of trade; this in turn depends to a great extent upon the number of customers or clients who buy the firm's goods or use its services. Companies therefore find it worthwhile to spend a considerable amount of time and money creating a favourable image which will attract the maximum number of customers and clients.

Even charities and other non-profitmaking bodies are concerned with what the public thinks about them and the work they do. In order to collect as much money as possible, they too depend upon their 'image' or their reputation for the worthiness of their causes and also for putting the money given to them to the best possible use.

Some companies have built up a sound reputation over the years so that today they are well-known for the consistently high quality of their products. Hotels work to acquire a good name for the excellence of their service and cuisine. A retail store can create a favourable image by building up a reputation for good customer relations, such as exchanging goods or giving cash refunds with the minimum of bother. Other stores, often long-established ones well-known for their reliability and respectability, change their 'respectable' image for a new and different one more in keeping with the times by setting up new departments where the very latest fashions are sold. These new departments have ultra-modern décor and *trendy** names; usually background music further contributes to the *way-out** or *in** image.

Within recent years image-making† has increased in importance to such an extent that it has become an industry in itself, using the professional services of public relations officers, research workers, sociologists, commercial artists, industrial designers, interior decorators and all those whose work is concerned with setting new trends and creating new styles and fashions.

The aspect of image-making which concerns us here is the appearance and quality of an organisation's typewritten work. It is often said that a firm's letters

* Have you noticed that there is even a fashion in the words which are used to mean 'fashionable'?
† If this subject interests you, you might enjoy reading *Image Men*, Vol. 1, 'Out of Town' and Vol. 2, 'London End', two novels about image-making, by J. B. Priestley, Penguin Books.

are its ambassadors and there is no doubt that the receiver of an attractive letter forms a good impression not only of the person who has signed the letter, but also of his office, his staff, the company he represents and the goods or services marketed by his company. In other words, your company's reputation in the eyes of potentially good customers can be made or ruined for ever by the first impact of the image portrayed by the letters you type.

As part of your secretarial training programme, you are undoubtedly learning to type or you may already be a typist. However, as a well-qualified secretary your knowledge of typewriting is not complete when you have achieved a fast and accurate copying speed and have learnt how to display letters, tables and other documents. In order to produce work of the highest quality, you must study all the factors which contribute to the good appearance of a typewritten page, such as: the quality of the paper, the design of the printed heading, the type-face of the typewriter, the density and clarity of the type, the various display styles, the way in which the letter is set out, the perfection of the typewriting, the correctness of the spelling, grammar and punctuation, not to mention the literary style of the writer of the letter and the kind of machine on which it is typed.

The final appearance of multi-copy typewritten work is also affected by the choice of typewriter ribbon and carbon paper, and by the typist making full use of the various aids and accessories available, such as copy-holders, backing sheets, erasers and erasing shields. Other items, usually grouped under the heading of *Office Sundries*, such as paper clips, tags, guillotines, paper fasteners, binders and staplers also contribute to the production of first-class work.

If you study these topics you will know how to produce work of the highest quality which is a credit to you, your chief and your organisation, and which portrays the image your company is seeking to promote.

You will also be able to advise your employer about the kinds of work which can be produced on the most up-to-date machines, such as automatic typewriters and those which are used for what is known as cold-type composing, that is, the typewritten composition of offset plates for lithographic work.

Two further reasons make the study of these topics a very important part of your secretarial training. Firstly, in small offices the secretary is frequently responsible for ordering stationery supplies and controlling the stationery stock—she should therefore learn the correct names and terms used in the stationery trade for the various kinds of paper, envelopes, filing folders and so on, and also the standard ordering units, for example, reams of paper, boxes of carbon paper, packets of cards and labels.

Secondly, the aspiring senior secretary should never forget that she may one day be in a position where junior staff will come to her for help and guidance. Bear in mind that you should never look down on the girl who spends most of her time typing long and complicated statistical tables, whilst you are concerned with the preparation of confidential documents at top management level. To be worthy of your position, you should be capable of tackling every typing and clerical job throughout the organisation; and you should welcome any chance

The Modern Carpet Company Limited,
10, Lode Lane, London, W.1.
Telephone 01–075 4753

ADP/CBH. 3rd January, 1973.

Mr. Howard J. Harmon,
Executive Vice-President,
Jet-Set Hotels Inc.,
119 East 61st Street,
New York, AMERICA.

Dear Sir,

We enclose our estimate for supplying and laying fitted carpets for your group of six hotels. Our usual price for this carpet, which is exceptionally hard-wearing, is £5 ($13.00) a square yard, fitted and laid; but in view of the quantity needed for six 300-room hotels we are making a special reduction and offering this to you at £4 per yard ($10.50). This price includes all transportation and insurance including the accommodation expenses of our staff who will, of course, need at least three weeks to fit and lay the carpet in each hotel.

We note that the Beirut hotel will be ready for carpet-laying to start on 20th May, 1973, and that the other hotels will be ready at monthly intervals thereafter. We can guarantee to have the carpet delivered to Beirut by 10.5.1973, provided that you place a firm order by the end of January.

We are sending you today, by air parcel post, a package of samples so that you can see the range of colours available. Should you need any further information, please do not hesitate to contact us.

We look forward to hearing from you shortly.

Yours faithfully,

Alan D. Prichard,
Sales Manager.

décor designs
10 Lode Lane London W1R 1AA 01 075 4753

ADP/CBH

AIR MAIL

3 January 1973

Mr Howard J.Harmon
Executive Vice-President
Jet-Set Hotels Inc
119 East 61 Street
New York, New York 10017
UNITED STATES OF AMERICA

Dear Sir

We enclose our estimate for supplying and laying fitted carpets for your group of six hotels. Our usual price for this carpet, which is exceptionally hard-wearing, is £5 ($13.00) a square yard, fitted and laid; but in view of the quantity needed for six 300-room hotels we are making a special reduction and offering this to you at £4 ($10.50). This price includes all transportation and insurance including the accommodation expenses of our staff who will, of course, need at least three weeks to fit and lay the carpet in each hotel.

We note that the Beirut Hotel will be ready for carpet-laying to start on 20 May 1973, and that the other five hotels will be ready at monthly intervals thereafter. We can guarantee to have the carpet delivered to Beirut by 10 May 1973 provided that you place a firm order by the end of January.

We are sending you today, by air parcel post, a package of samples so that you can see the range of colours available. Should you need any further information, please do not hesitate to contact us.

We look forward to hearing from you shortly.

Yours faithfully

Alan D Prichard
Sales Manager

Enc

Each of these letters has the same object: to get an order to supply, fit and lay carpet in six 300-room hotels—an important order. Which letter gives the better impression?
Apart from the difference in appearance, there are six points which you could criticise about the letter from The Modern Carpet Company Limited. How many can you find?

1 The postcode is not included in the letter-head.

2 The words *AIR MAIL* have been omitted, so there is a possibility that the letter might be sent surface mail. Would this matter?

3 The typist has left out the American ZIP code. * (*see facing page*) Perhaps she thought *New York 10017* was the phone number.

4 Do not put 'st', 'nd', 'rd', 'th' after the street number.

5 10.5.73 means October 5, 1973 to an American—never use the 'number only' method of writing the date.

6 As *Enc* is omitted, there is a possibility that the estimate will be left out.

you get to train and improve the work of junior staff if they ask for your help with an unfamiliar or particularly difficult piece of work.

Standard typewriters When we speak of a 'standard' typewriter, we generally have in mind an office machine, either manual or electric, fitted with a 'Universal' four-bank keyboard, a tabular mechanism, choices of line-spacing (1, $1\frac{1}{2}$, 2, $2\frac{1}{2}$, 3), four ribbon positions (top, centre, bottom and stencil), and a carriage length from 300 mm (approx. $11\frac{1}{2}$ in) to 350 mm (approx. 14 in).

PICA
Your letters are personal representatives of your firm a
legibility and distinctiveness. Our precision built type
print work.
WE OFFER A WIDE SELECTION OF DISTINCTIVE TYPE STYLES DES
NUMERALS: 1234567890

EXECUTIVE PICA
Your letters are personal representatives of your firm a
legibility and distinctiveness. Our precision built type
print work.
WE OFFER A WIDE SELECTION OF DISTINCTIVE TYPE STYLES DES
NUMERALS: 1234567890 AVAILABLE ON ELECTRICS ONLY

PICA CLASSIC
Your letters are personal representatives of your firm a
legibility and distinctiveness. Our precision built type
print work.
WE OFFER A WIDE SELECTION OF DISTINCTIVE TYPE STYLES DES
NUMERALS: 1234567890

PICA CUBIC
Your letters are personal representatives of your firm ar
legibility and distinctiveness. Our precision built type
print work.
WE OFFER A WIDE SELECTION OF DISTINCTIVE TYPE STYLES DES
NUMERALS: 1234567890

ELITE
Your letters are personal representatives of your firm and as such d
distinctiveness. Our precision built typewriters assure the finest c
WE OFFER A WIDE SELECTION OF DISTINCTIVE TYPE STYLES DESIGNED TO MEE
NUMERALS: 1234567890

EXECUTIVE ELITE
Your letters are personal representatives of your firm and as such d
and distinctiveness. Our precision built typewriters assure the fine
WE OFFER A WIDE SELECTION OF DISTINCTIVE TYPE STYLES DESIGNED TO MEE
NUMERALS: 1234567890 AVAILABLE ON ELECTRICS ONLY

---

* ZIP stands for Zoning Improvement Plan. The American ZIP Code system (a five digit code system instituted in 1963) is similar to the British Postcode system. The object of postal codes is to speed mail deliveries by cutting down the sorting time. A booklet entitled *ZIP Code* is available free from the Information Service, Post Office Department, Washington, D.C. 20260. This is how the envelope for this letter should be addressed—the city first, then the state in full, then the ZIP code three spaces after the end of the name of the state.

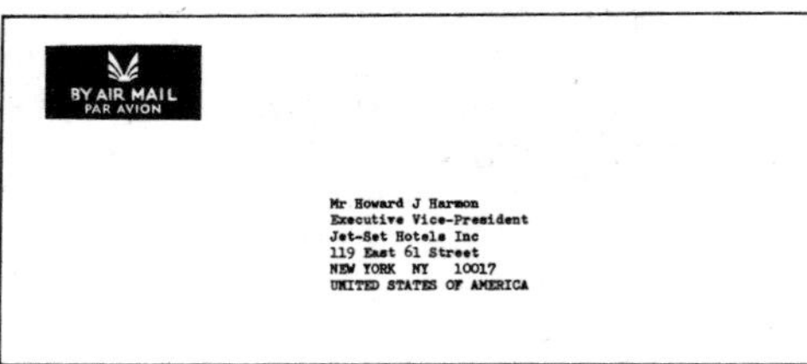

Most standard machines are available in a variety of carriage widths and *pitches* (the number of characters to the inch or, in the metric system, the width in millimetres of one character). The most usual pitches are pica (2·54 mm or 10 characters to the inch) and élite (2·12 mm or 12 characters to the inch). There is also a large selection of type styles, called *typefaces* or *founts*. Some examples are shown on pages 45, 70 and 72.

The Imperial Model 80 Mk II manual office typewriter is made in five carriage widths (13, 15, 18, 22 and 26 in) and four pitches (10, 11, 12 and 16 characters to the inch).

PORTABLE typewriters are light-weight machines which can easily be carried from one place to another. They take up very little room and are of great use to people who have to travel in connection with their work, e.g. reporters, journalists and representatives. Some portable machines have no tabular mechanism and this is a point to query if you are thinking of buying one.

LIGHTWEIGHT machines weighing about 7 kg—compared to about 4 kg for a portable and 16 kg for a standard machine—are used for general correspondence work in many offices. They possess nearly all the features of heavier machines but are cheaper and easier to carry about.

The Smith-Corona GT portable typewriter weighs 4·5 kg.

Lightweight machines are used for correspondence in many offices. They possess nearly all the features of heavier machines but are cheaper and easier to carry about. This HERMES 3000 with a 330 mm (13 in) carriage weighs 7·2 kg.

ELECTRIC typewriters are fitted with small electric motors. The typebars and carriage return are motivated by electricity. A very light pressure on a key which causes a depression of as little as 3 mm is sufficient to set the typebar mechanism in motion. The carriage is returned by depressing a key on the keyboard. Since variable finger pressure on the keys does not affect the momentum with which the typebars hit the paper, electric typewriters produce work of a very uniform appearance. An indicator at the side of the machine increases the typing impression and, with suitable paper and carbon paper, up to twenty legible carbon copies may be obtained at one typing. By extra pressure on the space-bar, hyphen and underscore keys, a repeat action is obtained.

The IBM golf-ball typing head on which the characters are mounted.

The IBM 72 electric typewriter has no typebars. The characters are mounted on a small typing head, like a metal ball, which moves across the platen when the keys are pressed. The typing head can be changed quite simply for another bearing a different type style.

The IBM 82, also a golf-ball model, is produced in a dual pitch version so that the typist can use both 10-pitch and 12-pitch type on the same machine. Like many other electric machines the IBM has some *typamatic keys* (for example, the hyphen, underscore, back space, space bar, carriage return keys) which repeat automatically when depressed slightly harder than normal and held down.

ELECTRIC PORTABLE typewriters are amongst the newest on the market. As their name implies, they are motivated by electricity and they are light enough to be carried fairly easily from one place to another. The Imperial 300 weighs only 6.13 kg (13½ lb).

Care of the typewriter

1 Keep the type faces clean by daily brushing with a stiff brush. To avoid straining typebars, brush backwards and forwards, not sideways. Always clean the type faces before and after typing stencils.

2 Use a long-handled soft brush to remove dust from the type basket, the ribbon vibrator and other exposed parts of the machine. Dust the platen.

The IBM 82 typewriter is made in a dual-pitch version so that the typist can produce both 10-pitch and 12-pitch type styles on the same machine.

The Imperial 300, an electric portable typewriter, weighs 6.13 kg and is 165 mm high, 356 mm wide and 333 mm deep.

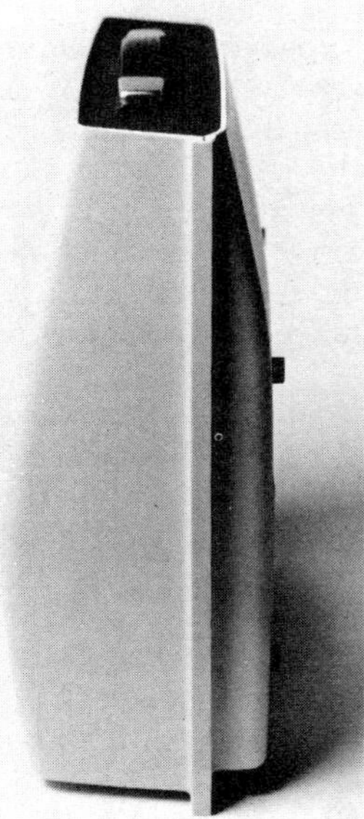

The ADLER *gabriele 5000* electric portable typewriter weighs 14.5 kg. The carriage width is 309 mm (12 in) and the length of the writing line is 277 mm ($10\frac{1}{2}$ in). Either pica (2.54 mm, 10 pitch) or élite 2.12 mm (12 pitch) type sizes are available.

3 When typing on a single sheet of paper, protect the platen by using a backing sheet.
4 Move the carriage clear of the type basket when erasing so that no eraser dust falls into the machine.
5 Cover the machine at night.
6 To move a typewriter, first lock the carriage by moving both margin stops to the centre and then place your hands under the base of the machine before lifting it. Lift a long-carriage machine from the back so that the weight rests against the body—this prevents the machine from overbalancing away from you.

Typewriter attachments There are a number of accessories and attachments available which increase the variety of work the typist can produce on an ordinary typewriter. Some of the attachments are permanent modifications, others can be taken on and off as needed.

DUAL RIBBON attachments enable the typist to switch from fabric to carbon ribbon in an instant. Instead of being wound with carbon ribbon, the second spool can carry a reel of correcting paper (see page 59).

The BTA CARBON RIBBON attachment enables almost any typewriter, portable, standard or electric, to produce the crisp black print-like typing normally associated with only expensive carbon ribbon electric machines or machines fitted with a dual-ribbon device. The BTA unit consists of a carbon ribbon container which has an adjustable ribbon guide arm with four slots and a universal take-up spool. The attachment holds one roll of 293 metres, 8 mm carbon ribbon and is fixed to the typewriter by means of a permanent adhesive pad. The carbon ribbon is fed through the appropriate feed-out slot on the guide arm and ribbon carrier in the normal way and wound on to the universal take-up spool on the left. When the spool becomes full, it can be lifted off, emptied over the waste-paper bin and the carbon ribbon wound on again ready for further use. The BTA attachment can be fitted to almost any typewriter. The switch-over from carbon ribbon to fibre ribbon for typing less important documents is quick and simple.

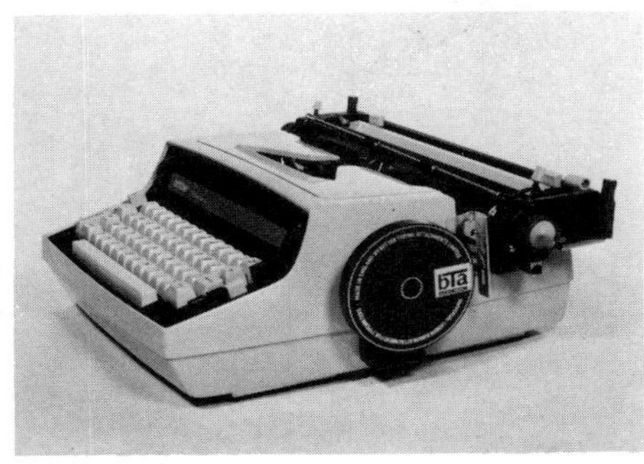

The BTA Universal Carbon Ribbon Attachment Mk 1 fitted to a portable typewriter.

The FORMALINER attachment is a continuous stationery attachment for feeding pre-collated sets of documents into the typewriter. If the time taken to interleave document sets manually is taken into consideration, it is obvious that a continuous stationery attachment can appreciably increase output.

The SPIRIT CARBON RIBBON attachment shown on page 52 produces spirit masters without a sheet of carbon being fed into the machine with the master sheet. The spirit carbon ribbon passes between the platen and the back of the master, so as the typist types the copy the carbon image is printed on the back of the master sheet.

The TYPIT attachment enables the typist to type symbols, letters or characters which are not included on the keyboard of her machine. This means that the professional appearance of technical documents is not spoilt by writing-in by hand special signs and symbols. Typits are separate typebars. The typist selects a typit symbol and inserts it into a modified typebar guide which has been fitted on to her machine. Then she strikes any key and the rising typebar forces a small slide into the platen and thus prints the symbol. Each typit is marked on the handle for identification. There are more than 1000 typit symbols available for both 10 and 12 pitch machines, ranging from scientific and mathematical letters and symbols to symbols used in pharmaceutics, astronomy, meteorology and linguistics.

The Hermes Ambassador Electric fitted with a spirit carbon ribbon. The spirit carbon ribbon passes between the platen and the back of the master, thus the image is formed on the back of the master sheet as the copy is being typed.

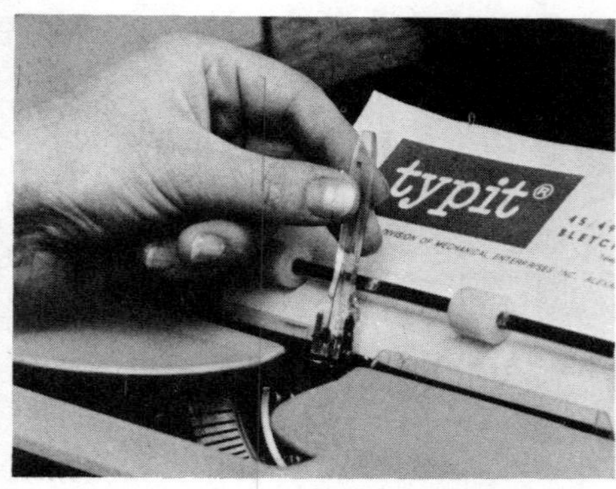

Striking a typit.

XV. DIACRITICS, ACCENTS, PUNCTUATION MARKS

´ 180 Acute accent	` 181 Grave accent	˘ 182 Breve	– 183 Macron	¨ 184 Diaerisis, Umlaut	^ 185 Circumflex
187 Modified macron	ˇ 280 Klicka	~ 282 Tilde	˵ 593 Double grave	776 Tone mark	° 322
396	⋯ 470 Dots over l.c.	⁄ 320 Bar for u.c. L	⁄ 321 Bar for l.c. l	⌢ 827 Superior bow	- 500 Bar for l.c. d
926 Dot over u.c.	927 Dot over l.c.	: 733 Colon	; 799 Semi-Colon	! 134 Exclamation	¡ 315 Exclamation (Sp.)
? 474 Question	¿ 314 Question (Sp.)	' 639 Apostrophe	" 318 Quotes	" 734 Bold quotes	“ ” 587 588 Quotes
¸ 279 Cedilla	˛ 281 Polish hook	· 496 Tick	∧ 137 Caret	⌣ 828 Inferior bow	. 829 Dot under letter

XX. FLOW AND DIRECTION SIGNS

△	▽	Y	⅄	⬡	∾	∩	µF
2200	2201	2202	2203	2204	2205	2206	2207

XXI. FORMULA DIMENSIONS (SIZES)

γ	ε	ϑ	ϱ	ς	τ	Ω
2300	2301	2302	2303	2304	2305	2306

XXII. MATHEMATICAL SYMBOLS (SIGNS)

≙	⌠ ⎮ ⌡	cos	.	≮	√	∛	—
2400	2401 2402 2403	2404	2405	2406	2407	2408	2409

XXIII. MEASUREMENTS AND WEIGHTS

mm	cm	cm²	cm³	qm	m²	m³	mg	gr	℔	kg	t°	Dz	hm	rm	km
2500	2501	2502	2503	2504	2505	2506	2507	2508	2509	2510	2511	2512	2513	2514	2515
ℓ	°C	№													
2516	2517	2518													

Some examples of TYPIT symbols.

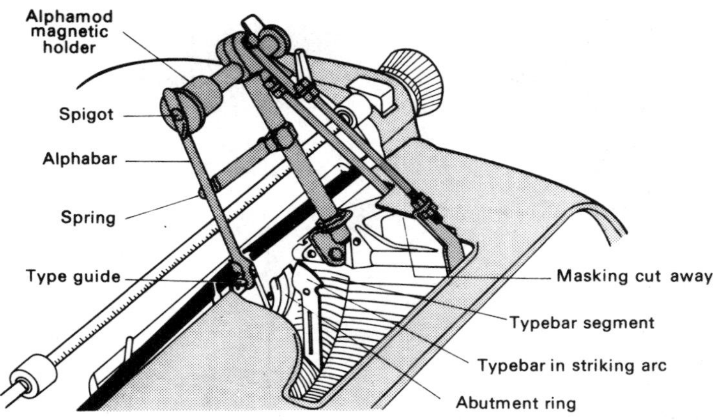

The ALPHAMOD, the BETAMOD, and the DELTAMOD, are three *Uneoprint* technical aids which can be fitted to the IBM Executive typewriter. The alphamod can also be fitted to the Olivetti Editor proportionally-spaced electric typewriter. The alphamod consists of a magnetic typebar holder above the type guide which is supported by a tripod attached to the typebar segment; thus it moves up and down with the segment when the shift key is used. Special typebars (called **alphabars**) placed on the alphamod are held in position by the magnet. A spring attached to the tripod holds the alphabars clear of the lifting ribbon before they are struck; after they have been struck, the spring pushes them clear of the ribbon and type guide.

Two characters (upper and lower case) can be fitted to each alphamod typebar and if only one or two extra characters are used in a whole piece of work, one typebar can be kept permanently on the holder and swung into position when needed. Alphabars are available for a wide range of foreign languages, fractions and mathematical signs and symbols. Alphabars may be kept in special holders. When a certain symbol or character is required, the typist

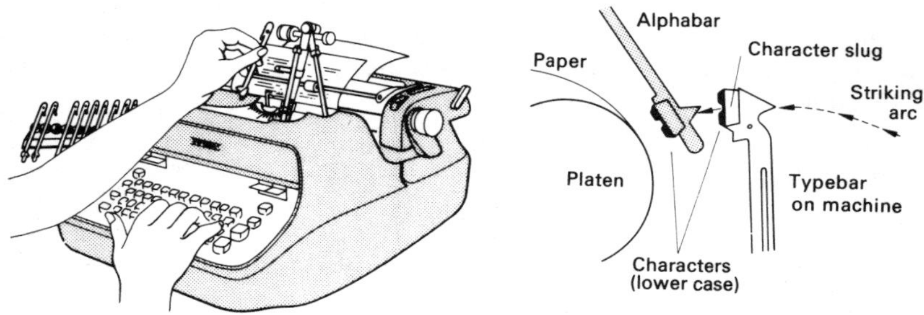

Operation of the alphamod.

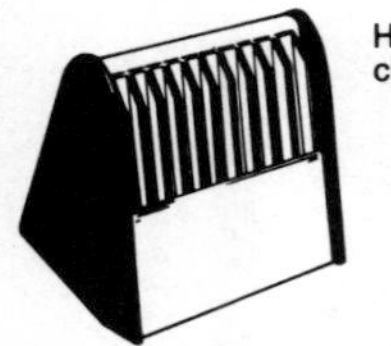

Plastic Alphabar Holder

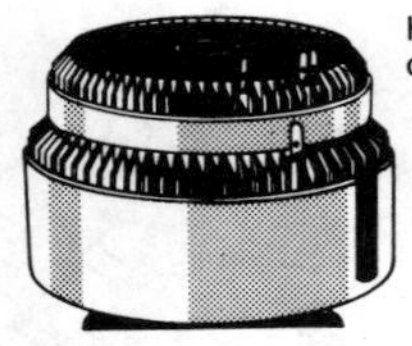

Carousel Alphabar Holder (double tier)
(Single tier also available,–holds 63 characters)

Plastic alphabar holders.

selects the alphabar, fits it into the holder and 'types' it by striking any key on the keyboard with the same unit width.

The BETAMOD enables the typist to produce **bold face** type. The betamod modification fits a lever to the left-hand side of the typewriter carriage; when the lever is pushed back, the platen (and therefore the paper too) are minutely displaced sideways. The words to be made bold are typed twice: the first time with the platen displaced, the second time with the platen in the usual position—the result is an overlapped image which gives the appearance of bold face type.*

Operation of the *betamod.*

The DELTAMOD attachment enables the typist to type characters and figures above or below the normal writing line; in other words, she can type inferior or superior characters. The amount of movement is controlled and need not be the standard half-line-space. A scale on the edge of the platen indicates the exact alignment position and reminds the typist to return to the normal writing line after the deltamod attachment has been engaged. The following example shows how the deltamod can be used:

$$\eta \mathrm{M} = \frac{\eta \mathrm{R}_{\mathrm{ex}}}{\mathrm{R}_{\pi \mathrm{in}}} \int \frac{(\mathrm{W}' - \mathrm{M}_{\pi})\mathrm{dW}^{\pi}}{(\mathrm{W}^{\epsilon} + \mathrm{Rd}_{\pi \mathrm{i}})\pi'} = - \epsilon^{1} \frac{\epsilon \mathrm{R}_{\mathrm{ex}}}{\mathrm{R}}$$

*With a little experience and practice, bold faces can be produced on any typewriter by first typing the words to be made bold, then moving the paper a minute fraction of an inch to the left or right by using the paper release lever, and then overtyping. As the movement of the paper has been so minute, it is unnecessary to return the paper to its previous position; after overtyping the words to be made bold, typing continues in the normal way.

Typists' supplies and accessories

RIBBONS Ribbons are made from carbon-coated paper or film (carbon ribbons) as well as cotton, silk or nylon (fabric ribbons).

Carbon ribbons are used only once.* They produce crisp, black impressions similar to normal printing. Carbon ribbons are also used to create offset-litho plates by direct typing, and they also produce excellent originals for copy by heat, photo or dyeline processes. There are several special carbon ribbon attachments which enable the typist to switch-over quickly and simply from carbon ribbon to fabric ribbon (see pages 50 and 51). Carbon film ribbons are also supplied on twin spools for easy ribbon changing.

As the ribbon acts as a buffer between the typefaces and the paper, the sharpness of the typed characters depends upon the weave and thickness of the fabric; the finer the fabric and weave, the sharper the imprint.

Silk ribbons are very strong and absorbent. They produce a fine impression and last longer than cotton ribbons.

Nylon ribbons are considered to produce work of excellent appearance. As the nylon fabric is very fine, it is possible to wind more on the spool, so instead of the usual ten metres, nylon ribbons can be made up to twenty metres long, so the typist does not have to change the ribbon so frequently.

When ordering typewriter ribbons, it is important to state: the make and model of the typewriter to ensure that the correct spool is supplied; whether a carbon-paper, carbon-film, cotton, silk or nylon ribbon is required; the degree of inking—this varies from light to medium and medium-heavy; whether a bi-chrome (two colour) or single colour ribbon is needed, and the length (if silk or nylon).

CARBON PAPER is made by coating a suitable paper with a mixture of waxes, oils and pigments; one of the best waxes is carnauba, a substance obtained from the leaves of the carioca tree which grows in Brazil. Carbon paper made in this way tends to smudge and the dye is not completely fast, so the colour may come off on to the typist's hands particularly in hot weather when the finger tips are slightly moist.

Solvent-coated copying sheets are a modern development of carbon paper. The solvent coating can be compared to a very thin layer of sponge saturated with ink which is applied to either a film or a paper base. With conventional carbon paper, the carbon coating breaks away at the point of impact, but when a typebar strikes a solvent copying sheet ink is squeezed out and immediately redistributed from the surrounding area when the pressure is released.

Solvent film copying sheets comprise two basic layers—the film base and the solvent applied coating. In addition there may be a primer or pre-coating, and a backing. The pre-coating or primer makes the film opaque; it also acts as a

* Carbon ('one-time only') ribbons are banned in offices of high security risk, e.g. some government departments, because the wording that has been typed can be read off from the used ribbons, unless their disposal and destruction is strictly supervised.

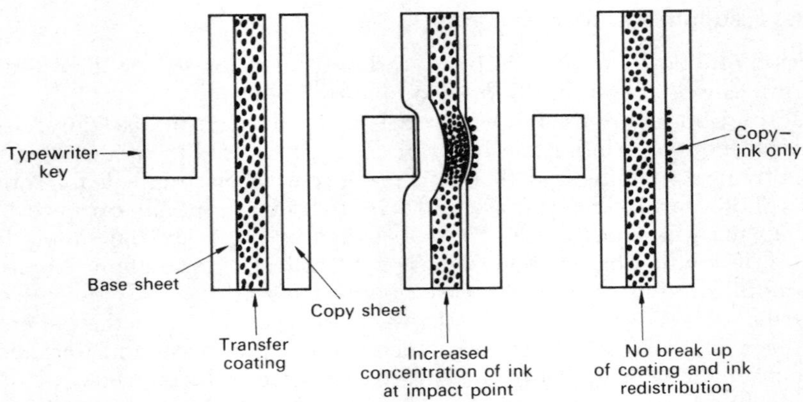

This diagram shows how the ink is redistributed at the point of impact when a typebar has struck a solvent coated sheet.

'key' to make the solvent stick to the film base; the backing usually carries a design and the brand name.

The finest film solvent carbon papers have a fifth or extra layer. This is made of a metallic substance; it makes the solvent sheets more durable and seals in the colour so that the carbon copies are very clear and sharp. In some cases copies produced by these carbons are so good that they are indistinguishable from the top or original copy.

Despite this difference between carbon-coated and solvent-coated sheets, the term 'carbon paper' is used colloquially to refer to either conventional carbon-coated paper or solvent-coated film or solvent-coated paper.

Film-base solvent carbons are exceptionally durable and it is claimed that they can be used well over a hundred times before being thrown away. Solvent carbons are clean to handle and the copies are easy to erase; the strength of the film base prevents curling, tearing and treeing.

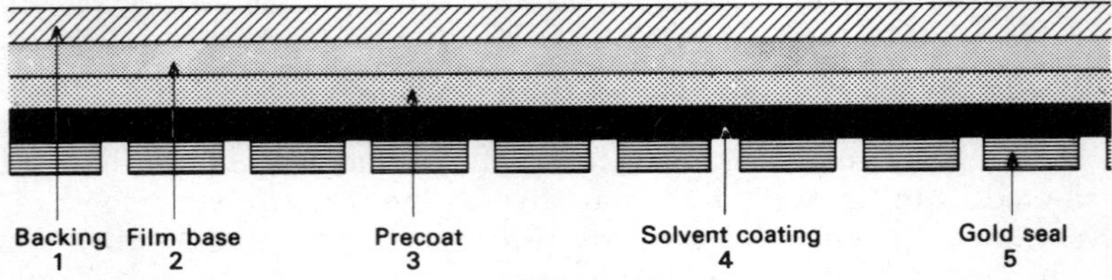

High quality film solvent carbon papers have five layers—(1) the backing, which may carry an ornamental design and a brand name; (2) the film base; (3) the primer or pre-coating which acts as a 'key' to make the solvent stick to the film; (4) the solvent coating which is the layer containing the colouring matter, and (5) a layer of metallic substance which seals in the colour.

Carbon paper and solvent-coated copying sheets are made in a variety of sizes, weights and finishes. The number of clear copies which can be made at a single typing depends upon several factors.

- a The weight of the carbon paper; more copies can be made using a thin, lightweight copying sheet.
- b The weight and finish (smoothness) of the typewriting paper, both original and copy; the lighter the paper, the more copies can be taken.
- c The hardness of the typewriter platen or cylinder—a hard platen enables more copies to be taken.
- d The hardness and density of the carbon or solvent coating; a hard coating gives a greyer but sharper image which is easier to erase than a really black copy.
- e The typist's touch—a firm, staccato touch is best for multi-copy work.
- f The action of the typewriter keys; most typewriters have an adjustable pressure control gauge and the harder the keys hit the platen, the more copies can be taken at one typing.
- g The style of type face or fount; sharp type styles such as 'standard' pica and élite give better copies than 'shaded'* styles.
- h The thickness of the ribbon material—the finer the ribbon, the more copies can be taken. A fine ribbon also gives sharper copies.

COLOURS Solvent carbons for typewritten work are usually black. Blue solvent carbons are manufactured for handwritten work. Purple solvent carbons in roll form are made for bill-writing registers such as those used in shops and garages. Wax carbons are made in black, blue and red; yellow is available for dyeline work and a special green carbon is produced for X-ray work. A two-sided carbon is made for use with translucent papers and for work of maximum security.

Special two-colour carbons are made for typing accounts; when the figures in red on the top copy are typed through the red area of the carbon paper, then those figures will of course appear in red on the carbon copies. Two colour carbon papers are made to order and are available in black/red only.

ONE-TIME CARBON as the name implies is carbon paper which is used only once. It is used in teleprinter rolls, adding and accounting machine tally rolls and in computer stationery. One of the most recent applications of one-time carbon paper is an aid for typists produced by Lamson Paragon which comprises two or three part sets made up with an extra top layer of carbon. The original is placed on top of the set and the whole pack is fed into the typewriter.

* By 'shaded' styles we mean those in which some parts of a fount are thicker than others, for example y (shaded) compared by y (standard).

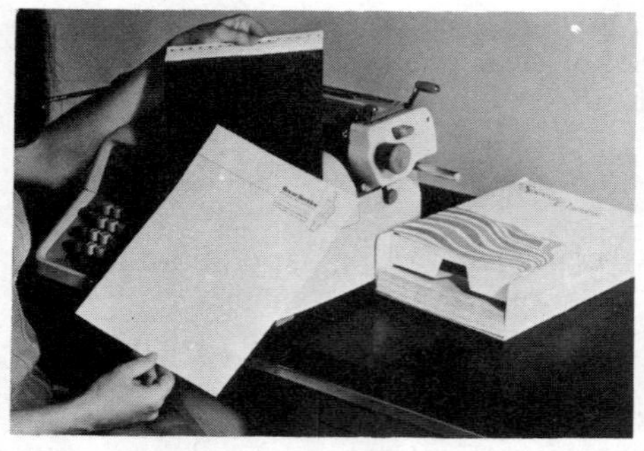

The typist in this illustration is placing an original or top copy on top of a three-part set before feeding the whole set into the typewriter.

One-time carbon sets such as these, which will give up to eight copies, eliminate assembling the carbon pack sheet by sheet. When typing is finished, all the carbons can be extracted in one movement.

SIZES Carbon paper and solvent film copying sheets are manufactured in conventional British and American paper sizes as well as A4. Special sizes can be cut to customers' requirements. Carbon papers are sold by the box. The most usual quantities are boxes containing 100, 250 and 500 sheets separated into individual folders or wallets containing 25 or 50 sheets.

PULL-TAB AND CUT CORNER carbons. Carbon sheets made with cut corners and half an inch longer than typewriting paper enable the typist to withdraw all the carbon papers in one action.

The typist holds the corners of the original and copy papers at the top left corner and separates all the carbons in one movement.

CHOICE OF CARBON PAPER The table below shows the best combinations of carbon paper weights and finishes used with electric and manual typewriters to produce up to twelve copies. There is a solvent-coated lightweight paper available which will give up to 16 copies when coupled with the correct weight copy paper. Nowadays, however, the wider use of office copiers if more than, say, six copies are needed and the improved performance of solvent-coated copying papers frequently enable one grade of carbon paper to be adopted for standard use throughout an organisation. The following weights in the Caribonum "PolyXtra" range will suit most office needs:

Solvent-coated film:	50-gauge weight	1 to 6/8 copies
	75-gauge weight	1 to 5/7 copies
	100-gauge weight	1 to 3/4 copies
Solvent-coated paper:	Lightweight	1 to 8/16 copies

Typewriter	Carbon Paper		
	1–4 copies	**5–9 copies**	**10–12 copies**
Electric	Standard weight Hard finish	Medium weight Hard finish	Lightweight Hard finish
Manual	Standard weight Sharp finish	Medium weight Sharp finish	Lightweight Sharp finish

ERASERS Typewriting erasers are made in various shapes and styles to help the typist to erase neatly and quickly. Some typists prefer the circular erasers, others prefer the pencil-stick types.

ERASING SHIELDS Erasing shields are made of thin plastic or metal, with differently shaped "cut-outs". The shield is placed over the incorrect letter or letters so that the typist can use the eraser without spoiling any of the surrounding words.

CORRECTION PAPERS These enable typing mistakes to be corrected without using an eraser. One side of the correction paper is coated with a white substance. The strip of correction paper is placed between the ribbon and the original over the 'wrong' letter, with the coated side against the paper. The 'wrong' letter is then typed again; this covers the mistake with the white substance, thus blanking it out. The correct letter is then typed. Different correction papers are normally used for correcting top copies and carbons. This method of correction is completely satisfactory only when the original (top copy) paper has the same degree and shade of whiteness as the coating on the correction paper.

It is possible to buy correction paper wound on standard typewriter spools

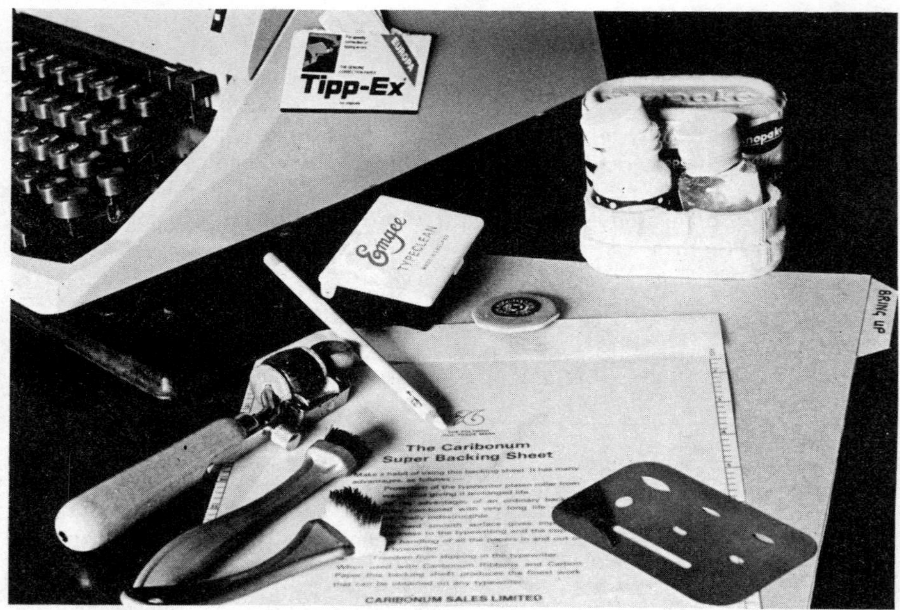

A selection of typists' aids. (1) erasing shield; (2) circular eraser; (3) pencil-stick eraser; (4) backing sheet; (5) correcting paper; (6) typewriter mat; (7) correction fluid; (8) brushes and type cleaners.

which can be fitted to machines with dual ribbon devices (see page 50). When the typist wants to correct an error, she engages the spool carrying the correction paper, backspaces, types the 'wrong' letter again, backspaces, switches to the normal ink ribbon and types in the correct letter.

BACKING SHEETS Backing sheets are used to place behind the paper in the machine. They protect the platen roller from wear and improve the quality of the copy by preventing the platen from absorbing some of the impact of the typebar. They also help the typist assemble and feed in the "carbon pack" as they have a turnover flat at the top which acts as a stay. Backing sheets marked with scales showing lines of typewriting and inches along the left-hand and right-hand edges help the typist to gauge when the work is approaching the bottom of the page. The use of a backing sheet marked off with line or inch calibrations is the best way to make sure that the lower margin is uniform on successive sheets of typing.

PLATEN RESTORER Sometimes the platen of a typewriter becomes pitted. This gives an uneven surface and produces poor carbon copies. Badly pitted platens can be improved by the use of a platen restorer. The typist inserts into the machine a sheet of paper wide enough to cover the full width of the platen,

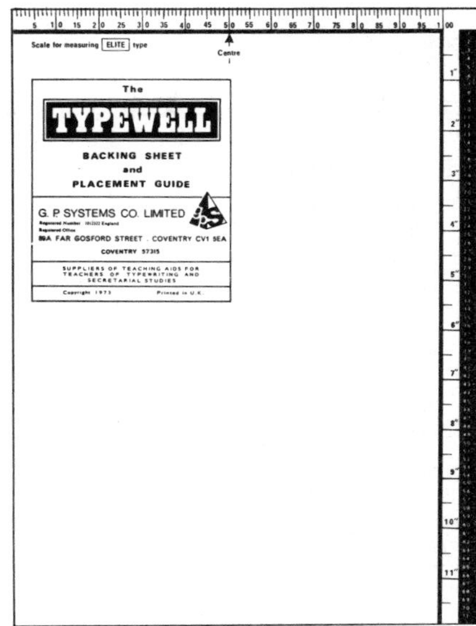

A backing sheet, calibrated in lines of typewriting and inches along the right-hand edge.

but sufficiently short to expose the front surface of the platen. Then, using the sponge from the top of the restorer container, the typist rubs across the platen, turning it until the whole surface has been treated. Very badly worn platens may need several applications, but if the restorer is used regularly on new machines the platens should keep in good condition. The restorer can also be used on other machines, such as teleprinters and accounting machines.

COPYHOLDERS Some typists like to place the copy from which they are typing or their shorthand notebooks on copyholders. The simplest copyholders are

Two simple copyholders—a shorthand notebook holder on the left, and the 'Lector Data-holder' on the right.

stands which hold the copy at a convenient height and enable the typist to work in a good posture, thus lessening fatigue and eye-strain. More sophisticated copyholders are suitable for copying statistical tables. The typist has a foot-control so that she can read the copy line-by-line; the larger copyholders are fitted with lights and can be fixed to the desk on either side of the typewriter or behind the machine.

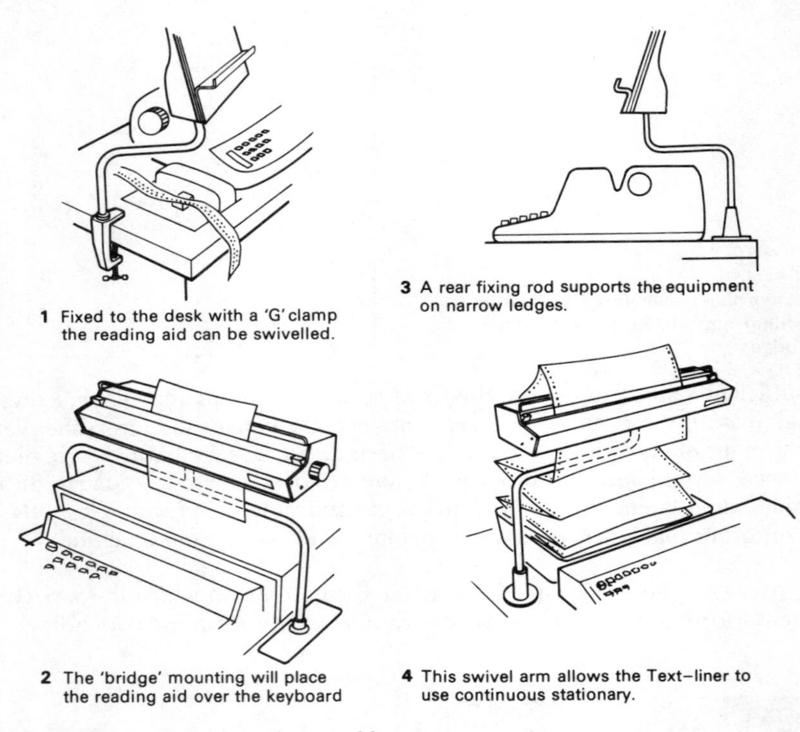

1 Fixed to the desk with a 'G' clamp the reading aid can be swivelled.

2 The 'bridge' mounting will place the reading aid over the keyboard

3 A rear fixing rod supports the equipment on narrow ledges.

4 This swivel arm allows the Text–liner to use continuous stationary.

Copyholders can be fitted in various positions.

Paper sizes, type sizes and type styles In addition to the typist's ability to type quickly and accurately and her knowledge of the theory of tabulation, effective display work also depends upon the ability to select the most appropriate paper size for the work in hand, bearing in mind that the total number of horizontal spaces available will depend upon the type size (or *pitch*) of the typewriter as well as the width of the paper, and the total number of vertical spaces will depend upon the length of the paper.

PAPER SIZES Until about twenty years ago, typewriting paper was manufactured in sizes which conformed to the first British Standard Specification BS 730 originally issued in 1937. The standard was revised in 1951 and again

The TEXT-LINER being used in conjunction with an Ultronic Data System 6000 machine. The typist is working from a corrected typescript. A 'record' of the document is being created on punched paper tape as she is typing; the tape will subsequently be used to produce automatically typed originals—see page 212.

in 1960. Until that time the most common sizes used in typewriting were foolscap, 8 in × 13 in,* and quarto (4to) 8 in × 10 in, which when halved provided an additional two sizes, sexto (6to) $6\frac{1}{2}$ in × 8 in and octavo (8vo) 5 in × 8 in. These sizes, together with two larger sizes (draft, 10 in × 16 in, and brief, 13 in × 16 in, convenient for legal and accountancy work) catered for almost all office requirements in the United Kingdom and other countries of the Commonwealth.

During this period the International Organisation for Standardisation (ISO) was studying the standardisation of paper sizes and its discussions revealed certain fundamental differences: not only were British sizes different from those used in 'metric' countries, but British practice was to use the untrimmed size as the basis from which the trimmed sizes were obtained by removing a variable amount of 'trim', whereas in many countries the trimmed size was fixed regardless of the untrimmed size from which it was obtained. Definitions between papermakers, printers and other users were eventually agreed and *trimmed size* is now defined as 'the final dimensions of a sheet of paper'.

*In quoting paper sizes, the first measurement refers to the width.

The ISO Recommendations (referred to as IPS—International Paper Sizes)* cover a system based on a series of three sizes all of the same proportion, designated A, B and C. The most widely used is the A series, ISO-A. The B series is intended for larger items such as posters and wall charts. The C series is a series of dimensions used for envelopes.

IPS sizes are based on metric dimensions and are in use in nearly thirty countries. Details of the sizes were published in British Standard Specification, BS 3176, in 1959 and the A series were adopted shortly afterwards by several large British firms and professional institutes.

During the 1960's an increasing number of British firms adopted the IPS-A series of sizes which is based on the AO sheet. AO has an area of approximately one square metre (841 mm × 1189 mm, approx. 33.1 in × 46.8 in). The A1 size equals half of A0 (that is, an A0 sheet folded in half with the two short edges brought together), similarly A2 is half of A1, A3 is half of A2 and so on. The relationship between the sizes is shown by the charts on page 65.

When it was suggested that the United Kingdom should adopt the metric system a further British Standard, BS 4000: 1968, was prepared under the authority of the Paper Industry Standards Committee. BS 4000 lists the ISO A, B and C sizes, defines the quantities for packaging (for example, 500 sheets to the ream, not 480 as formerly), recommends a g/m^2 (grammes per square metre) series of weights for paper and board, and states that as in using the Système International d'Unités (SI units) there was a preference for the millimetre rather than the centimetre as a submultiple of length, all dimensions will be quoted in millimetres. The compilers of BS 4000 recognised that there would necessarily be a period of transition from British to metric paper sizes but hoped that this would not last beyond the end of 1970.

This hope has not been realised. International paper sizes have not been universally adopted and paper and envelope manufacturers are still manufacturing Imperial sizes because of the big demand for them. In 1972 a representative of a leading paper manufacturer said that in his opinion, "Imperial sizes will be with us for a long time yet, although they will slowly be ousted by the International sizes. Meantime, we and the Stationer must make and stock both to meet all tastes."

Two further facts need to be mentioned:

1 Owing to the American influence in the computer industry and because the United States is a non-metric country, computer stationery remains non-metric. Computer print-out has been internationally adopted on a non-metric basis, viz. six lines to the inch down, and ten characters to the inch across.

2 The A sizes did not suit every office need. There were communications for which A4 was too large and A5 too small; so a new size, similar to the

**Paper at Work*, No. 4, International Paper Sizes, Spicers Ltd.

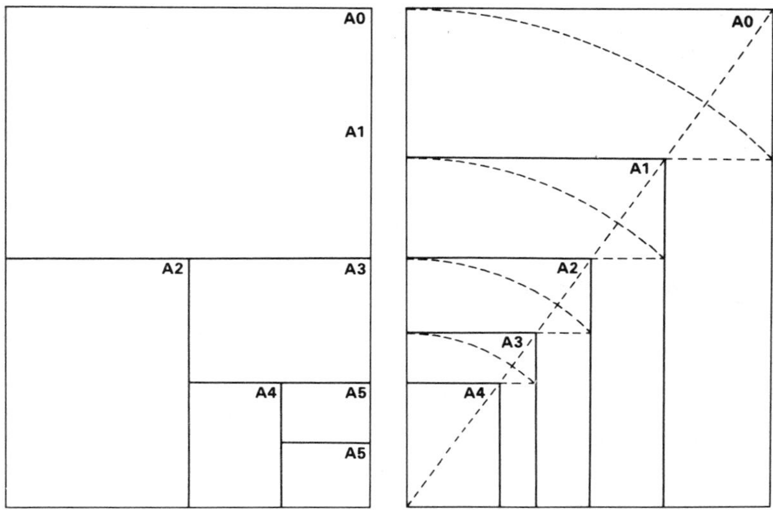

All International Paper Sizes are based on a perfectly proportioned rectangle whose longer side is the diagonal of a square, i.e. in the ratio 1 : $\sqrt{2}$ or 1 : 1.414. Following this formula, one can continue to halve the longer side or double the shorter one and still retain the same proportions. There are three ranges of sizes, prefixed A, B and C. The most widely used for general printing and stationery is the A series. The basic size A0 is approximately one square metre (841 × 1189 mm). A1 is exactly half A0 in the same proportions, A2 is half A1, and so on. (The B series is used for posters and larger pieces of print, the C range for envelopes.) The diagram on the left demonstrates the constant ratio between the long and short sides of each successive division. As the basic A0 size is approximately one square metre, the substance weight is expressed in grammes per square metre (gsm or g/m²). The diagram on the right shows how halving each size produces a division in exact proportion to the original sheet.

old sexto, has been adopted in a number of countries, including Great Britain. This is known as $\frac{2}{3}$ A4, 198 mm × 210 mm, approx. 7.79 in × 8.27 in. As you can see from the illustration on page 66, short letters can be attractively displayed on $\frac{2}{3}$ A4, which folded singly exactly fits into a DL envelope.

Whilst acceptance of the IPS-A series is increasing and accelerating, the traditional British sizes continue to be used particularly overseas in territories which were formerly under British administration. And yet another paper size—American quarto—is used in the offices of American companies and in large international organisations like UNESCO.

These anomalies are being studied by the ISO, which has established a committee* to discuss and recommend office machinery standards and the sizes of business forms, and hopes eventually to develop a modular system, that is a

* *Standards will trim a paper chase*, E. W. Pattle, Lamson Industries, 'The Times' Special Report on Decimal Currency and Metrication, 21 July 1969.

system based on a standard unit to which all paper sizes, type sizes and office machine spacings would have to accord.

The authors had hoped to omit all references to foolscap, quarto, inches and so on in this section, but in view of the present confused situation and also of the recent international adoption of ten letters to the inch in the computer industry,* all paper sizes are listed in both metric and British units.

this is ⅔A4

JEE/DLP 15 December 1973

C V Harper Esq
Office Manager
Smocks and Frocks
Stephen Street
London W1A 5EA

Dear Mr Harper

This is the new paper size I mentioned to you this morning. It has been developed to suit the needs of many offices in which it was found that for the majority of correspondence A4 was too large and A5 was too small. As you can see it is similar to sexto. Folded singly across the width, it conveniently fits into a DL envelope - which as you know falls within the POP range.

I am sure ⅔A4 will be ideal for most of your correspondence which as you mentioned consists mainly of fairly short letters to wholesalers and customers. May I give you a quotation per ream of 500 sheets, printed with your standard letterhead?

Yours sincerely

John E Edwards
Sales Manager

This is ⅔ A4, 8.27 in × 7.79 in (210 mm × 198 mm). This size has been developed in response to the demand for a size between A4 and A5. Folded singly across the width a ⅔ A4 sheet fits conveniently into a DL envelope 4.33 in × 8.66 in (110 mm × 220 mm).

* Information produced in typewritten form by computers is called **print-out**. The standardised pitch-ratio for computer print-out is ten letters to the inch.

PAPER SIZES*

Designation		Inches	Millimetres
A Series	A0	33.1×46.8	841×1189
	A1	23.3×33.1	594×841
	A2	16.5×23.3	420×594
	A3	11.7×16.5	297×420
	A4	8.3×11.7	210×297
	⅔ A4	8.3×7.8	210×198
	A5	5.8×8.3	148×210
	A6	4.1×5.8	105×148
	A7	2.9×4.1	74×105
	A8	2.1×2.9	52×74
	A9	1.5×2.1	37×52
	A10	1.0×1.5	26×37
B Series	B0	39.3×55.7	1000×1414
	B1	27.8×39.3	707×1000
	B2	19.7×27.8	500×707
	B3	13.9×19.7	353×500
	B4	9.8×13.9	250×353
	B5	6.9×9.8	176×250
	B6	4.9×6.9	125×176
	B7	3.5×4.9	88×125
	B8	2.4×3.5	62×88
	B9	1.7×2.4	44×62
	B10	1.2×1.7	31×44

Designation		Inches	Millimetres
British	Foolscap	8×13	205×330
	Quarto (4to)	8×10	205×254
	Sexto (6to)	8×6.5	205×165
	Octavo (8vo)	5×8	127×205
	Memo	8×5	205×127
	Draft	10×16	254×410
	Brief	13×16	330×410
American	Quarto	8.75×11	223×282

* When quoting paper sizes, the first measurement mentioned is the width of the paper.

BRITISH SIZES

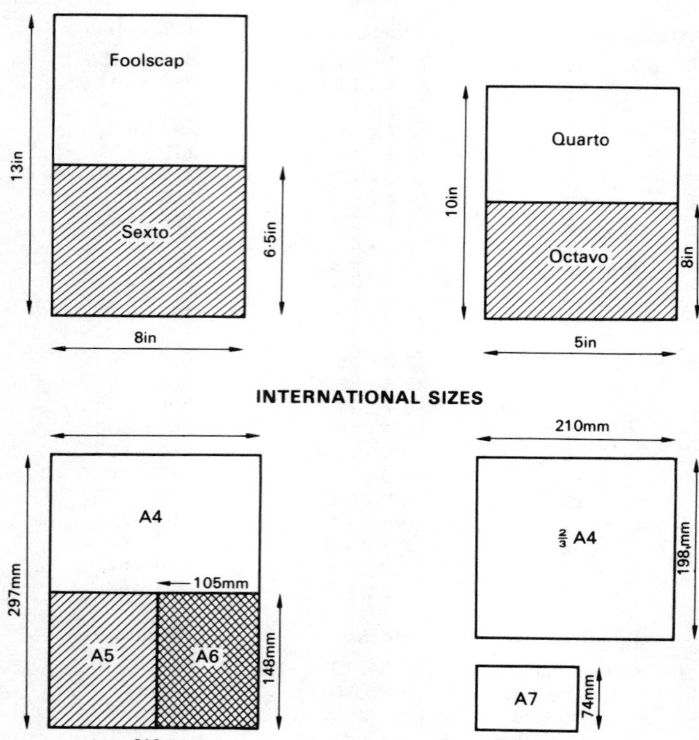

Use A4 for long or medium length letters
,, ⅔ A4 for medium length letters
,, A5 for short letters
,, A6 for postcards
,, A7 for compliment slips, business cards

LINE-SPACING This indicates the number of lines of type measured vertically, i.e. down the page. There are six line-spaces to the inch on all British typewriters, most Continental typewriters and all business machines. Some Continental machines were manufactured with a ratio of two line spaces to the centimetre, but now that six line spaces to the inch has been internationally agreed for computer print-out, all manufacturers of typewriters will now conform to this ratio.

To calculate the number of line-spaces available on any sheet of paper, simply take the length of the sheet in inches and multiply by six; round off to the nearest whole number.

Example: A4 = 11.7″ long $11.7 \times 6 = 70.2$ Answer: 70
A5 = 8.3″ long $8.3 \times 6 = 49.8$ Answer: 50

PITCH The term 'pitch' is used to indicate the size of type on a typewriter, i.e. the space occupied by a single letter, figure or character. When a typist plans a piece of columnar display such as a large complicated schedule composed mainly of columns of figures, she has to calculate the number of character spaces available across the width of the paper she is using. This is done either by multiplying the width of the paper by the pitch of the machine, or by dividing the width of the paper by the size of one character. It is obvious that the same units must be used for this calculation—you cannot multiply 210 mm (the width of A4) by 10 (the British pica size which gives ten letters to the inch) and expect to get the right answer.

Before the introduction of IPS into the United Kingdom and the decision to change to the metric system of measurements (which it is hoped will have been adopted by all industries by 1981) the two most common Imperial pitch ratios were:

1 British pica—10 letters to an inch
2 British élite—12 letters to an inch

These figures used in conjunction with quarto and foolscap paper—both 8 in wide—enabled typists to calculate simply and quickly:

Pica pitch and 8 in wide paper $10 \times 8 = 80$
Élite pitch and 8 in wide paper $12 \times 8 = 96$

During the 1960's as the A series of paper sizes was increasingly widely adopted and as attempts were made in some schools and colleges to metricate Imperial pitch ratios, a complicated situation developed which was further confused by the supply of increasing numbers of typewriters of Continental manufacture. Traditionally, metric type sizes are quoted in millimetres, the commonest being 2mm, 2.12 mm and 2.54 mm.

For a typist using a Continental 2 mm pitch machine it is a simple calculation to divide the width of A4 (210 mm) by 2; the answer—105—is the number of spaces available across an A4 sheet used in a Continental élite machine.

As we noted in the preceding section on paper sizes, whilst IPS is being used

	Spacing in mm	
Economic	1,5	The precision of HERMES typewriters and the perfection of their delicately engraved charac-ters, guarantees you a perfect impression year after year. 1 2 3 4 5 6 7 8 9 0
Script	2	*The precision of Hermes typewriters and the perfection of their deli-cately engraved characters, guarantees you 1 2 3 4 5 6 7 8 9 0*
Elite	2	The precision of HERMES typewriters and the perfection of their deli-cately engraved characters, guarantees you 1 2 3 4 5 6 7 8 9 0
Elite	2,12	The precision of HERMES typewriters and the perfection of their delicately engraved characters, guarantees 1 2 3 4 5 6 7 8 9 0
Hermes Special	2,5	The precision of HERMES typewriters and the perfection of their delicately engraved 1 2 3 4 5 6 7 8 9 0
Pica	2,5	The precision of HERMES typewriters and the perfection of their delicately engraved 1 2 3 4 5 6 7 8 9 0

These type sizes are quoted in millimetres. They show some of the styles available on Hermes typewriters which are manufactured in Switzerland.

by more and more businesses in the United Kingdom, British quarto and foolscap are still being manufactured and used in many offices; and ten spaces to the inch has been internationally adopted as the standard pitch for computer print-out. These two facts, added to the implications of Britain's entry into the European Economic Community, have caused some interesting developments:

1 Typewriters of European manufacture will in future be built with either a 2.12 mm or 2.54 type size. As you can see from the examples above, 2.12 mm looks the same as élite—12 letters to the inch—and 2.54 mm looks the same as pica—10 letters to the inch. The larger size will enable the machines to be used for computer print-out in connection with optical character (OCR) equipment.*

2 An increased range of type sizes (10, 11, 12 and 16 pitch) is available on machines marketed by British companies but "The use of 6 lines to the inch for vertical spacing and 10 and 12 characters to the inch horizontally (see BS 2481), has an almost world-wide acceptance and certainly is predominant both for office machines and computer printers, and present

> **Distinctive appearance without loss of versatility is the result Imperial has aimed to achieve with this 11 pitch type face called Oxford.**
>
> abcdefghijklmnopqrstuvwxyz ABCDEFGHIJKLMNOPQRSTUVWXYZ
> 1234567890-$\frac{3}{4}\frac{2}{3}\frac{3}{8}$=$\frac{7}{8}$;$\frac{1}{2}$., *"/@£?&'()_$\frac{1}{4}\frac{1}{3}\frac{1}{8}$+$\frac{5}{8}$:%.,

An 11 pitch type face available on Imperial typewriters.

* A 2.6 mm character pitch machine has been introduced in Germany. It is intended to be the nearest to 2.54 mm (10 to 1 in) pitch. There are typewriters imported from West Germany with this pitch in use in the United Kingdom. However, because of the requirements of OCR, most standard typewriters will be 2.54 mm (10 to 1 in) pitch with portable typewriters at 2.6 mm. The differences are small but could be meaningful over the width of a page.

international standardisation discussions recognise this established situation."*

It is hoped that the following recommendations will enable typewriting calculations to be made as quickly as possible using any paper size in any machine:

1 Using British pitch machines, multiply the decimalised inch width of the page by the inch-based pitch ratio.
Example A4 paper in an 11-pitch machine
Paper width: 8.3 in
$8.3 \times 11 = 91.3$ Answer: 91 spaces

2 Using Continental pitch machines with IPS paper, divide the width of the paper by the size of the type.
Example A4 paper in a 2.5 mm pitch machine
Paper width 210 mm
$210 + 2.5 = 80.4$ Answer: 80 spaces

3 Using Continental pitch machines with British paper, take the metric width of the paper and multiply by one of the following:
Continental pica 3.8 characters per centimetre
,, élite 4.5 ,, ,, ,, *or*
,, ,, 5.0 ,, ,, ,,
Example Quarto paper in a Continental pica machine
Paper width 205 mm (20.5 cm)
$20.5 \times 3.8 = 77.9$ Answer: 78 spaces

TYPE FACE The terms 'type face' or 'fount' are used to indicate the style of type. Many different type faces are available and the illustrations on pages 70 and 72 give some idea of the wide variety offered by different typewriter manufacturers. If you have the opportunity to choose your own machine, remember that 'shaded' type faces are not suitable for multi-copy work or for cutting stencils.

With standard type faces each letter occupies the same amount of space; for example, the letter 'i' occupies the same amount of space as the letter 'w' although the actual width of the letters is quite different. Machines are available with proportionally spaced type; on these machines the space occupied by each letter varies according to the size. *Proportional* spacing is often used in conjunction with a justified right-hand margin, that is a margin which is as even as the left-hand one. You will find more about proportional spacing and margin justification on pages 215 to 217 in Chapter 5, Reprography.

* *Metrication in Business Equipment.* A **beta** 'Guide to Users' publication. Pub. Business Equipment Trade Association.

Light Italic Type is a 'fine line' style that may be used alone or in combination with Pica or Elite typestyles to add impact and emphasis to many typing jobs.

Prestige Elite Type is a weighted type similar to the Prestige Elite typestyles offered with the IBM Standard D Typewriter. It meets a wide range of typing applications.

Courier Type, like Advocate type, is a square-serif design in the Pica family of typestyles. The open-spaced characters make it highly legible.

Delegate Type is a weighted type that conveys the feeling of printed material. It is recommended for text copy and similar typing jobs.

Bookface is a sharp, clean style which commands the attention of the reader. Eminently suitable for executive correspondence, it has a legibility which is unchallenged.

Windsor is specifically designed for the businessman who recognizes that his letters are personal representatives and must present the best possible appearance.

The 2 type styles below are used in connection with optical character recognition equipment.

Ocra	2.5	THE PRECISION OF HERMES TYPEWRITERS AND THE PERFECTION OF THEIR DELICATELY ENGRAVED 1 2 3 4 5 6 7 8 9 0
Ocrb	2,5	The precision of HERMES typewriters and the perfection of their delicately engraved 1 2 3 4 5 6 7 8 9 0

Some examples of type faces.

Paper weights and finishes The manufacture and classification of paper and the history of papermaking are both fascinating subjects; unfortunately they are outside the scope of our present studies but they could well form the topic for class or group research or for a secretarial project.

An important date in the history of papermaking in England is 1685 when the Edict of Nantes was revoked and non-Catholics were persecuted and expelled from France. Many of the master papermakers were Protestants or Huguenots; they fled to Holland and England. Henry de Portal, a Huguenot refugee, founded the Laverstoke Mill in 1718; he was granted a monopoly of making Bank of England notes in 1725 and banknote paper has been made at Laverstoke Mill ever since.

The first paper was made from rags and although methods for making paper from wood-pulp, bagasse,* esparto grass, straw, bamboo and other fibres were developed during the nineteenth century, the best quality writing papers today are made from one hundred per cent rag.

A sheet of paper can be thought of as a network of minute interwoven fibres bonded together to give the sheet a degree of strength. If a piece of normal writing paper is torn, the fibrous content can be seen at the torn edges.

In addition to being manufactured in a variety of sizes, colours, weights and finishes, paper may also be watermarked. Nowadays, paper is watermarked for

* Bagasse is the residue from sugar-cane and sugar-beet after the juice has been extracted.

In addition to its importance in the business world, paper plays a vital role in all aspects of life—books, newspapers and periodicals, examination papers and certificates, legal documents, birth and marriage certificates, to name just a few examples. In the basic process of making paper, fibres of wood, rag or grasses are pulped with water and then carried onto a moving wire belt. Most of the water is then drained from the belt and wet paper is formed. This wet paper is consolidated by large press rolls and the paper is finally dried by heated cylinders. This picture shows a computer controlled paper-making machine at Chartham Mill in Kent, England. Paper has been made at Chartham Mill since about 1730. In 1930 the mill was bought by Wiggins Teape Ltd.

security reasons, or for prestige purposes (i.e. company letterheadings, personal stationery), or as an advertisement, or to identify the quality or brand; originally, however, the watermark was the distinguishing mark of the papermaker. Each maker had moulds of a particular size and so watermarks gradually became associated with particular paper sizes. This explains the reason for the names of some British paper sizes such as Elephant (28 in by 23 in) and Grand Eagle (42 in by 28 in). Foolscap derived its name from a watermark of a jester with cap and bells.

Manufacturers classify paper under several headings: writing papers, printing papers, blotting papers, wrapping papers, speciality papers (for example, tracing paper, photocopy paper, carbon paper, carbonless paper, crepe paper), and boards. The kinds of paper in which we are interested are, of course, writing paper (including typewriting and duplicating papers), carbon paper (see pp. 55–57), and carbonless paper (see pp. 74–77).

Typewriting paper is divided into three grades (a) Bond, (b) Bank and (c) Airmail. These terms refer to the various substances or grammages that typewriting paper is available in; they do not indicate the material from which the paper is made. For example, bond paper may be made from 100 per cent rag, or from part rag or from all chemical wood.

In the Imperial system paper weights used to be quoted in pounds; for example, if a paper was quoted as "Large Post 18 lb" it meant that a ream* of paper of Large Post size ($16\frac{1}{2}$ in by 21 in) weighed 18 lbs. Now that the metric system has been adopted by the paper industry paper substances are quoted in grammes per square metre (g/m²); thus a paper substance quoted as 71 g/m² means that a square metre of the paper weighs 71 grammes. The International Organisation for Standardisation has issued ISO Recommendation R58, "Substances of Paper", which recommends a preferred series of basic weights for paper and board.

The minimum weight for *bond* paper, which is normally used for letterheads and top copies is generally accepted as 61 g/m². A good quality bond paper suitable for prestige stationery weighs 100 g/m².

Bank paper suitable for carbon copies and drafts weighs between 45 g/m² and 61 g/m².

Airmail weight is generally accepted as 28 g/m² or 30 g/m². *Onion skin* is a special type of airmail paper which has been manufactured with a cockled surface. It is particularly easy to erase neatly on onion skin paper.

Duplicating paper for use with ink duplicators must be fairly absorbent so that the ink dries quickly and does not offset on to the following sheet. Duplicating paper might have a substance as low as 56 g/m². The average accepted duplicating paper giving the best results is 71 g/m².

Uncoated paper can be manufactured in a variety of ways which produce different surfaces, such as *laid* or *wove*. These terms originated during the development of papermaking. The sieve of the papermaker's mould was originally formed by reeds; in the first half of the eighteenth century the reeds were replaced by wires which were sewn on to the supporting framework and produced what is now called a *laid* effect. The printing methods in use at that time could not produce a sharp image on the uneven *laid* surface; but about 1750 a Birmingham printer, named Baskerville, invented a woven wire sieve which solved this problem—hence the origin of the term *wove*.

Paper is also available with various finishes, such as onion skin finish and linen finish, which are applied when the paper has left the papermaking machine.

A paper with a matt surface is recommended for most typewriting work; erasing spoils the surface of glossy paper and it is almost impossible to avoid erasures being detected if the typist has to work with a shiny-surfaced or low quality thin paper.

Carbon-free copying paper Carbon-free or carbonless copying paper† enables anything written or typed on the top copy to be transferred to the sheet

* A ream of paper was formerly 480, 500 or 516 sheets; it is now generally accepted as 500 sheets.
† Formerly referred to as NCR paper, now marketed under the trade name IDEM by Wiggins Teape Limited.

THE FUNCTION OF PAPER AT DIFFERENT LEVELS The three companies we have invented represent an international, a national and a local organisation. The international company is a manufacturing group while the other two both offer a service. They chose three papers made by Wiggins Teape, all of which have particular advantages at different levels within one or other of the three firms.

The Barbican Group of companies is a large organisation. They operate a headquarters building in London run on a centralised system which contains servicing and marketing departments for the Group.

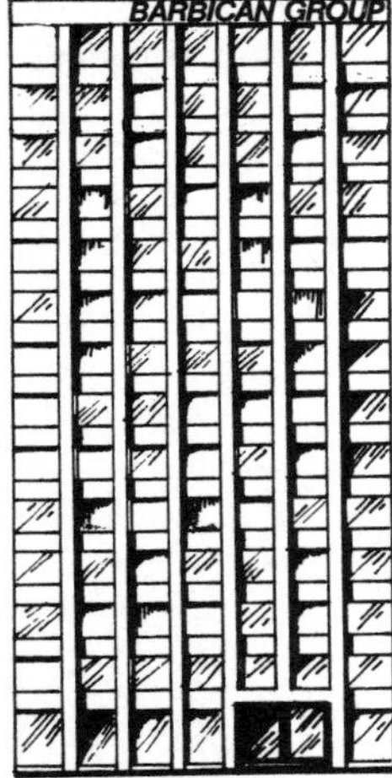

They chose to use all three papers—for letterhead and memorandums—giving an identity to the different levels of authority. The top quality paper—Optimum 100% Rag—is made from long rag fibres and is the finest writing paper. It will resist wear and show off the letterhead to full effect.

The architects work in a Georgian house. Four partners, a few associates, a typist or two, and several draughtsmen. The sort of firm where white paint never has finger marks and nobody kicks the furniture.

This firm chose Conqueror Grey Laid—by using a colour the firm can have an even more individual and complete identity. Conqueror has a lower rag content and is less expensive. It also has, especially in the blue-white shade, an appearance that appeals to modern management.

Home Removals are a smaller more down-to-earth company. They have branches in the larger cities and as one might expect, are mainly engaged in moving people's furniture. They have a lot of direct contact with the general public.

For smaller companies one paper can often cover every use. This means one watermark for every form and letterhead which helps to give a firm a well organised and complete identity.
They chose Abermill Bond, which is a reasonable letterhead and is economical on large runs. One major advantage is the large selection of tints for prestige forms and colour-coded memorandums.

or sheets underneath without the interleaving of carbon paper. Carbonless paper works by being coated either on the front side or on the back or on both sides with special chemical coatings which cannot be seen by the naked eye.

There are two types of coating. CB (Coated Back) is the coating on the back of the sheet; it is an emulsion composed of millions of tiny capsules containing two colourless dyes. CF (Coated Front) is the coating on the front of the sheet underneath the CB sheet; the front coating contains a clay material. When pressure is applied by means of writing or typing on the top sheet, the capsules at the point of impact burst and the dyes penetrate the clay surface below. A chemical reaction takes place and an immediate blue copy is formed by the first of the two dyes. A combination of light and air causes the second dye to appear later. The second dye is blue-green and is a permanent image. As the image is actually *in* the sheet, it cannot be altered without detection as the erased area is always noticeable. When erasures are necessary a medium-hard rubber should be used, although the manufacturers of carbon-free copying paper consider it better to cross out the error and put the correction alongside.

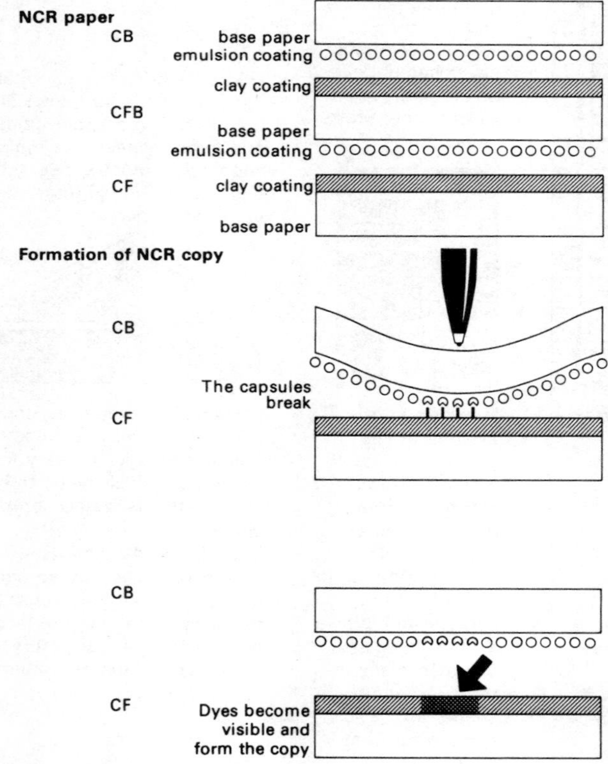

How carbon-free copying paper works.

There are three kinds of carbon-free copying paper:

CB (Coated Back)	Top or original copy
CFB (Coated Front and Back)	The middle sheet or intermediate sheets
CF (Coated Front)	The bottom or last sheet

A two-part set will consist of a CB sheet and a CF sheet. Multi-part sets consist of a CB sheet, a number of CFB sheets and a CF sheet.

Carbon-free copying paper is manufactured in a wide range of colours and substances; it can be printed by all conventional printing methods and is, of course, suitable for the production of pre-collated document sets such as are used in purchasing, invoicing and accounting procedures. As many as nine copies can be taken (depending on the thickness of the paper and the method by which pressure is applied).

The copies may fade slightly in extremely humid conditions but it is claimed that under good filing conditions the copy life of the paper is indefinite. Caution is advised when using IDEM paper in systems where a copy is designed to be photocopied, as its blue-green image may not at present give perfect copies on all photocopying systems.

Method of Processing	with use of the Middle Sheet	
	CFB 64	CFB 53
Handwriting		
Felt tip pen	0	0
Pencil	1 + 2	1 + 3
Ball-point pen	1 + 3	1 + 4
Manual typewriter	1 + 5	1 + 7
Electric typewriter	1 + 7	1 + 9
TELEPRINTER	1 + 4	
OUTPUT PRINTER (depending on model and setting)	1 + 3	1 + 5

Number of copies obtainable with IDEM Paper.

Envelopes Envelopes are manufactured in a variety of styles, shapes and sizes. There is also a wide choice of quality (weight), cutting and sealing.

STYLES AND SIZES Envelopes are divided into two main styles:

1. *Banker* envelopes have the opening on the longer side:

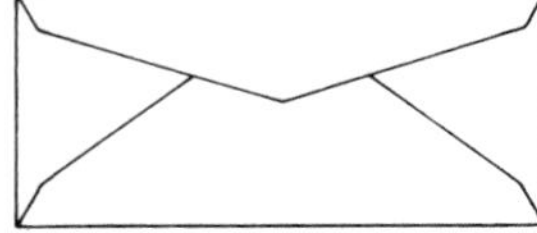

2. *Pocket* envelopes have the opening on the shorter side:

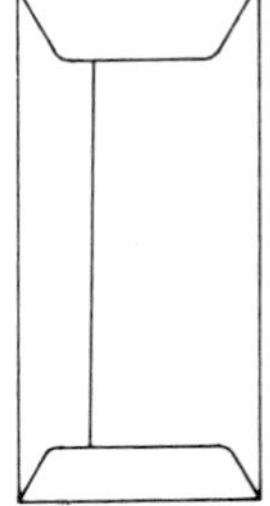

Envelope measurements are quoted to indicate the length and breadth in relation to the opening. The first measurement is that which is at right angles to the opening; in other words, the last measurement indicates the side which opens. Thus a 9 in by 4 in envelope would be a pocket envelope having the opening on the shorter, the 4 in, side.

There is a British Standard specification covering envelope terms and sizes* which suggests that with increasing emphasis on the standardisation of national specifications to conform with international recommendations, traditional British sizes will eventually be superseded by the sizes recommended by the

Envelope size symbol	Size in	Size mm	Envelope size symbol	Size in	Size mm
C3	$12\frac{3}{4} \times 18$	324 × 458	**B6**	$4\frac{7}{8} \times 7$	125 × 176
B4	$9\frac{7}{8} \times 13\frac{7}{8}$	250 × 353	**C6**	$4\frac{1}{2} \times 6\frac{3}{8}$	114 × 162
C4	$9 \times 12\frac{5}{8}$	229 × 324	**C5/6 (DL)**	$4\frac{1}{4} \times 8\frac{5}{8}$	110 × 220
B5	$7 \times 9\frac{7}{8}$	176 × 250	**C7/6**	$3\frac{1}{4} \times 6\frac{3}{8}$	81 × 162
C5	$6\frac{3}{8} \times 9$	162 × 229	**C7**	$3\frac{1}{4} \times 4\frac{1}{2}$	81 × 114
B6/C4	$4\frac{7}{8} \times 12\frac{5}{8}$	125 × 324			

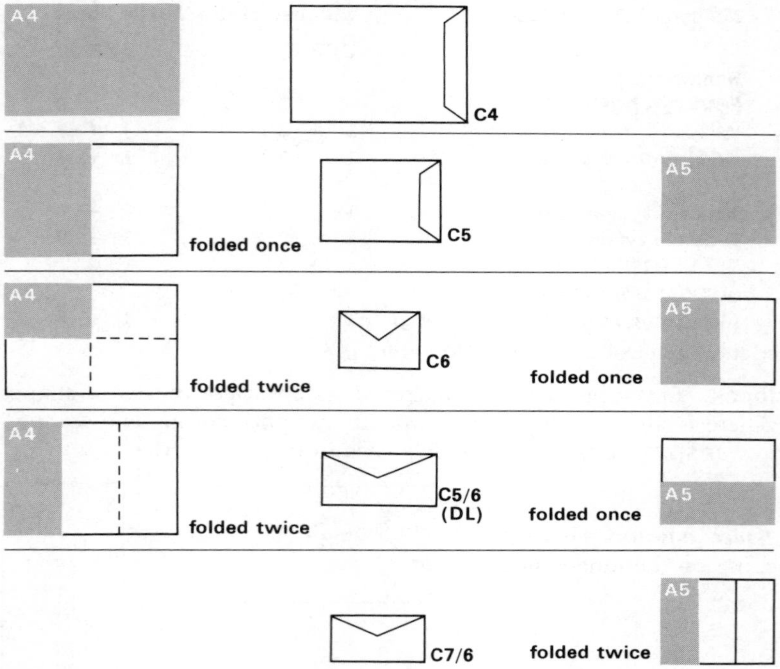

*British Standard 4264: 1967. Specification for Envelopes for Commercial Official and Professional use (terms and sizes).

International Organisation for Standardisation. As we noted when discussing paper sizes, ISO size C series is recommended for envelopes.

As you can see from the illustration opposite, an A4 sheet—

slides flat into a C4 envelope without folding
fits into a C5 envelope folded once
fits into a C6 envelope folded twice

One of the most popular envelope sizes is the C5/6 (DL)—usually designated DL—which will take an A4 sheet folded twice, and a $\frac{2}{3}$ A4 sheet or an A5 sheet folded once.

'Red Box' envelopes—sizes and styles.*

Pocket envelope sizes

No.	mm	inches	
1.	406 × 305 mm	16 × 12	
2.	381 × 254 mm	15 × 10	
3.	356 × 229 mm	14 × 9	
4.	330 × 279 mm	13 × 11	
5.	324 × 229 mm	$12\frac{3}{4}$ × 9	C.4
6.	305 × 254 mm	12 × 10	
7.	305 × 229 mm	12 × 9	
8.	292 × 235 mm	$11\frac{1}{2}$ × $9\frac{1}{4}$	
9.	270 × 216 mm	$10\frac{5}{8}$ × $8\frac{1}{2}$	
10.	267 × 203 mm	$10\frac{1}{2}$ × 8	
11.	254 × 178 mm	10 × 7	
12.	241 × 165 mm	$9\frac{1}{2}$ × $6\frac{1}{2}$	
13.	229 × 162 mm	9 × $6\frac{3}{8}$	C.5
14.	229 × 152 mm	9 × 6	
15.	216 × 140 mm	$8\frac{1}{2}$ × $5\frac{1}{2}$	
16.	194 × 127 mm	$7\frac{5}{8}$ × 5	
17.	178 × 114 mm	7 × $4\frac{1}{2}$	
18.	162 × 114 mm	$6\frac{3}{8}$ × $4\frac{1}{2}$	C.6
19.	381 × 152 mm	15 × 6	
20.	356 × 133 mm	14 × $5\frac{1}{4}$	
21.	305 × 127 mm	12 × 5	
22.	279 × 127 mm	11 × 5	
23.	235 × 121 mm	$9\frac{1}{4}$ × $4\frac{3}{4}$	
24.	267 × 114 mm	$10\frac{1}{2}$ × $4\frac{1}{2}$	
25.	220 × 110 mm	$8\frac{5}{8}$ × $4\frac{1}{4}$	D.L.
26.	229 × 102 mm	9 × 4	

Post Office Preferred

MAXIMUM POP SIZE
235 × 121 mm $9\frac{1}{4}$ × $4\frac{3}{4}$

Banker envelope sizes

No.	mm	inches	
1.	162 × 229 mm	$6\frac{3}{8}$ × 9	C.5
2.	121 × 171 mm	$4\frac{3}{4}$ × $6\frac{3}{4}$	
3.	121 × 197 mm	$4\frac{3}{4}$ × $7\frac{3}{4}$	
4.	121 × 210 mm	$4\frac{3}{4}$ × $8\frac{1}{4}$	
5.	121 × 235 mm	$4\frac{3}{4}$ × $9\frac{1}{4}$	
6.	114 × 162 mm	$4\frac{1}{2}$ × $6\frac{3}{8}$	C.6
7.	108 × 156 mm	$4\frac{1}{4}$ × $6\frac{1}{8}$	
8.	110 × 220 mm	$4\frac{1}{4}$ × $8\frac{5}{8}$	D.L.
9.	105 × 241 mm	$4\frac{1}{8}$ × $9\frac{1}{2}$	
10.	102 × 152 mm	4 × 6	
11.	102 × 229 mm	4 × 9	
12.	102 × 235 mm	4 × $9\frac{1}{4}$	
13.	95 × 146 mm	$3\frac{3}{4}$ × $5\frac{3}{4}$	
14.	95 × 165 mm	$3\frac{3}{4}$ × $6\frac{1}{2}$	
15.	92 × 149 mm	$3\frac{5}{8}$ × $5\frac{7}{8}$	
16.	92 × 216 mm	$3\frac{5}{8}$ × $8\frac{1}{2}$	
17.	89 × 140 mm	$3\frac{1}{2}$ × $5\frac{1}{2}$	
18.	89 × 152 mm	$3\frac{1}{2}$ × 6	
19.	89 × 165 mm	$3\frac{1}{2}$ × $6\frac{1}{2}$	C.7/6
20.	70 × 108 mm	$2\frac{3}{4}$ × $4\frac{1}{4}$	
21.	64 × 98 mm	$2\frac{1}{2}$ × $3\frac{7}{8}$	

Post Office Preferred

MAXIMUM POP SIZE
121 × 235 mm $4\frac{3}{4}$ × $9\frac{1}{4}$

*'Red Box' envelopes are manufactured by John Dickinson & Co, Ltd.

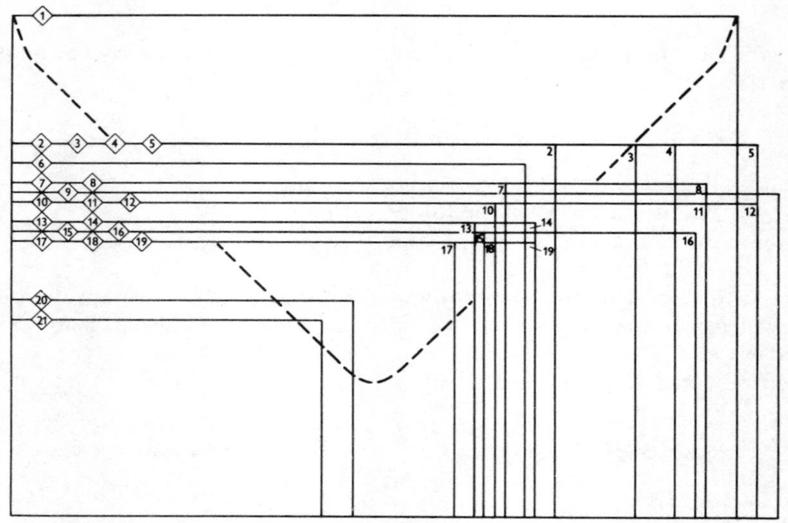

SHAPES, CUTTINGS AND GUMMINGS Envelopes may be bought in various shapes and cuts. Here are some examples:

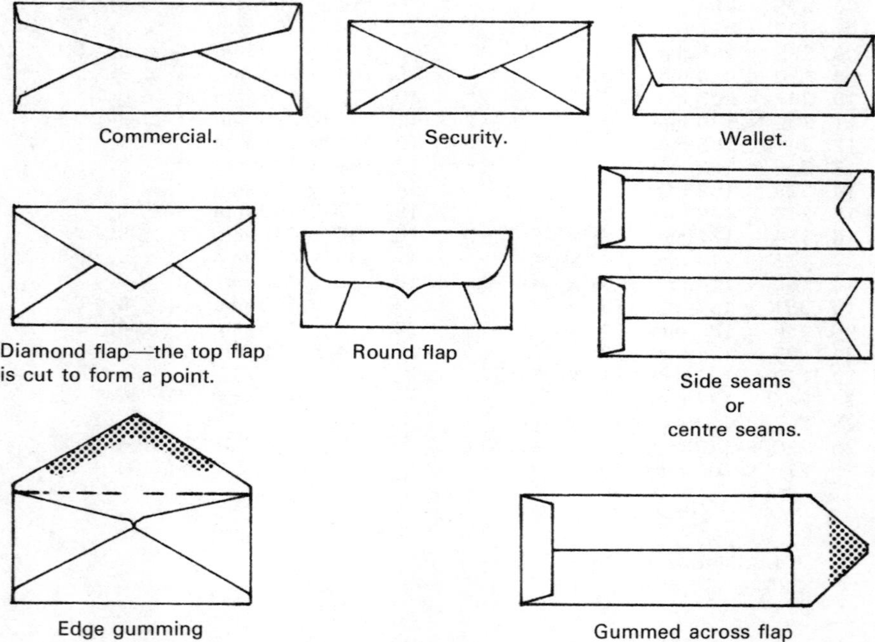

Commercial.

Security.

Wallet.

Diamond flap—the top flap is cut to form a point.

Round flap

Side seams or centre seams.

Edge gumming

Gummed across flap

These diagrams show some of the envelope sealing and fastening styles manufactured by Spicers Ltd.

Latex sealed. The two latex-treated surfaces on the flap and body of the envelope seal immediately they are pressed together. The method has been applied to both banker and pocket envelopes and is hygienic, quick and secure.

WINDOW, APERTURE AND ANTI-TRAP ENVELOPES.

Window envelopes have window panels made of some transparent material. *Aperture* envelopes have cut-out panels through which the address written on the letter can be read. The panels are not covered with any protecting material. *Anti-trap* envelopes are designed to prevent smaller items being entrapped, and to permit the contents to be examined.

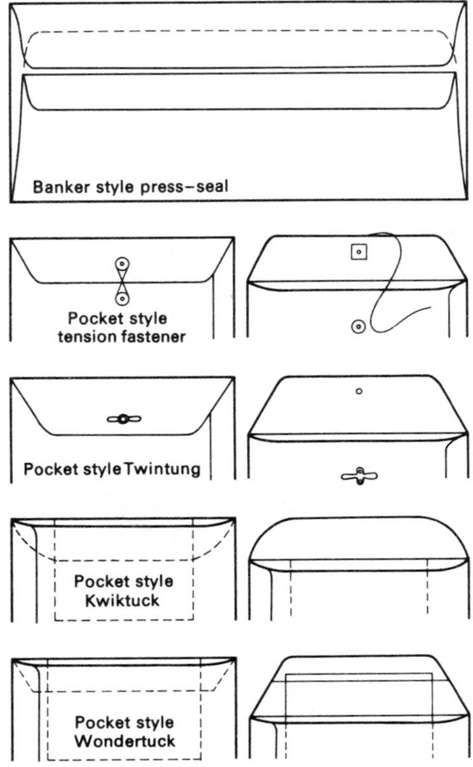

Examples of Anti-trap envelopes.

QUALITY As airmail postage rates are based on weight, airmail envelopes are made of very thin strong paper. Sometimes the paper has a faint pattern printed on the inside to ensure that the envelope is completely opaque. Most airmail envelopes have a red and blue border on both sides and are printed with the words BY AIR MAIL set in a solid blue rectangle in the top left-hand corner.

Business firms usually have envelopes of the same quality paper as their noteheads; they are frequently printed with the name of the firm either in the top left-hand corner or on the reverse side.

Manilla (buff-coloured) envelopes are cheaper than envelopes made from high-quality bond and cartridge papers. Manilla envelopes are frequently used for bills and general commercial correspondence.

Post Office Preferred (POP) Range. In March 1966 the Post Office announced a Post Office Preferred (POP) range of envelope sizes and asked the public to post their mail, whenever possible, in envelopes conforming to the Preferred range. At some future date inland mail weighing up to 4 oz posted in envelopes outside the POP range of sizes will be liable to an additional charge. POP regulations will not apply to Overseas Post. To fall within the range envelopes should be:

a at least $3\frac{1}{2}$ in $\times$ $5\frac{1}{2}$ in (90 mm $\times$ 140 mm) and not larger than $4\frac{3}{4}$ in $\times$ $9\frac{1}{4}$ in (120 mm $\times$ 235 mm)
b oblong in shape, with the longer side at least 1.414 times the shorter side
c made from paper weighing at least 63 grammes per square metre

The two most popular ISO size envelopes, DL and C6, are within the POP range. Packets and boxes of envelopes which fit in with the POP range are usually marked with a special Post Office Preferred symbol.

All *Aperture* envelopes, irrespective of their size and shape, will be classed as outside the POP range.

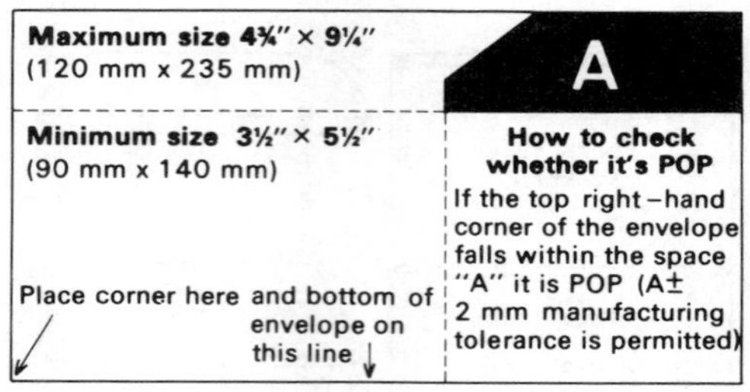

How to check whether it's POP.

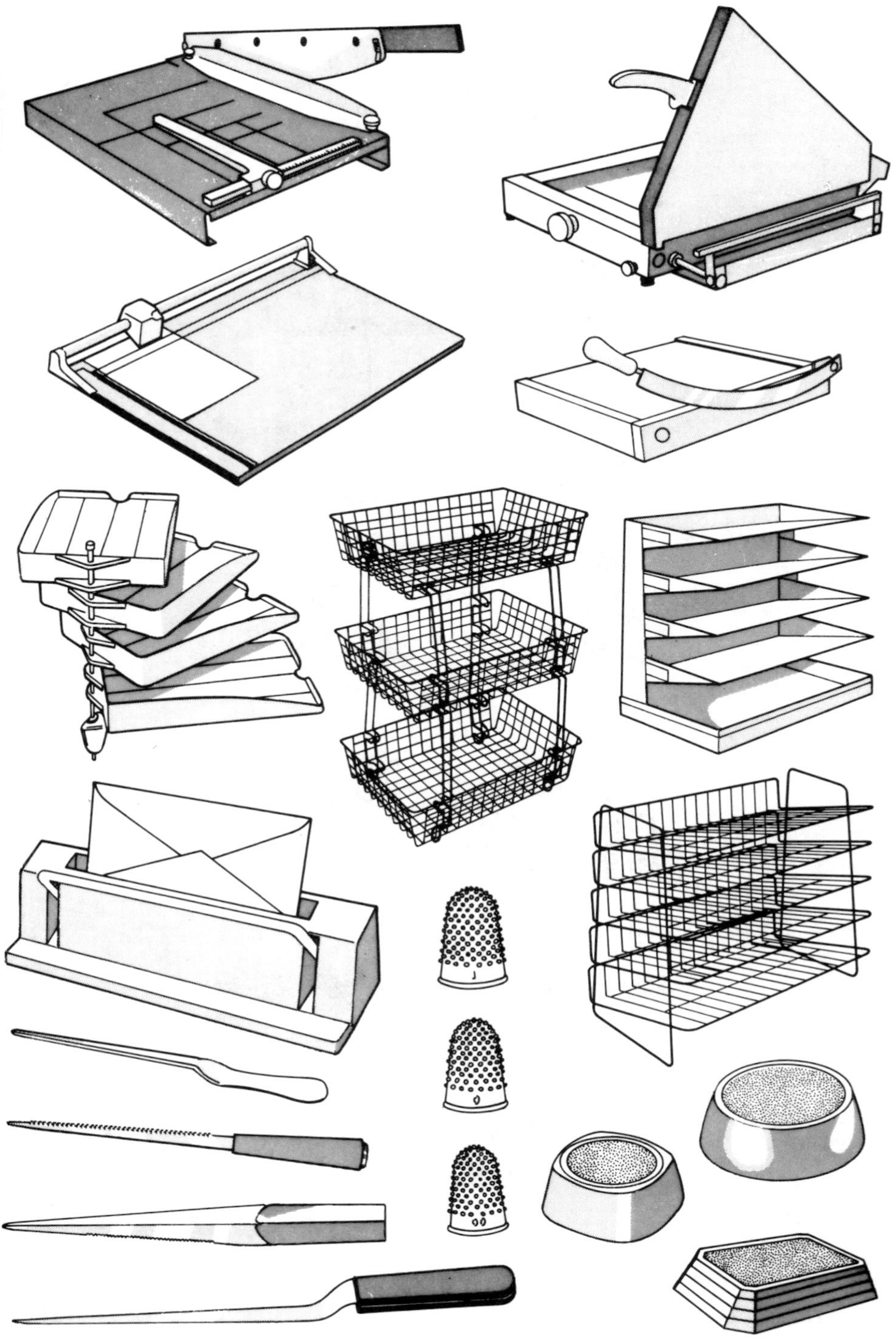

1. Items used for handling papers.

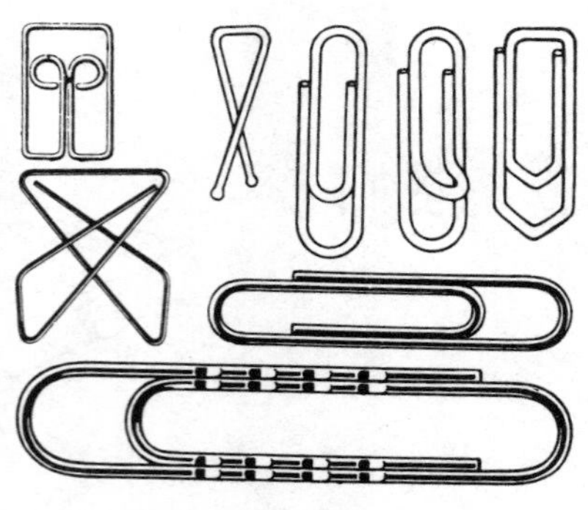

A selection of paper clips, letter clips and paper fasteners.

2. Fastening devices such as paper clips.

Office sundries There are a large number of small items used in offices, such as paper clips, tags and folders, which are usually termed *Office sundries.* They can be grouped in three sections:

1 Items used for handling papers, such as rubber finger stalls, guillotines, trays.
2 Fastening devices such as paper clips and staplers.
3 Items used in connection with the securing of papers, such as punches, rings and files.

There are many different kinds of machines used to staple sheets together. Some are very small (pocket or miniature staplers), others are more suited for thicker work ('heavy duty' and 'long-arm' staplers). Nearly all staplers work on the same principle and give two alternative fastenings:

1. PERMANENT FASTENING In this position the prongs of the staples are pinched inwards.
2. TEMPORARY FASTENING In this position the prongs are pressed outwards to produce a 'pin' which can be easily removed.

Temporary and permanent fastening.

The main difference between the various types of staplers is in the loading of the strips of staples. There are three main types: rear loading, top loading and front loading.

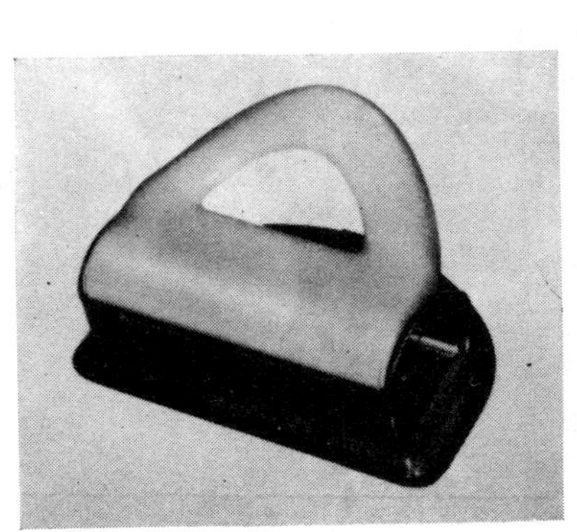

Punches cut holes a certain distance apart so that the punched sheets fit on to the prongs or rings of files and binders. The two commonest gauges are 70 mm ($2\frac{3}{4}$ in) and 80 mm ($3\frac{1}{8}$ in). The longer gauge is the more popular and is known as 'continental' gauge. Most punches are adjustable to both gauges; some punches cut holes in both positions at once so that the papers will fit on to any standard file.

There is a small gadget called a **staple remover** which takes staples out of papers without tearing them.

Reinforcing punch. There is a tendency for thin papers to become torn at the punch holes; other papers become worn if the files are allowed to become bulky or are handled very frequently. A reinforcing punch, as the name implies, reinforces the punch holes as they are cut, by automatically edging the holes with self-adhesive paper or plastic.

Reinforcement washers. Punched holes that have become worn can be strengthened or repaired by sticking on reinforcement washers.

Papers may be held together by **loose leaf rings** or **Treasury tags** (see Ch. 7).

Some types of files and folders

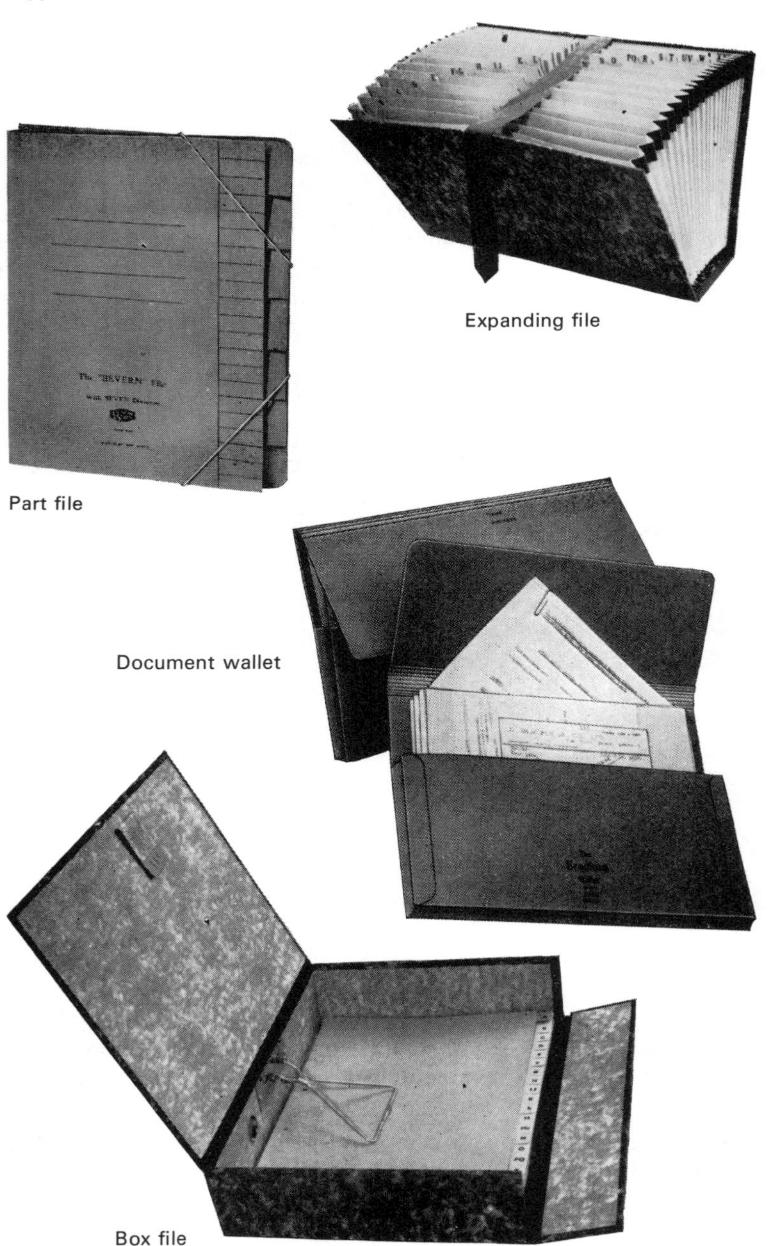

Expanding file

Part file

Document wallet

Box file

Style and display "The function of typed documents is not simply to impress people by their look; it is to convey information in the clearest and most readable form. The pursuit of style to the neglect of clearness and readability would defeat the document's purpose. Fortunately, however, no choice is called for. True style is the result, not the rival of clearness and legibility. At least where letters and reports are concerned, the document arranged for easy reading is always the best-looking, and the best-looking always the easiest to read."*

Before starting to type a document the typist must decide on the display style most likely to present the information in the clearest and most readable form. She should ask herself such questions as: Why has this document to be typed? Who is going to read it? How is it going to be used? The answers to these questions will help her to select an attractive, readable and functional style.

In recent years there has been a trend away from the conventional style of centring headings and indenting paragraphs. The reason for this is not only

NATIONAL INSTITUTE OF PUBLIC ADMINISTRATION, LODIKA

Department of Education
Secretarial Training Unit

PROPOSALS FOR THE ESTABLISHMENT OF A SECRETARIAL TRAINING CENTRE

Prepared by
Rima Munyari
Training Adviser
Nordic Foundation
Lodika, Kaganzia
September 1972

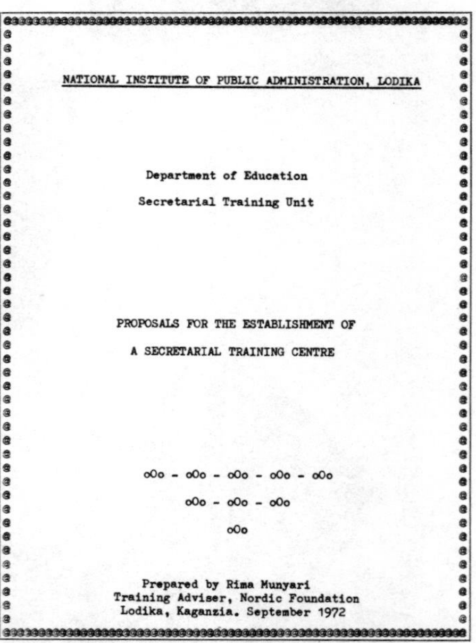

NATIONAL INSTITUTE OF PUBLIC ADMINISTRATION, LODIKA

Department of Education

Secretarial Training Unit

PROPOSALS FOR THE ESTABLISHMENT OF

A SECRETARIAL TRAINING CENTRE

oOo - oOo - oOo - oOo - oOo

oOo - oOo - oOo

oOo

Prepared by Rima Munyari
Training Adviser, Nordic Foundation
Lodika, Kaganzia. September 1972

Display styles Here are two versions of the title page of a report. Which looks the most up-to-date? Displayed work used to be decorated by ornamental borders and 'tail pieces' made by a special arrangement of typewritten characters and letters; modern design artists do not consider this to be in good taste. The example on the left is on the lines of the present trend in printed layout; such work is produced more quickly—the tedious stroke-counting or backspacing used for central designs is no longer needed.

**Paper at work, Number 3—Typing in style*. A series of Spicers Guides.

the current fashion in print lay-out but also the introduction of electric typewriters into many offices. With their speedy carriage return and repeating underscore key, electric machines encourage the typist to adopt display styles based on the "left design axis", i.e. with all lines starting at the left-hand margin. This achieves a crisp modern style and work is produced more quickly without the time-consuming stroke-counting or back-spacing used for centred designs.

Generally speaking, display fashions in typewriting follow display fashions in print. On page 88 you will see two versions of the title page of a report set out on the typewriter. One is centred in the conventional style; the other tries to give the same impression as a modern printed page.

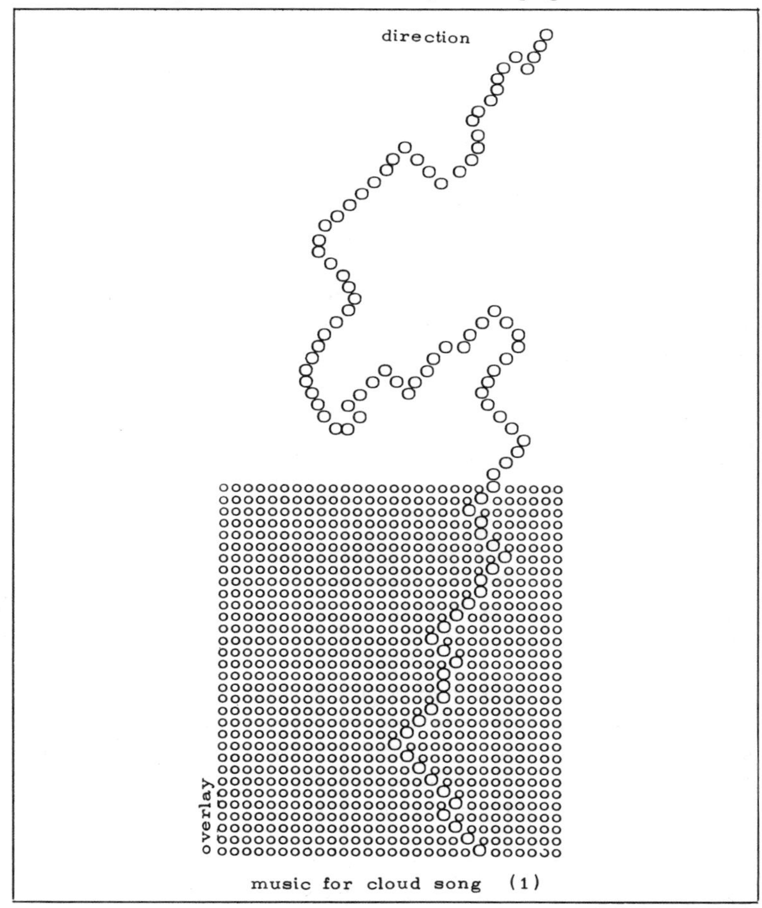

A typewriter poem by Peter Finch shows some work produced on the typewriter within the general medium of concrete poetry.

In this day of office-printing processes, the typist is very often the first person to "lay-out" a document subsequently to be printed and for this reason typists should study examples of modern lay-out with a critical eye. The present-day typist also needs a sound knowledge of the materials needed for the production, preparation and correction of master sheets for offset and photographic reproduction processes; she must also keep up-to-date with processes such as "cold type" composing. These processes are discussed more fully in *Chapter 4, Reprography* but they stand to be mentioned here as part of a modern typist's work, demanding creative ability as well as technical skill.

LETTERS We started this 'Typewriting' section by stressing the important contribution the appearance of a letter makes to the image of the office from which it originates. Many firms and large organisations like to adopt standard layouts for all correspondence and issue a "Typists' Handbook" or "Manual for Typists" which shows exactly how letters are to be displayed, how enclosures are to be indicated, how carbon copies are to be annotated, and so on. When a newcomer joins the organisation she is given a copy of the handbook and shown how her work is to be laid out. This is called the *Rule of the House* and she must follow it.

Some examples of letter layouts are illustrated on pages 98 and 99 and you will see that the lay-out no. 6 on page 99 is suggested as the one which will probably become the most commonly seen in coming years. There are no inflexible rules governing letter display but the style chosen should, of course, suit the printed letterhead.

PARTS OF THE BUSINESS LETTER It is usual to study letter lay-out by discussing the various parts of a letter each of which performs a definite function. For example, the printed heading serves to identify the company transmitting the letter and the subject line is a form of title indicating the content of the letter.

The *letterhead* or *printed heading* gives the name and address of the company or organisation, the telephone number, the telex number and the telegraphic address. There may also be a space in which the telephone extension number of the writer can be inserted. Sometimes the words OUR REFERENCE and YOUR REFERENCE form part of the printed heading, or they may be shortened to OUR REF and YOUR REF. Against YOUR REF may be typed the reference of the person to whom the letter is being sent, if this is known. Alongside OUR REF may be written the department reference or name of the person writing the letter. A common type of reference is the initials of the dictator followed by the initials of the typist; in the letters shown on page 99 the reference is shown as HLP/RS—HLP are the initials of H. L. Pincott who will sign the letter and RS are the initials of the typist. Sometimes the reference includes the name of a department and/or a file number, e.g. PERS/12212/GHB/CMB—this could mean that the letter originated from the Personnel Department, would be filed in file no. 12212 or concerned file no. 12212, was dictated by GHB and typed by CMB. If the printed heading provides no space for the reference it can be typed against the left-hand margin, either underneath the heading or at the foot of the page. In America and American companies overseas it is usual to type the initials of the typist in lower case, either GHM/cmb or GHM:cmb. The need to quote the names of directors on business letters is governed by the Companies Act, 1948 § 201, and applies to all companies registered after 22 November 1916. The gist of* the law is that:

> Every limited company, when quoting its name, must in all its trade catalogues, trade circulars, show cards and business letters state in legible characters the following particulars with respect to every director:
>
> 1 His present Christian names or forenames, or the initials thereof.
> 2 Any former Christian names or forenames and surnames.
> 3 His nationality if not British.

Any necessary information about directors can be included in the printed heading or along the lower edge of the sheet of paper.

Until 1 January 1973 the information to be shown on letterheadings was governed by Section 201 of the Companies Act 1948 and the Registration of Business Names Act 1916.

To comply with the European Communities Act 1972 and Value Added Tax legislation, additional information must now be given on business stationery, i.e. letterheadings, order forms, trade catalogues and circulars, tax invoices and credit notes.† Section 9 (7) of the European Communities Act 1972 which came into force on 1 January 1973 requires letterheadings to show:

a Registration number, i.e. the number appearing on the company's certificate of incorporation.
b Place of registration.
c Address of company's registered office.
d The words LIMITED LIABILITY in the case of a limited company exempt from the obligation to use the word 'limited' as part of its name.
e Reference to paid-up capital when reference is made to the amount of share capital.

You can see a selection of printed letterheads on page 92, and in *Appendix E, Forms of Address* you will find a selection of foreign letterheads with the key words translated so that you will know how to "read" them.

*Specification for Sizes and Recommended Layouts of commercial forms. Part 1—Letterheads and forms other than those produced on rotary presses. British Standard 1808: Part 1: 1970. British Standards Institution.

† *Business Stationery Must Meet EEC and VAT Requirements*, published by the British Federation of Master Printers.

Directors : A B Brown, C D Cobb, J D Green, R U Shaw (USA)

CLASSIC WHOLESALERS LTD

Registered number 000 000 England
Registered office 24 Market Street Anytown Anyshire

Telephone 00–123 4567

SCIENTIFIC PROMOTION ASSOCIATION

LIMITED LIABILITY

Registered number 000000 Scotland
Telephone 00–321 7654

10 High Street
Oldtown
Oldshire
(Registered office)

The date Every business document must be dated. The following form which starts with the smallest unit of time and progresses to the largest (day, month, year) is the most usual in Great Britain:

5 July 1973

Some offices still use the endings 'st', 'nd' and so on, but fully punctuated forms such as

5th July, 1973 July 5th, 1973

are rapidly becoming out of date. It is standard American practice to reverse the order of the day and the month, thus

July 5, 1973

for this reason you should never use a figure to replace the name of the month and if you come across an all-number date in an American transaction always query the meaning. For example—*5.7.73* means *5 July 1973* in London but *May 7 1973* in New York.

The date to use in transcribing a letter sometimes presents a problem if the letter was dictated one day and not typed until the following day. It is usual to date letters according to the day on which they are typed, but some officials may ask you to use the date on which they were dictated. Sometimes you may be asked to show both dates, thus:

Dictated: 4 July, 1973
Typed: 5 July, 1973

The date is usually typed a few lines underneath the printed letterhead at the right-hand side of the page. Firms who have adopted the full-block style as shown on page 99 have the date typed flush with the left-hand margin but many offices, after a brief trial of this style, decided to change the position of the date back to the right for the sake of clarity and to facilitate filing and reference work. In style no. 6 shown on page 99 the date is typed so as to end with the right-hand margin; in this position it is the first typed line seen when searching the files.

The reference We discussed the composition and meaning of the reference on pages 90 and 91 and mentioned that it could be typed either as part of the printed heading, or against the left-hand margin on the same line as the date, or above the date in a full-block style or at the foot of the page. The use of references facilitates filing and locating past correspondence in the offices of both the writer and the receiver of a letter; references also assist the Mail Room to sort the incoming mail and ensures that letters quickly reach the desk of the person to whom they are addressed.

The inside address The name and address of the person to whom the letter is being written (the addressee) is known as the inside address. It is usually typed in a fully-blocked style flush against the left-hand margin, three or four lines down from the reference or date line.

Organisations that use window-envelopes (to save the additional operation of typing envelopes) usually indicate where the inside address is to be typed by printing the outline or four "corners" of an oblong as part of the printed letterhead; some printed stationery also includes two small "fold" marks on the left-hand edge of the paper. When the address is typed within the outlined frame and when the letter is correctly folded and put in the envelope, the inside address aligns exactly with the window.

An individual who has no other titles may be addressed in one of the following ways:

W. F. Benton Esq
Mr. W. F. Benton
Mrs. C. M. Lavender
Miss S. D. Foxton

'Esq' is the abbreviation of 'Esquire'. In the United Kingdom 'Esq' is considered more courteous than 'Mr.' but the full form is never used. 'Esquire' is not generally used in the United States except for professional men, such as architects and lawyers. In official American correspondence 'Esquire' is written in full, but in social correspondence it is abbreviated.

Great care must be taken when addressing people who have titles, Orders and Honours. Decorations and honours must be written in their correct sequence and precede academic abbreviations; university degrees precede professional qualifications. A good general rule is "civil, academic, military", for example

Sir Nigel Paton KCMG MA MC

You will find further information on this in *Appendix E, Forms of Address.*

The word 'Messrs' is the abbreviation of the French 'Messieurs' and is used in the English-speaking world for the plural of 'Mr.'; Messrs should only be used when addressing a business partnership. Thus, if Mr. Elliott and Mr. Crocker trade together as *Elliott and Crocker* it would be correct to address the partnership as Messrs Elliott and Crocker. 'Messrs' should never be used before the name of a limited company. A limited liability company is a form of business organisation in which a number of people called shareholders have invested their money and appointed directors to run the business for them. When the company is registered it is given a 'life' or independent existence of its own, and in law it is the company and not the shareholders who are responsible for its activities. As it is an artificial person it is necessary for the company to act through one of its officers, usually the company secretary in official matters and this is why letters to the company may be addressed to him.

In actual practice, however, the contents of the letter usually indicate to which official the letter should be sent and if the name of the official is not known it is correct and acceptable to address the letter to him by his title, for example

The Marketing Director
Securiton Ltd
4 Park Crescent
BRISTOL
BS1 4BP

Sometimes an instruction such as 'All communications must be addressed to the company and not to individuals', is included in the printed letterhead, in which case it is best to mark the letter for the attention of the official who will deal with it by using a *For the attention of* . . . . line, for example

For the attention of Mr Philip O'Hea

Ansacall Ltd
Payton House
Fountain Lane
NEWCASTLE UPON TYNE
NE1 1TW

Every address in the United Kingdom has a *postcode*.* (The Isle of Man and the Channel Islands are not included as they have separate administrations.) The object of the use of postcodes is so that all mail can be sorted by automatic machines and reach its destination more quickly. Postcodes should always appear as the last item of information in any address. Leave one space between each part of the postcode. If it is necessary to restrict the number of lines used the post town, or the county name and postcode may be written on the same line, but the Post Office prefers that the code appears on a line by itself. If the postcode is written on the same line as the town or county, leave a space of an inch or so between the last letter of the town or county name and the first letter of the postcode.

	Salutation	**Complimentary close**
GENERAL BUSINESS	Dear Sir Dear Sirs Dear Madam*	Yours faithfully Yours truly
SEMI-PERSONAL	Dear Mr Wright Dear David† Dear Wright‡	Yours sincerely With kind regards Yours sincerely
OFFICIAL OR VERY FORMAL§	Sir Gentlemen Madam	I am, Sir, Your obedient servant, We are, Sirs, Your obedient servants,

*Women should be addressed as 'Dear Madam' in general business correspondence or, less formally, as 'Dear Mrs . . .' or 'Dear Miss . . .'. Should you wish to address more than one woman or a body of women, the correct form is 'Mesdames'. 'Mesdames' stands alone as a salutation without the word "Dear". If you are in doubt as to whether a woman is Mrs or Miss, use Miss or Ms.

† If there is a close personal relationship, the complimentary close may be "Yours ever".

‡ The omission of the courtesy title 'Mr' and the use of the surname alone between men is an indication of closer acquaintance. Thus 'Dear Wright' is more friendly than 'Dear Mr Wright'.

§ These very formal official forms may be seen in some newspaper correspondence columns, but otherwise they are rarely used.

The *salutation* is the greeting which commences the letter and precedes the message and the *complimentary close* is the closing remark of the letter. The choice of complimentary close is governed by the salutation which in turn is governed by the relationship between the two correspondents and the appropriate degree of formality. The plan above gives some guide as to the forms of salutation and close having similar degrees of familiarity. If the letter is semi-personal (see page 105) some executives like to write in the salutation and complimentary close by hand (this is usually called "topping and tailing"); if your chief wants to do this, be sure to leave sufficient space as handwriting normally takes up more space than typewriting. Remember to

* ZIP codes are used in the United States of America, see page 45.

note on the carbon copy the parts written by hand on the original. There are special forms of address for titled people, civic dignitaries, religious leaders and members of the diplomatic corps. Some of these are given in *Appendix E, Forms of Address* and further information is given in the reference books listed at the end of the Appendix and in *Chapter 10, Sources of information and research*

The *body of the letter* conveys the information or message to the addressee. It should be arranged in paragraphs and the paragraphs should be blocked or indented according to the style of display chosen. If the paragraphs are blocked and the letter is typed at double spacing, remember to leave an additional line-space between the paragraphs so that the beginning of each is clearly marked. When you start writing letters you may find the 'three-paragraph' rule helpful; the first paragraph is an acknowledgment or introduction; the second paragraph conveys information and is factual; and the third paragraph suggests future action. You will find more information about the actual composition of a letter in *Chapter 9, Correspondence and Communications.*

Signature The simplest way to finish a letter is to leave a space for the signature underneath the complimentary close and then type the name of the person who will sign the letter and his title or position in the company. This method is easy, practical and correct. The person who receives the letter knows the name of the person who has signed it (even if the actual signature is illegible) and his position. The letters shown on page 99 are closed in this way. Some companies like closures which show their names such as

Yours faithfully,
THE EXCEL DOMESTIC APPLIANCE CO., LTD.

Office Manager

and others prefix the company's name with 'for' or 'p.p.' or 'per pro.'; 'p.p.' and 'per pro.' are abbreviations for 'per procurationem' which is a legal phrase meaning that a power of procuration or attorney has been given authorising one person to sign on behalf of another or on behalf of the company, so strictly speaking 'p.p.' and 'per pro.' should be used only in cases in which legal power of attorney has actually been granted. If she is given permission by her employer, a secretary may sign letters on his behalf thus:

Yours sincerely

Angela Foxton
Secretary to John Mills
President

If your chief dictates some letters and asks you to send them off whilst he is away, he may give you permission to sign them on his behalf as shown here, or he may sign several blank sheets of headed letter-paper and leave you to transcribe and arrange the letters so that the complimentary close can appear to be naturally displayed around his signature. This takes a little practice but is generally considered preferable to the form 'Dictated by Mr Mills and signed in his absence'.

In addition to the standard parts of a business letter which we have just discussed, there are additional parts which the secretary may need from time to time.

One of these, *the attention line*, was mentioned in the section dealing with the Inside Address. Since it is part of the inside address the attention line is usually typed immediately above or below it, for example

The Channel Underpass Company
84 Welcome Street
BELFAST
BT2 8AY

For the attention of Mr G T Shaw

Dear Sirs

For the attention of Mr G T Shaw

The Channel Underpass Company
84 Welcome Street
BELFAST
BT2 8AY

Dear Sirs

Any one of the following forms is acceptable:

For the attention of Mr G T Shaw
Attention: Mr G T Shaw
Attention of Mr G T Shaw

The attention line is generally underscored and the position of the official may be added, thus

<u>Attention: Mr Q G Sandys, Marketing Director</u>
Tartan Products Ltd
14 Queen Street
EDINBURGH
EH2 3AR

The use of the attention line usually ensures that the letter will be opened by the official acting for the addressee, should he be on vacation, away from the office for any reason or no longer associated with the firm.

The development of letter layout

1

A *fully-indented* letter with *close* punctuation. In this style the lines of the inside address and the closing section are each indented five spaces from the line above. When strict rules of *close* punctuation were followed, a full-stop was placed at the end of the date line, a comma after each line but the last of the inside address and closing section, and a full-stop at the end of the last line of each of these sections. This style of display is considered old-fashioned and is rarely seen nowadays.

2

The *semiblock* or *semi-indented* style with *close* punctuation. The essential features of this style are the blocked inside address; the blocked closing section, each line of which starts at the centre of the page; the five-space indentation at the beginning of each paragraph; and the position of the date line, ending flush with the right-hand margin. This was the most common style in the post-war period until recently. The rules of *close* punctuation gradually gave way to *standard* or *mixed* punctuation in which the full-stops at the end of the date line and after the name and designation of the writer were omitted.

3

The *block* style with *standard* or *mixed* punctuation. In this style the inside address is blocked and the body of the letter is typed in block paragraphs. Each line of the blocked closing section starts at the centre of the writing line.

4

The *full-block* or *fully-blocked* style with *standard* or *mixed* punctuation. In this style all lines begin flush with the left-hand margin. This style was adopted by an increasing number of organisations during the late nineteen-sixties, frequently with *open* punctuation, that is, no punctuation marks after any of the lines above and below the body of the letter.

5

The American *NOMA* (National Office Management Association) *simplified style*. The NOMA letter is typed in the full-block style with open punctuation. There is no salutation and no complimentary close. A subject line is always used. Many business concerns consider this style too radical and it has not been widely adopted in Great Britain.

6

Many organisations, after a brief trial of the full-block style, decided to change the position of the date back to the right for the sake of clarity and to facilitate filing and reference work. The lay-out of this letter seems to be evolving as the 'style of the seventies' and could be termed *simplified British*. The essential features are *open* punctuation and every line, except the date, starting flush with the left-hand margin.

Our ref. HLP/RS 15th February, 1933.

Harold J. Short, Esq., M.A.,
"The Elms",
Links Close,
Perbury, S.W.27.

Dear Mr. Short,

Savings and Investment

Thank you very much for your request for investment details. I am delighted to send you the information you have asked for and hope that you will find this useful and helpful.

Savings and investment are very much a matter for the individual need and the importance we place upon this is demonstrated both by the wide range of schemes which we offer and the simple but personal service we provide.

Whether it is to open an account, or to discuss in more detail your personal requirements, I do hope you will get in touch with your nearest Priory Building Society office, or write to me for any further information you require.

Yours sincerely,

H. L. Pincott,
General Manager.

1

Our ref. HLP/RS 15th February, 1943

Harold J. Short, Esq., M.A.,
"The Elms",
Links Close,
Perbury, S.W.27.

Dear Mr. Short,

Savings and Investment

Thank you very much for your request for investment details. I am delighted to send you the information you have asked for and hope that you will find this useful and helpful.

Savings and investment are very much a matter for the individual need and the importance we place upon this is demonstrated both by the wide range of schemes which we offer and the simple but personal service we provide.

Whether it is to open an account, or to discuss in more detail your personal requirements, I do hope you will get in touch with your nearest Priory Building Society office, or write to me for any further information you require.

Yours sincerely,

H. L. Pincott,
General Manager.

2

Our ref. HLP/RS 15th February, 1963

Harold J. Short, Esq., M.A.,
"The Elms",
Links Close,
Perbury, S.W.27.

Dear Mr. Short,

Savings and Investment

Thank you very much for your request for investment details. I am delighted to send you the information you have asked for and hope that you will find this useful and helpful.

Savings and investment are very much a matter for the individual need and the importance we place upon this is demonstrated both by the wide range of schemes which we offer and the simple but personal service we provide.

Whether it is to open an account, or to discuss in more detail your personal requirements, I do hope you will get in touch with your nearest Priory Building Society office, or write to me for any further information you require.

Yours sincerely,

H. L. Pincott
General Manager

3

Our ref. HLP/RS

15th February 1967

Harold J. Short, Esq., M.A.,
"The Elms"
Links Close,
Perbury, S.W.27.

Dear Mr. Short,

Savings and Investment

Thank you very much for your request for investment details. I am delighted to send you the information you have asked for and hope that you will find this useful and helpful.

Savings and investment are very much a matter for the individual need and the importance we place upon this is demonstrated both by the wide range of schemes which we offer and the simple but personal service we provide.

Whether it is to open an account, or to discuss in more detail your personal requirements, I do hope you will get in touch with your nearest Priory Building Society office, or write to me for any further information you require.

Yours sincerely,

H.L. Pincott
General Manager

4

HLP/RS

15 February 1973

Harold J Short Esq MA
The Elms
Links Close
Perbury
SW27 4MJ

Savings and Investment

Thank you very much for your request for investment details. I am delighted to send you the information you have asked for and hope that you will find this useful and helpful.

Savings and investment are very much a matter for the individual need and the importance we place upon this is demonstrated both by the wide range of schemes which we offer and the simple but personal service we provide.

Whether it is to open an account, or to discuss in more detail your personal requirements, I do hope you will get in touch with your nearest Priory Building Society office, or write to me for any further information you require.

H L Pincott
General Manager

5

HLP/RS 15 February 1973

Harold J Short Esq MA
The Elms
Links Close
Perbury
SW27 4MJ

Dear Mr Short

Savings and Investment

Thank you very much for your request for investment details. I am delighted to send you the information you have asked for and hope that you will find this useful and helpful.

Savings and investment are very much a matter for the individual need and the importance we place upon this is demonstrated both by the wide range of schemes which we offer and the simple but personal service we provide.

Whether it is to open an account, or to discuss in more detail your personal requirements, I do hope you will get in touch with your nearest Priory Building Society office, or write to me for any further information you require.

Yours faithfully

H L Pincott
General Manager

6

A *subject heading* is frequently included in a business or official letter. As its name implies it states the subject of the letter and is of assistance when the letter is opened in the postal room and when the letter is being filed. Sometimes the word 'subject' is actually used in the heading, e.g. *Subject: Annual leave*, and sometimes the topic is introduced by the Latin word *Re* (given the meaning 'about' or 'concerning' in this context). Neither of these introductory words is really necessary; the wording and placement of the subject heading make its function clear. The subject heading is typed either flush with the left-hand margin or centred over the body of the letter, as shown in the examples on page 99.

Enclosures When catalogues, price-lists and other leaflets and documents are enclosed with a letter, the word 'Enc.' or 'Encs' or 'Enclosure' is typed at the foot of the page at the left-hand side. Some offices prefer to use a red sticky label, sometimes shaped like an asterisk with the word 'Enclosure' printed on it, for this purpose. Boxes of these labels may be bought from shops selling office sundries. Both these methods have two purposes: one, to remind the typist or the person responsible for despatching the mail to enclose the documents in the envelope; and two, to draw the attention of the person who opens the packet to the fact that something has been enclosed. When more than one item is enclosed, the number of enclosures may be indicated as follows:

```
Enclosures: 2   ENC.
3 Encls         ENC.
Enc 4           Enc.
Enclosures - 3
```

Important enclosures may be enumerated:

```
Enclosures:
 1 Cheque
 2 Contract
 3 Medical Report
```

Carbon copy notation When carbon copies are being sent to persons other than the addressee of the letter a note to this effect is typed on the original. One of the following styles is usually adopted:

```
c.c. B W Edwards

Copies to: B W Edwards
           G L Franks

CC: G L Franks
```

Carbon copy notations are usually typed at the bottom left-hand corner of the page. Sometimes it is considered discreet to send a copy of a letter to a second person but to make no reference to this fact on the original letter. Such copies are called *blind copies*. The notation is usually typed on the carbon copies at the top right-hand or bottom left-hand corner of the page and may be preceded by the abbreviation 'NOO' (not on the original). To type a blind copy notation, remove the top copy and first carbon by using the paper release lever and turn back the remaining carbon pack until the desired part of the page is aligned with the printing point of the typewriter.

Mailing instructions Sometimes letters are sent by methods other than normal surface mail. This fact should be recorded on the letters themselves (a) so that the person who despatches the mail is reminded to check that the special instructions are carried out, e.g. to make sure that a letter intended to go by air-mail is put into a clearly marked air-mail envelope and that the correct amount of postage is paid; and (b) to confirm the means of despatch if there are subsequent queries about the arrival or non-arrival of a letter. Special mailing instructions are usually typed immediately above the inside address:

REGISTERED

Mr A F da Costa
3 Kenyatta Buildings
Government Road
Nairobi
KENYA

Special instructions Letters containing confidential, personal or secret information are usually marked with special instructions so that they are not opened by the wrong person. These special instructions, such as CONFIDENTIAL, PERSONAL, and so on, are typed immediately above the name of the addressee (as in the case of special mailing instructions) to make sure that the words PRIVATE or SECRET are also typed on the envelopes. In some government departments confidential letters are placed in envelopes marked CONFIDENTIAL which are then put into unmarked envelopes (see *Chapter 3, Mail Handling*). Do not confuse the terms CONFIDENTIAL and PERSONAL. Only the addressee himself should open a letter marked PERSONAL or TO BE OPENED BY ADDRESSEE ONLY; but a deputy could open a letter marked CONFIDENTIAL and deal with confidential affairs if he had been authorised to do so during the absence of the official to whom the confidential letter was addressed.

Continuation sheets A plain sheet of bond paper may be used for the second page of a letter. The continuation sheet must be headed with the date, page number and name of addressee so that it can be identified if it becomes separated from the first page. The continuation details may be typed across the top of the page (semiblock, semi-indented or block style), or at the left-hand margin (full-block or NOMA style) or blocked at the right-hand side of the page (simplified British style).

Some organisations have pre-printed continuation sheets in which case the first continuation sheet is numbered CONTINUATION SHEET No. 1 although it is, in fact, the second page of the letter.

```
Mr Abdul Aziz          - 2 -          3 August 1973
```

```
2

3 August 1973

Mr Abdul Aziz
```

```
                                      Mr Abdul Aziz
                                      Page 2
                                      3 August 1973
```

The continuation particulars can be typed across the top of the page, or at the left-hand margin or at the right-hand top corner; the style chosen should be in keeping with the display style of the main part of the letter.

Start the first line of the continuation page about an inch below the heading and try to start the page with a new paragraph. As soon as you realise that you are going to need a second sheet to complete a letter, make a light pencil mark about an inch or an inch and a half from the bottom of the first page and stop typing when you reach this point; this will ensure that you have sufficient matter to give the continuation page a balanced appearance.

OFFICIAL LETTERS Until a few years ago official letters were displayed quite differently from business letters; for example, the inside address was typed at the foot of the page in an indented form, the salutation and complimentary close were 'Official', enclosures were indicated by a row of full-stops in the left-hand margin of the letter and the last word on a page was set underneath the last line of typing and was repeated again at the top of the next page, known as a catchword.

A suggested new format was recommended by the Civil Service Department O and M Division in 1969* and this has been adopted by most government departments. With two exceptions:

1 All numerals over *one* and all fractions to be typed in figures, except where a numeral is the first word of a numbered paragraph or sub-paragraph in which case it should be spelt out to avoid confusion.

2 Pages are numbered at the foot of each page when there is more than one sheet; the second page is typed on the back of the first.

the recommended display was identical to no. 6 on page 99. The list of simplifications included "blocking" the inside address, omitting all punctuation above and below the body of the letter, no indentation or paragraphs, no catchwords, enclosures to be indicated by typing 'ENCS' at the bottom left-hand corner of the page and the subject heading to be typed in block capitals, not underscored.

As you can see from the illustration on page 104, an official letter is now displayed in almost the same style as a business letter.

SEMI-PERSONAL LETTERS In these days of increasing informality business letters are frequently written in a friendly style particularly when the writer and the addressee are on first-name terms. As we mentioned on page 95 some executives like to write in the 'Dear So-and-so' and the complimentary close by hand (this is often referred to as *topping and tailing*); when your chief wants to complete a letter in this way remember to leave him enough space to do so, and also remember to note on the carbon copy what he wrote on the original.

In some companies it is the practice to type the inside address at the foot of the page on the left-hand side, and special paper is provided for semi-personal letters at boardroom level. A high quality heavy paper suitable for embossing, such as *Optimum* 100 % Rag Blue White Wove Smooth Finish 100 g/m²† in $\frac{2}{3}$ A4 size (7.79 in × 8.27 in) with matching envelopes, is suitable for semi-personal letters written from the Chairman's office.

REPORTS The acceptability of a report depends to a considerable extent upon the ease with which the person reading it can grasp the points made in the

* *Typing Topics—Towards a Simpler Letter Layout*, G. H. E. Fowler, O & M Bulletin, August 1969.
† g/m²—grammes per square metre;
100 g/m² means that one square metre of paper weighs 100 grammes
Optimum is the finest writing paper made by Wiggins Teape Ltd.

HER MAJESTY'S STATIONERY OFFICE
Establishments and Organisation Division
Sovereign House, St Georges Street, Norwich, NOR 76A
Telephone Norwich 22211 ext. 60

J Doe Esq
CSD
Sanctuary Buildings
Westminster
LONDON
SW1

Our reference
E 73/2
Your reference
MS(OM) 33/02
Date
June 1969

Dear Doe

PAPER PRICE ADVISORY SERVICE

I thought it might be helpful, in view of the forthcoming O & M investigation, if I set out very briefly the basic purpose of this Service. Its main functions are

a. to collect and process details of the paper prices currently, ie day by day, being asked and paid in each region, and

b. to pass this comprehensive information as quickly as possible to all regional trade associations.

I enclose 4 copies of a draft paper giving fuller details which has been specially compiled for you and the other members of the review team by the Secretary to the Service.

Yours sincerely

A N Other
Assistant Director

ENCS 4

An official letter. Note the blocked inside address, the *open* style of punctuation, the subject heading in block capitals, and the way the enclosures are indicated. The printed letterhead is completed by typing the telephone extension number, the references and the date in the spaces provided.

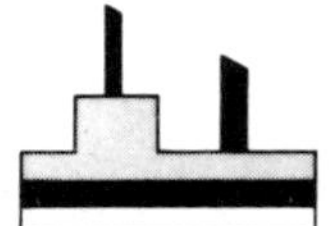

TECHNIK INCORPORATED

P.O. Box 146 Ankara Turkey

Cables: Techturk Tel: 506295

9 February 1973

Dear Omar

I was so pleased to hear that you are joining the Turkish Development Corporation as Administration Manager and look forward to having you in Ankara.

They are great people to work for and Ankara is a very pleasant town to live in. I'm sure you've made the right decision and that the move is in your best interests.

We have regular duplicate bridge sessions each weekend and there are several good clubs - let me know if you'd like some introductions.

With all good wishes
Sincerely yours,

George.

George Owens
Chief Designer

PERSONAL
Mr Omar Kasker
International Oil Inc
P O Box 893
TUNIS, Tunisia

A semi-personal letter. The inside address has been typed at the foot of the page on the left-hand side and the writer of the letter has completed the salutation and complimentary close by hand.

individual sections, and this in turn depends upon the clarity of presentation achieved by the judicious use of centred headings, main headings and sub-headings which act as sign-posts for the reader. Main headings may be centred but the sub-headings should be kept to the left so that as the reader runs his eye down the page he gets a quick summary of the contents.

An impression of conciseness can be given by a neat typing style; a 'fussy' style of layout may make a document appear unnecessarily complicated and longwinded. "Excessive use of capital letters, underlining, indenting and centring tends to break up the page and works against ease of reading. A crisp modern style will make the report appear briefer and more businesslike".*

Displayed work used to be decorated by ornamental borders and 'tail pieces' made by special arrangements of typewriter characters and letters such as these:

```
/_/_/_/_/_/_/_/_/_/_/_/_/_/

_____________________________
OoOoOoOoOoOoOoOoOoOoOoOoOoOoO
_____________________________

- oOo - oOo - oOo -

-:-:-:-:-:-:-:-:-:-:-:-:-:
```

Modern artists do not consider this to be in good taste.

Indentation should also be kept to a minimum and may be dispensed with altogether if the opening of new paragraphs is indicated by leaving additional space between the paragraphs.

Typists using special typewriters such as those mentioned on page 48 have a choice of typefaces and may select special founts for section headings and sub-headings. However, even on a standard machine there are several ways of typing headings and these give plenty of scope to the typist with a flair for artistic layout. Here are some forms which can be made on any typewriter:

Lower case	**Titles**
Lower case underscored	**<u>Titles</u>**
Lower case spaced	**T i t l e s**
Lower case spaced and underscored	**<u>T i t l e s</u>**

* *Paper at Work*, No. 3, 'Typing in style', Spicers Ltd.

Upper case	TITLES
Upper case underscored	TITLES
Upper case spaced	T I T L E S
Upper case spaced and underscored	T I T L E S
Upper case underscored and overscored	TITLES
Upper case spaced, underscored and overscored	T I T L E S

Bold face, a type-style slightly thicker and blacker than normal type, is very useful for headings or to give emphasis to special words or phrases or as an alternative to italics. The appearance of bold face can easily be obtained on any typewriter by typing the word or title in the normal way, moving the paper a minute fraction to the left or right by using the paper release lever, and then overtyping the word or title. This technique is suitable for the typist who occasionally needs to produce the effect of an additional typeface on a standard machine. If a complete second typeface is **frequently** needed there is a special device—the Betamod—which, when fitted to an IBM Executive typewriter, produces a simulated bold face thus giving the machine a complete second or alternative typestyle (see p. 54).

Reports frequently contain tabular matter and here again the style of presentation influences not only the ease with which the statistical information can be absorbed but also its acceptability to the reader. Headings should be either centred or blocked left; double spacing makes for easier reading and fine, light ruling gives complicated tables a neat and orderly appearance. Neither the ruling, nor the leader dots if used, should be allowed to dominate the page—they are intended to guide the reader's eye and must not be more prominent than the typed material.

Reports should always be typed with a wide left-hand margin (sometimes called a *stitching margin*) so that the typing does not disappear into the binding if the pages are stapled on the left-hand side or bound in loose-leaf form.

TRANSCRIPTION

The word *transcription* when used in connection with secretarial skills means typing either from shorthand notes (symbol, alphabetic or stenotyping systems) or from recorded dictation. For both audio-typist and shorthand-typist, transcription is a very important stage in the sequence of operations which starts

EXPLANATORY NOTES

Bilingual courses

The object of these courses will be to train typists to work in both languages. There will be a continued need for English-language clerks in offices dealing with importing and exporting where orders and documents have to be prepared in English. Bilingual typists will be trained to translate simple matter at sight directly on to the typewriter. They will not replace professional interpreters but they will lessen the time taken to produce typed translations of short routine letters.

Curriculum Development Unit

The Curriculum Development Unit will produce syllabuses for all subjects included in the curriculum and ensure that each subject syllabus is tailored to the needs of local commerce and industry.

A further function of the Curriculum Development Unit will be to produce training manuals, textbooks, teaching material and audio-visual aids for use in the Centre.

- 6 -

Practice Model Office

The Practice Model Office will play an important part in training students in office machines and methods. It will be equipped and laid out to simulate actual working conditions and all students will be given weekly assignments in the Model Office under the supervision of a teacher. The production of In-tray exercises using specially prepared documents and work sets will be part of the work of the Curriculum Development Unit.

Further planning and expansion

If the proposals recommended in this Paper are approved, more detailed plans can be prepared including lists of equipment and books, and job descriptions for all staff members.

Sabingo, Chad
October 1972

Alida M Baxter
Training Adviser

- 7 -

The last two pages of a report. The title of the section is centred in block capitals and the sub-headings are in underscored lower case. The report is typed in double spacing; four line spaces are left between the sub-sections and the blocked paragraphs. The date and place name are blocked in the bottom left-hand corner; the name and title of the writer appear on the right. The pages are numbered at the bottom to simplify collating.

ESTIMATED COST

Expenditure	£ Phase 1	£ Phase 2
Capital expenditure		
Equipment and machinery	20,000	---
Textbooks	5,000	500
Library books	2,000	300
Vehicle	1,500	---
Fellowships	---	10,000
Recurrent expenditure		
Salaries and Wages	44,000	60,000
Stationery and supplies	3,000	5,000
Consumable materials	2,000	1,000
Heat, light and water	1,500	1,800
Maintenance and repairs	500	750
Contingency Fund	1,000	1,000
Total	£80,500	£89,550

A statistical table. The main heading is in block capitals and underscored, the side headings are in lower-case and underscored. The use of double spacing makes each line easy to read. The fine ruling makes a frame for the table but does not dominate the page. The wide left-hand margin will prevent the typing from disappearing into the binding if the page is bound in loose-leaf form.

with dictation and ends with the mailing of the correspondence; transcription is the process of producing the end-product—the well-displayed and correctly typed letter—which is subsequently presented for signature and mailed.

Transcription is a complex skill which involves the use and co-ordination of many more intricate mental and physical processes than the two basic skills of shorthand and typewriting. The skill of transcription requires practice; to become proficient the shorthand or audio-typist needs to be trained in the component skills.

The skills required 1. Selection of paper and carbon pack. The transcriber must be able to judge the length of the letter so that she can select the appropriate size of notehead or paper; she must also select the correct weight of paper if the letter is to be sent by airmail; and she must decide what margins and spacing she should use to achieve an attractively displayed letter. The index or indicator slip (see page 33) tells the audio-typist the length of the dictation; after some practice the shorthand-typist learns to estimate the typed length of, say, twenty lines of her own shorthand notes. Having selected the correct size and weight of paper, the transcriber must look at her notes or at the index slip to see how many carbon copies she should take. She can then assemble the carbon pack and insert it in the machine.

2. Sense recognition. The transcriber needs to be able to recognise the sense of what she is reading or hearing. She, therefore, needs plenty of general knowledge and will be able to work more quickly and intelligently if she has studied the vocabulary of the dictator's specialisation. The word *dog* has a meaning in mechanical engineering which has nothing to do with a four-legged animal; another common engineering word is *cam*. The transcriber who has become acquainted with these terms will be able to cope with them without difficulty, but the first time she comes across them she may think she has mis-heard *cam* and that she ought to type *cat*.

3. Spelling and punctuation. The transcriber must be able to visualise spelling and punctuation quickly and correctly. Generally speaking, this aspect of transcription requires more practice than any other. As soon as the transcriber sees a shorthand outline or hears a word (or, to be more accurate, sees a group of shorthand outlines or hears a group of words, because the proficient transcriber works in meaningful phrases not word by word) she must grasp the meaning, divide it into its separate letter units and transmit these to her fingers so that the correct keys are struck in the correct order.

In order to do this quickly and accurately the transcriber needs to be an excellent speller and to have a first-class knowledge of punctuation. She must also follow the sense of what she is transcribing and always be on the alert so that she can immediately select the correct spelling for each homophone—and there are few sentences in the English language which do not contain at least one of the common homophones such as *their/there*, *no/know*, let alone those which occur less frequently, such as *compliment/complement*, *tray/trait*, *sealing/ceiling*.*

4. Quick and accurate typing. The ability to type quickly and accurately is probably *the* basic secretarial skill—this point has already been made in several

* *English in the Office*, Swift and Stanwell, Edward Arnold (Publishers) Ltd contains exercises in Chapters 1, 2, 3 and 4 to provide practice in this aspect of transcription.

preceding sections. It is mentioned again here because it is of course an essential component skill of transcription. The competent transcriber has "over-learnt" the skill of typewriting; in other words the physical process of striking the keys quickly and accurately is performed automatically, without conscious thought, so that the decision-making part of the brain is free to function simultaneously on problems arising from questions of display, spelling and punctuation.

5. Attractive display. In addition to the choice of paper size, margins and line-spacing, the transcriber will have to make other decisions regarding display whilst she is transcribing such as the indentation or centring of certain sections or the arrangement of items in columns. Here again, as we mentioned in the preceding paragraph, her mind must be free to decide "what should be typed where"—and she must not be pre-occupied with problems connected with locating the keys and manipulating the machine controls. This aspect of transcription can be compared to driving a car: the process of making the car move should be completely automatic, so that the driver's attention can be devoted entirely to the matter of steering and making judgments to pull in or overtake according to the amount of traffic, the road conditions and the behaviour of other motorists.

6. Proof-reading. Before she takes work out of the machine, the transcriber must proof-read and correct any errors. Typing mistakes must be corrected without detection; nothing spoils the appearance of typed work so much as obvious and untidy corrections. This aspect of typewriting is included in most typewriting syllabuses; there are many aids available (see *Typists' Supplies and Accessories*, p. 59) to help the typist erase neatly and 'invisibly', and there are several techniques such as *squeezing* and *spreading* which make use of half-spacing and enable the typist to change complete words almost without detection. If corrections or amendments have to be made after the work has been taken out of the machine, the typist must learn how to re-insert the original and copies, how to 'line-up' the type both vertically and horizontally, and how to type in the correction in exactly the right position and with the same density of blackness as the rest of the work.

7. Assembling work for signature. Before presenting work for signature, the transcriber should type an envelope if necessary and assemble any enclosures; she should select the correct weight and size of envelope and take care to include any special mailing instructions such as EXPRESS or CONFIDENTIAL. Enclosures, provided they are not too bulky, should be placed behind the letter and fastened with a paper clip. The envelope may be placed over the top of the letter with the address facing upwards.

Standards of attainment Typewriting speed is measured in words per minute; it is usually calculated by (a) counting the total number of key depressions including spaces in a piece of work, (b) dividing the total number by five (this is based on the assumption that five strokes constitutes an average word), and (c) dividing the total number of "words" by the number of minutes taken to type them, or by the time permitted for typing. Thus if a typist types 2500 strokes in 10 minutes, she has a speed of 50 words per minute:

$$\frac{2500 \text{ strokes}}{5} = 500 \text{ (words)}$$

$$\frac{500 \text{ words}}{10 \text{ minutes}} = 50 \text{ words per minute}$$

Typewriting speed in this sense is generally understood to indicate a typist's speed when she is working from straightforward typed or printed copy. Her *production speed* or *output speed*, that is the amount of work she can produce in a certain time, will of course be determined to some extent by her copy-typing speed; but it will also be affected by other factors such as her dexterity in handling paper, the number of times she has to stop typing to correct errors and the time she takes to decide questions of style and display.

TRANSCRIPTION SPEED means the speed at which a typist can produce mailable correspondence and documents from shorthand notes or recorded dictation. A transcription speed which is half the copy-typing speed is generally regarded as reasonable. A good standard of attainment for a transcriber is about two-thirds of her copy-typing speed. Thus a typist with a copying speed of 50 words per minute should have a transcribing speed of between 25 and 30 words per minute; a transcription speed of 35–40 words per minute would be very good.

There are many factors which affect transcription speed ranging from level of vocabulary and language to typewriting skill and general knowledge. These factors are listed here so that trainee shorthand-typists, audio-typists and secretaries may become aware of the areas of study to which they should pay especial attention during their secretarial training.

1. Typing accuracy and erasing skill. Use a stopwatch to find out how many seconds or minutes you take to erase and correct say two letters in a word, with an original and two carbon copies in the machine. Does it take you 30 seconds? If it does, and if your copying speed is 50 words per minute, you will 'lose' 25 words every time you stop to correct a mistake. Learn to type accurately and quickly so that you will not waste time in erasing and correcting. Of course, no-one types indefinitely without making a single error; all typists make mistakes, but you will increase your transcription speed if you do everything you can to minimise the number of mistakes you make; you should also practice speeding up the time it takes you to make a perfect correction.

2. If you are a shorthand-typist, take great care to write beautiful, well-formed shorthand notes, so you do not waste time trying to decipher bad outlines. Whilst you are training, do all you can to develop a neat, clear style of shorthand writing, so that even when your notes are 'cold' you can read them easily and transcribe them without hesitation.

3. Develop a nimble, alert mind. Practice reading or listening ahead of what you are actually typing so that you have time to settle points of punctuation and spelling involved in the phrases before you are ready to type them. For

example, suppose you read or hear 'the company's directors'; this could be transcribed as:

the company's directors
or
the Company's directors
or
the Company's Directors
or
the companies' directors
or
the Companies' directors
or
the Companies' Directors

Choices between homophones, questions of capitalisation, spelling, numbers (words or figures?)—all these problems are, or should be, thrown up and decided during the process of transcription. A well-informed, nimble mind is needed if transcription is to proceed smoothly and fluently, without wasting time by pausing to ponder over queries.

4. 'Collecting' non-dictated information. In order to get his work done more quickly, an employer often dictates like this: "This is a letter to Mr Johnson of Leeds—his initials are in the file, so's his address. Dear Mr Johnson, Thank you for your letter dated—whatever the date of his letter was—reference—that's in the letter too—regarding your account for £54.50 . . . ." and so on. Make a point of reading through every letter before you start to transcribe and collect all the information you need to complete the letter. This may also involve consulting reference books, diaries, calendars and possibly contacting other members of the organisation.

5. Become an expert speller by cutting down the number of times you need to consult the dictionary, although of course it is better to look up a word in the dictionary if you are not sure of its spelling rather than to take a chance and hope you have guessed correctly. You will be well on the way to becoming an expert speller if you know the words you cannot spell. Think of this as stage one; "*travelling*—one el or two? I'm not sure—must look it up". Look it up and make a note of it in your own spelling notebook; glance through the book when you have a few minutes to spare so that the next time you come across the word *travelling* you will know immediately that it has two el's. This is stage two, when you are perfectly sure how words are spelt, so the number of times you have to stop transcribing to consult the dictionary becomes fewer and fewer and, consequently, your transcription speed increases.

Presenting work for signature and mailing When the letter, enclosures and envelope have been assembled they should be placed in a Signature Book or in a folder marked 'FOR SIGNATURE'. Some firms use special signature books in which the pages are made of a heavy blotting paper and there is a circular hole in the centre of each page to show when the last letter has been signed. Carbon copies for other people, i.e. not the file copies, should also be attached for initialling by the dictator unless the name or signature is added by rubber-stamp. Envelopes should be prepared for these copies, unless they are non-confidential for internal transmission. Some employers like to see all the carbon copies and the envelopes. If your chief wants only the letters, keep the carbon copies, the enclosures and the envelopes in the same order as the original letters in a separate folder on your desk so that they are ready when the letters have been signed.

Your chief will probably tell you when he likes to sign his letters. The most usual practice is for the secretary to take in the Signature Book containing all the day's transcribed dictation and correspondence an hour or so before the office closes so that the letters can be sealed, stamped and despatched before the last postal collection.

Before sealing the envelopes for mailing,

a check that the name and address on the letter and envelope are the same;
b check that all enclosures have been included;
c check that any special notations such as "For the attention of . . . ." and any special mailing instructions such as BY AIR MAIL are clearly marked on the envelope.
d If the letter mentioned that certain items are being sent 'Under separate cover' make sure that they are being sent—it is a good plan to make a note in your desk diary for the following day to remind yourself to check that the 'under separate cover' items have been despatched.

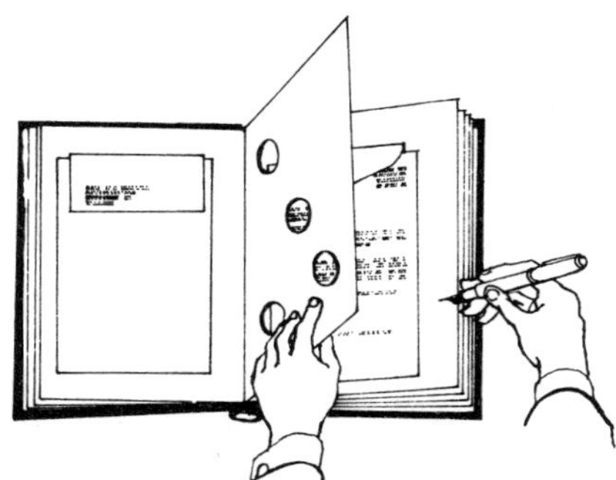

A Signature book.

FURTHER READING

The Art of Dictation, Eva Roman, Gower Press.
Manual of Stationery, Office Machines and Equipment, The British Stationery and Office Equipment Association.
Metrication in Business Equipment, Business Equipment and Trade Association.

Writing Out Loud, A. Donald Brice, Dictaphone Corporation.
How to be a Dictator, R. W. Bingham, Stenocord Corporation.
Teeline, James Hill, Heinemann Educational Books Ltd.
Glossary of Paper, Stationery and Allied Terms, BS 3203 : 1964, British Standards Institution.
Sizes of Papers and Boards, BS 4000 : 1968, British Standards Institution.
Envelopes for Commercial, Official and Professional Use (Terms and Sizes), BS 4264 : 1967 and 589 : 1970, British Standards Institution.
Specification for Typewriters, BS 2481 : 1961, British Standards Institution.
Metric Keyboards, PD 6462, British Standards Institution.
Specification for Sizes and Recommended Layouts of Commercial Forms, BS 1808 : 1970, British Standards Institution.
Paper at Work, No. 1, *House Style*, Spicers Ltd.
Paper at Work, No. 2, *Duplicating*, Spicers Ltd.
Paper at Work, No. 3, *Typing in Style*, Spicers Ltd.
Paper at Work, No. 4, *International Paper Sizes*, Spicers Ltd.
Paper at Work, No. 5, *An Office Guide to Buying Stationery*, Spicers Ltd.
Typewriter Poems, Second Acon Publications.
Titles and Forms of Address. A Guide to their Correct Use, Adam & Charles Black.
The History and Development of Typewriters, HMSO.
Paper, Its Making, Merchanting and Usage, Edited by S. Carter Gilmour, The National Association of Paper Merchants in conjunction with Longmans, Green & Co. Ltd.

GROUP DISCUSSION

A recurrent topic throughout this chapter has been image-making (defined on page 42). Discuss and list the ways in which the work of a stenographer or secretary can contribute to the image of a company, firm or organisation.

EXERCISES

1 Outline four methods by which a typist may be given the text of a letter. Discuss briefly the relative advantages and disadvantages of each method.

2 Dictating machines are to be introduced into your firm. Write some simple instructions for (a) dictators (b) transcribers.

3 You are working as secretary to a scientist. Much of the typing work includes scientific symbols which you have to insert by hand because they are not provided on the keyboard of your typewriter. You feel that this spoils the professional appearance of your work. Write a memorandum to your chief recommending the purchase of one of the typewriter accessories which makes possible the typing of symbols which are not on the keyboard.

4 In your position as senior secretary, you are asked to supervise the work of two junior typists. Both of them have difficulty in erasing errors neatly and without detection. You ask them to arrive fifteen minutes early one morning to come to your office for a demonstration of perfect erasing. Make a list of points which you would bring to their attention and comment briefly on each point.

5 Explain the meaning of the following terms and phrases:

transmission methods	alphabetic shorthand systems
non-recorded dictation	index slip
carbonless paper	tandem audio-typing systems
typefaces	portable electric typewriters
dual ribbon devices	backing sheets
platen restorer	copyholders
ISO	rag papers
onion skin paper	POP
postcodes	reinforcement washers
open punctuation	blind copies
transcription speed	cold notes

6 Describe the difference between conventional carbon paper and solvent-coated copying sheets; list the advantages of the solvent-coated sheets.

7 List the weights of paper you would normally expect to find in an office; write brief notes on each.

8 (a) What is the difference between a banker and a pocket envelope?
(b) When the dimensions of envelopes are quoted, which dimension is mentioned first?
(c) If you were responsible for ordering stationery for your office, which envelopes sizes and weights would you normally keep in stock?

9 You have to set up a small temporary office for your employer to use at a trade fair. Make a list of the basic stationery items (paper clips, folders, paper, etc.) you would include.

10 There is no consistency in the letter display styles used in the different departments of your company. One reason for this is that the typists have been trained at different schools and colleges in different parts of the country and at different times. As secretary to the Office Manager, you are asked to produce a recommended standard layout. Describe the layout you would recommend and point out its advantages in a covering letter to your chief.

11 Why is transcription considered a complex skill? List the component skills a typist needs to practice if she wishes to become a competent transcriber.

12 Your chief tells you that he likes to sign his letters at 12.00 noon and 4.00 pm each day. Describe how work should be presented for signature and the points to be checked before envelopes are sealed and despatched.

13 Is the use of correcting paper (either in the form of slips or wound on to a spool and carried by a dual ribbon attachment) a method of correcting typewriting mistakes that you would recommend? Can you see any connection between this innovation and the wider use of office copiers? Consider the comparative costs of (a) carbon copies and (b) photocopies when you are thinking about these questions.

14 What do you understand by 'continuation details' in regard to letter display? Describe four ways in which the continuation details can be shown.

3

Telephone Techniques

"She must be able to answer at least three telephones at once and sound equally charming to the caller at the other end of the telephone however harassed she might be."
Marjorie Proops

"Telephones are the bane of many an executive's life. They always seem to ring when one is concentrating, making awkward calculations, conducting interviews, meetings, etc. A good secretary can filter these calls and pass through only those which need urgent attention."
Godfrey Tyler, *Management in Action*. August 1970

It is scarcely necessary to comment upon the inclusion of a chapter entitled *Telephone Techniques* in a secretarial textbook. It is almost impossible to imagine an office without a telephone, or a secretary who is not expected to answer the telephone as part of her duties.

Nowadays more business is conducted on the telephone than ever before; this is partly due to higher postal charges and the increased costs of producing a letter;* it is also due to improved and automated telephone facilities. GRACE

* Taking every factor (e.g. overheads, salaries, machines) into consideration, the cost of producing a letter is now estimated to be in the region of £3+.

(Group Routing and Charging Equipment) enables telephone subscribers with all-figure numbers and STD (subscriber trunk dialling) to dial most trunk and many international calls direct, without going through a telephone operator.

The secretary must learn how to use the telephone correctly; she must also be aware of the telephone services available in her town and country; it is also important for her to cultivate a pleasant voice and manner when speaking on the telephone so that callers form an impression of courtesy and efficiency.

There are many different types and combinations of instruments available to suit the needs of every business. The Post Office Telecommunications Department is always willing to advise and assist a subscriber in choosing the right system for his organisation.

USING THE TELEPHONE

Switchboards Most businesses have a telephone switchboard which can vary from one main line with three extensions to hundreds of main lines with thousands of extensions.

Switchboards may be automatic or manual. PABXs (Private Automatic Branch Exchanges, often referred to as 'automatic switchboards') enable internal calls to be dialled direct from one extension to another. External calls are also made direct from any extension by first dialling a special digit (such as '9') to obtain 'an outside line' (that is, access to the national telephone network, indicated by hearing the dialling tone) and then dialling the number required. The operator or operators on the company switchboard can be contacted when needed by dialling a special code or set of digits or numbers.

PMBXs (Private Manual Branch Exchanges) are usually referred to as 'manual exchanges'. Like PABXs they may be either corded or cordless; but all calls from PMBX extensions have to be made through the switchboard operator. For example, if Mr Jones on extension 39 wants to speak to Mr Smith on extension 51, he must lift his receiver and when the operator answers he will ask her to connect him with the person and extension number he requires. External or outside calls are obtained through a PMBX switchboard either by asking the operator to get the number or by asking the operator for an outside line; in the latter case, as soon as the extension holder hears the dialling tone, he can dial the number he wants.

Organisations equipped with PMBXs usually supplement them by internal-only systems which can comprise either the small push-button intercom type or a PAX (Private Automatic Exchange) system.

The three main types of switchboard are *cord*, *key* and *pushbutton*. The advantage of cord-connected switchboards is that they can accommodate more extensions whereas the capacity of key and pushbutton boards can only be increased by the addition of further complete units.

Phillips Pushbutton Switchboard (top)

PMBX Key Switchboard (left)

PABX Cord Switchboard (right)

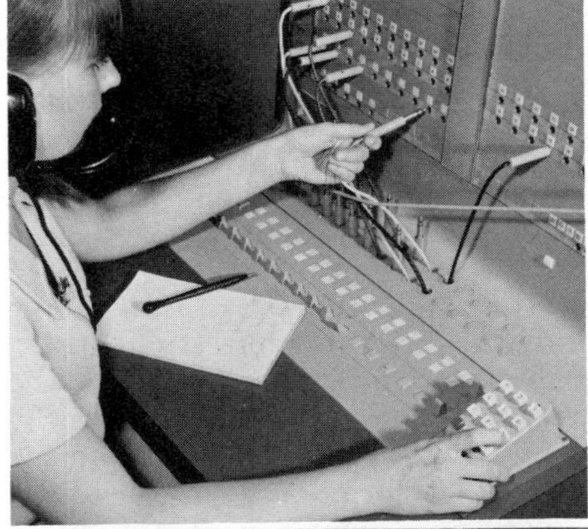

When answering a call the switchboard operator should greet the caller and identify the organisation. When the caller has said to whom he wishes to speak, the operator should make the connection accurately and quickly.

Receiving calls on an extension An extension is a telephone instrument wired to a switchboard or another main telephone. It is possible to have an extension of an extension and many secretaries use an extension to the switchboard while their bosses use an extension to the secretary's extension. This is known as Plan 107 (see the diagram below).

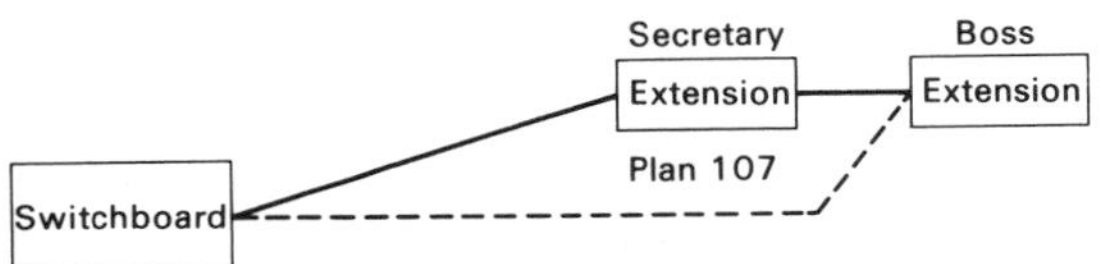

The main extension rings when called by the switchboard, unless it is 'switched through' so that the subsidiary extension rings. The secretary takes calls first and then connects callers to her boss. For details of how to operate a Plan 107 (or secretarial filter set) see page 135.

When the extension rings it should be answered as quickly as possible. It may be that you are already having a conversation with another person either face to face or on another telephone. If you are speaking face to face with another person you should finish the sentence or allow your visitor to do so, say, "Excuse me please", and then pick up the receiver. Never pick up the receiver and go on with your conversation keeping the caller waiting. If you are holding a conversation on another telephone, which may be an internal line, the same procedure would apply.

The exact procedure to be followed when receiving a call on an extension is dictated by the type of switchboard and the operator's method of connecting calls. If the switchboard is manual the operator may ring your extension and tell you that there is a call from Mr X. If this is the normal procedure you need only say your name and/or extension number when you lift the receiver. When the operator connects the caller to you, you will say: "Good morning Mr X. Mr Smith's secretary speaking."

If the switchboard is automatic you will be connected with the caller as soon as you lift the receiver in which case you will straight away give a greeting and identify yourself or the office—"Good morning. Chief Accountant's office."

At this point the caller should identify himself but in practice many callers forget to do so, particularly if they have already given their name to the operator, and do not realise that it has not been passed on to the extension user either because the operator has omitted to do so or because the switchboard is automatic. If the caller starts a conversation straight away do not interrupt him to ask his name; wait for a convenient pause. When you do ask his name and you don't catch it the first time, ask him to repeat it. If you don't catch it the second time, ask the caller to spell it for you. You should ask the caller to repeat any part of the conversation which you have not heard or understood.

When spelling out words it may be necessary to use the 'telephone alphabet' since certain letters sound alike, e.g. F and S. Only by saying "F for Freddie" or "S for Sugar" can the letter be identified. The alphabet used varies slightly from one English-speaking country to another. The alphabet used in each country is quoted in the national telephone directory.

If the caller wishes to speak to your boss there are several possible procedures.

a If the caller is a regular business contact ask him politely to hold the line, 'buzz' your boss, tell him who is calling him and when he agrees to take the call say to the caller, "Mr X, you are connected to Mr Jones."

b If your boss is engaged on another telephone line you would explain this to the caller and ask whether he will wait or would like to be rung back?" If he elects to be called back, take his name and number. As soon as your boss is free, tell him about the call and arrange the call back (see 'Making Calls'). If he elects to wait, keep in contact with him. About every minute say "I'm sorry, Mr Jones is still engaged" or "I am still waiting for Mr Jones to finish his conversation on the other line."

c If your boss is out, holding a meeting or has asked not to be disturbed say "I'm so sorry, Mr Jones is not available at present. Can I help you?" Depending on who is calling you might suggest that you ask your boss to ring back, or that you take a message.

d If the caller is someone you don't know, say you will enquire if Mr Jones is available, and add "May I tell him what you'd like to speak to him about?" Some callers may even have told you this. If they object say nothing but inform your boss accordingly. If he refuses to take the call you can act as for c.

e The caller finds that he has been connected to the wrong extension. You immediately apologise—the fact that he is calling your company means that he wants someone in it and is therefore an important person—and ask him to hold the line while you recall the operator. Move the rest gently up and down to attract the operator's attention and when she replies tell her who the caller wanted.

f If the call is for you, listen carefully and make notes of important points. If you have to ask the caller to wait while you get information, either from a file or on another telephone, say "Will you hold the line please?" Alternatively ask the caller if you should get the information and ring him back. This releases a line for use by someone else and saves the caller's time.

Receiving calls on a direct line Some senior officials have a 'direct line', i.e. a telephone on which calls can be received and made without being intercepted on a switchboard. Usually the secretary answers the call—"Good morning. Flag and Sail Company. Managing Director's office." The rest of the call will be dealt with in the same way as on an extension, depending on the circumstances.

It is possible that a caller has dialled the wrong number and may be somewhat nonplussed when he hears you answer. He may tell you the number or the organisation he wanted. A polite restatement of your own number will end the matter.

Screening calls It is an important part of a secretary's job to 'screen' telephone callers as well as visitors. Many people ask to speak to the boss over some detail which you could easily deal with. The caller must not be made to feel that he is not 'allowed' to speak to the boss. You must sound convincing when you say that he is 'not available'. Equally you must sound so anxious to help that he has no hesitation in putting his business into your hands.

Dealing with difficult callers Not all telephone calls run smoothly. As with visitors, there are the callers who for one reason or another are unpleasant, rude, in a hurry. Apply your knowledge of human psychology to the situation. Remain calm, imperturbable, efficient and helpful. A note of sympathy in the voice, an offer of help, an understanding comment can calm the ruffled nerves of the caller and smooth the way for your boss if he is to take the call. Always try to be positive; a negative approach only adds fuel to the fire of the caller's anger.

There are also the callers who refuse to give their names. Anyone who is telephoning on legitimate business should not be afraid to give his name, but usually in such a case the caller is afraid the boss will refuse to speak if he knows who it is. A polite but firm refusal to connect the call is necessary. "I'm sorry, but my boss refuses to take calls unless he knows the caller's name."

Taking messages Secretaries are frequently asked to take messages. If you are right-handed have the telephone placed on the left-hand side of your desk. Keep a notepad and pencil beside it so that you are ready to take a message at all times. As you listen to the message write down the main points—in shorthand. It is useful to repeat names, numbers, places, dates, etc as they are given. If the message is involved it should be read back at the end so that both you and the caller know that it has been taken down correctly and understood. Essential points to be written into the fair copy include:

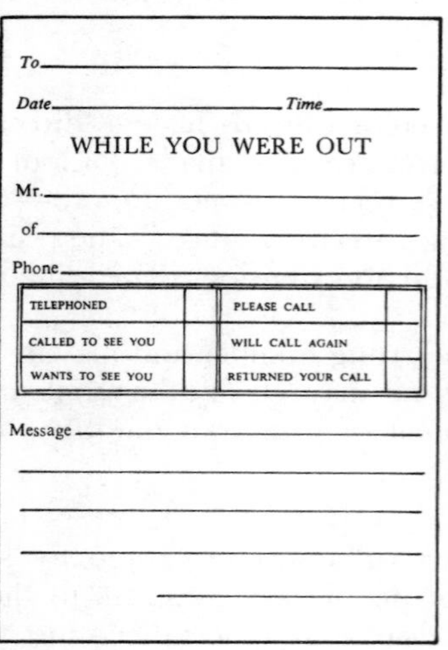
To ______

Date ______ Time ______

WHILE YOU WERE OUT

Mr. ______

of ______

Phone ______

TELEPHONED		PLEASE CALL	
CALLED TO SEE YOU		WILL CALL AGAIN	
WANTS TO SEE YOU		RETURNED YOUR CALL	

Message ______

name, organisation and telephone number of the caller; time and date when the message was taken; and the initials or signature of the person who took the message.

Numbers need especial care. Double numbers, ('teens and 'tys) should be called out separately. Seventeen, one seven; sixty, six oh or six zero. There are certain pairs of numbers which are difficult to distinguish on the telephone. One and nine; two and ten; five and nine; seven and eleven. These numbers need special emphasis.

Telephone numbers should always be read in pairs counting from the last figure. Thus, 67786 is read six, double seven, eight six. The number 68776 should be read six, eight seven, seven six. A double number at the beginning is always read separately, e.g. 88765—eight, eight seven, six five.

Speaking on the telephone When you talk with someone face to face you have a number of accessories to speech. Your facial expression, eyes, gestures all add meaning to what you are saying and so help the listener to understand. When speaking on the telephone the only means you have of communicating your words is your voice. It is essential that your speech be clear (not affected), that you do not speak too quickly and that you do not speak too loudly. Your voice is also the only means of communicating your personality and creating an impression. It is easy to wreck the image of a company by employing people who do not know how to speak on the telephone in such a way that they convey a smile, the desire to help, the ability to do a job efficiently. Female voices suffer most in transmission over telephone lines, so it is advisable to pitch the voice slightly lower than usual. Speak straight into the mouthpiece, not across it as this distorts the sound.

Girl sitting at desk holding hand set correctly and writing.

Making telephone calls To speed up calls and avoid delay keep an alphabetical index of the organisations you call listing the telephone number of each organisation and the name and extension numbers of the contacts in it. Before you make a call decide exactly what you want to say, and write down the main points so that you do not forget any of them.

MAKING CALLS ON AN EXTENSION TO A MANUAL SWITCHBOARD Write a list of the calls you have to make—numbers, names of people and reason—and cross off as each is dealt with. When you are ready to make the call lift the receiver. When the operator answers give the number you want, and the name and extension number (if possible) of the person. The operator may ask you to hold the line; this means that she is dialling your number immediately. If she tells you that you will be rung it means that she has no free lines and will call you as soon as she is able to make the connection.

When you are connected, identify your organisation and yourself, if it is your call. If the call is for your boss ask if Mr X is available to speak to Mr Jones. If so, the two secretaries can call their bosses simultaneously. This should happen whenever possible to save time and to avoid the discourtesy of keeping one boss waiting for the caller.

Some secretaries insist that their boss must be last on the line whether a call is being received or made. In this case the best thing to say is "Shall we go through together?"

If the person wanted is not available and his secretary has offered to help, you would ask her to hold the line while you find out from your boss if he wishes to speak to her.

When making a trunk call (either STD—subscriber trunk dialling—or through the exchange) or an international call it is essential that the person booking the call should be available to take it when it comes through. If there is some delay and the caller cannot wait, the operator should be informed so that the call can be either postponed or cancelled.

MAKING CALLS ON AN EXTENSION TO AN AUTOMATIC SWITCHBOARD Automatic switchboards allow direct dialling by the extension users. When the receiver is lifted there is no tone. By dialling 9 the extension is connected to a free line if there is one and the dialling tone is heard. If it is not heard it means that there is no free line. The receiver must be replaced and the procedure repeated. Make sure you know the number before starting to dial. If the line is engaged you will hear the engaged signal and should replace your receiver and try again a little later. If the number seems to be ringing for a long time it is almost certain that the number being called is an automatic switchboard with the 'queue' system. This means that incoming calls are taken in order automatically and if you replace your receiver and dial again you will be giving up your place and going to the end of the queue again. When you hear a reply give a greeting and identify your organisation and say the name and extension number of the person you or your boss wants. If you find you have the wrong number, apologise and ring off.

It may sometimes be necessary to make a call through the switchboard operator, in which case you must tell her your extension number because, unlike a manual switchboard, the automatic switchboard does not indicate which extension is calling, if it is the key or pushbutton type.

MAKING CALLS ON A DIRECT LINE The procedure is almost identical to making calls on an extension to an automatic switchboard except that it is not necessary to get a line by dialling 9. The dialling tone should be heard almost immediately when the receiver is lifted.

CO-OPERATING WITH THE TELEPHONE OPERATOR The telephone operator is a very busy person and has a great deal of responsibility. She is a part of the team and plays a big role in projecting the company image. She needs the co-operation of every extension user if she is to function with maximum efficiency. If you go out of the office and your boss is out as well take the trouble to let her know where you are going if it is within the building, or ask her to transfer your calls to another secretary or take 'ring back' messages if you are leaving the building. Call her as soon as you return to find out if there are any messages.

There may be times when the operator seems to be taking a very long time in getting numbers you have asked for. She should inform you when numbers are engaged or otherwise unavailable, but it is not her fault and criticism from you will only result in resentment and lack of co-operation from her.

Telephone facilities The facilities available vary from country to country but among those most usually available are:

(a) *Local calls* A local call is one made to another within the local call area. Exchanges within the local call area are shown in the telephone directories; they are also displayed in call boxes.

(b) *Trunk calls* Where subscriber trunk dialling (STD) is not available a number is dialled to obtain the exchange. The operator will make the connection to a subscriber outside the local area. Calls made through the exchange are charged on a time and distance basis. The minimum charge is for three minutes. Thereafter each minute is charged. STD is charged by units on the subscriber's exchange meter. The number of units for a given time depends on distance. Thus if a long-distance call is made by STD and the conversation is very short, say one minute, the charge is only for the time taken. On the other hand it may be necessary to call several times or wait while a wanted person is found. The call is being charged even though no conversation is taking place. If the call were made through the exchange it could be a 'personal' call.

(c) *Personal calls* Trunk calls can be made to a particular person and apart from the personal call fee no charge is made if the person is not available. In Britain the personal call fee includes efforts to contact the person wanted for up to twenty-four hours from the time of booking the call.

(d) *Transferred or reversed charge calls* A caller wishing to make a trunk call at the expense of the person being called can ask for the charges to be reversed. The operator asks the caller's name and will then ask the wanted subscriber if he will accept the call. If the answer is affirmative the connection is made and the cost charged to the account of the number called.

(e) *Credit Card calls* When a subscriber wishes to make a call or send a telegram from a telephone not his own he can ask for the cost to be charged to his own telephone account by having a credit card supplied by the area telephone manager. It can also be used to make overseas calls and send cables from the United Kingdom and to make calls (but not send cables) from certain countries abroad to the United Kingdom. A small charge is made in addition to the cost of each call. This is a particularly useful facility for businessmen who travel frequently.

(f) *International calls* International Subscriber Dialling (ISD) enables calls to be made to most European countries, and countries in other continents by direct dialling. Calls made through international exchanges are monitored and in some countries, recorded. The charges cover a minimum three minutes after which additional minutes are charged individually. If a call is requested but the subscriber in the country overseas cannot be contacted, a report charge is made. International calls can also be made from land to ships and aircraft up to a maximum radius, depending on the country.

(g) *Fixed time calls* A trunk call can be booked for connection at a particular time. A small fee is charged in addition to the trunk call charge.

(h) *Alarm calls* The operator can be asked to ring a subscriber at a particular time. This is used mostly for early morning calls.

(i) *Emergency calls* Fire, Police or Ambulance services can be called for accidents. Many countries use 999 as the emergency number.

(j) *Directory enquiries* When a subscriber's telephone number cannot be found in the directory a call can be made to ask the number. The name and address of the subscriber must be given for the number to be traced

(k) *Time calls* A number can be dialled connecting the caller to a 'speaking clock' which gives the precise time.

(i) *Faults* The engineers, or test room, can be contacted to report a telephone out of order.

(m) *Phonograms* A subscriber can dictate a telegram (inland or overseas) to the Phonogram operator. The cost is charged on the subscriber's telephone account.

(n) *Freefone* This service enables calls to be made to a number without cost to the caller. A firm that wishes to use the Freefone service pays a quarterly fee, plus the normal telephone charge and a transfer fee for each call it receives on the Freefone number. The caller is connected with the firm by asking the exchange operator to connect him with the Freefone number. The Freefone service encourages people to contact advertisers and place orders by telephone; it also enables representatives to speak to their head offices without the inconvenience of using telephone coin boxes. Many companies find it expedient to connect a Freefone number with a telephone answering machine (see page 133).

(o) *Advice of duration and charge (ADC)* The cost of a particular call made through the telephone exchange operator can be notified upon completion for a fee of 12p (1977). When the call is booked the operator must be asked for the ADC service.

There are a number of other facilities available in some countries, e.g. cricket scores during test matches, cookery recipes, entertainment in large centres, road conditions in bad weather and at holiday seasons, weather and shipping forecasts.

Full details of the facilities available in each country can be found in the national telephone directory.

Telephone reference books The *telephone directory* lists all subscribers in a given area in alphabetical order of surname. Similar surnames are then listed in alphabetical order of initials and first names. The subscriber's number is preceded by the exchange. In Britain a Code Book is issued in which are listed the code numbers for exchanges. Thus a subscriber in Bristol wishing to call a subscriber in Northampton will have to dial a code number for the exchange followed by the subscriber's telephone number.

In the United Kingdom the Post Office publishes the following types of telephone directories:

- a The main alphabetical directories printed on white paper. There are four directories (A–D, E–K, L–R and S–Z) for the London Postal Area.
- b Classified business (Yellow Pages) directories printed on yellow paper.
- c Business directories listing large businesses in alphabetical order over a wide area. These are printed on white paper.
- d Local alphabetical directories printed on white paper serving small communities.
- e Commercial classified directories listing in classified order businesses which are of predominant interest to the business community. These are printed on blue paper.
- f Where it is convenient, the main alphabetical directory is bound with a classified business directory; the book is then known as a combined directory.

Each subscriber is supplied with a copy of the alphabetical directory, the classified business (Yellow Pages) directory and, where issued, a local directory. Business directories are issued to each business subscriber in the area. Additional copies and copies of any directories for other districts may be purchased from the Telephone Manager.

INTERCOMMUNICATIONS

Telephone There are a great many systems of intercommunication, i.e. methods of holding conversations with other people within the same organisation. Some systems are connected to the Post Office telephone switchboard and internal calls may be routed through the switchboard. If the switchboard is automatic the extension users can dial each other independently.

Internal systems may be separate from the external telephones and may work by dial, key or pushbutton. The latter may be one of two kinds—either a buzzer to a pre-set number, or numbered buttons to be used instead of the digits on a dial.

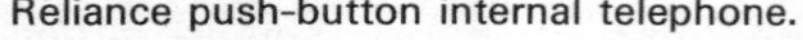

Reliance push-button internal telephone.

A Comtalk internal telephone.

There are many intercommunication systems which consist of box-shaped instruments. Some systems allow communication only between the master set and individual extensions; others have one-way calling from the master set, i.e. the extensions cannot call the master set; others allow intercommunication between and among master and all extensions. Many systems cater for 'private' calls by providing a handset. Normally the voice is heard in the room. Some intercommunication instruments can have a secretary's extension in the same way as a Post Office instrument.

When answering an internal telephone or other 'intercom' instrument it is necessary only to identify yourself by name, department and/or extension number, whichever style is used in your organisation.

(Left) Reliance Loudspeakercall master. (Right) Operating as a loudspeaking telephone, this Modernphone Triphone when held to the ear in the usual manner adjusts for private conversation. When laid face downwards it enables calls to be re-routed to a secretary.

COPING WITH SEVERAL TELEPHONES

Many secretaries have at least two and sometimes three or four telephones on their desks. It can happen that two instruments ring at the same time or, during a conversation on one instrument another instrument rings. It is useless to try to answer all at once. Deal with the first call, ask to be excused to answer the second call. Ask the second caller for his name and number so that you can ring back. Do not break off one call and deal with another leaving the first caller waiting for several minutes. Remain calm, courteous and helpful even if all four telephones ring at the same time!

FACSIMILE TELEGRAPHY

One of the latest developments to assist telephone users is a copying machine which can be attached to an external or internal telephone, or radio. If you want to discuss a document and your listener has no copy, you insert the original into your copying machine and almost immediately it is reproduced on your listener's copying machine. This is particularly useful in organisations with many branches or that cover a wide area. These machines are frequently called telecopiers, facsimile transceivers, transcopiers or remote copiers.

The machine is placed on a desk or table top and connected to an adjacent telephone. To transmit, (1) the document is put into the machine, (2) the SEND button is pressed, (3) the recipient is telephoned and told that a copy is being sent to him, (4) the recipient presses the RECEIVE button and switches through to the telephone line, (5) the transceiver signals when the transmission is complete and the two parties can then resume their conversation.

The Rank-Xerox 400 Telecopier sends facsimile copies by telephone. To send a copy of a document, put the original into the Telecopier, press the SEND button and telephone the recipient. Transmission begins immediately, and in a few minutes a facsimile of the original document emerges from the recipient's Telecopier at the other end of the line. By inserting a multiple-copy pack, the recipient can get up to four copies.

The Plessey "Remotecopier" facsimile transceiver operates over public or private telephone lines. It uses an electrostatic printing process to produce dry copy and is compatible with most other makes of facsimile transceiver.

When selecting a facsimile transceiver it is important to check that the model you decide to buy has what is known as "universal compatibility". This means that it can transmit and receive copies nationally and internationally through other makes of transceiver and is not restricted to being used only with models from the same manufacturer.* (See opposite.)

PAGING

As an accessory to a telephone system, some large organisations have a paging system. This may consist of sets of coloured lights placed at strategic points throughout the organisation. Each senior official has a particular light combination allocated to him, e.g. yellow still plus green flashing. When an official sees his own lights, he goes to the nearest telephone extension. There is also a system of paging by radio. This is a small instrument which can be used to cover areas up to 27 square kilometres. Each official carries his instrument and can be signalled from any telephone.

Modern Telephones pocket receiver.

PUBLIC ADDRESS SYSTEMS

Public address systems allow the announcement of messages over loudspeakers but there cannot be any intercommunication between speaking and listening stations. This system is frequently used for paging.

AUTOMATIC ANSWERING MACHINES

There are two kinds of telephone which will answer a caller automatically by pre-recorded message when the subscriber is unable to answer a call. The

* The difference between various makes of transceivers can be compared to the different kinds of television pictures, that is, 625 lines or 405 lines. Some transceivers in use in America are not compatible with transceivers of British manufacture.

answering set, which can be connected to most types of exchange lines and to extension lines connected to a private branch exchange, can be rented from the Post Office. It is not possible for the caller to leave any message, but it is suitable for people who wish to leave information about where they can be contacted, e.g. a doctor.

Telephone answering machines answer the caller with a pre-recorded message which invites him to leave his name and other details. His information is then recorded. Later the subscriber plays back the tape and hears the message.

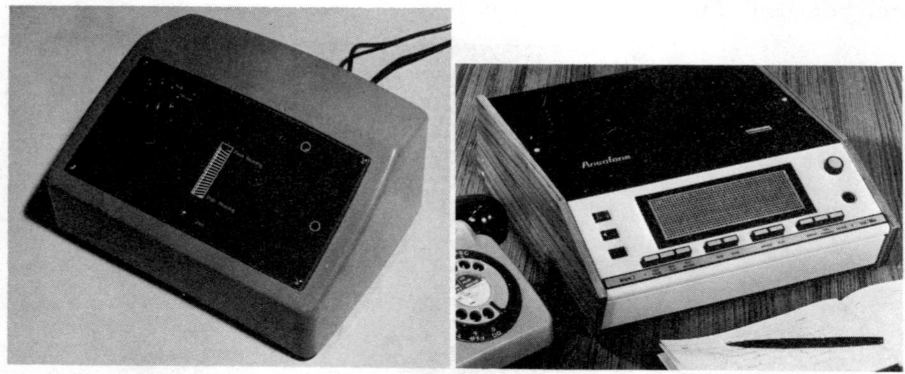

Post office answering set (left). (Right) The Ansafone Mark 7 telephone answering machine.

Most telephone answering machines are obtainable solely on rental because the equipment is connected to the Post Office telephone lines.

Basically, a telephone answering machine is a tape-recorder fitted with two sets of tapes and connected to the telephone. One tape is a continuous loop on which the subscriber has recorded his message or instructions to incoming callers; he can change the message or the wording of the instructions whenever he wishes to do so. The second tape is a standard blank tape; it is triggered into the RECORD position by the answering tape, and starts to record as soon as the message on the answering tape has been completed.

When a caller dials the subscriber's number, he will hear the ringing tone. After a few seconds the ringing tone will stop and the answering machine will 'answer' the caller by acknowledging the call with a pre-recorded announcement, such as: 'This is an automatic telephone answering machine. If you wish to leave a message for Mr Smith—*or whatever the name of the subscriber is*—you may do so as soon as you hear the bleep signal at the end of this recorded acknowledgment.'

The caller may then speak into the telephone and his message will be recorded on the answering machine attached to the receiving telephone. When the subscriber returns to his office a light on the machine will tell him that a call has come in; he will then play back the tape and listen to all the messages which have been recorded during his absence.

Telephone answering machines enable shop or store managers to offer a 24-hour service to customers; and for the business man with a small staff or none at all, they provide a method of accepting telephone messages at any time when he himself is not available.

Telephone answering machines have the great advantage that incoming calls can be routed directly to them, thus freeing the switchboard of the organisation for outgoing calls or incoming calls relevant to a different aspect of the business from that being handled by the answering machines. For example, 125 Ansafone machines installed at Television House were able to deal with 4000 calls made in response to summer holiday advertisements televised on Christmas Day and Boxing Day 1970. The messages were subsequently transcribed, envelopes prepared and mailed, and in most cases the caller received his brochure within 24 hours of phoning his enquiry.

This type of service is also useful for factories and head offices that are receiving continuous calls from dealers, agents and branches for spare parts or requests for new deliveries.

Some companies install telephone answering machines in the Telex or teleprinter room so that whilst the Telex or teleprinter operator is transmitting one message another may be received over the internal telephone and recorded ready for handling when the operator is free.

Some firms accept calls from their salesmen or representatives or regular customers by Transferred Charge Calls or by using the Freefone service. Calls through these services may also be connected to telephone answering machines; in this way orders are dictated at conversation speed and recorded without interruption, so that each call is cleared in less time than is needed for hand-written dictation.

There are several additional facilities which can be added to automatic answering. A caller can be *handed-on*, i.e. his conversation, started directly with a subscriber, can be recorded on the answering machine. Reporters wishing to dictate news copy might well be dealt with in this way; or salesmen reporting urgent orders.

On occasions it is considered advisable to record a telephone conversation between two people so a secretary is asked to listen in on an extension and take it down in shorthand. The *two-way recording* device records the conversation accurately.

Just as telephones can be connected to a central dictating system so some answering sets can be used as *dictating machines* via the telephone. Such a machine has transcribing facilities.

Many answering sets can now be operated by *remote control*. The subscriber who leaves his home or office for a considerable period may wish to know what messages the answering set has taken in his absence each day or so. He can dial his own telephone number and speak a code which is an instruction to the machine to rewind and play back. If it is wished to erase all or some of the messages this can also be done by operating another code.

Answering sets are put to a variety of uses to solve individual organisation

The Robophone Receptionist. The Robophone Secretary.

problems. One problem common to many different types of organisation is keeping a large number of clerks informed of up-to-date situations, e.g. airline clerks of flight information; spare parts clerks of stock holdings; bank clerks of computer service from head office when this is interrupted for any reason. In companies where a battery of clerks is needed to take orders, their time and that of the switchboard operators can be saved by automatic recording. The customer gets quicker service as well.

OTHER TELEPHONE FACILITIES

In addition to the telephone services and equipment already described, many other types of apparatus and extension arrangements are available, such as Extension Arrangement Plan 9, Keymaster sets and Loudspeaking Telephones. Further information on these and other specialised arrangements is available from Post Office Telecommunications Headquarters. Secretaries should ensure that they keep up-to-date in this important sphere of their work so that they can advise on the telephone arrangements best suited to their own office requirements.

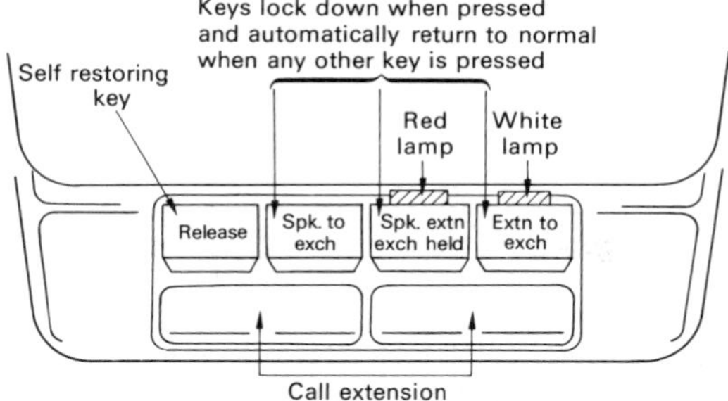

Plan 107:

The bell rings only on main telephone unless switched through to extensions. The main telephone can make and receive exchange calls and can call and speak to an extension whilst holding the incoming call. Incoming calls and outgoing calls can be dealt with by extension when a line is switched through ("EXTN TO EXCH" key depressed).

Key control operation on main telephone

SPEAK TO EXCH key depressed indicates that instrument is connected to the line and can be used as an ordinary telephone.

SPEAK EXTN EXCH HELD key depressed enables incoming call to be held and main to speak to extension. RED LAMP GLOWS.

Extension is called in by pressing CALL EXTN bar.

Conversation cannot be heard by caller being held.

EXTN TO EXCH key depressed enables extension to be connected to the line. RED LAMP GOES OUT AND WHITE LAMP GLOWS.

When WHITE LAMP goes out "RELEASE" key should be pressed—otherwise incoming calls will be connected directly to extension.

Depress "SPK TO EXCH" key after clearance.

IMPORTANT: If SPK EXTN EXCH HELD key remains depressed instead of pressing RELEASE key and the handset is off, no incoming calls can be received because the engaged tone will be heard by the caller. Make sure that you always depress keys firmly; a light tap could mean that the caller is cut off.

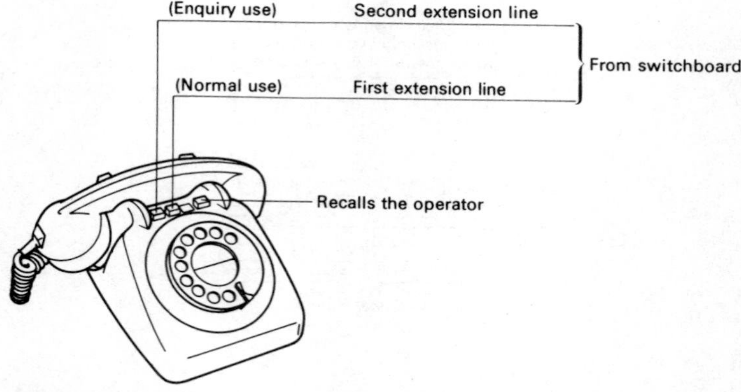

Extension Arrangement Plan 9 connects two extension lines to the same telephone and enables anyone with an extension from a switchboard to make telephone enquiries while holding the original call. The first extension line is obtained directly by lifting the handset. Pressing the ENQY button calls the PBX operator on the second extension line and holds the call on the first. The NORM (normal) button restores the telephone to the first extension line and clears the second. Calls are normally made on the first extension line; a call on the first line can be held while an enquiry is made on the second and the original caller cannot hear the enquiry.

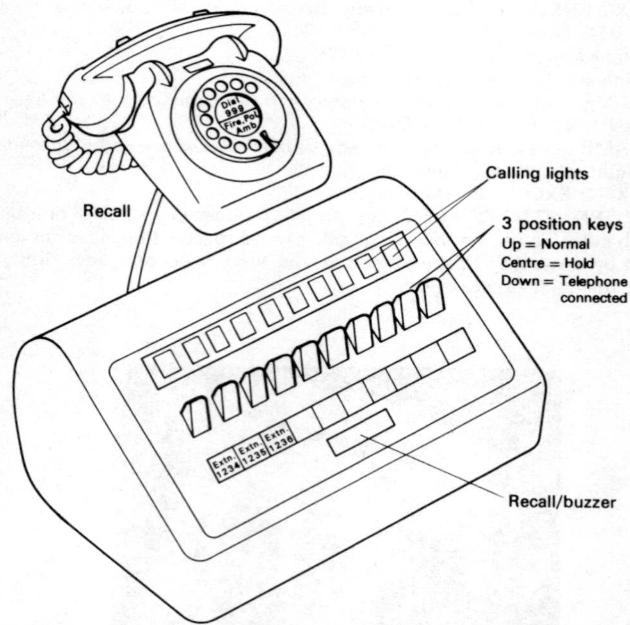

This is a *Key and Lamp Unit* containing 10 keys and 10 lamps, to which is connected a telephone. By the operation of the keys, it is possible to gain access to any of the lines connected. A flashing light indicates that there is an incoming call waiting to be answered and a continuous light indicates that the line is engaged. Any line can be held while an enquiry is made on another line.

Key and lamp units are used for two purposes.

1 Where different staff in a large office require access to the same extension, a key and lamp unit and associated telephone is provided for each member of staff, then anyone can answer an incoming call by pushing the key down under the lamp which is flashing. The same key may be operated simultaneously on several positions therefore allowing several people to speak in on the same conversation.

2 One key and lamp unit is provided in an office which is continuously staffed. Other members of the group are provided with Plan 7 or Plan 107 main units and the extensions of these terminate on the key and lamp unit. When staff vacate their offices they switch the line through to the key and lamp unit so that it can be answered in their absence.

Keymaster systems provide normal exchange lines plus intercommunication and conference facilities between a number of connected 'stations'. Keymaster 1+5 shown here provides one exchange line and five stations. External calls are made by lifting the handset and pressing the button marked EXCH. The left-hand lamp glows red while any station is connected to the exchange line. Incoming exchange calls flash the red lamp and ring the bell on each station telephone. The bell in each telephone other than the main one can be cut off by the locking switch BELL OFF. Any station is called by raising the handset and pressing the appropriate numbered button. Any number of stations can be called one after the other to join the internal call. Any station user can answer an exchange call and hold it while making an enquiry call to another station. The exchange line caller cannot hear the enquiry call. An exchange call from one station and an internal call between the other stations can be in progress at the same time without overhearing. Any number of stations can have a conference on an internal call but it is not possible to include an exchange line caller in the conference.

Loudspeaking telephone 1.

Loudspeaking telephone 4.

Loudspeaking Telephones such as those shown above allow a person to speak on the telephone and have both hands free to take notes or handle papers at the same time.

CONFRAVISION Although not strictly a telephone service the Confravision system is run by the Post Office and enables individuals or groups of people who are miles apart to exchange views. Those taking part in the discussions are accommodated in separate studios linked by two-way television. Confravision services enable discussions to take place in private, and save the time and expense of long-distance travel. Inter-city services are available between London, Glasgow, Manchester, Birmingham and Bristol and it is anticipated that international services may soon be developed.

AUTOMATIC DIALLING DEVICES

The **Card Callmaker** uses a punched card to dial calls. The callmaker is built into a small grey plastic box which is connected by one cord to the telephone set and by a second cord to a normal electric power socket. Telephone numbers are recorded on white plastic cards by pushing out the centres of the pre-scored holes with a guide and punch, as shown in the illustration on page 139. To make a call: lift the receiver of the telephone set and when you hear the dialling tone, drop the card into the slot at the front of the Callmaker. The card works its way through the slot, dialling the number automatically, then drops it into the tray below. The top of the Callmaker has storage space for thirty cards; a plastic box containing fifty cards and nine index dividers is provided with each set. The Callmaker card measures 89 mm by 57 mm and is about 1 mm thick. It has feed-holes down each side and spaces for writing down the name and number of the person to be called.

The **Tape Callmaker** can store up to 400 telephone numbers on magnetic tape and any one of the recorded numbers can be quickly located and called automatically without dialling. Numbers are recorded by connecting a dial unit to the Callmaker, writing the name and telephone number in pencil across the tape in the Callmaker unit, moving the entry between the guide lines and dial-

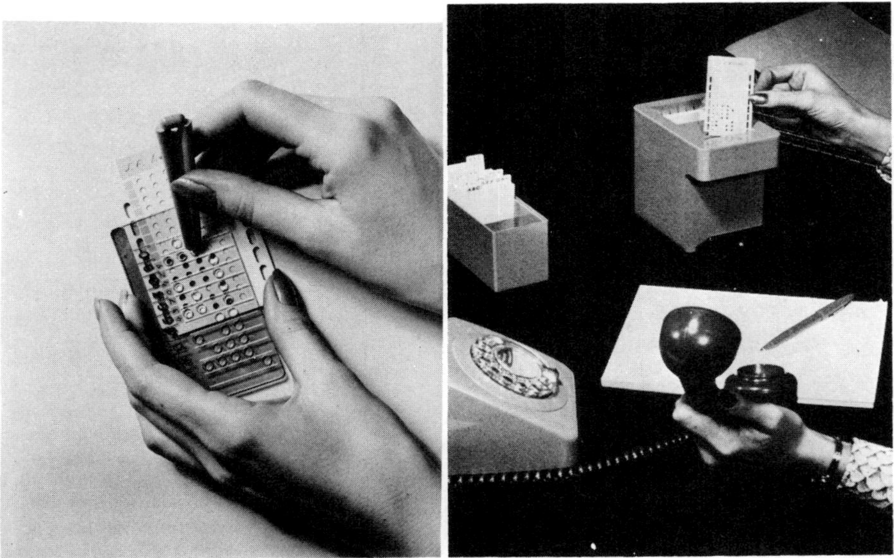

The Card Callmaker uses a punched card to dial telephone calls.

ling the number on the dial unit. The dial unit is then unplugged. A call is made by moving the tape to the required section of the alphabet indicated by the movement of a red line; the final positioning of the tape is made with the thumb-wheel. When the required number appears between the two guide lines on the window and when the dialling tone is heard on the handset, the "call"

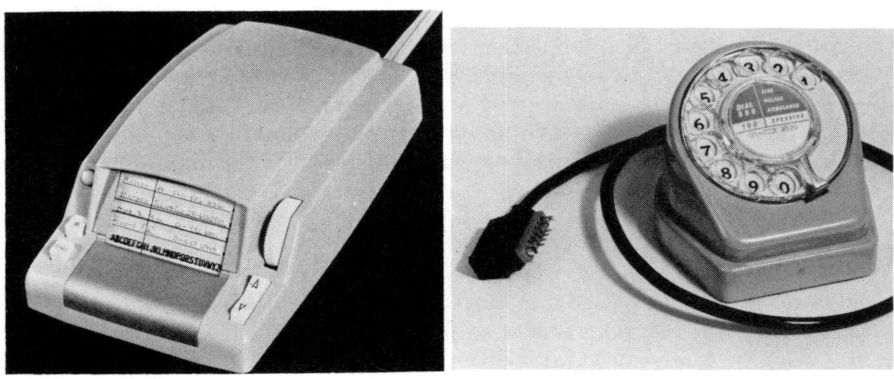

The Tape Callmaker unit stands near the telephone and can store up to four hundred numbers on magnetic tape. The dial unit is plugged into the Callmaker to record a number on the magnetic tape.

button is pressed and the number is automatically dialled. A call can be cancelled at any stage by replacing the handset. The Callmaker can be used on an extension from a PABX.

ATLAS, automated telephone line address system, enables thirty-two telephone numbers to be pre-recorded; the equipment dials the numbers automatically when the appropriate call-buttons are pressed.

Atlas—automated telephone line address system—is an electronic telephone number memory device being developed by the Shipton Automation Group for the British Post Office. Telephone numbers are fed into the machine's "memory" by pressing the appropriate push-buttons and call-buttons; the machine then dials the calls automatically when the call-buttons are pressed. If a called number is engaged or difficult to obtain, the call will automatically cancel after thirty seconds; it can be re-set by pressing the appropriate call-button. ATLAS has thirty-two call buttons, thus enabling thirty-two telephone numbers to be stored. A particular advantage of the device is that an executive can pre-programme all his business calls for the day and make them at any convenient time without further reference to directories or notes. If he is out of the office, his secretary can programme onto the equipment any numbers her boss should ring back; when he returns to the office he need only press the relevant call button and the machine will automatically dial the number.

GROUP DISCUSSION

Divide into groups and discuss in what ways you think the telephone extension user influences the company image. Consider carefully the role of the telephone in the work of a secretary. After group discussion, pool ideas and draw up a 'blueprint' for perfect extension user service.

EXERCISES

1 What differences are there between a private branch exchange and a private automatic branch exchange for an extension user receiving and making a call?

2 What is the telephone alphabet? Suggest occasions when you might use it.

3 You are a private secretary to a Managing Director and your work takes you out of the office frequently. Your junior takes calls in your absence and asks you to give her some guide lines for screening calls. What would you tell her?

4 What is the difference between receiving calls on an extension and receiving them on a direct line?

5 Write a list of instructions for taking messages.

6 What do you understand by the term 'smile in the voice'?

7 When making a call what is the first thing you would do when you have been answered?

8 In many countries most trunk calls are made by subscriber trunk dialling. There are, however, still occasions when you need to ring the exchange. State five such occasions.

9
 a What information is available in a telephone directory?
 b How does a classified directory differ from an ordinary subscriber directory?

10 What is an answering set and to whom do you think such a set would be useful?

11 What is a code number?

12 What is the advantage of STD over trunk calls routed through an exchange?

13 When would you book a personal call?

14 You are a private secretary to a Sales Manager. You answer the telephone to an irate customer who complains bitterly about the service he has received. Your boss is out for the day. How would you deal with this situation?

15 In connection with the telephone service, explain the following:
 a a fixed time call
 b an alarm call
 c a time call
 d a transferred charge call
 e a phonogram.

16 You take up a new appointment as secretary to the Chief Accountant and find that many of his telephone callers refuse to give their names. Suggest ways of dealing with this.

17 You overhear a junior using the following expressions on the telephone
 a Hold on.
 b Mr who?

c What do you say?
d Wait a minute.
e Who is it?
f Yes, I'll tell him.
g Hello (when answering)
h What do you want him for?
i He is out.
j O.K.

Write the expressions you would tell her to use instead of these.

18 Your boss asks you to carry out a survey to find out whether extension users are following the correct procedures when receiving and making calls. List the points you would look for.

19 When you are in the middle of a conversation on your internal telephone your external instrument rings. What action would you take?

20 What is meant by telephone personality?

4

Mail Handling

"Secretaries spend quite an amount of time in sorting and distributing mail and in compiling a mail register."

A. C. Pendlebury, *Technical Education*, January 1965.

In most large organisations there is a department responsible for handling all incoming and outgoing mail, and some or all of the internal mail; in government offices, public corporations and international organisations, the department responsible for this branch of the work is usually called the Registry. In industry and commerce, the 'department' may be called the Post Room or Mail Room or Department. Frequently centralised filing is also the responsibility of the Registry. In very large organisations there may be more than one registry.

MAIL ROOM FUNCTIONS

The functions carried out by the registry staff include the following:

1 Collecting mail from the Post Office at least twice a day, usually early

morning and early afternoon if a private post bag or box is rented at the Post Office.

2 Processing mail received from the Post Office.
3 Supervising messengers (internal postmen) who collect and deliver mail internally, and external delivery messengers.
4 Sorting and distributing internal mail.
5 Processing outgoing mail.
6 Delivering postal mail to the Post Office at the end of the day.
7 Processing 'confidential' mail.
8 Processing registered mail.
9 Arranging special deliveries of mail.
10 Processing incoming and outgoing telecommunications.
11 Filing—see Chapter 7.

Collection The mail may be collected from the Post Office by a messenger or other employee on the way to the office in the morning. Some large organisations have a private post bag. All mail for the company is sorted into this bag by the Post Office sorters and the bag is locked before being handed over to the collector. A key is kept in Registry where it is opened. (In countries abroad it is usual to have a Post Office Box Number as postal deliveries may be very limited or non-existent.) Where relatively small amounts of mail are involved, the organisation will receive its mail by normal postal delivery once, twice or three times a day, depending on the service given in the particular area.

Processing incoming mail When mail is received it must first be 'faced', that is, all envelopes placed in a pile with the address face up and the right way round. The addressee should be checked so that any mail wrongly delivered can be returned to the Post Office. Subsequent procedures are easier if envelopes are placed in order of size. During facing all envelopes marked 'Private', 'Personal' or 'Confidential' are set aside. 'Confidential' letters may be placed in a separate pile and sent directly to the registry which deals specifically with classified correspondence.

The envelopes are next slit. Assuming the person is right-handed, the pile of envelopes to be opened is placed near the left hand with the addressee's face down and the flap at the top. A paper knife is held in the right hand. The envelope is picked up by its left side and 'tapped' on the table to drop the contents to the bottom of the envelope, which is then flicked round so that the bottom of it is held in the hand; it is slit and placed in another pile.

When all the envelopes have been slit the contents are removed from the envelope. The envelopes should be set aside so that they can be checked before being thrown away to ensure that there are no enclosures left accidentally. The letters must be checked to ensure that:

the addressee is correct; (it is possible for the wrong letter to be inserted in the envelope);

enclosures mentioned in the letter are enclosed. They should be securely attached to the master document. If missing, the envelope should be checked and if the missing enclosure is not found, the fact should be noted on the master document. Special care should be taken with cheques or other monetary documents.

All the letters should now be stamped with the date of receipt. This proves that if there has been delay in delivery the company is not at fault. A 'distribution' stamp may also be used which enables the registry clerk or secretary to tick the appropriate designation.

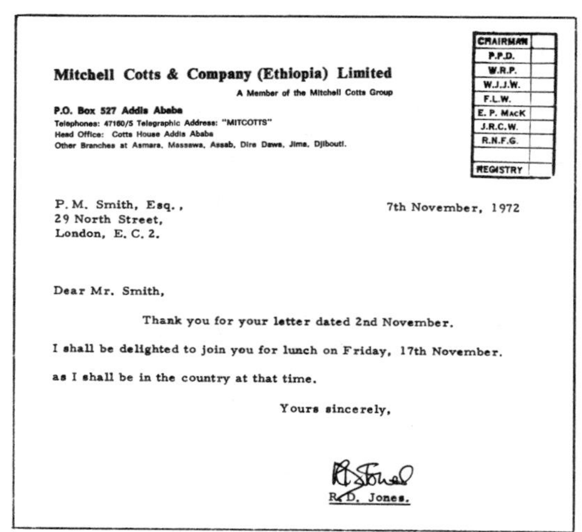

Mitchell Cotts & Company (Ethiopia) Limited
A Member of the Mitchell Cotts Group

P.O. Box 527 Addis Ababa
Telephones: 47160/5 Telegraphic Address: "MITCOTTS"
Head Office: Cotts House Addis Ababa
Other Branches at Asmara, Massawa, Assab, Dire Dawa, Jima, Djibouti.

CHAIRMAN	
P.P.D.	
W.R.P.	
W.J.J.W.	
F.L.W.	
E. P. MACK	
J.R.C.W.	
R.N.F.G.	
REGISTRY	

P.M. Smith, Esq.,
29 North Street,
London, E.C.2.

7th November, 1972

Dear Mr. Smith,

Thank you for your letter dated 2nd November.

I shall be delighted to join you for lunch on Friday, 17th November.

as I shall be in the country at that time.

Yours sincerely,

R.D. Jones.

Distribution stamp

At this point procedures vary in order, depending on the organisation. In private companies an incoming mail register is rarely kept. Many Government departments have also stopped keeping this record. If the organisation as a whole is efficient it is unlikely that such a record will be used frequently enough to justify the time spent in keeping it.

In organisations where it is kept the incoming mail should now be recorded in the Register. A typical ruling for a Mail Inwards Register is shown below.

In Government and International organisations the next step is to check the file reference where it is quoted and write on the reference where it is not quoted. The letters are then taken to the filing cabinets and as many files as are

Date	Sender	Subject	Attention	Replied

available are taken out, so that the letters can be either attached to the front cover with a paper clip, or actually filed. Where files have been loaned, they are retrieved as soon as possible, but this often involves long delay.

In some cases letters are placed loose in a file folder and circulated to one or more senior officers for a 'quick look' before filing, or even before registration. Letters needing urgent attention may be removed from the folder to avoid the delay involved in recording and filing.

In private organisations letters are not usually registered. They are sorted either according to departments or according to officers. A small organisation may have a number of mail trays, each marked with a personal or departmental name. Mail is then collected at intervals by the secretaries of individual managers and/or by a clerk from each department. In a big organisation it is delivered by the internal postman.

The senior secretary in a department may be responsible for receiving and distributing all the mail for that department. She must read it all and usually indicates to whom each document should be delivered, keeping only those which must be dealt with by her own boss and those with which she herself will deal. She may attach a 'Circulation' slip to a letter which should be passed around various officers.

Alternatively, if routine action is required she may attach a 'Routing' or 'Transmittal' slip, either on her own initiative or on the instruction of her boss.

		TRANSMITTAL SLIP	
To	Division	Room	Date
From	Division	Room	Extension

For ☐ Action ☐ Approval ☐ Signature ☐ Comment ☐ Information ☐ File
☐ Reply ☐ Reply for my sig. ☐ See me ☐ More details ☐ Investigate and report ☐ Note and return

Those for her boss must then be sorted into order of urgency, those which need immediate attention being placed at the top of the pile, e.g. telegrams, letters giving information which she knows he has been waiting for, letters requesting an urgent reply.

Internal postmen and messengers It is always advisable that internal post should be collected and delivered at specified times as this assists the boss and his secretary to keep to their work schedules. Incoming mail should be delivered to the offices as early as possible in the morning. When delivering, the messenger/postman will place letters in the 'In' tray in each office. Normally the postman does not enter the boss's office but will deliver all mail to the secretary. At the same time he will empty the 'Out' tray. He may sort through

Fiche d'accompagnement

A :

POUR

	Approbation		Plus de détails
	Réponse s.v.p.		Votre information
	Me voir s.v.p.		Retourné comme demandé
	Votre signature		Enquête et rapport
	Noter et classer		Pour action immédiate
	Noter et retourner		Réponse pour ma signature
	Vos commentaires		Initiales et faire suivre

Remarques :

Date	De

A French 'Routing Slip'.

the outgoing mail quickly so that he can deliver direct any internal mail, or he may take it all back to registry.

In addition to the main delivery/ies of incoming mail, there should be interim deliveries of internal mail, and mail delivered by hand from other organisations.

Processing internal mail Much internal mail is not enveloped unless it is confidential. If memoranda are placed in envelopes to ensure that they are not torn, the envelope should not be sealed (unless the subject matter is confidential) so that it can be used several times. Printed envelopes can be used to ensure that maximum use is made of each envelope (see illustration overleaf).

When an internal letter needs to be delivered immediately this is normally undertaken by a junior in the department, or by the messenger if there is one. In some cases the secretary may have to do this herself in a small organisation.

Processing outgoing mail Mail received in registry for despatch may or may not be already enveloped. In some cases the envelopes have been typed and attached, but in some organisations, especially Government departments, envelopes may be typed or written by a registry clerk.

It is most important that every outgoing letter is checked to ensure that it has the correct date, correct file references (the sender's and the addressee's), name and address of addressee correct, indication of enclosure, correct enclosure(s) attached, signature, no typewriting or spelling errors, correct size envelope, correctly addressed envelope.

A Despatch Register or Outgoing or Outwards Mail Register may be kept, in which case the letters are recorded in it at this point. Some Government

CIRCULATION INTERIEURE (Ne pas coller l'enveloppe)

NOM	DATE	ORGANISATION ou SERVICE	NOM	DATE	ORGANISATION ou SERVICE

departments also write the file reference of the letter on the envelope when it is to be delivered by hand.

Letters and enclosures are next folded to fit the envelope. See the diagrams on pages 78 to 80 which show varying sizes of envelope available and the correct way to fold the contents. Bulky things which need to be parcelled are set aside.

When the contents have been inserted all the envelopes are then sealed, the heavier letters being piled separately for weight checking. As the weights are checked the amount of postage required is written on. The requisite amount of postage is then affixed, either by postage stamp or by franking machine. The stamp or frank should be in the top right-hand corner of the envelope. All regular weight letters should be handled first and then all the heavier letters. On completion of stamping the letters are entered in the postage book. In the example shown on page 149 it will be seen that only the name and town of the addressee is recorded and that items such as invoices, circulars and statements are recorded in bulk. The postage book is usually kept on the Imprest system (see Chapter 12).

When articles are too bulky to be mailed in an envelope they must be parcelled. In some organisations a special Mail Room is used for packing and despatching parcels and the company may have its own delivery van. A secretary may have to pack a parcel for her boss. Hints on packing parcels are included in the *Post Office Guide*.

International organisations, Foreign Ministries and Overseas representatives (embassies and high commissions) send the bulk of overseas mail by 'Pouch'. The pouch has diplomatic immunity, i.e. it is not subject to customs inspection and is usually sent once a week on a specific day. International organisations send pouches by air freight. Some British embassies/high commissions have their pouches delivered and collected by Queen's

Dr.				Cr.
£	1973			
15.00	Jan. 1	Stamps in hand		
		Bloxon & Co. Ltd. Wellingboro		
		Pedigree Cattle Co. Stoke Poges		0.07
		56 Brochures @ $4\frac{1}{2}$p		2.52
	,, 3	Cheyne Building Co. B'ham		0.03
		Birmingham Plant Hire Ltd. B'ham (Recorded delivery)		$0.10\frac{1}{2}$
		24 Statements @ $2\frac{1}{2}$p		0.60
		Lebrun Shipping Co., Paris		0.05
	,, 4	27 Invoices @ $2\frac{1}{2}$p		$0.67\frac{1}{2}$
	,, 5	Baker, Line & Co., London Parcel)		0.45
		10 Brochures @ $4\frac{1}{2}$p		0.45
	,, 6	Johnson Bros. & Co., Bognor Regis		0.03
		Balance	c/d	9.99
£15.00				£15.00
9.99	Jan. 6	Balance b/d		
5.01	,, 10	To Cash		

Typical entries in a Postage Book.

Messengers. The pouch is sent to headquarters and the mail contained in it is transmitted onwards. To save weight, routine mail and forms intended for the headquarters are not normally enveloped. Embassy staff are allowed to send and receive personal mail by way of the pouch.

Delivering mail to the Post Office When a large number of letters are to be posted they should be faced, tied in bundles and handed over the Post Office counter, not posted into a posting box. Letters should be sorted into 'Town' delivery, i.e. the sender's own town; country delivery, i.e. places in the sender's own country but outside his own town; and overseas delivery.

Processing 'confidential' mail In private organisations 'confidential' mail is delivered unopened directly to the person to whom it is addressed or his secretary.

In Government departments any letters which are marked 'confidential' are sent to a special registry where the confidential files are kept. The procedures for opening and recording are the same as for ordinary mail. When the letter has been attached to the appropriate file, the file is enveloped for delivery to the officer concerned or is delivered by the registry officer.

Outgoing confidential letters may be enveloped by the secretary (or typists) or in the confidential registry. In some government departments such letters are placed in an envelope marked "Confidential". This is then placed in an unmarked envelope.

In the case of "Secret" documents, the inside envelope is marked "Secret" and this is placed in an outside envelope marked "Confidential".

All confidential and secret mail is termed "classified".

Registered mail Recorded delivery and Registered letters must be signed for by the recipient. Such letters are normally delivered to the registry of the organisation by the Post Office. A special Mail Inwards Register may be kept, or, more usually, a note made in the 'Remarks' column of the usual register that the letter was recorded or registered. The same applies to outgoing letters. If money (cash) is enclosed it should be carefully checked and placed in a sealed envelope. This, together with the letter, should be replaced in the registered envelope if possible, and sent to the appropriate officer.

Special deliveries Many organisations have their own messenger service for delivery of letters locally. This applies especially in developing countries where postal services may be rather slow. Each letter for hand delivery is recorded in a Delivery Book, which must be signed by the recipient of the letter. In some offices letters recorded in a Delivery Book are not recorded in the Despatch Register as this is an unnecessary duplication.

Telegrams, cables and telex messages Telegrams, overseas cables and telex messages are received in registry and processed in the same way as letters. They should, of course, be dealt with immediately on receipt, whether incoming or outgoing.

Incoming telegrams are usually telephoned by the Post Office and a 'confirmatory copy' sent later. The registry clerk may take the message or if it has been addressed to a specific person the company telephone operator may connect the Post Office with the appropriate secretary.

When telegrams are not first telephoned, the written message should be date stamped and marked with the time of receipt. A special time/date stamp may be used for this. If the appropriate file is immediately available the communication should be attached to it and delivered immediately. If the appropriate file is not available the delivery of the communication must not be delayed, but the file should then be obtained as quickly as possible and delivered to the officer concerned.

Outgoing telecommunications are usually given a reference number. Secretarial staff must ask the registry clerk for the next number before typing a telegram. The registry clerk thus keeps a record of all outgoing cables and telegrams. Inland telegrams are transmitted by the Post Office which accepts the messages at Post Office counters in written form, or by telephone. Overseas telegrams can be sent in the same way but can also be telephoned to one of the cable companies, such as Cable & Wireless Limited or Western Union, if the organisation has an account with such a company. It is

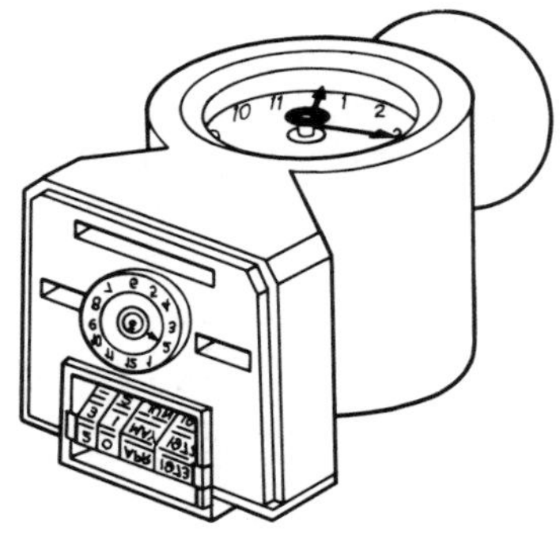

A time/date stamp.

also possible to send a telex message via these companies. This can be useful for a small company which does not rent a telex itself but wishes to communicate with a larger company that does.

THE SECRETARY'S RESPONSIBILITIES

A secretary may have to carry out some or all of these functions. In large organisations mail handling, filing and reprographic facilities are usually centralised so that a secretary is responsible only for those procedures related to her work for an individual manager. Frequently, however, she will find herself acting as a departmental registry (see page 143 ff.) and in many smaller organisations a secretary is the administrative kingpin and may well be responsible for the whole mail handling process. It is important that she has a strict routine and time schedule for mail handling since the work of many staff is connected with correspondence. Delay in receiving mail can completely disrupt an executive's programme.

A secretary may have one or more juniors under her to whom she can delegate mail handling duties. It may be necessary to arrange a rota so that juniors take it in turn to arrive early (collecting mail on the way possibly) to open and sort letters. Similarly a 'late' rota may have to be drawn up for posting mail at the end of the day. Staff must, of course, be allowed to leave early and arrive late when such duties are assigned to them.

Whether she has to carry out all mail handling procedures or not it is important that every secretary knows and fully understands the procedures carried out in the organisation. Even the best systems can have weaknesses due to unavoidable circumstances and a full understanding helps to achieve the teamwork necessary to minimise the effects of such weaknesses.

MAIL ROOM ORGANISATION

In order that the mail handling procedures can be carried out as quickly and efficiently as possible the room should be arranged to allow the work to 'flow' smoothly. The amount and size of furniture must depend on space available and the quantity of mail to be handled. A study of the plan of a mechanised mail room below will show how furniture and equipment can be arranged so that time is not spent in 'moving' mail from one place to another and back again. On page 153 is a plan of a registry/mail room which might belong to a medium size organisation.

Specimen plan for a mechanised mail room handling incoming and outgoing mail

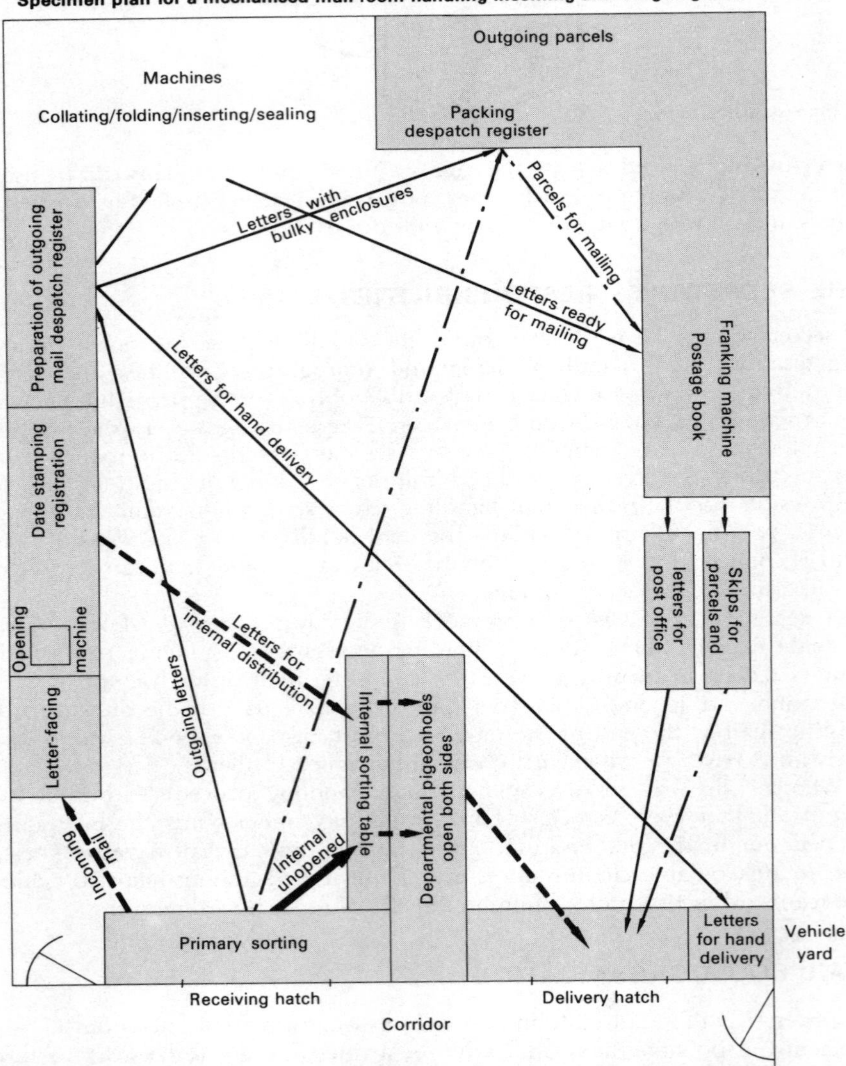

Specimen plan for a registry for all mail handling and filing

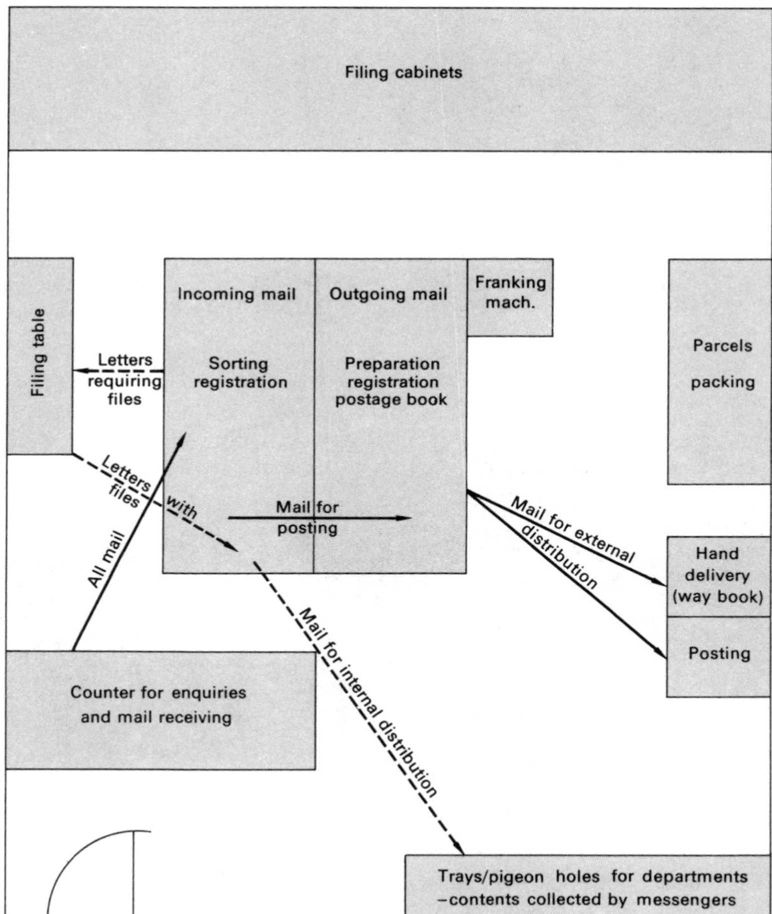

MAIL ROOM EQUIPMENT

Mailing procedures may be carried out entirely by hand but some of them can be carried out by machine.

LETTER OPENING MACHINE After facing and tapping, the envelopes are inserted into a machine which cuts a fractional slice off one side, usually the long side, of the envelope. Care must be taken to tap the envelope on the side opposite to that which is to be cut by the machine.

COLLATING MACHINE When a duplicated document consists of a number of pages which have been produced in piles a machine can be used to arrange the pages in sets in correct order—this is known as collating.

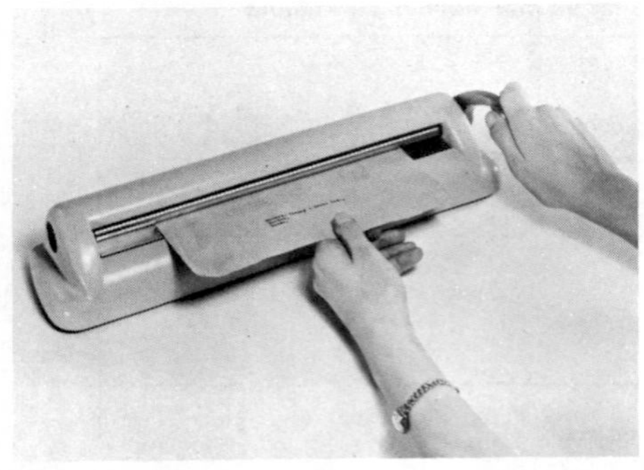

The Pitney-Bowes Model LH Mail-opener. This hand-operated machine is suitable for the secretary who opens her chief's mail and handles between 50 and 100 letters daily.

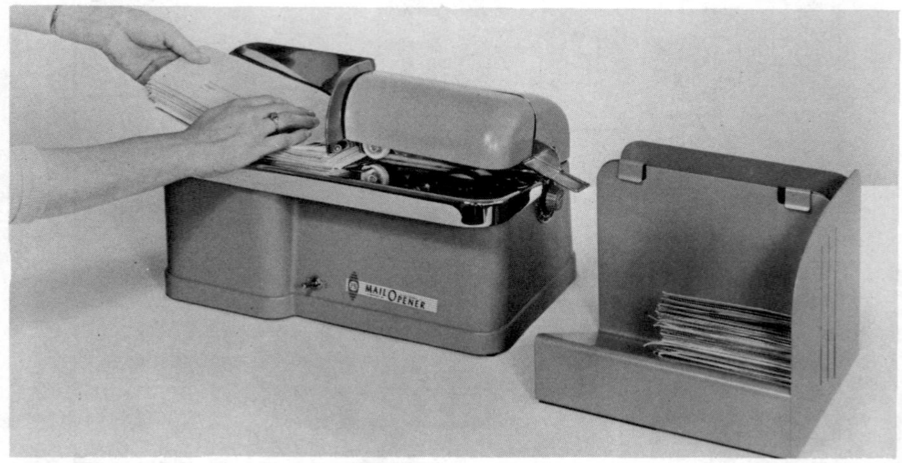

The Pitney-Bowes Model LA Mailopener. This is a high-speed electric machine suitable for a Mail Room where large numbers of envelopes, say more than 500, have to be opened each day.

FOLDING MACHINE Folding sheets of paper to fit into envelopes takes time. Machines are available which fold one or more sheets of paper, one, two or three times. The position of the fold(s) can be regulated to fit a suitable envelope.

FOLDING AND INSERTING MACHINE Some folding machines have an additional function—inserting the folded document into the envelope. The folding mechanism is pre-set to fit the size of envelope fed into the machine.

The Pitney-Bowes Model 3144 Collating/Mailing machine.

Folding/inserting machine.

ENVELOPE SEALING MACHINE The envelope into which the document has been inserted is passed through a sealing machine. The flap of the envelope is moistened as it passes sponge cylinders. The flap is then turned down and the envelope passes between rollers which stick the flap to the envelope. Most sealing machines take C6 and DL envelopes, but not the larger sizes.

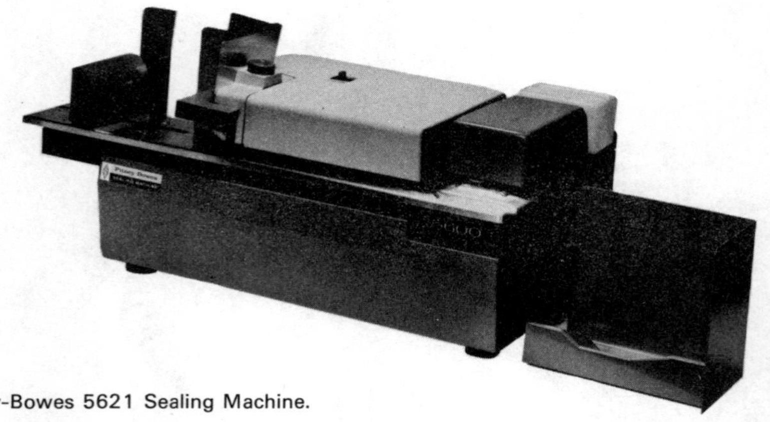

Pitney-Bowes 5621 Sealing Machine.

MAILING MACHINES These multi-operation machines take care of all operations from the collating of the papers to the sealing of the envelopes. When large quantities of circulars, invoices, etc. are despatched regularly such a machine can release several mailing clerks for more important work.

ADDRESSING MACHINES Addressing machines range from a small hand operated type to the highly sophisticated duplicating type. The basic principle is the same. A master is made by embossing a metal or plastic plate or by typing a spirit or stencil duplicating plate, and kept filed alphabetically, or possibly numerically if account numbers are included. The masters can thus form a card index which can be used for reference purposes by notching, punching or flagging. Colour coding can also be used to indicate sections or categories. This makes it easier to extract only the plates required at any one time.

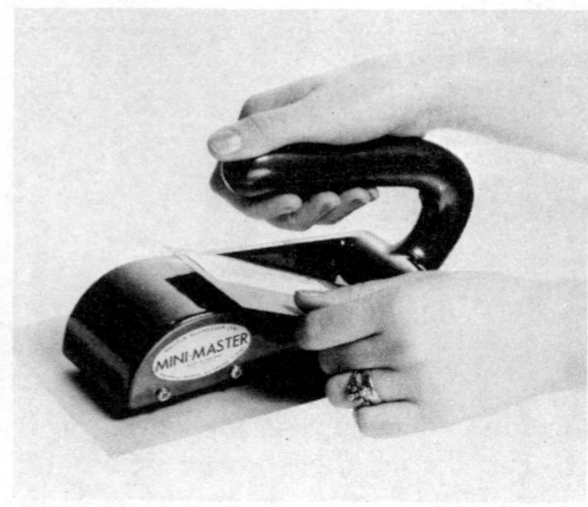

Miniature hand addressing machine.

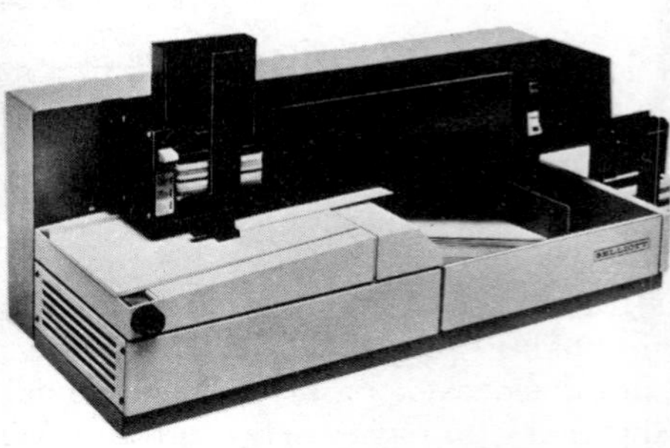

Automatic addressing machine.

The Elliott Addressall 6000 is an electric addressing machine with automatic print, skip and repeat controls. The address cards are prepared on a typewriter; it is claimed that each address card will give 10,000 impressions.

The plates to be used are placed in the addressing machine in a stack and the envelopes or cards to be printed are placed in the feed tray. As the printing lever is depressed the first plate is brought into contact with an envelope reproducing the details on the master, which is then passed to a receiving tray. The printed envelope is likewise passed to another receiving tray.

It may be that only selected masters in a batch are required. Those not required can be passed through without printing, either manually by use of a 'skip' lever, or automatically by using 'punched' masters which can be sorted by a special attachment on the addressing machine.

FRANKING MACHINE Many offices which have no other type of mailing machine, rent or own a franking machine. This obviates the necessity for keeping postage stamps. Before the machine can be used, money is paid to the Post Office, the amount being set on the meter. The total reduces as letters are franked. Before a letter is passed through the machine the amount of postage required must be set. This amount is then printed on the envelope as it passes through. Care must be taken to ensure that the frank will appear in the top right-hand corner of the envelope.

Some franking machines have an automatic feeding attachment which allows envelopes of varying thickness to pass through without adjustment. For large packets and parcels which cannot be passed through the machine, a piece of gummed paper is franked and then stuck on. "Flashes" can be incorporated in the machine so that as well as the frank, a slogan is printed on the envelope.

Franked envelopes may be posted only at main or sub-post offices. If the mail is late and the post office is shut, franked envelopes should be put in a large envelope (supplied by the franking machine company) which may then be posted in a pillar box.

POSTAL FACILITIES

Inland letters and packets Inland letters and packets may be sent by either First Class or Second Class services. (Packets are bulky envelopes and larger items which are paid for at letter rate—above a certain weight it is cheaper to send packages by parcel post but there are no express or registered parcel post services.) The cost of postage depends upon the speed of service required; the *First Class service* is the faster and costs 9p for up to 60 g. There is no weight limit in the First Class service, but in the *Second Class service* there is a weight limit of 750 g.

The **maximum size** for First Class letters and packets as well as for Second Class letters and packets, Registered Letters, Recorded Delivery Letters, Railex, Railway and Airway Letters is 610 mm long, 460 mm wide and 460 mm deep.

Franking machine with automatic feeder.

Envelope printed with frank and 'flash'.

Post Office Preferred (POP) envelopes and cards The Post Office asks all its customers to post their mail, whenever possible, in envelopes within a preferred range of sizes which have been recommended for use by postal administrations all over the world, so that much more of the mail can be handled by the latest electronic sorting machines. This will help to speed up the work, keep costs down and reduce demands on manpower.

At a later date only the Post Office Preferred range of envelopes (POP Envelopes) will qualify for the lowest rate of postage for inland letters. Mail weighing up to 60 g posted in envelopes outside the Preferred Range will be liable to an additional charge. A firm date from which the higher postage will be charged will be announced later. Mail weighing more than 60 g will be unaffected by the choice of envelope.

To fall within POP range, envelopes should be at least 90 mm × 140 mm and not larger than 120 mm × 235 mm. They should be oblong in shape (the longer side at least 1.414 times the shorter side), and made of paper weighing at least 63 grammes per square metre.

Postcards will be treated as letters and as if they had been posted in an envelope of the same dimensions as the card itself. Postcards outside POP sizes and those sent folded with the edges not sealed together will require the higher postage. Postcards must be not less than 1/100 in thick.

Irrespective of their size and shape, all *aperture* envelopes (that is envelopes where cut-out address panels are not covered with a transparent material) will be classed as outside the POP range.

Window envelopes (where cut-out address panels are covered with transparent material) will be treated as falling within the POP range provided they conform in size, shape and weight of paper.

All *unenveloped matter* weighing up to 60 g, except cards, will be classed as outside the POP range and will be liable to the higher postal charges. *Fold-and-tuck forms* and items enclosed in wrappers are in this category. Folders and lettercards with all the open edges sealed down will, however, be treated as falling within the POP range provided they conform in size, shape and weight of paper.

In order to make quite sure that a letter will arrive at its destination there is a *Recorded Delivery* service for inland letters and packets. The cost is postage plus a 9p fee which also covers the contents for reimbursement in the case of loss up to an amount of £2. This service may be by either First or Second Class mail; it is appropriate in such cases as sending final demands for payment, important documents, etc. Jewellery and money may not be sent by this service.

The more expensive *Registration fee* is a form of insurance. The fee ranges from 60p to 70p in Britain and covers the contents of inland letters and packets (not parcels) up to the value of £600. The fee is payable in addition to the normal First Class postage. When cash, uncrossed postal orders without payee's name or uncrossed bearer cheques are sent through the post, they must be despatched in a Registered Envelope, otherwise the amount will not be reimbursed in the case of loss. Letters and packets should be sealed, the latter with sealing wax. The registered parcel post service in Britain was withdrawn in 1972 and replaced by a Compensation Fee service (see page 164).

When the sender wishes to be informed that a Recorded or Registered letter/packet has been delivered he can pay an additional *Advice of Delivery* fee (12½p in Britain).

There are several ways of obtaining quicker delivery of mail than the normal first or second class post. These *Express Delivery* services include

a normal mail service as far as the delivery office and then delivery by Post Office messenger to the addressee (**Special Delivery**) either at the request of the sender or of the addressee;

b delivery of a packet to a railway station and collection from the train and delivery to the addressee by Post Office messenger (**Railway Letter, Railex** for packets or **Railway Parcel**);

c conveyance by Post Office messenger all the way from the sender to the addressee;

d acceptance of letters (not exceeding 450 g in weight) at some British Airways airports and terminals for transmittal on the next appropriate direct flight, either to be collected by the addressee or transferred to the normal mail delivery service.

If the last post has been missed there is a *Late Posted Packets Service*. A letter or packet may be posted in the mail box on a Travelling Post Office, i.e. a train to which a sorting office is attached, for a small amount of extra postage in addition to the normal first-class postage. Recorded delivery and registered packets are accepted at the Travelling Post Offices up to five minutes before departure time.

When companies wish to send goods to customers without requesting payment beforehand but at the same time ensure that they are paid for, the *Cash on Delivery* service can be used. This means that the cost of the goods, known as Trade Charge, is collected by the postman from the addressee. The sender pays a fee to the Post Office according to the amount to be collected.

Particularly useful for anyone who travels a great deal is the *Poste Restante* service which means that mail may be addressed to a Post Office from where the addressee can collect it. The Poste Restante service must not be used in the same town for more than three months.

Many organisations use the *Business Reply* service as an adjunct to advertising. A licence is obtained from the postmaster allowing the organisation to print Business Reply cards or envelopes, in a special format. The licence number is shown and every card or letter actually posted by the recipients is charged to the originator at the normal postage rate plus a small additional charge. This service is not available for letters sent from overseas.

Complementary to the Business Reply Service in Britain is *Freepost*. This service is a new reply method designed to encourage public response to advertising and sales promotion campaigns.

Although the FREEPOST service is similar to the Business Reply service in that it enables prospective customers to reply to advertisements without using postage stamps, it has the advantage that the licensee (the firm promoting the advertising campaign) has not first had to go to the expense of having Business Reply cards printed and mailed to prospective customers.

A firm wishing to use a FREEPOST address must first obtain a licence from the Head Postmaster of the district in which it is situated. The licensee pays an annual fee of £15 for a FREEPOST address; he also has to pay in advance a sum of money sufficient to cover the amount of postal charges likely to accrue during the period of approximately one month, and to make further payments to renew his credit from time to time. The licensee is charged the standard second-class mail postage (at present 7p) plus ½p on each FREEPOST item delivered to him. FREEPOST packets are treated as second-class mail.

The FREEPOST address is included in all the firm's press and television advertisements and prospective customers can send for further information by enclosing their replies in envelopes or using postcards on which they have

FIRST CLASS DESIGN

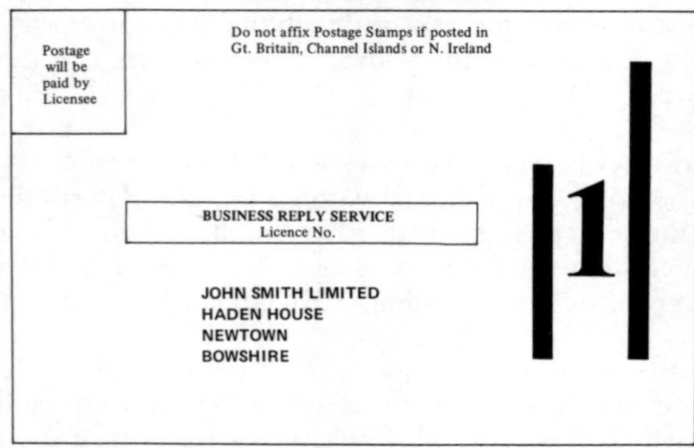

SECOND CLASS DESIGN

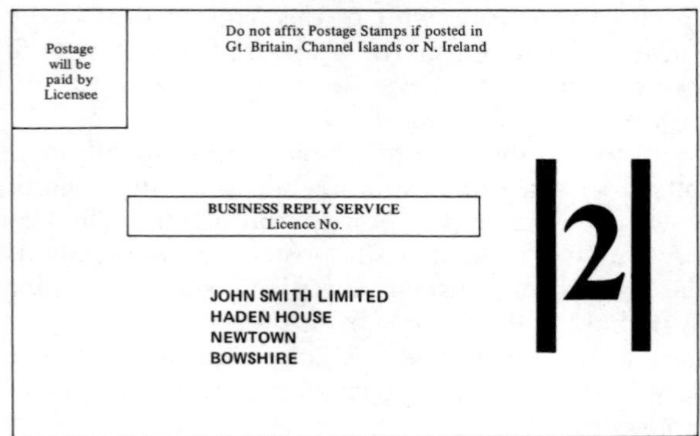

Reply-paid cards.

written the advertiser's FREEPOST address. No postage stamp is needed—the cost of postage is paid by the holder of the FREEPOST licence.

Selectapost is a useful additional service for large organisations which have departmental registries. Before delivery, mail is sorted by the Post Office into the different departments as required. The Selectapost charge is negotiated with individual organisations. The service may be used in conjunction with a private box, in which case no additional charge is made for the box.

Prepayment of postage charges. Many companies and firms take advantage of the facility by which postage on any postal packets may be prepaid, especially when a large number of packets must be despatched on one day. The conditions under which such packets may be posted are given in the Post Office Guide, and the arrangement is one which is convenient for both the Post Office and the senders. If the facility does not normally exist at certain post offices in the provinces, application for it can be made to the local postmaster, stating the exact date of posting and the approximate number of articles to be posted.

Certificate of posting. These may be obtained from post offices when the letters or parcels are posted. Certificates of Posting for Compensation Fee parcels are issued free of charge; for other parcels or for a letter or a packet, a Certificate of Posting costs 1p.

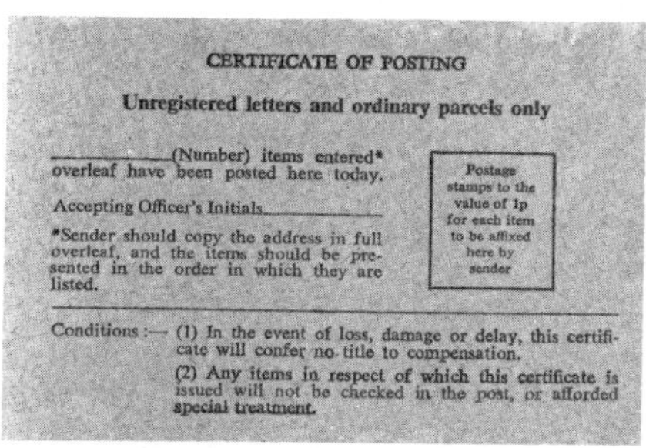

CERTIFICATE OF POSTING

Unregistered letters and ordinary parcels only

__________(Number) items entered* overleaf have been posted here today.

Accepting Officer's Initials__________

*Sender should copy the address in full overleaf, and the items should be presented in the order in which they are listed.

Postage stamps to the value of 1p for each item to be affixed here by sender

Conditions:—
(1) In the event of loss, damage or delay, this certificate will confer no title to compensation.
(2) Any items in respect of which this certificate is issued will not be checked in the post, or afforded special treatment.

Callers Services. The Post Office provides the following four Callers Services through which mail may be received earlier or at a more convenient time than normal delivery by the postman. Each service involves the addressee (or his authorised representative) calling at the post office which serves the address to which the mail would normally be delivered. All mail must bear the full address including the Box number if a Private Box is used, for example:

T Smith & Co Ltd
PO Box 100
9 High Street
HULL
HU9 1HF

1. The *Private Box Service* (town districts) allocates a Box number for use in the address. Mail is usually handed to the addressee when he calls at the post office but at some offices the mail is placed in a locked box to which the addressee holds a key. The standard fees for using this service during the daytime are:

Letters—£20 per year
Parcels—£20 per year
Letters and Parcels—£40 per year

2. *Private Bags.* The post office will sort mail into a lockable private bag ready for collection. The addressee must provide the bag. Although arrangements can be made for the Private Bag to be delivered to the addressee (provided it

is an acceptable weight when empty) it must normally be taken to the post office. The annual charge for a private bag is £20, irrespective of the number of times it is used daily for posting purposes. If the bag is used for collection and posting of mail both the private box and private bag fees must be paid.

If delivery of Bag by postman service is required an annual charge of £20 must be paid for each regular daily delivery.

3. *Callers Service.* In a rural district the addressee may call regularly at the post office for correspondence without the need to provide a Private Bag. The annual fee for this service is £20 covering both letters and parcels, but if the addressee needs to call after 6.00 a.m. and before the first delivery by postmen begins and when the public office is normally closed, an additional annual fee of £20 is payable.

4. *Registered and Recorded Delivery—Delivery to Callers.* The addressee may call regularly for Registered and Recorded Delivery packets during office opening hours on payment of a fee of £5 a year. This fee is not charged to Private Box or Bag renters.

Organisations can arrange for *free Collection of letters* from their premises if a minimum of one thousand first- and/or second-class letters are despatched at any one time or the total postage amounts to £70 or more.

A *Bulk Postage Rebate* can be obtained for a minimum of 4251 letters sent by second-class mail. The amount of rebate varies from fifteen to thirty per cent according to the number of letters despatched. The Head Postmaster should be consulted before a bulk posting and an official application must be made at least twenty-four hours before the posting is to be made.

The Post Office Parcels Services (Inland) *Compensation Fee (CF) Parcels.* The registered parcel service was withdrawn on 4 September 1972 and replaced by a Compensation Fee service. Under the new arrangements compensation for loss or damage can be claimed if a compensation fee has been paid at the time of posting. Compensation fees payable in addition to postage are:

12p	limit of compensation	£10
15p	limit of compensation	£50
25p	limit of compensation	£100
40p	limit of compensation	£200 maximum

A 'Certificate of Posting' form must be completed for each Compensation Fee parcel. Give the parcel and the Certificate of Posting to the counter clerk at the post office. When you have affixed stamps to the value of the fee you wish to pay, the clerk will initial and date stamp the top portion of the Certificate of Posting and hand it to you to keep.

Other parcels. If you are posting a parcel and do not wish to pay a compensation fee you may obtain a Certificate of Posting. There is a fee of 1p per parcel.

Parcels and packages may still be sent as first-class registered letters provided they conform to the size regulations for first-class letters (see page 158). The registration fees are:

60p limit of compensation £200
65p limit of compensation £400
70p limit of compensation £600 maximum

COMPENSATION FEE (C.F.) PARCELS
CERTIFICATE OF POSTING

Enter below in ink the name and full address as written on the parcel and tick the appropriate box at the bottom of the form

Name...

Address...

....

....

PLEASE SEE NOTES OVERLEAF
KEEP THIS RECEIPT – It must be produced if you need to make a claim.

STAMP(S) | Date Stamp

Inland COD form No.

Fee | Accepting Officer's Initials

COMPENSATION

Up to	£10	£50	£100
Fee	5p	10p	20p
Tick fee required ▶			

Date Stamp

PP 89B

How to post Compensation Fee parcels. Fill in the name and address of addressee and tick the appropriate box showing the fee you wish to pay.
Note: The form showing amounts of compensation and fees before revision is still in use.

The Postage Forward Parcel Service is useful for companies who run a 'free approval' service. The Postage Forward service enables customers to return goods at no cost to themselves. The cost to the company is £15 for a yearly licence and 6p per parcel over the usual rate.

Special Collections If at least ten parcels are despatched regularly a standing arrangement can be made for their collection, but in cases where bulk despatches happen irregularly a special collection can be arranged if the number of parcels is at least fifty.

Datapost is a door-to-door overnight collection and delivery service intended primarily for computer data, but it can be used for any other items. A contract for daily, weekly or monthly collection and delivery is made with the Post Office, the charges being negotiated. It is a particularly useful service for organisations which either use hired computer time in other organisations, or which have a number of branches using a centralised data processing department.

Under the *Railex* service packages (up to a maximum weight of 450 g) are collected and despatched on the first available train. At the arrival station, the parcel is taken straight to the addressee by Post Office messenger.

Parcels may also be sent by British Rail Parcels Service (see page 168).

Overseas Postal Services and Rates For overseas mail certain additional services are available. The contents of parcels may be covered by *Insurance.* There are specific packing instructions; a registration fee is charged in addition to postage. For articles which cannot be insured in an ordinary letter or packet, e.g. diamonds, *Insured Box Post* may be used.

First- and second-class *Airmail* services are available to most countries, second class being for such items as unsealed cards, printed papers, books, etc. Under the *All-up Service*, letters and postcards to Europe paid at the surface mail rate go by air at no extra cost when this speeds delivery. The letter rate of postage should be paid on other categories of mail sent to Europe if air transmission is required.

A special *Air Mail Leaflet*, obtainable from any post office, gives full details of all air services.

Air Letters, which can be bought at any post office for 10½p and 11p, may be sent to any address in the world outside Europe. They must not contain enclosures.

Blue air mail labels must be affixed to all letters and packets for transmission by air to destinations outside Europe. Air rates are assessed according to the weight of the letter or package (so much per 10 g), therefore special light-weight paper and envelopes should be used.

Printed papers sent in the *overseas post* must conform to the regulations published in the *Post Office Guide*. In particular, it should be remembered that they must not be sealed against inspection. The same applies to some other categories of overseas post (small packets and samples).

Especially useful for businessmen travelling abroad and wishing to send home recorded dictation for transcription is the *Phonopost Packet* service. Any sound recording may be sent by this service providing the weight does not exceed 2 lb.

If a writer wishes to prepay the postage of his correspondent's reply he may send a stamped addressed envelope. If the correspondent is overseas he cannot do this but he can send an *International Reply Coupon* which can be used in virtually any country in the world. The recipient takes the coupon to a post office in his own country and receives in exchange postage stamps for the cost of the appropriate surface mail charge.

If the sender of a telegram wishes to pay for a reply he may send a *Reply Paid Telegram.* This is applicable both in the home country and overseas. In Britain the Post Office messenger who delivers the telegram at the same time gives the recipient a stamped telegraph form and may wait for the reply.

THE POST OFFICE PARCELS SERVICE

Railex
The Post Office collect your package and despatch it on first available train. On arrival it is taken to it's destination by PO Messenger. (Up to 450 g in weight)

Special Deliveries
Urgent goods can have a Post Office Messenger to take them all the way, or they can be specially delivered on reaching the distant Post Office.

Special Collections
If you're regularly dispatching at least 10 parcels a day the Post Office will come and collect them. They will also make single collections, provided you have at least 50 parcels in each batch.

Datapost
A secure, overnight delivery service handling special classes of goods, e.g. urgent computer material. The Post Office will negotiate a contract to personally collect and deliver your consignment.

Postage Forward
A useful service for companies who run a free approval service. It costs £15 for a yearly licence and 6p per parcel over the usual rate.

Overseas Parcels
Once you have filled in the necessary declaration forms, the Post Office will take care of customs clearance.

C.O.D.
Cash on Delivery is still the most direct method of obtaining payment. The cost to you is 50 p a parcel, plus normal postage.

Weights & Dimensions
Up to 10 kg maximum weight. Length: not more than 1.07 m. Length and girth combined 2 m maximum.

Area Rate
Deliveries within the same group of counties qualify for area rate postal charges (see Post Office Guide).

UNION POSTALE UNIVERSELLE

GRANDE-BRETAGNE · GREAT BRITAIN

10p

Coupon-réponse international

Ce coupon est échangeable dans tous les Pays de l'Union postale universelle contre un timbre-poste ou des timbres-poste représentant le montant de l'affranchissement d'une lettre ordinaire de port simple à destination de l'étranger.

International Reply Coupon

This coupon is exchangeable in any country of the Universal Postal Union for a postage stamp or postage stamps representing the amount of postage for an ordinary single-rate letter destined for a foreign country.

COUPON-REPONSE INTERNATIONAL

Empreinte de contrôle du Pays d'origine (date facultative)

SPECIMEN

SPECIMEN

Timbre du bureau qui effectue l'échange

Express Delivery (Overseas) In many countries postal packets can be delivered to the addressee by express messenger as soon as possible after they are received in the office of delivery. A special fee of 60p must be paid in addition to the normal postage. The envelope or cover, and the despatch note in the case of parcels, must bear the word EXPRESS in capital letters in red ink or red pencil, above the address.

COD Parcels (Overseas) Many countries will arrange for the price of the goods (the '*Trade Charge*') to be collected before delivery and sent to the sender. The maximum trade charge collected by any country is £50.

Air Parcels Air parcels may be sent to almost all parts of the world from Great Britain. The maximum weight is 10 kg. A *Customs Declaration* is needed and in some cases a Despatch Note also.

Overseas Parcels The senders of parcels to some countries may arrange to pay all customs and other charges normally collected from the addressee. The service is known internationally by the title '*Franc de Droits*' (*Free of Charges*) or by the initials *FDD*. There is no additional fee for this service but the sender is asked to pay a deposit on account of the charges. The parcel must be marked 'To be delivered free of charges' or 'Franc de Droits' and applications for this service should be made to Postal Finance Department, Cashier's Section, Postal Headquarters, St. Martin's-le-Grand, London EC1A 1HQ.

BRITISH RAIL PARCELS SERVICES

Parcels may also be sent by the Red Star, TCF and C & D services provided by British Rail. The Red Star service is available from Monday to Friday, and Saturdays too by certain services. The parcel, clearly marked with the sender's name and address, the *name only* of the consignee and the name of the destination station, is taken to the Parcels Office of the nearest British Rail station. The consignor nominates the train on which the parcel must travel and pays the parcel fee plus the Red Star charge. The consignor then telephones the consignee and tells him the arrival time of the train so that the consignee can collect the parcel as soon as it arrives at the destination station.

British Rail also operate a *TCF ('to call for') parcels service* and a *C & D (collection and delivery) parcels service.* TCF packages, which are distinguished by a yellow label, can be collected or the consignor can take them to the British Rail parcels office himself. The package should be addressed to only one person; no postal address should be shown. The package will be held at the destination station until it is collected.

The C & D service covers the whole country. The average journey time is about three days.

POST OFFICE GUIDES

The facilities outlined above are but a few of all the services available. In every registry there should be a complete set of Post Office information books, the most important being the *Post Office Guide.* This contains full details of every service offered by the Post Office Corporation. In addition a lot of useful information is given on how to address envelopes, parcels, etc. The services available to every individual country in the world is given in the Overseas Postage and Telecommunications sections of the Guide. The Contents page gives the main sections and a very comprehensive index at the back of the book makes it easy to find any information required. (Most countries have their own Guide, Handbook or Leaflet.)

The Post Office Guide is issued annually and the cost is 60p in Britain. An 'Official Paid' postcard is inserted which should be completed and sent to the Head Postmaster of the town/city so that as Supplements are issued they are sent to the purchaser free of charge. The Supplements give details of changes in rates, new services, etc.

A secretary should know the principal services available from the Post Office so that in any emergency she can turn to the Post Office Guide and quickly find the details she needs to enable her to cope with the situation.

Another book issued by the Post Office lists all the Post Offices in the United Kingdom, showing those which give telegraphic services, etc.

FURTHER READING

Manual of Stationery, Office Machines and Equipment, Ed. F. G. Holliday (The British Stationery and Office Equipment Association), Chapter 25.
Post Office Guide (British Post Office Corporation).
The Postal Services can do more for Businesses than you Think (British Post Office Corporation).
Postroom Organisation (British Post Office Corporation).
How to cut your Post Office Costs (Editype Ltd).

GROUP DISCUSSION

You are a secretary in the area office of a selling organisation. The ten area salesmen call in at 0800 hours every morning with orders taken the previous day and wish to deal with mail before 0900 hours, i.e. read it, make necessary enquiries and dictate replies. The postal delivery service is very erratic and repeated complaints to the local postmaster have not resulted in any improvement. You are responsible for the entire mail handling process. Your office staff consists of a clerk and a typist. The clerk travels to the office from a village and there is no transport which can get him to the office before 0750 hours. The typist lives near the office. The Post Office is in town some two miles from your office. The salesmen live in various places around the area and all have cars provided by the company.

Discuss possible lines of action which might solve the problem. The aim is to have incoming mail on the salesmen's desk by 0755 hours every morning.

EXERCISES

1 State, in their correct order, the procedures involved in opening and distributing mail from the time when it is placed on your desk until it is delivered to the relevant officials.

2 Imagine that you are secretary to the Office Manager of the Vital Engineering Co. Ltd. and have taken the letters illustrated on pages 171 and 172 from their envelopes. You may, on checking, find some anomalies. State what you discover, then rule up a Mail Inwards Register and enter the five letters in it. Indicate to whom you would send the letters for action.

AFRICAN INSURANCE COMPANY LTD.

Tel: 67891.

P.O. Box 67, Cape Coast.
17th March, 1973.

Our Ref: 6178912/120–69.

The Secretary,
Vital Engineering Co. Ltd.,
P.O. Box 4711,
ACCRA.

Dear Sir,

Fire Policy G/6178912/F
Claim No. 120–69

We wish to inform you that the above claim made by you on 10th October, 1971 has been accepted by our Head Office. However, the surveyor considers the amount claimed is excessive and suggests that eighty per cent of your figure would be an equitable value.

I am, therefore, arranging for payment on this basis to be made to your bankers as requested by you.

Yours faithfully,

R. Smithson
Manager.

ACME COMMERCIAL COLLEGE

Tel: 21811.

P.O. Box 412, Accra.
13th March, 1973.

Ref. Sec/65.

The Personnel Manager,
Accra Engineering Co. Ltd.,
P.O. Box 4711,
ACCRA.

Dear Sir,

SECRETARIAL COURSE

I think you may be interested to know that a new Secretarial Course is to start at this College on Monday, 8th May, 1973. It is intended as an up-grading course and only those who are already employed as Stenographers Grade I will be accepted.

The course will last for two months and will be from 8 a.m. to 12.15 p.m. and 1.30 p.m. to 3.30 p.m. A programme is attached showing the contents of the course.

If you are interested in sending any of your employees to this course will you please contact the undersigned.

Yours faithfully,

James E. Mends
Principal.

Enc.

THE ABC BLANKET COMPANY LIMITED

Tel: 6701.

P.O. Box 678, Kumasi.

Your Ref. CE/6170.
Our Ref. JS/PC/14/11.

The General Manager,
Vital Engineering Co. Ltd.,
P.O. Box 4711
ACCRA.

Dear Sir,

We refer to your advertisement in the "Daily Graphic" and shall be glad if you will kindly let us have full details, including cost, of the small drilling machine you have for disposal.

Yours faithfully,

J. A. Quarshie
Chief Buyer.

GHANA MACHINE TOOL MANUFACTURING CORPORATION

P.O. Box 687, Accra.
Ref. PK/16-30/1. 14th March, 1973.

The General Manager,
National Engineering Co. Ltd.,
P.O. Box 4771,
ACCRA.

Dear Sir,

I shall be glad to know whether it would be possible for you to undertake some engineering work for us on a contract basis. As you may know, this Corporation is expanding considerably and at present is unable to cope with the volume of work. It is essential, therefore, that we contract out some of the work to reliable firms.

If you are interested in this proposal, will you please telephone me to arrange a suitable time for us to meet for a discussion?

Yours faithfully,

P. Kofi
Works Manager.

KINGSWAY SUPPLIES LIMITED

Tel: 62447

16 High Street,
NEWTOWN,
England.

Our Ref: Stores/6739/WPD

13th March, 1973.

The General Manager,
Vital Engineering Company Ltd.,
P.O. Box 4711,
ACCRA.

Dear Sir,

Your Order No. 6725/72

We confirm having sent you today the following telegram:—

"TWO CASES SPARES DESPATCHED BRITISH
CALEDONIAN AIRFREIGHT TODAY"

Our invoice No. S.2310 is enclosed, together with the Air Waybill.

Yours faithfully,
for: KINGSWAY SUPPLIES LTD.,

Sales Manager.

Enc.

INVOICE S.2310

KINGSWAY SUPPLIES LIMITED

16 High Street,
Tel. 62447 NEWTOWN,
England.

To: The General Manager,
Vital Engineering Company Ltd.,
P.O. Box 4711.
ACCRA.

Date: 13th March, 1973.

Cat. No.	Quantity	Description	Price	Cost	
200	6 dozen	Bearings	£1.71 per doz.	£10.26	
201	3 dozen	Bolts	£0.21 each	7.56	
				17.82	
		Less 20% Trade Discount		3.56	
				14.26	
		Plus Air Freight Charges		6.20	
				£20.46	

3 The following correspondence has been delivered to you. It is all to be placed on your boss's desk. Rewrite the list in the order (starting with the lowest and finishing with the uppermost) in which you would place the documents for his attention.

a Proof of a visiting card.

b An invitation to a cocktail party in eight days' time.

c A draft of the Company's Annual Report and Accounts being circulated among the managers.

d A letter asking your boss to become President of a business association.

e An internal memorandum from the Chief Accountant asking for the last quarter's sales figures as a matter of urgency.

f A letter marked 'Personal'.

g A memorandum from an outside representative of your firm saying that a customer has complained about the quality of goods supplied in his last order.

h An outside representative's monthly car allowance claim for authorisation.

i A confidential memorandum from the Managing Director asking for an explanation of the low sales in a certain area.

j Five routine letters to which you will type replies for your boss to sign, although he wishes to see all letters as they come in.

4 What action would you take if you opened an envelope addressed to your boss and found that the letter was addressed to someone else?

5 Which of the following letters do you think should be attached to a file before being placed on your boss's desk?

a An acknowledgement of a cheque sent for a personal purchase.

b A letter asking for further information about the goods supplied by your company.

c A letter from a contractor giving additional information to that given in a previous letter.

d A memorandum from the Chief Accountant asking for sales estimates for the next financial period.

e A cable informing your boss of the arrival of his deputy from a trip abroad.

6 You are secretary to the Chairman of a small business concern. You open and sort all incoming mail. To whom would you send the following?

a A query from the Inland Revenue about an employee's PAYE.

b An order for bulk delivery of goods.

c An account from the company's stationery suppliers.

d A complaint from a customer that the goods sold to him were received in bad condition.

e A letter from the company's solicitor giving advice about a contract.

7 A new regulation is enforced in a company to the effect that no internal mail should be enveloped unless it is confidential. Give three examples of internal documents which you think should be enveloped before transmission.

8 You suggest to your boss that as the volume of work is increasing a franking machine could be used so that the time spent by your junior in sticking on postage stamps could be better spent on other work. Your boss asks you to write him a memorandum, proving your case. Type the memorandum you would produce.

9 Your boss decides that as part of a major sales promotion campaign he will have several thousand circulars sent out. He asks you to find out the best way for them to be posted. Use the Post Office Guide and write a concise note giving him the required information.

10 State which of the following you would send by ordinary mail, recorded delivery service, or registered mail.

- a A letter to a customer making a final demand for payment of a long outstanding account.
- b A letter containing an open (i.e. not crossed) postal order for £1.50.
- c A parcel containing books value £15.
- d A letter containing a crossed money order.
- e A letter informing a supplier that a deposit of £50 had been transferred to his account by your banker.

11 What is the purpose of a Messenger's Delivery (or Way) Book?

12 You are working late with your boss in the office. At 8 p.m. he decides that he must telex his office in Turkey and asks you to find out how soon the message could be sent. Use the Post Office Guide to find the information.

13 A client has cabled from Okinawa. Your boss wishes to reply by any telecommunication service which will put him into contact with the client at his office at the earliest possible moment. The time is 10.30 a.m. What service would you advise him to use?

14 Describe briefly the function of a letter opening machine, a collating machine, an envelope sealing machine, a franking machine, a folding and inserting machine.

15 Using the Post Office Guide, find the following information:

- a The poundage payable on a Postal or Money Order value £10.60 to be sent to a town in your own country.
- b The cost of insuring a parcel value £150 to be sent overseas.
- c The cost of sending a postcard by airmail to Kenya.
- d The cost of sending a letter, which weighs 35 g, by airmail to Switzerland.
- e Is it possible to insure a parcel by surface mail to Malawi?
- f Can you send a Money Order to Somalia?
- g The cost of a letter telegram of 32 words to Germany.

- h The cost of sending a parcel, which weighs $4\frac{1}{2}$ kg to a town in your own country, outside the group county area in Britain.
- i The cost of registering a letter, which weighs 150 g, to a company in your home town.
- j The maximum compensation payable for the minimum registration fee.
- k The minimum amount of money which may be deposited initially when opening a Post Office Savings account.
- l The maximum amount of money which may be withdrawn on demand from a Post Office Savings account.
- m The annual rental fee for a private bag.
- n The minimum size of postcard which may be sent through the post.
- o The maximum weight allowed for parcels by surface mail to Nepal.
- p The cost of sending a telegram of 14 words to another town in your home country.
- q The cost of sending a phototelegram size 280 sq cm to Melbourne.
- r The cost of a telephone call lasting 12 minutes to Syria.
- s The maximum value for which a parcel to Brunei can be insured.
- t The cost of sending a Phonopost Packet by airmail to Norfolk Island.

16 Using the Post Office Guide if necessary, explain the following:

- a Report charge.
- b De Luxe Greetings.
- c Consular Invoice.
- d Express Letter.
- e Airway Letter.
- f Cash on Delivery.
- g Aperture Envelope.
- h Blind Literature.
- i Datel 600 Service.
- j Credit Card Call.

17 You are appointed secretary to the Office Manager of a very large organisation. One of your first assignments is to assist him in re-organising the mail registry. He asks you to suggest the furniture and fittings required, the layout and equipment necessary for the handling of between 1500 and 2000 incoming letters per day. Outgoing mail is never less than 1000 letters per day. The number of parcels mailed is negligible.

18 How can you ensure that enclosures are not inadvertently left in envelopes?

19 The Managing Director has decided to "automate" ruthlessly. At present the mail registry has only a franking machine; all other procedures are carried out manually. The average number of letters received daily is

about 700/800; the number of letters despatched is similar, many of them being routine replies to enquiries with brochures enclosed. Consider what machines you would consider to be necessary. Write a memorandum saying why you think they are necessary and why you do not recommend any others.

20 You are notified by the Post Office that a call from New York for your boss is to be connected in 30 minutes. Your boss is at a meeting in another town. What action would you take?

5

Reprography

The Rank Xerox 7000 reduction duplicator.

"Reprographics now covers an immense area, from the humble hand-driven offset printer to the fast transmission by wire of facsimile information. Most industrial needs dictate that the area must continue to expand."

The Financial Times, 8 May 1972

"According to the Institute of Reprographic Technology, reprography is the technology of producing and reproducing two-dimensional visual communication media in business and administrative operations—in short: the science of communicating graphically."

Management in Action, August 1972

Reprography includes the study of all machines and equipment used in the reproduction of documents, or in the production of many copies of reports, pamphlets and other work. As reprographic equipment has become easier to use, many companies have transformed their Duplicating and Photocopying Departments into Internal Print Departments (they are sometimes called In-plant Printing Departments) where a wide variety of work can be produced, some of which might previously have been sent out to a commercial printer. These new departments can produce from one up to a hundred copies of a single document "while you wait"; they can also produce publications such as house magazines or sales brochures with the appearance of having been bound and printed by a commercial printer.

In addition to knowing how to prepare offset, stencil and spirit masters, and knowing how to operate the copier in her own office, a secretary should also know of the equipment which is used in an Internal Print Department, so that she can say the best means of obtaining a specified number of copies of any document.

Reprography in its widest interpretation includes a knowledge of the various copying processes:

a taking carbon copies
b typing on carbonless copying paper*
c ink duplication
d spirit duplication
e offset lithography
f office copiers
g facsimile transceivers

when used in conjunction with

h the various kinds of typewriters and cold-type composing machines
i binding and collating equipment

The production of carbon copies and the use of carbonless copying paper were discussed in *Chapter 2, Dictation, Typewriting and Transcription*; and the use of facsimile transceivers (the machines which transmit and receive facsimile copies over ordinary telephone lines) was explained in *Chapter 3, Telephone Techniques*. In this chapter we shall study Reprography under the following headings: Ink duplication, Spirit duplication, Offset-litho duplicating and printing, Office copiers, Automatic typewriters, Office composing machines, including phototypesetters, Collating, Knocking-up, trimming, folding and fastening, Applications and Developments.

As the typewriter, the stencil and spirit duplicators are amongst the most frequently used office machines, and as the preparation of stencils and spirit masters and the operation of duplicators are fundamental skills for the stenographer and secretary, we shall study ink and spirit duplicating in some detail.

* Colloquially referred to as NCR paper, known also as *carbon-free* copying paper (see page 76).

INK DUPLICATION

The first step in ink duplicating is to prepare a stencil of the document to be duplicated. This may be done

- a by handwriting and/or drawing
- b by typing
- c using a thermal heat copier
- d using an electronic stencil-cutting machine

Kinds of stencils Special stencils are manufactured for each of these four methods. The *standard typewriting stencil* is suitable for ordinary manual and electric typewriters; extra fine stencils are made for use with the Vari-Typer machine, with IBM golf-ball machines, and with typewriters having shaded type-faces. *Thermal stencils* are "cut" by heat, by passing the stencil and document to be copied through a thermal heat copier, such as the Bandaflex Thermocopier.

A new kind of stencil had to be developed when the electronic stencil-cutting machine was invented; for this method the stencils contain special pigments—such as a form of carbon black—and there is no fall-out of letters because the "cutting" actually consists of a series of minute perforations. *Electronic stencils* should be handled with care as they are rather fragile. For handwriting and drawing a special *double-coated handwriting stencil* is made. There are also *tracing stencils* which are translucent so that the copy can be placed underneath them; the stencil is prepared by tracing over the outline of the original. Even standard typewriting stencils are slightly translucent; this feature enables the display typist to put the original under the stencil and make light pencil marks on the stencil to indicate the framework of the work to be displayed, before inserting the carbons and feeding the stencil set into the typewriter.

Stencil manufacturers will supply special *pre-cut stencils* to order. Stencils may be pre-cut with any design such as a company letterhead or a particular form layout or ruling. Pre-cut stencils are useful and economical if duplicated work is frequently required on headed letter-paper or in a standard display style, such as routine statistical and financial tables and periodic reports.

Parts of a stencil As you can see from the illustration, a stencil consists of three parts: the heading or headpiece, the stencil sheet and the backing sheet. The heading is perforated with a pattern of holes and slots which fits the pattern of pegs or slots on the duplicator and enables the stencil to be firmly fixed around the cylinder. The stencil itself is made of a thin, fibrous paper-based material. Handwriting stencils are usually ruled in squares similar to graph paper as a guide to the writer. Typewriting stencils are marked across the top with numbers corresponding to the scale on the typewriter; the line spaces are indicated on both sides of the stencil, and the centre of the page is clearly marked, as are the various paper sizes.

The backing sheet is made of thick paper and is attached to the stencil heading by a line of perforations. When the stencil has been typed and fixed on to the duplicator, the cylinder is rotated and the first impression appears on the backing sheet. This enables the operator to judge the density of the inking. The backing sheet is then torn off along the perforated line. When the stencil is taken off the machine at the end of the run, the backing sheet may be placed over the inky side as a protection during storage.

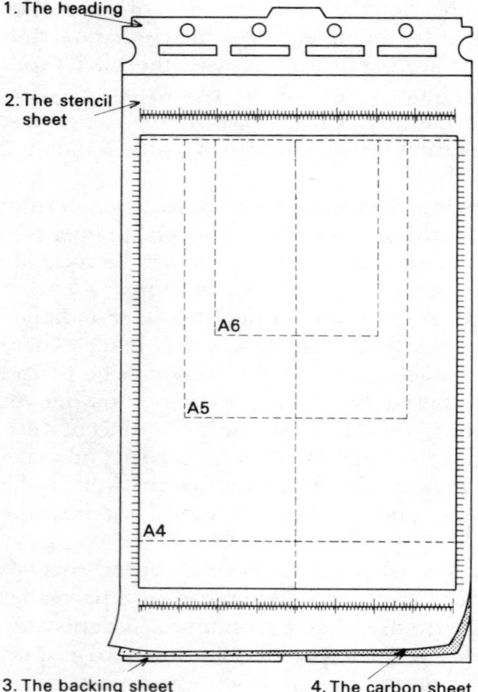

A typewriting stencil. 1. The heading. 2. The stencil sheet. 3. The backing sheet. 4. The carbon sheet.

Preparing a stencil by handwriting and/or drawing Special double-coated stencils are made for preparation by writing and/or drawing. The base coating is white and the top coating is coloured (usually blue) so that the person who is preparing the stencil can easily see what he has written or drawn. Special wheel pens and steel styli are made for this type of work and a hard backing sheet made of plastic should be put under the stencil. It is also possible to draw or write or sign one's name on a typewriting stencil; this needs a little practice to avoid tearing the stencil. A plastic backing sheet and stylus pen should be used.

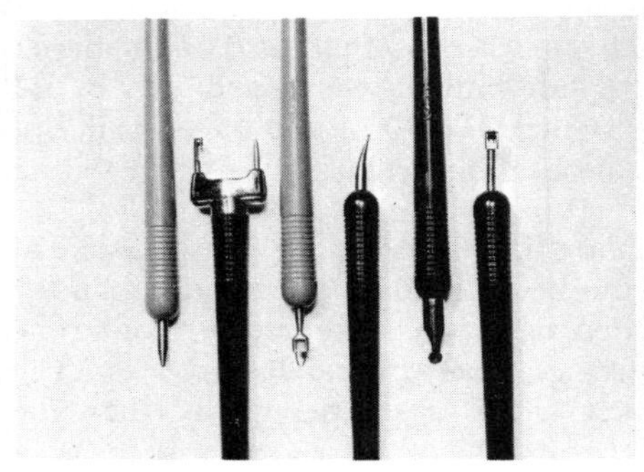

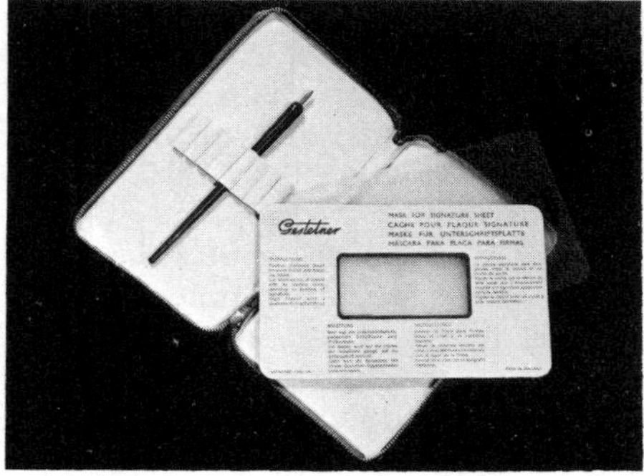

Gestetner pens and stylus, and signature set with plastic backing sheet.

The Gestetner Scope assists drawing, tracing, handwriting and ruling on stencils. It is fitted with a T-square and a built-in fluorescent lamp.

Typing a stencil Stencils are usually provided with a sheet of carbon paper between the stencil sheet and the backing, the carbonised side of the carbon facing upwards, that is next to the stencil, so that a reverse or "mirror" image of the typing appears on the back of the stencil. This assists the typist to read what has been typed; it also cushions the impact of the typebars on the stencil. Many people find it helpful to have an additional copy for checking, so they insert another carbon together with a sheet of plain paper between the stencil and the first carbon, and the backing sheet. Another method is to place a third sheet of carbon next to the backing, so that a copy is also taken on the backing sheet. This is particularly useful if the backing sheet is going to be used for storing the stencil.

Sometimes a thin transparent sheet of plastic film is placed in front of the stencil; this helps to keep the type-faces clean and avoids the fall-out of enclosed letters such as 'o'.

Before feeding the stencil set into the typewriter, push the paper guide as far to the left as possible, clean the type-faces with a stiff brush, and set the ribbon indicator to the stencil position (usually indicated by the letter S or a white dot) so that the ribbon carrier does not move up each time a key is struck. The stencil set should be fed into the machine so that the 0 on the paper bail scale is in line with the 0 on the guide-line of the stencil. If you are unable to do this, line up the 0 on the stencil with 10 on the paper bail, but remember to add 10 to all your calculations when centring or when setting margins and tabular stops.

Display your work within the outer guide-line frame printed on the stencil. Type with a firm, even touch, striking the keys slightly more heavily than for normal typing. The hardness of the platen determines the pressure of stroke needed—a medium platen requires a heavier touch than a hard platen. The letters 'm' and 'w' and the fraction keys need a sharper stroke than the punctuation keys, the letters 'o' and 'e', and the smaller letters such as 'l' and 'i'.

CORRECTING ERRORS Errors can be corrected by using a special correcting fluid. This is usually coloured pink or white, and is supplied in a bottle with a fine brush attached to the lid so that single letters can be neatly corrected without touching the adjacent letters. To correct an error, release the ratchet detent lever and turn up the platen until the error is easily accessible. Then loosen the stencil from the underlying carbon by moving the headpiece slightly forwards, and put a ruler or pencil immediately behind the stencil so that the part containing the error is free of the carbon sheet. Shake the bottle of correcting fluid and paint lightly over the error. When the fluid has dried (this usually takes a minute or two) replace the ratchet detent lever and align the former error with the printing point of the typewriter. The correct letter, or letters, can now be typed; use a fairly light touch because you are only striking through the fluid coating.

GRAFTING Correcting fluid should not be used over a very large area because it contracts as it dries and thus causes the surrounding parts of the stencil to pucker. Grafting is a better method for major corrections: the faulty paragraph or section of the stencil is cut out with a razor blade and replaced by a new piece of stencil trimmed off from the bottom edge or cut from another stencil. The 'insert' or 'patch' should be slightly larger than the original area. When the patch has been carefully lined up over the cut-out on the stencil, fix it in position by painting around the edges with correcting fluid. Then insert the stencil into the typewriter again and type in the correct words.

Using a thermal heat copier Thermal stencils, specially prepared stencils which are "cut" by heat, are prepared in a matter of seconds by passing them and the document to be copied through a thermal heat copier such as the Gestetner thermal copier (see page 185). Thermal stencils can be added to by overtyping and running through the machine again; parts of the original can be masked by covering with ordinary bond paper.

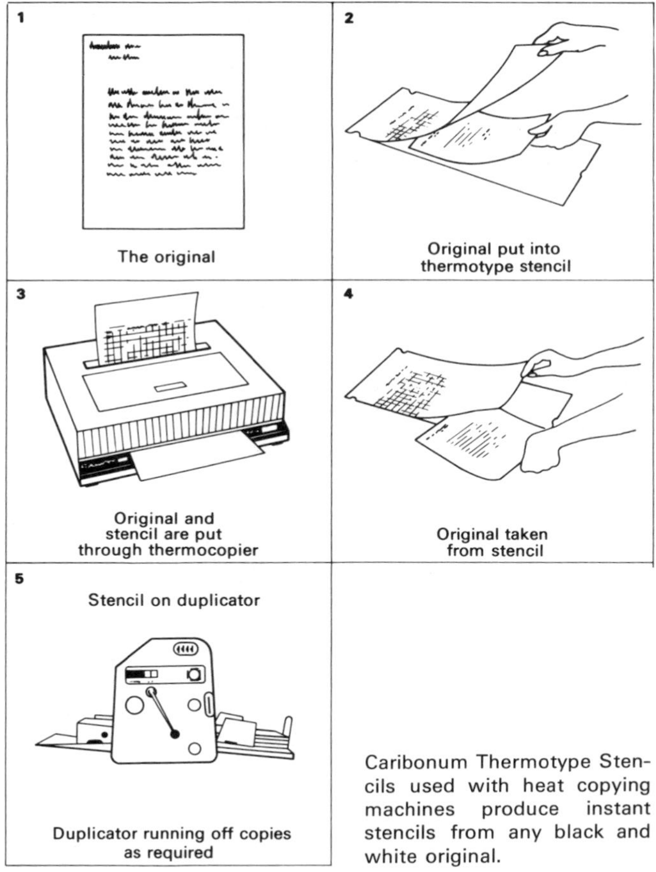

Caribonum Thermotype Stencils used with heat copying machines produce instant stencils from any black and white original.

Using an electronic stencil-cutting machine With the electronic stencil cutter a stencil can be produced from almost any form of document, even from photographs. The machine consists of a rotating cylinder on which the original to be copied and a specially coated electronic stencil are placed side by side. As the cylinder rotates, the original document is scanned by a photo-electric cell synchronised with a cutting stylus (an electrode) which travels backwards and forwards across the whole area of the stencil. When the photo-electric cell senses a dark area, a series of pin-point holes is burnt in the stencil thus forming the same pattern as the original.

Rotary duplicators Stencil duplicating was invented towards the end of the nineteenth century. At first the stencil was stretched over a wooden frame and a sheet of paper was placed underneath the frame; as an ink roller was passed

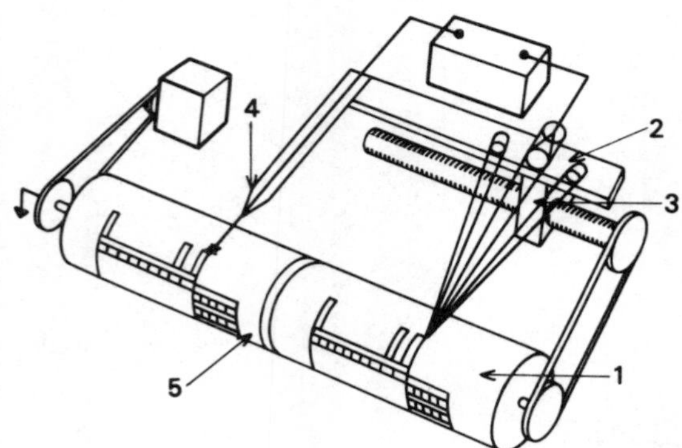

How an electronic stencil-cutter works. 1. The original. 2. The photo-electric cell. 3. The scanner, which travels backwards and forwards across the copy. 4. The stylus which is synchronised with the scanner and which burns a series of pin-point holes in the stencil whenever the photo-electric cell of the scanner senses a dark area. 5. The stencil.

over the frame, the image was pressed through on to the sheet of paper. The next development was the hinged flat-bed model and by the turn of the century the rotary duplicator had been developed.

In a rotary machine the stencil is fastened around an inked cylinder or drum, the image facing downwards. As each sheet of paper is fed into the machine, the cylinder rotates and ink is squeezed on to the paper through the cut or open areas (the image) of the stencil.

Rotary duplicators may be inked by either a two cylinder or a single cylinder system. In the *single cylinder process,* the stencil is secured around the drum or

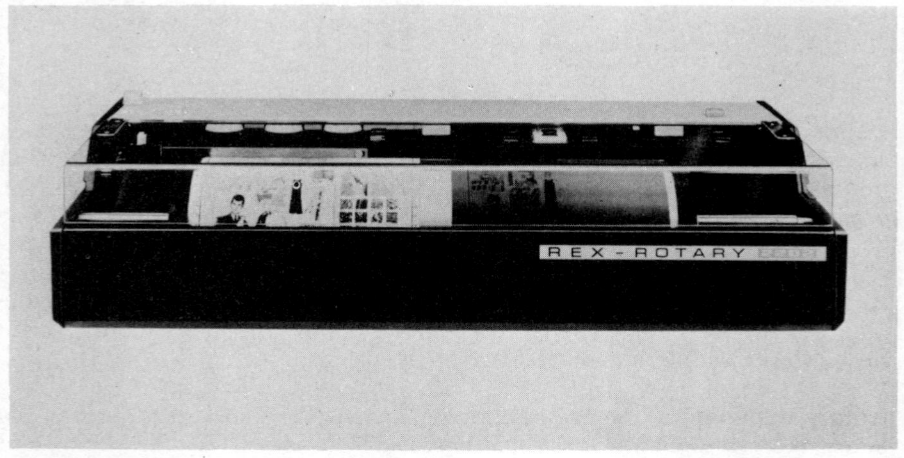

The Rex-Rotary 2002 electronic stencil cutter.

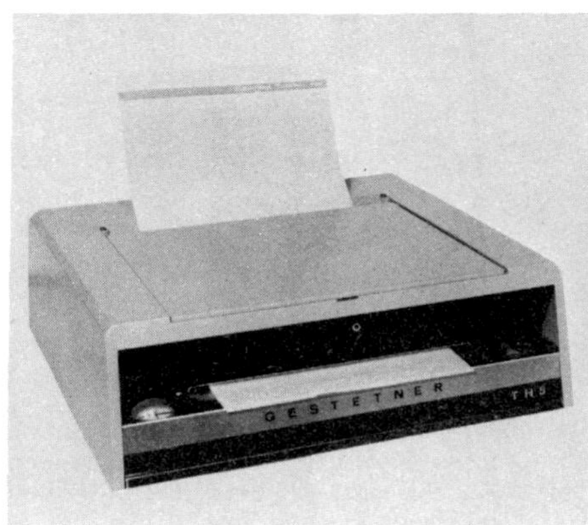

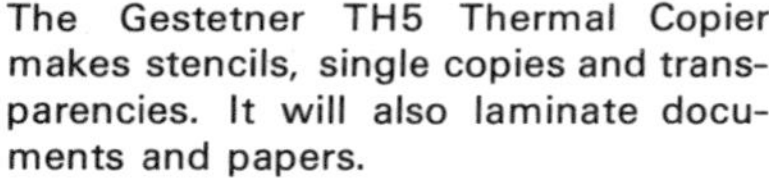
The Gestetner TH5 Thermal Copier makes stencils, single copies and transparencies. It will also laminate documents and papers.

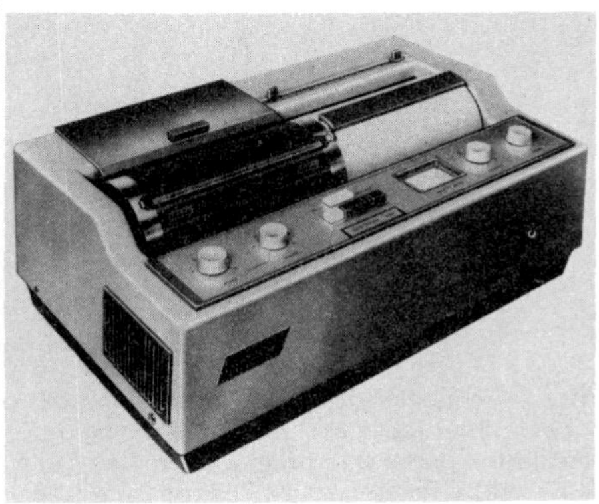
The Gestetner es456 Electronic Scanner produces facsimile stencils from a wide range of originals including photographs and half-tones, black and white or coloured.

cylinder which is made of finely perforated metal and covered with a cloth resembling flannel or lint. Duplicating ink is squeezed from a tube into the drum through the filler hole which is afterwards closed with a screw cap. (The contents of two tubes of ink are usually squeezed into a new machine before it is used for the first time. Thereafter the ink supply is replenished as needed; one tubeful of ink is usually sufficient for several thousand copies.) As the cylinder is rotated, the ink soaks through the metal perforations into the cloth covering and is evenly distributed all round the drum. The cylinder of a single cylinder machine can easily be taken off and replaced by another cylinder filled with ink of a different colour; this enables work to be produced in two colours. This rapid colour change facility is a feature of single cylinder machines.

On *two-cylinder duplicators* a silk belt carrying the stencil is fixed around two solid drums. The carrier belt is inked by a series of ink distributing rollers. In this system an ink paste is used and this is spread on to the stencil from the inking rollers via the cylinders and the silk carrier belt. The pressure roller forces the ink through the silk belt and stencil on to the duplicating paper. The actual tube of ink may be fitted into automatic inking machines and the ink is spread by suction or piston pressure.

To change to a second colour the silk belt, the inking rollers, the ink distributor and the tube of ink must be taken out; the cylinders must be wiped clean and new inking rollers, a new ink distributor as well as a new belt and a new tube of ink have to be fitted.

Rotary duplicators may be manually or electrically operated and many different types and models are manufactured. It is claimed that electric stencil

Two–cylinder duplicator

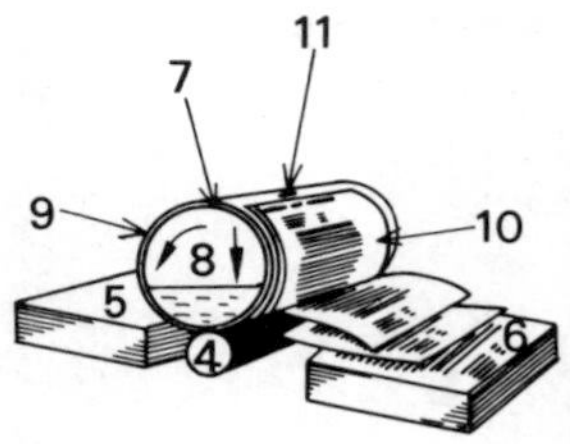

Single cylinder duplicator

The two-cylinder duplicator on the left uses paste ink which is distributed by ink distributing rollers. The liquid ink used in the single-cylinder process shown on the right is contained inside the perforated drum. 1. Ink distributing rollers. 2. The solid cylinders. 3. The silk belt covered by the stencil. 4. The pressure roller. 5. The stack of duplicating paper. 6. The copies being delivered into the receiving tray. 7. The hollow perforated cylinder. 8. The liquid ink. 9. The cloth which absorbs and distributed the ink. 10. The stencil. 11. The filler socket and locking nut.

duplicators can produce up to 7500 copies per hour. Up to 7000 good copies can be printed from one stencil.

The Gestetner and Rex-Rotary duplicators are two-cylinder machines. Roneo and Ellams duplicators use the single cylinder inking process.

Inks and colour work Duplicating ink is specially made so that although it dries quickly by absorption on the duplicating paper, it does not dry up in the machine itself if the duplicator stands for some time without being used. It is claimed that the ink paste used in two cylinder duplicators gives a sharper image than the liquid ink used in single cylinder machines; paste ink, however, does not dry so quickly. The consistency of liquid inks is important and is affected by extreme temperatures; a wide range of inks is manufactured to suit varying climates in different parts of the world.

Duplicating paper The paper used for stencil duplicating must be highly absorbent so that the ink on the copies dries very quickly and does not smudge or offset on to the back of the following copy in the receiving tray. Duplicating paper is available in many colours and in foolscap, quarto and A4 sizes; it is usually made from esparto grass. The best results are obtained from using paper weighing either 57 g/m^2 (lightweight) or 71 g/m^2 (thick) or 85 g/m^2 (very thick), although modern duplicators can copy on to a wide range of papers and even on to card.

Some machines can be fitted with an interleaving attachment; this enables copies to be taken on standard bond paper by interleaving each sheet with a piece of absorbent paper or thin card as it is delivered into the receiving tray. Another attachment will spray a drying powder on to each copy as it emerges from the feed rollers.

Operating a stencil duplicator When the stencil has been prepared it is fixed on the machine by fitting the pattern of holes or slots in the head-piece over the matching pattern of pegs on the cylinder and pressing the stencil firmly by hand against the silk carrier belt or the cylinder so that it remains secure. The cylinder is then rotated and the first impression appears on the inner side of the backing sheet. This enables the operator to see the density of the inking and make any necessary adjustments; special attention should be paid to letters or words that have been corrected on the stencil. The backing sheet can then be torn off at the line of perforations.

The next step is to prepare the duplicating paper for the feed tray. During the manufacturing processes of cutting and packing, the sheets of paper in a packet are tightly pressed together and they cannot be fed singly into the duplicator unless each sheet is loosened from its neighbours. This process of loosening the sheets from each other is known as 'fanning' and it plays a very important part in the subsequent smooth-running of the duplicator. A packet of paper can be fanned by rubbing the top gently in small circular movements with the knuckle of the first finger. Another method is to slap each end of the packet, after unwrapping, against the edge of a desk so that any bonding of the edges is broken—the sheets can then be fanned at each end by hand. A third method is to use a mechanical jogger. When each sheet has been separated from its neighbours, the pile must be carefully re-stacked and placed in the feed-tray.

When the paper in the feed-tray has been raised to the correct position against the feed levers or rollers, the machine switch may be turned to 'On' or 'Print'. Rotation of the handle will then cause printed copies to be delivered into the receiving tray. When one or two copies have been 'run off' they should be carefully inspected to check evenness of print-density and to see if

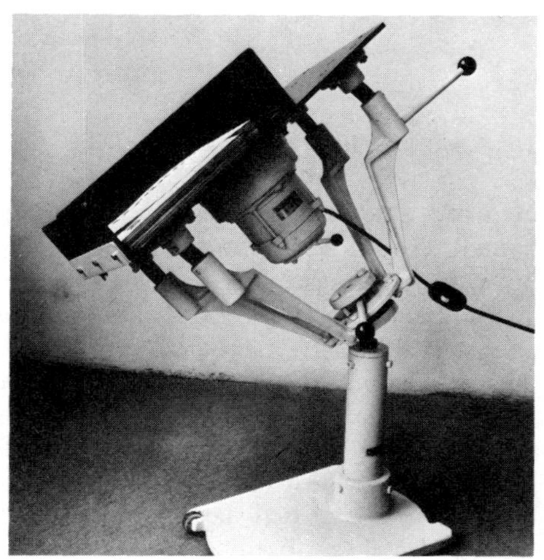

A Thomas heavy-duty jogger powered by electricity. In addition to knocking-up paper before duplicating or printing by offset-litho, the jogger can re-form sheets of paper into an even-edged stack ready for feeding through for a second run (as in two-colour duplication); it may also be used for squaring-up collated sets before they are stapled or bound.

the material is being printed too high or too low on the paper. On most machines there is an adjustment which enables the printed material to be raised or lowered an inch or two from the normal position. If the left-hand or right-hand margins are not even, the paper in the feed-tray may be adjusted.

When you are satisfied that all is well, set the counting mechanism to the number of copies required and adjust the guides on the receiving tray to fit the size of paper you are using so that the printed copies will be neatly stacked. Then start turning the handle (on a manual machine), or turn the switch to 'On' on an electric machine. When the required number of copies have been printed, the machine will stop feeding paper between the rollers.

The Gestetner 400 hand-operated stencil duplicator.

Storing stencils Stencils may be stored and used again when required. The stencil should be removed from the machine by loosening the lower edge and turning it back so that it lies along the top edge of the machine. The bottom of the backing sheet should then be placed exactly level with the lower edge of the stencil. If the edges of the stencil and backing sheet are grasped firmly together with the right hand, a sharp clockwise turn of the handle by the left hand will enable the whole stencil to be lifted off by raising the right hand. The backing sheet will automatically stick to the inky side of the stencil.

Most duplicator cabinets have trays in which stencils may be stored. The simplest method is to lay the stencil in a folder or book on which details of the stencil—subject, date, number of copies run off—can be recorded. The folders can be stored in a stencil box or in the cabinet drawer or tray. Stencils can also be stored on special suspension rails in filing cabinets or deep drawers, the head-pieces are numbered and an index is compiled to record full details of each stencil against the appropriate number.

SPIRIT DUPLICATION

In spirit duplicating (sometimes referred to as hectography and colloquially known by a variety of names such as 'Banda-(r)-ing', 'Fordigraph-ing', 'Ormig-ing' and 'Ditto-ing') a mirror or reverse-picture image is produced in carbon dye on a master sheet. The master sheet is a specially manufactured thick sheet of paper; the front is usually matt, the reverse side (which carries the carbon dye impression of the mirror-image) is white and shiny. As the carbon dye is soluble in alcohol, an impression of the reverse carbon image is transferred as a positive impression when the master sheet is brought into contact with a sheet of paper which has been dampened with alcohol.

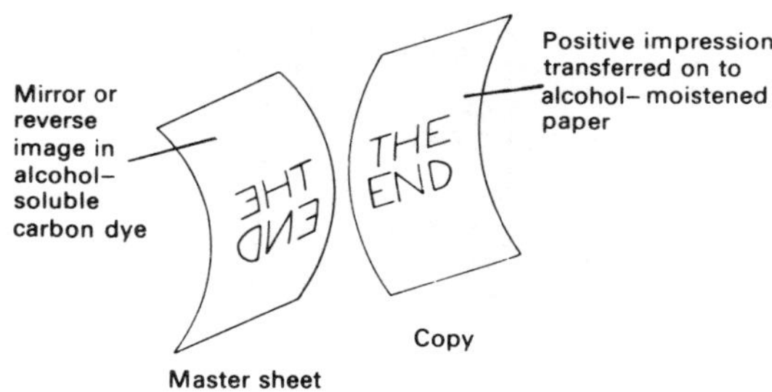

As a small amount of carbon dye is transferred from the master each time a copy is made, it follows that eventually all the dye will be removed and it will be impossible to make any more copies. The number of copies which can be taken from a spirit master is therefore limited and this method of duplication is not recommended for runs of more than 300 copies. It is most suitable for producing between 15 and 100 copies.

Although spirit copies are usually recognised by the well-known purple printing, the carbon or hecto-transfer sheets are also made in six other colours—black, blue, brown, green, red and yellow. A multi-coloured master which of course produces multi-coloured copies is easily prepared by changing the colour of the carbon sheets as required during the writing or typing of the master. The ease with which multi-coloured copies can be produced is one of the main advantages of spirit duplicating.

Another advantage of this method is that the copies do not have to be run-off on absorbent duplicating paper.

The spirit process is particularly suitable for documentation systems for in addition to being able to produce many documents from one master, certain portions can be masked or blanked off so that only selected parts of the original are transferred to the copies. This is often referred to as 'line selection'—Fordigraph produce a line selector duplicator. Thus the complete set of documents covering a transaction—acknowledgment, advice note, despatch and packing notes, despatch/delivery/consignment notes, sales copy, store order, representative's copy, labels and invoice—can be produced from one master.

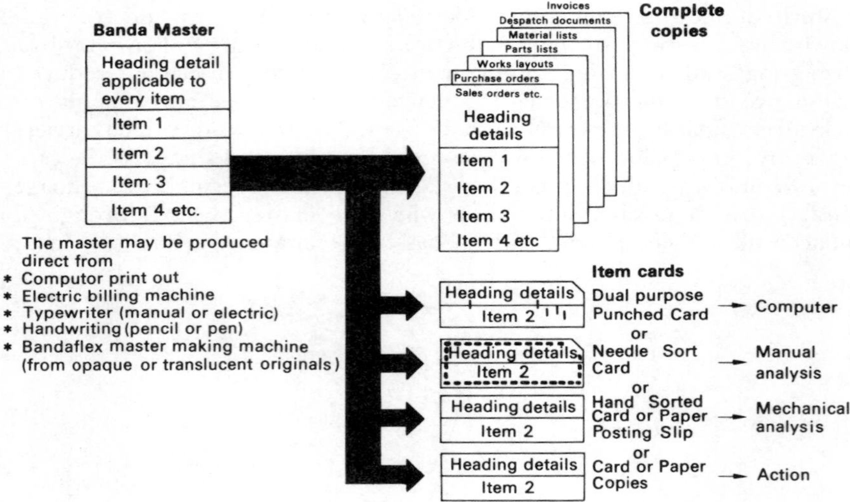

Spirit masters may be prepared:

a by handwriting and/or drawing
b by typing
c by using a thermal office copier such as the Bandaflex

Preparing spirit masters by handwriting and/or drawing Handwritten and/or hand-drawn masters should be produced by placing the master sheet and the carbon transfer sheet on a hard smooth surface and writing with a hard pencil or ballpoint pen. The master sheet with the matt side uppermost should be laid on top of the transfer sheet (carbon side up) so that the shiny reverse side of the master is in direct contact with the hecto carbon. Unwanted pressure marks from the hand may be prevented by resting the hand whilst writing on a pad of blotting paper or a folded handkerchief.

Mistakes have to be corrected on the back of the master. The carbon impression of the error can be gently rubbed away with a special eraser made of putty rubber, or painted over with a special correcting fluid; the carbon image can also be scraped off with knives specially made for correcting errors. Before the correction can be written in, a new piece of carbon sheet must be placed

In addition to its use as a standard spirit duplicator, the Banda Selectomatic A4 machine has push button controls which enable individual lines or groups of lines or items to be selected and reproduced from the master sheet.

against the erasure, as the carbon in that particular spot on the main carbon sheet has already been used. It is possible to buy pads of small carbon sheets, about 5 cm square, to slip behind erasures ready to receive the impression of the correction.

Preparing spirit masters by typing As with stencil duplication the type should be cleaned with a stiff brush. The master and the carbon should be

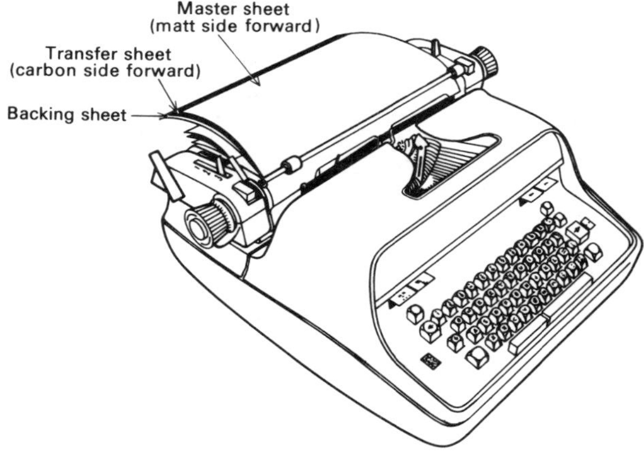

Banda Boards are ideal for Masters prepared by hand. The Masters and Transfer Sheets are held securely by a spring clip, and the graduations on the movable ruler and the board itself enable forms to be drawn accurately.

Banda erasers are made of 'putty rubber', these erasers absorb that part of the image it is desired to correct, leaving the china clay surface of the Master paper undamaged and ready to receive a further deposit.

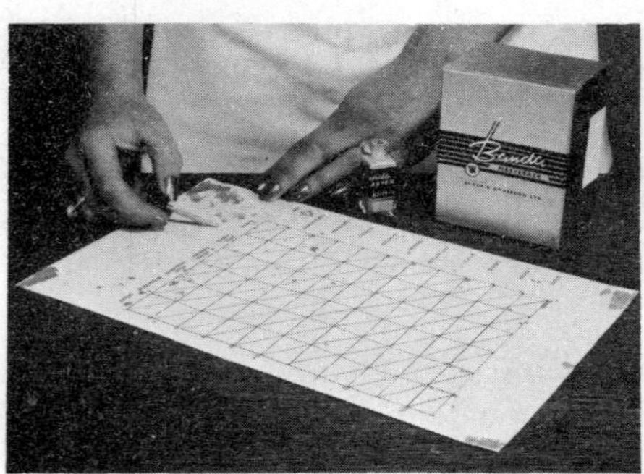

Banda Masteraze is supplied in small bottles complete with brush. Shake the bottle well and with the brush paint a small quantity evenly over the carbon deposit on the back of the master. Allow approximately 15 seconds to dry after which a perfect correction may be made. Ideal for minute corrections in confined spaces, e.g. a letter in the middle of a word.

Banda Thermopaks are available in two qualities. Type 'C' and Type 'D', both of which can be used on a Bandaflex to produce a spirit duplicator Master instantly from any black on white (faxable) original. Thermopaks will give copies in either purple or black. The purple is supplied in stock sizes quarto, Din A4 and foolscap and the black Din A4 only. Type 'C' (paper) comprises a lightweight paper Master and carbon paper suitable for runs of approx. 70/80 copies. Type 'D' (film) uses the same lightweight Master paper as Type 'C' but the carbon is on film instead of tissue. This gives the finest Master reproduction from a heat machine.

fed into the machine with a special backing sheet so that the typing surface is smooth and even. The ribbon is left in the normal position. Typewriting mistakes are corrected in the same way as handwritten errors: the mistake is erased from the back of the master, a new slip of carbon is placed behind the word to be corrected, and the right letter or letters are typed. It is not necessary to correct the typed copy on the front of the master, and corrections will appear as over-typings.

Spirit masters can also be prepared on typewriters which have been fitted with special attachments to take hectograph carbon ribbons or hectograph carbon rolls. Only the master sheet need be fed into the machine; as typing proceeds, the carbon image is automatically printed on the reverse side of the master.

Spirit masters as well as thermal stencils, transparencies for overhead projectors and single copies can be produced on heat copiers such as the Bandaflex Thermocopier shown here. Laminating (covering the surface of a document or leaflet with a thin film of glossy, transparent plastic) can also be done on this machine.

Preparing spirit masters by using a thermal copier Spirit masters can be prepared very quickly by passing the original and a special master-pack through a thermal copier. The original must be 'faxable', that is, black on white.

Operating a spirit duplicator Spirit duplicators are so called because the copy is transferred to the paper by means of a special spirit, instead of ink as with stencil duplicators. As we have already mentioned the copy paper must be moistened with spirit before it is brought into contact with the master sheet. There are two damping systems: one uses a pad, the second uses a roller. Having made sure that there is sufficient spirit in the machine to enable the moistening system to work properly, the master sheet is fixed to the drum with the carbon image facing outwards.

As in stencil duplication, the copy paper must be fanned and restacked before it is placed in the feed tray. When the cylinder is rotated a sheet of copy paper is first moistened by being drawn across the dampening device, and then passed between the pressure roller and the master sheet. The image is transferred in positive form on to the copy paper and the copy is delivered into the receiving tray. The spirit evaporates within seconds leaving the copy clean and dry.

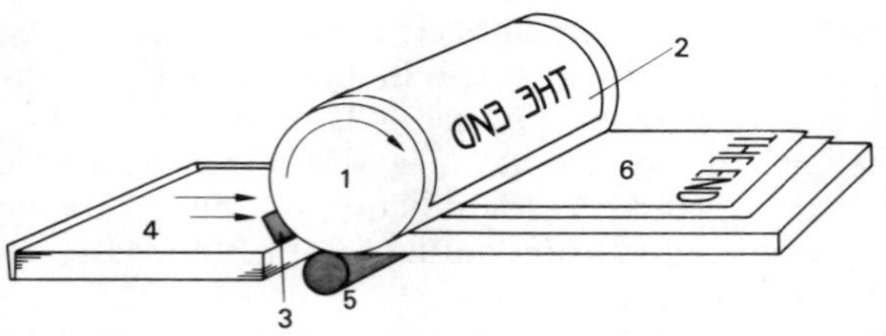

1. The cylinder. 2. The master. 3. The dampening device. 4. Copy paper in feed tray. 5. Impression roller. 6. Duplicated copies in receiving tray.

The Banda 'Junior' spirit duplicating machine is portable and manually operated. It weighs 9.5 kg (21 lb).

Copies made by this process tend to fade if they are left in strong sunlight or on a notice board for any length of time.

Many different kinds of spirit duplicators are available; some are simple manual, portable models, others are electrically operated and fitted with push button controls and automatic masking and selection devices suitable for sophisticated documentation systems, as illustrated on pp. 190 and 191.

Pre-printed master sets Pre-printed master sets such as those shown in the illustration on page 195 enable information to be added to the master either by handwriting or typing. The master can then be put on a spirit duplicator and the desired number of completed forms run-off.

Storing and mailing Spirit masters can be stored (preferably with the hectograph carbon against the image) and filed like ordinary papers; they can be used again and further copies taken until all the carbon dye deposit has been removed.

Masters can also be mailed from one office to another in the normal way such as from a branch office or works office to a head office, or from one overseas office to another or to the national head office.

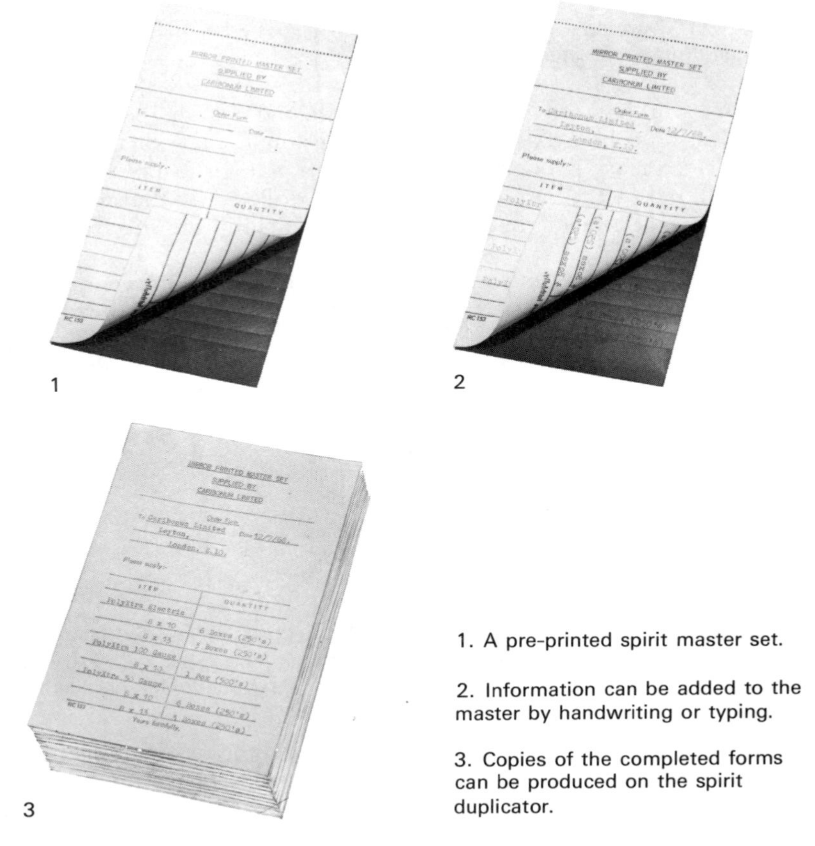

1. A pre-printed spirit master set.

2. Information can be added to the master by handwriting or typing.

3. Copies of the completed forms can be produced on the spirit duplicator.

OFFSET–LITHO DUPLICATING AND PRINTING

Offset-lithography, or offset-litho as it is more commonly called, is another method of producing many copies from one master.

Lithography is one of the three main printing processes: in letterpress, or relief, printing the raised surface of the type is coated with printer's ink and the ink impression is transferred to the paper; in gravure printing the image is recessed into the plate which is then inked and wiped, so that the ink remaining in the engraved or etched portions can be transferred to the paper; lithography is a flat printing process whereby the inked image is produced on the actual surface of the printing plate.

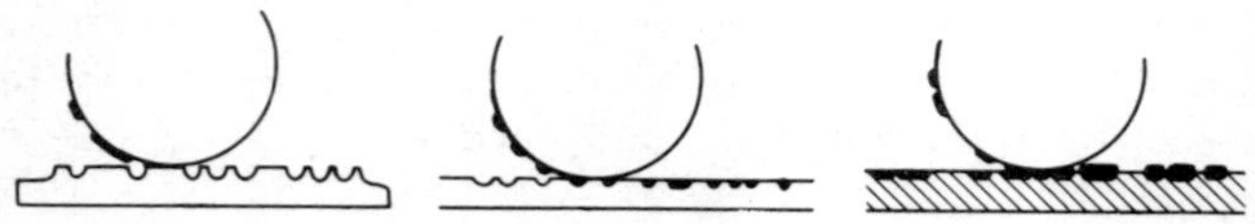

Letterpress (left) prints from a relief image, gravure (centre) prints from a recessed image, and litho (right) from a flat image.

The word 'lithography' means 'stone writing', and the process was discovered in 1796 by a Bavarian printer. He found that when he wrote on a stone with a greasy pencil, water would only adhere to the surface of the stone not covered by the writing. When ink was rolled over the stone, only the greasy crayon marks held the ink, the water repelling the ink from the rest of the surface.

Since then lithography has passed through many stages of development, and today light metal or paper plates are used for the master copy instead of stone. The process still relies on the fact that when the 'image' (the writing, typing or drawing) is made in a greasy medium and the remainder of the surface is covered with a film of water, the printing ink from the inking roller will only adhere to the image.

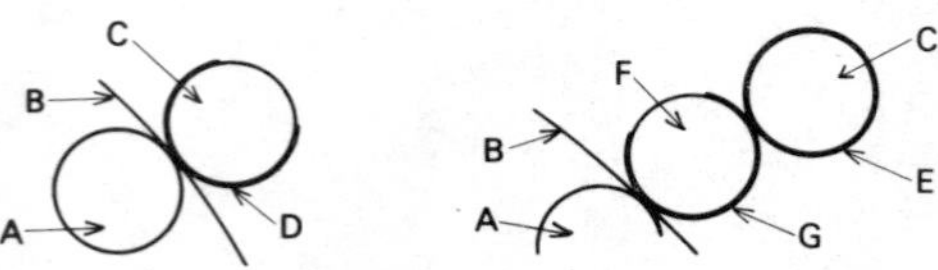

Lithography can use a direct method (left) with reversed image on the printing plate or an indirect, offset method (right). A. Impression cylinder. B. Paper. C. Plate cylinder. D. Litho plate. E. Offset litho plate. F. Blanket cylinder. G. Rubber blanket.

Lithography can be either a direct or an indirect, offset, method. The disadvantage of direct lithography is that the image on the printing plate must be in reverse—similar to the spirit duplication master. Although it is possible to make a reverse image direct litho master by typing on a thin plate with a sheet of greased carbon behind it, direct lithography has not become a popular office process.

Offset-litho plates may be prepared in a number of ways:

a by writing, drawing or typing through a litho ribbon or litho carbon paper

b by photographic or electrostatic processes, including heat type office copying machines utilising paper plates

c by electronic scanners and special paper plates

When the prepared offset-litho plate has been fixed to the cylinder of the machine, the ink rollers are brought into contact with it, thus inking the image. The inked image is then brought into contact with a second roller on

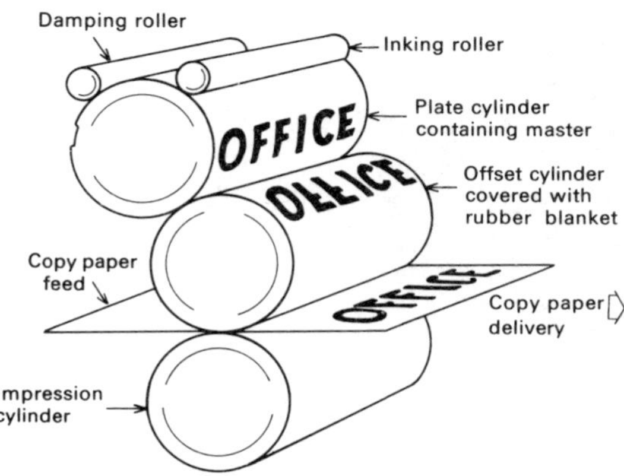

The principle of offset-lithography.

the machine, around which is wrapped a soft rubber sheet, known as a 'blanket'. In this way the image from the inked plate is 'set off', that is, it appears in reverse on the blanket roller. When the blanket roller is brought into contact with the running-off paper, the reversed image is transferred in a readable form. This process is known as 'offset', hence the term offset-lithography.

The Agfa–Gevaert copyrapid systems for making offset plates

MAKING METAL PLATES		MAKING PAPER PLATES	
Copyrapid aluminium offset materials	**Equipment**	**Copyrapid paper offset materials**	**Equipment**
Original +Copyrapid Offset negative paper CRSO (contact) CRSO (camera)	Printing box or camera e.g. SV 37 e.g. Repromaster	Original Copyrapid Offset negative paper DRSO	Printing box e.g. SV 37
Exposed negative paper +Copyrapid Aluminium Offset plate +Copyrapid Offset developer CR 165 C or B	Transfer processing unit for offset e.g. copy-rapid offset 0 40	Exposed negative + Copyrapid paper offset plate +Copyrapid offset developer CR 165 C os or B	Transfer processing unit for offset e.g. Copy-rapid offset 0 40
Offset plate: 1. Treat briefly with Copyrapid Offset fixer CR 610 B and copyrapid offset lacquer CR 612 B, or for very long runs CR 617 B 2. Mount on machine 3. Print	Aluminium offset master Offset machine	Paper offset plate 1. Treat briefly with Copyrapid Offset Etch DR 630 B 2. Mount paper master on machine 3. Print	Paper master Offset machine

The ROTAPRINT TTR desk-top, office offset duplicator is operated by a single lever which controls the main printing functions.

Offset-lithography can take the form of a large multi-coloured printing machine or a small office duplicator. The small office machine is capable of reproducing, in miniature, high-class work equally as good as the large offset machine, but it also has the added advantage of being capable of reproducing inexpensively most of the requirements of the modern office.

Typing offset-litho plates It is very important to use an even touch and to clean the typeface regularly when typing offset-litho plates, and no grease or dirt from the hands should be transferred to the image area. The plate must only be handled at the ends. When a manual typewriter is being used, the typist should use the same touch as when typing on ordinary paper so that the image lies evenly on the surface of the master. The pressure gauge on an electric machine should be adjusted so that it is light enough to prevent the typing being embedded into the surface of the master. The reason for this is that if the typing is deeply indented into the master, only the outer (or upper) edges of the letters will make contact with the ink roller of the duplicator as it passes over the surface. As a result the printed copies will have variations of ink density within the individual letters, the outer edges being blacker than the inner edges.

Another point requiring special attention is the correction of errors. Once matter has been typed on a plate, it is unwise to roll back the platen as grease can be picked up and transferred to other areas from the under-platen rollers. If a mistake has been made, it is best to finish and remove the plate. Re-insert it in the machine with a sheet of thin transparent paper over the image and re-align the typed matter. Roll up the plate slightly and tear away the paper to give access to the line to be corrected. An image on a metal plate can be erased with a glass brush or pumice block. Special rubber erasers free of grease or grit can be purchased from the litho supply companies for use with paper plates. The erasing must be done gently and the rubber must be kept perfectly clean. The re-typing of the character over an erasure should be done gently and repeated two or three times until the character is as black as its neighbours, but no blacker.

The number of copies obtainable by offset-litho depends upon the type of plate used. From 20,000 to 50,000 copies may be produced from a metal plate, and it is claimed that up to 10,000 copies can be obtained from the newest paper plates.

Plates using a variety of typefaces can be prepared photographically.

Offset-litho plates can be kept and used again when required. Copies can be

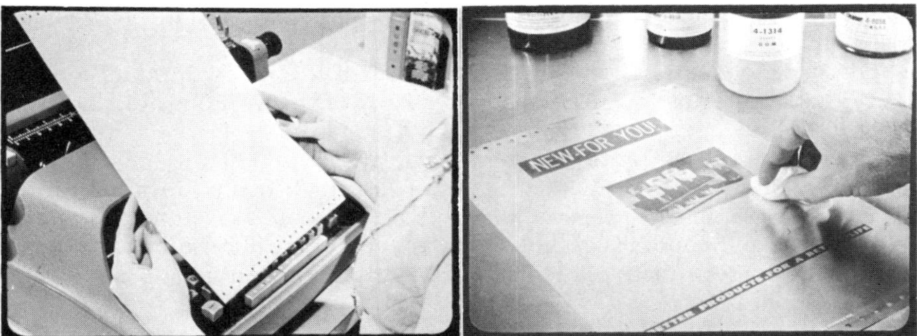

(left) The first stage in offset duplicating is the preparation of a paper master or (right) a plastic or metal plate.

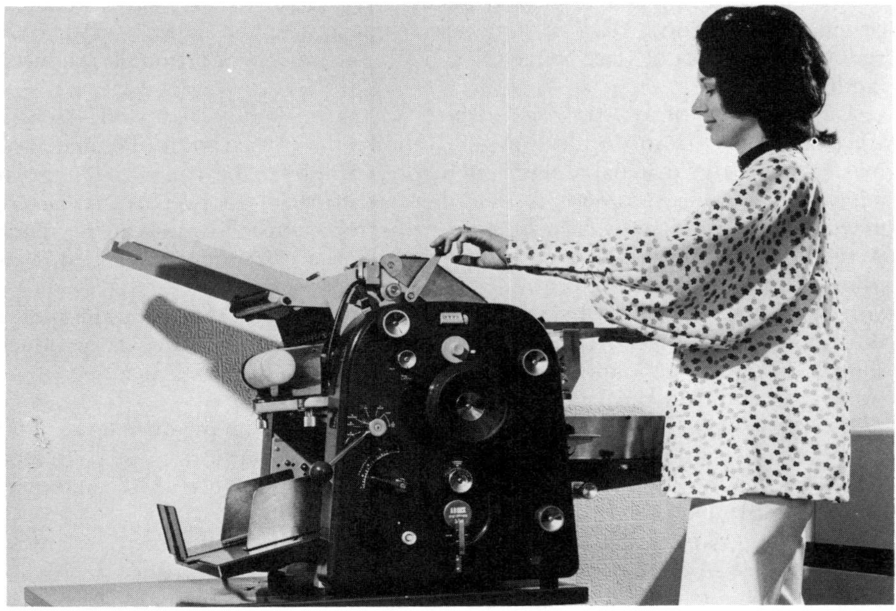

The A. B. Dick table top offset duplicator.

run-off on good quality bond paper, not absorbent paper as in stencil duplication.

Typing a paper master Paper masters are widely used for the reproduction of text and linework in quantities from 10 to 1500 copies. The paper master can be imaged in a number of simple ways: by typewriter, reproducing pencil, ballpoint pen, bookkeeping machine, computer printer, tabulator, teleprinter or addressing machine. Many types of electrostatic copier can directly image paper masters.

Offset paper masters can be pre-printed with a form or heading to which the variable information may be added by any of the methods described.

Preparing a metal plate for photography Offset is not only the most advanced duplicating method, it is also a fast, high quality printing process when photographically prepared metal plates are used. For large quantities of copies (tens and hundreds of thousands), photographic illustrations and quality colour illustrations these plates make more advanced printing as easy as paper master duplication.

OFFICE COPIERS

Office copiers are machines which produce facsimile, that is exact, copies of original documents. One of the newest machines, the Rank Xerox 7000 reduction duplicator (see page 177) will produce proportionally reduced facsimile copies.

The methods of reproduction which we have already discussed—stencil, spirit and offset-litho duplication—all require the preparation of a stencil or master from the original document before copies can be run-off. The great advantage of office copiers is that there is no need to prepare a master; provided the original is in a fit state to be reproduced copies can be made using one of the office copying processes which are frequently referred to as photocopying or photostatting.

In addition to their obvious use for making one or more copies of a document very quickly, some office copiers can also be used to produce stencils, spirit masters and offset-litho plates, as we have already noted in the previous sections of this chapter.

The latest machines are called *copier-duplicators*; they can produce up to 3000 or more copies an hour; the Rank Xerox 4000 copier-duplicator (see page 202) will turn over the copies and print a second image on the reverse side and then collate the printed sheets.

There are many firms manufacturing office copying equipment and most firms produce several models. Each process and each model is not suitable for all purposes, e.g. only flat-bed machines will copy pages of bound books. It would be an extremely long and complicated study to describe all the different machines and their applications so we shall classify them under four headings*—the electrostatic processes, the heat processes, the silver-halide process and the diazo process—and indicate the type of work for which each is most suitable.

Electrostatic processes During the past fifteen years there has been a rapid development in electrostatic copiers and their simplicity and convenience has caused them to become more widely used than almost any other process. There are two electrostatic processes: Xerography (sometimes described as indirect electrostatic) and Electrofax or direct electrostatic. The main difference between the two methods from the user's point of view is that Xerography copies on to plain paper, but specially coated paper has to be bought for use with the Electrofax process.

***Modern Office Copying*, S. B. Page, Andre Deutsch.

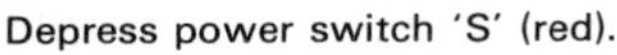

Depress power switch 'S' (red).

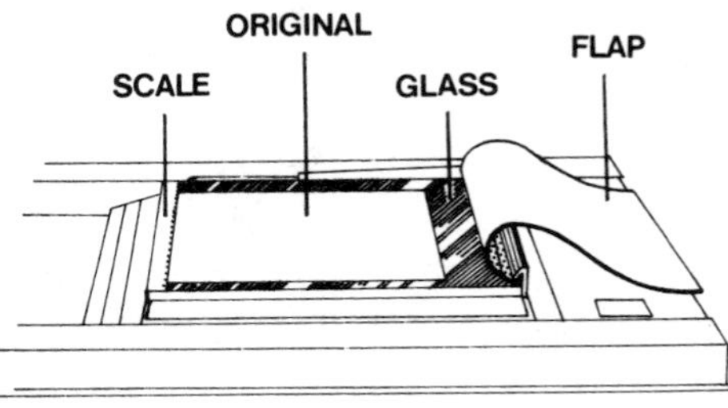

Raise flap. Lay original face down on glass with one edge against scale.

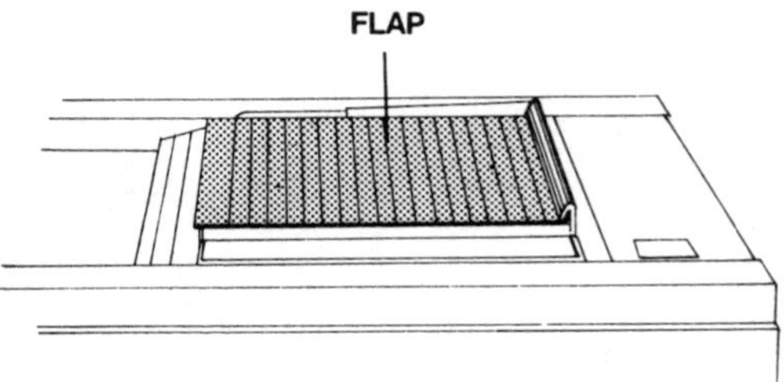

Set counter. Depress copy switch 'C' (green) and collect your copies from collecting tray. If amber light 'P' lights up, paper tray must be reloaded. If white light 'T' lights up, tissue must be replaced.

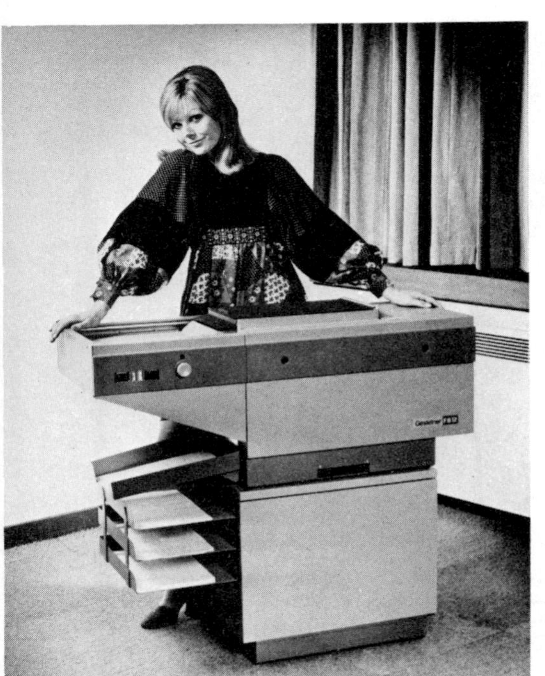

The Gestetner FB12 copier (left) produces dry copies at a rate of 12 copies per minute on plain paper. The right-hand diagram shows how to operate the machine.

XEROGRAPHY The Xerographic process was invented in America in 1938. The first popular model, the Xerox 914, was introduced into England in 1960 by Rank Xerox, the organisation which markets Xerox copiers in all parts of the world except the Americas and Japan.

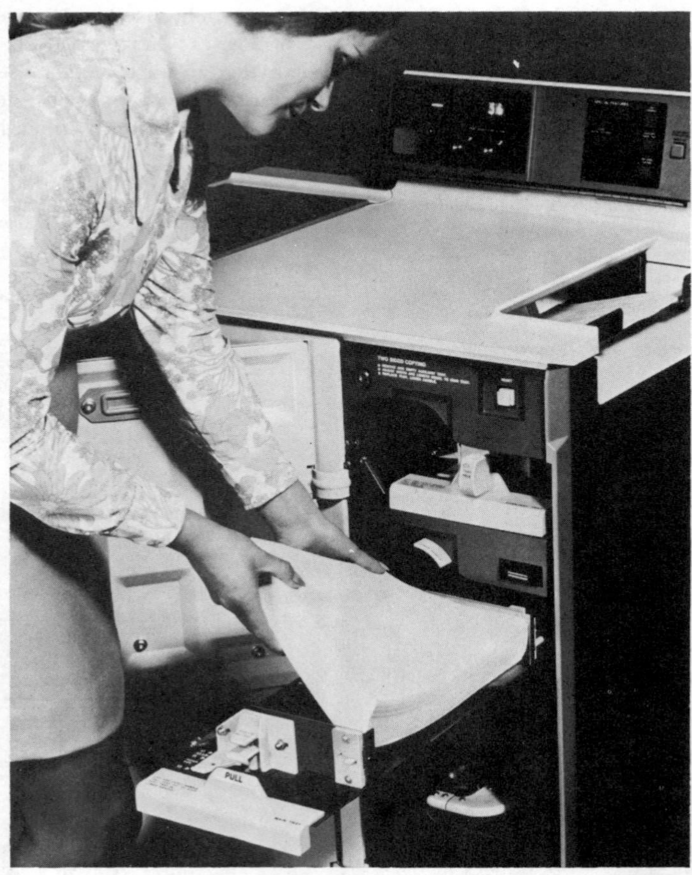

The Rank Xerox 4000 office copier produces copies of any original on plain unsensitised paper at the rate of 43 per minute. The machine can produce double-sided copies; this feature enables documents such as insurance policies and property deeds to be copied as single units rather than in two parts. Here the operator is inserting a supply of copy paper.

How xerography works

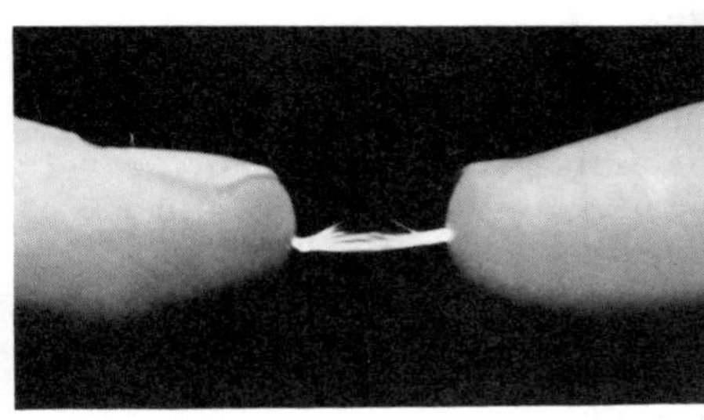

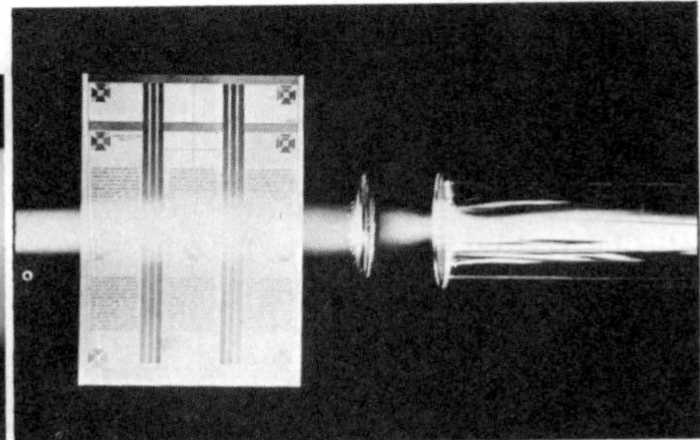

1 Remember the spark that snapped at your finger-tip after scuffing your slippers across a thick carpet? Or the way you could pick up bits of paper with a comb that had been run quickly through your hair?

Both of these familiar experiences are examples of static electricity, a natural phenomenon. This same electrostatic force is fundamental to the process of xerography.

2 The process starts with the three units displayed here. An image of the document to be copied is projected onto a light-sensitive surface. An electrostatic charge, placed earlier on the drum surface, disappears from the exposed areas, which were white on the original document. The charge is retained on the drum in the area which corresponds to the black or printed parts of the original document.

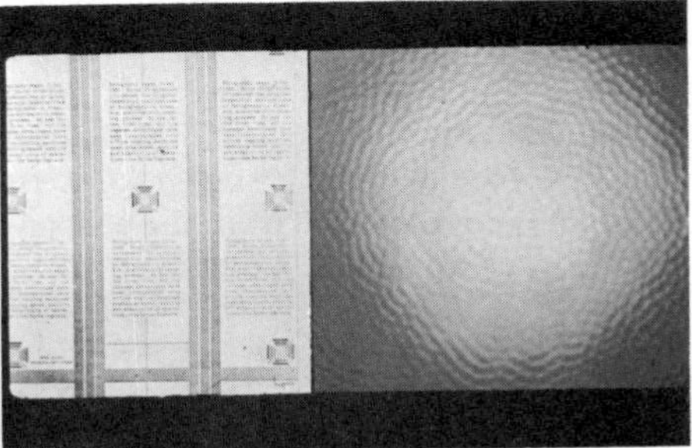

3 Special developer powder, poured over the drum, clings to the charged portion of the drum (just as the bits of paper adhered to the comb). A visible image of the original document is thus created on the drum. Ordinary bond paper is brought into contact with the drum and an electrical charge beneath the paper attracts the powder from drum.

4 The powder image is then softened and fused into the paper, usually by heat, creating an exact copy of the original document. The whole process takes only a few seconds from start to finish. The prints, on ordinary bond paper, are clean, dry and permanent.

The indirect electrostatic process (Xerography) produces copies on ordinary bond paper.

Developments during the following years increased the speed at which multiple copies could be made; in 1968 the Xerox 3600, a copier-duplicator, was introduced. The original document is placed on the platen, the required number of copies is dialled and the 'PRINT' button pressed. Any number of copies up to 499 can be dialled. Accessories for collating and feeding can be fitted. The Xerox 3600 produces copies at the rate of 60 per minute.

The Xerox 7000 will do the same work as the 3600 but it can also produce copies reduced to 85%, 75%, 70.7% and 61.5% of the size of the original, as well as same size copies. It will accept originals up to 14 in by 18 in, but the maximum copy size is 8½ in by 13 in.

The Xerox 4000 has two paper feed trays which enable it to produce double-sided copies; documents such as contracts and insurance policies can be automatically copied as single units rather than in two parts.

The latest Xerox office copier, the 9200, has a number of sophisticated facilities. Copies can be slight enlargements of the original (up to 102%) or reductions to any size down to 61%. The size required is dialled. There is also a facility for moving the image ½ in to the right or left so that it can be centred on the page. Double-sided copying and limitless sorting are two more features. Copies are produced at the rate of 7200 per hour, or 2 copies per second.

Xerox machines can be bought or they may be hired from the manufacturers. The user pays a fixed monthly rental and a small charge per copy made. The number of copies made is registered on a meter in the machine. If 100 copies are made per day, the cost per copy is approximately 2p.*

Xerography is a dry copying process; it will copy anything written, typed, printed or drawn, from originals in any colour. The finished result is always black and white. Both the xerographic and electrofax processes will make paper and metal offset plates for offset-litho machines.

As we have seen, the xerographic process uses a coated drum and copies on to plain bond paper. Within the past few years other copiers, such as the Gestetner FB12, have appeared which also copy on to plain paper.

The ELECTROFAX process, sometimes called direct electrostatic, uses paper coated with zinc oxide. The paper may be supplied in a roll and fitted into the copier which automatically cuts off the correct length for the document being copied. The electrofax process was developed by the Radio Corporation of America who have licensed over 200 copier manufacturers to use their process in one form or another. Electrofax copiers, like xerographic copiers, will copy anything written, typed, printed, or drawn, from originals in any colour. They will also make metal and paper offset plates.

* When 11 or more copies are made from one original the cost can be as little as ¼p to ½p per copy.

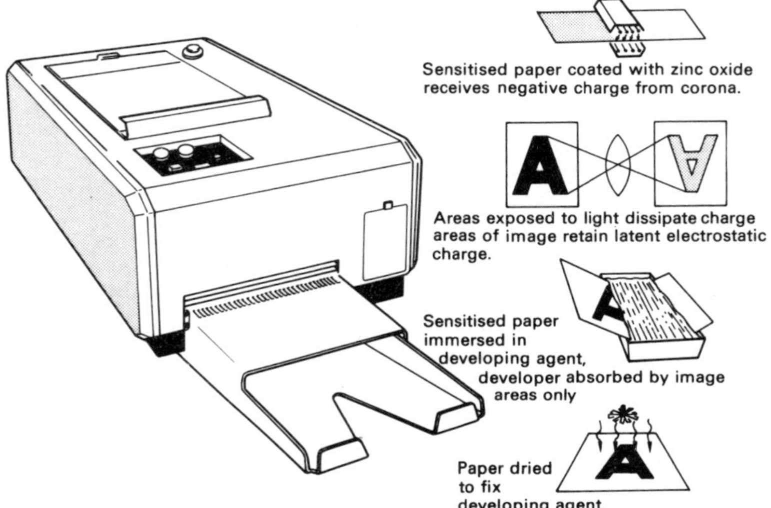

The direct electrostatic process (Electrofax) produces copies on special paper coated with zinc oxide.

The A. B. Dick 625 Copier. Up to 20 copies can be dialled. The toner (black powder) is supplied in an enclosed cartridge and the copy paper fits into a cassette for easy handling. Copies are produced at the rate of ten per minute.

Heat processes The office copier market today is dominated by electrostatic machines. Offices which do not have sufficient copying to justify the installation of an electrostatic machine tend to use one of the heat processes; these may be classified as: infra-red reflex, frequently referred to as *thermography* and known by the trade name *Thermofax*; infra-red transfer, used in the Bandaflex and Fordifax machines; or the Dual Spectrum process used in the 3M 051 machine.

The THERMOFAX process is based on the fact that dark colours become hot more quickly than light colours (because dark colours absorb more radiant energy, from which heat is generated). A copy is made by placing a sheet of copy paper on top of the original and feeding them both into the machine where they are exposed to an infra-red lamp. The heat generated by the dark areas (the image) of the original causes a colour change on the corresponding parts of the copy paper, and both copy and original emerge from the machine within a few seconds.

As Thermofax copiers are always rotary, they can copy documents of any length. The largest machine, Model 50, will copy documents 36 cm wide. Spirit masters and transparencies for overhead projectors can be made on Thermofax machines; because the process is dry, sheets of gummed paper can also be used in the machine. A wide range of copy papers is available including spirit master carbon sets, and gummed and perforated copy paper for address labels. The standard copy paper is usually buff.

The Thermofax process will not copy certain coloured inks (e.g. red) or inks or pencils without a graphite content. Originals should, therefore, be faxable,

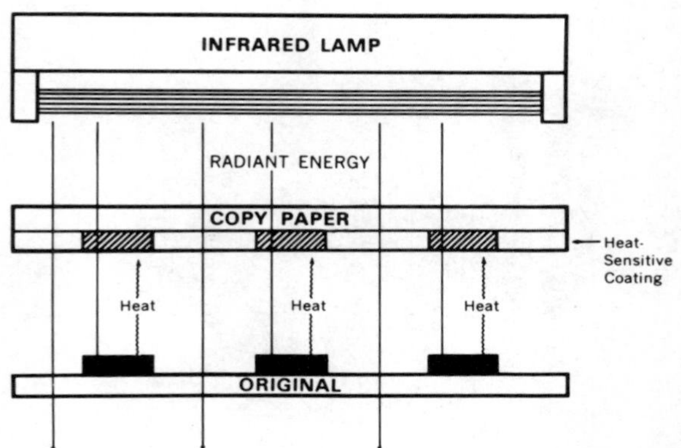

How the infra-red reflex process works. Heat generated in the infra-red-absorbing image area of the original is conducted to the heat-sensitive paper, forming a coloured compound in the image areas. This process is frequently referred to as *thermography* and known by the trade name *Thermofax.*

that is of black typing, pencil or black carbon copies. Signatures on letters, spirit copies or red typing cannot normally be copied because they do not cause the heat generation necessary to cause a colour change on the copy paper.

The BANDAFLEX (see illustration on page 193) and FORDIFAX machines, sometimes referred to as thermocopiers, use the infra-red transfer process. The copy is made on ordinary paper by placing a transfer sheet between it and the original. The sandwich of original, transfer sheet and copy paper is placed in a nylon folder and fed through the machine. As it is heated, the colour coating on the transfer sheet becomes tacky over the image area and sticks to the copy paper when the two are pulled apart. Machines using this process are usually rotary. In addition to making a single copy within seconds, the process is excellent for making spirit masters, thermal stencils and transparencies for overhead projectors. Thermocopiers will laminate, that is, cover the surface of a document or leaflet with a thin layer of glossy, transparent film. As with the Thermofax process, copies can also be taken on gummed perforated sheets.

The DUAL SPECTRUM process. When we were describing thermography, we noted that the process would not copy colours because only graphite-based images can absorb infra-red radiation and convert it into heat. The dual spectrum process relies upon the ability of an original to absorb visible light. Whilst many colour pigments and dyes are unable to be copied by thermography, they are able to absorb light, and for this reason virtually any image found on an original document can be copied by the dual spectrum process.

The process comprises two stages: in the first stage, called exposure, a pink Intermediate Sheet is placed on top of the original with the cut corner at the upper right-hand side. This ensures that the coated side of the Intermediate Sheet is facing the original. The combined sheets are placed on the exposure plate of the machine with the Intermediate Sheet underneath. The lid is closed. When the exposure button is pressed, the exposure lamps turn on. After a few seconds, the lamps turn off. The operator raises the lid and separates the original from the Intermediate Sheet. In the second stage, the Intermediate Sheet (with the cut corner at upper right again) is placed on top of a sheet of copy paper with the 'Flame' symbol underneath so that the sensitive surface is in direct contact with the Intermediate Sheet. The two sheets are fed into the slots and drawn through rollers into the machine. They emerge within seconds through the exit slot. The Intermediate Sheet is thrown away; the image has been produced on the copy sheet.

Flat-bed dual spectrum copiers, such as the 3M Dry Photo-copier 051, will also copy from bound books. The lid of the machine is hinged so that it can be closed over the thickness of an average book. For extra thick books, the lid may be completely removed. If the pages are thin or translucent, a sheet of white card should be placed behind the material to be copied.

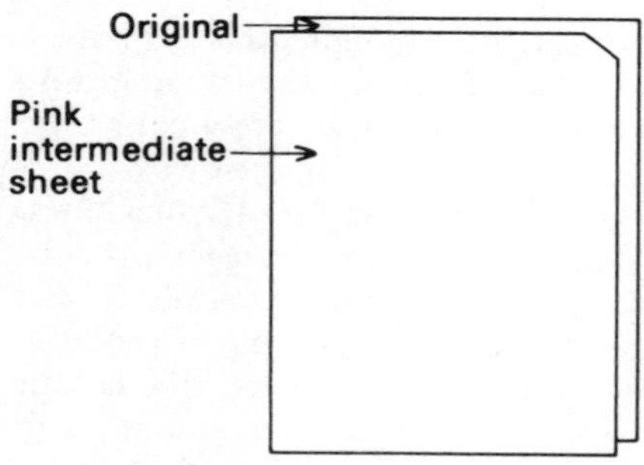

Exposure stage. The Intermediate Sheet with cut corner at upper right is placed on top of the original.

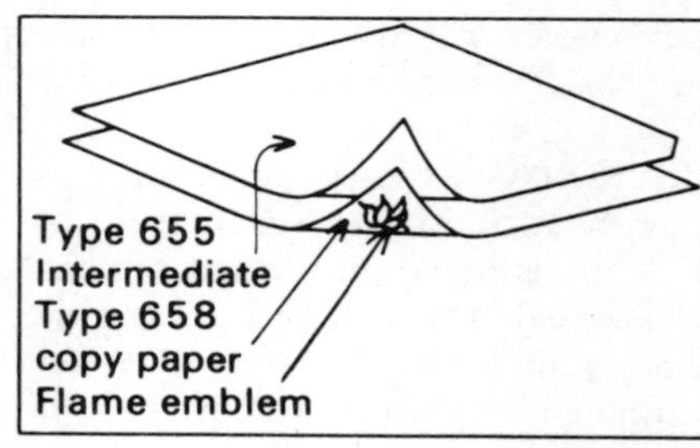

Development stage. The Intermediate Sheet (cut corner at upper right again) is placed on top of a sheet of copy with the 'Flame' symbol underneath.

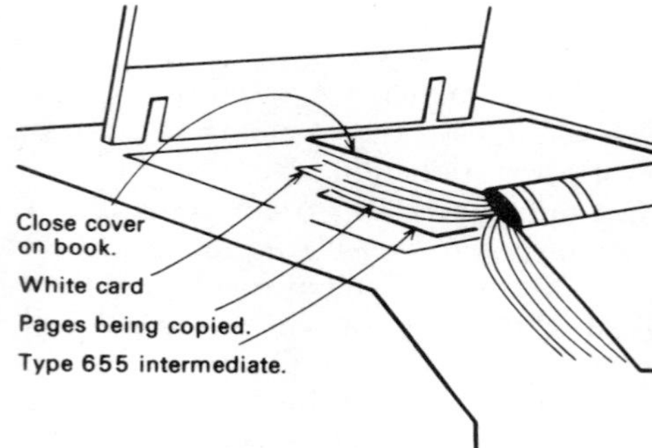

The 3M Dry Photo-copier 051 uses the dual spectrum process. 1. On/off switch. 2. Exposure lid. 3. Exposure plate. 4. Control knob. 5. Exposure button. 6. Copying entrance slot. 7. Exit slot.

1 Exposure (visible light)

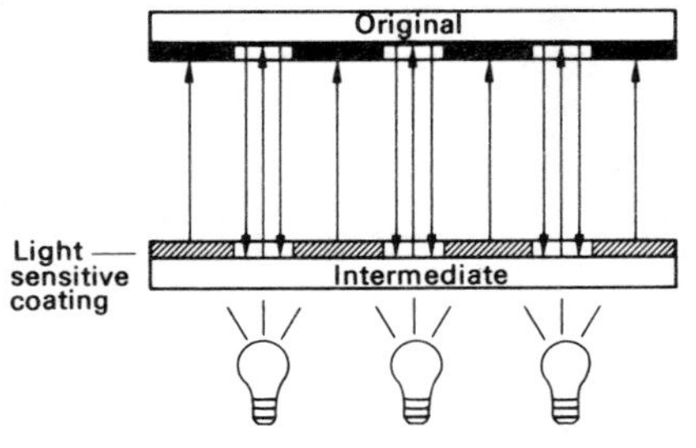

The light sensitive coating is destroyed by the visible light in the areas corresponding to the non-printed areas of the original, from which it was reflected. The coating remains in the image areas.

2 Development (heat)

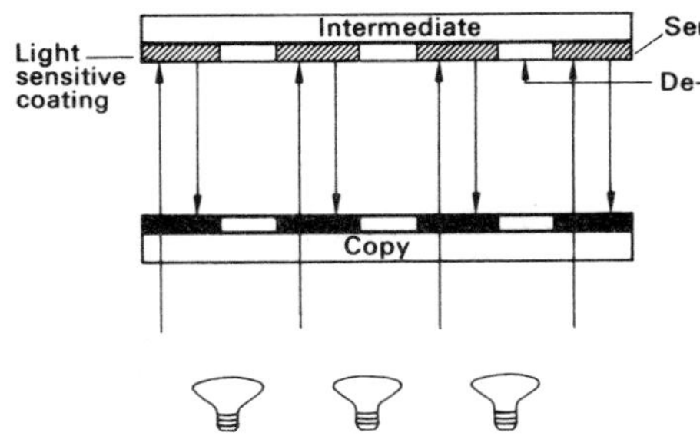

Application of heat to the "sand-wich" of light-exposed intermediate and receptor sheet causes imagewise transfer of reactant from intermediate sheet to receptor sheet

Heat source

The Dual Spectrum process relies upon the ability of an original to absorb visible light. As almost all colours are able to absorb light, virtually any image found on an original document can be copied by this process.

Silver halide processes The processes described under this heading are derived from orthodox photographic methods which depend on film or paper being coated with silver halide or similar materials to make them sensitive to light.

The DIFFUSION TRANSFER process is used by more than 100 machines on the British market; diffusion transfer machines can be recognised by two or three slots in the developing unit. The process is popular because the capital outlay is low; it comprises two stages—1. exposure to a light source, and 2. processing. The original is first exposed with a piece of sensitised paper to the light source; the light-sensitive paper and another sheet of special paper are then passed through a chemical solution, which transfers the copy from the light-sensitive paper to the other sheet of paper. The two sheets emerge from the machine slightly damp and in close contact. When they are peeled apart, the copy appears on the sheet of special paper. The diffusion transfer process is largely used for making plates for small offset-litho machines. Good single copies may also be made but the process is comparatively slow and expensive.

The GELATINE TRANSFER process is frequently known by the trade name Verifax. The process is similar in some respects to diffusion transfer but the method of transfer is different. The advantage of the process is that the positive paper, whilst being cheaper than photographic papers, has the quality of bond paper. The negative is called a 'matrix'.

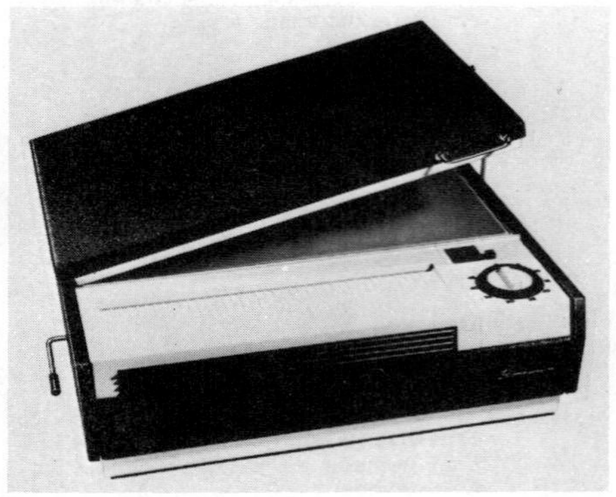

The Bandavelop Flatbed model uses the diffusion transfer process. There is also a rotary model.

The REFLEX process produces copies from opaque or transparent originals and also comprises two stages. It differs from the transfer processes in that the first operation produces a negative copy (white print on black) from which a positive print can be made during the second operation. The paper negatives can be stored and used to make as many positive copies as required. The positive copies are damp after processing and must be allowed to dry. Reflex is also capable of copying half-tones. Of all photocopying processes, the reflex process is the most similar to conventional photography.

The DIRECT-POSITIVE process is similar to the reflex process but produces a positive copy without first having to make a negative. A much stronger light source is necessary. Direct-positives, like reflex materials, have to be developed and fixed.

Diazo or dyeline process The diazo or dyeline process was used to reproduce engineering drawings from tracing paper or tracing linen for many years before it was incorporated into an office copier. The name 'diazo' is derived from 'diazonium salts'—the principal ingredients of the chemical coating the sensitised paper. The diazo process involves two stages. When the original and the sheet of yellow diazo paper are exposed to light, the chemical coating is bleached away from those areas not covered by the lines of the original image. During the second stage the diazo paper is passed through chemical liquid or vapour which develops the remaining yellow coating on the printing area, darkening the image, so that a positive copy emerges. The original must either be translucent or a translucent master must be produced in the first operation, from which copies can be taken.

It is possible to purchase good white diazo bond paper and some firms use this for their printed headed letter paper. If the receiver of a letter sees the note 'Suitable for making dyeline copies' printed along the lower edge he knows that he can take further copies by the diazo process.

Diazo, in spite of the low cost of materials and the introduction of heat developing materials, has not become very popular outside drawing offices. This is probably because only one-sided translucent originals can be copied. Almost all diazo copiers are rotary machines. A disadvantage of the diazo process is that copies tend to fade if exposed to light for any length of time.

Using the diazo process, the Ozalid 20A ozaprinter produces prints and sub-masters from opaque and semi-opaque single sided originals.

AUTOMATIC TYPEWRITERS

Automatic typewriters are operated by electricity; they type out prepared (that is, previously typed and recorded) information in a predetermined display style, without a typist striking the keys, returning the carriage or operating any of the standard machine controls.

The first automatic machine, the 'Auto-Typist', was made in America in 1932. The philosophy underlying the invention of the machine was that people react more favourably to typed originals (that is, letters which are clearly 'top copies' written personally to the addressee) than they do to duplicated or printed letters even though an attempt may have been made in a second operation to 'match-in' the name and address of the addressee.

As it is impossible to distinguish between a letter typed by an automatic typewriter and a letter typed by a typist, automatically typed 'originals' were found to be very effective when used for chasing overdue accounts, for direct mail advertising and for 'begging letters'. In addition to their effectiveness, automatically typed letters have three more advantages: 1. They can be produced at speeds ranging from 145–180 words per minute. 2. They need never be checked, and 3. They are very much cheaper to produce than hand-typed letters.

All automatic typewriters have a standard keyboard and, in addition, a number of function or control keys, which are used to give the machine instructions such as STOP, START TAPE, EDIT, PARAGRAPH. The function keys may be on the keyboard or front casing of the machine, or they may be built into a separate control unit.

All machines work on the same general principles:

1. The information to be automatically typed must first be 'recorded' or fed into the typewriter and the machine must be given the necessary display instructions. This is done by putting a sheet of paper in the machine and typing in the normal way; as this is being done, the whole document is being recorded—some machines record on punched paper tape, others use punched cards or magnetic tape or magnetic cards.
2. The machine is instructed to print-out the recording which is then checked for accuracy, edited and amended as necessary.
3. The 'record'—whether tape or card—is numbered, indexed and stored for future use.
4. When needed, the tape or card is threaded or put into the control attachment of the machine, top copy with carbon pack as required is inserted into the machine and the START key is depressed. When used for producing individual letters, the typist types the date (although some machines can be 'programmed' with the date at the start of the day's work) and the name of the addressee; she then instructs the machine to start. The machine can be programmed to stop so that the typist can type in variable information such as numbers or sums of money in the body of the letter, and then continue automatically when instructed.

The 'Auto-Typist' is controlled by a roll of perforated paper, similar to that used in old-fashioned pianolas. Standard paragraphs are typed automatically when the appropriate control buttons are pressed.

Following the success of the 'Auto-Typist', the next range of machines was marketed under the name of 'Flexowriter' and used edge-punched cards or punched paper tape or tabulating cards. Some of the newest machines use magnetic tape or magnetic card.

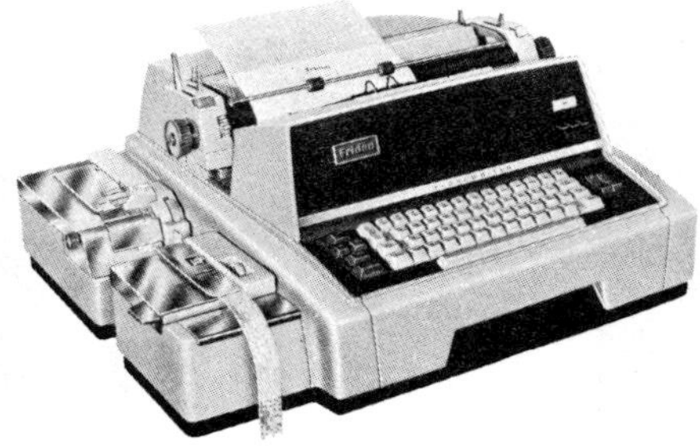

The Flexowriter 2345 automatic typewriter is operated by punched paper tape, edge punched cards or tabulating cards; the standard model has a 16 in carriage and types out error-free work at 145 words per minute.

The IBM Magnetic Card Unit which is connected to the typewriter and contains the read/record mechanism.

The IBM Magnetic Card 'Executive' typewriter consists of a modified Magnetic Card 72 typewriter and a Magnetic Card Unit which contains the read/record mechanism. The first typing of a document is recorded as it is typed on a reusable magnetic card—one track for each line of type and a card for each page. Alterations and amendments are made by locating the line and word on the magnetic card and then typing in the revision. Corrections may be overtyped. The machine types out the final copy at 180 words per minute.

The printing mechanism of automatic typewriters is either the IBM golf ball or the conventional type-basket with typebars. Typebars are claimed to be strong and reliable, and are used on moving carriage machines so that the positioning of the carriage can be programmed to form part of the machine's functions. On the other hand, a golf ball printer is usually quicker than a type-basket machine; it is also quieter because there is no carriage movement. The outstanding advantage of the golf ball head is that it can be changed very easily to give a variety of typefaces; this factor is of great importance in some display work.

Most manufacturers of automatic typewriters offer a variety of carriage lengths and the machines can be fitted with either carbon or fabric ribbons.

One of the most recent applications of automatic typewriters is known as *word processing* and is used in connection with the standardisation of business correspondence. It is claimed that up to 70 per cent of business correspondence is made up of repetitive phrases and similar sentences. When the correspondence requirements of a firm have been assessed by analysing and collating the contents of the filed carbon copies over a given period, it is possible to prepare a series of standard paragraphs, which can be fed into an automatic typewriter. Sets of handbooks are produced which contain the printed paragraphs, indexed by number and divided into subjects and sub-sections; for example, under the heading 'Accounts' might be sub-sections for reminders, covering-letters and so on. Instead of dictating full letters, the dictator gives his secretary the numbers of the relevant paragraphs together with any details which have to be inserted manually. It is claimed that this method reduces the total cost of each letter by as much as 90 per cent.*

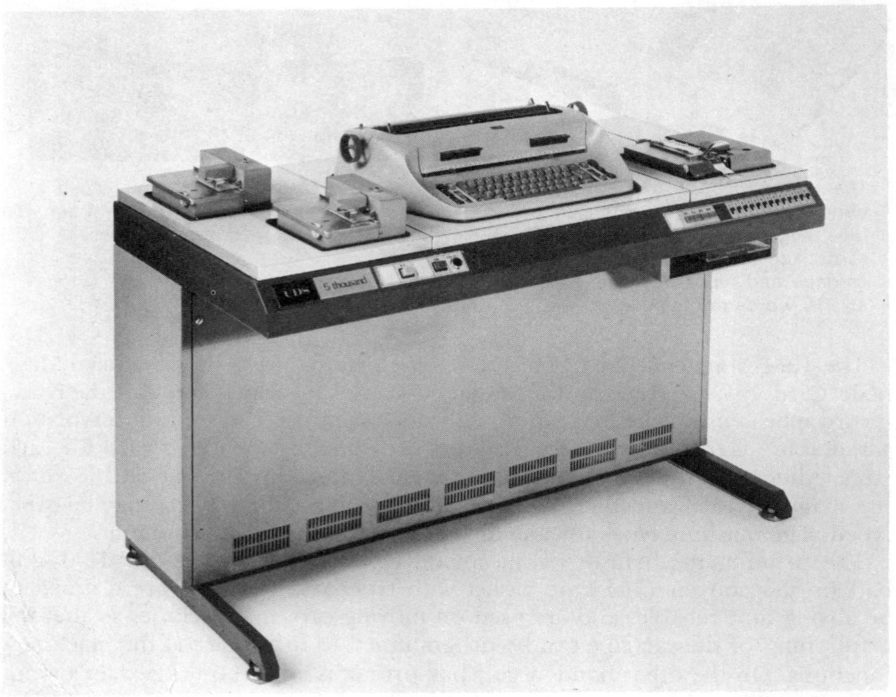

The UDS 5000, marketed by Ultronic Data Systems Ltd, comprises an IBM golf ball electric typewriter, a tape punch and a tape reader. It can be programmed to produce all sorts of commercial documents and correspondence. The output tape can be used for computer input.

OFFICE COMPOSING MACHINES

Cold-type composing The expression 'cold-type composing' was originally used by the VariTyper Corporation to distinguish the VariTyper from other typewriters. The phrase is now used to describe all composing systems which are not 'hot metal', that is, the conventional composing method used in the printing industry.

The function of office composing machines is not as with other automatic

*'In Europe—The Automatic typewriter', *Management in Action*, July 1970.

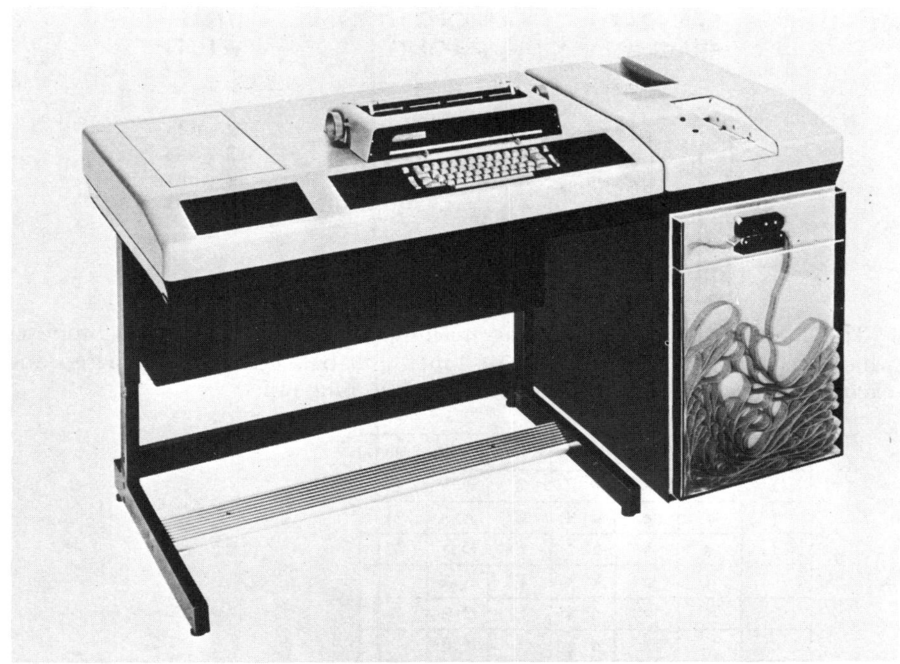

Supertyper manufacture a series of automatic typewriters using punched paper tape and edge-punched cards to record the data. The Selectograph shown here is suitable for routine correspondence; it types out perfect copy at 900 characters a minute.

typewriters to produce 'original letters' or correspondence; their function is to produce displayed copy (in a wide variety of typefaces and frequently with a justified, that is an even, right-hand margin) which may then be used for plate-making in Inplant Printing Departments.

There are three features which distinguish office composing machines from normal typewriters. These are the provision of proportional spacing, right-hand margin justification, and a choice of typefaces and sizes.

PROPORTIONAL SPACING With standard typewriters each letter occupies the same amount of space. Proportionally spaced type varies the space occupied by each letter or character according to its size by working on a unit system. Each character is allocated a certain number of units; for example, the letters i, l, f and j will be allocated less units than the letters m and w and the capital letters. The various machine manufacturers work on various unit systems. The IBM Executive and the Singer-Friden Justowriter work on a 5-unit system. The VariTyper and the Hermes Ambassador work on a 4-unit system.

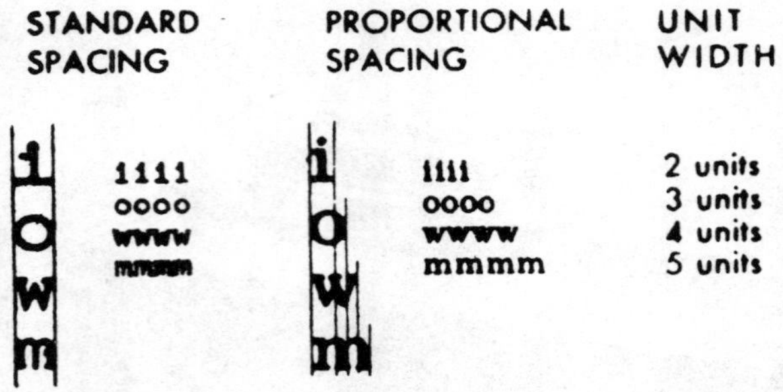

STANDARD SPACING	PROPORTIONAL SPACING	UNIT WIDTH
iiii	iiii	2 units
oooo	oooo	3 units
wwww	wwww	4 units
mmmm	mmmm	5 units

The latest proportional spacing machine is the IBM Selectric Composer which has a 9-unit system; the type fonts (golf balls) carry 88 characters and each character can vary in width from three to nine units.

3 Units	4 Units	5 Units	6 Units	7 Units	8 Units	9 Units
i	f	a	b P	B	w V	m
j	r	c	d S	C	A X	M
l	s	e	h *	E	D Y	W
.	t	g	k †	F	G &	
,	I	v	n $	L	H %	
;	:	z	o +	T	K @	
'	)	J	p =	Z	N –	
'	(	?	q]		O ¾	
-	!	[	u		Q ½	
	/		x		R ¼	
			y		U	
			All numbers			

IBM Selectric Composer character unit values.

Note: All characters in the Presswire Type Fonts have the same unit values as the "Selectric" Composer Type Fonts with the exception of the following:

All numerals = 4 units
Composite fractions = 8 units
$ = 4 units

With the IBM Magnetic Tape Selectric Composer a space of 9 units is allowed for the widest letter. The proportional spacing feature and the capacity for changing type styles, sizes and weights enables high-quality copy to be produced for reproduction. The copy is produced visually (hard-copy) and on to tape at the same time, corrections being made at this stage simply by back-spacing and overtyping. The copy is then checked or printed-out. Further or extensive corrections can be made by producing a second tape which is automatically merged with the first during the process of composing. Print-out can be on to paper or translucent masters or negatives from which plates are made. The whole process is very quick and error-free, because once the initial keyboarding and correcting phase is passed, the whole process including display is an automatic one. Operators do not have to type the final form of the master material.

The IBM Magnetic Tape Selectric Composer.

MARGIN JUSTIFICATION There are four methods of justifying the right-hand margin: those used on the Justowriter and the IBM Magnetic Tape Selectric Composer, the VariTyper, certain manual and electric machines, and the newest machines, phototypesetters and computertypesetters.

The Justowriter and the IBM Magnetic Tape Selectric Composer produce justified copy automatically after the first draft by means of tape. During the first typing the Justowriter punches a code into a paper tape and the IBM MT Selectric Composer produces a magnetic tape; both the text and the variation of spacing needed to make all the lines of type of equal length are recorded on the tapes. When the tapes are 'played back' by instructing the machines to 'PRINT OUT' all the lines are of equal length. Both these processes are automatic; during the second typing the machines increase or decrease the spaces between the words so that each line exactly fits the predetermined line-length.

With the VariTyper it is necessary to type the copy twice. Each line of the first typing has to finish within a 'justification area', as shown on a dial on the machine; this is adjusted before the second typing, and a special device automatically spreads out the spaces so that the line ends are equal.

Certain other manual and electric machines can produce justified right-hand margins but as with the VariTyper a second typing process is involved. When the required length of writing line has been decided, a draft is typed. At the end of each typewriting line a reading is taken from a scale. When the final copy is typed the justification lever is used in conjunction with the previous readings and the right-hand margin is automatically justified.

There are three methods of justifying on machine: those used on the Justowriter, on the VariTyper and on all other machines (manual and electric, fixed-width and variable-width). Basically, all involve a second typing and the principle is the same in each case: the amount of space by which the end of each line of typing and the predetermined right-hand margin differ on the first typing is, on the second, distributed (by adding or subtracting) over the spaces between words.

There are three methods of justifying on machine: those used on the Justowriter, on the VariTyper and on all other machines (manual and electric, fixed-width and variable-width). Basically, all involve a second typing and the principle is the same in each case: the amount of space by which the end of each line of typing and the predetermined right-hand margin differ on the first typing is, on the second, distributed (by adding or subtracting) over the spaces between words.

There are three methods of justifying on machine: those used on the Justowriter, on the VariTyper and on all other machines (manual and electric, fixed-width and variable-width). Basically, all involve a second typing and the principle is the same in each case: the amount of space by which the end of each line of typing and the predetermined right-hand margin differ on the first typing is, on the second, distributed (by adding or subtracting) over the spaces between words.

There are three methods of justifying on machine: those used on the Justowriter, on the VariTyper and on all other machines (manual and electric, fixed-width and variable-width). Basically, all involve a second typing and the principle is the same in each case: the amount of space by which the end of each line of typing and the predetermined right-hand margin differ on the first typing is, on the second, distributed (by adding or subtracting) over the spaces between words.

10 There are three methods of justifying on machine: those used on thelllll
7 Justowriter, on the VariTyper and on all other machines (manual andlll
-2 electric, fixed-width and variable-width). Basically, all involve a second
5 typing and the principle is the same in each case: the amount of spacell
10 by which the end of each line of typing and the predetermined right-lllll
11+3 hand margin differ on the first typing is, on the second, distributedlllllll
✓ (by adding or subtracting) over the spaces between words.

There are three methods of justifying on machine: those used on the Justowriter, on the VariTyper and on all other machines (manual and electric, fixed-width and variable-width). Basically, all involve a second typing and the principle is the same in each case: the amount of space by which the end of each line of typing and the predetermined right-hand margin differ on the first typing is, on the second, distributed (by adding or subtracting) over the spaces between words.

Examples of margin justification and setting by VariTyper (top), Justowriter (middle) IBM Executive (bottom). On the left, the first setting; on the right, the justified result. The VariTyper and Justowriter examples are reproduced same-size, the Executive reduced to 83% in the justified version. The first typing on the Executive shows the typist's workings; since it is only used for calculating, errors can be overtyped and left uncorrected.

The newest machines, phototypesetters and computer typesetters (see page 220), also produce justified copy in a second operation. The whole process is automatic and the typist has only to type the first version and use the function keys to give the machine the appropriate instructions.

VARIABLE TYPE STYLES AND SIZES The IBM Selectric Composer typewriter employs the IBM golf ball (sometimes referred to as the type font or printing head) principle which enables the typist to vary the type styles in a piece of work simply by changing one typehead for another. There are 130 type styles available including OCR (Optical Character Recognition) typeheads needed for documents which are subsequently to be processed by computer.

The VariTyper has no typebars. The characters are moulded on a curved metal segment and the segment swings to the printing point for the appropriate letter when a key is struck. Two segments can be fitted on the machine at the same time so matching italics or bold-face can be typed at will as the work proceeds.

The segments can also be changed at any stage during the course of a piece of work so that several different styles and sizes of type can be produced on the same document.

The IBM Selectric Composer. The standard keyboard layout makes typesetting an extension of the skill of typewriting; typists who are interested in display and graphic art can be trained as typesetters.

The VariTyper has no typebars. The characters are moulded on a curved metal segment which swings to the printing point for the appropriate letter when a key is struck. Two segments are in use at the same time. The segments can be changed at any stage during the course of a piece of work.

Line-spacing can also be varied from $\frac{1}{2}$ point to 18 points; the typist simply selects the desired spacing and the line advance lever automatically inserts the desired spacing.

Phototypesetting Computerised phototypesetting machines, such as the PHOTON Compositor, consist of a keyboard typesetter and a computer. They differ from other cold-type composing machines in that they produce automatically justified copy in a variety of type-styles and sizes on photo-sensitive paper or film (up to 10 in wide) which is then processed to make a printing plate.

The VariTyper 1010 desk-top typesetter.

The Photon Compositor, a keyboard entry phototypesetter.

As you can see from the illustration the typesetter comprises a standard typewriter keyboard and a number of peripheral function keys. The function keys are used to give the machine instructions regarding display (such as type-styles, type-sizes, line-lengths) and to make corrections.

Before the operator starts to type or "key-in", the copy should be "marked-up", that is, the required line-lengths, typesizes and display styles must be noted. At the present time, marking-up is usually done by a skilled compositor but it is anticipated that in future display typists will be trained to mark-up their own work.

The typist first depresses the appropriate function keys and then starts to type the copy. Whilst she is typing, the words and characters appear in red against a black background in an illuminated visual display panel on the front of the machine. The display panel can show 32 characters at a time. This enables the typist to check her work. Individual letters, words or whole lines can be corrected by pressing the KILL CHARACTER, KILL WORD or KILL LINE function keys which back-space and cause the characters or words to disappear from the display panel. The corrections can then be typed. The machine can be instructed to justify each line automatically or the justification and hyphenation can be controlled by the typist. As each line is completed, it is automatically stored in the computer and the display panel is cleared ready for the next line.

When the work is finished, the photo-sensitive paper or film is removed from the machine in a cassette and processed. It may then be used as it is or to form a paste-up from which a printing plate can be produced.

The PHOTON typeface images are drawn on to glass matrix discs. Each disc can accommodate eight typefaces (896 characters) and machines are available with four up to sixteen-point sizes.

Keyboard phototypesetters are already being used to print books and newspapers and it is possible that they may eventually take over much of the work that is at present produced by conventional hot-type printing methods. This development offers attractive career prospects to the display typist who is interested in printing and graphic art.

COLLATING

When a report running into many pages has been duplicated, the sheets have to be assembled into sets before they can be stapled or bound. The process of collecting the sets is known as **collating.**

Sometimes the piles of pages are placed in order around a table and all the office staff are summoned to help collate by walking round the table taking one sheet from each pile until all the sets have been assembled. This wastes everyone's time and is obviously not the best way to do the job.

1

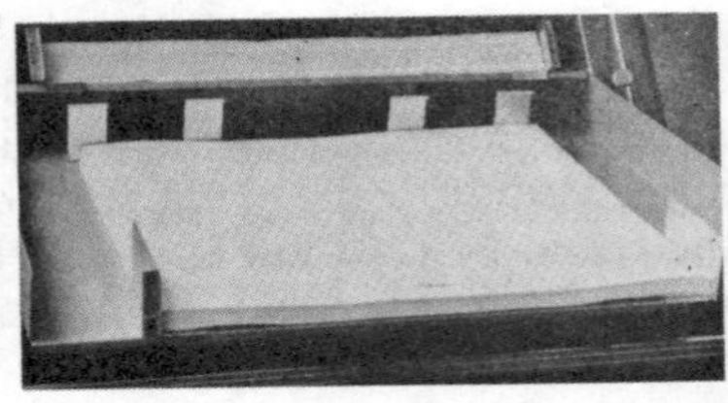

4

2

3

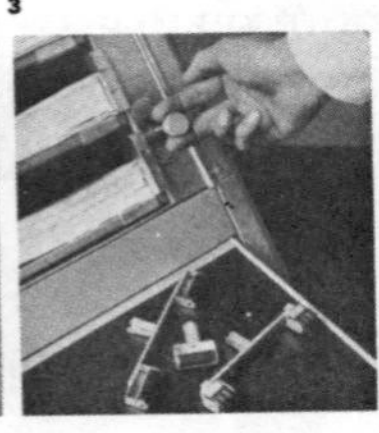

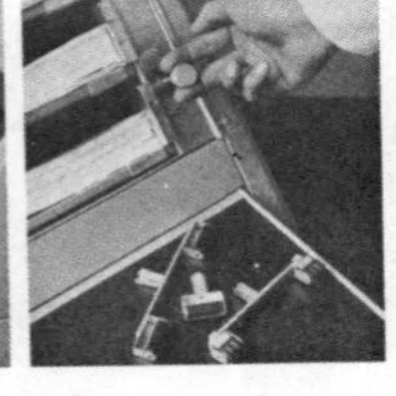

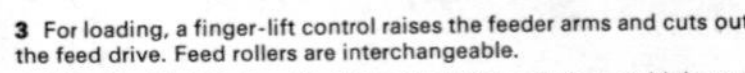

1 Each station is equipped with a sliding tray which is withdrawn and locked in a horizontal position for setting and loading.

2 Easily adjusted back stops, with a graduated scale, allow all stations to be set and loaded in less than five minutes.

3 For loading, a finger-lift control raises the feeder arms and cuts out the feed drive. Feed rollers are interchangeable.

4 Like the 10 RD, the 16 RD is ideal for collating multiple sets including one-time carbons, self-copy paper, bank and board.

The 16RD Thomas collator is semi-automatic and can handle 8–16 sheets at a variable speed up to 13,000 sheets an hour.

1

3

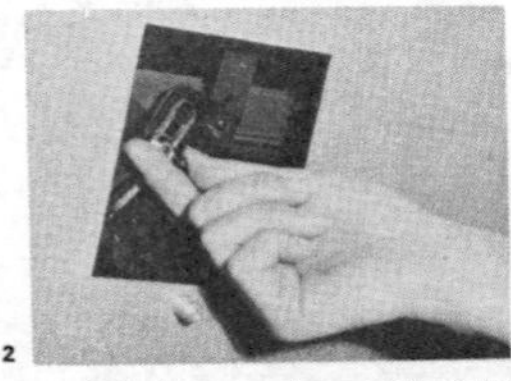

2

1 Adjustable back stop and side lays on each removable station facilitate setting up for any size of paper.

2 The length of stroke of the feeder arms is adjusted at the side of the machine.

3 The operator controls the Collarette Major with a foot pedal switch that activates the feeders for one cycle at each depression.

The Collarette Major Model T8 is an 8-station semi-automatic table top collator.

The first step in any collating operation is to square-up the separate piles so that the edges of all the sheets are in line. Even collating a short report of say six pages or less can be done more efficiently if the stacks of each page are set out in the order shown, and the operator uses both hands and wears rubber thimbles on the middle fingers.

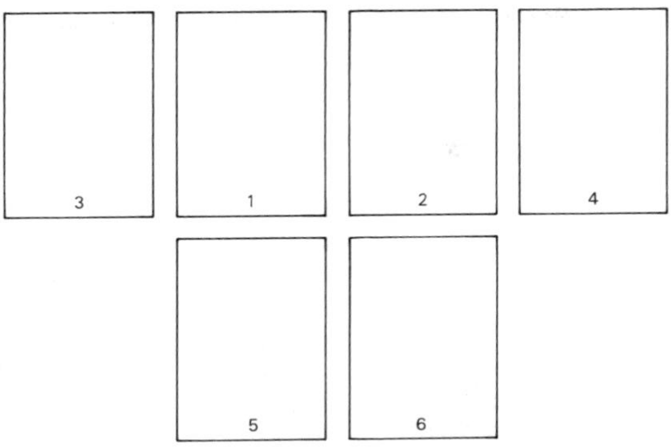

Collating frames or machines should be provided in any office in which collating long reports is a frequent task. A simple collator consists of a number of trays into which the stacks of each numbered sheet are placed. A foot or hand lever lifts the top sheet of each pile and allows the operator to use both hands freely for gathering up the papers in their right order.

More sophisticated collators will run for several hours automatically, delivering five or six sheets of paper in their correct order at a speed of several sets per minute.

KNOCKING UP, TRIMMING, FOLDING AND FASTENING

The final steps in the production of multi-page reports and leaflets are knocking-up, trimming, folding and fastening. There is little point in producing work efficiently up to the stage when the sheets have been collated, if bottle-necks are allowed to occur in the final stage, or if the remaining steps are done in an amateurish way. A wide range of auxiliary equipment is available which gives a professional look to the completed publication.

The first step is to make sure that all the sheets in a set are neatly aligned so that the corners are exactly square. This is known as *knocking-up*; it can be done by hand but it is quicker to use a mechanical *jogger* if hundreds of sets are being handled. A heavy-duty jogger is illustrated on page 187 in the section on Ink Duplication as joggers can also be used to loosen the pages in a packet of paper before duplicating or offset-printing.

Most offices have a hand guillotine for *trimming* sheets. Sometimes the sheets are trimmed before they are folded and fastened; professional printers guillotine after stitching. Mechanical guillotines with accurate adjustment to a fraction of an inch or millimetre are available and these should be used if more than say twenty sheets have to be trimmed in one cut, as the sheets tend to move slightly during the cut in the normal office hand guillotine.

There are machines which will stitch and fold, and staple and fold, and more complicated machines which will collate, jog, fold and stitch automatically.

The most usual method of *fastening* sets in the office is to *staple* them. Work can be stapled across the corner, or along the left-hand edge. Leaflets with a centre fold should be stapled along the fold, using a long-arm stapler.

Power-operated and hand-operated guillotines.

Booklets can now be bound simply and quickly with plastic binding. The DUO machine punches 21 holes in the first operation and fixes and secures the binding in a second operation. Up to 20 sheets of paper can be punched at the same time.

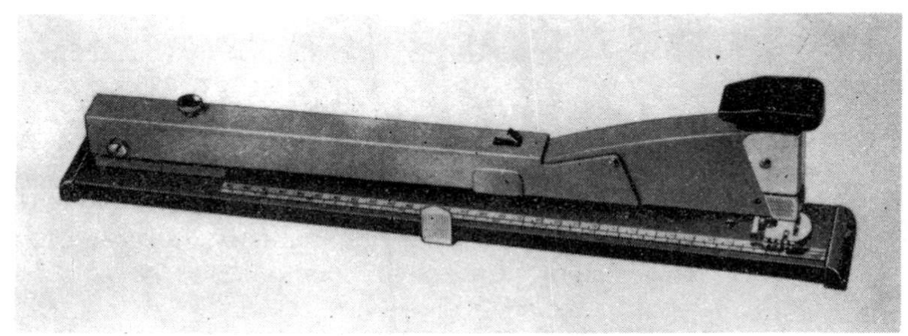

A long-arm stapler and an electrically-operated stapler.

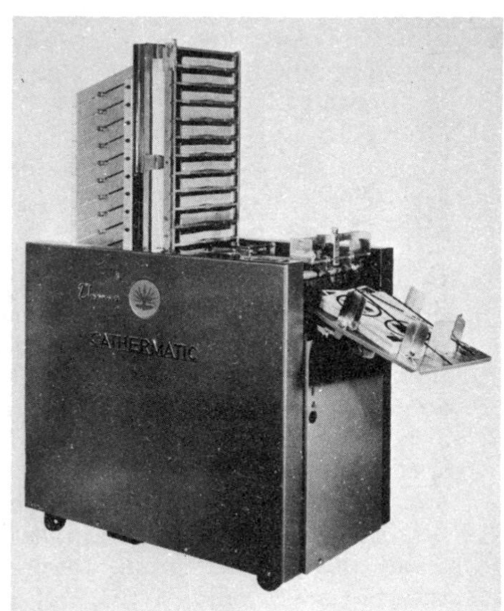

The Thomas Super Gathermatic Collator Model S12–1 fitted with a Stapler-Folder handles paper from 3×5 in up to 12.25×17.5 in at a variable speed up to 6000 sheets an hour.

APPLICATIONS AND DEVELOPMENTS

1 The factors to be considered when deciding which process is the most suitable and economic for getting a specific number of copies of a document are:

- a Is the original in a fit state to be reproduced? If it is, then it should be copied in one of the office copiers.
- b If there is no original document in a suitable state for reproduction, then an original or master must be created: the type of master depends upon the duplicating process which is selected for the job.
- c For short run work, where between 30 and 150 copies are required and cost is a primary consideration, spirit duplication is a very good method. It has increased in popularity now that spirit masters can be made so easily by thermal copiers.
- d How permanent need the copies be? Spirit and diazo copies fade in some conditions; stencil and offset-litho copies are permanent.
- e Will the master be needed again? What storage conditions are available?

2 Cost per copy is influenced by the following factors:

- a The purchase price or rental cost of the machine.
- b Depreciation of the value of the machine if purchased outright.
- c The costs of maintenance of the machine.
- d The number of copies made over a given period, e.g. per week, month or year.
- e The cost of the copy paper.
- f The cost of any other supplies needed, e.g. ink, chemicals.
- g The time taken to make a copy.
- h The cost of the operator's time.

3 Copier/duplicators will produce as many copies as are required from an original document. They are particularly suitable in the 10–80 copy range in which the cost of making a stencil or offset-litho master is disproportionate to the overall cost of making the copies.

4 Stencil duplicators are easier to operate than offset-litho machines and are a frequent choice where duplicating is to be done by non-specialist office staff. The introduction of the electronic stencil cutter and the thermal stencil which enables a stencil to be prepared from any original has increased the popularity of ink duplication.

5 Small offset is a simplification of a printing process and the most versatile of all office duplicating processes. Cheap paper plates can be made on an electrostatic office copier and the availability of professional plate-making services providing plates from which long runs of high quality copies can be produced has contributed to the popularity of

small offset as an office duplicating process. Where an Internal Print department is equipped with the more sophisticated small offset machines, it is also possible to print in full colour.

GLOSSARY OF TERMS USED IN REPROGRAPHY*

ARTWORK or ORIGINAL or COPY The original matter from which a reproduction is eventually made.

BLANKET A resilient rubberised blanket on to which the image is transferred from the inked lithographic plate in offset-litho printing.

BLEEDING The term used when the image runs off the edge of the paper, so that there is no white margin at the paper edge.

BLOCKING OUT The use of opaque, or other means, to delete areas on a master so that they do not print.

CARBON BACKING A carbon sheet (yellow or black) placed at the back of translucent masters to provide an opaque image for contact copying.

COLLATE Assembling together in correct sequence.

CONTACT PRINTING Printing by direct contact of a master, or of an intermediate copy, with the copy support.

COPY Frequently refers to a document to be reproduced (MASTER or ARTWORK or ORIGINAL) but more generally to the printed result from an original.

DIAZO BOND A paper visually opaque but translucent to ultra violet rays.

DIAZO (DYELINE) A process in which the print results from the effect of radiation on a diazonium sensitised material.

DIRECT-IMAGED MASTER A duplicating or printing master upon which the image has been directly typed, written or drawn.

DISPLAY-TYPE Comparatively large type used for headings, title pages, headlines and posters.

EM The square of the body of any size of type. Printer's unit of measurement.

FAXABLE An original having a 'black-on-white' image (i.e. black typing, pencil or black carbon copy) which can be copied by an infra-red process, either infra-red reflex (Thermofax) or infra-red transfer (Bandaflex and Fordifax).

FONT or FOUNT An assortment of type characters containing all letters (upper case, lower case, or both) and sometimes figures, punctuation marks and signs.

FORMAT The size, style, shape and general appearance of any printed material.

GRAVURE A commercial method of printing in which the image is etched in the printing plate.

GRAIN Paper fibres lie chiefly one way giving grain direction.

HALF-TONE A photograph which has been reproduced through a screen designed to break the transmitted image into small dots, which by variations in size, give the illusion of tonal values.

* Compiled from *Typewriting and Office Duplicating Processes*, A. W. Gardiner, Focal Press Ltd, and *Glossary of Terms used in Offset Lithographic Printing*, British Standard 4277 : 1968, British Standards Institution.

HECTOGRAPH *See* SPIRIT DUPLICATING.

HECTOGRAPH CARBON SHEET A specially prepared sheet of carbon used to back up a master sheet in the spirit process of hectograph duplicating.

IMAGE A likeness of the subject matter.

INFRA-RED Light having a longer wavelength than visible light.

INTERMEDIATE MASTER Prepared from the original or master, and made suitable for the process to be used.

JOGGING Mechanical movement on the delivery end of the printing machine or in a JOGGER to obtain accurate stacking of printed sheets.

JUSTIFICATION (JUSTIFIED MARGIN) Even right-hand margin.

LETTERPRESS Printing from a raised surface.

LITHOGRAPHIC RIBBON A special ribbon used for direct typing on lithographic plates.

LITHOGRAPHY Printing from a plane surface from a greasy image on a moistened background.

MASTER The prepared material from which copies are to be made.

MAT A paper specially treated to receive a typed, or drawn image for reproduction by offset. Also known as a paper plate.

OFFSET-LITHOGRAPHY A printing process in which the inked image is transferred from a printing plate to a suitably covered cylinder and then offset on to the material forming the print.

OPAQUE Having such resistance to the passage of light as to be unsuitable for processes using transmitted light.

PAPER PLATE A form of offset-litho duplicating master.

PASTE-UP Master copy made by sticking selected pieces of subject matter into a desired format; cutting, adding or deleting as necessary.

PHOTOCOPYING Producing copies by means of luminous radiation, in general with about the same dimensions as the original.

PHOTOLETTERING Preparing text by contact or optical printing on sensitised material.

PROPORTIONAL SPACING Allocation of space in the horizontal field appropriate to the width of the character.

REGISTER Exact alignment of type, especially when overlaying one image upon another.

REPROTYPING Preparing a master typed copy suitable for preparing a duplicating or printing master by a reprographic method; or typing an image which is then processed (usually by photographic methods, either by contact or via a camera) to produce the printing surface. The word REPROTYPING is coined from the phrase 'typing for reproduction'.

REVERSE READING Having the image left to right as in a mirror, also called *mirror reading*.

RIBBON, CARBON A continuous strip of carbon used in all forms of typewriter.

RUN The number of copies required from each master.

RUN-OFF The process of making copies on a duplicator or offset-litho machine.

SET-OFF The unwanted transfer of ink from a print to a facing surface.

SPIRIT DUPLICATING (HECTOGRAPH PROCESS) A type of duplicating which transfers the impression directly from the master to the copy by means of a fluid.

STENCIL DUPLICATING The process employing a stencil as the reproductive medium which permits ink to pass only through the perforations forming the image.

TRANSLUCENT Permitting the passage of light, the emergent light being diffused.

TRANSPARENT Permitting the passage of light without diffusion.

TYPOGRAPHY The art and technique of arranging printing. Appearance, arrangement and style of reading material.

UNIT-SPACING Allocation of equal space in the horizontal field to each character irrespective of character width.

WEB OFFSET Printing on a reel-fed machine by the offset process.

FURTHER READING

Modern Office Copying, S. B. Page, Andre Deutsch.

Typewriting and Office Duplicating Processes, A. W. Gardiner, Focal Press Ltd.

Methods of Test for Determining the Registration Obtained on Duplicating Machines, BS4588 : 1970, British Standards Institution.

Glossary of Terms used in Offset Lithographic Printing, BS4277 : 1968, British Standards Institution.

Typewriter Composition, Alistair McIntosh, The Gresham Press, Unwin Brothers Ltd.

Uneoprint Handbook, Alistair McIntosh, The Gresham Press, Unwin Brothers Ltd.

The Origin of Stencil Duplicating, W. B. Proudfoot, Hutchinson.

EXERCISES

1 Each of the following methods of reprography is advantageous in certain circumstances:

   a photocopying
   b spirit duplication
   c stencil duplication

   For each, state two circumstances, in which the one is to be preferred to the others.

2 List the steps you would take to produce copies by an ink duplicator.

3 State, with reasons, the methods you would use to obtain the following:

   a Fifteen copies of a three-page report which is required for internal use. It is in draft form and needs re-typing.

b 350 copies of a four-page report which is to be sent to all suppliers. It is already in its final form.

c Four copies of a page of a book which is required for internal use. The page must not be torn out of the book.

d A customer's letter which has to be dealt with by four departments.

4 Explain the difference between the infra-red transfer and the diffusion transfer methods of reprography. Give the advantages and disadvantages of each method and mention any other uses to which the machines can be put.

5 The new junior in your office can type, but she has never been taught how to cut a stencil. You are asked to teach her. Make a list of the points you would mention.

6 The ink duplicator in your office is used by several junior secretaries. When you want to use it yourself you frequently find it has not been used correctly or closed down properly with all the controls in the 'OFF' position. Type a list of INSTRUCTIONS FOR USE OF THE INK DUPLICATOR' which could be affixed to the wall at the side of the machine.

7 Your company is holding its annual Sales Conference at a hotel on the south coast. The conference will last a week and it will be attended by all 75 of the company's salesmen. A small room on the ground floor of the hotel has been allocated to you to use as the Conference Office. Your executive, the Sales Manager, has asked you to give him a list of the machines and stationery you would like to have available in the Conference office. List the items you would require and add a short note of justification for each item. An overhead projector will be available in the Conference Room for the use of lecturers.

8 Explain the meaning of the following words and phrases; briefly describe their use and significance in Reprography:

translucent	bleeding
format	key-in
set-off	run-off
function keys	justification
faxable	blanket
proportional spacing	collating

9 Taking into account as many factors as possible of those listed on page 226, calculate the cost per copy for producing copies on the various reprographic machines you have available under the following headings:

Less than 5 copies	From 100–500 copies
From 5–20 copies	From 1000–5000 copies
From 20–50 copies	From 5000–10,000 copies
From 50–100 copies	Over 10,000 copies

6

Appointments and Desk Diaries

Avoid double bookings by co-ordinating appointments and diaries. Most businessmen and women keep a pocket diary as well as a desk diary; set aside a few moments every day to cross-check that all appointments made by you or your boss in either diary are entered in both.

"How many executives have been hampered by secretaries who, although admirable shorthand-typists, lacked *nous* in an emergency, or failed in discretion, responsibility, or a sense of what needed to be done?"

"Much more than a shorthand-typist", article in
The Times Educational Supplement, 3 November 1967

Reception begins at the gatehouse of a manufacturing concern, or at the main reception desk in a commercial concern or a head office. In small organisations there may be no receptionist, and visitors are received in a general office. Alternatively, it may be a secretary who carries out basic reception duties. In any case, a private secretary is responsible for receiving the callers who wish to see her boss.

RECEPTION DESK

On arrival at the reception desk a visitor should give his name, the name of the organisation he represents and the name of the official he has come to see. If the visitor does not give this information, the receptionist must enquire so that she can check (from her list provided daily by each executive's secretary) whether he has an appointment. If the visitor is expected the receptionist should ask him to take a seat and immediately telephone the office concerned to announce his arrival. If the extension is engaged or there is no reply, she should inform the visitor and try the extension again within a few minutes; in the meantime she should reassure the visitor that she is trying to get an answer from the office he has come to visit so that he does not feel he has been forgotten.

When the executive's secretary is told of the visitor's arrival, she may do one of three things:

1 If she knows her boss is ready to see the visitor she may ask the receptionist either to send the visitor to her office, or she may go and meet him in reception, or she may ask the receptionist to tell the visitor that she will be waiting for him when he steps out of the lift at the appropriate floor.
2 She may check with her boss if he is ready to see the visitor and if so, she will take one of the courses of action outlined in the previous paragraph.
3 If her boss is not quite ready, she may tell the receptionist to apologise to the visitor and ask him to wait for a few minutes.

When visitors do not have an appointment, the receptionist might say, "Would you take a seat, please," while she telephoned the appropriate office, but the exact procedure to be followed is normally a matter of policy and in some organisations an unscheduled caller is always asked, firmly but politely, to write in for an appointment.

Sometimes the secretary can deal with the unexpected caller herself or, when she has found out the nature of his business, she will know what action to take. She may ask him to wait (while she discreetly finds out whether her boss is interested in seeing him), or she may ask whether there is anything *she* can do for the visitor, and if not perhaps make an appointment for him, or offer to telephone to make an appointment later. Neither receptionist nor secretary should allow a visitor to be given the impression that the official he is asking to see is, in fact, on the premises but is refusing to see him. Generally speaking, unexpected visitors should be carefully screened before being given any information about the whereabouts of an official or any other information about the organisation and its affairs.

Reception register Some organisations have a reception register in which are entered details of all visitors. Alternatively a card index may be kept. This is particularly useful to a secretary who may need the details for correspondence following a visitor's meeting with her boss. Many visitors

RECEPTION REGISTER

Date	Time	Name of Visitor	Description	Company	Address	To see	Business
16.11.73	16.30	Mr G P Jones	Sales Mgr	BHK oxidising	Public St	Chief Buyer	Routine Call
17.11.73	08.45	Mrs T Preston	Training Officer	Sec Services LTD	Main St Portsmouth	Gen. Manager	Appt.
17.11.73	09.00	Mr A L Smith	Buyer	Potteston	High St Berwick	Sales Manager	Appt.

present a visiting card which contains the information needed, but for ease of reference it is best to enter the details on a card to be inserted in the card index. It is advisable to cross reference visitors' names with the names of their organisations (see *chapter 7*, Storage and Retrieval of Information). Your boss may well say "We must write to that chap from the soap company." Since there are several "chaps" who call on your boss from that company it will be easier to get the card for the company and check which particular "chap" your boss is referring to.

Examples of a reception register, index cards and a visitor's card are shown on pages 233 and 234. Remember that your own boss will be a visitor to other organisations and should always have a small supply of visiting cards on him.

BLOGGS SOAP COMPANY LTD

46 Highway Road
Southampton SO2 IPQ
HAMPSHIRE

Tel 67891

General Manager Mr J T Phillips
Sales Manager   Mr T E Phelps

PHELPS T E (Mr)

see BLOGGS SOAP COMPANY LTD

Mr C.N.E.McDowall.

International Labour Office
Clerical Training Expert

National Vocational Training Institute
P.O. BOX M. 21 TEL. 64209
ACCRA

A visiting card.

Appointments list As mentioned above, a list of the day's appointments should be available to the receptionist first thing every morning. The same applies to the gatehouse in firms where this is a scrutiny point. In places where security is involved, e.g. a prime minister's office, an atomic power station, research laboratories, every visitor is checked before he enters the compound. A lot of time can be saved if the sergeant on duty knows who is expected. In top security organisations, a visitor is never left unaccompanied at any time during his visit and he will not be allowed to leave the building unless he can produce an "exit chit" signed by the official he has been visiting.

Typing the list of next day's appointments should be a secretary's last job of the day. At the same time she should get all files and papers which may be necessary for the interviews so that she can place them before her boss in time for him to refresh his memory on important points if necessary.

A typical appointments list is shown below.

APPOINTMENTS

Friday 30 November 1973

0930	Mr J T Peterson (Sales Manager, Petworth Machine Tools Ltd)
1100	Sales Staff Meeting (Conference Room)
1245	Lunch - Ambassador Hotel Mr S A Taylor (Managing Director, Training Organisation Inc, Ohio)
1500	Chairman (Agenda for Board Meeting)
1600	Training Manager (Report on Apprentices)

Scheduling of appointments When making appointments for your boss you must check certain points.

1 Whether he has made an appointment which you do not know about. If he is not engaged you can check his diary immediately, but if he is engaged you should make the appointment subject to confirmation as soon as possible.

2 How long the interview is likely to take. Trying to cram the maximum number of interviews into a day by allowing only minimum time for each is likely to result in the schedule getting completely out of hand.

3 Whether the boss has any particular work to do that day, e.g. reports to prepare, meetings. Never assume that a meeting will be over in two hours. It is usually safer to allow the whole of the morning or afternoon from the time it starts as meetings have a habit of lasting longer than anticipated.

4 If your boss already has appointments away from his own office immediately before or after the time of the appointment you are making, be sure to allow sufficient travelling time.

When making appointments be sure to get all relevant information: the name and organisation of the person concerned, telephone number in case contact is necessary before the meeting, the business to be discussed. If the appointment is to take place somewhere unfamiliar to your boss get all

PRIME MINISTER

10, Downing Street,
Whitehall.

THURSDAY 25 MAY 1972

10.30 a.m.	DOP Committee	No. 10
11.00 a.m.	Cabinet	No. 10
Afterwards	Trade and Industry Secretary Lord Privy Seal	No. 10
12.00 noon	Lord President	No. 10
12.30 p.m.	Member of the staff to say goodbye	No. 10
2.30 p.m.	Briefing	No. 10
3.15 p.m.	Questions	House of Commons
4.00 p.m.	Charles Wintour and Robert Carvel - Evening Standard.	No. 10
5.00 p.m.	Ministerial Meeting - Northern Ireland	No. 10
7.45 p.m.	Constituency Officials	No. 10
8.00 for 8.30 p.m.	Private dinner	No. 10 -

The Prime Minister's day.

details of the address—number and/or name of building, street, floor and room number. If he is driving, suggest a route, or inform the chauffeur in advance so that he is prepared.

When notice of a meeting is received check immediately to see if there are any appointments already arranged for that time. If so, consult your boss and contact the people, or their secretaries, for whom the appointments have been made; explain why you wish to alter the arrangement and apologise on behalf of your boss.

When scheduling appointments it is important to remember that your boss is a human being. Interviews are always tiring, some exhausting. The end of a day is not a good time for a difficult interview so try to ensure that those interviews requiring much mental concentration are early in the day. He must be left free time for his own paper work. If he likes to keep to a routine for such things as dictating, signing letters, etc. do not make appointments for those times except in an emergency and always check with him first.

As soon as you have made an appointment enter it in both your own diary and in your boss's. Keep checking his diary to see what appointments he has made himself. Most bosses make a point of telling their secretaries when they make appointments, but it is wise to cross-check each day.

Desk diaries There are various types of desk diary. For ease of reference it is best if a secretary has the same type as her boss. She may also find it useful to have two diaries; one for appointments and one for noting work that has to be done or prepared, etc.

APRIL 1971

TUESDAY **27**

9.00 Mr T Johnson (Discuss increase in scrap from 1.3.71)

12.30 Lunch (Palace Hotel) Rotary

3.00 Chief Accountant – Meeting re Budget

4.30 Blackwood Engineering – Mr C Baines (Sub-contract)

WEDNESDAY **28**

9.30 Seminar on Training
Conference Room

In diaries where times are not indicated space should be left for the insertion of appointments in correct time sequence. Brief details of the appointment should be indicated. It is advisable to note appointments in pencil, so that alterations can be made by erasing and not by crossing out which makes the diary look like a rough notebook.

A typical diary page is shown on page 236.

HANDLING INVITATIONS

Official invitations are normally written and your chief will indicate whether to accept or not. An official reply is then sent.

There may be last-minute or informal invitations made verbally through you in the absence of your boss. You should not make a definite acceptance on your boss's behalf, but if you think that he will accept you may make a provisional acceptance to be confirmed as soon as possible. Unless your boss already has an important engagement you should not make a definite refusal, even though he has another appointment. The invitation may be of such importance that your boss would wish to change an existing appointment. In such a case it is advisable to say simply that you will inform him of the invitation as soon as possible and let the host know his answer. Be sure to get all details as to function, time, place, formal/informal. The latter is particularly important if the invitation is social. In such a case your boss's wife may be included in the invitation. If your boss cannot be contacted quickly it may be possible to check with his wife and she may be able to give an answer for her husband.

Examples of an official invitation and reply are given below.

Major D. T. Agyemang

requests the pleasure of the company of

Mr. and Mrs. P. T. Beaumont

at lunch *at* 12.30 p.m.

on Sunday, 21st November, 1971.

R.S.V.P.

B6 Lewis Grove
Airport Residential Area

Telephone 66725 (Office)
Regrets Only

Mr and Mrs Beaumont

wish to thank

Major D T Agyemang

for his kind invitation to lunch

on 21st November 1971

but regret that they are unable to accept

owing to a previous engagement.

Princetown
10 November 1971

Reply to an official invitation centred on an A6 card.

RECEIVING VISITORS

Every visitor goes to an office for one or two reasons—either to give information or help, or to seek information or help. In either case, he is an important person, and must be treated as such. The customer placing an order for £100 today may be a back-street garage owner. In a few years' time he may be chairman of a several million pound manufacturing concern placing orders worth tens of thousands of pounds. His impressions and the service he gets as a small customer will influence his decisions as to where to purchase when his business grows. Every visitor must be treated identically—with courtesy, tact, and friendliness but not with familiarity.

Greet every visitor by name, so that he feels an individual rather than an unidentified person. A ready smile will make him feel he is welcome in your organisation. Never give the appearance of being busy to the point where visitors are a nuisance.

If the visitor has come from reception your boss will probably be ready for him by the time he arrives so that he can be shown in straight away. If he has come directly to your office you must inform your boss before showing the visitor in. Offer him a seat while you inform your boss that he is there. If he has no appointment, ask him to take a seat while you make discreet inquiries. If your boss is not willing to see him say, "I'm very sorry, Mr X is not available at present." This covers every situation. Then there are three possible courses of action which you may take to make the visitor feel that he is being looked after. It may be that you can help him yourself, or that your boss's deputy may be able to do so. You could offer to make an appointment for him. Or you might ask if your boss should telephone him.

Meeting visitors You may have to arrange transport to meet visitors at a railway station or airport; in some cases your boss might ask you to go yourself to meet someone. Always allocate plenty of time for the journey to the meeting point to allow for traffic congestion, punctures, difficulty in getting a taxi, etc. It is worthwhile checking (by telephone) the expected arrival time of aircraft with the appropriate airline information desk at the airport because flights are often delayed, and even early on occasions.

HANDLING VISITORS

Every visitor is an individual and therefore different from his fellows. Some are talkative, others taciturn; some are cheerful in appearance, while others seem to be permanently labouring under immense burdens. It is your job to be 'in sympathy' with each individual. The talkative man will feel snubbed if you answer his questions with nothing more than monosyllables; but the reserved man will be irritated by a flow of chatter. Beware of the visitor who tries to 'pump' you about your boss's business. The best ploy in this situation is to be ignorant. You simply don't know, or haven't heard. 'Stonewalling' will soon make the visitor realise he is wasting his time.

Refusing interviews There are visitors who demand to see the boss, i.e. the most senior person in a department or organisation, either because they like to claim intimacy with him or because they feel they will get better service from him than they would from someone lower down the scale. This type of visitor needs especially tactful handling. He must not be made to feel that he is not sufficiently important to see the boss, or that his business is too trivial for the boss to deal with personally. You might be able to point out that another official deals with that particular matter and the visitor would get much better attention and save a lot of time by going to him direct; or you might telephone the official and see if he can come to your office to speak to the visitor, if you feel that course of action would be more appropriate.

There are some visitors who keep calling in for no reason other than the desire to waste some of their time comfortably, but you will probably not want to encourage them to waste your time or that of your boss. The best way to deal with such callers is usually to assure them that you will tell your boss that they have called and pass on any messages or suggestions that they may call again in a few days' time.

In your capacity as a receptionist you have a dual role—(i) to receive all visitors courteously and deal with them efficiently; (ii) to screen visitors so that only those whom your boss wishes to see are admitted to his office.

Taking care of visitors If a visitor has to be kept waiting he should be provided with a newspaper or magazine. If the delay is likely to be more than a few minutes it is a pleasant gesture to offer a cup of tea or coffee if this is in accordance with company policy.

Some organisations have a waiting room for visitors, while in others the visitor has to wait in the secretary's office. In either case the room must be attractive. No dirty crockery or personal possessions should be lying around; the ashtrays should be emptied regularly; your desk should not be cluttered with files and papers. A vase of flowers or a pot plant add a note of colour and cheerfulness.

If you know that a visitor is likely to be long with your boss ask him discreetly if he would like you to offer a cup of tea or coffee. When you serve it make sure you have everything you need on the tray and serve the visitor first.

Try to notice if each visitor is carrying anything with him—a briefcase, an umbrella—and make sure he takes all his belongings away with him.

GROUP DISCUSSION

Discuss the following situations in groups and then pool ideas to find the best way to deal with each situation.

1 A gentleman has called twice to see your boss, who has been out each time. The visitor has refused to see anyone else. He calls a third time and seems annoyed that your boss is out again.
2 A man calls several times to see your boss, who has told you that he will not see this man. How would you deal with the visitor?
3 Your boss tells you that Mr Jones will be calling later in the day to collect some papers. He asks you to explain to Mr Jones that the papers are required for a few more days. When Mr Jones calls your boss is out and you pass on the message. He is very annoyed because he says they were promised and he needs them urgently. What would you do?

EXERCISES

1 Your boss is Chief Buyer in a large manufacturing organisation. Many salesmen call to see him without appointment trying to sell their firm's products. How would you deal with these visitors?
2 When someone who has never come to your office before calls and asks to see your boss, how would you find out his business?
3 A visitor calls at your office without an appointment. Your boss tells

you he is too busy to see anyone at present. Write the actual words you would say to the visitor.

4 You make an appointment for your boss in his absence. When he returns to the office you find, on checking his diary, that he has made arrangements to be away for three days, the first of which is the day for which you made the appointment. State step by step what you would do.

5 The receptionist at your firm telephones you to inform you that a visitor well-known to your boss has called. He has no appointment but wishes to see your boss on an urgent and highly confidential matter which has just arisen. Your boss is at an important meeting in the Chairman's office. What action would you take?

6 Your boss has two appointments—a visitor at 11.00 a.m. and a visitor at 11.30 a.m. Both gentlemen arrive simultaneously just before 11.30 a.m. The visitor due at 11.00 a.m. explains that he has had a slight accident on the way which delayed him. How would you handle this situation?

7 Your boss goes to a meeting half an hour's journey away. He tells you he expects to be back by 11 o'clock as he has an appointment at 11.15 a.m. The visitor arrives at 11.10 a.m. Your boss has not returned. At 11.15 a.m. he has still not returned. What would you do (a) when the visitor arrives at 11.10 a.m. and (b) at 11.15 a.m.?

8 What use can a secretary make of visitors' index cards?

9 Your boss asks you to make the following appointments for next Tuesday:

Mr S. Brown, Magnesium Products Ltd.—morning if possible in a town ten miles away.

Managing Director, Jackson Properties Ltd.—to have a short interview and then take him to lunch (Jackson Properties is about ten minutes' drive from your office and there is a good hotel in the area).

Mr A. T. Bamford, City Treasurer—morning or afternoon.

Mr C. Johnson, City Engineer—morning or afternoon.

(The City Treasurer and City Engineer are in different buildings about five minutes' walk from each other but about twenty minutes' drive from your office. The City Treasurer must be seen first.)

Type the Appointments List for the day concerned giving suitable times for the appointments.

10 An invitation to speak at an official function arrives for your boss while he is away on holiday. The date is the day after he returns to duty. What action would you take?

7

Storage and Retrieval of Information

". . . and a spike is a very good filing system in its way". The spike shown above is in the reception area of a highly-automated modern company in the middle of London's West End. The documents filed on the spike are the dockets received from the Post Office listing the quantities of Business reply envelopes delivered in a particular mail delivery. The spike method automatically keeps the dockets in chronological order, reference is never made to them until the end of the month when they are all removed in one operation; when they have been used to check the Post Office statement, the dockets are destroyed. This is also an example of one of the newest management techniques known by its acronym KISS—"Keep it simple, stupid."

"Filing is as fundamental to a business as paper. Every business has to have some sort of filing system even if it is only a spike—and a spike is a very good filing system in its way. At the other end of the filing spectrum is a computer store or microfilm; in between is a vast range. But whatever the system or the equipment, the basic aim is the same: to be able to retrieve stored information usually quickly and always at minimum cost."

Office Equipment News, May 1972

Information is the raw material of the office. Every day in all sorts of offices all over the world information is received and it has to be either processed or acted upon, or recorded, or passed on, or put on one side until it can be dealt with, or kept for future use in such a way that it can be quickly located when needed, or stored to comply with some legal requirements, or disposed of (by being thrown into the waste-paper basket, for example) or destroyed, by being incinerated, sold to a scrap dealer or torn into small pieces in a shredding machine.

Until recently, most information has been received in paper form such as an invoice, letter, cable or Telex message; or a written record has been created from an item of information received verbally, for example, the transcription of messages from automatic telephone answering machines or making a written note of the gist of a telephone conversation or a private radio telephone message.

Nowadays information may also be received in the form of punched tape, punched cards, magnetic tape, or on a belt, band, disc or tape such as are produced by sound recording machines, or on an illuminated visual display panel relayed from a computer, or as computer print-out in conventional form or as microfilm.

The form in which information is received is one factor to be taken into consideration when deciding how it should be recorded and stored. As information has most usually been received in paper form, the documents have been kept in folders and files and the process of putting paper into the folders is known as "filing". Conventional files, however, are not suitable for storing information recorded on magnetic tape or film or actually within a computer, so the term "filing" has been incorporated into the wider expression "storage and retrieval of information".

All businesses need a system whereby correspondence, documents and information can be safely stored and quickly found when needed. In some of the preceding chapters it has been necessary to make a distinction between the different methods and systems adopted by firms of differing size. In big organisations each function, for example buying, selling, accounting, engaging staff, is the responsibility of a separate department, and in very large firms the functions may even be allocated to individual divisions, each division being divided into several departments. In small firms a few people may share all the functions among themselves and it is even possible to have a very small firm in which all the work is divided between the owner, who directs the firm and "gets the business" and a secretary who will also handle some of the firm's financial records and take charge of the office whilst the owner is out. It follows from this that the systems adopted, the ways in which documents are processed, the methods by which the basic clerical processes of receiving, sorting, acting upon, storing and passing on information are carried out, the responsibilities allocated to each member of staff and the definition and scope of secretarial duties, will vary according to the size of the business unit or organisation. Nowhere is this distribution between large and small more marked than in the sphere of filing and the storage and retrieval of information. We shall study the topic under two main headings, 1 Document filing and retrieval, and 2. Data storage and retrieval.

Section 1: Document Filing and Retrieval

The *object of filing* is the *safe storage in an orderly fashion* of all the documents which circulate in a business so that they can be speedily found when required. *Safe storage* necessitates the provision of suitable *filing equipment,* e.g. folders, boxes, cupboards, drawers, cabinets, which will protect the documents from dirt and damage caused by extremes of heat and humidity, or fire; and *orderly fashion* demands some methods of classification which are usually referred to as *filing methods* or *systems.*

FILING EQUIPMENT

Folders The most usual file for general business documents is a folder made of pale fawn-coloured thick card, known as a manilla folder. Several types of manilla folder are available and they are manufactured in three sizes to take A4, quarto and foolscap papers.

The *Flush Cut* folder is simply a sheet of card folded exactly in half.

The *Square Cut* folder is folded off-centre so that the rear cover extends about 1 cm beyond the front one; the extension may be used for titling.

The *Tabbed* folder has a projecting tab on the rear cover which is used for titling. Tabbed folders are usually made in sets of five and the tab is in a different position on each folder so that all five tabs are visible.

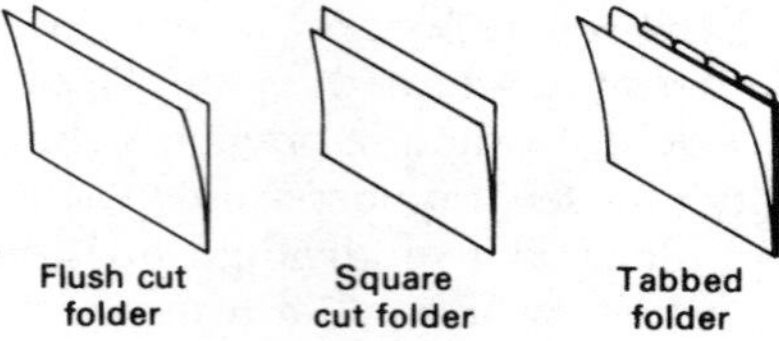

Fasteners Papers are usually secured in folders by means of fasteners. It is possible to buy files already fitted with fastening devices but *twin-prong fasteners* can be bought separately for use with standard manilla folders. The type illustrated here consists of two parts: a base, which is a strip of metal the ends of which are bent upwards to form prongs about 4 cm long; and a bar which has holes to fit over the prongs and two stays to slide over the ends of the prongs and keep the papers secure. The holes in the stay-bar are 7 cm ($2\frac{3}{4}$ in) and 8 cm ($3\frac{1}{8}$ in) apart to fit the standard punch gauges.

Papers may also be held in folders by *Treasury tags*. These are pieces of green cord with a metal tag at either end. Various lengths are available from 2.5 cm (1 in) up to 30.5 cm (12 in). They can be used in pairs or singly, as shown in the illustration.

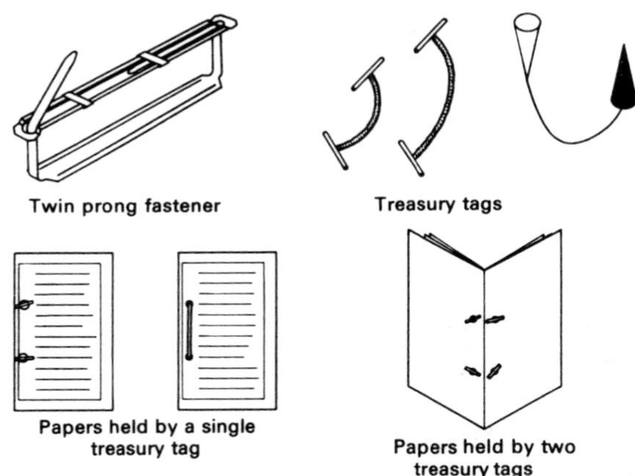

Punches An essential piece of filing equipment is a punch which makes holes in the papers before they are placed in the files. The standard **two-hole adjustable** punch makes holes either 7 cm ($2\frac{3}{4}$ in) or 8 cm ($3\frac{1}{8}$ in) apart; the gauge is selected by moving a bar which controls the small rods that move downwards through the papers when the hand-piece is depressed (see pages 85 and 265). Some punches can be adjusted to punch all three holes at once so that the papers can be filed on either 7 cm or 8 cm gauge file fastener.

There is a tendency for thin papers to tear at the punch holes. A *reinforcing punch* automatically sticks a ring of self-adhesive paper or plastic around the holes as they are punched.

Papers which have become torn around the punch holes can be repaired by sticking on *reinforcement washers*. These are made from cloth or plastic with self-adhesive backs. Reinforcement washers are available in a variety of shapes and sizes; the round 7/32 in diameter hole is the most popular.

Storage units Files may be stored either in drawers (*vertical filing*) or on shelves or in cupboards (*lateral filing*); and in both cases the folders or files may either:

a stand on their backs or spines or
b be hung from frames or rails *(individual pocket suspension filing)* or
c be placed inside a series of connected pockets which form a concertina of outer holders *(connected pocket suspension filing)*; when the files or folders are removed, the actual suspended pocket remains in the unit connected to its neighbours.

Files and folders may also be placed in piles, one on top of the other, on shelves or in drawers. One disadvantage of keeping folders in this way is that it is difficult to maintain any fixed or classified arrangement, and if one of the lower folders is removed some of the others may slide down or fall out of place. The method is really one of storage, although it is frequently described under the heading *horizontal filing*. This term is also used to describe the use of shallow drawers to house large charts, plans, prints and drawings, and to protect them from dust, damp or direct sunlight.

Lateral shelf or cupboard filing is generally preferred to cabinet or drawer filing because it occupies less space (see diagram on page 250). The conventional four-drawer filing cabinet actually takes up more room than twice its true

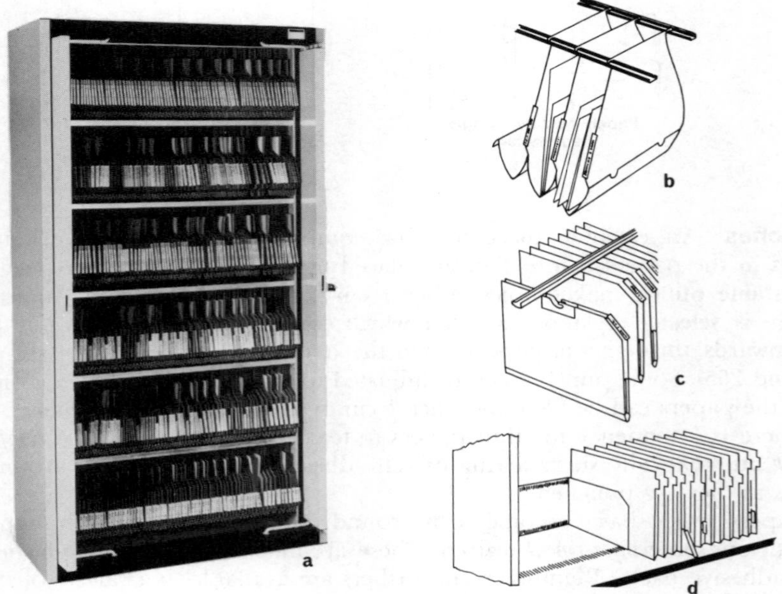

(a) In lateral filing the folders are arranged in rows on shelves. Notice that the whole unit is fitted with a shutter which protects the files from dust and enables the unit to be locked. (b) The folders can be suspended in a concertina of outer covers, or (c) hung separately from a centre rail, or (d) stood on their spines. Lateral filing takes up less space than the conventional four-drawer cabinets (see page 250).

dimensions because floor space has to be allowed for access to the fully extended drawers. There is also a safety consideration: if one of the drawers is allowed to become top heavy, it can overbalance as the drawer is opened; this risk can be reduced by placing wedges under the front edges of the cabinet so that the drawers slope slightly backwards and any drawer inadvertently left open will slowly close of its own accord.

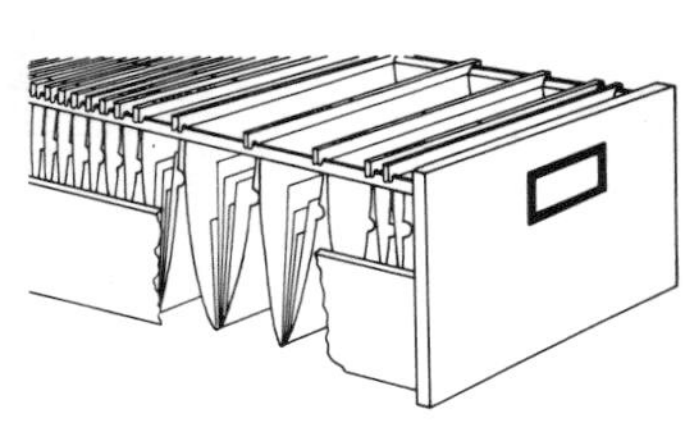

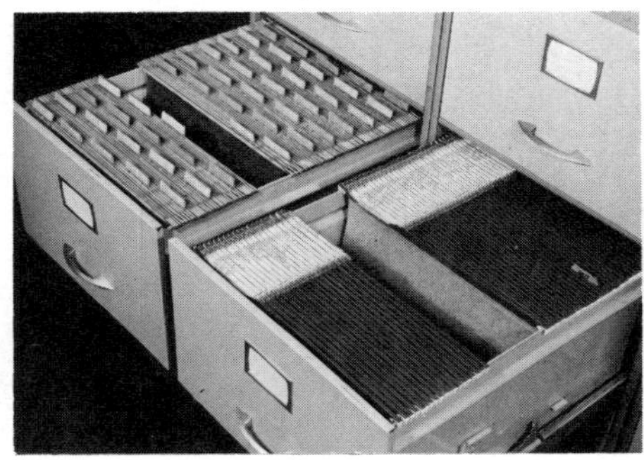

In connected pocket suspension filing, the files are placed in a concertina of pockets. The diagram shows how the folders are joined by metal slides on which are fixed the name tabs.

Dividers and tabs DIVIDERS Whether they are kept in drawers or on shelves, the files may be clearly labelled and arranged in sequence so that they can easily be found. For ease of reference the files are divided into sections and arranged in either alphabetical or chronological or numerical order (see pages 252–256, *Methods of Arrangement*). The sections are marked by guide cards which are made with stepped tabs, either plain, or printed A–Z for alphabetical classification and January–December and 1–31 for chronological classification, or numbered consecutively for numerical classification systems.

When a file is taken out, an *OUT* guide card is put in its place; OUT guide cards may be fitted with pocket corners to hold a card giving details of the folder that has been removed and its present location. A pocket on the reverse side of the OUT card houses papers which accumulate for filing whilst the file is absent.

Very large filing systems frequently find it convenient to use more than one set of guide cards: *primary guides* on the extreme left indicate main divisions and *secondary guides* on the right-hand side of the primary ones indicate sub-divisions; the actual file titles are arranged centrally leaving the far right-hand side available for OUT cards.

TABS There are various ways of labelling files and folders. Individual labels are made in a series of perforated strips either (a) to fit into the projecting metal carriers or (b) to slide under the plastic covering of flat-top systems.

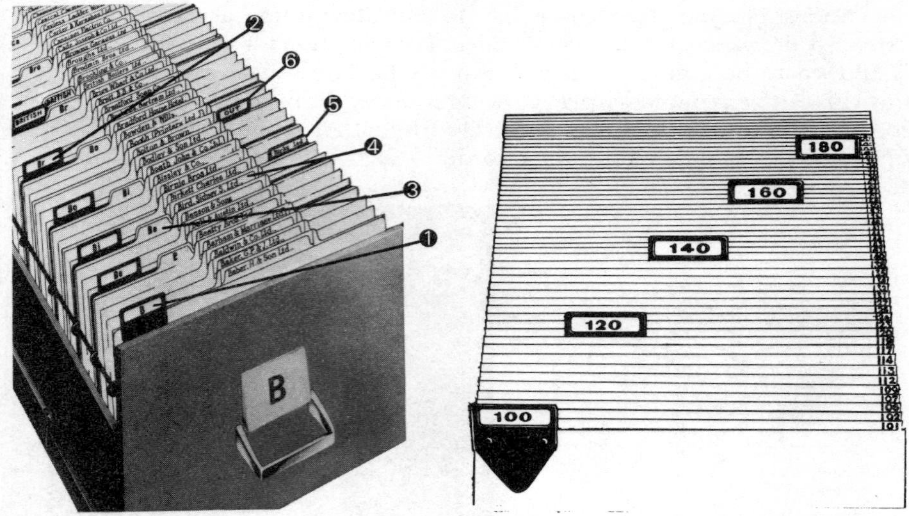

(Left) The Remington Rand VARIADEX system showing the use of primary and secondary guide cards. 1. The main alphabetic guides. 2. Secondary guides. 3. Miscellaneous correspondence folders. 4. Individual folders. 5. The extreme right position can be used for special cases. 6. An OUT guide card. (Right) A set of numerical guide cards.

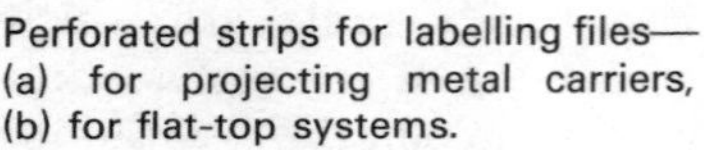
Perforated strips for labelling files—
(a) for projecting metal carriers,
(b) for flat-top systems.

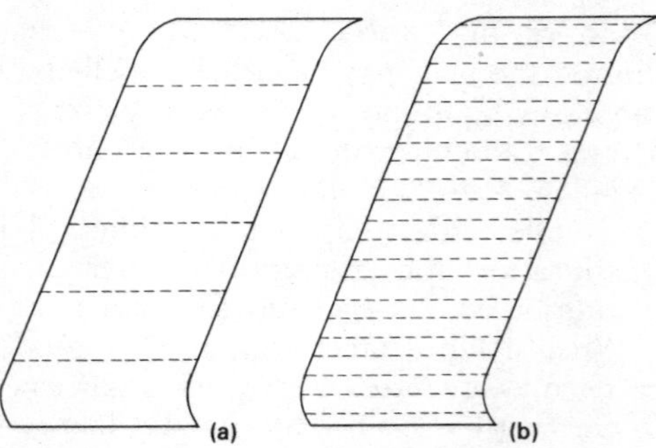

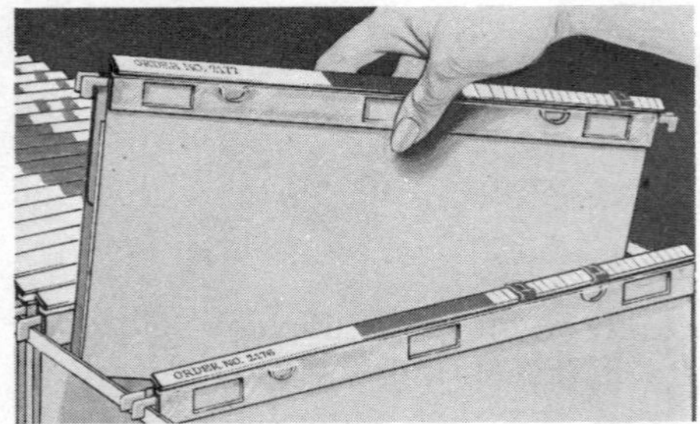

'Shannoblic 40' flat-top strip tabs which have sliding coloured index signals.

Triumph Fastvue (left) and Clearvue projecting tabs. The metal tab carriers can be covered with transparent coloured plastic for colour-coded signal systems, and a series of holes at intervals along the frame of the outer pocket enables the tab carriers to be fixed in any position across the width of the pocket.

Files In addition to folders suitable for dealing with one topic or person, there are other types of files and binders (illustrations see page 87).

LEVER ARCH FILES secure papers on two arch-shaped metal rods which are opened and closed by raising or lowering a lever. The rods are a standard 7 cm or 8 cm apart and the files are made in quarto, foolscap, octavo and A4 sizes, they can be obtained with the arches on either the long edges ("upright" files or short edges ("oblong" files). One advantage of lever arch files is that single sheets may be easily inserted or removed in any position, as the papers can be turned over like the pages of a book and the arches remain closed until the lever is raised. This enables lever arch files to be fitted with guide cards such as an A–Z index set, stepped letter by letter similar to an address book, and they often suit the correspondence requirements of smaller offices or club secretaries.

A disadvantage of lever arch files is that they are equally bulky whether they are full or empty and so frequently occupy more space than the letters they contain.

BOX FILES have a spring clip to keep the papers secure. They can be fitted with A–Z guide sheets. Papers do not need to be punched as there are no prongs, rings or rod fasteners. Box files are made in a variety of sizes and can be obtained with fixed or drop front edges.

EXPANDING FILES consist of a number of pockets or gussets connected together in the form of a concertina. The divisions are tabbed alphabetically. Papers are filed in the pockets and the whole file can be fastened with a strap.

PART FILES consist of a number of heavy manilla sheets folded and fastened to form a cover divided into seven or nine parts. The open edges are cut to form a series of tabs which can be used for labelling. Papers are placed loose between the manilla sheets and the whole file is fastened by two pieces of elastic across the corners.

Other types of files to suit various purposes are: document wallets, spring clip files, flat files and spring back files.

Rotary filing units Filing space is saved by storing lateral files on double-sided racks which are controlled mechanically or electrically. These installations save space and lessen physical fatigue. The operator can quickly and easily bring any rack of files within reach by rotating a wheel or dial.

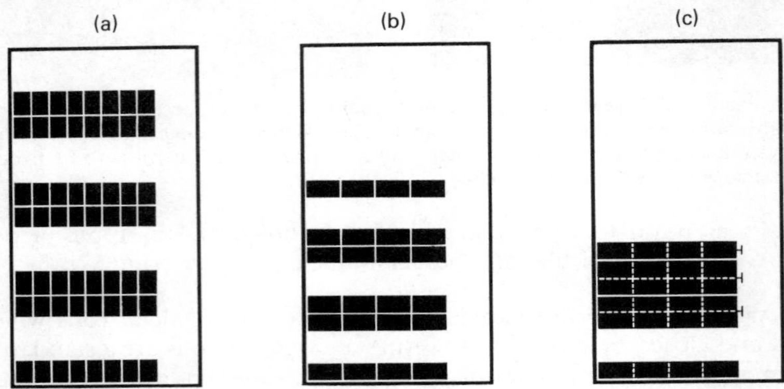

A comparison by Frank Wilson (Filing) Ltd. of floor space needed and file capacity of (a) 56 four-drawer filing cabinets, (b) 24 lateral filing cabinets and (c) 24 Railex Mobilfile units. The lateral filing cabinets contain the same number of files as the Railex units but occupy considerably more space. The four-drawer cabinets take up more space than either of the other two units and provide less capacity.

Automatic retrieval systems Remington Rand make several items of equipment which store files and retrieve them automatically within seconds. The Lektriever One stores lateral files on a conveyor belt which can rotate in either direction. Several models are available; the largest units can store up to 160,000 records. The shelf containing the file required is brought to hand by pushing a button. It is claimed that any file can be located within 8 seconds. The Randtriever is a more automated system. The Remstar system enables users to contact a central registry and view the documents on a remote monitor as soon as the operator locates the file and places the document into the transmission station.

Filing accessories

TROLLEYS can be used to collect filing from a large number of offices. They can also be used for pre-sorting, or to hold files beside a desk whilst the contents are being worked on.

The Railex Mobilfile rotary filing unit for lateral files.

The "Expandex" rotary filing system for lever arch files. Each tier holds 24 files.

The Remington Lektriever I.

A filing trolley.

Transfer or storage boxes.

TRANSFER BOXES When files are no longer active, they can be moved into transfer or storage boxes if the original documents have to be retained.

FILING SYSTEMS

Methods of arrangement Documents can be stored in (a) chronological order, (b) numerical order, (c) alphabetical order.

The CHRONOLOGICAL method of arrangement means filing in date order. In its usual form, each day's papers are filed on top of existing papers, thus the most recent documents are in the front of the file; if the pages are also numbered and entered in an index book, the first page (page 1) is the bottom page. This system is suitable for a Mail Book in which all copies of outgoing letters are kept in date order; the copies are sometimes referred to as "chron copies" and the file may be called the "chron file" or "letter book". A chron file may also be kept in book order, that is with new material placed at the end of the file so that it reads in book form with the oldest page as the first page in the front of the book. Tickler files and follow-up systems (see pages 261 and 262) are also arranged chronologically.

The NUMERICAL method has several forms (see Numerical Classification, pages 258 to 260) such as putting numbers in serial order or in order according to the last digit. It is usual to work in book form although the method sometimes referred to as "reverse book" is more convenient for classifying some documents such as the chron copies mentioned in the previous paragraph.

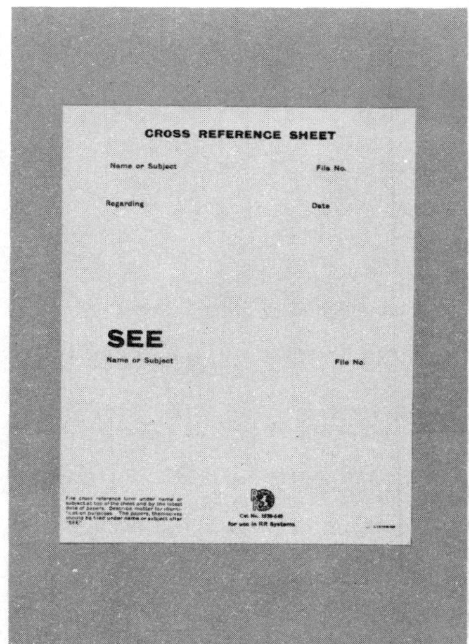
CROSS REFERENCE SHEET

Name or Subject — File No.

Regarding — Date

SEE

Name or Subject — File No.

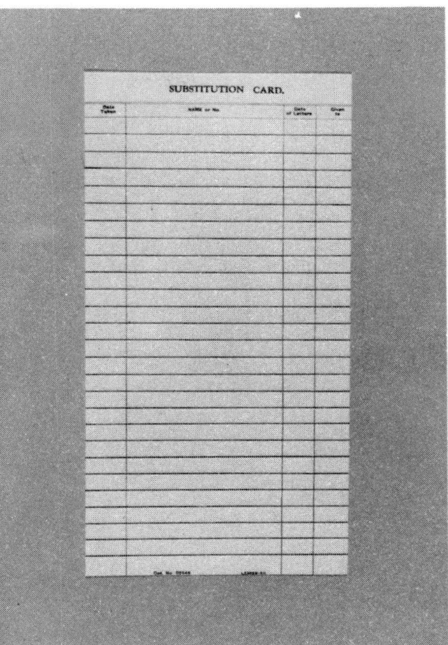
SUBSTITUTION CARD.

NAME or No.

(Left) *A Cross Reference Sheet.* Whenever a letter could be correctly filed under more than one heading, a cross reference sheet indicating the file in which it will be found should be put under the alternative heading or headings. (Right) *An Absent or Substitution Card* should be inserted in a file whenever a single document is removed. The location of the document should be noted on the Substitution Card.

ALPHABETICAL arrangement is the basis of most filing systems. Alphabetical order means the order in which words in a dictionary or names in a telephone directory are arranged; it is the basis of all indexing systems. Indexing is the process of dividing names and titles into indexing units and deciding upon the order in which they should be arranged. The technique of indexing is a basic step in filing; it is also used for indexing books, committee minutes and reports, and for keeping records on visible and strip indexes.

Indexing A number of rules have been developed for arranging names or items or files or cards in alphabetical order. The application of these rules includes the division of names or titles into one or more *indexing units*. Each initial letter and every word included in a name is treated as a separate indexing unit. Thus in the names *Alfred John Smith* and *The Daily Recorder* there are three units; the first important word is the first indexing unit and the remaining names and words are indexed in the order in which they occur, thus:

	Unit 1	Unit 2	Unit 3
Alfred John Smith	Smith	Alfred	John
The Daily Recorder	Daily	Recorder	The

Names and topics are first indexed by their first units; if the first units are the same, the second units must be considered; if the second units are the same, the third units must be considered. If two names are identical, then one must be distinguished from the other by the addition of a number or a place name, for example:

	Unit 1	Unit 2	Unit 3	Unit 4
James Brown	Brown	James		
Peter Brown	Brown	Peter		
Peter William Brown	Brown	Peter	William	
William Edward Brown	Brown	William	Edward	
William Frank Brown	Brown	William	Frank	(London)
William Frank Brown	Brown	William	Frank	(Manchester)

The following indexing rules should be borne in mind when files and cards are being arranged in alphabetical order:

1. File according to the initial letter of the surname and each subsequent letter, e.g.

	Unit 1	Unit 2	Unit 3
E. H. Parker	Parker	E.	H.
M. W. Parkinson	Parkinson	M.	W.
N. V. Parsons	Parsons	N.	V.
S. O. Partridge	Partridge	S.	O.

2. If the surnames are the same, file according to initials, e.g.

	Unit 1	Unit 2	Unit 3
B. D. Chapman	Chapman	B.	D.
C. M. Chapman	Chapman	C.	M.
C. P. Chapman	Chapman	C.	P.
H. A. Chapman	Chapman	H.	A.

3. Ignore titles, but include these on the flap or tab of the folder, e.g.

	Unit 1	Unit 2	Unit 3
F. G. Price	Price	F.	G.
Dr. H. J. Price	Price	H.	J. (Dr.)
Col. P. R. Price	Price	P.	R. (Col.)
Mrs R. W. Price	Price	R.	W. (Mrs.)
Capt. T. D. Price	Price	T.	D. (Capt.)

In the case of identical names, personal titles may be used to distinguish one from the other, e.g. Dr. R. T. Brown before Prof. R. T. Brown.

4. 'Nothing' comes before 'something'—a surname alone precedes a surname with an initial; and a surname with an initial precedes a surname with a first name, e.g.

	Unit 1	Unit 2	Unit 3
Wilkinson	Wilkinson		
H. J. Wilkinson	Wilkinson	H.	J.
N. E. Wilkinson	Wilkinson	N.	E.
Albert J. Wilkinson	Wilkinson	Albert	J.
Alfred H. Wilkinson	Wilkinson	Alfred	H.
Alfred John Wilkinson	Wilkinson	Alfred	John

This rule, common in offices, deviates from the order in most telephone directories, where initials and names are sorted together, alphabetically.

5. Consider the surname prefix as part of the surname, and treat names beginning with M', Mc and Mac as if they were all spelt MAC—that is, file according to the first letter of the next syllable, e.g.

	Unit 1	Unit 2	Unit 3
M. N. De Gruchy	De Gruchy	M.	N.
A. R. De Haan	De Haan	A.	R.
De Havilland Ltd.	De Havilland	Ltd.	
De Hems Restaurant	De Hems	Restaurant	
Mrs C. De La Motte	De La Motte	C. (Mrs)	
B. D. McAdam	McAdam	B.	D.
F. P. MacAdam	MacAdam	F.	P.
A. S. McAllister	McAllister	A.	S.
Mrs D. Macalpine	Macalpine	D. (Mrs)	
M. R. McAlpine	McAlpine	M.	R.
Harold W. MacAlpine	MacAlpine	Harold	W.

6. Ignore 'The', '& Co' when filing names of firms and companies, e.g.

	Unit 1	Unit 2	Unit 3
Metal Alloys Welding Co Ltd	Metal	Alloys	Welding Co Ltd
The Metal Box Co Ltd	Metal	Box	Co Ltd (The)
Metal Containers Ltd	Metal	Containers	Ltd
Metcalfe & Mulligan Ltd	Metcalfe &	Mulligan	Ltd
The Metropolitan Carriage Co Ltd	Metropolitan	Carriage	Co Ltd (The)
Metropolitan Vickers Ltd	Metropolitan	Vickers	Ltd

7. File names consisting of initials, before whole words, e.g.

	Unit 1	Unit 2	Unit 3
AA Duplicating Co Ltd	AA	Duplicating	Co Ltd
ABC Valet Service	ABC	Valet	Service
AJP Gown Manufacturers	AJP	Gown	Manufacturers
A–Z Enquiry Services Ltd	A–Z	Enquiry	Services Ltd
Mrs E. Aaronson	Aaronson	E. (Mrs)	
Abbey Court Hotel	Abbey	Court	Hotel

8. File all names with the prefixes 'St.' or 'Saint' under SAINT, e.g.

	Unit 1	Unit 2	Unit 3
St Agatha's School	St Agatha's	School	
Saint Catherine Press Ltd	Saint Catherine	Press	Ltd
St Pancras Hospital	St Pancras	Hospital	

9. Treat any number in a name as if it were written in full, e.g.

	Unit 1	Unit 2	Unit 3
The 51 Restaurant	(FIFTY-ONE) 51	Restaurant	The
The 2 Arts Society	(TWO) 2	Arts	Society

10. File government departments and ministries under the key words, e.g.

	Unit 1	Unit 2	Unit 3
Ministry of Defence	Defence	Ministry of	
Department of Health and Social Security	Health and	Social Security	Department of
Department of Trade and Industry	Trade and	Industry	Department of

11. Subdivide files for county councils and local authorities into departments, e.g.

	Unit 1	Unit 2	Unit 3
Greater London Council Architect's Department	Greater London Council	Architect's	Department
Greater London Council Establishment Department	Greater London Council	Establishment	Department
Greater London Council Housing Department	Greater London Council	Housing	Department

12. Always file letters under the name of the firm, company or institution, and not under the name of the individual to whom you are writing.

Cross-referencing Even if all these rules are followed there may occasionally be difficulty in deciding which word should be the first indexing unit. For example, should *British Red Cross Society* be filed under B for British or Red for Red Cross? When you have to make such a decision, put a note in the section where the folder is *not* filed indicating where it will be found. This is called making a cross-reference. It is useful because you may not remember under which letter the correspondence was filed, and if you are absent from the office the cross-reference slip will assist anyone who is looking for the file.

If you decided to file letters from the Philippa Fawcett College under 'P', you would put a cross-reference note under 'F'.

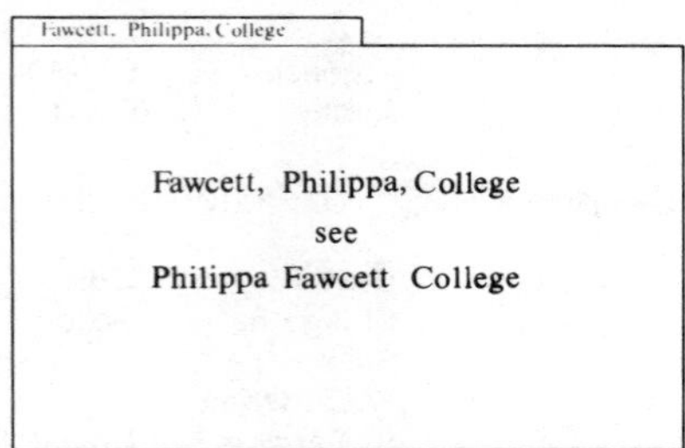
Fawcett, Philippa, College

Fawcett, Philippa, College
see
Philippa Fawcett College

A cross-reference slip.

Methods of classification BY NAME This is one of the commonest and simplest methods of classification. A folder is labelled for each firm or individual with whom the organisation corresponds and the folders are arranged in alphabetical order. In a small filing system the sections are separated by one guide card for each letter of the alphabet. A larger filing system will require some subdivision between the letters, especially the letters B, C, H, S and W, as many more English names begin with these letters than, say, the letters Q and Y. The sections are then subdivided into B–Be, Be–Bi, Bi–Bo, Bo–Br etc. (see page 248).

Sometimes the correspondence with one firm will be too small to justify the making out of a separate file. For this purpose a miscellaneous folder is made out for each letter of the alphabet and letters which have no files of their own can be filed in the miscellaneous folder. For example, if there were no file for Taylor Enterprises Ltd letters from this firm could be filed in the 'T Miscellaneous' folder.

GEOGRAPHICAL CLASSIFICATION Sometimes it is convenient to arrange files in alphabetical order according to location and then subdivide by name. In the illustration below the main guides indicate counties, the subsidiary guide cards indicate towns and the individual folders for correspondents in each town are placed behind the appropriate guide cards.

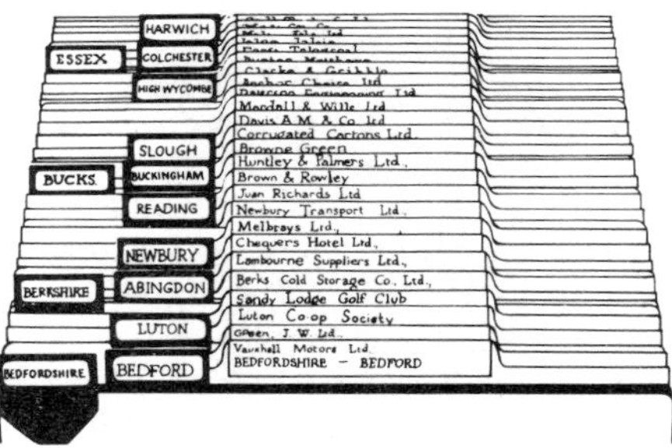

This method is frequently used by the wholesale distributors who deal with many small firms. It is also used by gas and electricity boards, insurance companies, sales offices, mail-order firms, laundries and firms employing travellers.

A firm corresponding with agencies abroad often finds it more convenient to file under the name of the country and town, than under the name of the individual agent. Travel agents and shipping companies have agencies all over the world and they nearly always file under the name of the port or town rather than under the name of the agent which is often difficult to remember. Furthermore, the name of the agent may change but the name of the town will remain the same. It is, for example, easier to look under 'T' for Tenerife, than under 'M' for Miller y cia SA, the Tenerife agent.

CLASSIFICATION BY SUBJECT Professional people such as architects, builders, engineers and lawyers often find it convenient to have a file relating to each project or case; sub-divisions may be made for each particular aspect of the subject as in the example shown below. This method is also frequently used in personnel departments, and offices dealing with schools and colleges. A logical scheme of subject headings divided into sub-headings co-ordinates and groups all relevant documents. Subject filing concentrates information very effectively.

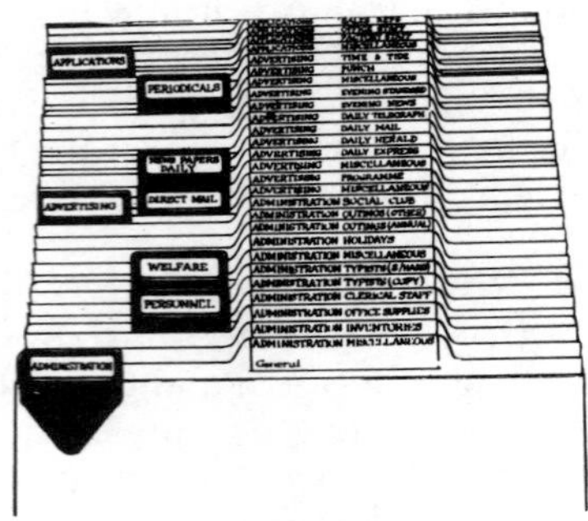

NUMERICAL CLASSIFICATION Most large filing systems adopt a system of numerical classification in which each folder is given a serial number and the guide cards and folders carry numeric captions.

The first point to note about numerical filing is that it is *indirect*; in other words it must be used in conjunction with an alphabetical card index control system—to find a file reference number it is necessary to refer to the A–Z card index.

A second point to note is that an *Accession Book* or *Accession Register* or File *List* is needed to keep a record of assigned numbers. Each new file is given the next available number in the Accession Register; the name is entered in the register, and an index card bearing the name and assigned number is filed in the alphabetical card index box. The usual size for these index cards is 125 mm by 75 mm (5 in by 3 in), and they can be used to record other information such as the address of the correspondent. A society or association might also record on the index cards whether the member had paid his subscription, whether he was a 'Town' or 'Country' member and any other personal information which was relevant to his membership. It is important to note that both the *File List* or *Accession Book* and alphabetical card index must be kept up to date and in order—the alphabetical index is essential for tracing files and finding file numbers.

Thirdly, a numerical system can be expanded indefinitely. A new correspondent will be allotted the next available number, his folder will be placed at the back of the existing folders, and an index card is made out and filed. A further advantage is that the file number will be quoted on correspondence so the filing clerk does not need to read through all the correspondence; as soon as he has seen the reference number he knows the number of the folder in which the papers must be filed.

Numerical classification may be either consecutive, terminal digit or alpha-numeric.

In *consecutive number* filing the folders are arranged in strict numerical sequence. This system is particularly suitable for large projects; each section or division or department may be allocated an initial number or block of numbers which can then be sub-divided, for example:

100–199	Project Manager's Office
200–299	Senior Management Department
300–399	Middle Management Department
400–499	Higher Clerical Department
500–599	Clerical Department

Each department can then add new sections to suit its needs, e.g.

500.0.0	Clerical Department			
	500.1.0	Courses		
		500.1.1	Clerical Upgrading	
		500.1.2	Bi-lingual Clerks	
	500.2.0	Syllabuses		
		500.2.1	Clerical Duties	
		500.2.2	Office Machinery	
	500.3.0	Examinations		
		500.3.1	English Language	
		500.3.2	Office Practice	

New files are assigned the next number within the section or sub-section. In the scheme given above, for example, a new section—*Textbooks*—would be assigned the number 500.4.0, a new course—*Office Supervisors*—would be assigned the number 500.1.3, the next number in that sub-section. In addition to permitting infinite extension, this system also enables papers to be immediately identified, thus any document commencing 100 would belong to or have originated from the Project Manager's office.

The *terminal digit method* of numeric classification is based on dividing large numbers (five digits or more) into groups of two or three and reading the numbers in groups from *right to left*. The terminal numbers, usually the farthest right pair of digits, form the primary indexing unit, the next two figures to the left are the secondary units and so on.

For example, if you wanted to find file number 540921 you would read the number from the right in pairs, thus "21 . . . 09 . . . 54", meaning file drawer 21, guide card 09, folder 54. You would first locate the shelf or drawer containing folders ending in 21, then you would look for the guide 09, finally you would find the folder labelled 54 09 21.

A new folder would be given the next number, that is 55, so the next available number would be 55 09 21.

This method may also be used for individual document numbering within each folder. For example, the number 60 92 73 would mean document number 60 in file number 92 in drawer (or on shelf) number 73. A new document would be given the number 61 (61 92 73) and a new file would be given the number 93 (60 93 73)—they would both be kept in drawer 73, or behind the primary guide 73.

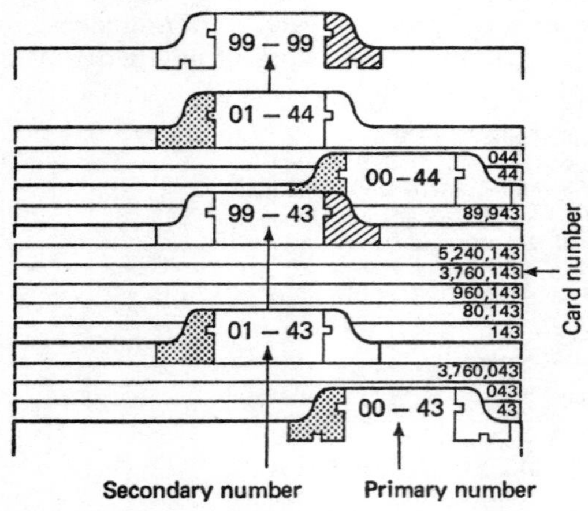

The terminal digit method of numerical classification in use.

The advantages claimed for this system are (a) that filing folders according to their terminal digits ensures even distribution throughout the filing installation, (b) it is simple to add new files or remove old ones, (c) that it reduces the possibility of error as the filing clerk needs remember only two digits at any one time and (d) it is easy to pick out any folders filed in the wrong place.

Terminal digit filing is used by building societies for savings accounts and mortgages, by hospitals for case records, by insurance companies and many other organisations who deal with large numbers of customers or clients each of whom has an identifying account or policy number.

Numbers of fewer than six digits can be made up to six by adding noughts to the left of the number. When larger numbers are dealt with, they can be divided into groups of three digits, thus 123 456 789.

The *alpha-numeric system* as its name implies is a combination of numerical sequence and alphabetical order. Some alpha-numeric systems are highly specialised and are used in centralised filing departments staffed by specially trained personnel. One application of the alpha-numeric system is to assign blocks of numbers to topics arranged in alphabetical order, and then to sub-divide the topics also alphabetically and numerically. For example:

48 Post Office
    48.1 Parcel services
    48.2 Telegraph services
49 Production
    49.1 Control
    49.2 Experimental
    49.3 Market surveys

Another system combining numerical and alphabetical sequences is the *Dewey Decimal Classification* system which is used in libraries (see *Chapter 11, Sources of Reference and Information*, pages 446 to 448). Whilst the alpha-numeric system can be extended indefinitely, the Dewey system is closed, i.e. there can be no more than ten main categories. If the Dewey Decimal Classification were to be adopted as an office filing system, the material to be filed would first have to be divided into ten sections; it is, of course, necessary to have an alphabetical card index to find out the numbers of each sub-section and individual subject.

FILING PROCEDURES

In non-governmental organisations and private offices, documents are normally never filed until some action has been taken upon them. Filing is primarily storing documents for future reference and, although a letter may be attached to the cover of the relevant file if reference has to be made to previous correspondence, the letter will not be placed 'on file', i.e. actually clipped into or secured inside the file, until action has been taken on it and until it has been released for filing.

The procedures that are described here are written primarily for filing in this sense, i.e. storage filing. However, it should be mentioned that in government departments and the offices of many public, national, international and supra-national organisations, filing is the first step in the action stage of a document, and no action is taken on a document until it is 'on file'. When a letter is received in the Registry, it is placed on the respective file and flagged with either an ACTION or INFORMATION flag; the whole file is then routed to the appropriate official or officials. This type of *pre-action filing* is rarely found in the business world and differs from the *post-action filing* procedures described in this section.

A document passes through several stages during the course of its life. It is created when it is written or typed and signed or initialled by the originator; it is then sent to the person who needs the information it contains or the person who has to act on the message the document conveys. This action stage of the document may be accomplished within a few hours (such as a reply to a routine enquiry) or it may take a few days or it can take weeks or months. Various bring-up and reminder systems have been devised (a) to prevent papers from being filed away and forgotten before they have brought about the action or results for which they were originated, (b) to ensure that the papers will be regularly brought to the attention of the person who is waiting to deal with them—in other words, they will not be allowed to remain in abeyance indefinitely, and (c) to act as a reminder that the matter to which the papers refer should be followed-up at some future date.

Work in hand Work which can be completed within a reasonably short time (say up to ten days or two weeks) may conveniently be kept in a WORK IN

HAND or WORK IN PROGRESS folder. If the case or incident to which the document refers has to await further developments or actions in another sphere, the matter may be said to be pending, or in abeyance; in such cases the document may be put in a PENDING, or IN ABEYANCE or BRING-UP file. The object of all these practices is the same: to keep in one place all the pieces of paper relating to work which is in the process of being performed. In some offices a date is handwritten on carbon copies indicating when a reply may be expected, or a remark such as 'Bring up in two weeks' is noted on the papers; sometimes the carbon copies are kept in a REPLIES AWAITED file. With all these methods, part of the secretary's daily routine is to look through the BRING-UP folders each morning and take whatever further steps are required since the various matters were last being dealt with.

For example, letters which have not produced a reply within a reasonable period may have to be followed-up by a reminder or an enquiry as to whether they were actually received by the addressee; another instance is when a telephone call fails to reach either the person required or someone authorised to speak on his behalf (because of holidays or illness) and the caller must have some kind of reminder system so that he can telephone again at a later date.

Sometimes *desk diaries* or *desk calendars* form part of a reminder system. A note to make or to expect a phone call, or to check that some action has been taken, can be entered against the appropriate date in the desk diary.

Reminder systems The procedures mentioned in the preceding paragraph are suitable for work which is actually being performed or which will probably be completed in the near future.

Some matters may have to be put aside for longer periods, or they may not need following-up for several months. A sales representative, for example, needs to know which prospective customers he must visit again three or six months from the date of his original call. Reminder systems for cases such as these usually take the form of FOLLOW-UP or TICKLER files which consist of 12 month guide cards and a set of 31-day guides for the current month. Documents for future action are filed immediately behind the cards bearing the dates of the days upon which the action must be taken.

Follow-up systems may also be used to store carbon copies of letters awaiting replies, so that if replies have not been received within a reasonable time, enquiries can be made to find out whether the original letters were safely delivered.

Filing steps 1. COLLECTION Material for filing may be placed in a tray labelled FILE. There will probably be a filing tray or wire basket on your boss's desk and one on your own desk too. Clear your boss's file tray several times a day; most secretaries do this as a matter of routine whenever they happen to be in his office. Sometimes it may be necessary to look through the papers on your boss's desk to sort out any that can be filed—you would, of course, ask his permission before doing this.

Filing should be done daily; some secretaries find it convenient to file the previous day's correspondence while the post is being read first thing in the morning and before they are called in to take dictation, or while letters are being recorded on a dictating machine, other secretaries consider the end of the afternoon the best time for filing—they find that it rarely gets done if it is left until first thing in the morning because all sorts of unexpected things crop up.

2. INSPECTION If you work for a large organisation in which some papers are filed in a central registry or central filing department, separate the papers that will be filed in your own files from those that will be sent to the central filing department. Inspect each document that is to be filed to check that it has a *release mark*, that is, a mark which indicates that the necessary action has been taken and the document has been released for filing. The release mark usually takes the form of the initials of you or your boss. It is not necessary to put release marks on carbon copies, but it is usual to underline the file reference in red as an indication to registry staff that it is the file copy; in offices where a "master" or "chron-file" copy is kept by the secretary, this practice distinguishes the registry copy from the secretary's copy. Some firms use coloured paper for carbon copies; others have the words FILE COPY printed in large letters on the copy paper.

Examine any correspondence that is pinned or clipped together to make sure that it is complete. Remove the pins or clips and mend any torn papers; keep small slips of paper secure by stapling them to the documents to which they refer.

3. INDEXING AND CODING The next step is to index the document, that is to decide how it is to be filed. This will, of course, depend upon the method of classification used. Names and titles have to be divided into indexing units rules for indexing are given on pages 254 to 256) and cross reference sheets must be prepared where necessary.

When you have determined the indexing units, mark or code the document by underlining or numbering the units with a coloured pencil; should the document be removed from the files at any time the coloured coding shows clearly to which file it must be returned.

Put a cross at the end of any words or titles which should be cross-referenced and prepare the cross-reference sheets or take a photocopy of the original. The cross will indicate that the copy is a cross-reference and where it should be filed; the coding will indicate where the original is filed.

4. SORTING As soon as they have been coded the papers should be sorted into indexing order so that they are ready to be placed in the appropriate folders or files. This process is assisted by the use of sorters or sorting trays which can

be equipped with alphabetical, numerical, geographical or chronological dividers. When the documents have been *rough sorted*, that is placed behind the appropriate dividers, they can be *fine sorted*, that is placed in exact indexing order.

An Ambidex sorter.

Sorters and sorting trays enable the documents to be placed in filing order so that each folder is handled only once, and so that the folders come to hand as they are needed, that is in the order in which they are arranged in the drawer or on the shelf. Another advantage of using a sorter is that documents can be easily found if they are needed before they are filed.

5. PUNCHING AND STORING Papers should be placed "squarely" in the folders so that they do not become creased. Projecting papers make a set of folders look untidy or inefficient and may hide the tab or card carrier. To punch paper correctly, make a small crease in the middle of the left-hand edge and align the crease with the centre point of the punch. Some punches have adjustable metal guides which can be pre-set for various sizes of paper.

Folders are usually manufactured with eight pairs of punch holes so that the metal clips can be threaded through to hold the papers in any one of eight different positions.

The diagram on page 266 shows six ways in which papers can be placed in folders. Each method has certain advantages and disadvantages and the system adopted in most offices seems to be mainly one of personal preference.

TIME-LIFE INTERNATIONAL (NEDERLAND) N.V.   OTTHO HELDRINGSTRAAT 5   AMSTERDAM-1018

File
JS

8 July 1973

The Librarian
Hotel and Catering School
47 Avenue St Pierre
Marseilles FRANCE

Dear Sir

Thank you for your remittance of $5.75 in settlement of our invoice for the book "Cooking of the British Isles" from our FOODS OF THE WORLD LIBRARY. Your account for this volume has been credited.

We also confirm that your account for the entire series is completely up to date and that payment has been received for all books sent so far.

Thank you for your continued interest in our publications.

Yours faithfully

Edward Pearson

Edward Pearson
Customer Service Department

EP/bs

Trade Register Amsterdam 104120

Letter released, indexed and coded ready for sorting.

CROSS REFERENCE SHEET

FIRM, NAME, SUBJECT ....FOODS OF THE WORLD LIBRARY....

Remarks ....acknowledges $5.75 for 'Cooking of the British Isles....

SEE ....TIME-LIFE BOOKS (8 July 1973)....

Cross-reference sheet.

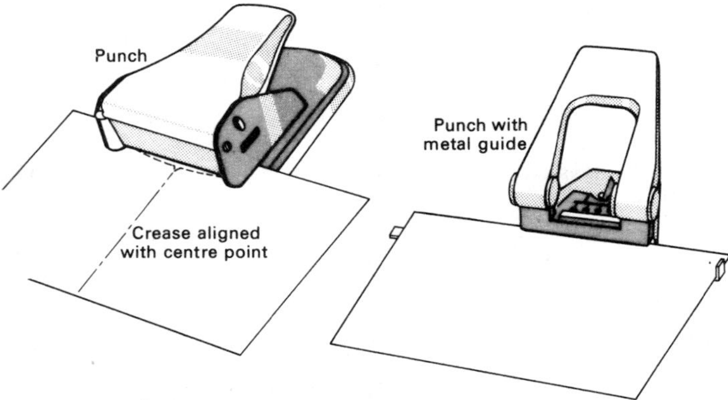

Punching papers before placing them in folders.

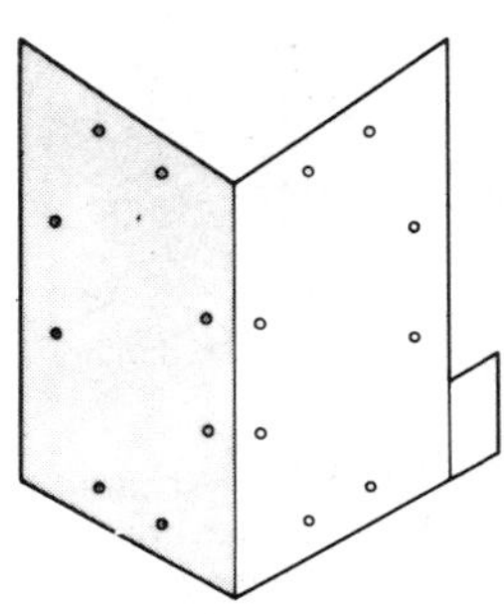

Filing folders are usually manufactured with eight pairs of punch holes.

VARIOUS WAYS IN WHICH PAPERS CAN BE PLACED IN FOLDERS.

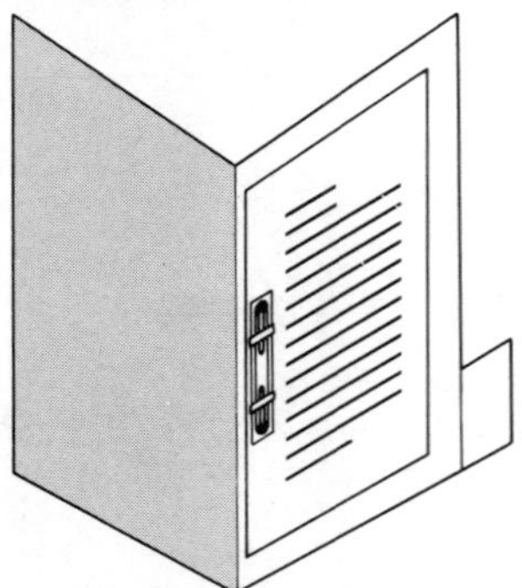

1. Papers secured by left-hand edges against centre fold of file. If the file hangs in a suspension unit or stands on its spine in a drawer, the papers are held by their lower edges and the top edges may curl downwards and crease, but the papers open for reading in familiar book form.

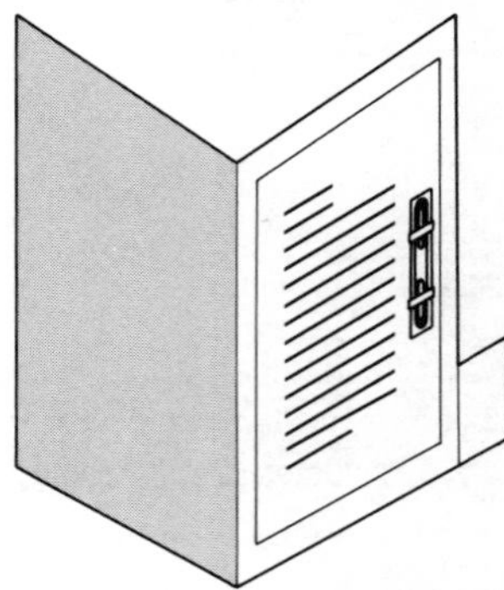

2. Papers secured by their right-hand edges against the top edge of the file. If the file hangs in a suspension unit or stands on its spine in a drawer, the papers will naturally hang downwards and keep flat—but they will open in reverse book form.

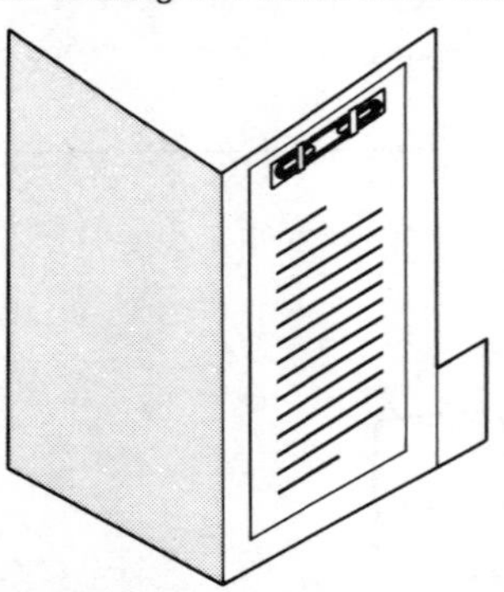

3. Papers secured by their top edges on the right-hand side of the folder.

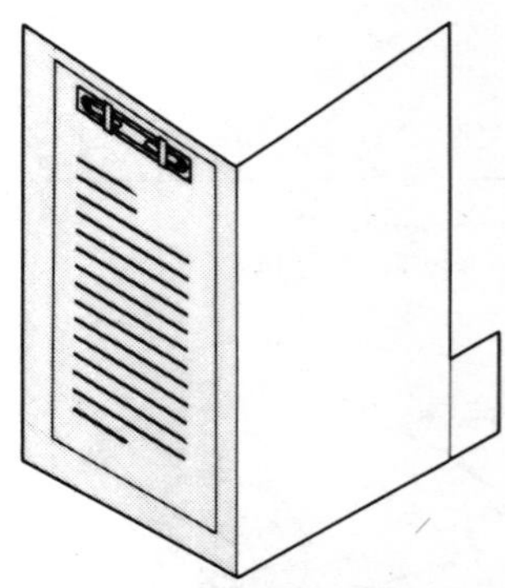

4. Papers secured by their top edges on the left-hand side of the folder.

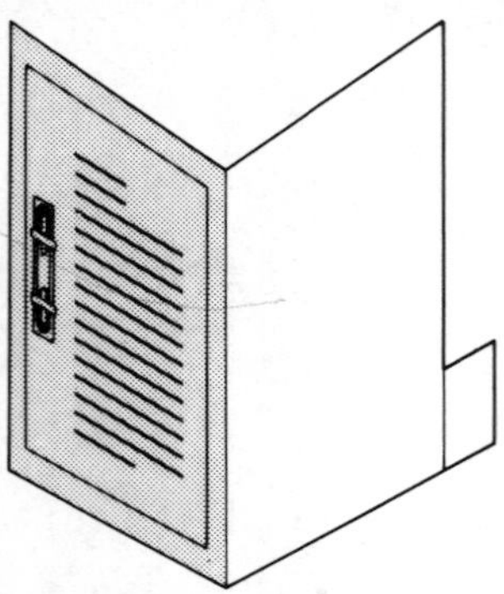

5. Papers secured by their left-hand edges on the left-hand side of the folder. If the file hangs in a suspension unit or stands on its spine in a drawer, the papers will naturally hang downwards and keep flat, and they can be referred to in the familiar book form.

6. "Split" filing enables documents to be separated within the folders, e.g. internal documents on one side and external documents on the other.

In the Civil Service three different systems may be found. These are known as "book", "reverse book" and "split".... Some five years ago the matter was brought to the attention of the Treasury O and M, as it then was. A small survey was carried out and the sensible if uninspired conclusion was reached that none of the three main systems could claim any conclusive advantage over the other. Users, for the most part, tended to prefer the system they were "brought up with".*

Papers which have been typed horizontally (that is, with the longer edge as the width) should either be punched along the left-hand side—in which case the projecting edge can be neatly folded inwards—or they should be punched along the top edge so that the reader need only turn the file through a ninety degree angle to bring the document into view "the right way up".

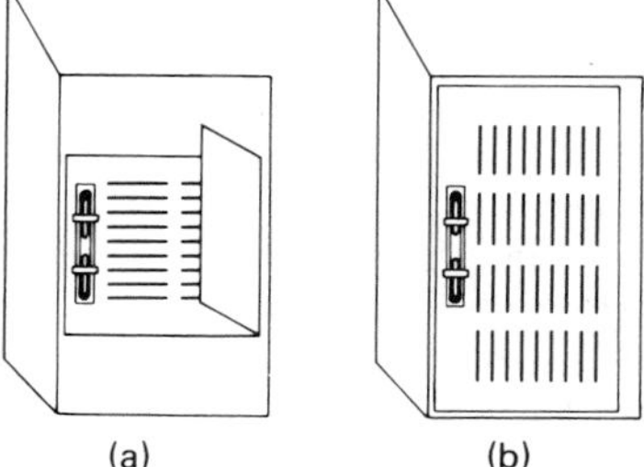

Filing papers which have been typed with the longer side as the width—(a) the projecting edge is folded inwards, (b) secured by the top edge.

Removing files and documents When a file is taken out of the office, an *OUT card* should be inserted in the place where the file is normally kept. Some OUT cards such as the one shown below have a frame into which can be fitted a card giving details of the location of the missing folder; a pocket on the reverse side houses papers which accumulate for filing whilst the file is absent.

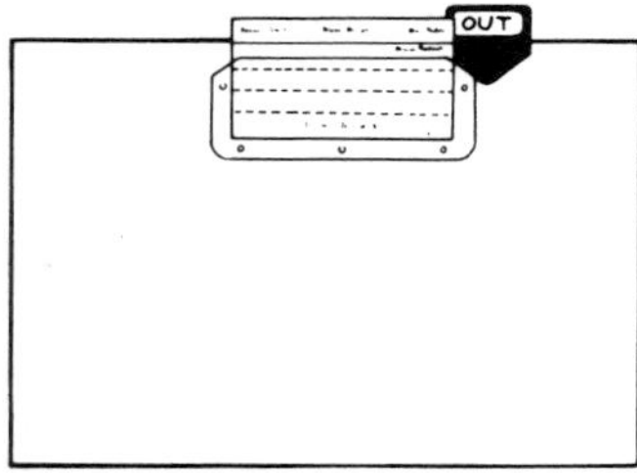

The folder should be "charged out" to the person who has borrowed it and and an entry should be made in the *File Register* (page 268) showing the date, the name of the file, the name of the borrower and the department or office where he works. The date on which the file is returned can be entered in the last column. The person responsible for the files should make a daily check through the "Returned" column and follow-up any files which have been out for an unreasonable length of time.

* *How Should We File?* D. D. Wellmann, O. & M. Bulletin, Civil Service Department, August 1969.

Date	File	Name and dept.	Returned
1973			
3 June	Dreamy Tours	F. Dyers, Accounts	
4 June	Pix Captions	M. Fellows, Management	

Ruling for a File Register.

The methodical use of OUT cards and daily updating of file registers does not prevent files being mislaid unless some procedure is established to prevent (in theory) the uncontrolled movement of files between one officer and another or one department and another. There are two ways to do this: either files must always be re-routed through the Registry so that their most recent location can be noted, or each officer has a supply of *file movement slips* on which he writes the file number, the name of the person to whom he is passing the file, the date and the time. The file movement slip is sent by internal post to the Registry where the clerk-in-charge amends the OUT card and the file register.

Generally speaking, single documents should not be removed from files and taken away. Nowadays this is rarely necessary as most offices have a copying machine and a photocopy can easily be made of any document. If it is necessary to remove an original document from a folder and lend it out, it must be replaced by a *substitution card* or an *absent card* which gives details of the document taken out (date, subject, name of originator) in addition to the name and department of the person who has removed it, and date.

Use of colour We have already mentioned that some firms use coloured paper for taking carbon copies of letters so that these can be easily identified. Colour can also be used to distinguish other aspects of filing, e.g. sets of folders can be in one colour or the metal tab carriers can be covered with coloured plastic to identify certain groups of folders. A manufacturing firm making a wide range of products could use colour coding for files for each group of products within the range, e.g. blue for cosmetics, pink for baby-care products, yellow for kitchen cleansers, purple for men's products.

Active files We started this section by stating that a document passes through several stages during the course of its life. Reference to the diagram on page 269 will show that we have so far traced the history of a document up to stage five, the point at which the document is stored in active files after action has been taken upon it and it has been released for filing.

Active files, as their name implies, are files in daily use containing documents still needed at operational level.

From this point onwards a number of different methods are available to store documents which are not needed for current work but which must be kept for a certain time, sometimes for statutory reasons,* sometimes in accordance with the firm's retention policy.

**The Disposal and Retention Of Documents*, The Chartered Institute of Secretaries.

Documents can either be microcopied (see page 270), or transferred to semi-active files, or transferred direct to non-active files. Microcopying, or microfilming as it is sometimes called, was originally used for storing inactive records; nowadays, however, the quality of the film and equipment used has improved to such an extent that microcopying can be used for active records in everyday use. Some documents, having been microcopied, may be destroyed; others will need to be kept.

Each organisation will choose the method best suited to its needs. We shall now discuss the different methods bearing in mind that the order in which the topics are mentioned (as indicated on the diagram) does not necessarily reflect their time-sequence, their importance or their frequency of occurrence.

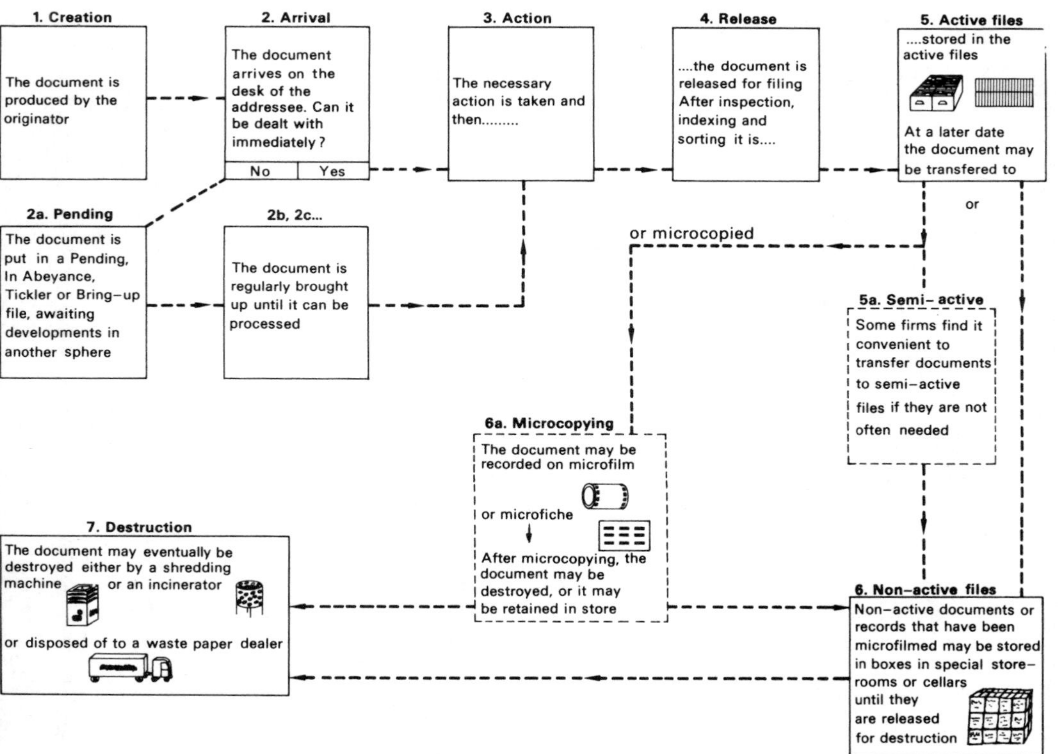

The life history of a document (From creation to incineration)

Transfer of files As the documents in a file gradually become out of date and as the files themselves become thicker with the continual addition of new material, most companies have a system for thinning-out files by transferring material from the active to the inactive files. *Inactive* or *storage files* are those which contain obsolete papers and the documents all businesses are obliged, by law, to preserve for a certain number of years.

Many companies find this division of files into active and inactive or storage suits their filing requirements. Some firms find it expedient to separate the most recent papers and most frequently used files from those which are less frequently referred to; under this system, all documents are transferred to *semi-active files* as soon as the transactions or events for which they were used have been completed.

Inactive files may be kept in boxes which are clearly labelled with the contents and dates, and stored in a basement or store-room.

Microcopying Miniature photographs of documents were first produced during the Franco–Prussian war of 1870. The technique, which subsequently became known as microfilming, developed during the Second World War when many companies microfilmed their records and put them into safe storage.

After the war, as office accommodation became more and more expensive and as paperwork systems increased in size and volume, the use of microfilm was recognised as a way of saving space. Many large firms and institutions such as hospitals were able to save valuable floor-space by microfilming their records.

As we have already mentioned microfilming was originally used for storing inactive records. Nowadays, however, the quality of the film and the equipment used, particularly the retrieval/readers and the reader/printers have improved to such an extent that microfilming can be used for active records in everyday use.

The word 'microcopying' is now used in preference to 'microfilming'. The terms 'micrographics' and 'microfiling' are also in current use. "Microfilming has been defined as 'the application of photographic processes to reproduce copy in sizes too small to be read by the unaided eye' but many of the newer techniques do not employ conventional photographic methods and microcopying is now the accepted term."*

Various microforms are available—16 mm and 35 mm roll film, aperture cards, microfiche and film jackets. There are other less frequently used microforms such as 70 mm film for some engineering drawings and micro-opaques (opaque versions used for some publications in various microfiche sizes).

Thousands of documents can be recorded on a 30 m roll of 16 mm film and stored in a 7.5 cm diameter container; and thousands of pages of information can be recorded on microfiche.

MICROFICHE is a sheet of film about the size of a postcard on which a number of microcopy images have been recorded in a standardised format. The British Standards Institution (BS4187 : 1967) recommends International Paper Size A 6 (105 mm by 148 mm, or approx. 4 in by 6 in) as the standard

**Methods in miniature. An introduction to microcopying*, HMSO.

size for microfiche; this size can provide 72 microcopy images each 15 mm by 11 mm. There is usually a title at the top of the microfiche indicating its contents; the title is readable with the unaided eye. Microfiches can be stored in labelled envelopes and filed in a card index box; they are suitable for storing related documents such as all the documents referring to a particular transaction or incident, and they are also suitable for storing reports—each page will occupy one frame so a 72-page document could be copied on one microfiche.

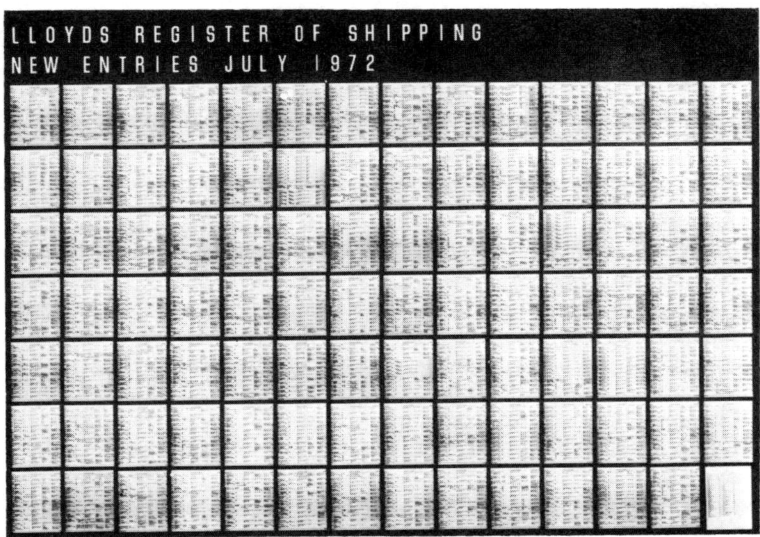

A sheet of microfiche produced on the Remington Rand Automatic Camera Processor. There are 98 micro-images. Each micro-image is an A4 page reduced 24 times.

An *aperture card* is similar to a standard computer punched card with a rectangular cut-out hole specially designed to hold a single microcopy on 35 mm film. The information is recorded visually on the microcopy and also in coded form on the punched section of the card; the punch-coded information can be used for retrieval and for further processing in a subsequent operation.

FILM JACKETS are transparent holders usually the same size as microfiche into which can be inserted strips or individual frames cut from roll film. The strips or frames can be inserted in rows in any order to produce a form of master which can be updated, sorted, read and duplicated, and from which prints can be taken. Microfiche in its conventional form is not updateable but equipment to produce an updateable microfiche has been developed.

A wide range of cameras has been developed which enables almost any form

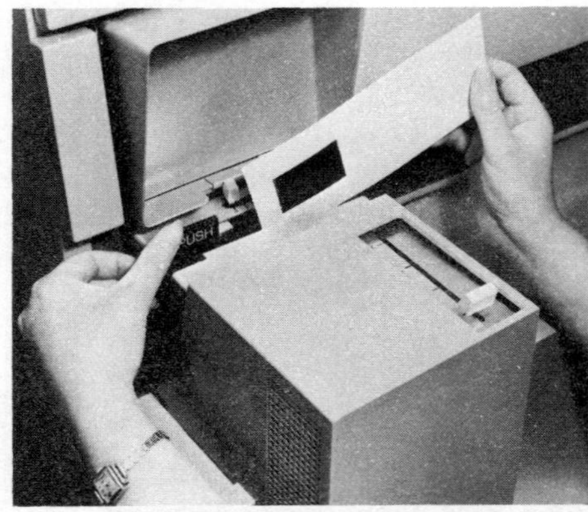

The Rank Xerox 1824 Universal Printer makes sharp prints from all forms of microfilm. In the illustration, an aperture card is being inserted. A dry, permanent print, magnified 14.5 times can be produced within seconds.

The MTC Model 750 Microfiche Camera/Processor marketed by Remington Rand. Originals are microcopied at reduction ratios of 20, 24, 27 or 42. The finished microfiche is delivered within 90 seconds of the last exposure frame.

of documentation to be microcopied. There are three main types of camera: planetary and flow cameras which copy on roll film and the *microfiche camera* sometimes called a 'step and repeat camera' because of its action in copying the first document in its appropriate position on the sheet film and automatically moving the film into the correct position for the next document. a *planetary camera* can be moved up or down on its stand to provide a variety of reduction ratios for different sized originals; a *flow camera* is so-called because the paperwork flows in front of the camera in synchronisation so that no shutter is needed. The more sophisticated models cater for the simultaneous filming of the front and back of documents side by side on the film. There are also special flow cameras for microcopying continuous stationery including computer output.

Microcopies are viewed through *readers* which project a readable enlargement of the copy on to a self-contained illuminated panel.

The most sophisticated automatic machines provide a complete system of information storage and retrieval; the microcopies are electronically coded enabling electronic sensing systems to locate and project a required frame almost immediately and *reader–printers* will produce a 'hard copy' (that is a photocopy) within seconds; the operator has only to press a button when the selected frame comes into view on the screen.

In a comprehensive microcopy system a reader is needed at every user-point.

Microform is suitable for the issue of publications such as reference and maintenance manuals which need frequent amendment, for libraries, reference files, transaction records and engineering drawings.

Microcopying applied to Publications.

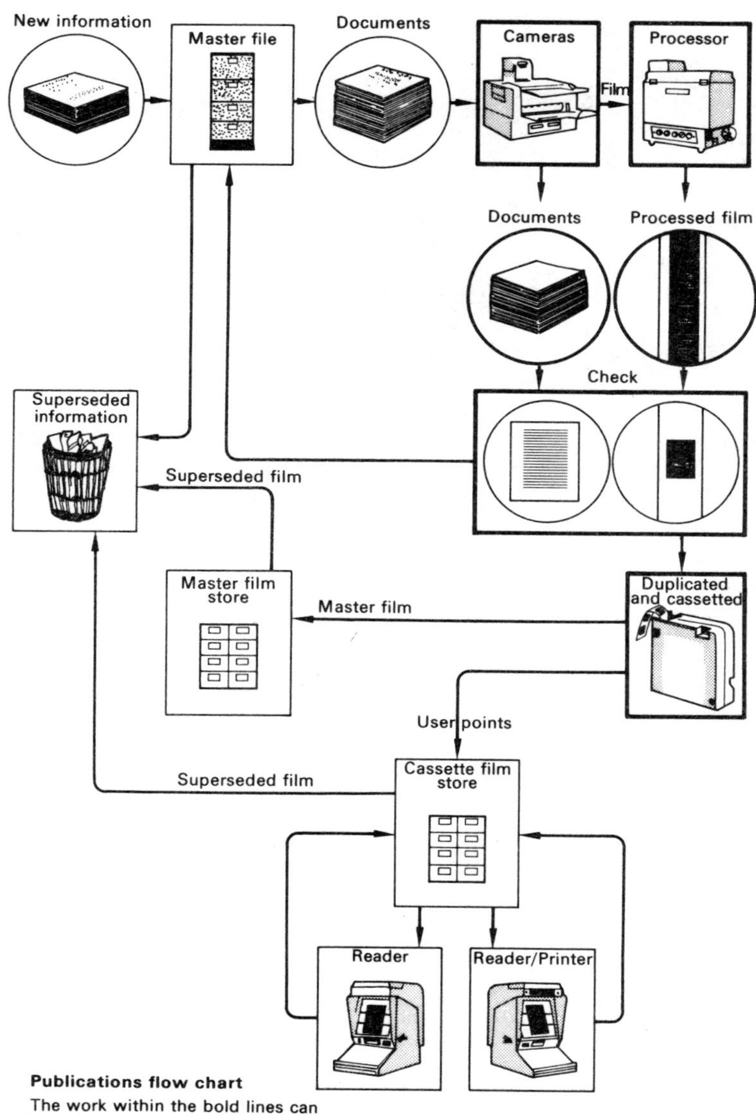

Publications flow chart

The work within the bold lines can be undertaken by an outside agency

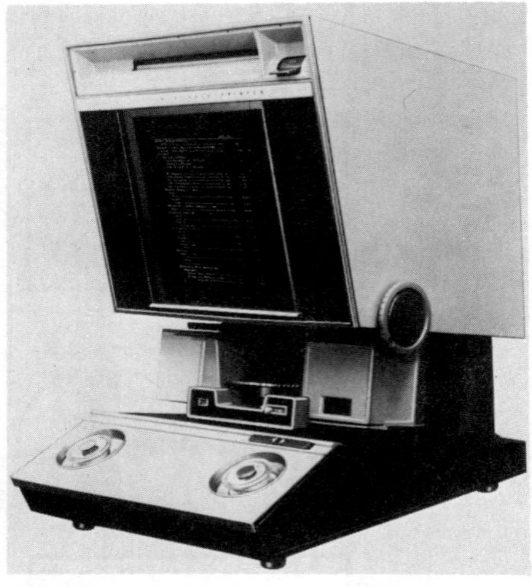

A 3M Microfilm cartridge reader–printer.

Documents should be sorted into correct order before they are filmed. Once microcopied in roll form, the documents never lose their sequence. Suppliers of microcopying materials provide indexing indicators which assist in locating frames in equipment which is not provided with electronic sensing. The microcopies of all documents should be certified by a senior official so that they may be produced as evidence if required at a later date.

Name of Company

Date

Certificate of Intent

Roll No. ....

This is to certify and declare that the MICROFILM records which appear on this roll are accurate and true records of the following category of documents of the above company, and that these records are photographed in the ordinary course of business and are preserved by microphotography on this roll of microfilm, exactly as in the original.

(Here list category of documents)

These records are microfilmed with the specific intention to destroy or otherwise dispose of the original records and to retain in their stead permanent film images in order to save time, space, personnel and filing equipment.
We also certify that the original records recorded on this roll of microfilm will be destroyed or disposed of only after an inspection of the film has ensured the accuracy and completeness of these records and their film images.

....
Camera Operator

....
Senior Executive

Name of Company

Date

11

APPENDIX B

Certificate of Authenticity

Roll No. ....

This is to certify that the MICROFILM images appearing on this roll of microfilm starting with:—

START

ROLL NO.

CERTIFICATE OF INTENT dated

and ending with:—

THIS CERTIFICATE OF AUTHENTICITY dated

ROLL NO.

END

are true and accurate images of the categories of documents referred to in the Certificate of Intent.
These documents were photographed in the ordinary course of business and as a regular part of current office procedures.

....
Camera Operator

....
Senior Executive

March, 1970.

Microcopies of documents should be certified by a senior official. The Chartered Institute of Secretaries suggests that the Certificate of Intent (left) should be filmed first, then the documents, and finally the Certificate of Authenticity (right).

Disposal and destruction, or retention When documents have been micro-copied some of them can be destroyed; others will need to be kept as permanent records in fire resistant cabinets, safes or store-rooms.

There is no statutory obligation as such under the Companies Act (1948) for the permanent retention of any documents and this is a matter upon which each organisation will decide its own policy. A company is, however, required to make its statutory books available for inspection and these books should not be destroyed during the life of the company. Under the Civil Evidence Act 1968 both microfilm and computer records may be produced as evidence, subject to certain conditions.

A list suggesting the types of document, the numbers of copies to be kept and the periods of retention is given in Appendix A of *The Disposal and Retention of Documents* published by the Chartered Institute of Secretaries, e.g.

Certificate of Incorporation	1 master copy to be kept permanently
Patent reports and records	10 years
Banking Records, including cheques, statements, Giro	6 years
M.O.T. vehicle test records	2 years after vehicle disposed of
Customs and Excise returns	5 years
Payrolls	12 years
Tax returns	Permanently

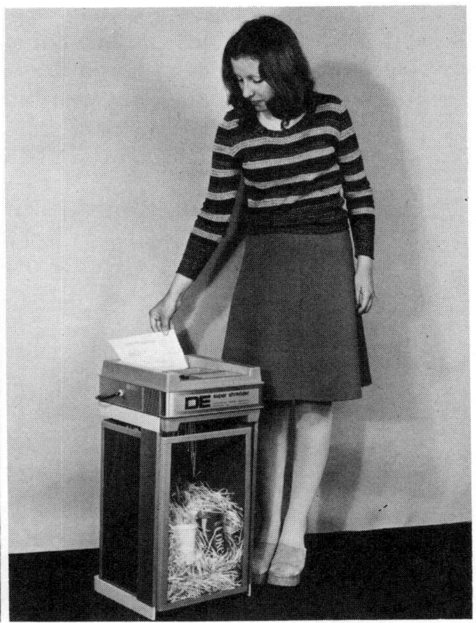

The document-shredder on the left is mobile and can reduce up to 22 sheets of multi-part continuous stationery to unreadable shreds at a rate of 98 feet per minute. Output is collected in disposable plastic bags. The model on the right disposes of single documents.

Unwanted documents can be disposed of (a) as salvage, or (b) by shredding, or (c) by burning. Waste paper can be sold to *salvage companies* who pay a price based on the weight of the paper they take away. Salvage companies frequently provide security arrangements for the disposal of confidential papers.

There are many different *shredding machines* available ranging from small models which will take single sheets of paper to large models which can shred complete files.

Special *incinerators* for office use can also be purchased or arrangements can be made with outside companies for the incineration of confidential and secret documents.

CENTRALISED AND LOCALISED OR DEPARTMENTAL FILING

In a large organisation the storage and retrieval of information may be the responsibility of filing clerks in a centralised department or registry under the supervision of a records manager or head of registry. The advantages and disadvantages of centralised filing may be summarised as follows:

ADVANTAGES

1 Saves space and makes full use of equipment and staff.
2 Uniform methods can be adopted.
3 Specialist staff can be trained.
4 As only filing staff are permitted to handle the files, the files are kept tidily and in good order.
5 Standardised equipment can be installed.

DISADVANTAGES

1 Papers which are needed quickly, for example during a telephone conversation, cannot be immediately brought to hand.
2 Sometimes a person may not be able to give an exact description of a document but he would recognise it if he were allowed to look through several files.
3 Files are not kept near the people who need to work with them.

Many organisations find that a combination of centralised and departmental filing is best suited to their requirements. Individual department heads, managers and executives require their secretaries to handle confidential information, specialised documents and those which are active. Information of a general nature may be kept in the centralised filing department.

In other organisations, current papers may be stored at departmental level and the completed files can be passed to the central filing department at the end of each year.

RECORD-KEEPING

Kinds of records As well as storing papers and documents in files, every office needs to keep records. Whereas files generally group together all the papers relating to particular incidents (such as transactions or projects—**Classification by Subject**) or particular firms or people (such as clients, customers, members of staff—**Classification by Name**), information in the form of records concerning other aspects of an organisation's activities may be stored and classified separately.

All organisations have to keep records of their accounts, but other kinds of records kept depend on the nature of the business. All businesses record the names and addresses of their customers; schools and colleges keep records of students' names, addresses and dates of birth; dentists and doctors keep records of their patients; libraries keep records of all the books they own, as well as keeping separate records of the books on loan and when they should be returned; manufacturers keep records of sales by product, area and representative, and some offices keep a record of all the letters received and those despatched.

The methods of keeping some of these records are described in the chapters on *Finance and Statistics*, *Business Background* and *Mail-handling*, but they are mentioned again here to emphasise the fact that they all form part of the sum total of information which has to be stored in an orderly method so that it can be quickly located. We should also note that the methods and equipment used for keeping these records differ from those used for general filing in which all the various pieces of paper—letters, orders and copies of forms and documents, etc.—are collected together in files or folders allocated to the topics, firms or people to which they refer.

Document Filing One method of record-keeping (sometimes referred to as **Document Filing**) sorts and classifies material according to the type of document, e.g. copies of telegrams and cables, copies of requisitions, advertisements, press releases. A firm's sales records may comprise copies of all the orders received and/or invoices sent out. In these cases, the first classification will be into types of document (orders, invoices, etc.) and the second classification may be chronological, each day's orders being placed in the file on top of the previous day's; the second classification can, of course, be by name of customer, by name of salesman, by sales area or by product—the point to note is that the first classification is by type of document.

When records of this type are kept, it is not uncommon to produce two "office copies" of documents and letters; one copy is kept with the document records and one copy in the file relating to the transaction or customer.

The same principle applies in offices where a complete record is kept of all outgoing correspondence, two copies are taken of each letter, one is the file copy, another (frequently on a special coloured copy paper) is put in a file with all the other outgoing communication.

Record cards Another method of record-keeping uses *record cards*, such as stock control cards, on which new information can easily be entered either by hand or machine so that new facts can be quickly recorded and the up-to-date position immediately noted by glancing at the card (see p. 532).

Visual records A third method of record-keeping uses wall charts, graphs, bar charts, pictograms, etc. These are known as *Visual Record Systems* (see *Chapter 13, Finance and Statistics*, pp. 525–531).

Index cards Many record-keeping systems incorporate indexing. An index is an alphabetical list of subjects or names; some indexes (like the card index used in connection with Numerical Filing or the index at the back of a book) tell us where to find further information on the subject we have looked up. Other indexing systems give all the information needed on the actual index card; a stock card, for example, states all the issues from stock, the deliveries of new stock, maximum, minimum and re-order levels, etc. (see page 532).

Indexes, whether they are in list or card form, must be arranged according to the rules given for dividing titles into indexing units and sorting into alphabetical order given on page 253.

Equipment LOOSE-LEAF BOOKS The pages in loose-leaf books are not permanently fixed; in other words, although the pages are held together by devices such as rings or thongs, they may be taken out and rearranged in any order, and new pages can be inserted as required. Loose-leaf systems are flexible and provide facilities for expansion, but pages can be taken out and may not be replaced. When loose-leaf books contain valuable or confidential records this is a serious disadvantage as pages can be lost. For this reason some loose-leaf books can be locked and only the person holding the key can remove or insert pages. A further disadvantage of loose-leaf books is that the ring-holes sometimes get torn; when this happens the holes should be reinforced.

CARD INDEX DRAWERS keep records in alphabetical or numerical order. The cards can be separated by guide cards and OUT cards should be used to indicate when a card has been taken out. This method is capable of indefinite expansion but it has several disadvantages: the cards are thicker than the sheets in a loose-leaf system, therefore the drawer is heavier to move; loose cards can be easily removed and not returned; and if the drawer is upset all the cards can fall out and it takes a considerable time to put them all back correctly.

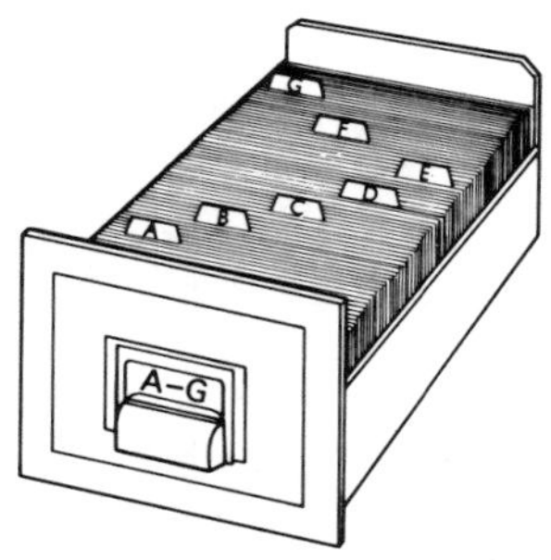

A card index drawer.

VISIBLE CARD INDEXES In this system between fifty and sixty cards are held in a flat metal drawer which fits into a cabinet. The names on all the cards are immediately visible. The cabinet shown in the illustration below has fifteen drawers and will therefore hold over seven hundred and fifty cards. The firms who manufacture these visible card systems will print cards specially designed to suit the requirements of a particular office.

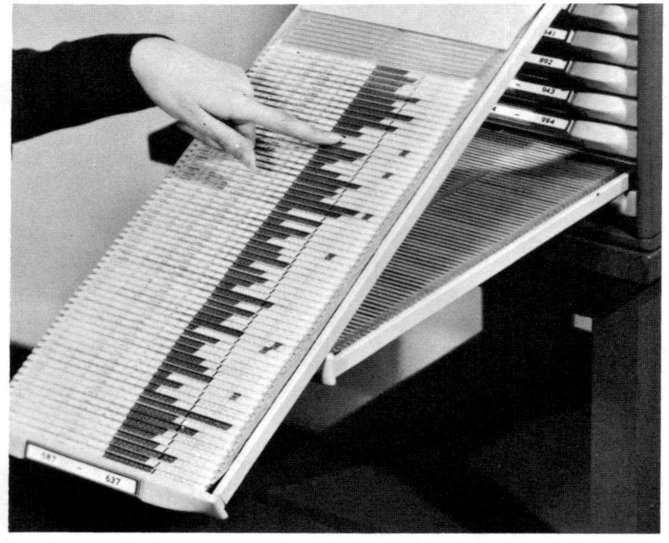

Visible card index showing signals.

Additional information can be recorded by clipping coloured metal or plastic signals to the edges of the cards. These *coloured flash signals* form a pattern as shown in the photograph above.

STRIP INDEXES In a visible card index, only the edges of the cards appear, giving the appearance of a number of strips. A further development of visible indexing is the strip index which does, in fact, consist only of strips, giving information such as a mailing list. Strip indexes are easily kept in alphabetical order. They may be stored in drawers or on stands.

ROTARY SYSTEMS In rotary systems the cards are stored on wheels which revolve and enable any card to be quickly located.

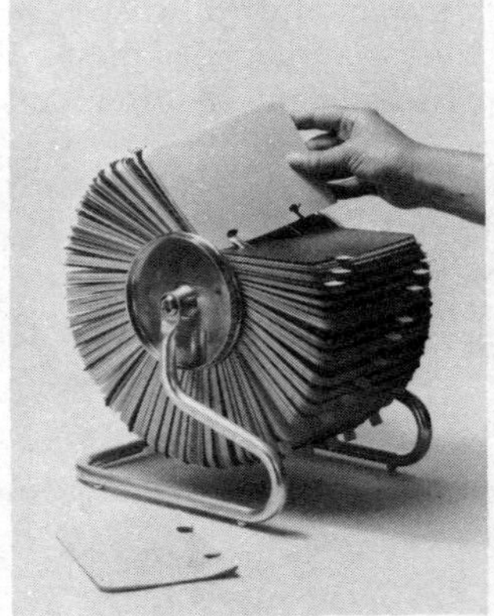

Rotary card index systems may be large (as shown on the left) or small. The illustration on the right shows a wheel holding very small cards; it is called the 'Mini-Cardwheel' and is suitable for keeping records of addresses, membership, credit ratings. Various models are available, holding from 600 to 4800 cards.

PUNCHED CARDS Sometimes it is necessary to select quickly from a number of cards all those marked with the same item or items of information. A simple way is to punch information instead of writing it on to a card. Holes are put in the appropriate sections to denote certain items such as department, age group, sex, etc. If you wish to pick out, for example, all the female employees in any one department, a rod is slid through all the punched holes for 'female' and another through the hole for the appropriate department. In one method, all the cards so punched are lifted; in another method, all the cards except the ones wanted are lifted clear, so that the required cards can be examined and listed. The photograph on p. 281 illustrates this latter method.

The Paramount punched card sorting system.

APPLICATIONS AND DEVELOPMENTS

When you take up your first appointment and whenever you change your job and start work in a new office, you will almost certainly find that there is a filing system already in existence. Your first task, of course, will be to study the existing filing system until you have thoroughly mastered its principles.

When you have learnt how to operate it without undue anxiety or hesitation, you may find you are able to suggest ways in which it can be improved. You may even feel that a strong case could be made for scrapping the entire system and setting up a new and more efficient one of your own invention. You might submit a report to this effect to your executive as a result of which he might give you authority to go ahead and implement your proposals.

Or your executive might say to you when you have been working for him for a few months, "I'm not too happy about our filing system. It's not particularly efficient; it really does take up a lot of valuable space and it's years since anyone took a critical look at it. Now that you've had time to learn something about our business and the type of information and documents we have to file and find, perhaps you'd jot down any ideas you have about how the system can be improved. If you think we should scrap the whole thing and start a completely new system, please don't hesitate to be completely frank."

Bearing in mind what we have already learnt about filing and record-keeping, the following notes on applications and developments may help you to assess the efficiency of a filing system, to suggest changes and improvements, or to propose a completely new system.

1 Consider the most suitable method of classification, bearing in mind,

   a the type of information to be stored (folders, carbon copies, brochures, pamphlets, stencils, business reply dockets),

b the amount to be stored, i.e. the physical volume,
c which officials and the number of different people who will seek the information,
d how often the information will be needed—generally speaking, the more recent the information, the more frequently it is needed; in other words, frequency of access decreases with age.

2 Choose the most suitable equipment, bearing in mind points 1a–d above, and also,

e risk of fire, theft, flood, damage by extremes of temperature and humidity,
f risk of espionage,
g cost of storage equipment and floor space.

3 Consider the most suitable location, bearing in mind,

a floor space available,
b cost of floor space,
c the numbers of users,
d proximity of users.

4 Institute a cross-reference system if the same information will be needed by different users because the captions under which people seek information differ according to the work the people do, e.g. a scientist and an advertising manager might need the same information but they would probably look under different headings.

5 Establish a control procedure for

a issuing or "charging out" files and folders,
b using a File Register,
c using ABSENT or OUT cards to replace files and folders,
d using SUBSTITUTION or OUT sheets to replace documents (although the withdrawal of a document from a folder should be discouraged and can be avoided if a copying machine is available).

6 Produce a List of Files showing main classifications and subdivisions.

7 Establish a procedure for transfer from active to semi-active or non-active by considering the type of record and the space available. Transfer can be either *continuous*, e.g. when a folder is full, or *periodic*, e.g. at the end of every three or six months.

8 Consider the economics of microfilming and decide which documents can be microfilmed and at what stage in their life. Consider, according to the policy laid down by the Company Secretary, which documents can be destroyed and the methods of disposal.

9 Recommend how archives and inactive documents should be stored, and where and how the storage cartons should be marked.

10 Establish a Retention Sequence in card index form for each type of record showing,

- a where it is kept at each stage of its life,
- b how it is classified,
- c when and how it is transferred,
- d its retention or disposal.

11 Make sure filing cabinets are not allowed to become top-heavy and that the drawers are always closed after use.

12 Consider the use of colour. Different coloured paper for carbon copies, coloured signals and tabs assist sorting and retrieving.

13 Remove paper clips before filing papers. Single sheets are easily trapped by clips and pins. If it is necessary to attach carbon copies to the letters answered, staple them together.

14 Place papers 'squarely' in the folder so that they do not become creased. Projecting papers make a set of folders look untidy and may hide the tab or index flap.

15 Before you go home in the evening, make sure the filing cabinet is locked, if this is the practice in your office.

16 Do not make the mistake of thinking that the most expensive equipment is always the best. Sometimes the simplest device as well as being the cheapest is also the best, because it is the most suitable for the circumstances. Filing methods and equipment must be selected to suit (a) the physical size of the documents, (b) the reason why they are kept, (c) the length of time they must be kept, and (d) the frequency of referral.

Section 2: Data Storage and Retrieval

COMPUTERS

Computers have the capacity to store, retrieve and manipulate information at great speed. All operations performed by a computer are specified by a series of instructions known as a *program*, which is usually initially input to the computer on punched cards. The program is stored on a *peripheral* (see page 287 and diagram on page 286) and may be called into *core store* and executed when desired.

Information processing by a computer can be illustrated by an airline ticket booking system. The booking clerk sends the customer's request for a flight to the computer by *keying-in* (typing) the required information, e.g.

flight no./date/number of seats/class/single or return

on the keyboard of a console on his desk. The computer program will check the request against data files which contain up-to-date information of all flights. If the request can be met, the details will be repeated on the visual display unit of the booking clerk's console for customer confirmation, and the data files will be immediately updated with the booking when the confirmation is keyed-in. If the request cannot be met, a message will be displayed and the booking clerk may request alternative flights which he can offer to the customer.

A Burroughs TC500 Branch Terminal.

A second illustration is the clearing banks' computer system. Each transaction will be recorded at the banks' computer centre so that accounts can be updated with debits and credits as is appropriate by the type of transaction. A customer's balance may be recalculated after each posting. In the illustration above, information is being keyed-in on a Burroughs TC500 Branch Terminal. The operator is transmitting data from a bank headquarters to a computer centre where it will be stored until it is needed. When a customer wants to know his balance, the information is produced by the computer centre and relayed back to the branch within a very short time.

These examples show the use of computers in two aspects of life with which almost everyone is familiar. The well-informed businessman or woman will want to understand these operations in more detail in order to appreciate the increasing importance of computers in industry today and the ways in which electronic data processing can improve business efficiency.

A computer can be divided into two functions—a Central Processing Unit (CPU) and a number of other units and devices, usually referred to as *peripherals*. The relationship between the CPU and the peripherals is shown in the diagram below.

ICL 1901A computer installation.

Central Processing Unit The Central Processing Unit consists of a Control Unit, a Core Store and an Arithmetic Unit.

The CONTROL UNIT manipulates data within the Core Store, controls the Arithmetic Unit and all the peripheral units and devices, and orders and co-ordinates the whole system so that it functions according to the *program*, that is the list of operating instructions which the computer has been instructed to perform.

The CORE STORE, also known as the *Memory Unit* or *Immediate Access Store* (IAS), is used as a short-term memory and holds data which is to be processed.

The ARITHMETIC UNIT performs the actual calculations. All operations performed by a computer can be reduced to adding, subtracting and comparing two values to distinguish whether they are equal, greater or smaller.

CENTRAL PROCESSING UNIT (CPU)

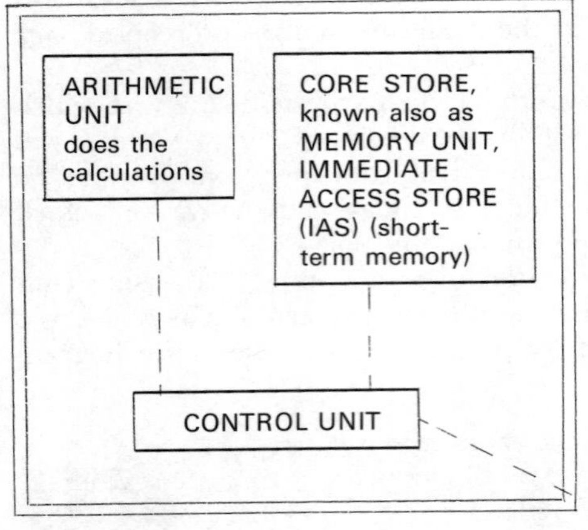

PERIPHERALS

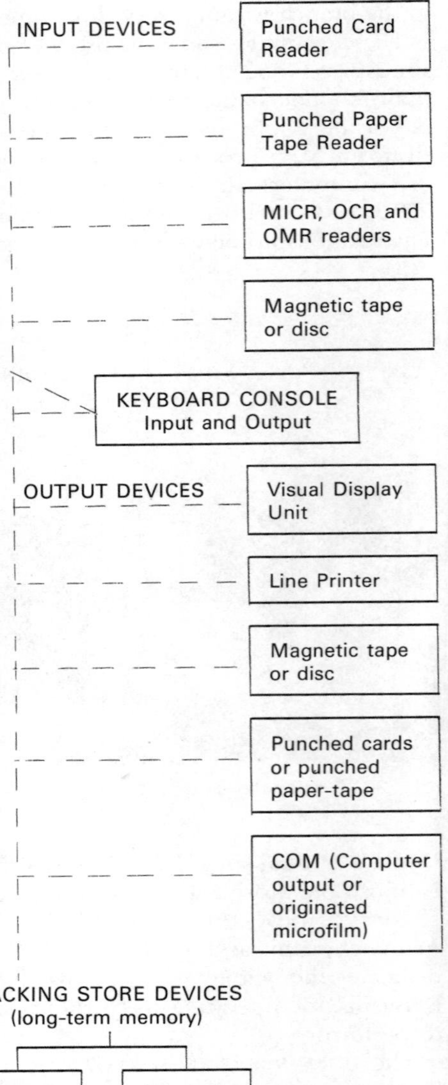

A computer installation consists of a Central processing Unit (CPU) and a number of peripheral units on which data may be stored, either as input or as output (*backing store devices*). The CPU and the peripherals may be in one room or building or many miles apart, e.g. users of a computer bureau or organisations such as banks where branch terminals are connected to a main computer centre. Terminal units are connected to computer centres and bureaux by the Post office Telecommunications Datel services.

Computer Peripherals Peripherals may be input, backing store or output devices.

1 INPUT DEVICES

a Card Reader which reads data recorded on punched cards.
b Paper-tape Reader which reads data recorded on punched paper-tape.
c Magnetic Ink Character Reader which can read characters written in magnetic ink.
d Optical character Reader which uses light to recognise characters.
e Optical Mark Reader which scans documents to locate and identify marks.
f Console unit keyboard.

2 BACKING STORE DEVICES

a Magnetic tape } These are used for long-term storage and fast input and
b Magnetic disc } fast output.

3 OUTPUT DEVICES

a Line-printers which produce sheets of print-out.
b Visual display units where the output is displayed in a temporary form on a screen similar to a television screen.
c Magnetic tape and disc.
d Punched cards or punched paper-tape.
e Computer originated or computer output microfilm.
f The Console.

4 CONSOLE

The console is a communicating unit which can be used for both slow input and slow output.

INPUT DEVICES Of the four main types of input device the character reader has the highest speed:

Character reader	up to 1500 characters per second
Card reader	up to 1333 characters per second
Paper-tape reader	up to 1000 characters per second
Keyboard entry	up to 10 characters per second

Punched cards are at present one of the most popular methods of input to computers. The cards are prepared by **keypunch operators** and checked by **verifiers**.

When the cards have been punched and checked, they are presented to the computer system in batches which are placed in the hopper of an input device called a **card reader**. Card readers can read at rates from 300 to 1000 cards a minute; as each card has eighty columns of data, this means that data can be transferred at a rate of between 24,000 and 80,000 characters per minute.

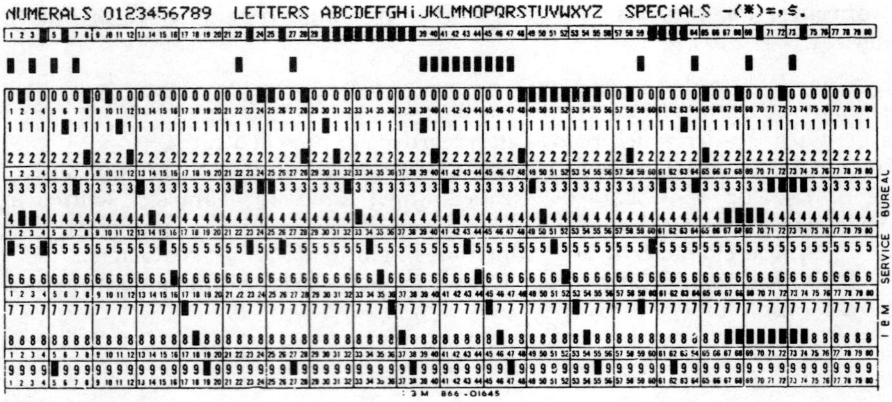

A punched card.

As its name implies, *punched paper-tape* consists of a very long strip of paper in which characters of data are recorded by punching holes across the tape.

A typical reel of paper-tape is $8\frac{1}{4}$ in (200 mm) in diameter, approximately 300 m (1000 ft) long and capable of containing up to 120,000 characters of data in continuous form. The tape may have either five, six, seven, or eight tracks. In the illustration you can see a sample of eight-track paper-tape code; the eighth track is used for checking purposes by making sure during the reading stage that all holes punched in the tape have been detected.

The tape to be read is placed in a bin and fed by roller into the reader at speeds of up to 250 cm (100 in) per second. As data is recorded on tape at ten characters to the inch, the reading speed is 1000 characters per second.

Paper-tape is prepared either by manual punching and verifying, or as a by-product of another system, such as an accounting machine, a teleprinter or an automatic typewriter (see page 212).

Paper-tape and punched card inputs function at similar speeds; the punching and verifying methods are also similar, although paper-tape has the advantage that it can be prepared as the by-product of another operation. Punched cards are durable and can be easily sorted; tape is cheaper, but less durable; it is easier to store, but as the records are held on a strip they are in a fixed sequence and cannot be re-arranged.

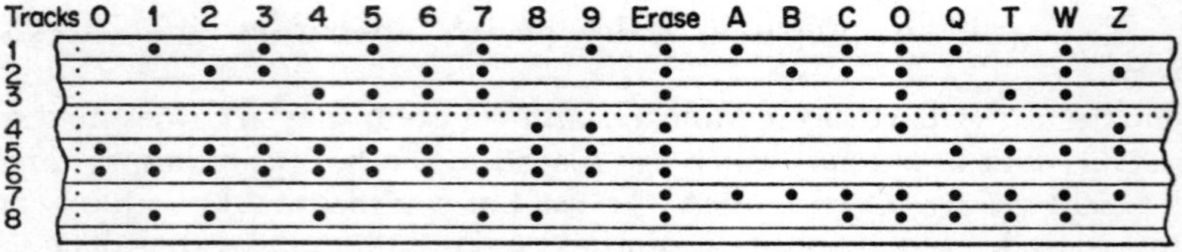

Sample Eight-Track Paper-Tape Code.

Magnetic Ink Character Recognition (MICR) has been developed primarily for use in banks where the cheque is the "original document" bearing the information or data to be processed. The basis of MICR is the use of specially designed characters which are printed in a ferrous-based ink which enables them to be magnetised prior to reading. When the document is fed into a magnetic ink character reader, the pattern of the characters is detected and transmitted in the form of impulses to the computer processor.

Before a new cheque book is issued to a customer each cheque in the book is printed with the bank branch number, the customer account number and the cheque number in MICR fount. When the used cheque returns to the bank, the amount the customer has written on the cheque is encoded ('post-coding') so that all the necessary data is magnetically recorded on the cheque. The cheques can be 'read' by a *reader/sorter* which can handle 1200 documents a minute—reading the documents, feeding the data into a computer and sorting the documents into a pre-determined order. An add-lister can be attached to the reader/sorter which lists and totals each cheque as it is read.

Optical Character Recognition (OCR) reads alpha-numeric characters in a special fount by scanning them with a beam of light; the light is reflected on to a lens where it is focused on a photo-electric cell and the cell produces a unique electric current for each character, which generates input signals for the computer.

Optical Mark Recognition (OMR) also utilises light scanning. A series of photo-electric cells scan a document looking for a mark or the absence of a mark within a pre-determined area or grid; when the mark is detected, its position and value is identified and a unique input signal is generated.

The slowest way of putting data into a computer is from the *keyboard of the console unit*; it is, however, a direct operation. The operator types, or *keys-in*, the data which is transmitted to the control unit, where it is retained until the operator presses an 'END OF MESSAGE' key. The data can then be processed or the entire record can be stored away on magnetic tape or disc in the backing store. Several keyboards can be connected to the same control unit as the control unit works very much more quickly than the keyboard, but because of this limited typewriting speed, keyboard entry is not normally used for bulk input, but mainly for interrogation, e.g. the airline clerk who wants to find out whether seats are available on a particular flight or by a computer bureau user working *on-line*, that is, directly connected to the central processing unit (see page 300).

BACKING STORE DEVICES Once information has been fed into the computer and processed by the Central Processing Unit, the data which is required for temporary or permanent storage can be recorded by the computer itself on magnetic tape or magnetic disc. These fast input and output media are known as backing store devices.

Just as *magnetic tape* can record sound on a standard tape-recorder, it can also record data. Magnetic tape is usually seven or nine-track. To record, for example, the records of 10,000 employees on magnetic tape, a card would be punched for each employee and the computer would then be instructed (programmed) to record all the information on to magnetic tape. As the cards were read by the computer, the information from each card would be recorded in **serial form** on to a reel of magnetic tape.

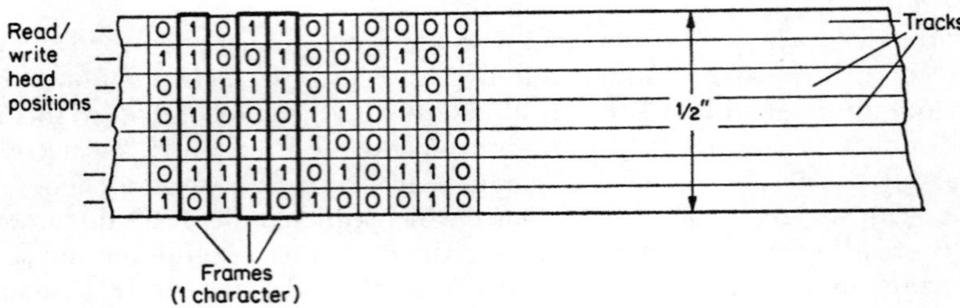

Data Recording on Tape.

The international standard for magnetic tape lays down that data should be recorded with 800 frames to the inch (32 to the millimetre). The **transfer rate** (the rate at which data is transferred between the store of the processor and the tape unit) is obtained by multiplying the frames to the inch by the tape movement speed in inches per second. The result is in characters per second. Transfer rates can be between 60,000 and 200,000 characters per second (abbreviated to 60 Kch/s and 200 Kch/s).

Using a 60 Kch/s tape unit and a 1000 card/min reader the record cards of the 10,000 employees referred to in the example above would be read in 10 minutes and transferred on to magnetic tape in about 120 seconds. As tape reading and writing are done at the same speed, this means that any subsequent searching of the tape containing the complete file of 10,000 employees would take about two minutes.

Files recorded on magnetic tape can be updated by creating a tape of amendments and programming the computer to produce a new updated master file on a separate reel of tape from the old master file tape and the amendments file tape.

Magnetic tape is a **serial processing device**, this means a file must always be processed by reading every record—that is, running through the whole tape; and every alteration requires making a new tape.

In the same way as magnetic tape may be compared to tapes which record sound on tape-recorders, *magnetic discs* may be likened to gramophone records, as information on magnetic discs is recorded on tracks. The great advantage of discs over tapes is that information does not have to be read sequentially, but records may be directly (or randomly) accessed. This makes discs suitable for files of information when the volume of records to be accessed is low in comparison to the total number of records, or where the accessing cannot be sorted into a defined sequence. It is possible to locate any point or track on a magnetic disc within ten or twenty milliseconds (a millisecond is one-thousandth of a second). This speed of location is known as **access time** and the fact that discs offer **direct** or **random access** makes them a suitable storage medium for information which is required very quickly, e.g. prices of stocks and shares.

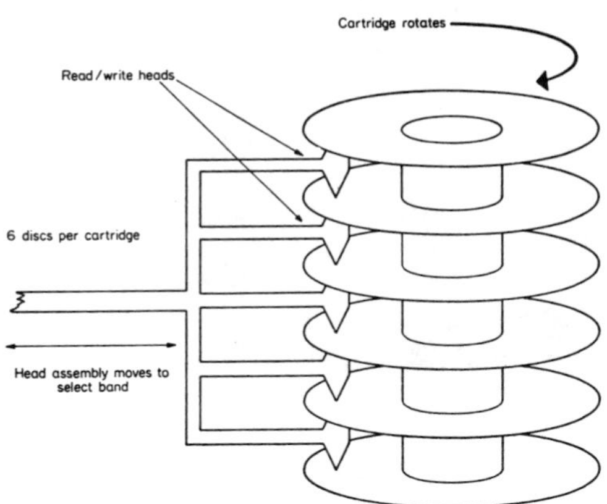

Disc Cartridge.

The disc units are usually provided as a pack, or cartridge, of six discs and a transport of cabinet with read/write heads. When information is wanted from a disc, the cartridge is loaded on the transport and the read/write head is programmed to locate and read the specified information. A cartridge can contain up to eight million characters of data; the access time is about one hundred milliseconds and the transfer rate is approximately 200 Kch/s.

OUTPUT DEVICES As the purpose of computers is to provide information, the output must be in the most useful form for the person who needs the information. There are several different methods of computer output; each of them originates from electrical impulses in the central processor.

Line-printers operate on the same principle as the typewriter and are the most usual method of output because the print-out can be read directly by the user. Continuous stationery is used for line-printers; the print-out can be produced at speeds of up to 1500 lines of print per minute.

Another familiar type of output is the *visual display unit* where the output is displayed in a temporary form on a screen similar to a television screen. More sophisticated Visual Display Units incorporate a camera which records the data in a permanent form and enables the user to alter the displayed matter, e.g. a drawing, by moving a **light pen** over the surface—the light pen electronically erases existing lines and makes modifications.

Computers used by BEA's booking services.

It is possible to record output directly from the processor on to peripherals such as *magnetic tape or disc*. As the line-printer works so very much more slowly than the Central Processing Unit, it is often more convenient to record directly on to magnetic tape or disc from the CPU. The tapes or discs can subsequently be used to pass the results to the line-printer *off-line*, that is, not connected to the central processing unit. The advantage of using peripherals in this way is that the CPU is available to work on other programmes during the (comparatively long) print-out time.

Another output device is the direct production of *punched cards* or *punched paper-tape*. This is a relatively slow method and not very commonly used unless the output in the form of cards or tape is needed as input for some other equipment.

The newest output device is *computer output microfilm* or *computer originated microfilm* (COM). This is the direct generation of microfilm from a computer with no intermediate paper print-out. It is an extremely efficient method of handling vast quantities of data and occupies considerably less space than the equivalent amount of paper.

There are several COM methods. One method uses computer-produced magnetic tape and converts it into human readable data on microfilm by producing the images on a cathode ray tube and photographing them. In another method the output from the converter is projected from an electron beam gun which shoots the characters in microform directly on to film.

Until the introduction of COM the hard-copy output of a computer was restricted to the speed of the output printer and occupied a considerable amount of space. COM enables computer output to be produced direct on

The Kodak KOM90 Computer Output Microcilmer converts computer-produced magnetic tape directly into human readable data on microfilm. The computer information on the magnetic tape is translated on to microfilm at rates of up to 90,000 characters per second.

microfilm; copies that can be read with the aid of a reader can be made as required. The latest microfilm reader-printer will produce a readable full-size copy of any selected microfilm frame simply by having the 'PRINT' button pressed when the required document is in view on the screen (see page 292).

The CONSOLE has a typewriter keyboard and can be used to feed instructions directly into the computer. Information from the computer can also be received and printed out directly in the same way as Telex, teleprinter or teletype machines receive messages. The console is a slow input and slow output device.

USING COMPUTERS

Many computer systems operate on a method known as *batch processing* whereby the punched cards are submitted to the computer centre and processed at a time determined by the manager or supervisor. The user has no contact with the job whilst it is being carried out, but the supervisor can ensure that the computer time is fully utilised.

The method known as *time-sharing* enables a large number of users to communicate directly and also simultaneously with a central computer. Each of the users has a unit called a **terminal** from which he can communicate with the central computer. The terminal can be a teletype or visual display unit or both. Each terminal has a **buffer store** and the central processing unit of the computer is continuously scanning all the buffer stores and dealing with their individual instructions. A request for information keyed-in from a terminal is transmitted to a buffer store where the central processing unit of the computer deals with it—that is, accepts the instructions and produces the information—within microseconds (a microsecond is a one-millionth of a second). As this speed is millions of times faster than the keying-in or print-out speed of the terminal, the central processing unit can deal with each terminal simultaneously.

INSTRUCTING THE COMPUTER

Some firms have their own computers and data processing machines, others use computer bureaux. Bureau-users are connected with the computer bureau from teletype terminals by the public switching network using the Post Office Telecommunications Datel services (see page 428).

When a firm opens an account with a computer bureau, it is given an account number and a user's handbook. When the user wants to use the computer he must follow a prescribed routine known as the **logging-in procedure**, e.g.

a Dial the telephone number of the computer bureau.

b When the user hears the whistling note (which is the sound generated by the computer's modem*) he knows he is connected to the computer.

c The user switches on his own modem which converts his telephone from a speech carrying medium into a data link and thus completes the connection between his terminal and the computer.

d The user then keys-in his name (which can be a contrived name such as a telegraphic address), his account number and a pass-word. These particulars prevent the system from being used illegally (for example, they prevent industrial espionage such as one user assessing another user's information) and ensure that the correct user is invoiced for the computer time used.

Whether the computer is being used in a time-sharing mode or for batch processing, it must be given certain basic information:

a The 'language' which will be used must be defined. There are about ten commonly used international computer languages; each language has been devised for a specific area of operations, e.g. mathematics, accountancy, stock control. The language designed for business use is COBOL, COmmon Business Oriented Language.

b The computer is told
   (i) where it is going to find the input data, e.g. from a card reader, a paper-tape reader, a magnetic tape or disc reader,
   (ii) the format, that is the identity of each item of input data. For example, if the user wishes to store in the computer the population of each town in the British Isles, the data could be entered in blocks

* See page 300

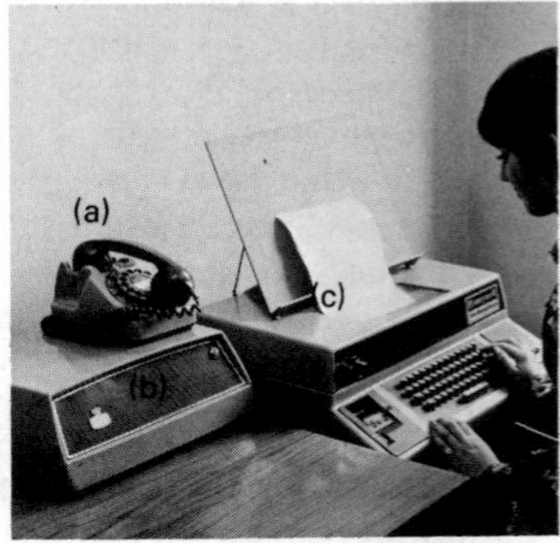

A time-sharing terminal at Honeywell's London centre. (a) the telephone, (b) the modem, (c) the paper tape unit.

of three items—town, county, population. In the format instruction the computer would be told that, reading across the line, the three numbers would represent town, county, population,

(iii) where the user wants the output data, e.g. line-printer, teletype or back on to magnetic disc or tape for future use,

(iv) how the user wants the output displayed or stored, e.g. in columns, on specially prepared business forms (pre-printed stationery) which would have been previously fed into the output printer.

c The computer must be provided with a set of instructions telling it how to manipulate the input data; this is the **program**. The program may have been previously written and stored in which case the user merely has to tell the computer which program is to be used; or the program can be part of the input information.

For certain specialised applications where the situation is constant and the computer is always required to carry out the same operation, e.g. the airline booking system or a pay-roll operation, the information will be permanently pre-programmed.

Television-type display in the office of a stockbroker's client allows direct access to the broker's central computer for up-to-date share and company information.

To summarise, the computer can accept data in the form of punched cards, punched paper-tape, magnetic ink characters, optically readable characters or marks, magnetic tape, magnetic disc or by direct keyboard entry. The computer is given a set of instructions, called the program; the program is usually prepared on punched paper-tape or punched cards or magnetic tape or disc.

Computers can be used on-line in a time-sharing system, or off-line in a processing system.

The computer can be instructed to retrieve and produce information in readable form by (i) visual displays, e.g. the television display shown in the illustration on page 299 and the consoles in airline offices, or (ii) hard-copy print-out on line-printers or teletype machines, or (iii) microfilm which can be put into a reader/printer which will produce copies of selected frames.

Accessories Special accessories and storage equipment has been designed to house the cards, tapes and discs which have to be filed for future retrieval.

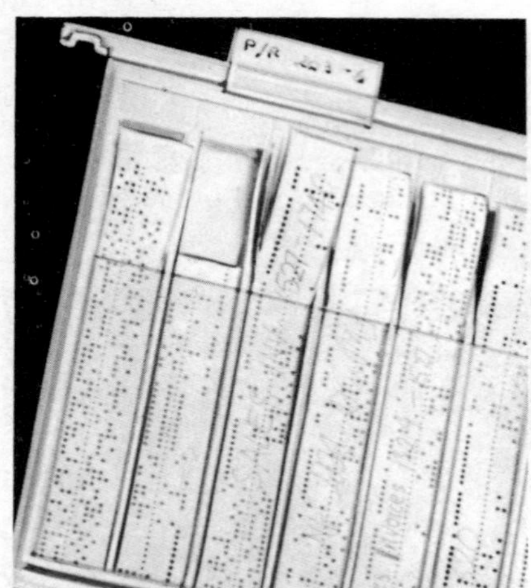

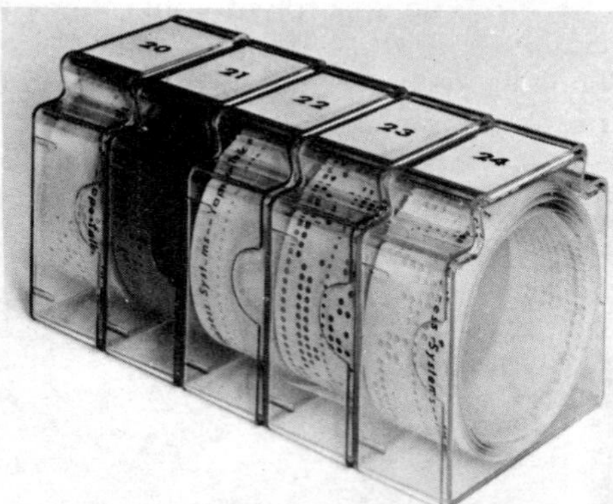

Two methods of storing punched paper tape. (Left) Twinlock runners for suspension filing cabinet. (Right) Paper Tape Storage Boxes produced by Data Efficiency Ltd.

As shown in the illustration above, punched paper tape can either be stored in a suspension filing cabinet in a runner fitted with twelve clear plastic pockets designed to hold lengths of tape, or it can be stored in transparent plastic boxes identified by numbered labels, as shown above.

Magnetic discs and tapes can be stored on racks and in fireproof safes as shown in the illustration on page 297.

APPLICATIONS AND DEVELOPMENTS

1 Recorded information which will be used in the order in which it has been recorded, such as lists of names and addresses, is most usually stored on magnetic tape because information is retrieved from magnetic tape by *serial access* (starting at the beginning of the tape until the required part is used). For example, lists of names which are required once a month would be stored on magnetic tape.

(Left) Fireproof safe for storing magnetic tape reels and disc packs. (Right) Disc storage unit.

2 Magnetic discs are used in cases where *random access* (widely scattered references) is required. For example, stock market prices which are being continuously updated and referenced.

3 In addition to adding, subtracting and storing information, the computer can also make comparisons. For example, a computer calculating salaries and wages can calculate how much tax should be deducted for the month or week by comparing the 'tax due' amount with the 'tax paid' amount; if the tax paid is greater than the tax due, the computer calculates the amount of the refund and adds this to the salary for the month.

4 An important use of computers is to provide management with accurate forecasts of the position of the business in the future, e.g. how much stock will be required at certain times, what additional staff and materials will be required for particular tasks, how many machines will lie vacant or be occupied.

5 A computer can be thought of as a man sitting at his desk planning his work and carrying some of it out. He has his files for reference, his IN tray and his OUT tray, and his mind or calculating machine. He may also have some last-minute reminders as rough notes scribbled on his blotting pad. The computer has files or 'storage units'; it has an 'input' and an 'output' and an arithmetic or calculating system. The information is fed in; the machine works upon it in the manner directed by the programme; and the results are printed out either by tabulators or by electric type-

writers, teleprinters or high-speed printing devices. The results may be stored on magnetic tape or disc, or in the machine itself, or on microfilm, and the files of the future may well look like the illustrations on page 297. Instead of pieces of paper, files and cards, businesses will gradually become accustomed to records which cannot be looked up at present, but which will have to be interpreted or read by a computer, which will then print out the information required.

6 Computer magnetic tapes and discs cannot be recommended at present for the retention of permanent records for long periods because there has not yet been sufficient time for ageing tests to be carried out, and there is the possibility that the recording codes used may not be legible to computers of the future.

7 Magnetic tapes and discs must be very carefully stored and handled, e.g. tapes should be kept away from areas of electrical disturbance, such as a transformer above ground or the motor compartment of an underground train, as the magnetic flux emitted from these sources can demagnetise the tapes and thus destroy the records!

GLOSSARY OF COMPUTER TERMS

ACCESS TIME is the time taken to locate data stored on a PERIPHERAL DEVICE.

ACCESSING means retrieving information (data) from a PERIPHERAL DEVICE.

ARITHMETIC UNIT is the part of the CENTRAL PROCESSING UNIT which performs the actual calculations.

BACKING STORE DEVICES are magnetic tapes or magnetic discs on which data is stored either temporarily or permanently. The backing store supplements the main memory of the CENTRAL PROCESSING UNIT. Backing store devices are fast input and output media on which data is recorded by the computer itself.

BATCH PROCESSING is the method of processing in which all the input intion is prepared beforehand and submitted to the computer centre in the form of punched paper tape, punched card and file references of any magnetic disc or tape required for the program. The batches are processed at a time determined by the supervisor who is responsible for the efficient use of computer time. Batch processing is suitable for the daily processing of orders; it contrasts with REAL-TIME PROCESSING in which data is received, acted upon and a response is transmitted within seconds or possibly minutes, as in the case of airline seat booking systems.

BUFFER STORE is an intermediate store between two units, e.g. the CENTRAL PROCESSING UNIT and a TERMINAL UNIT.

CENTRAL PROCESSING UNIT (CPU) is the centre of the computer installation which controls all the peripheral units. It consists of a Control Unit, a CORE STORE and an ARITHMETIC UNIT.

COMPUTER OUTPUT (or ORIGINATED) MICROFILM (COM) is microfilm generated directly from the computer with no intermediate paper print-out.

CORE STORE also known as the MEMORY UNIT or IMMEDIATE ACCESS STORE (IAS) is part of the CENTRAL PROCESSING UNIT. It is used as a short-term memory and holds data which is to be processed.

DATA is the computer term for information.

DATEL SERVICES are the services provided by the Post Office Telecommunications for the transmission of data between terminal units and computer centres. Datel Services use telephone or telegraph lines to transmit electronic signals. (See page 428, *Chapter 10, Correspondence and Communications.*)

DIRECT (or RANDOM) ACCESS is the location of data as it is required regardless of the sequence in which it is stored. It applies to data stored on magnetic discs and contrasts with SERIAL ACCESS necessary for magnetic tapes which have to be read sequentially. Random access enables any point or track on a magnetic disc to be located within ten or twenty milliseconds—a millisecond is one-thousandth of a second.

HARDWARE is the word used for the machinery used in data processing and contrasts with SOFTWARE, i.e. the program.

IMMEDIATE ACCESS STORE see CORE STORE.

INPUT is the word used for data which is fed into a computer.

KEY-IN to type information on the keyboard (QWERTY) of the console which is part of a unit in a computer installation.

LEASED NETWORKS are private networks allocated to a customer to enable him to communicate with another office, e.g. branch office or factory with head office; printed messages use a leased telegraph line and a teleprinter line and a teleprinter machine; spoken messages use a leased telephone line.

LOGGING-IN PROCEDURE is the routine a user must follow when he wants to use the computer bureau with which he has an account. The logging-in procedure prevents one user being able to gain access to another user's information.

MEMORY UNIT see CORE STORE.

MICR (MAGNETIC INK CHARACTER RECOGNITION) is the name given to the process by which a computer can 'read' information printed on cheques using a special fount. The characters are printed on cheques in a ferrous-based ink which enables them to be magnetised prior to reading.

MODEM is a machine which converts the signals from the teletype or computer into a form which can be transmitted over the telecommunication lines. The word *modem* is made up from two words *modulator* and *demodulator*; the modulator encodes the information which is to be fed into the telecommunication line and the demodulator decodes the information received from the line. (See page 428, *Chapter 10, Correspondence and Communications.*)

NETWORKS or CIRCUITS are the systems of wires and cables developed by the Post Office Telecommunications to transmit messages (telegraph) and the human voice (telephone).

OCR (OPTICAL CHARACTER RECOGNITION) is the process by which alphanumeric characters in a special fount can be 'read' by scanning them with a beam of light.

OFF-LINE is not directly connected to the computer, that is, not physically connected at that point of time when it is being used.

OMR (OPTICAL MARK RECOGNITION) utilises light scanning to detect the presence or absence of a mark within a pre-determined area or grid.

ON-LINE means that the operation is being carried out in direct connection with the central processing unit at that actual point in time.

OUTPUT is information which is produced by or retrieved from a computer.

PERIPHERALS or COMPUTER PERIPHERALS or PERIPHERAL DEVICES are the various units which are used (a) to input data to the computer, (b) to produce output or (c) to house the storage media.

RANDOM ACCESS see DIRECT ACCESS.

REMOTE TERMINAL SYSTEM is a system in which the terminal is far from the computer.

SERIAL ACCESS is the method of locating information by searching for it in the order in which it has been stored. Magnetic tape is serial accessed. Serial access is slower than random access used for searching magnetic discs.

SOFTWARE is the word used for the programmes which are fed into the processing machines.

SWITCHED NETWORKS are public circuits which enable a customer to communicate with any other customer; the switched service for written messages is known as Telex; the service for spoken messages (i.e. the normal telephone system) is known as the Public Switched Network (PSN).

TELETYPE MACHINE is an input/output terminal unit with a QWERTY keyboard, paper tape punch and paper tape reader, connected to a computer;

the teletype machine and the computer can be in the same room or thousands of miles apart, e.g. a teletype machine in England can communicate with a computer in America. (International data transmission services are being co-ordinated by the International Telecommunications Union, a specialised agency of the United Nations Organisation. There are Datel services to the United States of America and 17 European countries and by using satellite circuits intercontinental services include Australia, Canada and Hong Kong.)

TIME-SHARING is a system by which a large number of users can communicate on-line simultaneously with a computer. This is possible because the CENTRAL PROCESSOR of the computer works much more quickly than the terminal units; it can, therefore, accept and produce information much more quickly than any one terminal can transmit or receive it.

VISUAL DISPLAY UNIT is an input/output device which has a television-type screen on which data can be displayed, and a keyboard on which the operator can key-in data.

FURTHER READING

Understanding Computers, T. H. Crowley, McGraw-Hill Inc.

Methods in miniature—An introduction to microcopying, HMSO.

The Disposal and Retention of Documents, The Chartered Institute of Secretaries.

How Should We File? D. D. Wellman, O. & M. Bulletin, August 1969, Civil Service Department.

Modern Filing Methods and Equipment, G. Continolo, Business Books Ltd.

Guide to the Universal Decimal Classification (UDC), BS.1000C : 1969, British Standards Institution.

Recommendations for the Preparation of Indexes, BS.37000 : 1964, British Standards Institution.

Specification for Alphabetical Arrangement and the filing order of numerals and symbols, 1749 : 1969, British Standards Institution.

Staff Titles and Job Descriptions in Commercial Data Processing, HMSO.

Electronic Data Processing and Computers for Commercial Students, E. A. Bird, Heinemann.

GROUP DISCUSSION

Divide into four groups. Each group will consider the filing and record-keeping requirements of a specific type of organisation and draw up a list of the kinds of records which would be kept, a Retention Sequence for each type of record, the most suitable methods of classification and recommended equipment.

Group 1 The national headquarters of an employers' federation.

Group 2 A construction company with civil engineering contracts in most parts of the world but mainly in oil-producing countries.
Group 3 A national examining body.
Group 4 A residential conference centre.

EXERCISES

1 What is microcopying? What reasons would cause you to recommend the installation of a system of microcopying in an office?

2 Describe four different methods of placing and securing papers in folders. Point out the advantages and disadvantages of each method.

3 Draft some 'Hints on filing' for the guidance of junior staff in your department.

4 Type or write each of the names listed on a 125 mm by 75 mm (5 in × 3 in) card:

Bennett and Solstice Ltd.
The Manyara Country Club
Lady Mary Howard
The Countess of Rutland
Emil Khoury (Tissues) S.A.
Antonio Garibaldi
Jamal Abdul Sukka
Department of Posts and Telecommunications
Ye Olde Logge Restaurant
Darenthe Dyers and Cleaners
Ministry of Transport
Madame Eva, Astrologist
The Hon. Angela Smythe-Peters

Sort the cards into alphabetical order.

5 Make up an address for each of the cards prepared in the previous exercise and write or type the addresses in the correct position.

6 Sort the cards into geographical order and make out the necessary guide cards.

7 In connection with filing and record-keeping, explain what you understand by:

a cross-referencing
b guide cards
c a substitution sheet
d a part file
e a visible strip index
f punched cards
g inactive files
h automatic retrieval systems
i reinforcing washers
j periodic transfer

8 In connection with data processing, explain the following terms and expressions:

a keying-in
b hardware
c on-line
d MICR
e COBOL
f batch processing
g random access
h COM
i teletype machine
j in-house system

9 Describe suitable systems of filing classification and record-keeping for:

a An import agent who communicated with firms in many parts of the world.
b The despatch office of a warehouse.
c An architect employed by a local authority to design housing estates.
d A dentist.
e The personnel department of a factory with 10,000 employees.

10 Name four media which can be used to input data to a computer.

11 Explain why a time-shared computer can appear to retrieve information for a large number of terminals simultaneously.

12 Batch processing is one way of using a computer. Explain (a) how the method works, (b) its advantages, and (c) the sort of work for which it would be used.

13 Arrange the following names in order in geographical classification. The names of counties should be the primary guides; the name of towns, the secondary guides.

West Malling, Kent	Chelmsford, Essex
Faversham, Kent	West Mersea, Essex
Chatham, Kent	Harlow, Essex
Elsenham, Essex	West Wittering, Sussex
Faygate, Sussex	Hockley, Essex
West Horndon, Essex	Holland-on-Sea, Essex
Horsham, Sussex	Tenterden, Kent
Teynham, Kent	Thaxted, Essex
Tilbury, Essex	Thorpe-le-Soken, Essex
Thorpe Bay, Essex	Tonbridge, Kent

14 Describe briefly each of the five steps in filing.

15 Describe a control procedure for charging out files.

16 Describe three methods of disposal for documents. Where could the secretary find guidance on the question of document disposal or retention?

17 By what factors would you judge the efficiency of a filing system?

18 Describe four methods of classification used in filing and indicate the types of offices for which each method is suitable.

19 Explain the following terms and expressions used in connection with filing:

a	Treasury tags	f	square cut folder
b	connected pocket suspension filing	g	reinforcing punch
		h	a sorter
c	primary guides	i	indexing units
d	a lever arch file	j	Dewey Decimal Classification
e	transfer boxes		

20 Describe a Work in Progress/Follow Up system which you think would keep efficient control of papers during their action stage.

Part III
Secondary Secretarial Functions

8

Business Background and Management Techniques

"Possibly the most interesting and useful finding which emerged from the research was that both bosses and secretaries feel the need for secretaries to be taught more about the organisation and procedures of the corporation."

BEA Secretarial Training, A. C. Pendlebury

Although a secretary works for a particular official or group of officials, she must know her own organisation thoroughly in order to assist effectively in the running of its affairs. She should also understand the background against which it functions and its role in the national economy.

Section 1: Organisation

PRODUCTION

The chart below shows the three major sub-divisions of production and some examples of what they comprise.

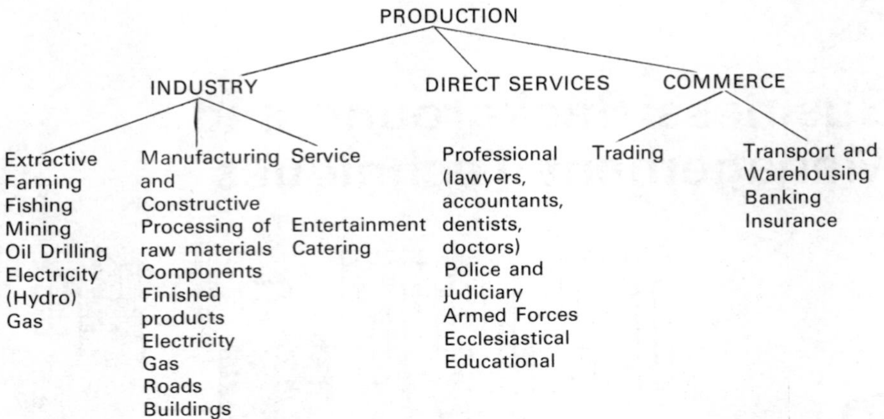

Only 2.5 per cent of British firms employ five hundred workers or more. Well over half of the remaining 97.5 per cent have less than twenty-five employees on payroll.

OWNERSHIP

There are two main sectors of employment—that which is publicly owned and that which is privately owned. The public sector can be subdivided into state (civil service) and public corporations (public service). Employers in the private sector can also be subdivided into corporate ownership and personal ownership.

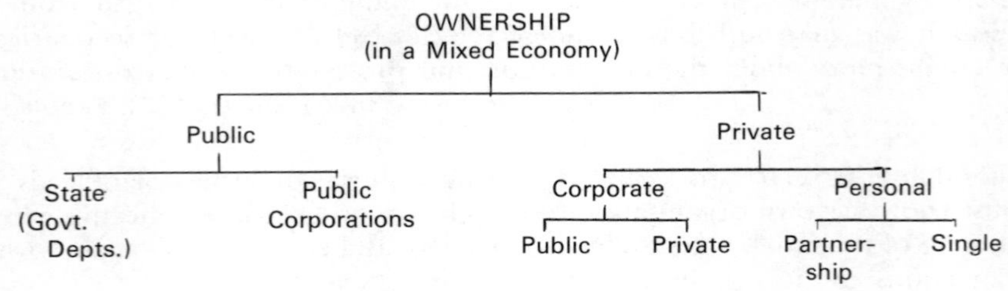

State ownership State organisation takes the form of Ministries and Departments, each headed by a Permanent or Principal Secretary. He is responsible for advising his Minister or Secretary of State and for implementing the policy laid down by the Government, which may be an elected body, such as Parliament, the United States Congress or a military appointed body, as in some non-European countries. Whatever the government, the civil servants must implement the policies it dictates, but they should also advise those in power, for example on the practicability of proposals.

Local authorities in Britain are organised on similar lines. The councillors are elected but the day-to-day work is carried out by employed staff headed by a group of officers, such as the town clerk, borough treasurer, borough engineer.

Some governments, e.g. the States of Jersey Government, delegate certain aspects of policy-making to management committees. Such committees are usually headed by a member of the governing body.

When the central government is a military regime, local authorities are usually headed by a management committee appointed by the government.

Public corporations Public corporations in Britain are generally created by Statute (an Act of Parliament) although a few have been established by Royal Charter. They may produce goods, such as electricity, gas and coal or provide services, such as airlines, broadcasting and research. Most public corporations which sell goods or services are obliged by the terms of their Acts or Charters to make sufficient income to offset expenditure which may include interest on loans raised to finance expansion programmes. They are not strictly profit making in the sense that profits are distributed, but profits must be made to cater for normal production expansion. These corporations are headed by a Chairman and Board of Directors appointed by the government. The executive structure, that is the functions and personnel, is similar to that of a company in the private sector (see page 310). In some countries corporations are graded, the salary structures varying according to the grade.

A non-selling organisation, such as the British Broadcasting Corporation, is usually headed by a Director appointed by the government. Since such organisations may be somewhat specialised their executive structures may vary to meet particular needs.

Private ownership Private ownership may be either corporate or personal. *Corporate ownership* consists of public and private companies, also known as joint stock companies. They may be incorporated in one of three ways—by Statute, by Royal Charter, or by Registration. The famous overseas trading companies of the past, such as the Hudson Bay Trading Company, the East India Company, were created by Royal Charter.

Registered companies may be either public or private. (Public companies are different from public corporations, the former being owned by shareholders, the latter by the government of a country.) Before a company can be established the Registrar of Companies must be informed of the proposed name of the company and its business aims. If approval is given the company must be legally constituted under Articles of Association in accordance with the Companies Acts. It has a *Certificate of Incorporation* which bears the *seal* of the company. This gives the company an identity of its own. The seal is used on all legal documents to which the company is a party.

Public companies require a *Trading Certificate* in addition to a Certificate of Incorporation and special provisions apply to certain types of businesses, such as Insurance.

Public companies, the shares of which are negotiable on the stock market, are of two types: groups of companies and individual companies. A group may consist of a holding company owning a number of companies which produce goods or provide services. The holding company may be purely financial, not itself producing anything, or it may be a parent company which produces goods or services and at the same time owns, either wholly or partly, subsidiary companies. If its ownership is partial, the holding company owns the majority of the voting shares, the remainder being held either by other subsidiary companies in the group or by the public, which includes investment companies, unit trusts, etc. The other type of public company is the single company with no subsidiary. Many companies own shares in other organisations in which they have some interest. For example, a printing company may own shares in a paper producing company. There are public companies in which the government also has an interest both in Britain and in many developing countries. In this case the government is a shareholder and the national exchequer receives dividends appropriate to its shareholding.

The capital which a public company issues is approved by the Stock Exchange and is known as 'Authorised Capital'. It may not be necessary, however, to raise the full amount of capital, at least in the early days of a company's existence, and so shares will be offered for as much capital as is required. The nominal (stated) value of shares bought is 'Issued Capital'. Shares are often bought and sold at prices below and above nominal value but it is the shareholders involved in these transactions who lose or gain, not the company.

A private company is normally owned by a small number of shareholders (up to fifty)—there must be at least two directors but not more than seven. The shares are not available on the stock market. Private companies may own subsidiary companies.

Public companies are normally 'limited'; private companies may be limited or unlimited, although unlimited companies are rare. Unlimited liability means that the shareholders are responsible for debts incurred by the organisation. In the event of its being unable to pay its debts, it would have to go into liquidation (see Chapter 13), and the shareholders would be obliged to pay the debts to the limit of their resources both in the company and held privately.

Limited liability means that the shareholders are not called upon to use their private resources to pay the debts of the company in the event of bankruptcy. They stand to lose only their investment in the business.

Some organisations are 'limited by guarantee'. This means that there is no capital investment from which debts may be redeemed but the members of the organisation guarantee by membership to meet its commitments by contribution of a nominal sum (usually £1) in the event of liquidation. Organisations which use this form of incorporation are non-profit making, for example professional bodies, such as the British Society of Commerce, and clubs.

All registered companies are required to produce annual audited accounts, which must include details of turnover, exports, directors' fees and subscriptions to political parties. Public companies usually publish with the accounts a statement from the chairman giving the main points about the company's achievement during the year, such as major policy proposals, profits/losses and dividends (interim and final).

Personal ownership may be either a partnership or single. A partnership may consist of not less than two and not normally more than twenty owners. Since a partnership does not have limited liability, the partners would be called upon to settle debts from their own resources in the event of bankruptcy. In a limited partnership at least one partner must be unlimited, but the other partners who have limited liability stand to lose only the amount of their investment in the business. Partners may be 'active', that is working in the business, or 'sleeping', that is financially interested only, not working. Only sleeping partners may have limited liability.

One person owning a business is known as a *sole trader*. The financial responsibility for the business is his alone and he is responsible for all debts in the same way as partners.

Businesses owned in any of these ways are normally functioning with the object of making a profit for the owners who have invested capital on which they require some return. There are various forms of investment in a business—shares (ordinary and preference) stock (ordinary, preference and debenture), debenture loans. The proportion of the profits paid to shareholders is known as dividends, and the part of the profits paid to stockholders and debenture holders is known as interest.

Finally mention must be made of Co-operative ownership. Members of the public form 'Societies' for manufacturing, wholesale or retail trading. Each 'member' contributes towards the setting up of the business and a Management Committee is appointed to control it. The manufacturing organisations sell to the Co-operative Wholesale and Retail Societies, where members can buy their requirements at very competitive prices. This is possible because of the facilities for bulk buying. The profits are distributed to members in direct proportion to the amount of money spent during a given period. They also receive a fixed annual interest on their capital.

KINDS OF EMPLOYER

Employers in both public and private sectors may be either profit-making or non-profit making.

Profit making employers may belong to any branch of industry or the services. Such businesses exist by selling goods or services to the consumer for more money than they cost to produce or buy. The excess of income over expenditure, or profit, is then used partly to expand the business, that is to increase capital investment, and to give a return on the original investment in the form of dividends or interest.

Professional employers may be either individual owners or private companies. The firm may consist of the owner and his secretary or it may be a full organisation with a chief executive and various departments depending on the nature of the business.

Non-profit making organisations may receive their finance in the form of government grant, or public subscription, or both. The revenue is intended to cover the expenditure involved in achieving the aims for which the organisation was established. For example, it might be decided to establish a council to encourage some particular form of art. This would involve the employment of a number of people who would have to be paid salaries, and expenses would be incurred for the work.

ORGANISATION STRUCTURE

Public corporations and joint stock companies have a similar organisation structure, because they are in business producing either goods or services for profit. The policy of an organisation is decided by a Chairman and Board of Directors. In the case of public corporations, the appointments are made by government; in companies the shareholders elect the Board, as the team of directors is known.

Directors may be either 'executive' or 'non-executive'. Executive directors are salaried members of staff and may or may not own shares in the organisation. Non-executive directors are usually elected for some specialist knowledge or ability. For instance, a banker may be a non-executive director of a public company and the financial advice he is able to give will be valuable to other members of the board in deciding financial policy.

The Chief Executive of a business is usually the Managing Director, who is responsible for the implementation of the policies decided by the Board. Together with the Company Secretary he forms the liaison between the Board and the executive of the organisation.

The Board's policy decisions will include finance, production and marketing, in their major aspects such as expansion, changes and diversification.

Functions The exact structure of any organisation depends on the particular type of business being conducted and its size. However, the basic functions have to be performed whether by one man or a large staff. In a small business one man may perform several functions. The diagram below sets out the basic structure of a business organisation and shows the departmental functions. Some of the functions included would not be applicable to all types and sizes of business, but the four main functions—finance, production, marketing and administration—must be carried out to a greater or lesser degree in every organisation.

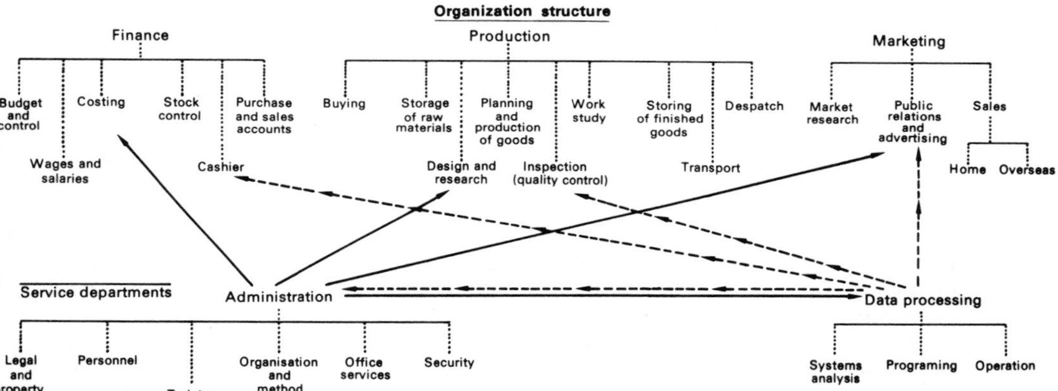

Responsibility relationships No one department in any organisation can function in isolation. It may depend upon, and is certainly related to, the work of other departments. The Sales Department cannot function effectively unless the Production Department does its job properly.

The General Manager, or Managing Director, if there is no General Manager, co-ordinates the work of the various departments. The final responsibility for the effective functioning of the organisation is his, and his alone, but since it is not possible for him to do everything himself, he must delegate responsibility. This he does by appointing a head of each department, generally known as a Departmental Manager. The Departmental Manager in turn delegates his responsibilities to subordinates such as Supervisors and Section Heads. Below are two diagrams showing the personnel pyramid and the responsibility pyramid from which it can be seen that the fewer the personnel the greater the responsibility.

Lines of responsibility and communication Lines of responsibility are always vertical, i.e. an employee is responsible to his immediate superior in accordance with instructions. This is direct responsibility. He is also indirectly responsible to all those senior to his immediate superior in the line

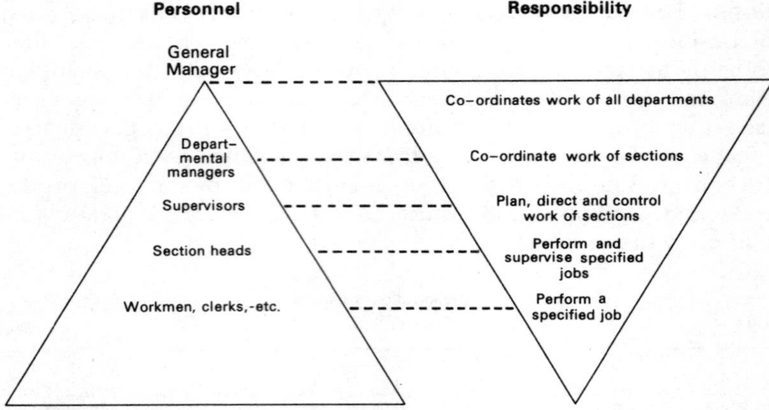

The personnel pyramid shows that the number of employees decreases at the top of an organisation. The responsibility pyramid is the other way up—the responsibility increases for the personnel higher up in the organisation.

to the top. An accounts clerk in the cost accounts section of an organisation is directly responsible to the assistant accountant in that section, and indirectly responsible to the cost accountant, the chief accountant and the managing director. He is *not* responsible to any of the assistant accountants in the sales or purchases accounts sections, although they are senior to him.

There are certain types of job where an employee may be responsible to more than one superior. In this case one superior will be in overall command subject to supervision of a certain aspect of the work by another superior. This may occur when technical work is involved, but is to be avoided if at all possible. Such dual responsibility is shown on an organisation chart by a dotted line. In the chart shown below the sales staff might be involved in the installation of equipment for which part of their work they would have to report to the technical manager, while being directly responsible to their area managers.

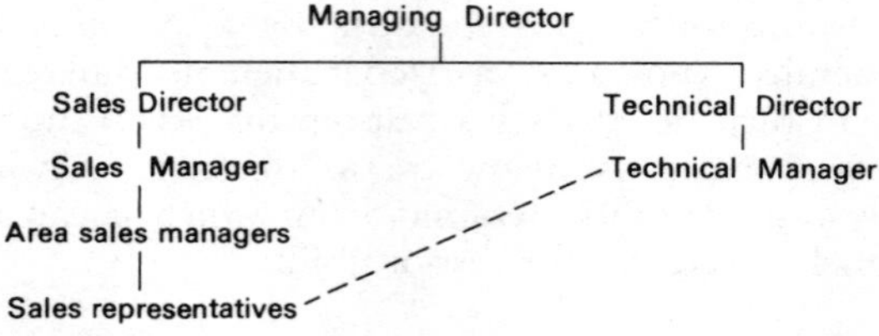

The communication of instructions must be from the top 'down the line'. The managing director may not give an instruction direct to the cost accountant—it must go through the chief accountant. The chief accountant could not possibly do his job if instructions were given directly to his subordinates without his knowledge.

Similarly if an employee wishes to communicate with anyone senior to his immediate superior he must do so through his superior, not directly. If the accounts clerk were able to go directly to the sales accountant the assistant accountant to whom he was responsible would not be informed and would consequently have his authority undermined.

Horizontal communication is necessary to ensure proper integration and co-ordination of activities. It might be necessary for the chemists and the workshop foremen to consult each other. This should be done through the respective managers. Suppose a workshop foreman wishes to discuss a problem with a chemist. He informs the works manager who may either speak to the chief research chemist or give the foreman the authority to do so. The chief research chemist will then either tell his chemist to discuss the matter or give the foreman permission to approach the chemist direct.

THE OFFICE

Most departments have a certain amount of paper work, the actual amount depending on the type and volume of work. If the amount of paper work involved is small it may be carried out by the technical staff in a small office situated in or near the place of work. If the volume is great, staff are employed specifically to deal with it.

In big organisations an office manager is responsible for ensuring the smooth running of the administration which includes mail registries, information storage and retrieval sections, secretarial pools, reprographic rooms, and possibly clerical sections covering such things as office equipment and supplies. He must ensure that the work of all the sections is properly co-ordinated, that work is produced on time, that the administrative services are meeting the needs of the other departments in the organisation and that costs in his department are kept to a minimum. He will keep his organisation chart under constant surveillance, and ensure that every employee in the department has a job description (see page 560). He should also assess training needs in his department. For maximum efficiency he must see that proper lines of communication are maintained.

Each section is controlled by a supervisor who is responsible to the office manager for the productivity of his section. He must direct his staff as to the work they have to do, ensure the quality of work done and give on-the-job training as necessary.

It is impossible to be specific about the designations and gradings of office workers because they vary so greatly from one organisation to another. In the private sector clerical and secretarial staff may be graded simply as junior and senior. In the public sector they may be graded by number, Grade I being the most senior. In the civil service in Britain and in countries which follow the

British system the gradings are clerical assistant, clerical officer, executive officer, higher executive officer, senior executive officer, principal executive officer. Above this grade are the administrative grades, which are the equivalent of management in the private sector.

It was mentioned that secretarial pools came within the orbit of the office manager. However, secretaries who work for specific people in the organisation do not because they do not fit into the "line" of responsibility. A secretary is responsible to her boss only, although she is subject to the conditions of employment of her employer. She takes instructions only from him and unless she has some assistants to whom she may give instructions, she may not give instructions to any other employee. She may, and of course frequently does, pass her boss's instructions to other employees, but she is only transmitting instructions, not giving them. The diagram below shows the position of a personal secretary on the organisation chart of a technical department.

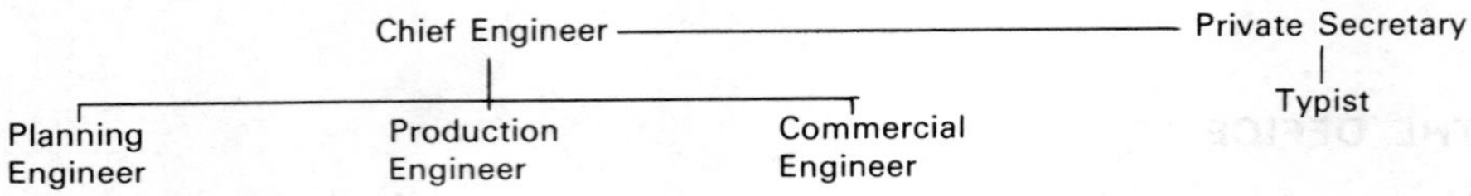

FURTHER READING

Basic Business Studies—Commerce, Swift & Warson, Edward Arnold.
Basic Business Studies Supplement S4—Government Departments, Local Authorities and Their Functions, Regan, Edward Arnold.
Supplement S5—Commerce and the State, Swift & Warson, Edward Arnold.
The Manager and the Organization, Eric Moonman, Pan Books Ltd.
The World of Industry and Commerce, J. L. Hanson, Macdonald & Evans Ltd.

GROUP DISCUSSION

1 Divide into four groups and make investigations in your city, town, or area to find as many examples as possible of

public non-profit making organisations,
public profit making organisations.
private non-profit making organisations,
private profit making organisations.

List the organisations in categories, for example, public corporations, public companies, and show the business functions of each.

When investigations have been completed discuss how all the organisations provide the goods and services required by the population in the city, town or area.

2 Each group visit a different type of organisation to find out the functions of the various departments. Finally discuss and compare the findings.

EXERCISES

1 Describe

- a a holding company
- b a private limited company
- c a subsidiary company
- d a partnership
- e a non-profit making organisation.

2 What is the difference between authorised capital and issued capital?

3 Who is responsible for deciding the policy of a company, and who is responsible for ensuring that it is carried out?

4 How are directors appointed to the boards of public corporations and public companies?

5 When a company is registered it becomes a corporate body with an individual identity. What are the legal requirements to achieve this status?

6 The following is an extract from a Chairman's statement. "The year under review has been a difficult one for your Company owing to stringent credit restrictions. The capital reserve fund was not large enough to meet expansion demands without the assistance of a substantial loan and this was aggravated by the general price increase in all building materials and engineering equipment. Only a substantial contingency reserve has enabled the directors to recommend a final dividend of 15%, which with the interim dividend of 5% already paid, brings the total dividend to 20% as last year. Warning must be given that if credit restrictions are not relaxed in the near future, the company's trade will continue to drop, since without expansion it cannot meet customers' demands which in turn results in loss of customers to our competitors."
What is meant by

- a stringent credit restrictions?
- b aggravated?
- c substantial contingency reserve?
- d total dividend?
- e relaxed?

7 Explain the function of the following departments of an organisation:

a Sales
b Administration
c Public relations
d Purchasing
e Personnel.

8 Explain 'the responsibility pyramid'.

9 You are a private secretary to a Manager and you have a typist working for you. She wishes to have a day off to attend to personal matter and goes to your boss to ask permission. Is this correct? If you think not, say why and state what action you would take.

10 Your boss, a General Manager, asks you to pass his instructions to a departmental head. When you do this, the person concerned objects, saying you have no right to give him orders. Is he correct? What would you do in this situation?

11 Summarise the duties expected of an office manager.

12 There are the following workers in an administration department:

Office Manager	5 typists
Stenographer Secretary	2 senior clerks
3 stenographers	6 junior clerks.

Between them, these workers have to do all registry duties, provide secretarial services for all senior officials of the organisation and look after a small accounts section. Produce an organisation chart showing the personnel in relation to functions.

Section 2: Commerce

In Section I we saw that Commerce was divided into two major parts, Trading and Commercial services such as Banking and Insurance, which are auxiliary services, necessary to industry.

TRADING

In the same way that no individual person can be completely self-supporting, so no nation can exist without trading, that is exchanging what it does not want for something it does want. Most countries produce certain raw materials in larger quantities than they need. This surplus can be exchanged for the surplus of some other items produced by another country, either as a raw material, a processed material or a manufactured commodity.

Some countries are basically industrial; others are basically agricultural. Some countries are fortunate in having a variety of raw materials or agricultural products; others may be virtually one commodity/crop traders. More and more developing countries are trying to diversify their national production so that they can produce a greater variety of goods both for use on the home market, thus reducing imports, and for export, thus increasing import potential.

Home market Two parties are involved in a 'transaction', as the process of buying and selling is called, and both have to take certain steps, some of which have legal implications.

The chart below sets out what has to be done by whom, at each step, and the document involved. Not all steps are taken in every transaction.

Step No.	By whom taken	Details	Document involved
1	Buyer	Ascertain full details of goods available—quantity, quality, size, colour, price, delivery dates, payment terms, credit terms, special specification requirements.	Letter of enquiry.
2	Vendor	Give full details to prospective buyer including all those requested and any other relevant details.	Letter, catalogue, quotation, tender or estimate.
3	Buyer	Place order for goods required stating full details.	Purchase Order.
4	Vendor	Despatch goods.	Advice Note or Delivery Note.
5	Buyer	Receive goods.	Goods Received Note.
6	Buyer	Check goods received to ensure that they comply in all details with goods ordered. If there is any discrepancy the buyer may legally refuse to accept the goods. Any shortages or damage must be notified to the vendor within a maximum period, usually stated on the Advice or Delivery Note.	Letter.
7	Vendor	State cost of goods as agreed, including delivery charges and Value Added Tax (VAT).	Invoice.
8	Buyer	Check invoice against purchase order.	
9	Vendor	Correct shortages, losses or wrong delivery either by replacement or by crediting the amount involved.	Credit Note.
10	Vendor	Request payment due.	Statement of Account.
11	Buyer	Check Statement of Account against invoice and credit note. If accurate, pay amount due.	Cheque or National Giro.
12	Vendor	Acknowledge Payment.	Receipt if requested.*

*Cleared cheques act as receipts since the Cheques Act of 1957. Most businesses do not send receipts unless the customer requests them to do so.

VAT

Britain's entry into the European Economic Community meant that on 1 April 1973 purchase tax was abolished and replaced by Value Added Tax (VAT).*

Value Added Tax is a system of adding tax to the value of the goods at each stage of production until the goods reach the consumer. When a producer buys raw materials he pays tax on the value. At each subsequent stage the trader involved pays the difference between the amount of tax that he has paid to the previous trader and the tax due on the sales value of the article. The consumer pays the whole amount as he or she cannot be paid VAT by reselling the goods. The diagram below illustrates how the system works.

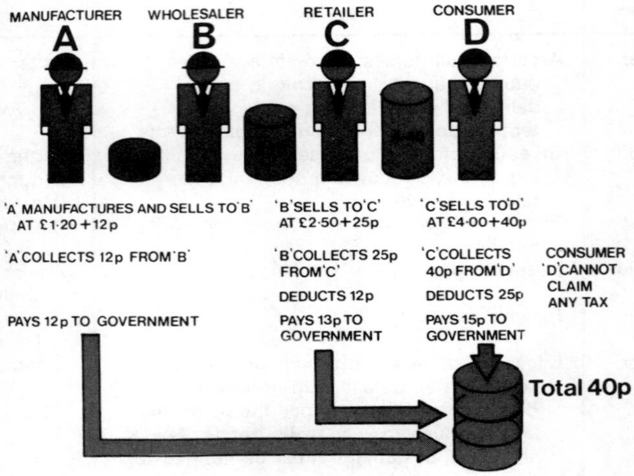

MANUFACTURER A
WHOLESALER B
RETAILER C
CONSUMER D
'A' MANUFACTURES AND SELLS TO 'B' AT £1·20+12p
'A' COLLECTS 12p FROM 'B'
PAYS 12p TO GOVERNMENT
'B' SELLS TO 'C' AT £2·50+25p
'B' COLLECTS 25p FROM 'C'
DEDUCTS 12p
PAYS 13p TO GOVERNMENT
'C' SELLS TO 'D' AT £4·00+40p
'C' COLLECTS 40p FROM 'D'
DEDUCTS 25p
PAYS 15p TO GOVERNMENT
CONSUMER 'D' CANNOT CLAIM ANY TAX
Total 40p

Chart showing how VAT is collected.
Note: When first introduced in 1973 VAT was set at 10 per cent. The percentage has since been varied.

Any individual, company, partnership or body supplying goods or services at a total turnover rate of £5000 per annum† or more *must* register with H.M. Customs & Excise who collect VAT. Smaller businesses may do so if it is to their advantage. Registered traders are known as *taxable persons*.

The VAT regulations compel such registered traders to:

1 Keep copies of all documents concerning the taxable aspects of every transaction for at least three years—this means the retention of docu-

*It is estimated that nearly two million traders are concerned with VAT, compared with 70,000 who were concerned with Purchase Tax.

† The introduction of VAT has even caused a new word *vatable* to be coined, to describe goods and services on which VAT is levied.

ments such as invoices, credit and debit notes but not, of course, documents like delivery notes; the records may be stored in any form including storage on microfilm or in a computer.

2 Be able to produce for visiting Customs and Excise officials documentary evidence of

   a Outputs (sales)—there is a list of ten items of information which 'must be clearly shown' for every taxable supply to 'another taxable person', and
   b Inputs (purchases)—six details of each transaction must be recorded.

3 Return a form VAT 100, showing total input tax and total output tax for each tax period (normally three months).

The ten details which must be shown on invoices for sales are:

1 Identifying number and date.
2 Date of supply—this determines the *tax point*, i.e. the date when the tax is officially chargeable.
3 Supplier's name, address and VAT registration number.
4 Customer's name or trading name and address.
5 Type of supply, e.g. sale, hire purchase, credit sale.
6 Description sufficient to identify the goods or services supplied.
7 Quantity and amount payable (excluding VAT) for each such description.
8 Total amount payable, excluding VAT.
9 Rate of any cash discount offered.
10 Rate and amount of VAT charged.

The six details of each purchase which must be recorded are:

1 Number and date of supplier's invoice.
2 Date of supply, the *tax point*.
3 Supplier's name, address and VAT registration number.
4 Description sufficient to identify the goods or services.
5 Quantity and amount payable excluding VAT for each description.
6 Rate and amount of any VAT charge.

The introduction of VAT legislation has meant that not only must businesses keep detailed records of every taxable transaction, but also that the information must be stored in such form that it can be speedily retrieved when needed, for example, when required by a visiting Customs and Excise official. Traders have, therefore, had to redesign their invoices to provide space for the entering of VAT rates, amounts and registration numbers; they have also had to improve their record-keeping systems to make sure that an office copy of an invoice can be retrieved within seconds.

An example of a VAT invoice is shown below. Note that VAT is calculated on the discounted price, that is, the gross price less discount.

A. Wholesaler Ltd.
22 North Road, London N12 4NA
VAT Registration No. 912 3456 78

INVOICE NO. 3654
DATE 3 January 1974

To: Messrs. Fashion Retailers Ltd,
High Street, Newtown.

Delivery Note
No. 1234

Tax Point
3 January 1974

Consignee:
Fashion Retailers Ltd,
NEWTOWN.

Terms 2½% seven days, otherwise strictly net

Quantity	Size	Goods	Cost	VAT Rate	VAT Amount
20	12	Dresses style 1056 @ £5·25 each	£105·00	10%	
10	14	Dresses style 2014 @ £5·55 each	£55·50	10%	
			£160·50	10%	£15·65*
		Delivery Charge (Strictly net)	£3·73	10%	£0·37
		Total goods	£164·23		£16·02
		Total VAT Strictly NET	£16·02		
SALE		TOTAL	£180·25		

* This is calculated on the discounted price.

A VAT Invoice

If the amount payable does not exceed £10 (including VAT) a less detailed tax invoice may be issued showing only: supplier's name, address and VAT registration number; date of supply; description of goods; amount payable, including VAT; rate of VAT in force at time of supply.

To calculate the 'net of tax' sale price, deduct one eleventh from the total amount payable.

International trade In all countries there is a government department or ministry responsible for formulating the national trading policy and for issuing import and export licences. In Britain the Department of Trade and Industry performs this function.

Usually certain restrictions must be placed on the import and export of goods. In Britain most goods can be imported without a licence, that is under *Open General Licence*. However, the government of a developing country may restrict the import of a commodity from a foreign country if its own country is trying to establish an industry to produce it. Local producers may be hard hit if similar products are imported from overseas at cheaper prices. For such items *Quotas* are set by agreement between governments. Certain goods may also require a licence before they can be exported. In Britain export licences are required for some items, such as works of art and guns.

The state of a country's currency also affects the government's policy on international trading. Imports may have to be restricted and exports given special encouragement in order to achieve a favourable Balance of Payments situation (see page 330).

The Commonwealth and EFTA Before Britain joined the European Economic Community on 1 January 1973 she belonged to two groups of trading nations, the British Commonwealth and the European Free Trade Association. In matters of trade, Britain had a special relationship with the Commonwealth countries that allowed most of their exports to enter Britain free of customs duty. In return, about half of the British goods exported to Commonwealth countries had preferential tariffs, that is lower customs duties than the same goods from other countries. Britain's entry into the EEC would normally mean that these special privileges would be completely ended. However, during negotiations for entry into the EEC, fears were expressed that certain Commonwealth countries would suffer considerable economic damage if they lost their favourable trading position with Britain. These countries are the developing nations that produce sugar and New Zealand which had been exporting most of her dairy produce to Britain. Under Community regulations which allow for special trade agreements with non-member states, a continuation of favourable treatment for these countries has been negotiated.

Before 1 January, 1973 the European Free Trade Association (EFTA) consisted of Britain and eight other European countries – Austria, Denmark, Finland, Iceland, Norway, Portugal, Sweden and Switzerland. Much of Britain's trade was with the other members of EFTA which aimed to remove trading restrictions, such as import quotas and customs duties, among member countries. Now that Britain and Denmark have left EFTA and joined the EEC, it is hoped that favourable trading arrangements between the two groups may be developed.

The European Economic Community In 1958 six European countries, France, West Germany, Belgium, Holland, Luxemburg and Italy, signed the Treaty of Rome which established the European Economic Community (EEC) also known as the Common Market. These countries, often called The Six, agreed that over 12 to 15 years they would abolish customs duties on goods traded among themselves and set up a Common External Tariff (CET) on dutiable goods (commodities on which customs duty is charged) imported from any other countries. The Rome Treaty also made provisions for a common agricultural policy, banking, insurance, transport and the free movement of labour and capital within the EEC. Member countries agreed that their representatives would meet together to make certain decisions on these matters that would affect the whole Community.

Britain did not wish to join the EEC at that time. Later she changed her mind and made applications for membership which were rejected in 1963 and 1967. At the end of June, 1970, Britain, Denmark, Ireland and Norway opened negotiations with The Six for membership of the EEC. All four applications were accepted but the people of Norway rejected membership in a referendum held in 1972. On 1 January, 1973, Britain, Ireland and Denmark became members of the EEC. The Six became The Nine.

In the same way as the Rome Treaty allowed The Six a number of years to abolish customs duties among themselves, Britain negotiated that her tariff barriers to the other members would be removed in stages. The transition period agreed ended on 1 July, 1977. From that date there have been no customs duties on Community goods imported into Britain. Britain now has to charge the full Common External Tariff on dutiable imports from non-member countries.

Marketing The basis of marketing both at home and overseas, is buying raw materials and/or components to process into commodities or finished products, to sell at a profit. We said earlier that two parties are involved in a transaction; therefore the man with something to sell must find a man who wants to buy it. Alternatively the prospective vendor can find out what people are wanting and produce it. Finding buyers for goods available may be achieved by various forms of advertising and many other methods of sales promotion including appointing representatives to contact potential buyers directly. Producing what people want necessitates marketing research, which is explained in 'Management Techniques' in Section 3 of this chapter.

Many countries have *national standards* to which manufacturers must conform. In Britain the British Standards Institution lays down specifications which are given numbers.

There is an International Standards Organisation to which member countries send representatives. The national standardisation body of each country is normally that representative. The object of the ISO is "to encourage the development of standards in the world with a view to facilitating international exchange of goods and services and to developing mutual co-operation in the sphere of intellectual, scientific, technological and economic activity". It is therefore in its own interests for any country wishing to export goods to adopt the appropriate international standards.

There are various other considerations which the vendor must bear in mind. His prices must be *competitive*; that is to say he cannot expect to sell goods at a higher price than that charged by a competitor for similar goods. A higher price may, however, be competitive if the quality of the goods is comparatively far better. A vendor may attract customers if he can deliver the goods more quickly than other producers and consistently prompt delivery is often a major factor in influencing a buyer to continue trading with a particular supplier. The condition of goods when received is yet another point and proper packing and choice of transport (see below) are important points.

After sales service, either at home or abroad, is a very important factor. It has occurred that a car manufacturer has advised a potential customer against buying a car for use in a particular country because of the lack of servicing facilities there.

The *presentation* of goods is another factor which influences buyers. The design of containers and wrappers is an important aspect of sales promotion.

Distribution is a fundamental aspect of marketing. Manufactured products are not normally sold direct from the manufacturer to the customer. There is a fan-shaped process which ensures a larger number of buyers at each stage. Producers may sell to wholesalers, distributors or overseas agents; they in turn sell to retailers or agents; from this source the consumer buys. Thus distribution costs are kept to a minimum as large consignments can be supplied by the manufacturer to a small number of wholesalers in various areas. Each wholesaler can supply to a large number of retailers in his own area and retailers are located where the consumers are concentrated.

Consumers buy in small quantities according to individual needs.

Retailers keep moderate stocks of a variety of goods to suit consumers.

Wholesalers keep large stocks of selected goods to supply in quantity to retailers.

Manufacturer sells his products to wholesalers in very large quantities.

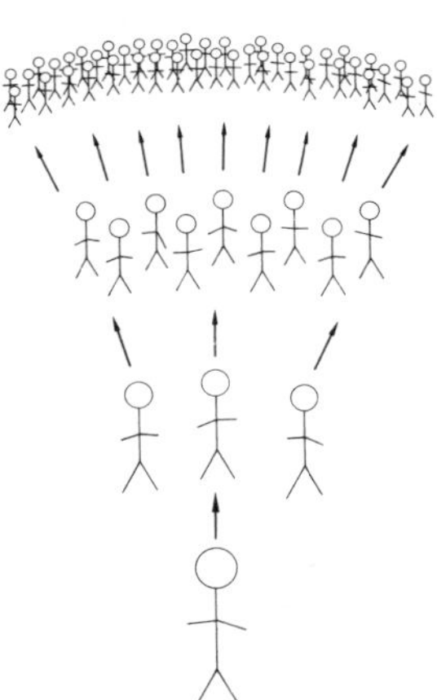

COMMERCIAL SERVICES

Transport The need to move raw materials, agricultural products and manufactured products both within a country and between countries gave rise to the development of various national and international transport systems. The growth of trading automatically encouraged the improvement and enlargement of transport systems.

Goods can be moved over land, by road or rail, over water by canal barge or sea-going vessel, and by air.

Various considerations must be taken into account when choosing the method of transport to be used.

1 The nature of the freight—for example, fragile, perishable, bulky, heavy.

2 The packaging requirements for different types of transport.
3 The time factor.
4 The cost.
5 The co-ordination of different types of transport involved in any one shipment, for example, delivery to the port to coincide with the sailing date of a ship.

The chart below indicates the various transport facilities available, how the freight is charged, and any special advantages and disadvantages.

Type of transport	Types of carrier	Facilities available	Freight charges	Remarks
Road	Bus	Small packages from terminal to terminal.		Generally more expensive than rail.
	Lorry, Truck, Van, Tipper	Door to door delivery within home country; loading at and unloading at door; delivery from Britain to places in Europe and Ireland without off-loading; container handling; loose loads, e.g. sand, which need tipping.	According to distance.	
	Dray (horse drawn)	Delivery to and collection of goods from barges.		
Rail	Wagon Truck Vans	Loading at door where special lines are laid to factories; complete wagon/truck/van can be consigned; container handling; collecting depots or small export consignments; Export Express freight service to industrial centres and ports; Rail Star service; road service from door to railhead; International Express Parcels Service.	Weight	Choice of most suitable vehicle for goods being transported, for example, van for goods affected by atmosphere, wagon for heavy loads. Guarantee of next-day delivery to ports.
Water	Passenger Boat Cargo Boat	Hold or deck stowage; container handling; delivery to any port in the world; charter of complete ship for bulk loads, such such as grain, oil.	Cubic capacity or tonnage. Ships chartered charged according to length of time and cargo.	Cheaper than air transport for heavy goods, such as machinery and vehicles, service subject to dock strikes, delay in loading and unloading caused by congestion at ports; pilferage is relatively easy except from containers.
	Ferry Hovercraft	Small packages; road and rail vehicles carried without unloading.		Arrangements necessary for delivery to and collection from terminals.
	Barge			Slow; limited routes.
Air	Passenger aircraft	Small packages; unaccompanied baggage.	Weight	Quick service; ideal for perishable goods; less risk of damage to fragile goods; high security resulting in lower insurance rates; costly for heavy goods; other arrangements necessary for delivery to and collection from airports.
	Freighters	Regular all-freight services between major international cities; charter of a complete aircraft.		
	Helicopters			

Finance and banking The use of banking services for making payments is dealt with in Chapter 13, Finance and Statistics. In this section we discuss the role of the banks in providing finance for industry and the operation and control of credit generally.

To review the activities of the financial institutions it is convenient to divide them into two groups: one, those which form the short-term money market, namely, the Joint Stock Banks, the Discount Houses and the Merchant banks when performing that part of their function which deals in the supply of short-term loans; two, the long-medium term or Capital market, consisting of the Issuing Houses (including merchant bankers performing this function), the Finance Corporations and Finance Houses, the Insurance market and the Stock Exchange.

Until recently, each institution specialised in a particular type of operation but over the past few years all financial institutions have widely extended their activities so that today they participate in many types of financial operation.

Later in this chapter there is a short survey of the changes which have been brought about by the new credit policy which has developed since the consultative document "Competition and Credit Control" was published by the Bank of England in May, 1971. First, certain of the financial institutions and their functions and roles are described in simple terms.

The Bank of England is the Government's banker. It maintains accounts for the Exchequer, national loans and government departments. It is also banker to the joint stock banks; it grants loans to Discount Houses and thus to the whole banking system; issues bank notes and coins; controls foreign exchange; and formulates and exercises a policy of credit control, for example, by calling for special deposits from clearing banks. The Bank of England also acts as Registrar of government and nationalised industries' stock, also the stock of some local authorities.*

The Commercial, Joint Stock, or Clearing Banks, such as National Westminster, Barclays, Lloyds, Midland, Williams & Glyn's, and the Scottish banks, provide the following services: Deposit, Savings and Current accounts; Bank Giro and cheque clearing; loans and overdrafts; payment of standing orders; distribution of notes and coins; issuing credit cards and cash dispenser cards; safe custody of customers' valuables; buying and selling shares through stockbrokers for customers; arranging insurance; dealing in foreign exchange—cash, travellers' cheques, letters of credit, international money conversion; acting as executors and trustees; managing customers' investments; dealing with customers' income tax; keeping up-to-date on economic, financial and trade conditions all over the world; keeping up-to-date information on individual business organisations (their credit worthiness, for example); acting as Registrars for companies and handling new issues of stock and shares.

The Merchant and Industrial Banks, such as Hambros, Rothschild, Baring,

* Many developing countries have in recent years established a national bank to perform similar functions to the Bank of England.

Lazard, Hill Samuel, have two functions—one in the short-term market and the other in the capital market. In the short-term market they act as Accepting Houses—accepting Bills of Exchange on commission—and some are members of the Discount Houses Association. Their second function is that of issuing houses, and this function is also discussed in the next paragraph. They also act as advisers on investment both to private and corporate customers and specialise in advice and finance for mergers and take-overs.

The Issuing Houses are firms whose business is the promotion of public limited companies, for whose shares the public is to be asked to subscribe. There are about 50 members of the Issuing Houses Association. Their chief functions are to advise capital borrowers and lenders and to sponsor new issues of shares. A frequent method adopted by issuing houses is to purchase outright all the issued capital of an existing company and offer it to the public on different terms. The difference represents the charge made by the issuing house for its services, and this method is known as an 'offer for sale'. The more usual method is for the issuing house to invite public subscription for shares *by prospectus* which gives full particulars of the history and financial standing of the company being floated. Institutional investors (Insurance companies, building societies, etc.) may *underwrite* a public issue by purchasing shares at a discount, thus guaranteeing that the new company will receive the capital it seeks. Issuing houses do not normally cater for small-scale capital requirements. A firm requiring, say, £250,000, would probably first approach its friendly bank manager, a merchant bank, or the Industrial and Commercial Finance Corporation (ICFC). This corporation was formed in 1946 by the Bank of England, the London clearing banks and the Scottish banks, in order to provide credit for smaller businesses.

Discount Houses. The Discount market is a part of the British banking system whose job is to connect those who have money to lend for short periods with those who wish to borrow. Discount houses do not deal with the needs of small, or personal, borrowers and lenders, but with the needs of institutions and the Government. The twelve discount houses borrow from the clearing banks and other financial institutions, at short notice or 'at call', at comparatively low interest rates. The banks do not borrow directly from the Bank of England but obtain cash from the discount houses by calling in part of their loans. A large part of the money borrowed by the discount houses is used to buy British Government Treasury Bills, and the discount houses meet the needs of the government by tender each week. The banks buy for their customers Treasury Bills from the Discount market. The Discount houses also deal in commercial bills and local authority bonds.

Industrial bankers, finance houses, investment trusts and unit trusts. There is often confusion about the institutions bearing the above names, but they all form part of the very complex machinery known as the capital market, raising capital from the public and directing it into investment and other channels.

The term *industrial banker* has been used loosely to cover Finance Corporations and those firms engaged in financing instalment buying. There are about

30 members of the Finance Houses Association, many having links with the joint stock banks, and about 900 members of the Hire Purchase Trade Association, including retailers giving credit. Altogether there are about 2000 firms engaging in finance for credit transactions, but the Finance Corporations are distinct from the hire-purchase firms in that they deal in the provision of medium and long-term capital.

Institutional Investors. Small savings find their way into many channels which result in funds which are far from small. The term *institutional investors* covers the National Savings Banks, the Trustee Savings Banks, Insurance Companies, Investment Trusts, Unit Trusts, Building Societies, Co-operative Societies, Trade Unions and Pension Funds, the National Giro and the Government itself, all with very large sums at their disposal. These sums are reinvested in 'gilt-edged' stocks and shares by the institutional investors.

A growing form of investment is the Unit Trust. The investor buys shares in the trust which in turn buys and sells shares on the stock market. Some trusts specialise in "capital appreciation"; this means dealing in shares to get maximum increase in value, so safeguarding the capital originally invested against inflation. Other trusts specialise in high income yield, that is investing to get maximum dividends or interest.

Control of Credit. In May 1971 the Bank of England published its revolutionary consultative document 'Competition and Credit Control', and its recommendations were generally welcomed by the banks.

One of the most marked changes introduced through this new credit policy was the relaxation of restrictions on bank lending and the freedom given to individual banks to fix competitive lending rates. Not only the large clearing banks but smaller and foreign banks, merchant banks and finance houses, all took advantage of the easing of restrictions and offered varied and attractive schemes—credit cards, personal loans, budget accounts—to attract new customers. They have also, through subsidiary companies, undertaken *factoring* functions, which enable company customers to sell their unpaid invoices at a discount to the factoring company which will collect the monies due.

Other recommendations in the document for the control of credit were:

a the end of quantitative ceilings on lending and the end of the banks' own agreement among themselves on minimum lending rates,

b the day-to-day maintenance by the banks of a uniform reserve ratio of $12\frac{1}{2}$ per cent of eligible liabilities,

c the right of the Bank of England from time to time to call for special deposits.

Certain banks were given time to build up their reserve assets as were finance houses who were required to maintain a reserve ratio of ten per cent. Several well-known finance houses applied for, and were given, full banking status.

The banks began implementing the recommendations of the document in September 1971. In the same month Bank Rate was abolished and the banks were allowed to fix their own *base rate* which, in theory, could vary with individual banks but has tended to remain uniform throughout the banking system. When one bank alters its base rate, other banks follow. Interest rates on loans to customers are charged at varying percentages above base rate, at the discretion of the bank manager.

Borrowers were quick to take advantage of easier money from the banks, and it was soon necessary for the Bank of England to exercise its right to call for special deposits. This meant that the clearing banks had to deposit a percentage of their money with the Bank of England, and this money was 'frozen' in special accounts. These calls for 'special deposits' (which are additional to the clearing banks' cash reserves normally held at the Bank of England) have the effect of reducing the amount of cash available for lending by several hundred million pounds. Special deposits are released back to the banks when the economy allows. In December 1973 the controls on hire purchase and on bank special deposits were re-imposed in order to control the inflationary situation caused mainly by problems resulting from the supply of oil and the fuel crisis.

MONEY SHOPS One of the most recent developments in banking services is the money shop. Money shops are open six days a week during normal shopping hours and provide many banking facilities. Some money shops offer only personal loans, savings and insurance facilities; others provide comprehensive banking and financial services.

The main appeal of money shops is their personal loan service, but the banking facilities offered by some of them are designed to extend banking methods of payment to a greater number of people.

The current accounts available at some money shops work like those at

banks. Account-holders have cheque books for making payments and cheques pass through the bank clearing system with one of the clearing banks acting as the money shop's agent. Statements are sent to account-holders at regular intervals and standing orders are available for paying regular amounts, such as rent, mortgage payments or club subscriptions. Although overdraft facilities are not available, customers are offered a variety of personal loan plans.

INVESTMENT Both joint stock and merchant banks lend money to business organisations and to individuals. The money they lend is either earned through interest and other charges made by the banks, or is borrowed from customers who deposit money with them. Depositors earn interest on their savings or deposit accounts (but not normally on current accounts), and thus become investors. This is the simplest form of investment, and building societies offer similar opportunities. Investment in public companies is made through the *Stock Exchange* where stocks and shares are bought and sold. Governments borrow money from the public by issuing bonds or stocks which will normally be redeemed (repaid) at some specified future date. When first issued the price is sometimes lower than the nominal value (usually £100). Interest is paid regularly during its term until the redemption date, when the nominal value is repaid plus, in some cases, a cash bonus. Some government stocks are 'undated', that is, they have no fixed redemption date. Examples of these are 'Consols' and War Loan, and although interest continues to be paid on these stocks, the prices have fallen well below the original purchase prices.

Companies issue shares (see page 326) and stocks and raise loans, called debentures. These are bought and sold by brokers acting on behalf of clients, who may be individuals or organisations. Unit Trusts (see page 327) use the money invested in them to buy and sell stocks and shares. (Only jobbers buy and sell at the Stock Exchange from and to brokers. The public must deal through stockbrokers.) Shares may be 'ordinary'; 'A', which usually, but not always, means that the holder has no voting rights as an ordinary shareholder has; 'preference', which means that dividends are paid to the holders of these shares before payment is made to others. People may buy stocks and shares for 'capital appreciation' in the hope that the price will rise and that the value of the money they have paid for the shares will not decrease due to inflation. Alternatively, they may buy shares offering a high income return. In this case, there may also be an element of capital appreciation over a long period.

Many of the national daily newspapers carry 'Closing Prices'. This is a list of the prices of stocks and shares at Stock Exchange closing time on the previous day. Fuller information is given in "The Times" and "The Financial Times", the variation in prices throughout the day's trading being shown. There are two indices, based on the rises or falls of a specified list of shares—the Financial Times Index and the Extel Indicator Index, and these are reliable pointers to the state of the Stock Market. They rise and fall by 'points' and are affected by many economic considerations both national and international.

A 'credit squeeze' (limiting of loans) by a national bank means that industry may find its expansion inhibited. It is possible, however, for large organisations to borrow money from abroad, particularly through the Eurodollar market. This, briefly, is a pool of currencies held by the central banks in Europe, and is available for borrowing by business organisations in other countries.

The study of the Stock Market is fascinating, and those interested in learning their way about the financial pages of newspapers will find a good guide in "Basic Business Studies Supplement S3—Understanding the Financial Section of Your Newspaper" by Rawcliffe.

Balance of Payments In the section on 'Trading' we saw that a country runs into financial difficulties if its imports cost more than the value of its exports. Like Mr Micawber, we can say "Exports £101, Imports £100—Result: Foreign Exchange Surplus (Happiness). Exports £100, Imports £101—Result: Foreign Exchange Deficit (Misery)."

This difference between the value of imports and exports is known as the *Balance of Payments*. When a country has a large foreign exchange deficit its economy may be seriously affected if foreign countries refuse to extend credit facilities, with the result that even essential imports have to be stringently curtailed.

Exports are divided into two categories—'visible' and 'invisible'. Manufactured goods and commodities (coal, steel, copper) are examples of visible exports. Tourism is a good example of invisible exports; the attractions of a country bring people to it, and these people spend collectively a great deal of money. Other examples of invisible exports are banking services, shipping and insurance.

International Finance The national bank in any country is the watchdog of that country's economy. It is the responsibility of its Governor and Board of Directors to advise the Government on the steps necessary to ensure stability and progress. A careful watch must be kept on the economies of other countries, particularly those with which trade is conducted to any extent.

In overseas countries, particularly developing countries, the functions of merchant and industrial banks are carried out by 'development banks'. In some cases these are related to specific areas of the country's economy, e.g. agriculture.

There are four banks associated with the United Nations—the International Bank for Reconstruction and Development (IBRD or the World Bank), the International Development Association (IDA), the International Finance Corporation (IFC) and the International Monetary Fund (IMF). The first three of these banks lend money made available by various countries to countries in need of financial aid. The IBRD makes long-term loans available to member countries for agreed development projects and encourages private capital investment. The IDA (an affiliate of the World Bank) provides similar help to less developed countries by making loans, but on a more flexible basis and generally at lower interest rates than is the case with other finance. Closely associated with the World Bank, but a separate legal body, the IFC lends money to developing countries in the form of investment in private enterprise.

The IMF was established to promote international monetary co-operation and exchange stability. When member countries are in difficulties over balance of payments they may buy foreign exchange from the Fund.

With international trade competition becoming keener every year British bankers are rapidly expanding their overseas activities. Barclays have had overseas branches (under its DCO subsidiary) for many years, and other British joint stock banks are already established in Europe, United States, Africa, the Far East and many other parts of the world. Similarly, many foreign banks have opened branches in Britain, mainly in London, but these operate independently and are not members of the London Clearing Banks.

Insurance The main purpose of insurance is to safeguard against damage or loss by possible misfortune. Anyone wishing to insure himself against a 'risk' pays to do so, but if he does not suffer damage or loss he cannot claim back the amount paid, known as a 'premium'. It will go towards paying the claims of other insured persons who do suffer loss. Thus, the claims of the few are met by the premiums of the many.

Principles of Insurance Insurance is based on three main principles.

UBERRIMA FIDES or 'utmost good faith' is the first of these principles. This means that the information given by the person wishing to be insured is taken by the insurers to be fair and accurate. This is necessary because only the proposer, that is the person wishing to be insured, knows the material facts. If the insurers discover later that the information given was not correct, they will not accept claims and may refuse to insure the person for any risk.

The second principle is INSURABLE INTEREST, which means that the risk to be covered must be of direct consequence to the insured, that is the insured will sustain damage or loss in the event of the risk occurring. You cannot insure someone else against personal accident unless that person is in debt to you. In this case you have an insurable interest in the subject of the insurance.

INDEMNITY is the basis on which claims are accepted and paid. It means that when a claim has been met the insured is in the same position as he was before the risk, for which he was covered, occurred. If you have an accident in your two-year-old car and it is 'written off', that is cannot be repaired, the insurers will pay you the value of the car, not buy you a new one. Thus you do not profit from the misfortune.

Insurance Divisions Insurance is treated in four main divisions—*fire*, *accident*, *marine* and *life*. Insurance originated in the seventeenth century to cover the risk of losing ships and rich cargoes at sea because trade was developing rapidly at that time, but the high seas were still infested with pirates, Spanish and French privateers were legion and storms played havoc with the small sailing ships of the time. Thus marine insurance is the oldest form of cover.

Lloyd's Register, though not marine insurance, may be complementary to it.

It is quite separate from Lloyd's (see below). Surveyors all over the world supervise the construction of ships to ensure that they are built to Lloyd's standard which is 100 A1. The repair of ships is also their concern. There are nine other major organisations of this kind set up by various countries to classify ships.

Fire and accident insurance covers most kinds of risk other than marine and life.

Life cover, generally called life assurance, is of three main types: endowment, term, and mortgage protection. For Endowment Assurance the insured pays premiums regularly (monthly, quarterly or annually) for a set period. At the end of the period, or at death if this occurs before, a lump sum is paid by the insurers. (The lump sum is more than the total premiums paid.) The money can then be used to buy an *annuity* which pays a pension either for a pre-determined period or until the death of the annuitant.

Term Assurance and Mortgage Protection premiums are lower because if the insured survives the set period the insurers make no payment. Term Assurance is the payment of a lump sum to stated beneficiaries if the insured dies before the term expires. In the case of Mortgage Protection the money is paid to the building society which made the loan, so that the balance of the insured person's mortgage owing at the time of the insured's death does not have to be paid from his estate or by his dependants.

Insurers invest the premiums paid by the insured in many ways, both at home and abroad, thus accruing dividends and interest which pay the endowment sums. This capital investment is also a valuable aid to industry and agriculture, particularly in developing countries.

INSURERS There are three types of insurers. Lloyd's syndicates, groups of wealthy men, known as 'underwriters', accept risks. The word 'underwriter' means literally that under a statement of the risk the person willing to accept the risk, or a part of it, writes his name. To belong to a syndicate a member must deposit a minimum amount of capital with the Committee of Lloyd's. These syndicates are represented at Lloyd's by Underwriters agents who do the work on their behalf. Lloyd's itself is merely a place—one of the largest commercial rooms in Europe. Lloyd's started as a coffee house in the seventeenth century where marine insurance business was transacted.

Insurance companies, some of them very large commercial groups, do similar work. Among the best-known are the Commercial Union, Pearl, Phoenix, Prudential, Royal and Sun Alliance. One of the main differences between a member of Lloyd's and an insurance company is that the member has unlimited, and a company normally has limited liability. There are tariff and non-tariff companies, though the division is now less marked. Rather, some types of insurance are based on a tariff, for example fire in the United Kingdom, motor and workman's compensation in many developing countries. This means that the companies who operate the tariff charge about the same premiums for the same cover.

Mutual societies are rather like co-operative societies in that they are formed by groups of people who share the profits as there are no shareholders.

Insurance brokers are used by many people. They do not themselves insure, but place the risk with either a company or a syndicate at Lloyds on the most favourable terms they can get—not necessarily the cheapest, but the most suitable for the insured's needs. With the growing complexity of insurance offered, the intermediary broker or agent is becoming more important. Solicitors, bank managers, estate agents, etc., act as agents and there are many firms of specialised insurance brokers who are highly skilled professionals and well placed to advise on the best type of policy and the company offering it.

GETTING INSURED Any person or organisation wanting to 'take out an insurance policy' must first complete a *proposal form.* Full details of the risk and the party to be insured must be given. Where a risk is very large no one insurance company or syndicate will accept it in total, so the risk is *spread* among several, each stating what percentage they are prepared to accept. Some risks run into many millions of pounds, for example, a hydro-electric power station and dam. In the event of a claim being made, one insurer alone would be unable to meet it.

If the risk is accepted, a *premium* is requested. An insurer may refuse a risk if he does not wish to accept it, although this is usually confined to certain circumstances, such as a motor vehicle driver who has had a lot of accidents. The premium is usually charged on a percentage basis, for example, £2% means that for every £100 of cover required a premium of £2 is charged. Discounts are given on certain policies and enquiries should always be made by potential insured persons. The amount of the premium is based on the amount of the claims which are made annually on the type of insurance in question. In recent years fire and motor premiums have increased considerably because of the increase in claims. Insurers are profit-making organisations, so that income from premiums must exceed expenditure on claims, and of course, the expenses of conducting the business.

When the premium has been paid, cover is given by the insurer who issues a *policy*, which sets out in detail the risk to be covered and all the conditions of cover. Also 'exclusions' are stated, these are specific circumstances under which the cover is not effective, for example, ordinary wear and tear on an All Risks policy covering a fur coat. The insured should read the policy carefully and ask for an explanation of any clause he does not understand.

TYPES OF RISK The chart on pages 336 to 339 summarises the types of risk which are commonly insured by individuals, business organisations in general, manufacturers and retail traders.

There are some risks which are uninsurable. A person who invests his money in shares cannot insure against the risk of losing his money if the company goes into liquidation. This is a calculated risk which must be taken after a decision is made taking all known facts into consideration.

FURTHER READING

Basic Business Studies—Commerce, Swift, Edward Arnold.
Basic Business Studies Supplement S3—Understanding the Financial Section of your Newspaper, Rawcliffe, Edward Arnold.
Bank Education Service Study Booklet Series (Booklets 1 to 12), The Bank Education Service, 10 Lombard Street, London EC3V 9AT.

GROUP DISCUSSION

Divide into groups of not less than four and not more than six in each group. Discuss how each of the commercial services—trading, transport, banking and insurance—affects us in our daily lives. Each group may take one particular service.

EXERCISES

1 Explain the difference between industry and commerce.
2 What is meant by "diversify the economy"?
3 What documents may have to be used by (a) the buyer and (b) the vendor, when a transaction takes place?
4 Briefly explain the following:

   a transaction;
   b open general licence;
   c quota;
   d proposal form;
   e unit trust;
   f after sales service;
   g distribution;
   h Common External Tariff (CET)
   i finance house;
   j clearing bank.

5 What considerations must a vendor take into account when finding buyers for the goods he wishes to sell?
6 What is VAT, how is it calculated, and what records are businesses required to keep to comply with VAT regulations?
7 Discuss the purpose of national standards for goods produced.
8 There are five people involved in the making, selling and buying of a pair of shoes—the tanner, the manufacturer, the wholesaler, the retailer and the customer. The tanner imports and processes the hide, then sells it to the manufacturer for £2.00. The manufacturer makes the

shoes and sells them to the wholesaler for £3.50. The wholesaler sells them to the retailer for £4.00. The retailer sells them to the customer for £5.00. What will the Value Added Tax amount to at each stage and to whom will it be paid?

9 You are asked to despatch a small crate to a country overseas. State the possible methods of despatch, the basis on which freight would be charged in each case, and in what circumstances you would use each method.

10 "The national bank is the watchdog of the nation's economy." Explain.

11 As a business owner what services would you expect to find available at a joint stock bank?

12 Bills of Exchange are 'discounted' by merchant banks and discount houses. What does this mean?

13 Explain the difference between 'capital investment' and 'income investment'.

14 There are four international banks. Describe their functions.

15 Explain the following:

   a balance of payments;
   b foreign exchange;
   c invisible exports;
   d spreading risks;
   e uninsurable.

16 Name five essential imports in your home country.

Type of policy	Risk covered	Usual premium rate	Remarks
PERSONAL Fire	Loss of property by fire.	Per £100 value of property.	A Fire policy is commonly extended to cover certain additional perils, storm, water damage, flood, earthquake, aircraft, riot, strike, impact.
Motor Vehicle	Third Party—necessary by law—accident to any person injured by the car insured. Fully Comprehensive—third party, damage to or loss of vehicle by accident, fire or theft.	According to type of car, age and driving experience of driver, locality in which used.	Certain areas are more hazardous than others from the point of view of accident probability, for example, London compared to the North of Scotland.
All Risks	Loss or damage to any property, usually valuable such as jewellery, photographic equipment.	Value of property per £100.	Insurers may ask for an official valuation of items of high value unless newly purchased, when a receipt must be produced.
Householder's Comprehensive	Loss or damage to contents of a house by fire or burglary or other risks.	Value of property per £100.	
Personal Accident	Medical expenses, loss of salary, compensation for loss of eye(s), limb(s), or in the event of death, due to accident.	Per £1000 of death benefit.	
Baggage	Loss of suitcases, etc. and contents while travelling.	Per £100 value of baggage.	This policy commonly includes cover for medical expenses and is often combined with a Personal Accident policy for travel purposes. The premium depends on the duration of the policy which may vary from three days.
Sports, such as Golf	Third party, loss of equipment, personal injury.	Value of equipment, per £1000 compensation value.	
Mortgage Protection	Balance of mortgage due in the event of death of the property owner.	Value of mortgage and age of assured.	No moneys payable if assured is still alive at end of period of insurance.

Type of policy	Risk covered	Usual premium rate	Remarks
Endowment Assurance	Payment of a lump sum to assured at end of a stated period or to stated beneficiaries in the event of death of the assured.	Term of policy, age of assured and amount of lump sum.	
Annuities	Provision of a pension at the end of a stated period for remainder of life of the assured (and his wife in some cases).	According to pension required and age of annuitant at commencement.	
Education	Payment of children's school fees for a stated number of years at a specific cost.	According to duration and size of payments.	
Private Aircraft	Third party, accidental damage to or loss of aircraft.		
Medical	Expenses incurred for hospitalisation including surgery.	According to amount of expenses required to be covered.	A typical policy can be obtained for short period when travelling overseas.
Domestic Servants	Accidental injury to or death of servant while on duty.	According to type and number of servants.	
Combined	A number of insurers are issuing very comprehensive policies under which most of the above types of cover can be incorporated under one policy.	According to types of risk included.	
BUSINESS			
Fire	Loss of property by fire.	Per £100 value of property.	An extension to a fire policy allows compensation for loss of revenue during the period of repairing and/or rebuilding.
Burglary	Loss of property by theft following entry or exit by violent and forcible means.	Per £100 value of property.	Insurers may inspect the premises to ensure that security is adequate.
Motor Vehicle	Third Party or Fully Comprehensive.	According to type of vehicle, age and driving experience of the driver, locality in which used and type of use.	

Type of policy	Risk covered	Usual premium rate	Remarks
Pedal Cycles	Third Party, accidental damage to or loss of cycle.	Value of cycle.	
All Risks	Loss or damage to any portable property of high value, e.g. instruments.	Value of item on a percentage basis.	
Cash in transit	Loss of money being moved between business and bank or vice versa, or between branches.	Per £1000 on the amount annually at risk.	Insurers may insist on certain precautions, for example, that the person(s) carrying the money must be accompanied by a guard.
Cash in Safe Overnight	Theft of cash left in a safe on business premises.	Per £100.	The safe must be approved by the insurer, and a maximum value is set.
Fidelity Guarantee	Employees who handle company's cash who could embezzle.	Per £1000.	
Public Liability	Amount that the insured may become legally liable to pay as a result of his own or his employee's negligence.		
Employers Liability	Any amount which the employer may be legally liable to pay in respect of claims by employees injured at work.	According to number of employees and claims made during previous year.	In countries where no national insurance scheme exists this policy is usually referred to as ''Workmen's Compensation''.
Personal Accident	Medical expenses, loss of salary, injury or death on employees while on duty.	Per £1000 death benefit.	This type of cover is more usually taken for partners and directors than for general employees.
Pensions	Provision of pensions to employees when they retire for the remainder of their lives and, in some cases of their wives' lives if husbands predecease them.		
Engineering	Damage to goods or materials during handling from the first stages of manufacture to delivery to the consumer or user, and the equipment used for handling.	Sum assured and type of machinery.	This type of insurance requires highly specialised knowledge and is usually handled by specialist companies.

Type of policy	Risk covered	Usual premium rate	Remarks
Marine 'Cargo'	Damage to or loss of goods being transported by sea, or air including road and rail journey at beginning and end of voyage.	According to value and type of goods and distance of movement.	
Marine 'Hull'	Damage to or loss of ship.	According to tonnage.	
Goods in Transit	Damage to or theft of goods while being transported.	Per £100.	
Plate Glass	Damage to plate glass, either showcases, display windows or doors.	Value of glass.	
Aircraft	Third party; damage to or loss of company's aircraft by accident, fire or theft.		
Credit	Buyer's failure to pay for goods sold and delivered, work done or services rendered, on credit terms.	Percentage of turnover.	For goods exported on credit the Exports Credit Guarantee Department of Trade give wider cover than the normal credit insurance policy.
Export "Seller's Interest" Contingency	Loss or damage to goods in transit should they be returned to the exporter for any reason.	Per £100 value of goods.	
Anticipatory Credit	Supplier's failure through insolvency to supply goods for which a deposit or advance payment has been made.		
MANUFACTURERS			
Products Liability	Claims from consumers for compensation as a result of buying defective products.	Negotiable.	
RETAIL TRADERS			
Perishable Stock	Deterioration of perishable stock, such as frozen foods, through circumstances beyond the retailers control, such as failure of electricity supply.	Per £100 value of stock.	

17 State and briefly explain the three basic principles of insurance.

18 State five types of risk which each of the following might insure against:

- a a manufacturing organisation;
- b a transport organisation;
- c a retail organisation;
- d an architect.

19 If a particular type of insurance cover is based on a tariff in your country how will this affect you if you wish to take out a policy?

20 Discuss how insurance benefits the individual.

Section 3: Management Techniques

As a personal secretary your work is complementary to that of your boss. It is essential therefore that you know what his work involves and can understand easily when he explains situations to you. You may have to attend various kinds of meetings where discussion revolves around management policy and methods of implementing policy. You must recognise the terms used and the general sense of the discussion if you are to produce accurate and meaningful reports or minutes, and take appropriate follow up action for your boss.

There are two major functions involved in the running of an organisation—*planning* and *control*. When the policy-making body (Board, Council, Committee) has decided a policy, it is up to the chief executive to decide how it can be implemented.

Planning must cover *all* aspects of the business. It would be useless to plan to produce a million pounds worth of goods without planning how to sell them. This would cover such items as capital requirements, suppliers and supplies, storage, machine capacity, manpower requirements both for production and service departments, control procedures, distribution, sales promotion. There are various techniques for planning which will be explained.

Managers are responsible for achieving specified results. The *Control Theory* sets out the stages by which control is achieved.

Stage 1. Objectives (targets) must be set.
2. Staff must be informed of the objectives.
3. The resources (men, money and materials) must be obtained to enable the objectives to be achieved.
4. Action must be taken, that is the plan must be put into operation.
5. The results of the action must be observed and measured.
6. The results must be constantly monitored for comparison with the objectives.

7. Failures of results as compared with objectives must be reported.
8. Action must be taken to counteract the failures.

It is very rare that a plan can be implemented without change, either due to unforeseen circumstances or developments, or naturally progressive developments. Control is therefore essential not only to detect and correct mistakes as soon as possible after they occur, but to adapt procedures to changing circumstances.

To enable them to plan and control as efficiently as possible, managers use a number of management techniques. No one manager will use them all. He will select only those which will provide the relevant information for effective decision-making.

TECHNIQUES FOR FINANCIAL CONTROL

Estimates and Budget Towards the end of a financial year each department is required to produce estimates, which are a broad statement of expected revenue and expenditure for the following financial year. (The financial year is not necessarily a calendar year.) The main areas of expenditure are shown but a detailed breakdown is not included. Managers are expected to justify the estimates, that is explain the inclusion of increases in certain areas, and possibly explain why reductions are not possible in those and other areas. Supporting facts and statistics may have to be produced.

When the estimates have been agreed in principle (the policy-making body will not necessarily accept the figures given) a detailed *budget* must be produced. This may be done by departmental heads or it may be done by the financial department in consultation with the departmental heads. These individual budgets are known as "functional budgets", that is each one covers a particular function of the organisation. The central feature is the sales forecast, which usually shows a monthly figure for each product. The volume of sales for each product may vary from month to month if it is a seasonal item; the figures will be based on past sales experience and possibly on market research. The other budgets follow in sequence from the sales forecast. They normally include *production*, related to the sales budget and production capacity, as well as funds available for stock requirements; *plant utilisation*, that is the capacity of the plant in relation to required production; *capital expenditure*, such as additional machinery required for increased output; *cash*, estimating the amount of cash available each month related to expected receipts and payments of cash—this will depend on the production and sales budgets; *selling and distribution costs* related to the sales budget; *administrative costs* covering all overhead expenses.

These "functional budgets" are summarised into a "Master Budget" which shows the total budgeted costs, the total budgeted sales and the projected results, that is profits, which will be achieved at the end of the year's business. It might be necessary to adjust the selling price of some or all products in the light of the anticipated profit or an effort might be made to reduce the production budget without loss of output. The diagram below shows that all the functional budgets are related directly or indirectly to the sales budget, although this also may depend upon capital to enable the production required to meet the sales forecast to be achieved.

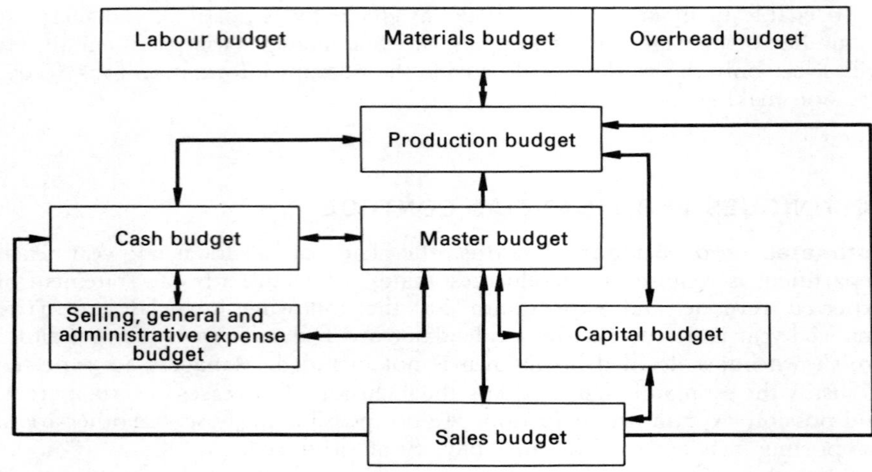

Budgetary control Each departmental manager is given a copy of the final budget for his department. The Finance Department allocates revenue and charges expenditure to the departments and should produce monthly statements showing an up-to-date financial situation. For effective budgetary control there must be constant comparison of the actual figures with budgeted figures. The difference between the two is called a 'variance'. A plus variance means that the budgeted figure has not been expended in full; a minus variance means that it has been exceeded. Over a period of time plus and minus variance offset each other, but immediately a significant variance appears an investigation must be made to find the reason.

Suppose that in the Administrative Budget is a figure of £2000 per month for stationery and office equipment. After four months a budgetary control statement might look like this:

	Budget	Actual	Variance
Month 1	£2000	£1400	+ £600
2	£2000	£2300	– £300
3	£2000	£2850	– £850
4	£2000	£1200	+ £800

At Month 3 an investigation would be made because the total variance is – £550.

Stock control When stock is bought, whether it is for re-sale or raw materials for production, it represents capital. If the capital has been borrowed it is costing money in the form of interest. If the money has not been borrowed it still represents a cost as the money could have been invested to earn interest. The storage space necessary to keep the stock is also costing money for such items as maintenance, rent, rates, heating and lighting. Consequently stocks must be kept to a minimum consistent with flow requirements. In mass production organisations the inwards flow of materials is tied as closely as possible to production flow so that minimum storage is required. For example, tyres for motor vehicles are being received throughout the day at a car manufacturing plant and after checking, proceed to the assembly lines.

Precise re-order levels should be set to ensure that orders for goods are placed in time for them to be received when required. Average consumption rate and delivery dates must be taken into consideration when setting re-order levels. Maximum levels must also be set, again determined on availability of the goods. In large organisations where stocks are being received and issued in large quantities at all times, stock control is carried out by data processing. This means that the computer print out automatically indicates when re-order levels have been reached.

Credit control Probably the vast majority of sales are on a credit basis, the terms varying with the type of goods, the selling organisation and the particular customer. No business organisation can give unlimited credit since it has had to pay for, or will soon have to pay for, the goods or the cost of their production. The credit-worthiness of new customers should be carefully investigated and the credit of slow-paying customers should be limited. Payment dates should be set and debtors who do not pay in accordance with the terms agreed should be followed up. A 'black list' of customers who are not credit-worthy should be kept under review.

The operation of credit control on individual customers should start when an order is received. It is first checked by the Credit Control Section of the Finance Department. If it is within the pre-determined credit limit the order is then passed to the factory or warehouse to be processed; if it exceeds the limit it will be returned to the customer with a request for payment of money owing from previous transactions. This control may be incorporated in a computer system so that when the order and despatch documents are being processed a check is automatically made that the value of the order does not exceed the allowed credit limit.

Costing In order to make a profit a business makes or buys an article at a certain price and sells it at a higher price. The difference between the two prices is not all profit. From this, overheads must be paid. To work out realistic selling prices, costing is necessary. This means that the costs of production (that is materials and labour) are allocated to the work done. Selling costs must be added with a percentage of the overheads e.g. salaries of office workers and depreciation of machinery. If there is a change in the cost—this could result from an increase in the price of raw materials or a wage increase—management must consider whether the selling price is still realistic. If the increase in cost price reduces the profit margin too much the selling price will have to be increased. If the selling price required to maintain the percentage profit margin would be unobtainable in a competitive market the product would be discontinued.

Cost analysis and cost control Costing produces figures which indicate how much the production of goods or a service cost, taking into account overheads and other factors. By analysing the figures it is possible to see whether the costs are realistic in terms of cost/profit ratios, that is whether the cost of producing goods is bringing in sufficient return in terms of profit. The ratio of direct (production) to indirect (overhead) costs is another important factor and may well be influencing the profit figure considerably.

Cost control is possible only when a cost analysis has been carried out. Decisions may have to be taken affecting certain factors shown up by the analysis. There may be controlling factors such as maintenance labour charges which have to be kept under strict surveillance.

Breakeven analysis When fixing the selling price for a particular item the "breakeven point" (B/E pt) must be taken into consideration. That is the point at which the income from sales less variable costs will cover the fixed costs of production. To give a simple example, if the basic annual expenditure of a factory is £20,000 (that is the fixed cost of keeping the factory whether anything is produced or not), that much income from sales, plus the cost of production, that is variable costs such as labour, raw materials, the portion of the electricity bill applicable to running the machines, must be received. If the item costs £2 in labour and materials and can be sold for £3 there is £1 towards the £20,000. Thus 20,000 items must be sold to offset the fixed cost. If he produces and sells 50,000 articles, he should make a profit of £30,000.

Revenue:	50,000 articles at £3 each		£150,000
Less:	Cost of labour and materials		
	(50,000 at £2)	£100,000	
	Expenditure	£ 20,000	£120,000
Profit:			£ 30,000

In fact, breakeven analysis is not as simple as this. Production costs are not static. The more goods that are produced, up to a certain point, the less the cost. Beyond that point they may increase again owing to various factors. For example, the capacity of a plant may be to produce 100,000 articles in an eight-hour shift. To produce 120,000 would necessitate overtime work which immediately increases the labour cost usually by fifty per cent (if the overtime is worked on a week day) for the extra 20.000. Since all goods must be sold at the same price the increase will have to spread over the 120,000. However, 200,000 would necessitate two eight-hour shifts. If shift rates were paid the cost would be different again.

A simple breakeven chart shows clearly the production point at which revenue covers costs and the amount of loss or profit to be made for a given output. The chart below illustrates the example given above.

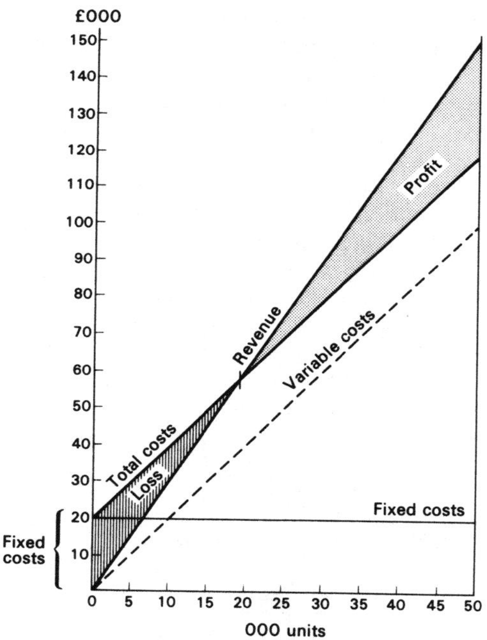

Internal audit Large organisations usually have an Internal Audit Department which is responsible for checking the accounting systems to ensure that controls are effective, that there is no misappropriation of funds or stock. One of its objectives is to detect and prevent fraud. It also ensures that information presented to management is not only accurate, but that it gives a true picture of the financial state of the organisation. By omitting a seemingly trivial point, the real state of affairs can be completely falsified.

Internal auditing does not take the place of the annual external audit which is demanded by law and which must be carried out by independent professional auditors. Internal auditors can go into much greater detail because they are continually on the job, whereas external auditors normally spend only a few weeks in an organisation. Co-operation between the internal and external auditors can save a considerable amount of money because much of the necessary routine work can be incorporated in the continual auditing. Internal auditors should also work closely with the Organisation and Methods Department to ensure that new systems are 'safe', that unsatisfactory systems are changed and to control and assess the effectiveness of existing systems.

TECHNIQUES FOR OVERALL PLANNING AND CONTROL

Corporate planning Corporate planning involves looking at all the major aspects of the organisation as a whole, setting and assessing objectives taking into account each entity as it relates to the overall picture. Such considerations as the 'shape' of the organisation, its structure and the relationship of subsidiary groups, companies and departments, its venue in relation to its potential markets, the advantages and disadvantages of potential markets when relating products/services to each other, the effect of social changes on the present company potential, should all come under review not for the immediate future but for five, seven, ten years ahead.

Corporate planning, like any other form of planning, should be a continual process in that adaptation and reassessment is necessary at regular intervals to make sure that changing conditions are taken care of, and continued effectiveness is achieved. This is the 'broad' planning, the 'general direction' of the organisation, which guides management in the more detailed planning for individual companies, departments and projects.

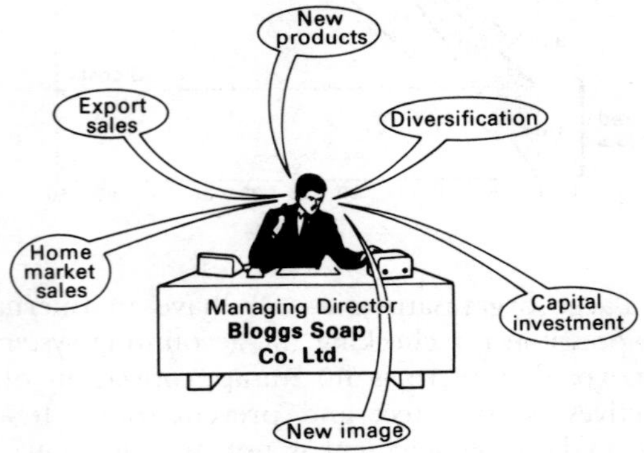

Company appraisal Management control is aimed at getting information about problems as quickly as possible after they arise, finding the reasons for deviations from plans, such as a rise in costs, and at correcting the faults, and assessing the effectiveness of operations in relation to pre-determined objectives. Company appraisal is the co-ordinating factor by which corrective techniques can be applied to remedy fundamental weaknesses. By looking at the overall picture of company aims, functions and methods it should be possible to assess where the basic causes of failure lie—and these will not necessarily be where they appear to be on a departmental basis. For example, the failure of the Sales Department to achieve the sales target may be blamed by the Sales Manager on the Production Department for not producing goods on schedule. In fact, perhaps the real reason is delay in the administrative processes involved in the requisitioning of raw materials, caused by a checking procedure.

Statistics Statistics are dealt with in Chapter 13. Generally speaking, statistics are only useful if they are kept up-to-date. The production cost schedule is not much use after a week because any detectable fault has either disappeared, or has continued, probably getting worse. The object of statistics is to bring to light any deviations from the norm, so that investigations can be made and corrective action taken if necessary.

Management by objectives Not to be confused with management objectives (targets of the organisation as a whole), management by objectives is the setting of specific aims for individuals which will stimulate them to improve their own performance, thus contributing to the attainment of the overall objectives of the organisation. A manager might decide that he can produce next year as much as he did this year with ten per cent less staff by improving certain systems for example.

Objectives must be realistic and when assessing achievements consideration must be given to factors which may have affected results but which were unforeseeable when objectives were set.

Planning Programming Budgeting Planning Programming Budgeting (PPB), also known as Programme Budgeting, is used by some Government Departments and in Local Government, but is still in the exploratory stages to a large extent. The system consists of three stages—(i) programme budget, which sets down the expenditure of the immediate past years and the estimated expenditure for the next five to ten years, relating expenditure to objectives (activities) instead of items; (ii) programme review which is normally carried out annually when the detailed budget for next year is being drawn up; the objectives will be reviewed to see if they are being achieved and if still valid, whether there are better/cheaper ways of achieving them; the programme budget is extended by a year at this time also; (iii) special studies are called for to make a detailed analysis of areas shown by the programme review to be faulty or weak; the feed-back from the analysis will enable management to decide whether to change or modify objectives, whether the methods are correct, whether resources are being allocated to best advantage.

Systems analysis Basically systems analysis (SA) is the analysis of facts in relation to the company objectives. Facts which usually come under such scrutiny fall into four main categories—the information required by managers to enable them to make decisions; accounting processes; calculating systems for research and development; control systems, such as stock control and sales analysis. Systems analysis could be considered as an extension of Organisation and Methods in that it includes the designing of systems, but may probably (though not necessarily) use computers.

There are seven stages in the creation of a system.

1 *Feasibility study* to assess the existing system/s and see if improvement is needed and if so, whether SA is the right way to achieve it.
2 *Analysis* which includes defining the system's objectives, investigating existing systems to find out where they fail, drawing a specification of the system needed to produce the required results taking all relevant factors into consideration.
3 *Design*—the creation of a new system which will achieve the objectives, at the same time being sufficiently flexible to allow changes to be made either to correct faults or to meet varying conditions. This is achieved by designing the system in sections, or modules, so that any one part can be changed without altering the whole system.
4 *Detailed creation*—the detailed specification for each module either by expressing requirements in computer language for the programmers* to work on and/or by drawing up detailed instructions for non-computer work. The required output will be forthcoming only if the input is accurate and adequate.
5 *Implementation*—putting the system into operation.
6 *Evaluation*—assessing the effectiveness of the system, that is whether it is giving the information required, reducing costs as estimated, saving time as required. This may be done six to twelve months after implementation.
7 *Maintenance*—changing the system as necessary either when faults occur and/or when requirements change.

Marketing research Any company in the throes of change needs information on which to base decisions. A change of product, extension of services, increase in production should only be undertaken if some definite information indicates that such a step will be profitable. Marketing research covers all aspects of marketing (products, markets, distribution channels, pricing, etc.) and includes market research, opinion research, field research, advertising.

There are various techniques which can be used to get information.

1 *Information from publications*—statistics and reports produced by government departments, trade associations, chambers of commerce, banks, embassies, newspapers, technical and professional journals, libraries (professional and national).

*A computer programmer 'translates' the information (data) to be fed into the computer into computer language in the correct sequence to give the required information output.

2 *Random sampling*—taking people as they come, for example, in the street, in their homes, alphabetically.

3 *Quota sampling*—taking a selection of people covering known factors, such as salary level, geographical area, age group, occupational category.

4 *Personal interviews*—the interviewer asks the interviewee specific questions and records the answers on a form designed for the purpose. (The forms may be data processed.) This technique is expensive to operate but the results are usually more reliable than those from other techniques.

5 *Postal questionnaires* contain questions which may require Yes/No answers or more specific information. The results may be disappointing because of poor response.

6 *Telephone interviews* are conducted in a similar manner to personal interviews.

Information obtained from marketing research should not be used as a deciding factor in taking a course of action but is a valuable component in the total material for assessment.

The personal interview usually gives the most reliable information.

Data processing The basic principle of data processing is that certain information is 'programmed', that is translated into a form acceptable to a machine as instructions to perform certain functions and make certain calculations and produce in a specific format the information required. A simple example is the production of electricity bills. The programme 'input' consists of an account number, the date of the latest meter reading, the previous meter reading, the latest meter reading and the tariff rate. The computer or accounting machine calculates the number of units consumed, selects the unit price applicable under the tariff, calculates the cost of units consumed. It will pick up from its 'storage' unit the name and address applicable to the account number, arrears, fixed charges. Finally it will calculate the amount due. The 'print out' will be in the form of a bill (which will be mailed to the consumer) with a duplicate which forms the accounting document. Payments from customers will be processed in a similar way so that the 'storage' unit is the ledger account for the customer.

A computer has standard programmes for constant use for such processes as wages, billing, stock control, sales analysis, but programmes must be specially written for new and specialist applications. It is possible to computerise almost any job, but unless a real saving in time/money will result, there is little point in doing so. The fact that a computer performs calculations in a tiny fraction of the time it would take a man to perform them does not necessarily mean that savings will result. Only standard large volume jobs or lengthy specialist processing jobs are suitable for computerising. (For additional information on computers, see pages 292–301.)

Network analysis* It is essential to plan any job so as to get the best possible results at minimum cost. Very few jobs fall into the 'straight line' category, that is one step after another, each step dependent upon the previous one. Each job may possibly consist of a vast number of components, many of them interdependent, but at different points. Suppose a production job consists of three parts—the first part must be done before the second part, but the third part is much smaller and can be done any time provided it is ready when the second part is finished. In this case the time schedule for the whole job is dependent upon the time needed for the first and second parts.

Network analysis is a way of scheduling the components of a job to find what is called the 'critical path', that is the minimum time necessary to get all components of the job done. The allocation of machine time, materials and human resources to individual jobs within the time and cost schedule follows. It is a tool for control because it can be used to keep track of the course of the different components of the job and make adjustments as and when necessary.

Consider the drawing of a network for producing a printed report. First list all steps that you can think of. They need not be in sequence.

1 Request to Departments for draft report—engineering, accounts, legal, administrative, sales, stores, transport, purchasing.
2 Preparation of draft by sections.
3 Compilation of statistics.
4 Collating of sections of report.
5 Preparation of draft (four copies) for consideration of Chairman.
6 Consideration by Chairman.
7 Alterations and preparation of duplicated draft for Board members.
8 Submission to Board members at least a week before a specially convened meeting.
9 Preparation of diagrams by printing department.
10 Photographs to be obtained for final document.
11 Alterations—retyping of individual sheets or whole report.
12 Printing department—production of proof copy.

*Network Analysis is also referred to as Critical Path Analysis (CPA), Critical Path Method (CPM) and Programme Evaluation and Review Technique (PERT). Although started as different techniques they now all serve the same purpose.

13 Proof-reading.
14 Final printing.
15 Individually typed covering letter to go with each copy.
16 Envelopes.
17 List of addressees.
18 Preparation for despatch of copies.

The network for the job is shown below. Each oval represents an event, that is the completion of an activity. Each activity is shown by an arrow. The numbers in the left half of the ovals are the activity numbers. For ease of reference these have been shown as corresponding with the numbers on the list above, but this would not normally be so.

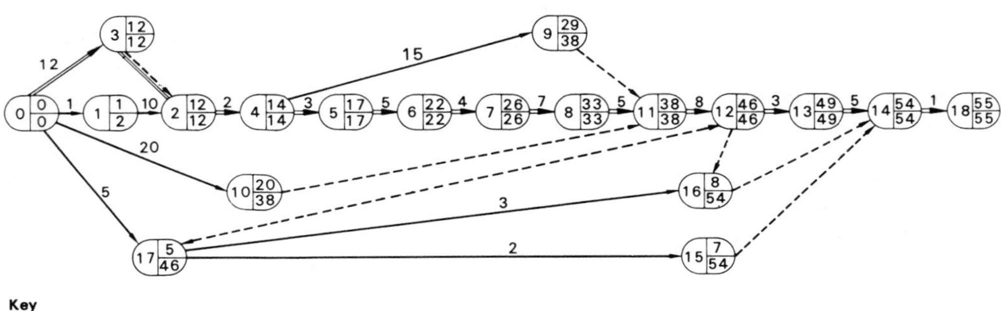

It can be seen that activities 1, 3, 10 and 17 can be started immediately. Activity 4 cannot begin until activities 2 and 3 have been completed. The dotted line from activity 3 shows this. It is called a 'dummy' activity because no work is required. Activity 12 cannot begin until activities 9, 10 and 11 have been completed. Activities 15 and 16 can begin when activity 17 is completed, but in the case of activity 16, activity 12 must also have been completed. (The size of the report would have to be known before envelopes could be prepared.) Finally activity 18 can be undertaken when activities 14, 15 and 16 are completed.

Stage 2 is to decide how long each activity will take. The numbers above the arrows are the time units—these may be hours, days or weeks. In the example the time unit is a day.

Now the time for each activity is known, Stage 3 is to calculate the minimum time required to reach each activity point. The largest number of days is inserted in the top half of the right-hand side of the ovals. So activity 1 takes 1 day, activity 3, 12 days. Activity 2 takes 12 days because activity 3 has to be completed before activity 4 can begin.

Stage 4 is to find the latest starting times for each activity. Although activity 17 can be started at the beginning it is clearly not necessary to do so since it takes only 8 days to finish it and activities 15 and 16, while activity 14, (the other activity which must be completed before the final activity 18) needs 54 days. Starting at the last figure (55) the time required for each activity is deducted. Where two or more activities meet the lowest figure is taken, for example, activity 4 shows 14, because activity 5 shows 17 – 3 = 14, although activity 9 shows 38 – 15 = 23.

Stage 5 is to find the 'critical path', that is the activities which *must* keep to schedule in order not to disrupt the whole time schedule. The activities which show the same time factor in both time to be taken and latest starting time are the 'critical' ones. This means that if there is any delay in completing activities 3, 2, 4, 5, 6, 7, 8, 11, 12, 13, 14, 18 the total time will be extended.

When a network has been completed it can be used to see if time units can be cut, perhaps to reduce costs, or to complete orders more quickly. It can also be used to allocate machine time and human resources. As the job progresses there may be unavoidable delays which will necessitate re-scheduling and may change the critical path. This can apply to activities outside the critical path as well as on it. In the network example, if activity 9 was started fifteen days before completion of activity 11 but took 17 days to complete (instead of the planned 15 days) the rest of the schedule would be delayed by 2 days.

TECHNIQUES FOR EFFECTIVE USE OF HUMAN RESOURCES

To produce anything it is necessary to have materials and manpower. In the same way that the best use of materials is made, so men must be used to the best advantage. There are various ways of doing this.

Manpower planning An essential component of corporate planning, manpower planning aims to make sure as far as possible that the right people are available for every category of job at the right time and in the right place. It is necessary to study the company objectives and possible future changes to assess the human resources which will be required. The existing manpower is reviewed in terms of ages (how many people will have the necessary experience and/or potential for management? how many people will be retiring each year in which fields?); skills (will new skills be needed?); qualifications (will more or different knowledge be required and if so, by whom?). It is then possible to see the gap between what will be required and what presently exists. To fill the gap it might be necessary to recruit new staff, either trained or to be trained; to up-grade by training; re-train in cases where present skills are likely to be redundant; transfer staff to gain insight into new fields. The decisions made will depend on many factors such as finance, the state of the employment market, whether salaries and fringe benefits offered are adequate to attract the right calibre of staff, whether required training facilities exist within the organisation or externally, whether the company policy aims to promote from within exclusively, and so on.

No planning can be foolproof, but it can prevent major crises arising unheralded, by showing up likely points of difficulty. It also enables control to be kept on recruiting and training.

X and Y Theory In order to get the best out of people they must be handled in the right way. There are a great variety of ideas and opinions on how this should be done and basically it depends on the character and personality of the manager and the characters and personalities of those being managed. The X Theory and the Y Theory are diametrically opposed. Theory X assumes that people have to be told what to do and be made to do it. Theory Y assumes that people are keen to participate and take responsibility and therefore should be consulted and integrated into the managerial system. As with most such concepts, the best system is probably somewhere between the two. Consideration must be given to workers as people—they should be kept informed, be given a pleasant working environment, proper reward, but a certain amount of direction and control is essential to mould a group of human beings into a team which will achieve predetermined objectives.

Job evaluation The process of deciding the reward value, that is wage or salary level, of each job is called job evaluation. There are four main methods of evaluating jobs: all require a job description (see Chap. 15) as a basis for assessment.

The RANKING method, regarded as suitable for small organisations only, consists of arranging jobs in order of difficulty, or importance, or value. It is not suitable for large organisations because of the difficulty of equating jobs in different departments, though by computerising the comparison technique, that is ranking each job against every other job in the organisation, the method has been used successfully. Its weakness lies in the fact that only rough criteria are used and the ranking of a job depends to a large extent on the judgment of the ranker, who may be biased. No specific answer can be given to an employee who questions the ranking of his job.

The POINTS RATING method involves analysing each job from a detailed job description into factors such as skill, mental requirements, physical requirements, responsibility, working conditions. Points are then allocated to each factor, a points system having first been devised covering all aspects. The total number of points for a job dictates the pay level.

The FACTOR-COMPARISON method is based on an analysis of each key job into factors as for the points rating method. Each factor is allocated a pay rate which can then be applied to the factor analysis of all other jobs. In other words, all jobs related to a key job are compared with it.

The GRADING (OR CLASSIFICATION) METHOD* is based on job functions. Tasks

* The Institute of Administrative Management publication *Job Evaluation* contains detailed specifications for all aspects of office work common to the majority of commercial and industrial organisations. (Available from the Publications Department, Institute of Administrative Management, 205 High Street, Beckenham, Kent BR3 1BA.)

are graded from A to F depending on the amount of supervision required, degree of responsibility, and the complexity of the work. For example preparing cash book entries and receipts by simple copying under the close direction of a clerk of a higher grade is a Grade C task. Private secretarial work in a complete sense for a senior executive is a Grade F task. This system is widely used for salaried jobs including those in Government organisations.

Job interest or job enrichment People should be given the kind of work and responsibility for which they have aptitude, ability and capacity. If a person is bad at his job it may be because he is unable to cope with it, it is too easy and therefore boring, or it is too narrow to hold his interest. Job enrichment aims to give people more interest in their work. This may be achieved by automating routine work, thus freeing people for more interesting jobs; or if this is not possible, by distributing the routine work among more people and giving them additional duties of greater interest; keeping people informed of policy decisions so that they see their own role in the overall plan can motivate them; making them aware of the function of the section/department so that they see how their own activities form an integral part of the whole; giving them a sense of responsibility to see that their own work is well done in order not to upset some other activity carried out by a colleague.

Work study The aim of work study is to attain greater efficiency, that is less input to achieve the same output, or greater output with the same input. For example, the aim may be to produce the same volume of products with fewer men. The two means used, method study and work measurement, can be applied to almost any form of human activity.

METHOD STUDY sets out to find the best way of doing a job and to streamline the processes. For example in a factory the progress of a product during assembly should require as little movement as possible of materials and personnel. Paper work may cause delays. Positioning of tools because stacking facilities are inadequate may mean more movement for the worker, thus causing greater fatigue, which reduces productivity.

TIME STUDY is one of the techniques of work measurement. It is used to determine as accurately as possible from a limited number of observations, the time necessary to carry out a given activity. To arrive at a time for a particular activity it is necessary to rate as well as to time. Rating is an assessment of performance for which there is a British Standard scale of 0–100. A trained operator of average ability is expected to work at 75 performance on hourly or basic payrate. 100 performance is 'standard' or 'incentive' performance which normally merits $33\frac{1}{3}$ per cent bonus on basic pay.

A complete work study project sets out to investigate every facet of the work involved in a particular section or department. Frequently such a study highlights the necessity for further studies in other areas, since any section or department must work in conjunction with others.

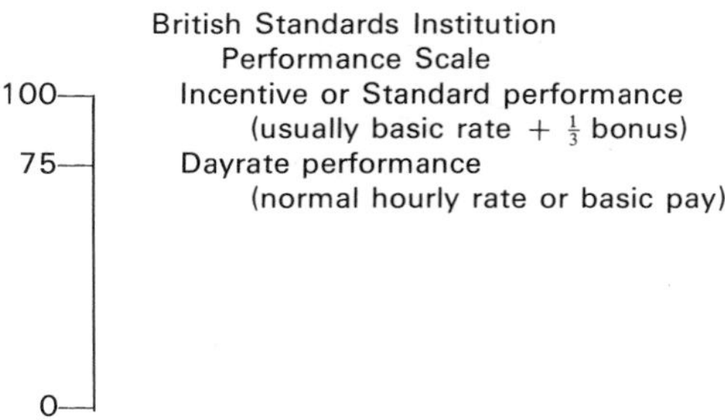

ORGANISATION AND METHODS

Work study when undertaken in an office is called Organisation and Methods, or O & M. An O & M project consists of six stages:

1 Preliminary discussion with management and employees concerned.
2 Survey of the present situation.
3 Production of a full report.
4 Discussion of recommendations with management.
5 Implementation of recommendations.
6 Monitoring.

Preliminary discussion It is essential that full discussions are held with all concerned, both staff and management, before the survey begins to ensure the necessary co-operation during the survey. The smoothness with which a survey can be conducted by the O & M personnel depends to a large degree on the co-operation of the staff in the department concerned. They must be reassured on the question of redundancy, and that they will be consulted before major changes are made.

Survey There are two parts to an O & M survey.

(i) Method Study is conducted to find out what systems are in use and how they can be improved. Various charts may be used in the course of the survey.

a *Specimen chart* shows specimens of the documents involved in a particular procedure. When amplified to include movement lines (that is lines drawn to show where each document is taken or sent) it becomes a *Procedure Map*. It is particularly useful for comparison if charts of both the present and proposed methods are prepared.

b *Work Distribution chart* analyses the activities being carried out. There are three stages. *Stage 1* is concerned with cost. It is necessary to check with every person involved in the activity so that the following questions can be answered:

a What is the activity and why is it done?
b What does this activity accomplish?
c Why is this activity necessary?
d What are the benefits and costs?
e What is the cost order, compared with the importance order?
f What contribution does this activity make to the objectives of the department?

The aim is to reduce cost; the answers to these questions will show what unnecessary activities can be eliminated and identify high costs of minor activities.

Stage 2 is concerned with the location of operators and the time factor.

g Where should the activity be carried out, when and by whom?
h Where (in which department) should this work be done?
i When (day of week or month) should this work be done?
j When (how often) is it required?
k Who has the skill needed?
l Who duplicates or overlaps?
m Who should specialise?
n Who will stand in when necessary?

The answers to these questions should result in assigning the work to a department where it can be done at the least overall cost. Productivity can be increased by balancing the daily workload, arranging batch work to save 'make ready' and 'put away' time, using trained operators and planning for flexibility by providing 'stand in' operators.

Stage 3 is concerned with the method of operation and its effect on the operators.

o How is the activity carried out?
p How are skills utilised?
r How much checking is done?
s How many monotonous tasks are there?

The answers should show where skills are wasted and/or mistakes are being made through lack of skill. It can also be seen how monotonous tasks can be spread either by dividing them among several operators or by rotating the operators.

c *Departmental distribution chart* shows the distribution of the paperwork involved in a procedure, highlighting unnecessary movement of documents and those not used at all.

d *Flow chart* shows the actual stages in a process or a procedure. It analyses the nature and number of operations involved and shows how the work flows. A procedure chart is primarily intended to show movement (a document may be passed from one department to another for various processes to be carried out on it); a process chart highlights the individual operations involved in the procedure. If the procedure or process chart is very complex it may be necessary to have a written explanation to be read in conjunction with the chart.

Symbols are used to indicate

operation ○ produce work
inspection □ checking or verifying
transport ⇨ movement
storage ▽ filing
delay D temporary retention

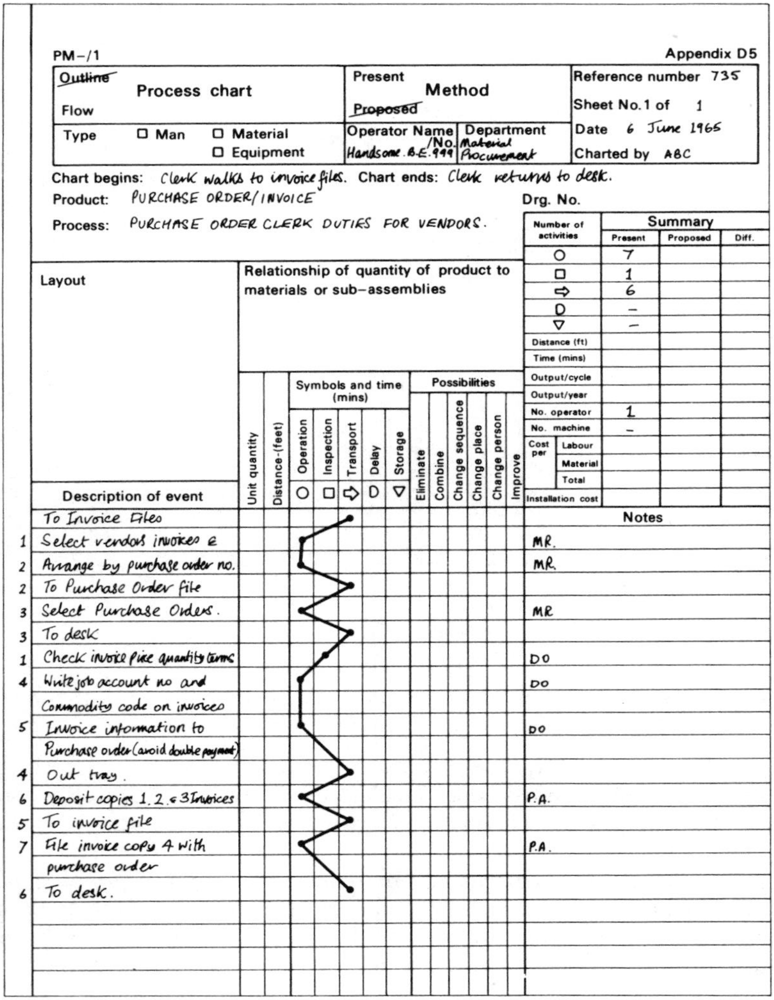

PM–/1 Appendix D5

~~Outline~~ Process chart Flow	Present Method ~~Proposed~~	Reference number 735 Sheet No. 1 of 1
Type □ Man □ Material □ Equipment	Operator Name/No. Handsome. B.E. 999 — Department Material Procurement	Date 6 June 1965 Charted by ABC

Chart begins: Clerk walks to invoice files. Chart ends: Clerk returns to desk.

Product: PURCHASE ORDER/INVOICE

Drg. No.

Process: PURCHASE ORDER CLERK DUTIES FOR VENDORS.

Layout

Relationship of quantity of product to materials or sub-assemblies

Number of activities	Summary Present	Proposed	Diff.
○	7		
□	1		
⇨	6		
D	–		
▽	–		
Distance (ft)			
Time (mins)			
Output/cycle			
Output/year			
No. operator	1		
No. machine	–		
Cost per Labour			
Cost per Material			
Cost per Total			
Installation cost			

	Description of event	Unit quantity	Distance-(feet)	Operation ○	Inspection □	Transport ⇨	Delay D	Storage ▽	Eliminate	Combine	Change sequence	Change place	Change person	Improve	Notes
	To Invoice Files					●									
1	Select vendors invoices &			●											MR.
2	Arrange by purchase order no.			●											MR.
2	To Purchase Order file					●									
3	Select Purchase Orders.			●											MR
3	To desk					●									
1	Check invoice price quantity terms				●										DO
4	Write job account no and			●											DO
	Commodity code on invoices														
5	Invoice information to			●											DO
	Purchase order (avoid double payment)														
4	Out tray.					●									
6	Deposit copies 1, 2 & 3 Invoices			●											P.A.
5	To invoice file					●									
7	File invoice copy 4 with			●											P.A.
	purchase order														
6	To desk.					●									

computer. Special symbols are used for the various stages involved. On page 357 is an example of a flow process chart for the production of an invoice.

Flow charts can be used to show the stages in a procedure which uses a computer. Special symbols are used for the various stages involved. On page 357 is an example of a flow process chart for the production of an invoice.

e *Outline process chart* is a simplified flow chart showing only main operations and inspections.

f *Multiple activity chart* is used to show ineffective and non-productive time of one or more people and machines involved in jobs which consist of a number of activities. The chart below shows the ineffective time of a duplicating machine operator and the non-productive time of the machine.

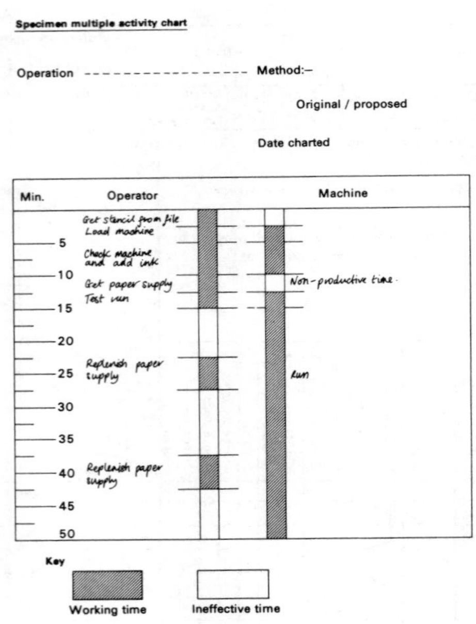

g *Volume chart* is produced in graph form to show the amount of production achieved for a specific activity during certain periods.

Charts should show clearly the subject; whether it is of an existing procedure or a recommended one; scales used (time, distance) when appropriate; key to show abbreviations, symbols, colour coding; date; originator.

In addition to the charts, diagrams and models may be used. A *flow diagram* shows the movement of people and/or documents. (The diagram of the mailing room in Chapter 3 is an example of a flow diagram.) A *string diagram* shows the actual distance of movement. To illustrate layout a *scale model* is useful.

(ii) Clerical Work Measurement (CWM) is the second part of a survey to assess the effectiveness of the human resources. There are various techniques used in work measurement.

a *Time study* is the timing of activities or component parts of activities with a stop watch. In conjunction with time study, rating is used (see page 358). In office work the British Standard rating of 75 is accepted as the norm for purposes of work measurement.

b *Pre-determined Motion Time System* (PMTS) is the building up of established times for the basic human motions involved in a job, at a defined level of performance. All PMT systems are based on the fact that skilled workers, who have had sufficient practice, will carry out a motion in approximately the same time.

c *Activity sampling* means taking random observations of a group of machines, workers or processes to find out what is happening at the moment of observation. There must be a large number of observations over a considerable period at all sorts of times. This kind of measurement does not give an accurate assessment but may be sufficient for a particular purpose.

d *Synthetic data* is produced for a certain operation or part of an operation as a result of direct time studies. The standard times for the basic elements of a job are combined to arrive at a total for a job, such as typing a letter. This particular operation involves collation of a carbon pack; insertion of pack into the machine; typing the letter including the operation of various parts of the machine; removal of pack from the machine; checking; decollation of pack; preparation of letter for signature.

On page 360 a letter is shown with a grid placed over it. (The grid is a template of transparent material such as plastic.) To measure the time which should be taken to do this piece of work the body of the letter is measured in square inches by placing a square-inch grid over it as shown. Depending on the kind of machine (electric or manual) and the size of type there are established times for typing a square inch. The specimen below measures 10 square inches and an addition of 2 square inches is made for the inside address, etc.* The machine has pica type and we assume it was typed on a manual machine. The time per square inch has been established as 0.37 mins. The time for this specimen is therefore $12 \times 0.37 = 4.44$ mins. There must be added to this the time for collation and decollation (which includes insertion into and release from the typewriter and assembling typed papers ready for signature). Assume one carbon copy, the time is 0.93 mins. An allowance must also be made for the correction of errors. (The time allowed is based on an average of one error in every 900 key strokes.) The error correction time for an original plus a carbon copy using pica type is 0.035 mins per square inch, that is

*Usually paragraph spaces compensate for the address, etc. and no allowance is made, but in this case the grid fits the body of the letter exactly so a standard allowance of 2 square inches is made.

0.42 mins for the specimen. The total time which should be taken to type the letter should therefore be 4.44 + 0.93 + 0.42 = 5.79 minutes. Typewritten work may also be measured in words, lines or pages, or in Treasury Units. (A Treasury Unit is equivalent to approximately 24 single spaced six-inch lines of élite type.) Output varies considerably but an average performance of about 400 lines a day may be expected of any typist. Some typists achieve as much as 800 lines per day. Synthetic data are available for operating machines including typewriters; calculating machines; punch card machines; addressing, mailing and record-housing equipment; reprographic machines; and for clerical operations, such as completing documents.

It would not, of course, be fair to apply such work measurement times to odd pieces of work. It must be done over a considerable period of time to allow for all contingencies. Such an exercise is usually carried out with other methods of recording work done, some of which cannot be measured.

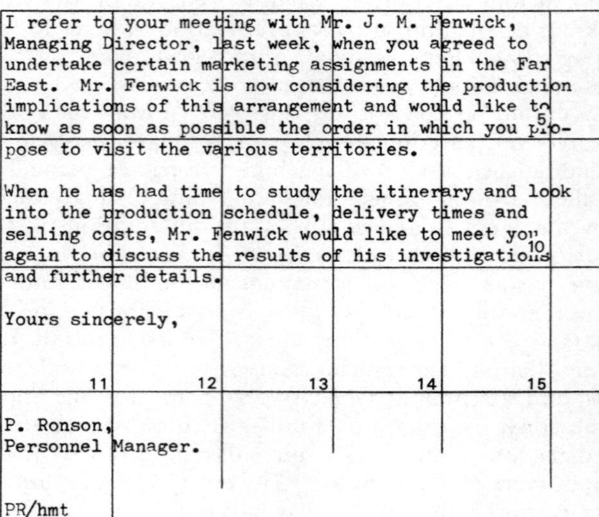

PERS.1052/72 10th September 1972

John D. Rose, Esq.,
15 Waverley Drive,
OFFCHURCH ON4 6PD

Dear Mr. Rose,

I refer to your meeting with Mr. J. M. Fenwick, Managing Director, last week, when you agreed to undertake certain marketing assignments in the Far East. Mr. Fenwick is now considering the production implications of this arrangement and would like to know as soon as possible the order in which you propose to visit the various territories.

When he has had time to study the itinerary and look into the production schedule, delivery times and selling costs, Mr. Fenwick would like to meet you again to discuss the results of his investigations and further details.

Yours sincerely,

11 12 13 14 15

P. Ronson,
Personnel Manager.

PR/hmt

e *Commercial packages* which are available from various consultants include Group Capacity Assessment (GCA), Clerical Work Improvement Programme (CWIP) and Variable Factor Programming (VFP). All include some method study and one or more techniques of work measurement, although not usually the most accurate. Consultants usually train staff to operate and control new systems when they are implemented.

Report The report produced by the O & M team must include details of the methods used in making the survey, the findings with conclusions relating to existing situations, recommendations for improvements and/or changes explaining what results can be expected.

Discussion Management will certainly need further details of what is proposed and what the changes will do to improve productivity. These days staff are also usually involved in the discussions. It is essential that full agreement be reached on what is to be done. Once approval has been given the staff must be fully informed to ensure that they co-operate in implementing the changes. It is for management to make sure that adequate training is given.

Implementation The approved changes must be carried out in logical sequence, possibly in conjunction with a training programme.

Monitoring To ensure the continuation of higher productivity, a system of monitoring must be carried out. This is usually achieved by keeping records of work volumes and hours worked, which, when related to the times established for an activity during the original work measurement exercise, provide a constant measure of efficiency.

As part of the O & M project two points often need attention.

1 OFFICE LAYOUT Space must be used to maximum effectiveness. Arrangement of cabinets, furniture and machines must take into consideration the movement of people (in some cases it will be considerable, in others very little), ease of access to constantly used documents/files and machines, volume of materials in use, noise, lighting, heating, frequency of visitors.

The open plan office is becoming more common because an area arranged in this way can accommodate far more people than the same area divided into individual offices.

The open plan is frequently used for large secretarial pools, accounts sections, correspondence departments. However, people react to their environments, and the landscaped office, referred to as Bürolandschaft because it originated in Germany, is being used more and more. Instead of being arranged in rows the desks, although remaining in sections, are placed at different angles in non-uniform groups. At the same time acoustic screens are used to divide one section from the other to give privacy and deaden noise. Wall to wall carpeting, shrubs and plants are used to create a more relaxed atmosphere. Many companies are now producing special filing cabinets, and other equipment to suit this type of office. Experiments have been carried out to find out whether the people work better with quiet background music and this has been confirmed for certain types of work. In such cases piped music is provided.

Any office layout must take into consideration the provisions of the Offices, Shops, and Railway Premises Act 1963. Each individual must have a minimum area in which to work; the rooms must be of minimum height; ventilation, heating and lighting must be adequate; fire escapes must be provided and easily accessible; fire prevention and the siting of fire fighting equipment must also be considered. (More details of the Act are given in Chapter 15.)

2 FORM DESIGN The objective in producing a written or typewritten document is to communicate information. There must be some way of ensuring that every piece of information is transmitted in the right form to the right person at the right time. It is also necessary to make sure that information is not transmitted to people who do not need it. Much routine information can be transmitted by means of a form, and if several people need the same information, the appropriate number of copies can be made at the same time. If the people concerned do not need to refer to the information but must merely be kept in the picture, the communication can be circulated.

When designing a form, it is necessary to decide who needs the information, where, for what purpose and in what detail. A form can then be designed to accommodate the required data in logical sequence. At the same time the production aspect should be considered and printing should be arranged in a way that line spacing on the typewriter is catered for, and that adequate space is provided for the information that has to be typed. It should be possible to pick off any single piece of information at a glance from a well designed form. Most forms are numbered consecutively, either on pads or joined to each other with perforations (continuous stationery). Many forms are produced in sets, each copy being in a different colour to facilitate distribution. It is possible to create a complete system with each set of forms interrelated, so that the pink copy, for example, of every set is sent to the Accounts Department. If one particular form in the system is not required by the Accounts Department, that set does not contain a pink copy. Many sets of forms are now produced by the spirit duplicating process either using masks or line selectors (see Chapter 5) so that each copy has on it only the information required by the person/department to receive it. Certain photocopying machines can also be used for this purpose.

When designing a form the company 'image' must be kept in mind. Some organisations have a symbol or emblem which appears on all stationery, packaging, advertisements, delivery vans, buildings. The laurel wreath used by all United Nations organisations and agencies is an example. Wavy Line Food Distributors is a commercial example. This is known as 'house style' and should be carried on all forms.

For the secretary O & M is really the application of common sense to any job to find the quickest way of doing it accurately, which is another way of saying efficiently. A typist having a thousand envelopes to address can place the new envelopes in a pile, face upwards, with the bottom of the envelopes towards her. With her left hand, she takes hold of the bottom edge of the envelope from the top of the pile and inserts it into her typewriter using her right hand to operate the platen knob. Having pre-set the left margin (and tabulation stops, if indented style is used), and line space regulators, she types the address; with her left hand she extracts the envelopes from the machine, using the right hand to operate the paper release lever. From the O & M point of view, it will be quicker for her to use block display instead of indented display because this will eliminate the time for operating the tabulator bar.

Clerical Work Management (CWM) A very sophisticated form of reorganising an office, Clerical Work Management involves a survey of the organisation structure of the department/s, staffing, organisation and methods including a very detailed analysis of work done, procedures in operation, and time study. The interrelation and interdependence of the department with other departments is carefully investigated and may be reorganised by directive from top management.

Multi-Aspect Data Correlation and Presentation MADCAP is a highly sophisticated computer-assisted system of measuring creative and managerial work, the sort of work which cannot be measured by any of the usual measurement techniques. Its aim is to provide factual information which can be used to improve organisational weaknesses in the creative and managerial areas of administration. It can be used on a wide range of people from junior clerks to senior managers.

MANAGEMENT RESOURCES

Management resources is a term used for services available to management, which though usually expensive, can be well worth using if carefully selected for a specific purpose with a definite objective.

Management services A number of large and medium size organisations have a Management Services Division (MSD). This is staffed by various specialists in such fields as Organisation and Methods, accounting, systems analysis, work study. When it is felt that a company within a group, or a department within an organisation is not as efficient as it should be—if profits are decreasing, turnover is falling, labour costs are rising, overhead costs are increasing—a team consisting of appropriate specialists carries out a survey. A report is made setting out the details of the survey, a clear assessment of the situation and recommended action. It is then for management to decide whether or not to implement the recommendations. The MSD staff will be expected to assist departmental heads in whatever reorganisation is necessary.

Management consultants Organisations which are not large enough to have their own Management Services Division can call in management consultants to do such work. The consultants charge fees usually on a weekly basis depending on the size of the team necessary. They may or may not be asked to implement their recommendations.

Computer consultants When an organisation is considering the possibility of installing a computer there are many points to be considered. First of all it is essential to examine carefully what benefits will result from installation. If it can be proved that the exercise will be worthwhile, the most appropriate type of equipment for the work to be done must be selected. Equipment consists of hardware (machines) and software (the programmes and systems). Systems which will give the required information in the required form must be designed. The planning and control of systems to improve management performance, that is designing systems which will provide adequate information accurately for decision-making, must be prepared. Staff must be trained to operate the computer and staff not directly employed for computer operation must be trained to use its output. Their work may have to be adjusted so that it fits into the entire system of which the computer is a part. Finally, trained staff will have to be recruited.

Genuine computer consultants will undertake a feasibility study to investigate the potential benefits. If they find it would be worthwhile to instal a computer, and if their recommendations are accepted by management, they will proceed with the next stages.

Public Relations, Advertising, Marketing, Design Consultants Some firms have an 'account' with an advertising consultant, that is to say they put all special jobs in the hands of specialists. The launching of a new product may involve the design of wrappers, design of advertisements for different media, market research to assess the most profitable media. However, not all use consultants on a continuing basis; they may employ them for a special promotion only. It is reckoned that firms that have an account change their consultants every two or three years. This could be to give a 'lift' to the company's image, or to get a different angle on products.

Selection Consultants and Agencies Since advertising vacant positions, reading and sorting written applications, short-listing and interviewing candidates once or even twice, and finally selecting the person for the job can be a time-consuming and difficult task, many firms use selection consultants. A number of management consultants perform the function as an additional service. Usually they advertise specific jobs and do the initial sifting and interviewing. They short-list the most suitable of the interviewees to be interviewed by the employer.

There are also selection agencies which may have a list of people wishing to change their employment. Such people may be included in the selection process.

Institutions There are a number of professional institutions to which directors and managers can belong. Services provided include journals, training courses, advisory bureaux. Such institutions include The Institute of Directors, the British Institute of Management. There are also the specialist professional bodies for such fields as engineering, accounting, marketing, personnel managers.

SOME MANAGEMENT TERMS

Brainstorming—A meeting of people, ideally twelve, called together to get as many ideas as possible in as short a time as possible on a particular subject. Everyone throws in his contribution and it does not matter how ridiculous or wild it may appear. One idea often leads to another—cross-fertilisation. All worthwhile ideas are afterwards scrutinised from every angle. An important practical point is that everything said must be recorded because such uninhibited talk is easily forgotten and some of the best ideas may be lost.

Cost Benefit Analysis (CBA)—Comparing the costs of a proposed or existing course of action or system with the resulting effects, which may be either good or bad, tangible or intangible, short-term or long-term. The cost of setting up and running a public relations department in a company could be analysed in relation to the amount of business which would be acquired, directly and indirectly, as a result of the department's activities.

Cost Effectiveness Analysis—Analysing the result of expenditure to see (a) whether the desired objective has been or will be achieved, and (b) whether the expenditure could be reduced without impairing the result.

Cybernetics—The study of communications and control between men and machines in complex systems.

Delegation—The art of passing work to subordinates so that all detailed and routine work is done and the necessary information passed back to the manager, leaving him free to analyse situations and make decisions.

Discounted Cash Flow—Money invested yields its return, the amount of which can be pre-determined, later. Money becomes of less real value in time, so a given amount in three years will be worth more than the same amount in five years. Discounted cash flow is a system of assessing the real value of return on investment.

Ergonomics—People react to situations and environment. Ergonomics is the study of these reactions and the design of instruments, tools and machines to facilitate work. For example certain types of work may be more easily done if a desk is specially designed for it.

Fatigue Study—All work involves fatigue, physical and/or mental. The greater the fatigue the less productive the worker. The fatigue factor is an important element in work study (see page 358).

Forecasting—Predicting future production, sales, capital investment, etc. from data compiled over a period, which will vary with the accuracy and/or length of forecasting required.

Incentive Schemes—Usually, though not always, incentive schemes are introduced into factories. Workers are paid a set wage for a certain amount of production. Workers producing more than the minimum required will be paid more on a pro rata basis. Incentive schemes may be on an individual basis or on a group basis, i.e. extra production by a section or group of workers resulting in a bonus for all. The latter is most likely to be used in an office.

Industrial Relations—The relations which exist between management and other employees, usually represented by trade unions. On a formal basis industrial relations cover the machinery for consultation, worker participation in management, effective shop floor communication.

Line Management—The line by which work is delegated from the top to the bottom. The manager delegates to his deputy, who delegates to his supervisors, who delegates to his section heads, who delegate to their workers. A section head should not go directly to the deputy manager with a complaint; the manager should not give an instruction directly to a worker.

Lines of Communication—Communication must be both upwards and downwards and also horizontally. That is to say instructions must be passed down the line and information must be passed up the line. It may also be necessary to pass information between sections/departments/companies within a group. A Sales Manager cannot give instructions to a foreman in the workshop, but he needs information from the Production Manager.

Long-term planning—Similar to corporate planning, long-term planning involves reviewing all aspects of an organisation's activities as they are expected to develop in the next five years or more. Objectives are reviewed first and then the factors on which achievement of those objectives depend, such as capital investment, market expansion, staff, etc.

Management by Crisis—When a problem arises which cannot be solved because two people refuse to compromise or one to give way, a manager can create a situation in which action will have to be taken. A Production Manager might say he needs new machinery costing £100,000. The Finance section say such an amount cannot be spared. The Production Manager threatens that if he cannot have the machinery he cannot produce the required output. Either Finance must give him the money he wants or lower production must be accepted. This is a dangerous technique because the one who threatens might find himself displaced to make room for someone more co-operative.

Management by Exception—This is really another way of saying proper delegation. Each person in the line from manager down picks out the important issues on which to concentrate, passing down the routine and detailed work. In reverse it means that only exceptional cases are referred to management, others being dealt with down the line in accordance with pre-determined instructions or general guide-lines. Exceptions might be a considerable increase/decrease in production, or in costs.

Operational Research—In small organisations a procedure necessary for stock control is fairly simple to establish. In large organisations with mass production units it can be a very complex problem, as can production planning, scheduling, sales forecasting, distribution, etc. Operational Research sets out to solve highly complex problems by using mathematical and other scientific techniques to identify the significant facts, their interrelationship and interdependence, and thus their relative importance.

Performance Appraisal—Assessing the effectiveness of a manager's performance in relation to objectives.

Qualitative Analysis—Determining the elements which contribute to the final degree of quality required.

Quality Control—Assessing the quality of work done in comparison with predetermined standards. Quality control is the responsibility of supervisors. In large organisations inspection staff ensure that standards are maintained. It also involves the examination of sub-standard work with the object of eliminating errors by training, improved methods, etc.

Risk Analysis—It is very seldom that a manager will have concrete information on every facet of a situation about which he must make a decision. There will be probable conditions and possible conditions and variable conditions. The extent of risk will depend on the ratio of known information to unknown and the seriousness of the unknown. Decisions are usually based on forecasts which invariably contain some uncertain elements. The degree of uncertainty is analysed and the various possibilities worked out to see their likely effect on the forecast. The extent of the variations show the extent of risk involved in a decision based on the forecast.

Sales/Operation Planning Control (SOPC). This technique is used mostly in America and to some extent in Europe. It is based on a corporate approach. The aim is the closest possible co-ordination and integration of all systems in the organisation to achieve greater profitability. The focal point of the system is the customer. Going back up the line come the product, resources needed to produce and distribute the goods to the customer, use of resources, controlling the pre-determined plan.

Sensitivity Analysis—Nothing can be done without human agency at some point. In modern commerce and industry changes are frequent and sometimes radical. Human beings cannot be treated like machines but must be taken into account when changes are to be made. The right attitudes can be achieved by consultation, training, communication.

Value Analysis—Costs are made up of a number of factors whether they be material costs, production costs, overhead costs, information costs. In relation to production the design, methods of production, materials, etc. are systematically investigated to see if costs can be cut without impairing the value, or the value can be increased without increasing the cost. This technique can also be used to find out whether a service or procedure, for example accounting, is costing more than it should in terms of its value to the organisation, or could be done as effectively at less cost.

FURTHER READING

Essentials of Management, Joseph L. Massie (Prentice Hall).
Factories Act 1961.

Glossary of Management Techniques, Her Majesty's Stationery Office.
Management in Action (monthly publication), MacLaren.
Management Techniques, John Argenti (Allen & Unwin).
Offices, Shops and Railway Premises Act 1963.
Personal Assistant and Senior Secretaries, Janet Moore and Gloria Neal (The Industrial Society).
Procedure and Process Charts for Office Use, The Institute of Administrative Management.
Procedure Charts for Administrative Work, The Institute of Administrative Management.
Work Measurement in Typewriting, Burke & Watts (Pitman).
Work Study in the Office, Harry P. Cemach (MacLaren & Sons Ltd).

GROUP DISCUSSION

Discuss which management techniques can be of use to a personal secretary

a in her dealings with junior staff, and
b in taking her full share in the manager/secretary team.

EXERCISES

1 i What is a "master budget"? When is it prepared?
ii Why is such a budget necessary?

2 Below is a budgetary control statement. Explain what information this statement gives an office manager and how it is useful to him.

Telephone Account—Calls

	Budget	Actual	Variance
Month 1	£65	£68	– £3
2	£65	£72	– £7
3	£100	£136	– £36
4	£150	£141	+ £9
5	£65	£92	– £27
6	£65	£80	– £15

3 Why is it necessary to control stock levels? Explain briefly how this is done.

4 What are the main items of expenditure included when costing a product?

5 Explain the following terms:

costing
cost/profit ratio
company appraisal
programmer

job evaluation
method study
activity sampling
implementation
house style
computer hardware
cost benefit analysis
delegation
line communication
performance appraisal
sensitivity analysis.

6 Below is a breakeven chart. What does it tell you?

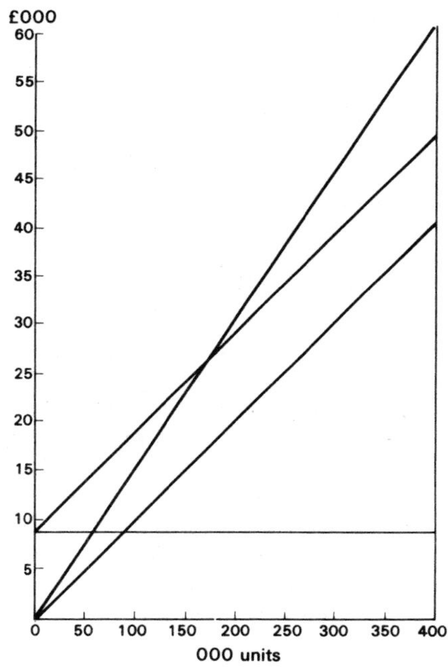

7 What is the purpose of internal audit? Does it take the place of external audit? Explain your answer.

8 What is meant by corporate planning? What sort of points must be considered?

9 Explain the difference between 'management objectives' and 'management by objectives'.

10 The following abbreviations are frequently used for certain management techniques. Give their full titles and briefly explain what they are.

(i) PPB (ii) SA (iii) CPA (iv) O & M (v) B/E pt.

11 What is the difference between 'random sampling' and 'quota sampling'? Which is the more accurate technique?

12 Below is a network analysis. Reproduce it and indicate the critical path in red.

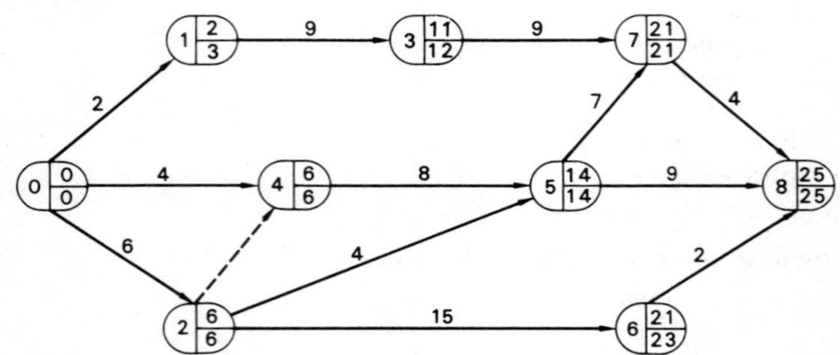

13 What are your personal views about the X and Y theories of management?

14 Suggest ways in which greater job interest can be created for a typist who complains about the monotony of her job.

15 There are six principle stages in an Organisation and Methods project. List them with a brief explanation of each.

16 During an O & M survey a number of charts may be produced. Name five and illustrate at least two of them.

17 Name three office procedures, other than typewriting, to which clerical work measurement techniques can be applied.

18 You are told that you and your staff of a stenographer, two typists and a clerk are to move into a new landscaped office. You will be allocated an area of 250 square feet. Draw a diagram (to scale) showing how you will position the necessary furniture and equipment.

19 On page 371 is an example of a badly designed form. Study it and say why you think it is bad and how it could be improved.

20 CWM can stand for Clerical Work Management or Clerical Work Measurement. What is the difference?

21 You are secretary to the Marketing Manager of a company which is developing a new product. On behalf of your boss write to the Advertising Consultant telling him about the new product (which can be imaginary) and the services you will require from him.

22 You are asked by your boss to attend a brainstorming meeting with him to take notes. What will you expect?

ORDER FORM

OFFICE SUPPLIES CO. LTD.

16 Park Street,
Bournemouth,
Hants. BH2 6AC

Tel. 74810

To:

Code No.	Unit Price	Description	Qty. Ordered	Qty. Despatched	Total Price

Date:
Delivery:

9

Planning Journeys

"If you are flying solo, your secretary can still make or mar the trip."

How to win the Business Battle, Eric Webster

"For the businessman, travelling hopefully is no substitute for arrival, but competence and survival do depend on travelling sensibly."

Dr. H. Beric Wright, "Keeping the globe-trotters healthy and happy," *The Director*, June 1972

Whether your boss asks you to arrange a journey to a one-day conference in the next town or a round-the-world trip lasting four months, the same attention must be given to detail. Every journey has to be given individual treatment because although the approach is basically routine, the details are different and it is perfection in detail that makes a journey a success or a nightmare.

Travelling is tiring and your boss must be at his best all the time. He will probably be meeting far more people in a day than would normally be the case and frequently the profits of his company are at stake. You can ensure that he can give his undivided attention to his job by preparing meticulously the mechanics of the trip.

Planning Take a new folder for every journey. On a sheet of foolscap paper make a check list of the arrangements which have to be made for the particular journey being planned. These are best arranged by headings, leaving plenty of space between each for details. The main headings are likely to be:

> Travel; Hotels; Companies to be dealt with; Meetings/Conferences; Documents; Money; Insurances; Itinerary.

Staple this sheet inside the front cover of the folder and add the details to each heading as they are decided.

Into the folder will go all papers connected with the journey, such as correspondence, papers for meetings, notes on people who will be met and business to be discussed, reminders for last minute details, etc.

If the trip is to be a short one it may be possible to make firm arrangements immediately, but in the case of travel abroad, especially on a long trip when arrangements will have to be carefully dovetailed, it may be necessary to make provisional reservations and arrangements for meetings, etc. to be confirmed later.

Itinerary The first step is to plan a draft itinerary in accordance with the wishes of your boss as to methods of travel, and duration of stay in each place. This may have to be redrafted several times according to trains, flights or ships available. To help you make the first draft use the general books of reference for travel.

Air travel:	*ABC World Airways Guide*	
Rail travel:	*ABC Railway Guide*	
	British Railways Regional and Continental Time-tables	
Road travel:	*Automobile Association Handbook*	British Isles and Continental
	Royal Automobile Club Handbook	
	Maps	
Sea travel:	*ABC Shipping Guide*	
Hotels:	*AA and RAC Handbooks*	
	Courtney Edwards Hotel Guide, etc.	

It is important when drafting itineraries for long trips that sufficient relaxation time is allowed to offset the strain of long flights and time changes. It is possible for a man to step off a 'plane and drive straight to a high-powered meeting but highly undesirable. Quite apart from wanting to bath and change he needs a good night's sleep in a comfortable bed and a good meal at a table before heavy mental concentration. He may also wish to meet people unofficially before real business begins to be 'sure of his ground'.

Having drafted the itinerary, check with a travel agent or the appropriate air or shipping lines. When planning flights it is important to find out which routes connect with each other because often a lot of time can be saved by taking connecting flights rather than direct flights which may only take place once or twice a week. As some countries have a considerable number of public holidays,* this point should be checked so that your boss does not have to spend time in a place on days when he cannot do business. Find out how much time he will need for writing reports, and be sure to allow sufficient free time for this.

Reservations Having checked the draft itinerary (see p. 379) with your boss you can start making reservations, for which you will need some information from him.

AIR Some airlines allow passengers to choose seats before the flight and in any case are likely to allocate in accordance with the wishes of an important traveller. Try to get to know the seating preferences of your chief—window seat, front or rear of plane if the class he is travelling allows a choice, smoking or non-smoking section of the cabin. In many types of aircraft seats A and F in each row are window seats.

Certain people are recognised as VIPs, in which case the airline must be informed so that arrangements can be made for the VIP lounge at the airport to be available. If the flight involves an overnight stop, the airline usually arranges hotel accommodation but the point should be checked. If the company's own aeroplane or helicopter is to be used for part or all of the journey, the chief pilot must be notified of details well in advance so that he can make all necessary arrangements for landing, refuelling, etc. His advice should be sought as to flight duration and most suitable times.

RAIL It is always advisable to book a seat and you will need to know whether your chief prefers a seat facing or back to the engine, window seat, in a smoker or non-smoker carriage. Depending on the time of travel it may be more suitable to book a seat in a dining car, or even both in a carriage and dining car. A sleeper can be arranged for overnight travel.

ROAD Arrangements must be made for your boss to get to and from the place of departure. He may prefer to be driven to the airport rather than the air terminal. If he is to drive himself to the airport arrangements must be made with an airport parking service to meet him and take over his car, and to have it waiting for him at the airport on his return. If his wife wishes to see him off and meet him on his return, transport must be arranged for her.

* See Appendix F.

If he is travelling to his destination by road it may be necessary to book garage facilities either at the hotel where he will stay or in a local garage or covered car park.

Your boss may wish to hire a car in the town/s he will be visiting and he may like to have this available for him at the station or airport where he is to arrive. Some car hire firms allow the hirer to take over the car in one town and leave it in another.

SEA Most passenger-carrying ships have several decks with staterooms, inside and outside cabins and varying number of berths, some with shower or bath.

HOTEL Reservations for accommodation in hotels are usually made from the day of arrival to the day of departure. You need to know the type of accommodation your boss requires, e.g. a room with private shower or bath, air-conditioned if abroad, a suite, time of arrival and departure (very late arrivals should be intimated); whether transport is required from the point of arrival to the hotel; notice of any entertaining your boss may wish to do with as many details as may be available; any special dietary requirements. Arrangements must also be made for those who may be travelling with your boss—chauffeur, pilot, personal assistant or other staff members. When hotel accommodation is being reserved in the home country it can be done by telephone to be followed by a letter of confirmation.

When all the details have been worked out you will insert them on your check list. On the right-hand side of the paper rule two narrow columns, one to indicate when you have taken necessary action and the second to indicate when it is finalised. On page 376 is an example of a checklist at this point.

Most large organisations and government departments have a section in the Administration Department which is responsible for travel arrangements. In this case they will make the sea/air/rail bookings in accordance with the schedule your boss has approved. They may or may not make hotel reservations.

Arranging contacts If your boss is going to visit companies and make contacts you may have to arrange dates and times of meetings with various people. In the first place it is advisable to write to potential contacts as soon as possible giving proposed dates of visits, so that they can keep the time available. At this point arrangements can often be only tentative since one arrangement may depend upon another. For instance, if your boss wishes to hold a meeting with several senior civil servants he may wish to meet them individually first and possibly in a certain order. There is also the question of protocol. Certain 'courtesy' calls may have to be made before real business meetings begin. It is important that these are included in the right order because an official who feels he has been affronted may prove unco-operative. Some re-arranging may have to be done before a final programme can be drawn up. If possible it is best if someone on the spot can make the arrangements following general guide-

CHECK LIST		Initial Action	Final Action
TRAVEL:	Car—office to airport 3 pm 18.11.71 airport to office 11.15 am 24.11.71 Flight—London/Paris 4 pm 18.11.71 Paris/London 10.15 am 24.11.71 Paris Office—car		
HOTELS:	Champs Elysees Paris } 18.11.71–20.11.71 21.11.71–24.11.71 La Mer, Nice 20.11.71–21.11.71		
COMPANIES:	Lebrun et Cie (M. Jacques Lefévres) arrange meeting 19.11.71 (p.m.) Paris Office—meeting of senior personnel 9 a.m: 19.11.71		
DOCUMENTS:	Passport Driving licence		
INSURANCE:	Baggage/Personal Accident (£5000) 18.11.71–24.11.71		
MONEY:	Francs (£25) Dollars ($100) Travellers' Cheques (£250–£50 units)		

lines provided by your boss, so that time will not be wasted in corresponding backwards and forwards.

In overseas countries the commercial attachés at the High Commissions or Embassies would make contacts on behalf of your boss, possibly through local Chambers of Commerce and Employers' Associations.

Documents You must make sure that your boss has all necessary documents. Those he has already must be checked for validity and those he needs must be obtained.

PASSPORT Forms for a new one or for renewal of an existing one can be obtained at the national Passport Office, at any Labour Exchange in the United Kingdom or a travel agent. See that it is valid for all the countries to be visited. Special endorsements may be necessary for such countries as those in Eastern Europe, Russia and China. The form of application for a British passport is accompanied by "Notes for Guidance" which should be studied carefully. Three weeks should be allowed to obtain a new passport. Renewal takes less time but it is advisable to allow two weeks.

LAISSEZ PASSER This diplomatic passport is not usually valid for the holder's home country and in the case of United Nations it is usually valid only for developing countries. A *laissez passer* holder should carry his national passport as well.

VISAS A British passport holder does not need a visa to visit West European countries and many others. In most English-speaking African countries an entry permit is needed and if the traveller's stay is to be more than a certain period an exit permit may also be needed. This is often related to payment of income tax. It is always advisable to check with the appropriate High Commission or Embassy in the home country what the requirements are for the countries to be visited.

Many countries do not have embassies or consulates in every other country in the world. In some cases other embassies act for them or a consular agent is appointed. If your boss is to visit more than one country, obtain the addresses of the representatives of subsequent countries on his itinerary in each place. It may also be useful for him to have the address and telephone number of the representative of the home country in each of the countries to be visited.

HEALTH A *smallpox* vaccination certificate is required for returning to the United Kingdom from most countries except those in Europe. It is valid for three years and if due to expire during the course of the journey it is wise for the traveller to be revaccinated before leaving. *Yellow Fever* inoculation is needed for all countries outside Europe and is valid for ten years. *Cholera* inoculation is now required for all countries outside Europe and is valid for only six months. *TAB* inoculation is compulsory only in Middle East and Far East countries, but is advisable for all countries outside Europe. It also is valid for only six months. If in doubt about regulations the World Health Organisation local office can be consulted. Information about medical treatment for visitors to countries of the European Economic Community is given in leaflet SA28, available from the Department of Health and Social Security.

CAR If your boss is travelling by car abroad certain documents may be required, for example, an International Driving Licence (a British Licence is acceptable for a certain period in some countries); an International Fiscal Permit, an International Certificate for Motor Vehicles, and an insurance cover note for the countries to be visited.

MONEY Depending on the countries to be visited and the amount of time to be spent in each country it may be necessary to obtain the approval of the national bank before foreign currency (cash, traveller's cheques or letters of credit) can be bought. Many countries have regulations concerning the amount of home currency and total amount of cash which may be taken out of the country. In certain countries foreign travellers may not take out any local currency, e.g. Morocco, Ghana.

When arranging the purchase of travellers' cheques you need to know whether your boss wishes to have them in US dollars or in sterling, and the denominations. He will have to sign the cheques at the time of purchase and you may have to arrange with his bank to send a clerk to his office. The numbers of the cheques should be typed out, one copy to be carried by your boss, one copy to be retained by you. If the cheques should be lost the bank should be notified immediately.

It is possible to arrange for additional funds to be made available either by asking for cashing facilities at a branch of his own bank in another town of the home country or abroad, or, if there is no branch abroad, at a corresponding bank.

The validity of credit cards must be checked. In addition to Diners Club, American Express and Eurocard, credit cards for general use, there are now certain specialised cards for car hire, petrol, air travel (especially useful for excess baggage), telephone use. Certain bank credit cards can be used in Europe for obtaining a limited amount of cash in the currency of the country. Credit cards can only be used abroad for amounts within the foreign exchange allowance. If the full allowance has been taken in travellers' cheques, a credit card could not be used by the traveller.

For a small premium Diners Club cards can now be insured against the holder's responsibility for any amount incurred by anyone finding a card and using it illegally in the event of the owner losing it.

A letter of credit can be obtained instead of or in addition to traveller's cheques. The traveller presents the letter to a prescribed bank and can obtain cash up to the amount stated.

Insurances Many companies insure their employees travelling on business but your boss may wish to take out additional policies. It is possible to arrange for personal accident cover, baggage cover (the two can be combined if both are for the period of the trip only) and, as mentioned above, cover must be obtained for a car being driven to an overseas country.

Final preparations

FOLDER/S A new folder should be prepared, one for each town, region or country, if the trip is to be a long one. Each folder should contain all appropriate documents, etc.

ITINERARY The final itinerary must be typed, preferably on octavo or A5 sheets, one for each day. A specimen itinerary is shown on pages 379 to 380. from which it will be seen that full details must be given. If the trip covers several places a summarised itinerary for each place can be stapled inside the front cover of each folder, see the example on page 380.

DOCUMENTS All papers should be sorted into the order in which they will be required and flagged for easy reference. Confirmation letters from hotels, etc. should be included.

BAGGAGE LABELS Prepare stick-on and tie-on labels for each section of the journey, putting them in small envelopes clearly marked. Provide sufficient labels for hand baggage, including portable typewriter, etc.

TICKETS Check all tickets and see that there is a note either on the ticket or attached to it of the departure point (station and platform numbers; air terminal; dock and quay letter/number) and check-in times. Check that all flights are marked OK on the ticket; RQ means that the booking is not confirmed and the traveller's name is on the waiting list. Prepare a list of shipping/airline, car hire offices in each place as appropriate and place at the back of the relevant file.

VOUCHERS Some companies provide a voucher for rail travel. This has to be exchanged for a ticket at a railway booking office. Hotel vouchers are issued in booklet form by the travel agent. They should be very carefully checked to make sure that dates and type of accommodation are shown correctly. Hotel vouchers (or coupons) are issued when the fixed amount for accommodation is paid to the travel agent instead of directly to the hotel.

DOCUMENT HOLDER All the documents required for travel—passport with health documents, permits, etc. attached inside with a rubber band, tickets, vouchers, travellers' cheques, money—should be placed together in a wallet.

ITINERARY

	Time	
18.11.71	15.00	Office to London Airport
	16.00	Check in at Airport
	17.00	Flight BE 625 (London/Paris)
	18.10	Arrive Paris (car from Paris office)
		Hotel Champs Elysées
	19.30	Mr. Peterson (drinks at hotel)
19.11.71	08.30	Hotel to Office
	09.00	Meeting of Senior Personnel
		(Company long range planning)
		Arrangements for next week.
		Lunch
	15.00	Office to Lebrun et Cie
	15.15	Meeting with M. Jacques Lefévres.
		Dinner with Mr. Peterson at his house.
20.11.71	06.15	Hotel to Le Bourguet Airport
	07.00	Check in at Airport
	07.45	Flight AF 210 (Paris/Nice)
	08.20	Arrive Nice
		Hotel La Mer
21.11.71	18.00	Hotel to Nice Airport
	18.30	Check in at Airport
	19.15	Flight AF 217 (Nice/Paris)
	19.50	Arrive Paris
		Hotel Champs Elysées
22.11.71		
23.11.71		
24.11.71	08.30	Hotel to Airport
	09.15	Check in at Le Bourguet Airport
	10.15	Flight BE 629 (Paris/London)
	11.15	Arrive London (car from office)

SUMMARISED ITINERARY

18.11.71	15.00	Leave office
	17.00	Flight BE 625 (London/Paris)
	18.10	Arrive Paris
	19.30	Mr. Peterson
19.11.71	09.00	Meeting at Paris Office
	15.15	Meeting with Mr. Jacques Lefévres at Lebrun et Cie
		Dinner with Mr. Peterson
20.11.71	06.15	Leave Hotel
	07.45	Flight AF 210 (Paris/Nice)
	08.20	Arrive Nice
21.11.71	18.00	Leave Hotel
	19.15	Flight AF 217 (Nice/Paris)
	19.50	Arrive Paris
24.11.71	08.30	Leave Hotel
	10.15	Flight BE 629 (Paris/London)
	11.15	Arrive London

A6 card is a suitable size for summarised itineraries—one can be stapled inside the travel folder and another kept in the pocket.

Since there is inevitably a lot to do before the departure on a long trip of any boss you will be well-advised to make yourself available in the evenings and at the weekend preceding your boss's departure. The more preparatory details you can deal with in advance the easier your last minute preparations will be.

If your chief asks you to travel with him to the departure point be ready and willing to do so, but do not suggest this. If you do, you can assist by getting a porter to handle the baggage, directing him as to flight or train and holding small items such as raincoat, umbrella, briefcase, etc. while your boss checks in, or gets into the train. Check that he has sufficient reading material. Most stations and airports have bookstalls.

It is not necessary to wait with him until departure time; leave him with courteous good wishes for a pleasant trip as soon as he is comfortably settled.

In the Boss's absence While your boss is away work has to go on. Various situations will arise which you must handle in such a way that his absence does not cause inconvenience to others, particularly customers.

CORRESPONDENCE Deal with routine correspondence in the usual way. Seek advice from your boss's colleagues on technical matters or pass letters to them to be dealt with. A letter which must be dealt with by your boss should be acknowledged with an explanation and assurance that you will put it before him on his return.

VISITORS AND TELEPHONE CALLERS If you cannot deal with the matter yourself ensure that all visitors and telephone callers are referred to someone capable of attending to their requirements. Follow up if necessary.

MEETINGS If your boss is a member of a committee the Secretary and/or Chairman should be informed as soon as practicable of his intended absence. This is not necessary for short periods unless a meeting is notified to take place while he is away.

REQUESTS FOR TALKS, INVITATIONS, ETC. Contact the person who has made the request or issued the invitation. If it is official you may be asked to suggest an alternative person.

EMERGENCIES Situations may arise in a boss's absence which cannot possibly be foreseen. Each situation has to be handled according to the circumstances and people involved at the time. Use your common sense and if you act in what you believe to be the best interests of your boss it is unlikely you will be doing anything wrong.

While your boss is away you have an excellent opportunity to catch up on all those jobs which can never be fitted in when he is in his office—sifting files, renewing file covers, dusting and reorganising bookshelves (your own and your boss's), long range planning and so on. Make the most of the time and be ready when your boss returns to ease the burden of dealing with backlog. If you have done your job while he has been away this will be as small as possible.

Travelling with the Boss There may be times when your boss needs your assistance during the whole or a part of his trip. If he asks you to accompany him the arrangements you make beforehand will include provision for yourself. Remember you will be 'on the job' while travelling. Your boss may expect you to attend some, or all social activities—or none. If meetings are held frequently during the trip your evenings will probably be fully occupied with drafting minutes and preparing for the next round.

Consider your wardrobe well in advance. Find out what the weather will be like in each country to be visited—BOAC issue an excellent booklet giving details of weather, the dress required for various social activities, places of interest, etc. You may need this information for your boss's wife whether you are travelling or not. Take clothes which will look crisp and fresh for as long as possible—and ensure that they are really non-iron so that you can wash overnight and manage with a minimum amount.

During the trip you are there to 'look after' your boss—not the other way round. You cannot relax very much because you have to carry the burden of detail which will leave him free to concentrate on the major issues which have necessitated the trip.

GROUP DISCUSSION

Your boss is scheduled to visit Europe in two months' time. The object of his visit is to see methods used in medium and large scale industries in France, Germany and Italy. He wishes to leave the home country during the first week of the month and to be away for not more than one calendar month. If possible he would like to have a little time for private sightseeing in each country.

Your boss asks you to find out the best companies for him to visit and plan a draft itinerary. He would wish to entertain the Chairmen and Directors of the companies. In addition he would like to meet someone very senior in the Ministry of Trade (or its equivalent) in each country.

By discussion decide what information you would have to get for planning the itinerary and how you would get it. Decide what arrangements would have to be made and what would be involved in making them, e.g. letters, telephone calls, etc. List the arrangements in correct order—some arrangements may depend upon others—not forgetting follow-up.

EXERCISES

1 Following the group discussion type a draft itinerary. When this has been approved by your instructor make a check list and then type all necessary letters.

2 Arrange the itinerary and prepare the necessary letters for your boss (the Deputy Permanent Secretary, Ministry of Education) to visit Towns A, B, C, D and E. He will leave his home town on Monday morning in three weeks' time and is prepared to give up six days to the tour if necessary.

The order in which the towns are to be visited is flexible except that Town D must be visited before Town E. The minimum time possible should be given to travelling. A car can be made available at any centre for onward travel if necessary, and your boss has no objection to using domestic airline flights.

The purpose of the tour is to visit Chief Education Officers, Polytechnics and Technical Colleges. The reason for visiting Town D before Town E is that the Deputy Permanent Secretary wishes to find out whether technical training facilities in the area are being fully utilised before taking a decision on the setting up of a technical training centre in Town E.

In Town D the Deputy Permanent Secretary would wish to have a meeting of all principals and heads of department of technical training institutions and representatives of employers. The Chief Education Officer in the area would have to arrange this.

3 When your boss tells you he wishes to travel abroad what arrangements do you expect to make to ensure the smooth running of his trip?

4 Your chief is to visit Hong Kong on business, stopping off in USA—New

York one way, Los Angeles the other. He asks you to find out the following details for him.

a What vaccinations/inoculations are required.
b What regular airline services are available.

Explain briefly how you would get the information and in the case of (b) do so.

5 What reference books would you use to find information on travel

a by air?
b by sea?
c by car?
d by train?

6 Your boss is abroad when a business associate of his from another country telephones. He refers to a letter he wrote saying that he would make contact as soon as he arrived in your country. The letter has not been received. What would you say to the caller, and what action would you take, if any?

7 You work for two partners who own a small business manufacturing lead pipes. One of the partners is abroad for a month trying to increase export sales. One day the other partner's wife telephones to say he has been rushed to hospital for an emergency operation. You have the keys to the premises and a little petty cash but no money to pay the weekly wages of the ten workmen. State the steps you will take when you receive the information.

8 Your boss is due to arrive from Paris at 15.00 hours. He has asked you to meet him at the airport with certain papers and he is booked to fly on a domestic flight ready for a meeting next day. When checking the flight arrival you learn that all flights from Paris have been cancelled due to fog. Flights may resume the following day but this is not certain. You yourself are due to travel the next morning to attend a meeting on behalf of your boss. What action would you take?

9 You work in a small firm not far from your home. The office staff consists of you and a junior typist. Your boss has asked you to take charge of the office, including dealing with the mail, while he is away on business for a month. You become ill during this time and the doctor tells you that you must be away from the office for at least a week. Consider the implications of this state of affairs and say what you would do.

10 Your company has a private aeroplane which your boss frequently uses. He is scheduled to fly to a town 200 miles away to which there is no airline service. The day before the trip you are informed that the pilot is ill. Your chief is away all day at a Conference. What action would you take?

10

Communications and Correspondence

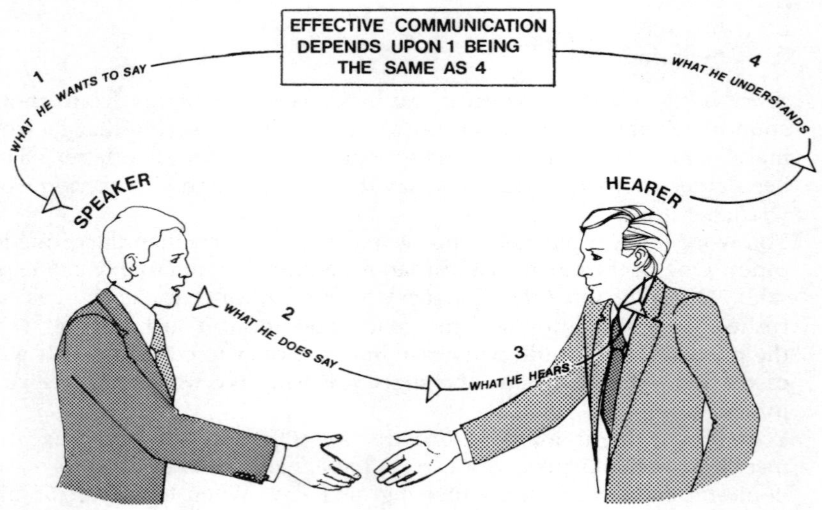

How misunderstandings can occur: the speaker does not always say exactly what he wants to say; sometimes he is unable to find the right words and phrases to express his thoughts. The hearer does not always listen carefully and sometimes misinterprets what he hears.

"In Promotion we have to communicate our thoughts to others; that is our whole business, communication. If you cannot communicate with me, how can I expect you to carry out your work and communicate with others? Now, please try to answer my question more fully."

The Executive, Michael Fisher, New English Library

'The horror of the moment,' the King went on, 'I shall never, never forget.' 'You will, though,' the Queen said, 'if you don't make a memorandum of it.'

Through the Looking Glass, Ch. I, Lewis Carroll.

In order to do our work properly we have to communicate. 'Communicate' in this sense means either to convey our wishes to others in such a way that they will do what we want them to do, or to pass on information which has been requested or which is needed.

The diagram on page 386 shows that we can identify four areas of communication—mass media, spoken, written and telecommunications. A detailed study of mass media is outside the scope of this book but the heading has been included to indicate the various media which can be used for mass-communication (press, radio, television and posters/hoardings) and to emphasise the important part played by them in promoting an organization's total image, its policies, products or services.

In all branches of communications words are the instruments and tools of the trade; therefore before proceeding to a detailed study of spoken, written and telecommunications, we should consider the importance of choosing and arranging words "in such a way as to get an idea as exactly as possible out of one mind and into another".*

LANGUAGE

In the section on TYPEWRITING in Chapter 1 we discussed how the appearance of a typewritten document affected its acceptability. In this section we shall discuss various aspects of vocabulary, style and usage and note the contribution which the correct choice and arrangement of words makes to the overall effectiveness of any form of communication.

The cuttings from advertisements shown on page 387 illustrate some of the effects that can be produced by the skilful choice of words. Although the copywriter's motives may not meet with universal approval, there are few who would not admit to a grudging admiration for his ability.

Whatever you happen to be reading—a daily paper, a modern novel, a classic, a weekly magazine or a circular inviting you to subscribe to a new publication—take note of the writer's skill and the effect his words have upon you. If you study style, widen your vocabulary and consciously note how words can be used to provoke certain reactions, you will gradually find yourself acquiring the ability to use language in a variety of different ways.

This ability will be of great use to you in your business career. If you can imitate your boss's style of writing,† or write in a style which he finds acceptable, he will probably hand over an increasing amount of correspondence for you to answer yourself. A study of advertisements will show you how "hard sell" or "soft sell" copy is written; and a study of the prose style of recognised writers and professional columnists and journalists will help you to

* *The Complete Plain Words*, Sir Ernest Gowers, Penguin Books.

† "The best secretary I ever had could accurately anticipate my responses to much of my incoming correspondence. Although her style of expression was quite different from my own, she had carefully studied my characteristic expressions and sentence structure, and could write a reply uncannily like one I might have dictated. Sometimes, when signing the outgoing mail at the day's end, I had to read a letter twice before I could decide whether she or I had originally written it." *Survival in the Executive Jungle* by Chester Burger, The Macmillan Company.

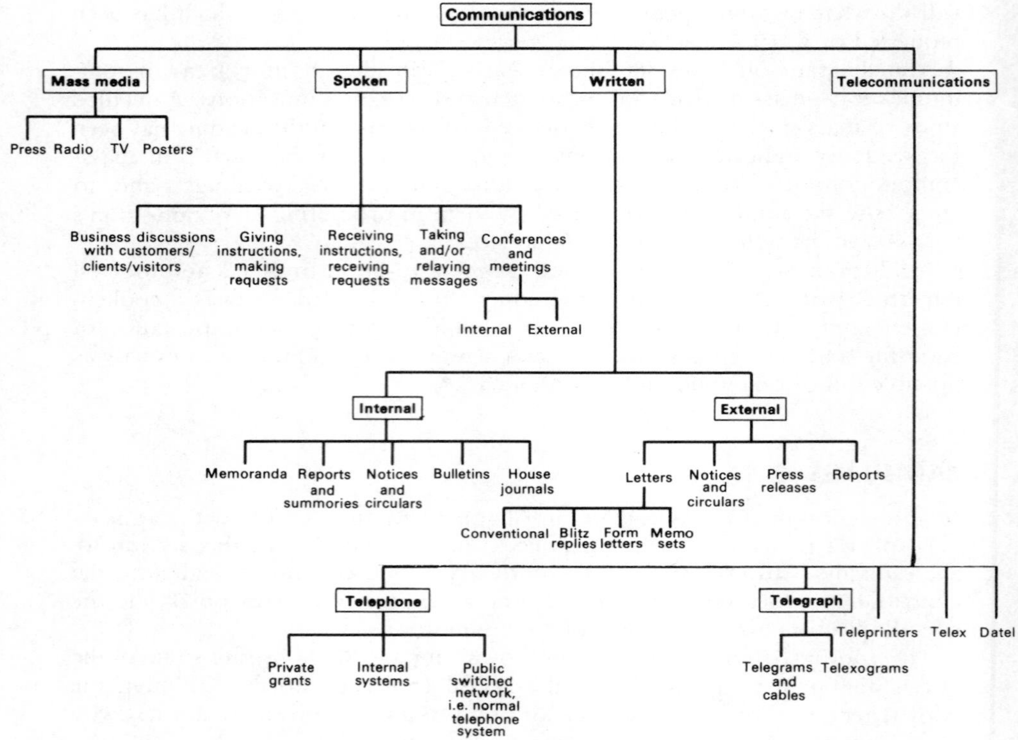

vary the style of your writing to suit whatever type of communication you are writing.

Generally speaking, business communications should be written in a direct unambiguous style because "time is money" and busy people do not want to waste time reading through unnecessary verbosity; on the other hand, there are occasions when a tactful, rather vague letter is best suited to the occasion. The following sections may help you to become aware of various aspects of language and this awareness may in turn help you to become a versatile and competent writer.

Vocabulary JARGON is the special terminology of a subject or a trade or profession. The word is now used contemptuously for any speech which a person does not understand, but there is nothing wrong with jargon in itself. If you consider the purpose of your communication and the person it is addressed to, you will not be accused of writing or speaking jargon if you avoid using technical terms that are not commonly intelligible. On the other hand, every profession has its special vocabulary. In the chapters on Reprography, Management, Data Storage and Retrieval of Information, and Committee

These examples of the copywriter's skill show the importance of language in advertising; words are carefully chosen to provoke a positive and favourable reaction.

Work, we have included lists of specialised terms, and there is a glossary of business terms in Appendix B.

NEOLOGISMS are new words. The cuttings collected in the illustration on page 389 show some new words that were coined during 1972 and the extracts from the latest edition of *Chambers Twentieth Century Dictionary* contain some words which English people who have not lived in England or who have not seen many British newspapers during the past ten years might not be able to understand. New words are continually being coined to meet new conditions and to describe new inventions. A new word which will always be associated with 1973 is *vatable*, meaning 'subject to the levy of VAT' and the word *vatman* is being used to describe the official responsible for the administration and collection of VAT.

ACRONYMS are words made from the initial letters of words comprising names and titles and definitions, such as NATO, North Atlantic Treaty Organisation. These words were formerly typed with a full-stop between each letter (U.N.E.S.C.O.) but now it is more usual to see them typed in block capitals (UNESCO), or simply with an initial capital (Unesco). What might be termed "marketing English" is a fertile source of acronyms as they are easy to remember and sound slick and modern.

VOGUE WORDS As well as widening her vocabulary and noting the introduction of new words into the language, the secretary should also be aware of vogue words, the term for words which enjoy a short spell of popularity and then become dated. There are fashions in words just as there are fashions in appearance and dress; *psychedelic, swingeing, grassroots* became fashionable within recent years and at the time of writing *arcane* seems to stand a reasonable chance of being the *in-word* for 1973. Vogue words should be noted, but they should be used with caution, particularly when communicating with people for whom English is a second or foreign language; there are also regional differences or differences in the meaning of words as they are used by various social groups; *chuffed*, for example, is understood to mean "very pleased" by some people, whereas others interpret it as meaning "displeased, fed-up".

1

convenient, *adj.* . . . . – **convenience food,** food (partly) prepared before sale so as to be ready, or almost ready, for the table. **convention,** *n.* . . . – **conventional weapons,** weapons that are not nuclear. **cool,** *adj.* . . . – **keep one's cool** (*coll.*), to remain calm and unflustered, keep one's head. **corridor,** *n.* . . . – **corridors of power** (*fig.*), higher reaches of government administration. **courgette,** *n.* a small marrow. **crease,** *n.* . . . – *adj.* **crease-resistant.** -resist-

2

The Daily Telegraph, Wednesday, May 3, 1972

Couple due to marry gazumped

Daily Telegraph Reporter

A COUPLE due to marry on Saturday have had their house "gazumped."

3

Bludget, doll, doxie, mugger...now read on

SOMETHING new has happened under the Sun. The people who since time immemorial have been waylaid, knocked down, held up, jumped, rolled, assaulted, robbed, reived and marauded, are now being *mugged*. In the past, he who mugged studied very hard, made faces, bribed people with liquor, took photographs or ate hugely. It mugged occasionally when it drizzled or rained slightly. What a mugger is now (besides a hawker of earthenware or the broad-nosed crocodile of India) is beyond a mere lexicographer's power to determine.

The Home Office has come to our aid, where the Oxford Dictionary cannot. Mugging is "robberies by gangs of two or more youths on people walking alone in the open." The footpads who for centuries infested th heaths and commons thro which city-bound travellers to pass would be puzzled their ancient arts descri newly-spawned in 1972. brigandage has its own tradition, a whole culture language, not to be set aside the first flash of an American monosyllable.

4

nick, *n.* . . . – **in (very) good nick** (*coll.*), in (very) good health or condition. **non,** a Latin word used as a prefix, not: sometimes used of someone or something with pretensions who, which, is ludicrously unworthy of the name mentioned, e.g. **non-hero, non-event.** The words given below include the most common words with *non-* but the prefix is living and many other words using it may be formed . . . – *adj.* **non-aligned,** not aligned: not taking sides in international politics. – *ns.* **non-alignment;** . . . **non-fiction,** of a literary work, without any deliberately fictitious element (**non-fiction novel,** one whose material is entirely drawn from people and events in real life). . . . – *adj.* **non-profit-making,** not organised or engaged in with the purpose of making a profit. . . . – *n.* **non-starter,** a horse which, though entered for a race, does not run: a person who has no chance at all of success. – *adj.* **non-stick,** of e.g. a pan, treated so that food or other substance will not stick to it. **nosh** (*slang*), *v.i.* to nibble, eat between meals: to eat. – *n.* food. **nut,** *n.* . . . a crazy person (also **nutcase,** *slang*). **off,** *adv.* . . . – *adj.* **offpeak,** not at time of highest demand; . . . **off-street,** of parking, in a car park. **op art,** art using geometrical forms precisely executed and so arranged that movement of the observer's eye, or inability to focus, produces an illusion of movement in the painting. **open,** *adj.* . . . – **open-end(ed),** not closely defined, general and adaptable to suit various contingencies: (of question, debate, etc.) allowing free unguided answers or expressions of opinion; . . . **open university** (earlier called **university of the air**), a university (1971) whose teaching is carried out by correspondence and by radio and television.

5

girl, *n.* . . . – **Girl Friday,** a young woman who acts as secretary or personal assistant in a business office. **Giro,** *n.* a banking system by which money can be transferred direct from the account of one holder to that of another person (or to those of others). **glass,** *n.* . . . – **glass fibre,** glass melted and then drawn out into extremely fine fibres, which are later to be spun, woven, etc. **gnome,** *n.* . . . – **the gnomes of Europe, Zurich,** etc., the big bankers. **goggle,** *v.i.* . . . – **goggle-box** (*coll.*), a television-set. **good,** *adj.* . . . – **goodies and baddies,** characters in a drama regarded respectively as definitely good and definitely bad. **goof,** *n.* . . . – *v.i.* to make a blunder. – *adj.* **goofy.** – **goofball** (*slang*), a barbiturate pill used as an exhilarant. **grace,** *n.* . . . – **gracious li ing,** (living in) conditions of ease, plenty, and good taste. **graffito,** *n.* a mural scribbling or drawing, as by schoolboys and idlers at Pompeii, Rome, and other ancient cities (*ant.*): (in *pl.*) **scribblings** or **drawings,** often indecent, found on public buildings, in lavatories, etc.: **sgraffito**: – *pl.* **graffiti.** **grass,** *n.* . . . hashish (*slang*). **groove,** *n.* . . . – *adj.* **groovy** (also **in the groove;** *jazz slang*), in top form, or in perfect condition: up to date in style: a general term of approval: following a set routine. **grotty,** (*slang*) *adj.* ugly, in bad condition, or useless. [**grotesque.**]

1, 4 and 5. Some new words in the 1972 edition of Chambers Twentieth Century Dictionary. 2. Cutting from *The Daily Telegraph*, 3 May 1972. 3. Extract from article by Germaine Greer, *The Observer*, 5 November 1972.

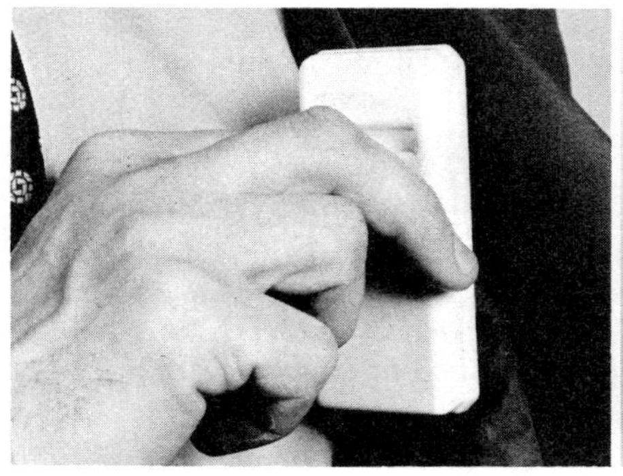

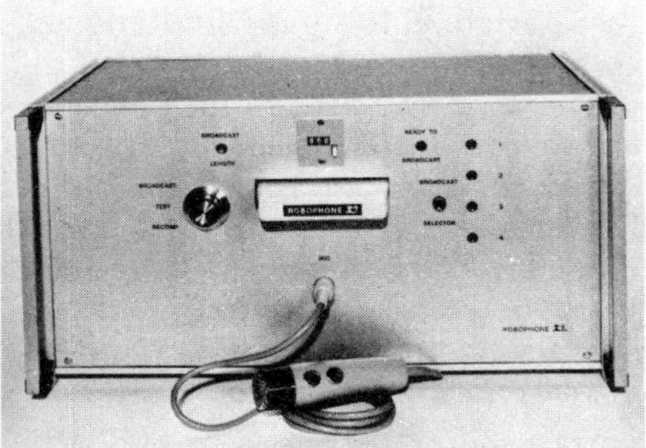

Two acronyms invented in 1972: (left) MASTIFF—Modular Automated System To Identify Friend from Foe, an electronic device carried in the pocket which allows the wearer to enter areas of maximum security by automatically opening locked doors (Lewis Security Systems Ltd), and (right) Mabus—a multiple access broadcasting unit system, an automatic device from Robophone Ltd for dealing with a large number of telephone calls.

Style COMMERCIALESE is the term given to the stilted, old-fashioned and often meaningless expressions which used to be written in business letters. This is now universally condemned and such words as *inst.* (this month), *prox.* (next month), *ult.* (last month) and phrases such as *we beg to acknowledge receipt of your esteemed favour* and *your good self* are rarely used. Nowadays business letters are written as simply and clearly as possible and there is no need to hide the message of the letter behind strange, unfamiliar phrases. There is, of course, a business vocabulary and there are conventional, accepted ways of writing business, as opposed to personal, letters. Some examples of letters which the secretary can compose herself are given in WRITTEN COMMUNICATIONS on pages 406–410.

OFFICIALESE is the name given to the kind of writing which is seen on official documents and in pamphlets and notices written by government departments such as the Inland Revenue. The object of "explanatory notes" is presumably to explain, but the writer of officialese obscures his meaning in a mixture of vague phrases and abstract nouns with the result that the communication is rarely effective and usually very difficult to understand. The main characteristics of officialese are that it is verbose, woolly and pompous. The Americans call this style of writing *gobbledygook.* Perhaps the outstanding feature of officialese is that it fails "to get an idea as exactly as possible out of one mind and into another" which is the main purpose of communication.

HACKNEYED PHRASES AND CLICHÉS are expressions that have become worn out by excessive use. They are often spoken or written by people who have a poor command of language and who do not consider the actual meaning of the words they are using. The person who starts a sentence with "I tremble to think" is rarely thinking and hardly ever trembling. Because they have lost their original freshness and impact, clichés contribute nothing to effective communication.

The excessive use of *colloquialisms* and the unnecessary use of *slang* and *dialect* are further aspects of language which have a bearing upon the effectiveness of our spoken and written communications. Because slang words frequently have their origin in specialised groups, such as the Armed Forces, they may not be understood outside these groups, and the meaning of dialect words is restricted to the people of a certain region or district. Colloquial expressions frequently add colour to the language but may be considered out of place in formal communications.

Usage The customary practice of the best writers and speakers is normally referred to as 'usage' and there are many reference books (listed at the end of this chapter) to guide the unpractised writer.

There are a number of differences between English and American usage, for example, 'a lift' in English is 'an elevator' in American, and certain differences in spelling, for example, colour/color, theatre/theater. A useful list of differences in word usage is given in *Business in English,* Sydney Stevens, Chatto & Windus, and any secretary working for an American organisation would find useful *A Dictionary of American–English Usage*, Margaret Nicholson, Oxford University Press, based on Fowler's *Modern English Usage*. American usage tends to be less relaxed than English and a typical American custom seems to be to prefer the more important sounding word to the simpler one; these differences reflect the different tempo and psychological outlook of British and American business, the American ambience being distinctly more dynamic and bracing. This can cause some American business letters to read more like spoken than written English; is there any reason to condemn this effect if it conveys the exact meaning the writer intended?

It is relevant here to glance back at the advertisements we looked at on page 387 at the beginning of this section and to notice the usage of emotive words and phrases by the people who write the texts for advertisements. 'Emotive' in this sense is used to describe words and phrases which make people feel emotional and excited. Copy-writers use emotive language to make people act in a certain way, e.g. buy certain products or support certain political parties. If you study language and realise the power of words, you will not only learn to look critically at the persuasive endeavours of advertisers and politicians,* you will also improve your own ability to communicate.

SPOKEN COMMUNICATION

The diagram at the head of this chapter illustrates four stages of spoken communication and attempts to indicate how misunderstandings can occur. The

* *The Hidden Persuaders*, Vance Packard.

first stage is in the mind of the speaker when he thinks he has something to say. If he is not perfectly clear in his own mind about what he does want to say, it is unlikely that he will express himself accurately and coherently. Discrepancies between what the speaker wants to say and what he actually does say can be caused by lack of fluency in speaking, poor articulation, weak vocabulary, illogical thought processes, lack of concentration and all those shortcomings in the use of language which are frequently summed up in the simple phrase "unable to express himself". If the speaker is aware of this inability and attempts to rephrase his meaning by saying, "I'm sorry, I'm not expressing myself very well. Let me try again," he stands a better chance of conveying his thoughts to his audience. On the other hand, the speaker may be under the impression that he has spoken lucidly and clearly—and he may well have done so. But this is no guarantee that he has communicated effectively, because his words now have to be interpreted into meaning by the hearer.

The third stage is what the hearer hears; the chances of misunderstanding at this stage arise from three causes—(a) the hearer may not be paying full attention and may not catch all the words spoken, or (b) the hearer may only hear what he expects or wants to hear, or (c) the speaker may be using words which the hearer does not understand properly. In other words, unless the hearer is consciously listening, he will not hear the whole of the speaker's utterance, and if he does hear the whole utterance he may not understand it.

Even if he does hear and understand all the speaker says, there is still the possibility of misunderstanding at the fourth stage, when the hearer interprets what he has heard. The words used by the speaker may mean something different to the hearer, or they may have a slightly different connotation or implication. We do not all use words in exactly the same sense and some people may think they can infer certain attitudes from our use of words which they consider derogatory or complimentary. An obvious example is the use of 'strong-willed' and 'obstinate'. If we talk about a person being 'strong-willed' we usually imply approval; 'obstinate' is not normally used in a complimentary sense.

So far we have discussed only the difference between the actual words used by the speaker to express what he wants to say and the hearer's understanding of those words. But there are other aspects of spoken language which can strengthen or weaken or slant the effect of our communications, and these are aspects in which the spoken language has advantages over the written; intonation, stress, hesitation, emphasis, pitch, accent, pauses, gestures, are a few of the devices we use when we speak which cannot be represented in writing, and their use (for example, a patronising tone, an unacceptable accent, a deliberate stress, a pause for effect, a wink) plays an important part in the way our hearers interpret what we say.

Effective spoken communication depends upon our ability to convey meaning as exactly as possible from our own minds to the minds of our hearers. To be aware of all the possibilities that exist for misinterpretation and misunderstanding, may help us to take more care when talking and listening.

Although formal negotiations are not usually the responsibility of the secretary, she may be asked to have preliminary discussions before her boss comes on the scene "to prepare the ground" or "to get the gist of the general feeling" before the main business meeting begins. A secretary's duties at committee meetings and conferences have been discussed in Chapter 12, Committee Procedure, and Chapter 14, Human Relations, but the areas of spoken communication with which the secretary is primarily concerned are those of giving instructions, receiving instructions and taking messages.

The secretary will communicate on a variety of different levels and in several different directions. Some of these are indicated in the diagram below; internally, the secretary will communicate with her boss, she may convey her boss's instructions to other executives and managers, she will communicate with other secretaries and give instructions to clerical and other staff who may be under her supervision. The secretary's main communication with the outside world is normally through the telephone (see Chapter 3, Telephone Techniques and pages 416 to 419), but she will also speak to visitors who have appointments with her boss, and other callers who wish to see her boss or make appointments or whom she has been authorised to handle (see Chapter 6, Appointments, Desk Diaries and Reception Duties).

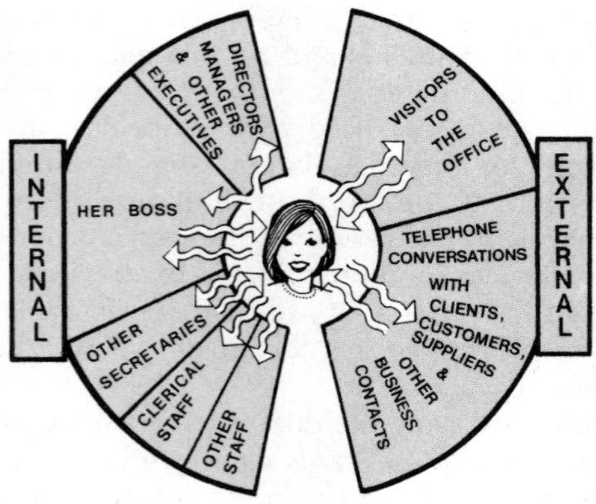

The secretary's areas of spoken communication.

Receiving instructions Whenever you are given instructions, first of all make quite sure that you understand what you are being asked to do, and secondly make a note of what you have to do and how you are to do it. It is essential that you understand the information clearly; if you are not sure of anything, always ask. It is much better to ask a question than to spend time doing something incorrectly. Then write down the instructions in your notebook. Never rely on your memory and never make notes on odd pieces of paper which can easily be mislaid. If you have no notebook at hand when you are given an instruction and have to make a note on scrap paper, transfer the message to your notebook at the first opportunity.

Try to keep all the instructions given to you on the same day on the same page (dated, of course) and "flag" with an asterisk or red pen those instructions which take priority. Put a line through each job as you complete it, and make a new entry if, as the result of doing one job, another job has to be done.

Deal with your work in accordance with your boss's priorities and whenever you have a spare moment, check through your list of instructions to make sure that you are as up-to-date and up-to-the-minute as possible. If a person you had to telephone was not available, a glance through your check list should remind you that the call has still to be made.

Giving instructions When you are giving instructions, it is important for you to remember the points made about spoken communication at the beginning of this section. If you have to explain a job of work to a colleague or assistant, make quite sure you know exactly what you want to say and how you are going to say it. Find out how much she knows and then explain to her in the simplest terms. Try to begin by telling her the reason for the job, so that she is able to work intelligently.

If you have to give instructions make quite sure that you can express yourself clearly in words that will be understood by the person who has to carry out the instruction, and use a tone of voice which is polite but carries a hint of authority. A request is always better than an order, and most people react more favourably to a polite request made in a pleasant tone. If the person to whom you are giving the instruction appears not to understand or seems not to be listening, attract her attention and repeat the instruction patiently and carefully. There is little chance of your instructions being correctly carried out if you have not taken the necessary time and patience to ensure that they are fully understood.

With junior staff it is quite a good idea to ask them to "recap" the instructions you have given them. Often people answer "Yes," to the question "Do you understand?" when in fact they haven't understood or don't realise that they haven't understood. Asking for instructions to be repeated back to you, or asking one key question the answer to which will indicate whether the whole message has been "received and understood" is more effective than a vague, "Ask me if there's anything you're not sure about"; although of course, just as you yourself ask if you are not sure of anything, show those whom you instruct that you welcome relevant questions and are never too busy to deal with queries which will enable the person to carry out your instructions more intelligently.

Taking and relaying messages Nearly all that has been said about receiving instructions, giving instructions and taking telephone messages applies to taking and relaying messages, i.e. make sure you understand the message to be conveyed, write it down, relay it as soon as possible, and check (if you have been asked to) that the message has been acted upon.

Some of the messages may be from your boss's directors, such as calling him to another office for an urgent discussion. For this reason alone, apart from other obvious reasons, you should always make a point of knowing where to locate your boss.

On other occasions, you may have to transmit messages from your boss to his colleagues through their secretaries, or to other business clients. Here again a similar procedure of making a note of the message and relaying it as soon as possible applies, with the added precaution of asking for further instructions should you be unable to get the message through to the person concerned within the relevant period of time.

WRITTEN COMMUNICATIONS

Internal Communications

MEMORANDA Officials working for the same firm or organisation—not necessarily in the same building or even in the same town or country—use memoranda forms to communicate with each other in writing. No salutation or complimentary close is used and it is customary for internal 'memos' to be initialled, not signed in full.

Memoranda are not put into envelopes unless they contain confidential information. They are usually sent through the internal post; if they are particularly urgent they will be taken by hand if the recipient's office is in the same building or precinct. Memoranda for offices in other towns and countries are usually collected in the Central Mail Room and despatched daily in a large envelope or bag.

Most firms have printed memo forms on A5 or $\frac{2}{3}$ A4 size paper. There is no need for a printed letterhead; the forms usually have the words INTERNAL MEMORANDUM printed at the top and ruled sections with the words FROM, TO, DATE, SUBJECT or REFERENCE as shown in the examples on page 395.

A memorandum should deal with only one point which can usually be covered in two short paragraphs or possibly two sentences: first, make a statement or explanation or indicate the importance or relevance of the subject; second, state the basic point of the memo—the request, the instructions, the reminder, order or message.

Memoranda addressed to more than one official are known as *multiple memoranda*. Either a separate copy is sent to each individual concerned or one copy may be routed to each person in turn. In the latter case the memorandum is usually routed with an attached circulation slip (see page 396). When a separate copy is sent to each official, the names of all the recipients are listed in the 'TO' section of the memoranda and each recipient's name is underlined or ticked on one of the copies.

M E M O R A N D U M

TO: Chief Designer SUBJECT: "Sprite" Mk.6

FROM: Production Manager DATE: 8 April 1973

I attach letter from one of our customers, Mr O D Kelway, who bought a new "Sprite" from Woodard and Griggs Ltd, our dealers in his area.

As this is the fourth complaint we have received about water leaking into the tool box, I should be glad to have your comments on the matter.

I am inclined to think that the fault is due to careless assembly rather than to bad design.

MEMORANDUM

TO: Mr R K Doyle Mr J S Hunt Mr R Foster-Hayes cc Mr J Rogers

FROM: Miss Stella Foreman

13 May 1973

POST ARRANGEMENTS

With effect from 1 June 1973 outgoing post will be collected for despatch twice a day at 1200 and 1645 hrs. Parcels for despatch, eg computer tabulations, should be placed in the open boxes with labels typed ready. Packing will be carried out by the mailing clerk.

Incoming post will be distributed to Departments by depositing items in the appropriate trays at the mailing point. Collection is the responsibility of the Departments. At present we have 3 deliveries a day.

SF.AK.104.May 73

Two examples of Internal Memoranda—the one on the right is fully blocked.

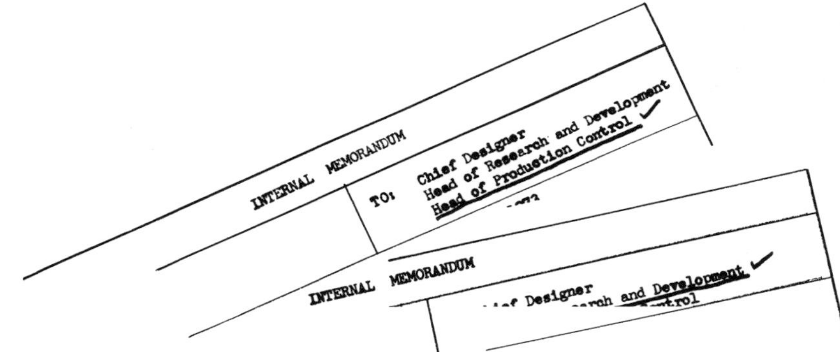

INTERNAL MEMORANDUM

FROM: Chief Engineer	TO: Chief Designer ✓ Head of Research and Development Head of Production Control
SUBJECT: Modifications to fuel pump, no. RCV/937	DATE: 12 July 1973

We are still receiving complaints about the poor performance of our fuel pump, no. RCV/937.

Would you please attend a meeting in my office at 10.30 a.m. on Tuesday next, 17 July, to discuss possible modifications.

A multiple memorandum. Note how each recipient's name is underlined or ticked on one of the copies.

There are several ways in which the name of the recipients may be listed: (a) alphabetically, (b) by location, (c) according to rank, (d) according to job priority, and (e) for information only. The alphabetical method is simple, makes no allowance for rank and no one need feel slighted. Routing by location saves time, but pays no attention to job priority. The advantage of routing according to job priority is that the person who must act on the memorandum's contents sees it first. Sometimes memoranda are routed to certain officials who are not directly affected by their contents; this may be classified as 'informational routing'. It is usual to type the initials FYI (for your information) or FIO (for information only) next to the name.

Possibly the best method of routing is by job priority combined with information routing as this allows the person who has to act to see the memorandum first and also helps executives to keep in close touch with company operations. In most offices, the office manager will decide which method is to be used; he will, of course, choose the method best suited to the requirements of the organisation.

Very short messages may be written on *action slips.* These small slips, frequently brightly coloured for prominence, are used to initiate action within an organisation; they may also be used to accompany a document upon which action is requested.

ACTION SLIP	
TO Chief Transport Officer	FROM Cashier
SUBJECT Travel Claim	DATE 17.2.73

Please authorise payment of attached & return.
Thankyou.
RMW.

An action slip.

CIRCULATION SLIP

FROM:	DATE
SUBJECT:	
	INITIALS
CHIEF OF PROJECT	
DIRECTOR, N. V. T. I.	
IN-PLANT TRAINING EXPERT	
APPRENTICESHIP TRAINING EXPERT	
INSTRUCTOR TRAINING EXPERT	
OFFICE & CLERICAL (1) EXPERT	
OFFICE & CLERICAL (2) EXPERT	
TRADE STANDARDS & TESTING EXPERT	
VOCATIONAL TRAINING PLANNING EXPERT	
PLEASE RETURN TO:	FILE No.

A circulation slip.

In Government departments and ministries 'a memorandum' is an official document setting out matters relating to policy which is presented to ministers for their consideration. Communications between officials in Government offices and international organisations are known as *minutes.*

REPORTS Reports can be classified according to the restrictions placed upon their distribution (SECRET, CONFIDENTIAL, etc.) or they may be classified according to the official from whom they originate, or by the department or purpose for which they have been written.

It is convenient to discuss the writing of reports under *three* subheadings, *routine reports, research reports,* and *progress or periodic reports.*

A *routine report* may be written on a special report form and may be simply a factual account of a single incident, such as an accident; or it may be an account of a visit or business trip. It can be divided into the following parts:

1 Title or heading.
2 Introduction, which should state the date, time, place, number of people involved, purpose, upon whose orders or at whose request the visit was made (where relevant).

3 Information, divided into sub-sections.
4 Conclusions.
5 Name of writer, signature and date.

If the report is not to be transmitted by a covering letter or memorandum, it should also be addressed to someone.

F.B.6.

F. H. BROWN LIMITED

ACCIDENT REPORT

NAME OF INJURED PERSON: ....

OCCUPATION: .... DEPARTMENT: ....

TIME AND DATE: .... PLACE: ....

DESCRIPTION OF ACCIDENT: ....
....
....
....
....
....
....
....
....
....
....
....
....

NAMES OF WITNESSES (Block Caps) ....
....
....
....

REPORT BY (Block Caps) ....

SIGNATURE: ....

REF. NO.: DATE:

REPORT ON VISIT TO WISEMAN OPTICAL COMPANY LIMITED

1. INTRODUCTION

Messrs P A Jones, Lighting Consultant, and E F Overton, Design Engineer, visited Wiseman Optical Co Ltd., Surbiton Works, on 9 February 1973. Mr A Watson, Chief Engineer, represented the Wiseman Optical Co Ltd.

The purpose of the visit was to discuss a modification in the focal length of condenser lens, part no. 3640/0073, used in a film-strip projector.

2. INFORMATION

(a) Mr Watson was rather perturbed that it has been found necessary to change the focal length at such a late stage in negotiations as jigs and tools had already been ordered for producing the lens as originally specified.

(b) He stated that our Company would be liable for the additional tooling charges which his Company would be called upon to pay by their sub-contractors.

(c) The effect of this alteration upon delivery dates was discussed. It was decided that delivery would have to be delayed by about two weeks.

3. CONCLUSION

As other components are not expected until the end of March, this later delivery date will not affect our production schedule.

10 February 1973
Ref. EFO/cb/95/0073

E F Overton
Design Engineer

(Left) An example of a routine report form. (Right) An example of a short routine report (not on a printed form).

A research report is a report which gives an account of an investigation and the way in which the investigation was carried out. A *short research report* can consist of:

a Title or heading.
b Terms of reference, which should state
  i who commissioned the investigation or research
  ii the person/s authorised to make the investigation
  iii the object of the investigation
c Procedure, how the investigation was carried out.
d Findings.
e Conclusions.
f Recommendations.
g Names of authors, signatures, office, place and date.

A *long research report* can contain all or some of the following parts:

I INTRODUCTION

Title page—the name of the report, the author's name, title and department, date of issue.
Circulation list—those readers for whom the report is intended.
Preface—why the report was written, background information.
Acknowledgments—people and organisations who have helped the author.
Table of Contents—listed in the same order as in the report, giving page numbers.
Summary.

II BODY OF THE REPORT

Terms of reference.
Procedure, methods of investigation.
Findings.
Conclusions.
Recommendations.

III APPENDICES

Statistical Tables.
Bibliography.

IV INDEX (only necessary in a very long report).

Progress or periodic reports are usually written to sum up work that has been accomplished during a given period and to indicate future plans. Examples of reports of this type are (a) those written by sales representatives reporting to their head offices on the calls they have made during the period covered by the report, potential new customers, increases or decreases in sales, new orders, criticisms from customers about the quality and standard of goods, packaging, delivery dates, special promotions, enquiries about new products, and (b) reports made by experts to their headquarters on survey trips or technical missions. Progress or periodic reports can usually be written under some or all of the following headings:

1 Title—to include name of official, job title, date, period covered by the report, date of previous report, area covered by report, name of mission or assignment.
2 Object of trip or mission or assignment.
3 Work Contacts—name of people visited, their positions, relevance to object of mission, summary of discussion.
4 Work carried out—description of accomplishments during period covered by report.

5 Difficulties encountered—any difficulties of which headquarters may not be aware or which headquarters may be able to solve.
6 Future work plans.

Everything that has been written in this chapter about Communications and about the appearance of typewritten work applies to the writing and presentation of reports—the appearance of a report has a great bearing upon its acceptability, and the writer must select his vocabulary and style to suit those for whom the report is intended. If the report is upon a very technical subject outside the field of specialisation of the people who are being asked to approve its recommendations, the author will have little chance of success if he uses technical terms without explaining their meaning.

Statistics are more easily understood if they are presented in neatly displayed tables; double spacing is easier to read than single spacing; allow fairly wide margins and decide upon a clear division and numbering of headings, section headings, sub-sections, such as:

```
I HEADING

  A - SECTION HEADING
      1 Sub-section heading
      2 Sub-section heading

  B - SECTION HEADING
      1 Sub-section heading
      2 Sub-section heading
        a Paragraph heading
        b Paragraph heading
           i Sub-paragraph heading
          ii Sub-paragraph heading
```

You will not be asked to write reports at the beginning of your business career but you will be able to make a great contribution to the acceptability of the reports you produce by selecting an attractive typing style and layout, the most suitable paper size and weight, the best method of reproduction, and the most suitable form of stapling or binding. If the report is to be handled by many people over a fair period of time, it is important that it is bound with a durable cover and that the binding allows the report to open easily for reading. Make sure that the final version of the report is free from typographical errors, that the pages are correctly numbered and that each set is correctly collated. The appearance of a duplicated report is greatly enhanced if the registration of the lines on all the sheets of paper is identical; uneven registration on successive sheets causes "greying" or "shading" to show through and this produces an unattractive, unprofessional effect which can be avoided by starting each new page on the same typing line and double-checking the registration of the first sheet of each new "run".

Unless you decide to specialise in another branch of work in the office it is unlikely that you will ever be asked to undertake the type of investigation which requires a long research report. You may, however, be asked to go to an exhibition, such as an exhibition of office machines to find out about some new items and their prices, if your employer is thinking of buying a new machine which you will use, such as an office copier, a duplicator or a collator. You would then prepare a report on the lines of a short research report. The stages for preparing such a report are as follows:

1 Get all the information you require.
2 Arrange the information and your recommendations (if asked for) under suitable headings.
3 Draft a report, writing as briefly and clearly as possible, using the headings you have prepared.
4 Check your draft against the REPORT-WRITING CHECKLIST on pages 400 and 401, and make any amendments or additions.
5 Type the report, place it in a folder with any accompanying papers such as leaflets or brochures, and hand the whole to your employer.

REPORT-WRITING CHECKLIST

What are the preliminary questions to consider when preparing a report?

1. Why have you been asked to write the report?
2. Do you fully understand your terms of reference?
3. What type of information is required from the report?
   (a) Factual information based on observation or research?
   (b) Conclusions drawn from observation or research?
   (c) Recommendations as to future course of action?
4. If you are writing the report on your own initiative, have you defined exactly what you hope to achieve?
5. Has the reader any prior knowledge, or formed opinions on the subject? How much will this affect the writing of the report?
6. How much information on the subject is already available? Will you incorporate any of this?
7. Will your report have any financial or legal repercussions?
8. Have you considered security precautions for confidential report?

Have you planned how to compile and present the report?

9. Does the title immediately identify the subject matter?
10. What are the most effective lines of enquiry to obtain reliable information?
11. Have you ensured that you obtain a balanced picture of the subject and that the information you have collected is wholly pertinent?

12. Is it arranged logically so that the basic message and main topics of argument emerge progressively?
13. What is the most suitable format (a routine report, a short research report or a long research report) and how many headings will you need?
14. Is the style and method of analysis suited to the subject matter and the reader?
15. Have you avoided the use of generalisations?
16. Have you used any technical language which might be unfamiliar to the reader?
17. If any specialised terminology is unavoidable have you provided a suitable explanatory key?
18. Is any of the information more suitable for presentation in diagrammatic or graphic form?
19. Will it be necessary to provide a reference list for further reading?
20. If the report is long or detailed, will an index help the reader?
21. If the report is based on original research, should you include descriptions of the standards and enquiry methods which you adopt?
23. Is it as simple and easy to read as you can make it?

Are your conclusions and recommendations correctly presented?

24. Do the conclusions and recommendations match the terms of reference of the report?
25. Do the conclusions follow logically from information and discussions in the main body of the report?
26. Are they based solely on information incorporated within the report?
27. If not, have you referred to the outside evidence which has influenced the conclusions reached?
28. Should you point to any wider significance which your conclusions might contain, even though this might be outside your immediate terms of reference?
29. Have you taken account of any minority or dissenting opinions? Should these be included in an Appendix?
30. Have you distinguished between:
    (a) Conclusions from information presented in the report?
    (b) Your own personal comments on this information?
    (c) Recommendations as to future action based on the report findings?
31. Has the report been fully checked before presentation?

SUMMARIES A secretary who has mastered the art of summarising can relieve her boss of much time-consuming, non-productive but nevertheless necessary work by (a) making précis of articles in newspapers, journals and magazines, (b) summarising reports, (c) summarising correspondence, and (d) reporting meetings which her boss is unable to attend.

Most businessmen have to keep up-to-date with national and international developments which affect their sphere of operations, and nearly all trades and professions have their own journals and magazines. If you can scan the daily papers, particularly *The Financial Times*' special supplements, and periodicals relevant to your boss's specialisation, and produce *summaries of articles* your boss will not have to spend his valuable time reading every paper and journal page by page. He will be pleased to rely on your judgment to indicate those articles which he should study in depth, and appreciate having been made aware by your summaries of the existence and main points of other articles which have a less direct bearing upon the main purpose of his work.

To summarise an article you would use the précis techniques you have learnt in your English lessons. Read carefully through the article, and make notes of what seem to you the most important points. Your summary may be in note form and should state:

1 Title of article, source (name of paper or journal), date and/or edition number, name and title of author.
2 Main points, written in paragraphs under sub-headings, to help the reader look over the page and assimilate the main facts at a glance.
3 Further comments, such as if the article is one of a series, when the next article will appear, reference to any other work being carried out simultaneously, physical location of original article.

A *précis of a report* can be written under similar headings. Your firm may have large overseas contracts and your representatives in other countries may send in reports on the business being done in their areas. Some of these reports may be models of precise writing, but others may be verbose and contain material which has no real importance to executives in England. If your boss receives reports of this nature from his assistants, you will save his time if you can produce a list of reports received, the names of the authors, the areas of work covered and the main points of each report.

A third application of summarising which the secretary will find useful is the ability to *summarise an exchange of correspondence*. Suppose that you had been working for a senior executive who has recently left the company. A new man has been brought in from outside the company because of his special qualifications. He has only been employed a fortnight when he is told that he is to attend a meeting with all other heads of departments to discuss moving the company's headquarters from London to the country. He finds that there is a thick file in existence consisting of notes of previous meetings, correspondence with estate agents, and advertisements cut from newspapers, of possible premises. He realises that he cannot possibly read everything and also carry on with his other work; yet he does not wish to go to the meeting knowing nothing of the background of the matters to be discussed. He asks you to take a day off your normal work, and to make him a summary of the contents of the file. You would provide him with something like the summary illustrated on page 403. You will note that a summary of this type is not complete in a grammatical sense. There are few verbs. What is required is a series of points divided by punctuation.

Fourthly, the secretary may be asked to *summarise the proceedings of a meeting*. Suppose, for example, your boss is an editor in a firm of educational publishers

SUMMARY OF CORRESPONDENCE AND REPORTS

from 7 January to 10 September 1973, dealing with the transfer of the Company's headquarters to the Home Counties.

<u>7 January 1973</u>

Confidential memorandum sent by Managing Director to all heads of departments pointing out the overcrowded condition of the present building, the problem of finding suitable premises in London and the possible advantages of moving to the Home Counties.

<u>21 January 1973</u>

Report on meeting between the Board of Directors and heads of departments.

Points put forward in favour of moving:

Problem of finding and cost of premises in London.
Congested travelling conditions.
Expense of housing and travel to staff.

Points against moving:

Damage to business to be away from a centre where clients could easily call.
Possible effect on prestige.

From staff point of view:

Unwillingness to move from existing homes.
Cost of removal.
Loss of friends.
Loss of accustomed leisure-time pursuits.
Change of children's schools.
Objection by wives.

<u>5 February 1973</u>

Letter from estate agent in Amersham describing large country house which could be converted to office premises. Cost £150,000.

<u>20 February 1973</u>

Report on house by Mr James. Well situated but cost of conversion at least £25,000.

Suggested layout for a summary of correspondence.

and she wishes to attend a meeting of, say, mathematics teachers, but is unable to do so owing to a previous engagement which cannot be changed; she is anxious to know what is said at the meeting and asks you to go on her behalf. Before going to the meeting you should make sure you appreciate the relevance of the meeting to your boss's work: Why is she interested in the proceedings? What aspects are of particular interest? What would she hope to get out of it if she were able to attend herself? When you are at the meeting, note carefully the names of the speakers, the main points of their lectures, the questions asked afterwards, the names of the people asking the questions (if possible); be on the look-out for any issues which provoke strong feeling, and take a note of any future developments (such as new policies and structures) and future meetings or promotions which your boss might like to attend. Your summary of the meeting should be written under the following headings:

1 Introduction—title of meeting, date, time, place, approximate number of people present.
2 Lectures—name of each speaker, main points of the lecture (plus, if relevant, brief description of appearance and presentation).
3 Questions.
4 Conclusion—attempt to summarise "the feel of the meeting" and indicate any issues which aroused strong feelings.
5 Future plans—date of further meetings, new developments or points to be followed up.
6 Attachments—programme of meeting and any printed hand-outs.

NOTICES Many organisations have notice boards where matters of interest to staff are pinned. Notices are a way of communicating which enables those in authority to convey information to staff at every level.

A notice must be easily understood by the most junior employee. It should have a heading, it should be signed, and it should be simply and clearly worded in an appropriate tone. Badly worded notices can cause disruptive reactions.

Although people are usually eager to know what is going on in an organisation, they may not bother to read notices unless they are attractively displayed, so if you are involved in the production of notices, try to produce something bold and eye-catching which will stimulate curiosity. There are many transfer devices available for producing captions in large letters in a variety of colours, and the use of line-drawings or pictures attracts attention.

Notice boards should be conveniently sited and a ratio of one notice board to every fifty employees is a reasonable suggestion. The general effect of a notice board can be improved by using narrow coloured ribbon to divide it into boldly titled sections and grouping the notices in sections according to their content or department of origin. Securing notices by pins in each of the four corners keeps the notice board looking tidy, by making sure that the notices hang square and by preventing them from being torn or blown about in the wind.

Interest will be stimulated if the lay-out of the notice board is changed from time to time; and it is important to remove dead material—a notice board is not likely to be effective if it is cluttered with dog-eared, out-of-date material. A sensible policy is to appoint one person to be in charge of the notice board;

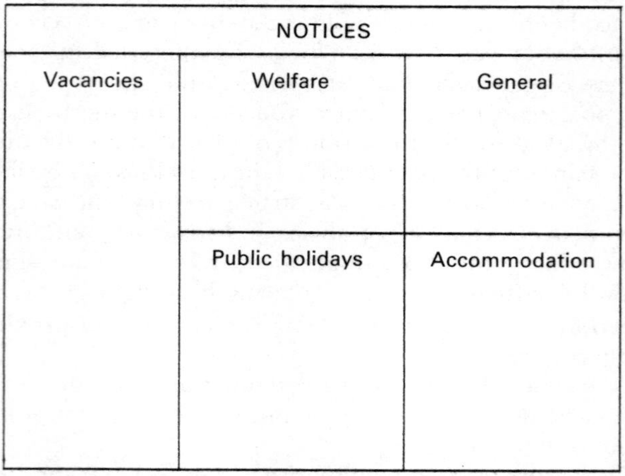

NOTICES

Vacancies

Welfare

General

Public holidays

Accommodation

A notice board divided into sections. Staff will be more inclined to read the notices (a) if the board is attractively displayed, (b) if the layout is changed from time to time, and (c) if the board is regularly cleared of out-of-date material.

notices should only be pinned up by the authorised official to whom all notices should be submitted so that they can be checked for accuracy and content. Notices which are going to remain on the board for a fair length of time should be laminated or protected by a sheet of transparent plastic from dust (and from the gratuitious addition of graffiti).

CIRCULARS Organisations with a small number of employees sometimes communicate with them by issuing circulars, in which every member of staff is given his own copy. This method may also be used by large companies if the matter is of such importance that every staff member should have his own copy in writing, or if there is a statutory obligation upon the employer to communicate certain information in writing to every employee. Circulars should be headed, signed, simply and clearly worded and written in an appropriate style. As with any piece of typewritten work, circulars should be attractively displayed, but there is no need to make them as eye-catching as notices because, by definition, a circular is a letter or notice which is distributed to every person concerned with the content or message.

BULLETINS In some companies, notices are circulated by means of a weekly or monthly Staff Bulletin. This is frequently prepared, typed and duplicated by the senior executive's secretary and a copy is distributed to every member of staff. The staff bulletin is a convenient means of communicating regularly with every employee; as you can see from the example given on page 406, the staff bulletin keeps everyone in the firm informed about new appointments, promotions, transfers, staff rules and entitlements and general information. A regular, reliable staff bulletin written in a frank, informative and affable style has many advantages: it can prevent gossip and rumour by making early announcements of impending changes and innovations, and it can improve morale by fostering a good working spirit amongst employees and making all members of staff feel that they are "in the know". If your boss were the official responsible for producing the staff bulletin, you could help by collecting all items of news in a folder and sorting them into individual points so that all the information was ready prepared before he started to compose and dictate; after a little while you would probably become accustomed to the type and source of information to be included and you might try your hand at producing a draft bulletin yourself. You would start by looking through previous bulletins and noting the individual items, then telephone other officials who might have points they want included and then list these points with any you had collected yourself. Before submitting the draft to your boss you would check that what you had written was (a) factually correct, (b) correct from the point of view of grammar, spelling and vocabulary, (c) in an appropriate style and (d) simple to understand and unambiguous.

HOUSE JOURNAL Large companies frequently produce house journals similar in appearance and format to glossy magazines. Professional journalists and

WEEKLY STAFF BULLETIN

57. Our new branch in Halifax will open on 1 October 1973. Mr C E Field, at present West End Manager, has been appointed Manager of the Halifax branch and will take up his new appointment on 1 September 1973.

58. Mr O R Newton will join the firm on 15 August 1973 as West End Manager. For the past six years Mr Newton has been District Manager in East Anglia for a well-known construction company.

59. All members of staff are now entitled to a third week's holiday. This may be taken in either October or November, or in February or March. Each department head is requested to prepare a rota for his own department.

60. Offices will be closed for Christmas from 5.30 p.m. on 21 December until 9.0 a.m. on 27 December.

61. Complaints have been received from Kleenwell Ltd, our window-cleaning contractors, that their men have difficulty in cleaning some office windows because of obstruction. Staff members are reminded that windows are cleaned on the last Friday on each month and are requested to move any files, books, parcels, pot plants from the sills, so that the cleaners can do their work with the least possible delay.

62. As from 1 September all internal memoranda will be typed on the pre-printed memo sets now obtainable from the Office Manager's office. Top and blue copies should be sent to the addressee; the yellow copy is the file copy. Further instructions are given on the memo sets.

16 August 1973 Office Manager

Example of a staff bulletin.

photographers are responsible for the tone and appearance of the house journal and the use of modern colour and lay-out techniques ensures that the production reflects credit upon the organisation and all its employees. House journals are given to all members of staff and sometimes they are also distributed freely outside the company as part of its public relations policy.

The contents may be divided into sections for new products, new members of staff, births, engagements and marriages, news of sports activities, articles of general interest, interviews with executives or directors, stories of success and promotion and reports from representatives in exotic and remote parts of the world.

Wealthy corporations usually spare no expense to produce house journals which have the look and feel of quality periodicals because it is realised that the appearance and contents play an important role in promoting the organisation's image and in instilling loyalty and "pride in belonging" amongst the employees.

External

LETTERS The majority of external written communications are carried out in the form of letters. Letters requiring skilful composition will usually be dictated to the secretary or even drafted in manuscript, because the information to be conveyed or the specialised wording required is part of the executive's expertise. There are many letters which only the executive can compose by virtue of his position, his authority, his background knowledge, his technical training or his professional competence.

We are not concerned here with letters of this type. Our purpose is to discuss

47 Lode Lane

Hurst Park, HA8 6DW

6 April 1973

The Production Manager
The Imperial Motor Company
Imperial Works
COVENTRY CV1 5HA

Dear Sir

I have recently bought a new Imperial "Sprite" and am writing to complain about the following faults on the car:-

1. The windscreen demister on the off-side is not operating.

2. The tool box at the rear of the car fills up with water in wet weather owing to the lack of sealing between the body and the valance sections.

3. The heater fan inside the car is out of balance and vibrates when it is switched on.

I am, of course, returning the car to the dealer to have these faults corrected, but I am bringing them to your notice as I feel that, in view of your national advertising campaign "Buy Imperial - never a better car", more care should be taken in checking cars as they come off the production line and before they leave the factory.

Yours faithfully

O D Kelway

O D Kelway

1. Please write usual letter to customer.

2. Send copy to dealer and ask for comments.

3. Send copy to chief Designer and ask for comments.

SWB.

Instructions to the secretary written by the boss on the incoming letter.

1

8 April 1973

O D Kelway Esq
47 Lode Lane
Hurst Park
HA8 6DW

Dear Sir

Thank you for your letter of 6 April listing the faults you have found on your new Imperial "Sprite".

Although every case is taken to ensure that new cars leave the factory in perfect condition, it is not always possible to prevent one or two small faults becoming apparent during the running-in period. It is, indeed, rare to produce a car which does not require one or two minor adjustments when it is brought in for its first service and these are, of course, carried out free of charge under the terms of our guarantee.

We have asked your local dealer to carry out a thorough inspection of your car whilst he is attending to the faults you have listed, and upon receipt of his report we will write to you again.

Yours faithfully

S W Ballard

S W Ballard
Production Manager

1. The letter to the customer.

2

8 April 1973

G R Woodard Esq
Woodard and Griggs Ltd
83 High Road
Hurst Park
HA8 6DW

Dear Mr Woodard

I attach copy of letter from Mr O D Kelway which is self-explanatory.

Whilst you are making the necessary adjustments, would you please carry out a thorough inspection of the car and send me a detailed report on its condition. Please include the engine and chassis numbers.

We are inclined to think that the water seepage into the tool box is due to faulty assembly rather than bad design, but we are asking our Chief Designer for his comments on this complaint. In the meantime, would you please do what you can to remedy the condition.

When we have discuss this complaint (which is one of several received during the past three weeks) we will write to you again.

Yours sincerely

S W Ballard

S W Ballard
Production Manager

2. Letter to the dealer.

3. Memorandum to Chief Designer (see page 395, upper left).

letters which the secretary may write and to indicate how they can be composed; four types of letter can be distinguished:

1 Letters passed over to the secretary with a brief verbal instruction such as, "Please acknowledge this letter and send them the pamphlets they are asking for."
2 Notes dictated to the secretary for expansion into a properly worded letter, such as, "Please write to this man and explain that we have had to increase our costs by ten per cent owing to production delays caused by the industrial troubles at the factory. Tell him that I hope to be in the Midlands next month and will call and see him. Remind me to let him know the exact date of my visit when the trip is fixed up."
3 Brief notes written across the incoming letter which can be incorporated into a complete reply, such as in example shown on page 407.
4 Letters which the secretary can compose on her own initiative.

The first three types require the secretary to *compose letters from brief instructions* and to type them ready for her boss's signature. In the examples shown on page 407, the first paragraphs are the introduction, the second paragraphs convey the information and the last paragraphs are the conclusion. Most routine letters fit into this framework and you may find it helpful to use the three-paragraph arrangement when you start writing business letters.

Opening paragraphs may be acknowledgments or introductions of the writer or topic of the letter such as:

> Thank you for your letter dated 4 June 1973, regarding your order for wood block flooring.
>
> We should like to draw your attention to the fact that our account no. 786, dated 3 March 1973, for £105.75 is still outstanding.
>
> We are pleased to announce that on 1 September we shall be opening a new branch office at Hadley Corner, Roxham.
>
> I am a student at Fairley College of Further Education taking a Bi-lingual Secretarial Course.
>
> We are interested in purchasing a quantity of crockery for use in our Staff Canteen.

Middle paragraphs amplify the topic and convey the message of the letter.

Closing paragraphs usually suggest future action or state what the writer proposes to do or hopes will be done, for example:

> **I shall very much appreciate any help you can give me.**
>
> **We look forward to hearing from you soon.**
>
> **If you should need any further information, please let us know.**

There are three main *types of letter which the secretary composes and signs herself.* These are:

a Letters written on behalf of her boss which can start

> **Mr Jackson has asked me to thank you for your letter of ... and to say that ...**

and finish

> **Yours faithfully**
>
> Angela Ford
>
> **Secretary to Mr F C Jackson**
> **Information Officer**

b Letters written in her boss's absence, such as

> **Thank you for your letter dated ... to Mr ... inviting him to speak to your Society on ...**
>
> **Unfortunately Mr ... is away from the office/out of town/away on business/out of the country/on holiday ... and he will not return until ...**
>
> **Your letter will be brought to his attention as soon as he returns. I hope that this delay will not cause you any inconvenience.**

c Letters written on her own initiative such as follow-up letters,

On ... we wrote to you concerning/regarding/ asking ...

Unfortunately we cannot trace having received any reply and therefore enclose a copy of our earlier letter.

We hope we shall have the pleasure of hearing from you shortly.

CHECKLIST FOR LETTERS

1. Is the information complete? Does the letter contain all the information the correspondent requires? Have you covered all the points mentioned?
2. If you have been unable to answer all the points, have you indicated where the correspondent might look for further information?
3. Is the meaning clear? Are there any sentences or phrases which are ambiguous or could be misunderstood?
4. Is the letter correct as regards facts and figures and detailed information?
5. Are the following correct—spelling, punctuation, names, initials, dates, decorations, qualifications, forms of address?
6. Is the wording simple and direct? Is the letter free of slang, commercialese and the unwarranted use of jargon?
7. Is the style or tone appropriate?
8. Are all the enclosures mentioned in the letter included in the envelope?
9. Have any special mail notations been indicated?
10. Has the letter been signed?

The letters we have been discussing are typical of conventional correspondence or what may be called "normal business practice" at the time of writing. A letter produced in one of these ways may cost a surprisingly large sum of money (£3 per letter has been estimated, taking into account all the factors involved—total office costs, the executive's and the secretary's time, depreciation, cost of stationery supplies, postage, etc.). It is possible that an increasing number of firms may try to lessen their office costs by adopting some of the time- and money-saving correspondence methods, such as Blitz Replies, Reply Memo Sets and Form Letters,* already used by a few leading companies.

* The authors are grateful to Mr H. P. Cemach for permission to quote examples and ideas under these three headings. These are more fully described in *The Reduction of Correspondence Costs* by H. P. Cemach, Anbar Publications Ltd.

The *Blitz Reply* method can be used if a letter requires only a short reply such as "Yes", "No", or "Noted". These words are handwritten in the margin or at the foot of the original letter and initialled. The letter is then photocopied and the copy is sent to the writer of the original letter. It is obvious that this type of reply can be produced in a matter of seconds and saves time as well as stationery. It is not uncommonly used with internal correspondence; for example, an internal memorandum requesting a day's leave can be authorised by the responsible official writing "Approved" and his initials in the margin or at the top or bottom of the page. The memorandum is then photocopied; the copy is sent back to the staff member and the original is filed.

Blitz Replies may also be used for external correspondence. The method is particularly useful for acknowledging receipt of correspondence when it will take some time to get the necessary information to reply to all the points raised in the letter in detail. A photocopy of his original letter with a handwritten comment such as "Will reply in full within ten days" assures the writer that his letter has been received and that it is being dealt with. The term "Blitz Reply"

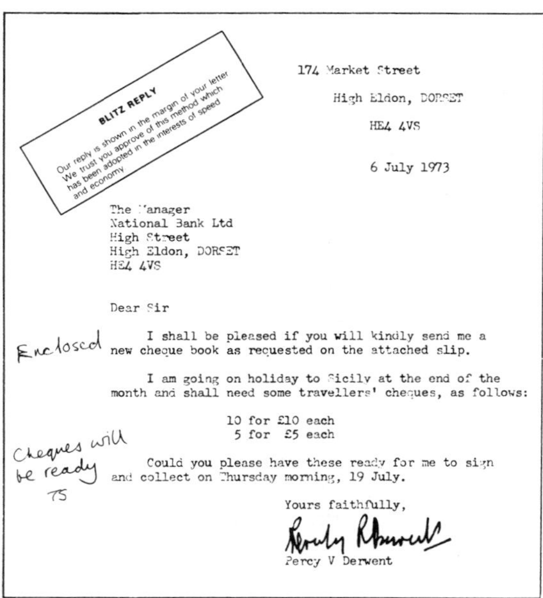

BLITZ REPLY

Our reply is shown in the margin of your letter. We trust you approve of this method which has been adopted in the interests of speed and economy

174 Market Street
High Eldon, DORSET
HE4 4VS

6 July 1973

The Manager
National Bank Ltd
High Street
High Eldon, DORSET
HE4 4VS

Dear Sir

Enclosed — I shall be pleased if you will kindly send me a new cheque book as requested on the attached slip.

I am going on holiday to Sicily at the end of the month and shall need some travellers' cheques, as follows:

10 for £10 each
5 for £5 each

Cheques will be ready TS — Could you please have these ready for me to sign and collect on Thursday morning, 19 July.

Yours faithfully,

Percy V Derwent

A Blitz Reply letter. The bank official has written his reply in the margin so the customer knows that the matters are being dealt with, and the 'reply' acts as a letter of transmittal for his new cheque book. The rubber-stamped comment explains the use of this type of 'reply' and helps to remove any impression of impersonal service which might possibly have been conveyed. Fears that Blitz Replies may be considered impersonal are not really warranted—on the contrary, as they are handwritten it could be argued that they have a more personal touch than a conventional business letter.

originated in Germany; the word 'Blitz' means 'lightning'. Sometimes the letter is rubber-stamped with a comment such as:

> Our reply is shown in the margin of your letter. We trust you approve of this method which has been adopted in the interests of speed and economy.

Quick Reply forms as shown in the illustration on page 413 are prepared in triplicate: (1) the original, (2) the reply, and (3) the temporary file copy. For external correspondence they can be pre-printed with the originator's name, address and company particulars as in a normal printed letterhead. (Quick Reply forms designed for internal use usually omit the address but are usually pre-printed with the name of the organisation and/or blank spaces where the names of the originator and recipient and their departments may be inserted.) On the reply copy the positions of the words 'TO' and 'FROM' are reversed. The three copies are in distinguishing colours, e.g. the original white, the reply copy pink and the temporary file copy yellow. The originator inserts carbon (unless carbonless copying paper is used), writes his message on the white top copy and sends it together with the pink reply copy to the recipient; he keeps the yellow copy, the temporary file copy. The recipient inserts carbons (unless carbonless copying paper is used) writes his reply on the white copy, sends the pink copy to the originator and keeps the white. Copies for third parties can be taken if need be. If the originator wishes to send a copy of his memo direct he does so and indicates it by typing "c.c. ABC" at the bottom of the left-hand portion. If he wishes the third party to have a copy of the memo and reply he types his "c.c. ABC" at the bottom of the right-hand portion and sends the extra copy (for which another colour, such as blue could be chosen) to his correspondent who will pass it on after inserting his reply.

The advantages of reply memos are considerable, the main point being that replies can be very short; often 'Yes' or 'No' or a short reference or a figure will be enough. The originator's reference, number, subject, etc. need not be repeated. The address need not be typed again. Answers can be given without repeating or referring to what the originator has said. A further advantage is that when the reply is received the originator then has his own message and the reply in front of him and further file references are unnecessary. Quick Reply forms also economise on filing space as the temporary file copy can be destroyed when the reply is filed. If this is conscientiously done, yellow copies on files then draw attention to overdue replies.

Form Letters are pre-printed replies which list all the comments that experience has shown may reasonably be needed in a certain office situation. Those that apply are indicated by writing a cross or tick in the space provided. The code letters make it possible to keep a record of what has been "written" without retaining a copy. Form letters are useful for situations in which correspondents have not complied with certain regulations or stipulated requirements, such as completing a form correctly, enclosing the correct documents or writing a cheque correctly. The example shown below was

CAUTION-Tear off three-part set before use, to avoid show-through

Quick Reply Form

MESSAGE	REPLY
To Type the name and address of the addressee here.	Date
Date Type the date here.	
1. This is a specimen of a Quick Reply form.	
2. The set comprises a white original, a yellow copy and a pink copy.	
3. The sets are pre-printed on carbonless copying paper so no time is wasted interleaving carbon paper.	
4. The originator keeps the yellow copy and forwards the white original and the pink copy.	
5. The addressee writes his answer in the REPLY column, retains the white original and returns the pink copy to the sender.	
6. Both sender and addressee have the message and reply on one sheet of paper.	
7. Typing addresses in the marked spaces enables window envelopes to be used by both parties.	
Please address your reply to: A further saving of time is effected if the originator has his name and address pre-printed in this space.	

Can be mailed in a window envelope by the sender and the addressee

Notes for the Sender:
1. Please retain the yellow copy
2. Please forward the white original and pink copy

Notes for the Addressee:
1. Please write down the answer
2. Retain the white original
3. Return the pink copy to the sender

© Leviathan House Ltd. 1973 mls forms

Illustration of Quick Reply form.

obviously produced as a result of receiving a considerable number of incorrect or defective sets of documents for goods being imported into Ghana. There are many office situations in which the production of form letters could reduce the volume of correspondence—two situations are suggested in the exercises at the end of this chapter.

CIRCULAR LETTERS Notices and circular letters differ from the letters discussed in the previous section in two respects, (a) they are not written to one particular addressee, and (b) they are unsolicited. Apart from notices such as printed notices of annual general meetings sent to all the shareholders of a company, circular letters usually announce a new product (sales letters), or an event, such as a public meeting, or they are from charities seeking support for their activities. Because their aim is to persuade people to act in a certain way and because they are written to a large number of typical people rather than to one specific person, circular letters are written in a tone and style which is different from the normal business letter. As they are unsolicited and as their production and mailing has cost a considerable sum of money, their composition is especially important, particularly the opening sentence which is most carefully

Our Reference: SJ/DD/1
Our Order No.
Date

Dear Sirs,

DEFECTIVE DOCUMENTATION

We regret that your Invoices No.
do not comply with our requirements as set out on our Order. The omissions are those marked by a cross below:

A ○ SIX copies are required, you have sent only	B ○ The Invoices are not on the approved form for West Africa/ Ghana.
C ○ All copies must be signed.	D ○ For GHANA facsimile or carbon copy signatures are not acceptable.
E ○ Discounts must be shown on the invoices.	F ○ Discounts must be described as 'TRADE DISCOUNT' or 'CASH DISCOUNT'.
G ○ Weights and Measurements of all packages must be shown.	H ○ Exact Width, composition and square yardage must be shown. If pieces differ in width, square yardage for each piece.
I ○ Alcoholic Beverages require: Total Gallonage, Percentage Spirit.	J ○ C.I.F/F. & F. Invoices must show: Freight and shipping charges, Insurance, and for GHANA Freight Rate.

ACTION REQUIRED

1 ○ Please send a fresh set of Invoices.	2 ○ Please supply.............................. additional copies of Invoice.
3 ○ Please sign/complete Invoices and return to us.	4 ○ Please note for future reference only.

5 ○ Please sign/complete Invoices and send them by First Class Air Mail to ( ) Ltd., P.O. Box

○ YOUR IMMEDIATE ATTENTION IS REQUESTED
Delay may involve our Associates in Africa in heavy expenditure.

○ PLEASE RETURN THIS LETTER WITH THE INVOICES

Yours faithfully,

A Form Letter.

and skilfully worded to make sure that each recipient continues reading the letter and does not throw it away unread as "just another circular". The aim of the letter is to make the reader gradually adopt an increasingly favourable attitude towards the underlying theme so that by the time he reaches the end of the letter he feels he wants to "complete and return the enclosed business reply paid card" or do whatever else the promoters have been trying to persuade him to do.

Circular letters usually start with a salutation such as Dear Parent, or Dear Colleague, or Dear Householder, or Dear Sir or Madam. They may be mailed or delivered by hand either to every house in an area, or to only those households which the promoters have selected as being most likely to be interested and respond favourably. Although the circulars are usually composed and produced by the sponsoring organisation, the actual addressing and mailing can be done by specialised agencies who compile mailing lists according to the promoters' instructions, that is, by area, by income group, by profession, age, number of children in the family, whether the house is owned or rented and so on.

As a circular letter is going to hundreds and probably thousands of people, its appearance and the image it conveys are even more important than that of a normal business letter. Because of this, every effort is made to give a circular the appearance of an individually typed letter. This may be done by using good quality paper and envelopes and an automatic typewriter (see page 215 ff.) which produces apparent "originals"; letters appear to be even more "original" if the actual name of the recipient has been typed in manually before running through the punched paper tape or magnetic tape or card which produces the body of the letter.

There are many books on the market which suggest ways of writing circulars and sales letters and give examples; the names of some of these books are given at the end of this chapter.

PRESS RELEASES are announcements which companies distribute to the press about new products or developments in the hope that the topic of the announcement will be included in a news item on radio or television or in the national press. This aspect of an organisation's communications with the outside world has such an important bearing upon the whole business of image-making, that it is usually the responsibility of a Public Relations Officer (a PRO) who may launch the press release at a special press conference to which editors of newspapers and journals have been invited to send reporters. Further information on this topic will be found in Chapter 14, Human Relations, pages 543–545.

REPORTS Reports produced for external, that is public, distribution are slightly different from the reports we considered in the *Internal Communications* section. Internal reports, as we discussed, are usually written for a person or group of people within an organisation and describe an incident, or a piece of research, or work achievements over a given period of time. External reports are commonly of two types (a) a company's annual report which is circulated to all shareholders with copies of the accounts for the year, or (b) a government report which may be a small booklet of twenty to thirty pages or a full-size book of over two hundred pages. It is unlikely that the secretary will be directly involved in producing the final versions of these reports as they are almost always printed; she may, however, be involved at the type-script stage in which case she should bear in mind that she is preparing work for the printer and not typing the publication in its final form. This means, for example, that she should indicate type-styles and layout needed (in the case of a company's annual report the style and format will probably be the same as in preceding years) and follow other guide-lines she has learnt in typewriting under the heading "Preparing Work for the Printer" such as typing footnotes on the line immediately following the reference and not at the foot of the page.

In government reports all the paragraphs are numbered consecutively in Arabic numerals from one right through to the end, and the whole report is usually divided into sections indicated by Roman numerals; the sections generally follow the layout suggested for internal reports, i.e. introduction stating terms of reference and names of members of the council or committee who have compiled the report, the main body of the report, summary of conclusions and recommendations, and annexes or appendices.

TELECOMMUNICATIONS

Under this heading we shall study the facilities using telegraph and telephone circuits which form the telecommunication services of the British Post Office. Cable and Wireless Ltd is a British company whose cable network connects many parts of the Commonwealth and foreign countries. Through close association with Cable and Wireless Ltd, the Post Office is able to provide a world-wide range of telecommunication services from Great Britain.

The telephone The correct use of the telephone and the variety of equipment available were discussed in Chapter 3, Telephone Techniques. The telephone is mentioned again here, partly because any survey of communications must include reference to it, and also to list the specific uses of the telephone by the secretary as one of her methods of communication.

TELEPHONE CIRCUITS In addition to the normal telephone service controlled by the Post Office in the whole of Great Britain (except the local system in the Hull district) and known as the Public Switched Network (PSN), and internal telephone systems which can be separately wired or part of Private Manual Branch Exchanges or Private Automatic Branch Exchanges (see pages 118 and 119), it is also possible to rent private telephone circuits from the Post Office to provide, for example, direct connection between a head office of a firm and its factory or factories. Private circuits are independent of the public services. They can also be used to transmit pictures, alarm signals, music and signals representing data for computers (Datel services, pages 428 to 429). Private equipment which is to be used in conjunction with Post Office circuits must be approved by the Post Office. Details of the equipment, of the permission needed before it may be connected, and the charges can be obtained from the Post Office Telecommunication Headquarters. The charges vary according to the kind of service and the distance between the places to be connected.

TELEPHONE MANNER All that has been said throughout this book about the importance of creating an appropriate image and the role of language in effective communication applies with equal force to the use of the telephone in business. Frequently the telephone is the first contact a would-be client has with an organisation and this should never be forgotten by all who answer and handle telephone calls. Earlier in this chapter we mentioned an important difference between spoken and written English: that the use of pauses, intonation, stress, winks and gestures enables us to vary the implication and impact of the actual words we speak and that the effects created by these devices cannot be conveyed in writing. When we speak on the telephone, we should remember that although we are using spoken English we cannot rely on facial expressions and other gestures to aid our communication; until we have videophones, for example, we cannot soften with a wink a harsh word spoken on the telephone.

However, the tone of voices is affected by facial expressions such as frowns and smiles—this is one reason why people who earn their living by telephone

Videophone, one of the interesting new telephone facilities in the course of experiment. A small TV screen associated with the telephone enables the two parties to see each other.

selling are told to "put a smile in your voice". The secretary should practise this too so that her telephone manner conveys a good image of herself and her office and thus of her boss, the organisation and the products or services it provides.

The secretary should also make sure that callers are never left 'high and dry' without explanation while they listen to a background of other conversations, possibly personal, going on in the office. If a caller has to wait on the telephone, explain why there is a delay and reassure him from time to time that he is still connected and that you are still trying to find the person or information he wants. Do not forget that the caller is paying for the call, so if you anticipate a considerable delay in attending to him, ask whether he would prefer you to ring him back or to call again himself later on. Similarly if a caller has to be transferred to another extension, explain what is going to happen and do not replace your receiver until you are sure the call has been transferred.

RECEIVING INFORMATION An example of a telephone message form was given in Chapter 3, Telephone Techniques. If you are receiving information yourself, you will not need to complete a message sheet, but you should make a note of the information in your notebook, particularly any proper names and numbers, such as dates, times and reference numbers.

GIVING INFORMATION The secretary will use the telephone either to convey her boss's instructions or to make calls on her own initiative. In the former case, she may say something on these lines: "Good morning, this is Marion Wilson, Mrs Harper's secretary. Mrs Harper has asked me to confirm that she will be catching the ten o'clock train from Euston on Wednesday. She very much appreciates your offering to meet her off the train and looks forward to meeting you at Bisham Station at eleven-thirty."

When you start initiating calls yourself, it is helpful before actually making the call to write down the information you want to communicate or the points you want to cover in the call, as it is easy to be side-tracked during a conversation and find you have rung off before accomplishing all the purposes of the call. Have the list in front of you when you are speaking, tick off each point as it is dealt with and write down any new information or ideas that come to mind during the conversation. A telephone call can be divided into parts similar to the paragraphs of a letter: (a) introduce yourself, (b) deliver the message or deal with the points on your list, and (c) conclude the conversation. It is a convention that the person originating the call should bring the conversation to an end. A good plan is to summarise the points covered, concluding with a statement that indicates future action such as "I'll look forward to hearing from you towards the end of the week", or "I'll put it in the post tonight", or "Good, I'll expect your mechanic here first thing in the morning", or "I'll call you again when you get back from the States"—and then say, "Goodbye".

Another telephone convention is that if a call is cut off, the person who originated the call attempts to re-establish the connection.

If difficult words have to be spelt out confusion can be avoided by using names for letters. The following 'telephone alphabet' is suggested by the British Post Office:

A	Alfred	G	George	M	Mary	S	Samuel	Y	Yellow
B	Benjamin	H	Harry	N	Nellie	T	Tommy	Z	Zebra
C	Charlie	I	Isaac	O	Oliver	U	Uncle		
D	David	J	Jack	P	Peter	V	Victor		
E	Edward	K	King	Q	Queen	W	William		
F	Frederick	L	London	R	Robert	X	X-Ray		

CONFIRMING CALLS Some telephone calls, particularly those regarding bookings or orders, have to be confirmed in writing. An example of how to do this is shown below.

4 August 1973

The Manager
Eaton Arms Hotel
Eaton CARDIFF
CF1 4LT

Dear Sir

I am writing to confirm our telephone conversation this afternoon when I booked a single room with bath for Mrs Joan Sawyer, Divisional Sales Manager, for the night of Friday, 17 August 1973.

Mrs Sawyer will be travelling by car and hopes to arrive about 6.30 p.m.

I look forward to receiving your acknowledgment of this booking.

Yours faithfully

Angela Foxton

Angela Foxton
Secretary to Mrs Joan Sawyer
Divisional Sales Manager

Example of a letter confirming a telephone call.

As we pointed out in the section on Written Communications, *time is money* and business people do not like to waste time reading unnecessarily verbose communications. It is equally important to be brief on the telephone—as the calls themselves cost money (the charges being related to the duration of the calls) in addition to the cost of the working time of the two parties to the call. An unnecessarily long telephone call may also waste the time of other people who are trying to get through to one of the telephone numbers engaged in the call. In addition to being polite, firm and efficient, the secretary should also make her telephone calls as brief as possible.

This is a convenient point to mention the use of the office telephone for personal calls. Nowadays few firms forbid their employees to receive or make private calls in cases of necessity, but this is a privilege which should not be abused. The senior secretary may find herself having to mention this point to junior staff who spend too much time on personal calls; the points to mention include: that they come to the office to do a job of work, not to chat to their friends on the phone; that there is no reason why the firm should bear the expense of their personal calls; and that whilst they are using the phone the line will be engaged to people who are trying to contact the firm for genuine business purposes.

Telegrams and cables In everyday speech we scarcely discriminate between the words 'telegram' and 'cable' because we do not know by which telegraphic means our messages are going to be transmitted—by radio waves, by overhead wires, by cables laid underground or under the sea, or via an artificial satellite, Telstar, and the Post Office earth station at Goonhilly Downs. Throughout this section the word telegram is used, therefore, to include the terms 'cable' or 'cablegram', and we should note *en passant* that many of the services offered by the Post Office use the cable network of the British company, Cable and Wireless Ltd.

The inland and international telegraph services provide a quick and reliable method of sending brief written communications throughout the world. The secretary must be aware of the various telegraphic services available and the time and cost factors involved, so that she can select the most appropriate method in any given situation. She also needs to be able to judge under what circumstances the sending of a telegram is to be preferred to sending a letter or making a phone call.

Telegrams are normally used to communicate very quickly with someone who is not available by telephone, e.g. a person who does not have a home telephone number and cannot be contacted on a business number, or a person who is travelling, or if the matter to be communicated consists of a large number of figures or data which it would be difficult to dictate over the telephone but which should be transmitted more quickly than the time taken by a letter.

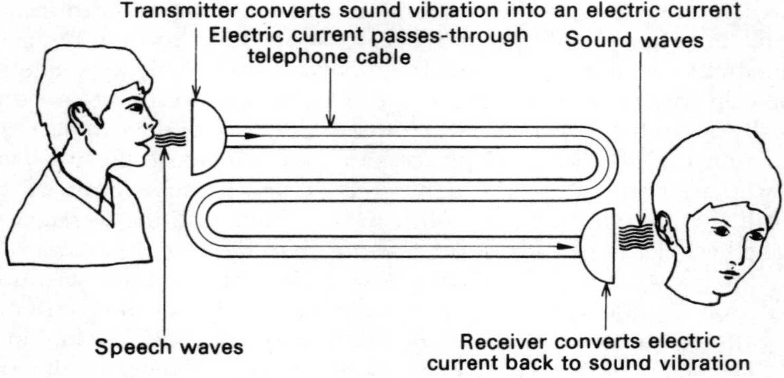

How the sound of speech travels
When you speak, the vibration of the vocal chords causes minute changes in air-pressure in your mouth. These changes in pressure radiate from you in waves comparable with ripples on the surface of a pond. These radiations, known as 'sound waves', make impact on the listener's ear. If the waves are strong enough, impulses are sent to the nerve centres of the brain, and your voice is heard.

In ordinary speech, air is the medium of transmission of the sound. The pressure as the 'waves' leave your mouth, may be comparatively heavy, and the sound loud, but as the waves extend over a wider distance their force, or 'amplitude', becomes smaller, until—at no great distance from you—they become inaudible. Air is not a good medium for the transmission of sound waves over a long distance.

An electric current can be transmitted over wires to a relatively great distance without much loss. If, therefore, speech sound waves can be converted to a similarly fluctuating electric current to be later changed back again to sound, the distance over which speech can be transmitted is greatly increased. This is the principle on which the modern telephone works.

A simple telephone consists of a transmitter, which converts the sound waves to a varying electric current corresponding to them; and a receiver which changes the electric current back into sound waves of the original form.

Before deciding whether or not to send a telegram, consult the time zone column in Appendix G so that you will be able to form some idea of when (local time) the telegram will be delivered.

INLAND TELEGRAMS may be sent between places in Great Britain, Northern Ireland, the Channel Islands and the Isle of Man. Telegrams sent to the Irish Republic are also sent as inland telegrams, but there is a higher basic charge. Telegrams may be (a) written or typed in block capitals (with three or four spaces between the words) on special forms and handed in at a post office counter, or (b) dictated from a private telephone or public call box, or (c) sent by telex.

The charge* for a telegram is made on the number of words used, the standard charge is 70p per telegram plus 7p for each word. Because it is important to use as few words as possible, most firms have a special abbreviated address for use on telegrams. These *telegraphic addresses* must be registered with the Post Office. The fee is £3 a year. The telegraphic address is usually included in the printed heading of a firm's letter paper and may be formed from parts of the words in the firm's name, such as BRITSTEEL for the British Steel Corporation.

It is important to make a file copy of all telegrams sent, and to note on the copy the date and time of handing-in, and the cost.

Telegrams can be delivered (a) to the addressee's address, or (b) by telephone, or (c) by telex. If telegrams are to be delivered by telephone or telex, the addressees' telephone or telex numbers should be included in the address. If a telegram is addressed to a telephone subscriber, only the name, telephone number and town need be given—the address is not necessary. Telegrams addressed to telephone subscribers are not delivered after 11 p.m. A telegram to be delivered by telex will be delivered at any time provided that the addressee's telex machine has been left switched on.

Greetings telegrams may be used for sending messages of congratulation or good wishes. They are delivered on decorative forms in colourful envelopes. The charge is the same as for an ordinary telegram (see above) plus a surcharge of 40p.

Overnight telegrams may be sent between 8 a.m. and 10.30 p.m. for delivery by the first post the following morning, except on days (Sundays and public holidays) when there is no postal delivery. Overnight telegrams cost 50p per telegram plus 4p for each word. The word 'Overnight' must be written before the address.

Reply-paid telegrams. A sender may prepay the reply to his telegram when he sends it. A reply form, showing the amount prepaid, is delivered with the telegram to the addressee.

INTERNATIONAL TELEGRAMS may be sent to most parts of the world, to ships in port, to aircraft at airports and to trains at railway stations abroad. They are sent either by wireless or cable. When the route is not specified by the sender, the Post Office selects the route. International telegrams may be written on an International Telegram Form and handed in at a post office or Post Office international telegraph office or dictated by telephone or sent by telex.

Ordinary international telegrams are charged by the word in accordance with the rules for counting words (see pages 423–4). There is a fixed charge of 70p

* The charges mentioned here and on the following pages are the current rates in Great Britain. Students studying overseas are recommended to refer to their own Post Office guides (or the national or local departments responsible for Posts and Telegraphs) for current local rates.

per telegram. Details of the charges for telegrams to all countries in the world are given in the Post Office Guide.

Urgent telegrams are transmitted more quickly; the rates are double the ordinary rates. The notation URGENT (which is charged as one word) must precede the address.

The *Letter Telegram service* enables international telegrams to be sent at half the rate for ordinary telegrams, with a minimum charge for 22 words including the notation ELT or LT plus a fixed charge of 70p per telegram. *Letter Telegrams* (LT) may be sent to most places outside Europe. LT telegrams take longer than ordinary telegrams but are normally delivered the day following the day of handing in.

GLT (Commonwealth Social Telegrams) may be used to send greetings and family and personal news to most places in the British Commonwealth and to territories under British Trusteeship. GLT telegrams are charged at half the ordinary rate per word plus a fixed charge of 70p per telegram.

The principal supplementary facilities available for international telegrams are indicated by the following notations, which should always precede the address:

= RP = Reply paid, followed by the amount to be prepaid, e.g. = RP 75p = means that a reply costing up to 75p has been prepaid.
= TM = indicates a multiple address telegram, that is, a telegram addressed to several addresses in the same town or the same addressee at different addresses in the same town. The notation should include the number of addresses, e.g. = TM5 =.
= LX = indicates delivery on an ornamental form at a supplementary charge of 40p.
= Jour = indicates that if a telegram reaches its destination during the night it should not be delivered until day-time.
= Nuit = indicates to the office of delivery that if the telegram arrives during the night it should be delivered at once; this service is not available on Letter Telegrams or Commonwealth Social Telegrams.
= Remettre ... (date) = asks for delivery on a specified date.
= TF = asks for the telegram to be delivered by telephone and should follow the name of the addressee and precede the name of the exchange (if any) and the telephone number.
= TLX = requests that the telegram should be delivered by telex; the telex number should follow the notation, then the name and address of the addressee.
= TR = indicates a telegram to be called for at a telegraph office.
= GP = indicates a telegram to be called for at a Poste Restante.
= GPR = indicates a telegram to be called for at a Poste Restante, registered. The supplementary charge for this is 3p.
= FS = may be used when it is not certain that the addressee will be found at the address given. The notation FS asks for the telegram to follow the address, that is to be sent on; it is not necessary for the

sender to indicate the address to which the telegram could be forwarded.

The *preamble* of an international telegram is the series of letters and figures which precede the address of the recipient on the delivery form. The order of the preamble is fixed by international agreement and contains the following information: the reference number, the office of origin, the number of words, the date of handing in, and the time of handing in. In the example shown below these are two reference numbers. The United Kingdom reference number is CLG/30JGD395 and that for the place of origin is CLN108 WG49. The telegram was sent from Wynberg, Cape Town, contains 14 words and was handed in at 11.15 on the 18th day of the month.

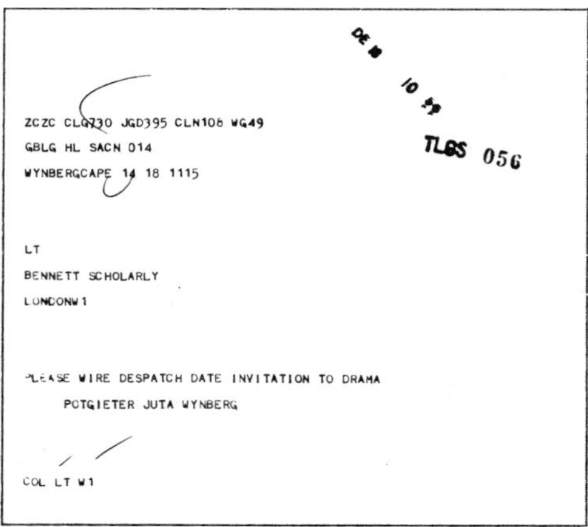

ZCZC CLG730 JGD395 CLN108 WG49
GBLG HL SACN 014
WYNBERGCAPE 14 18 1115

TLGS 056

LT
BENNETT SCHOLARLY
LONDONW1

PLEASE WIRE DESPATCH DATE INVITATION TO DRAMA
POTGIETER JUTA WYNBERG

COL LT W1

A telegram received from abroad.

Regulations for counting words in telegrams are laid down by the Post Office, as follows:

1 Words in the address, other than the name of the office of destination, are counted at the rate of 15 letters to a word.
2 Personal names and other names and titles may be combined to form single expressions, for example, *Delarue*.
3 House numbers are counted at the rate of five characters to the word but an oblique stroke or fraction bar is not charged for.
4 Post box numbers, for example, Postbox 876, are counted as two words; but if the address is written Postoffice Box 876 or PO Box 876 the charge is for three words.
5 A telephone number and the name of the exchange, together with the notation =TF= is counted as one word.
6 The name of the office of destination is charged as one word even if the name contains two or three words, but they must be written as one, e.g. MILFORDONSEA; if it is necessary to add the name of a country or

district for purposes of distinction, the additional name is not charged for, nor are district indicators added to the names of large towns.

7 Groups of initials in common use such as HMS may be written without full-stops and are counted as five letters to the word.

8 Groups of initial letters representing organisations such as UNESCO may be combined as a group and are counted as 15 letters to the word.

9 An underlining, a pair of brackets or a pair of inverted commas count as one word.

10 Figures are counted at the rate of five figures to a word.

11 Punctuation marks are counted as one word.

12 Compound words joined by a hyphen may be charged and sent as a single word, that is, without the hyphens. However, if they do not appear in a standard dictionary, they are treated as separate words.

We mentioned that one of the most important uses of telegrams was to contact travellers. It is, therefore, useful to note how telegrams to travellers should be addressed:

A telegram for delivery to *a railway passenger* should be addressed c/o Stationmaster. If the telegram is for a passenger on a train calling at a station en route, full particulars of the train by which the passenger is travelling should be given, e.g. ANN PATTISON, 10.20 a.m. SOLIHULL–EUSTON C/O STATIONMASTER WATFORD.

Telegrams for the *passengers or crew of an aircraft* are not delivered by the Post Office but handed to the airline company concerned which is responsible for delivery. The address should include:

1 The name of the addressee followed by the word PASSENGER or CREW.

2 The name of the airline.

3 The flight or trip number and date if known.

4 The name of the airport (the suffix HEATHROW or GATWICK should be added to *London Airport*).

Examples:

AHMED KHALIL
PASSENGER BA
BA561
LONDON AIRPORT
HEATHROW

JOYCE REDMAN
CREW SWISSAIR
SR832
LONDON AIRPORT
HEATHROW

Telegrams can also be addressed to passengers or crew on board ships in port, to personnel serving in HM ships and HM forces, to passengers in aircraft in airports abroad, and to passengers in trains in railway stations abroad. Full details of how these telegrams should be addressed are given in the *Post Office Guide*.

PHOTOTELEGRAPH SERVICES Pictures, photographs, drawings, typed or written documents and plans may be telegraphed in facsimile from London to many places in the world. The charges are calculated on the size of the item to be transmitted, which must be printed on one side only of the paper. Phototelegrams are accepted at the more important post offices throughout the country and at International telegraph offices. They are forwarded by post to London for onward telegraphic transmission. Alternatively the sender may post his phototelegram direct to London with the necessary remittance. They are delivered from the office of receipt by post.

RADIOTELEGRAMS may be sent to ships at sea. They may be written on an International Telegram form and handed in at a post office, dictated from a telephone or sent by telex. Radiotelegrams may also be sent from ships for delivery to addresses ashore.

CONFIRMING TELEGRAMS As soon as a telegram has been sent it is usually followed by a letter of confirmation. Such a letter usually starts with a paragraph such as

> We confirm having sent you today the
> following telegram:

The full text of the telegram is then quoted, usually in block capitals, and further details of the situation that required the sending of the telegram are given. An example of a telegram and a letter of confirmation are shown below.

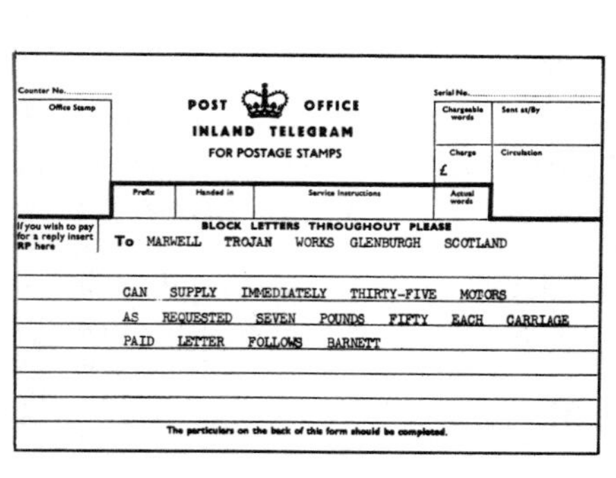

Counter No. .... Serial No. ....

Office Stamp

POST OFFICE
INLAND TELEGRAM
FOR POSTAGE STAMPS

Chargeable words | Sent at/By
Charge £ | Circulation

Prefix | Handed in | Service Instructions | Actual words

If you wish to pay for a reply insert RP here

BLOCK LETTERS THROUGHOUT PLEASE

To MARWELL TROJAN WORKS GLENBURGH SCOTLAND

CAN SUPPLY IMMEDIATELY THIRTY-FIVE MOTORS
AS REQUESTED SEVEN POUNDS FIFTY EACH CARRIAGE
PAID LETTER FOLLOWS BARNETT

The particulars on the back of this form should be completed.

3 August 1973

G R Marwell Esq
Trojan Works
Glenburgh
SCOTLAND

Dear Sir

We confirm sending you the following telegram in reply to your advertisement for ½ HP electric motors in today's "Daily Recorder":

CAN SUPPLY IMMEDIATELY THIRTY-FIVE MOTORS AS REQUESTED SEVEN POUNDS FIFTY EACH CARRIAGE PAID LETTER FOLLOWS BARNETT

These motors are 240/250 V AC, 50-cycle and run at 1425 RPM. They comply with your specification in every respect and are in very good second-hand condition. They were originally fitted to some hydraulic pumps but have had little use as the pumps were unable to do the job for which they had been installed and were withdrawn from service.

We feel that the price at which we are offering these motors, £7.50 each, straw-packed and crated, carriage paid, represents excellent value. Upon receipt of your order we can despatch the motors immediately by road transport.

Yours faithfully
for GENERAL EQUIPMENT DISTRIBUTORS

K C Barnett
Executive Director

Example of a telegram and a letter of confirmation.

Teleprinters A teleprinter resembles a typewriter in appearance and can easily be operated by a typist after a little practice. When the typist types a message on the teleprinter, an identical message is typed on a distant teleprinter with which her machine is connected. Teleprinters enable two separate premises of one business firm to exchange information and messages instantaneously. It is not necessary for the typist to sit at the teleprinter machine all day, as messages received are printed automatically. As soon as a message is received, however, it should be taken from the machine and sent to the appropriate department. If the operator at the transmitting office wishes to attract the attention of the operator at the receiving office, she can press the figures key and a key marked 'BELL' which will ring a bell on the receiving machine. Teleprinters operate by means of private circuits rented from the Post Office.

Telex The telex service is an extension of the teleprinter system. Whereas the teleprinter connection is a private circuit, the telex service uses a network of public circuits both nationally and internationally. A teleprinter can exchange messages with only those machines (usually one, but there can be more than one) to which it is permanently connected. The telex service provides a public teleprinter system and subscribers connected to the system can communicate direct with any other telex subscriber in the United Kingdom and in many overseas countries.

Providing the telex machine is switched on, it will receive messages even though it is unattended; the service therefore is continuous and operates day and night. Each subscriber has a telex number, which is shown on his printed letterhead, and is provided with a telex directory giving the numbers of all the other United Kingdom telex subscribers.

As you can see from the illustrations on page 427, a dial similar to a telephone dial is attached to the telex machine. The operator dials the number and as she types the message it is automatically typed immediately on the receiving machine. If you study the keyboard shown in the illustrations, you will see that it is very similar to a typewriter keyboard. The rental for the teleprinter and the line to the telex exchange is charged quarterly. Inland and dialled international calls are charged in units. The charges in force can be found in the *Post Office Guide*.

Using punched tape to send messages. A machine which translates information into a series of holes punched in tape can be attached to a telex teleprinter. The typist can prepare intricate messages or tabulations on punched tape by typing the matter before a call is made. The machine will then transmit the information to the selected subscriber.

Telegrams by telex. Telex subscribers can send inland or overseas telegrams directly to the Post Office, including Post Office overseas telegraph offices, for transmission. Incoming telegrams can be received on the teleprinter from the telegraph office.

The telex operator dials the distant subscriber with the dial connected to her machine and types her message.

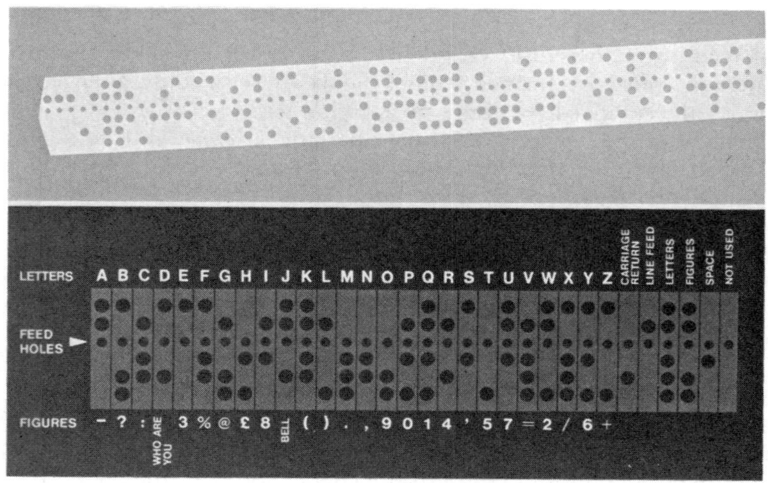

(Top) A piece of perforated tape. (Bottom) The teleprinter alphabetic code.

Datel Services In Chapter 7, Storage and Retrieval of Information, we mentioned that data is electronically transmitted by the Datel services of the Post Office Telecommunications. Datel services use certain public telephone and telegraph lines and circuits (usually referred to as 'networks') to transmit data between computer centres and terminal units. Electronic transmission is quicker than all other means of communication; the fastest Datel service, Datel 48K, can transmit data at the rate of 48,000 bits per second. In order to have some idea of what this means, we must try to define 'a bit' and give an elementary explanation of how information can be converted into electronic pulses or signals which can be transmitted by telephone or telegraph lines.

Computers process information by means of a *binary digital process.* (*Binary* means involving a choice between two items, figures or units; *digital* means relating to numbers or digits.) The binary digital process uses an electronic element which has two states—on or off, positive or negative—and the computer is able to distinguish between these two states. In other words, it can make a decision when presented with a 'yes/no', 'this or that' type of question. Each decision the computer makes is known as a *bit* (from *bi*nary digi*t*), which can be defined as a unit of information. The expression *bits per second* (bit/s) refers to the number of bits that can be transmitted in one second.

The information which is sent to the computer will be of various kinds: letters of the alphabet, decimal digits 0–9, punctuation marks, mathematical symbols, other symbols such as currency signs and special 'function' or instruction symbols like 'carriage return' and so on. Each of these symbols or signs may be made up of any number of bits. That is to say, the computer will have to make a certain number of decisions (bits) before it can understand any single item of information such as a letter of the alphabet, a number or a symbol.

Characters are, therefore, encoded in a series of bits (0 or 1) and in data transmission codes are formed from five, six or seven bits. There are several internationally standardised codes in common use.

In the illustration on page 284, the operator is *keying-in* or typing information on a teletype machine for transmission to a central computer. Before the information (the *input*) can be transmitted, it must be *encoded*, that is, changed into electronic signals which can be transmitted over the telecommunications network. Similarly, computer output must be decoded. The machine which performs the technical processes of encoding and decoding is called a *modem*, a word made up from the two words *modulator* and *demodulator*. Modems for use on the public telephone network are provided by the Post Office; on private telephone circuits either Post Office modems or permitted private modems may be used. The modem is shown on page 294 and the illustration below shows modems mounted in racks. Before the operator can key-in data she must follow a prescribed routine, known as "the logging-in procedure" to establish the identity of the user and establish the connection with the computer centre. Part of the logging-in procedure is when the user switches on his modem to convert his telephone line from a speech carrying medium into a data link.

Datel services are rented from the Post Office. For example, the Datel 200 service transmits data at 200 bits per second; the modems for this service are rented at £100 per annum and the terminal equipment is obtained from the manufacturers.

Datel services are used by many businesses whose operations depend upon rapid communication. One large manufacturer of a well-known range of foodstuffs such as tinned cream, soup and instant coffee, has 600 salesmen working around the country in nine sales regions. As the firm manufactures

Modems mounted in racks in the computer terminal installation of a national bank.

nearly 900 products there are always a lot of orders being processed and the company has to keep track of every transaction. So they have a central computer linked to each of their sales offices. The rapid transmission of information between the offices and the computer enables orders and invoices to be sent out very quickly and the Head Office always knows the up-to-date stock position and the sales records of all its products and salesmen.

As data can be transmitted over ordinary telephone lines, the Datel service is nationwide. Large cities are connected to computer centres throughout the United Kingdom and international services are co-ordinated by the International Telecommunications Union, a specialised agency of the United Nations Organisation. There are Datel services to the United States of America and 17 European countries, and by using satellite circuits intercontinental services include Australia, Canada and Hong Kong.

Plans are being made for a digital data network which would not require the use of modems in the transmission of data. The diagram below shows the possible location of the specialised exchanges required for this work.

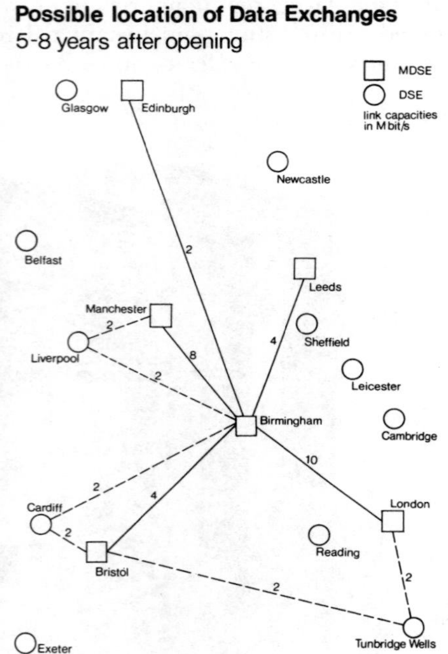

The diagram shows possible future locations of Data Exchanges. The numbers against the transmission links show the probable capacity in Megabit/s (million bits per second) of the routes between exchanges.

FURTHER READING

Business in English, Sydney Stevens, Chatto & Windus.
The Complete Plain Words, Sir Ernest Gowers, Penguin Books.
Our Language, Simeon Potter, Penguin Books.
Words Words Words, Andrew Scotland, Cassell.
English in the Office, Swift and Stanwell, Edward Arnold (Publishers) Ltd.
Written Communication for Business Students, C. J. Parsons and S. J. Hughes, Edward Arnold (Publishers) Ltd.
Report Writing, A. E. Darbyshire, Edward Arnold (Publishers) Ltd.
Better Business Letters, Reid & Silleck, Addison-Wesley Publishing Co.

Personal Letters for Businessmen, Mary Bosticco, Business Publications.
Good English: How to Write It, G. H. Vallins, Andre Deutsch.
Better English, G. H. Vallins, Andre Deutsch.
Best English, G. H. Vallins, Andre Deutsch.
Modern English Usage, H. W. Fowler, Oxford University Press.
An ABC of English Usage, H. A. Treble and G. H. Vallins, Oxford University Press.
A Dictionary of American–English Usage, Margaret Nicholson, Oxford University Press.
How to Write Successful Sales Letters, J. W. W. Cassels, Business Publications.
English and American Business Letters, Eckersley and Kaufman, Longmans.
Instant Business Letters, Mary Bosticco, Business Publications.

GROUP DISCUSSION

You are secretary to a shipping agent, Mr. T. B. Johnson of 168 Newton Road, ACITY, tel. 61234. There is a branch office at 21 Princes Road, BETOWN. It is the 26th of the month. Mr Johnson is away from the office because of sickness. He has told you to handle everything in his absence.

You receive information from the INTERCOUNTRY Shipping Line that a consignment of goods ordered by a firm in SEETOWN is due to arrive at FREEPORT on the 1st of next month. The consignment, motor vehicle spares, has been consigned by the Tiaf Motor Company, Rue de la Liberté, Marseilles, to Messrs Jones & Bannerman, 41 Short Street, SEETOWN. The goods are required by the consignee not later than the 5th of the month. This means that loading for inland transportation must be completed by the 3rd. All labour is recruited through the Labour Exchange at the port. The supplier wishes to be informed when the goods are received by the consignee, and payment is to be made immediately.

Divide into groups and discuss what communications are involved and how they would be made. Not all the communications will be made by you.

EXERCISES

1 You are working in a travel agency and part of your work is to check the booking forms for holiday reservations received from clients. The forms are frequently not fully completed, sometimes they are unsigned, sometimes no deposit is enclosed, sometimes the cheque is incorrectly written. Design a form letter to suit these circumstances, the use of which would avoid your having to write so many letters on the same lines.

2 The junior who assists you in your work receives and makes too many personal telephone calls; even when she is giving a business message on the telephone she takes the opportunity to "have a chat" as well. You decide you must talk to her about her telephone manner and using the office telephone for personal calls. What would you say?

3 Your company has decided to institute a suggestion scheme. The procedure to be followed has been agreed and must now be communicated to the employees, about 100 people who work in an office block of three floors and an adjacent factory. Compose a notice or letter informing employees of the procedure to be followed and suggest the best way to communicate the information to all concerned.

4 "*The Globe* costs only 3p—the same price as an ordinary newspaper." Comment on the use of language in this advertisement and suggest improved "copy" for advertising a newspaper.

5 Write out notices, suitable for display on a notice board, for the following:

a The introduction of flexible working hours in your office.
b Announcing the visit of a distinguished guest to your organisation.
c Announcing the proposal to form a Bridge Section of the Sports Club, and asking all who are interested to attend an inaugural meeting.

6 Write telegrams for the following situations. Supply additional details where necessary, and write letters of confirmation where necessary.

a To Mr Hafez Ibrahim arriving at London Aïrport, Heathrow, on a Middle East Airlines flight ME891 from Beirut, to say that accommodation has been reserved for him at the London Hilton and that a Company car will drive him to the hotel from the airport. The driver will be waiting to meet him when he has passed through the Customs Hall.
b To your boss who is flying to Rome on Alitalia flight AZ974, asking him to ring the office as soon as he can as there have been important developments which he should be aware of before he starts negotiations the following day.
c You are secretary to the Principal of a private college. He tells you to type a cable to Marcel Lanvin, Les Berges, Annemasse 74420, France, offering him an appointment as French language teacher, one-year contract with possibility of extension, £1600 per annum, approx. 25 hours teaching a week, fare paid, medical scheme for staff. The cable should be confirmed by letter.

7 Your boss is responsible for producing a weekly Staff Bulletin which is distributed to all members of the staff. He thinks that this is a routine job which you should be able to take over and suggests that you produce

your own draft of the following week's bulletin. During the course of the week you have noted the following items:

a The Managing Director is leaving for a three-week tour of West Africa in ten days' time.
b The firm's football team has reached the semi-final of the district league.
c A clerk in the Accounts Department has announced his engagement.
d The Offices will be closed for the usual four days at Easter, that is from Good Friday to Easter Monday inclusive.

Supply another six items of news and suitable names and other details and draft the bulletin. The last item in the previous bulletin was numbered 147.

8 Your employer asks you to attend a lecture on his behalf. The topic of the conference is "Great Britain and the European Economic Community"; the lecture in which your employer is interested is on the subject of courtesy and acceptable behaviour. Your employer believes there is more to doing business abroad than learning languages. The following is the text of the lecture. Produce a summary of reasonable length, say, three or four pages of A4, double-spaced. (You may find it convenient to write in note form making good use of side headings.)

Excuse me, monsieur le directeur, but your prejudices are showing

Once upon a 1971 there was an energetic and enterprising British business executive Somewhere in Central Europe who lost an important contract for sale of electronic equipment when, during a pause between negotiations, he didactically lectured a roomful of local officials on the Thirty Years War. His only problem was, he believed that to be another name for the Spanish Civil War and, emboldened by his host's hospitality, stoutly defended this view and shouted down opposition.

When Mr Christopher Soames suggested at the Institute's annual conference in November that joining the European Economic Community increased the need to learn their languages, he was only touching the tip of a very considerable iceberg—the overwhelming necessity to get along on amicable terms with anybody one hopes to do serious business with. And this, among other factors, includes an element of natural reticence —particularly when venturing on uncertain ground.

To suggest that the British businessman abroad, or for that matter the diplomat, is distinguished for his courtesy, smooth manners or consideration for the sensitivity of foreigners is to raise a hollow laugh. On average he may not shape up badly by comparison with some nationalities, but as often as not he will leave behind him a roomful of distinguished foreigners perplexed and dumbfounded by his beautifully-poised arrogance.

It was Rebecca West who once wrote: "while everybody knows that Englishmen are sent to Public Schools because that is the only place where they can learn good manners, it unfortunately happens that the manners they learn there are recognised as good only by people who have been to the same sort of school, and often appear as very bad indeed to everybody else".*—particularly, one might add, to the non-English.

Generalisations are, of course, invidious and this is not to say there is any monopoly of good manners by the Americans, French, Germans, Scandinavians, Kikuyu or what you will. One can only record that it can frequently be acutely embarrassing to witness the negative impression left behind by one's compatriots, as they retire smugly cocooned in their self-assurance.

If anybody ran an opinion poll in Continental Europe today on slogans that come to mind upon mention of the word "British", the poll would probably be topped by something like "technical sophistication, quality and resourcefulness". Next on the list would most likely be "personal arrogance". For (Dame Rebecca again), the casual offhand, hands-in-trouser-pockets approach acceptable in Belgravia or Bembridge looks, from Calais onwards, like rank bad manners.

Equally, the extreme clannishness of the British rep. abroad who consorts only with his own tribe and, for example, is to be found at the Industrial Fair skulking in a cubby-hole behind his stand cuddling the inevitable bottle of Scotch or sucking on his gin and tonic. This reputation is in sharp paradox to the other distinction for niggling inhospitality. Now, I would be the last person to advocate turning offices or conference rooms into smoke-filled café houses, but there is, to the "outside" observer, a yawning chasm between the normal minimal civilities (a coffee, mineral water, soft drink), automatically extended to visitors by most Continental officials and executives, and the bleak reception meted out in a British office. There are, naturally, degrees of hospitality and generally speaking, the further east one goes from the Rhine, the more insidious it becomes. (In Middle East bureaucracy, one is tempted to guess that national budgets could conceivably be balanced if the endless cups of coffee were abolished.) There are excesses, of course, such as the very senior Jugoslav government official who opened a 7.30 a.m. conference by offering Jumbo glasses of *slivovitza* and, when the interpreter and myself prudently declined, gaily knocked off the three—just to steady his hand. However, to the foreign trade official or representative, it is painfully noticeable how long he can be left languishing in a waiting-room or thirsting at a conference without the simplest cup of tea or coffee. "If you happen to catch your man", one Italian executive joked to me, "as his secretary brings in his 10.30 or 4 p.m. tea and

*The Meaning of Treason.

digestive biscuit he may grudgingly mumble—'You wouldn't care for one too, would you?' Otherwise you're out of luck."

Casualness in business and social relations is a feature of British good-breeding little valued in Paris, Brussels or Düsseldorf. Failure to introduce people articulately and carefully on first meeting, or at a reception, may have been acceptable convention in 18th century drawing-rooms when one could safely assume everyone was "one of us" or would not have been invited; it does not go down well in a company of mixed nationalities and languages. How often has one floundered for hours at cocktail or dinner parties until forced to resort to the commendable American technique of introducing oneself . . . "and would you mind telling me your name?" General hand-shaking is, needless to say, customary everywhere outside Britain and to avoid it, however strongly one may disapprove, is churlish.

Granted, any itinerant businessman can quote you instances enough of appalling shortfall in manners among other nationalities: the point is that it comes as a particular shock from the British who historically are, or were, reputed to be ultra-courteous. Another characteristic that sends the European executive up the wall is what we might call Big Business Inefficiency.

Enough has been written about failure to meet delivery dates and specifications for which there may often be valid explanations: but what your European counterpart cannot grasp is gross inefficiency or slackness in details, such as prompt handling of correspondence. True, letters do occasionally go astray in the post, but it is noteworthy how frequently British firms have recourse to this palpable excuse for unreplied letters. One European executive of my acquaintance, nonplussed by his inability to inspire any reaction to his correspondence with London on an important business deal, and bending over backwards to be Anglophile, once pleaded with me: "But I just don't understand—after all, he is a *Sir*." Sloppily produced letters, pockmarked with errors and obviously dictated on the run to a lengthy luncheon and signed (uncorrected) "For Mr Smith in his absence", do nothing to inspire mutual confidence. Nor do repeated "pacifiers" from secretaries, explaining that "Mr Smith is at present abroad" (that magic word) "and will give the matter his attention upon his return"—which he frequently does not. One Central European business director showed me a file of correspondence from London on a highly technical issue that embraced letters signed by at least half a dozen ladies all bearing elegant names and impressive titles; a file that proved nothing except that the ladies in question knew nothing of the technicalities involved and had manifestly not read any of the preceding correspondence on the subject. Such a bizarre pantomime is not calculated to put up export figures.

Not at home . . . Again, it is astonishing to one with considerable experience of working in Europe how much time a busy Continental executive or official is prepared to devote to assisting the visiting Englishman and smoothing the way for him; somehow he almost always seems to make room, even in the busiest schedule, and is often a little dumbfounded later, as a stranger in London or Manchester, to discover everyone to whom he has been given fulsome introductions is far too busy (doing *what* he never discovers), to afford him reciprocal treatment.

Mr Soames is absolutely right. The basic essential is surely some workable understanding of the more common languages. Few Hungarians, for instance, expect anybody (apart from a few million "overseas" Hungarians) to correspond or conduct negotiations in their own language. But there is no reason why one should not do them the courtesy of conducting business in their second fluent tongue, German. There is little excuse for that frequent spectacle—a tableful of mixed nationals—all perfectly articulate probably in the major European languages, being obliged to hobble along in English, due to the presence in their midst of one monolingual but condescending British diplomat or businessman.

Over the years I have discovered that perhaps 90%, or more, of difficulties between nationalities on a personal level stem from language barriers. On countless occasions one has been told the people of this or that city "are abominably rude and offensive", only to discover that the complainant is unable to grasp even the simple basics of their language and, human reactions being what they are, a person unable to understand another—whether in a rush-hour bus queue, restaurant or at a negotiating table—tends immediately to become offensively defensive. Courtesy and custom aside, there is also the purely practical consideration that anyone conducting business negotiations entirely in English with foreigners, is at a permanent disadvantage and will understand just as much of the cross-talk as they wish him to, and no more.

There are numerous other solecisms, some minor in themselves but collectively adding up to a bad image, to which the British abroad, even experienced diplomats, seem curiously prone: witness, for example, the subdued and controlled rage of foreign ladies as wisecracks are bandied to and fro across their heads, *sotto voce* in a clipped English *patois* they could not possibly, and are not intended to, understand.

And from linguistics we come back to the original theme—the essential of sound background knowledge when dealing with peoples to whom, for instance, history is not a curious alternative subject in a sketchy school syllabus but something they live with and breathe. One does need to know, to put it at its lowest, the difference between the Quai d'Orsay and the Elyseé, and not be obliged to demand in a loud whisper, as one British business visitor did in Vienna several years ago: "Who *are* these Habsburg people everyone keeps talking about?" That one stopped the conversation dead in its tracks.

A command of one's own brief also helps: I was once required, some years ago, to expedite a meeting with the then President of the West German Federal Bank, the late Professor Karl Blessing, for a very senior London executive who believed he knew about finance. Dr Blessing (who stayed behind in his office long after 8 p.m. for this express purpose) spoke fascinatingly and fluently in English for over an hour, then suddenly looked horrified at his visitor's glassy stare and demanded: "Mr X, you *do* follow what I am talking about, don't you?" The meeting was abruptly terminated shortly thereafter.

KENNETH AMES

9 Write brief notes on the following Telecommunication services:

Datel
Telex
Telegrams

10 Send multiple memoranda to the heads of the Business Studies, General Studies, Home Economics, and Modern Languages departments, telling them that the summer examinations will start on 5 June and last for three weeks. Draft question papers should be prepared ready for discussion at the next meeting of the Board of Studies on 24 April. The memoranda will be initialled by the Director of Studies. Supply suitable names, type and annotate the memoranda.

11 You are secretary to the Sales Manager of a large organisation. While he is away on holiday, you receive a letter from a customer complaining that the washing machine bought from you six months ago is still not working properly. He has been unable to obtain any satisfaction from his local dealer. What action would you take? Compose and type any letters you would send.

12 Write a report to the Office Manager of your Company on the duplicator in your office which is very old and needs frequent attention no matter how carefully it is operated. Assume that you have visited several office equipment showrooms in the town, and recommend the model which you suggest should be bought to replace the existing machine.

13 You are secretary to the Manager of the Mail Order Department of a large store. He hands you a letter from a customer complaining that two cups and a milk jug (part of a 21-piece tea set) were broken when she took them out of the crate in which the tea set had been packed and delivered, and says, "Write a letter to this lady, apologise for the breakages and say we are having replacements sent off immediately. Then send a memo to the Head of Packing and Despatch and ask him to tell his people to take more care when they're packing china and glass—this is the third complaint about breakages we've had this month." Write the letter and memorandum. Supply suitable names and addresses.

14 You are secretary to the Regional Marketing Director of a firm of cosmetic manufacturers; he is responsible for sales in the south-west region of the country, and has just returned from a 10-day tour of the area. You find the following message in your IN tray on the morning of his return:

Fenella –   8.45 a.m.

Arrived back from S.W. late last night. Am now on my way up to see Div. Manager. Whilst I'm with him, would you please:

1. Write to the hotel I stayed at in Bristol and ask them to post on my black shoes – think I left them in the room probably under the bed – better send a P.O. to cover cost of parcel.
2. Write to Bernard Edgar of Edgar's of Exeter and thank him for his hospitality. Tell him I was most impressed with his point of sale display for our new spring range. Say we'll send advance notice of new colour range of lipsticks for autumn promotion by end of July.
3. Send a memo to John in Special Promotions & tell him to go ahead with printing the Free Offer cards for the new perfume which Plummers of Plymouth are offering as part of their special Birthday Week promotion.
4. Write to the Organising Sec. of the Penzance Summer Fair & say we will donate a leather vanity case fitted with our products as one of the prizes in the annual Beauty Queen competition.

Expect me down around 10.0

DD

Compose and type the communications. Supply suitable names and addresses.

15 Type memoranda to J. B. Fawcett, Production Control, C. H. Lawyer, Test Bay, B. W. Everest, Chief Chemist, from A. G. Smith, Sales Liaison, saying that F. C. Harmer, Chief Engineer, of Howell Aviation Ltd will be visiting the factory on Monday week and so they should arrange to be available for consultation if required.

16 Type a notice for display on the company notice board informing all staff that summer working hours will start on 1 May and continue until 31 October. Summer hours are:

Core-time	9.00–3.00	
Flex-time	2 hours at either end,	
	that is, 7.0 a.m.	earliest start
	5.0 p.m.	latest finish

Staff are required to work an 8-hour day, including an hour for lunch.

11

Sources of Information and Research

No-one is expected to remember everything. People keep diaries to note forthcoming events and address books for the addresses and telephone numbers of their friends. These are reference books for our personal lives. If we are asked whether we are free on a certain evening the following week or if we are asked for a mutual friend's telephone number, we know where to look to find the information.

KNOWING WHERE TO LOOK

An efficient secretary should also know where to look to find accurate and complete information when any query arises in the course of business. Part of her secretarial skill is knowing what sources of information exist and how to use them.

Answers to certain questions can be found in the office address book or in the files. Questions such as "What is Mr Howard's phone number?" or "When did Jones and Company first write to us?" should cause no difficulty. Other questions can be answered only by looking in reference books or contacting an organisation in the relevant field.

HOW TO START

With a little practice anyone can become skilled in ferreting out information, but both the beginner and the skilled researcher have to ask themselves, "Where do I start?" Before opening a book or asking anyone a question, the practised researcher first thinks about what facts she is looking for. Sometimes the answer to the question is not the same as the facts to be obtained, for example:

Question: Does Italy have a larger population than Great Britain?
Facts: What is the population of Great Britain? What is the population of Italy? Which is the greater?

At other times there may be more than one possible approach to a question. One method of approach should be tried first and if it proves fruitless, then another method can be tried. Attacking a problem from all sides at once only leads to confusion and a waste of time and energy.

Question: What countries sell their oil to Britain?
Approaches: Find statistics of Britain's oil imports broken down into countries of origin *or* find a list of oil exporters and then look up the export information of each one.

Obviously the first approach is simpler. Once she has decided on this approach, the researcher must not be diverted until she has found the answer or been informed by a knowledgeable person that the second approach is the only possible one.

Once the facts have been considered and the approach has been chosen, the time allowed must be taken into account. If the boss asks, "How many banks are there in the City of London?" and he wants an answer the same day, a letter to the Banking Information Service would take too long. The answer must be discovered through a telephone call or research into reference books on banking.

WHERE TO START

The major problem of research is that there are so many sources of information. This means:

1 Finding out what sources exist for any particular subject.
2 Deciding which of the available sources to use.

Unfortunately, more time is often spent on the first task than on actually obtaining the information from the source. Unless a variety of sources springs to mind, it is unwise to spend much time trying to think of a list of people or books to try. If one book or organisation suggests itself, try that one. A reference book may give a list of books for further reading and one organisation that cannot help may suggest another organisation or a book that can.

The important thing is to make a start. If no sources on the subject can be thought of, a general reference work or an organisation related in any way is a beginning. The following section gives some hints on ways to start.

GENERAL SOURCES

1 All government departments, such as the Department of the Environment, and public enterprises, such as the National Coal Board, are willing to help the public with queries concerned with their own area of responsibility. If they are unable to help, they can usually suggest another organisation or an appropriate reference work.

Queries can be made by letter or by telephone. Departments are listed in the London telephone directories under their names, e.g. *Trade and Industry, Department of.* Addresses of government offices are also given in Whitaker's Almanack (see page 443). If you are telephoning a government department or public enterprise to obtain information, ask the switchboard operator to put you through to Enquiries.

2 Embassies or High Commissions, trade delegations and national tourist offices exist to represent their countries. Embassies have information on regulations of their governments, trade delegations can be approached on matters of trade and economics, while tourist offices have general information and can answer queries about travel.

Most of these offices are in London, although some governments may also have representatives in other cities. The offices are listed in the London telephone directories under the name of the country and addresses are also given in the London Diplomatic List (published by HM Stationery Office and available in the reference section of public libraries).

3 *The Daily Telegraph* maintains an information service at its library which answers queries by telephone or letter. They can supply many facts and suggest other sources of information. *The Daily Telegraph*, 135 Fleet Street, London EC4, 01.

The Financial Times Library is also willing to suggest sources for queries on finance, business and economics, both British and international. *Financial Times* Library, Bracken House, Cannon Street, London EC4.

4 Most large and medium-sized firms maintain a public relations department that can answer queries about that firm over the telephone or by letter.

Firms in one type of business often form trade associations which, amongst other work, handle queries from the public and may also publish a magazine.

The address of the trade association can be discovered from trade directories and yearbooks in the public libraries or from the trade journals which are sometimes kept at public libraries.

A trade journal is a specialist magazine or newspaper for a trade or profession, such as *Tailor and Cutter*, *The Bookseller*, *The British Medical Journal.* A list of trade journals and their addresses is given in Willings Press Guide which can be found in reference libraries.

Professional institutes, such as the *Institution of Electrical Engineers*, and the *Institute of Bankers* are concerned with the standards and work of the professions. They are also willing to help the public with queries in their field. A list of the addresses of professional bodies is given in Whitaker's Almanack (see below).

5 General reference works are full of useful information and refer the reader to helpful organisations and other books for further research. It is a good idea to have at least one of these general works in the office for easy reference, but they are all available in the reference section of the public library.

Encyclopaedia: Subjects in an encyclopaedia are listed in alphabetical order. A good encyclopaedia, such as Britannica or Chambers, can be relied upon to give accurate and essential information on most subjects.

Pears Cyclopaedia: As it is published annually, Pears gives up-to-date information on many subjects in one volume. Sections include world events, local and central government, law, international organisations, dictionary, foreign phrases and business dictionary, first aid, medical dictionary.

Whitaker's Almanack: Published annually, Whitaker's is full of useful information on Great Britain and all other countries. There are statistical tables as well as articles on trade unions, insurance, building societies and income tax. Lists of the Peerage, Members of Parliament, government offices and professional bodies are included with information on post, forms of address, world events, sports results and many other subjects.

The Statesman's Year-Book: This volume is published annually in four sections:

Part I: Statistical tables on commodities, such as sugar, and information about international organisations, such as NATO.
Part II: Information on countries of the Commonwealth.
Part III: The states and territories of the United States.
Part IV: All other countries.

The information includes names of books for further reference.

6 The reference section of the public library is described fully in a section below but it should be mentioned here that the reference librarian is always willing to give advice about sources of information that can be consulted.

SOURCES OF INFORMATION WITHIN EACH FIRM

The efficient secretary knows how to use the resources in a firm to answer queries. She has her own records and knows about the records of other departments and the specialist knowledge of certain members of staff, such as the staff of the Salaries and Wages Department who will have a detailed knowledge of PAYE and income tax.

A secretary's own records To be efficient and save her own time a good secretary keeps records of useful information, such as names and addresses of customers and suppliers, telephone numbers of restaurants for her chief's business lunches and of the electrician, the typewriter repair man and other necessary services. As information changes, the secretary keeps her records up to date so that she can produce the required name or telephone number quickly without searching through all her files.

Files An employer often requires the information from previous correspondence to handle a current letter. Neat files in the correct order make retrieval of information an easier and more pleasant task. The files of other departments in the firm often hold useful information; a member of staff in another department may be asked for the information or permission to look through the files and records should be sought from the departmental head or his deputy.

Specialists In large firms specialists, such as accountants and lawyers, are often employed by the company. These specialists can be asked politely if a query in their field arises. If they have not the time to give a complete answer, they can suggest books of reference.

Reference books Every secretary needs a set of basic reference books to answer queries which arise in the day-to-day running of the office.

Dictionary: a good dictionary, such as the Concise Oxford Dictionary, in addition to telling you how to spell words, also gives information on:

a the plural of the word, if it is an exception to the general rule,
b the pronunciation of the word,
c the part of speech,
d the derivation,
e the prepositions which must follow certain words,
f the meaning,
g if the word is slang, vulgar or old-fashioned.

Vocabulary and Usage: A book on English usage gives guidance questions such as, "Which is to be preferred **spelt** or **spelled**?" and "Is it **neither of the men was** or **neither of the men were**?" The standard work of reference on English usage is *Modern English Usage* by H. W. Fowler. An *ABC of English Usage* is a very similar book to *Modern English Usage*. The decisions on usage are mostly taken from Fowler, but the language is simpler and the reasoning easier to understand. From the point of view of the office worker who wants a quick decision on correct usage, the book by Treble and Vallins is more practical; Fowler, however, is more interesting as he gives reasoned explanations in addition to decisions. *Usage and Abusage* is one of many books written by Eric Partridge. The ground covered is similar to Fowler's MEU. *Roget's Thesaurus of English Words and Phrases* arranges words in groups according to their meanings. Each page is printed in two columns; one column lists synonyms, the other lists antonyms. The *Oxford Dictionary of Quotations* contains all well-known and many not-so-well-known quotations.

Postal regulations and telephone services: The *Post Office Guide* published by HM Stationery Office gives detailed information on postal, telephone, telegram, telex and other services of the Post Office.

The Post Office supplies each subscriber with a telephone directory for his own area. Directories for other areas and foreign directories are available from the Post Office. Classified Directories (Yellow Pages) list local firms under types of business.

General: Whitaker's Almanack, *Pears Cyclopaedia* and *The Statesman's Year-Book* are described in detail on page 443.

Shorthand, typewriting and secretarial: Pitman's *English and Shorthand Dictionary* is, as its title suggests, a combined shorthand and English dictionary that gives the meanings of words and their shorthand outlines. In one respect it is more useful than an ordinary dictionary: as each word has a different shorthand outline, the derivatives as well as the root words are listed in alphabetical order. For example, if you want to know whether the word 'ferreted' has one or two t's, an ordinary dictionary gives no assistance. In a shorthand dictionary, however, 'ferreted' is listed after 'ferret' because the shorthand outline is different.

The standard work of reference on typewriting is *The Dictionary of Typewriting* by Edith McKay. Information on all aspects of typewriting and typewriters is arranged alphabetically for easy reference.

Figure work: A secretary who has to do any figure work should have a *Ready Reckoner* in her desk for quick calculations.

Gazetteer: The *Oxford Atlas* has two sections: the atlas with detailed maps of the world and the gazetteer which lists place names in alphabetical order. The correct spelling of place names, as well as their county, state or province can be found quickly by referring to the gazetteer.

Forms of address: Both the *Dictionary of Typewriting* and *Whitaker's Almanack* contain information on the correct forms of address. *Titles and Forms of Address* published by Adam and Charles Black and *Debrett's Correct Form* gives complete details on the forms of writing and speaking to people with titles or in official positions.

Specialised reference books: Each industry, profession or type of business has its own reference works, some of which appear in the specialised lists on pp. 449 to 450.

Abbreviations: British Initials and Abbreviations, Ian H. Wilkes (Leonard Hill). *World Guide to Abbreviations of Organisations*, F. A. Buttress (Leonard Hill). *A Dictionary of Acronyms and Abbreviations*, Eric Pugh (Clive Bingley).

Sources of further information: Facts at your Fingertips, K. C. Harrison (Kenneth Mason), and *How to Find Out*, G. Chandler (Pergamon Press).

The Company library Many firms have a library of books about their own type of business or even a small reference library. In some cases the library is just a corner of a room where the books are kept, while in others full-time librarians are employed. The librarians are trained to find information quickly and can give advice on sources within the firm's library and outside.

SOURCES OF INFORMATION OUTSIDE THE FIRM

The Reference Library The reference section of the public library contains only non-fiction books, that is books that deal with facts and not invented stories. These books cannot be borrowed from the library but they can be used for reference at the desks in the library.

All the books in the reference library are listed on cards which are kept in file drawers. The cards are filed in two ways: in one set of drawers the cards are filed under subject headings and in the other set they are filed under the name of the author. Some books with a large number of contributors, such as *Whitaker's Almanack*, are filed in the author index under their title.

The author index is useful only if the author is known. Books by one author are grouped together, each on a separate card. However, in the case of most queries, only the subject is known. Subjects are filed in alphabetical order, with books on each subject grouped together. If the subject of the query is not one of the headings in the subject index, it may be under a more general heading.

The librarians are very helpful in locating books on any subject. They should be informed of the steps already taken to prevent duplication of effort.

Dewey Decimal Classification: Finding the name of a book in one of the card files is only the first step. It then has to be located among the thousands of books in the library. This would be almost impossible if the books were on the shelves in no order, but libraries have a system called the Dewey Decimal Classification, which is a method of arranging and classifying non-fiction books according to their subjects. All the books on one subject are together and related subjects are nearby. In this way if someone goes to the section on Insurance, for example, and finds the particular book he wants is being used by

650 LOC

Locke, P J Ed.

European Business Correspondence and Practice

Batsford 1967

Contains glossaries of business terms in French,
Italian, Spanish and German.

Example of an author card.

COMMERCIAL PRACTICE

650 LOC European Business Correspondence
and Practice

Locke, P J Ed.
Batsford, 1967

Contains glossaries of business terms in
French, Italian, Spanish and German.

Example of a subject card.

someone else, he can see what other books are available. Since Dewey Decimal Classification is used in most libraries, a person can find her way around any library once she has learnt the system.

Each book has its own number which is printed in the corner of the file card and on the spine of the book. If the card has 622.122, the book is in the 600 section. Within the 600 section all the books are in numerical order. The system is called a decimal system because it is based on the number 10. There are ten major divisions from 000 to 900.

000 Generalities of Knowledge
100 Philosophy, Metaphysics, Psychology
200 Religion, Theology
300 Social Sciences
400 Philology
500 Mathematics and Natural Sciences
600 Applied Sciences, Medicine, Technology
700 The Arts, Recreation, Entertainment, Sport
800 Literature, Belles-Lettres
900 Geography, Biography, History

Each of these divisions is divided again into ten divisions: 600–610, 611–620 and so on. The tens are then divided into units, and divided again into decimal places. In this way the large divisions are for general subjects headings and each smaller division is more specific:

600 Applied Sciences, Medicine, Technology
611–619 Medical Sciences, Health and Disease
612 Physiology, human and comparative
 612.1 Blood and circulation
  612.11 Properties and groups

It is not necessary to memorise all the heading of the system. As a person uses the system, she will become familiar with the sections and therefore soon be 'at home' in the library.

When the library does not have a particular book If the library does not have a particular title, the librarian can arrange to borrow the book from another public library. This takes time and is therefore not suitable for most queries in the office, but it is useful to know that there is a system whereby almost any book is available.

The librarian applies to borrow the book through the Regional Library which has a list of all the non-fiction books in the co-operating libraries in the region. If the book is not in one of these libraries, the request can be sent to the National Central Library which can arrange for the book to be borrowed from a library in one of the other regions or from a specialist library or from its own collection.

HOW TO USE A REFERENCE BOOK

Since most reference books are rarely read straight through from cover to cover, there are methods of extracting quickly just one piece of information from a large book. Here are some suggestions for approaching works of reference:

1 See how the book is arranged. If entries are made in alphabetical order, as in dictionaries and encyclopaedias, look up the subject under the first letter. A lot of time is wasted flipping through books.
2 Books that are not in alphabetical order have a Contents page which is usually immediately after the title page. However, in certain directories, there are pages of advertising before the Contents page and it can easily be missed. The Contents page lists the subjects in the book in the order in which they appear. Usually only the major divisions are listed.
3 All reference books have an index which lists the subjects mentioned in the book in alphabetical order with the page numbers on which they appear. Subjects in the index are usually much more detailed than the Contents page. The index is often at the end of the book, although it can be near the beginning. Some books have more than one index, each index covering one classification of subject.

4 If the information required must be recent, it is wise to check the date of the book. This is usually printed on the reverse side of the title page.
5 Make use of cross-reference. A cross-reference is a reference to another page or another subject heading. It is usually in the form "see also p. . . . ".
6 Keep an eye out for lists of books for further reference. Such a list of books is called a bibliography and may come at the end of a book or at the end of each chapter or section.

SPECIALISED SOURCES

Although the following list is grouped under subject headings, all books and organisations in each list cannot help with all problems. However, they can give helpful suggestions.

British business and finance

ORGANISATIONS

Financial Times Library, Bracken House, Cannon Street, London EC4

Local Chambers of Commerce

The London Chamber of Commerce and Industry has an excellent reference library and produces a wide range of bulletins, journals, surveys and reports, e.g. *COMMERCE International*, the monthly journal of the Chamber, *Digest*, a bulletin of commercial and economic information, published fortnightly in five regional editions, Africa and the Middle East, Asia and Pacific, Eastern Europe, Western Europe, and Western Hemisphere; and market reports and surveys on individual countries based upon the reports of trade missions to those countries

Confederation of British Industry, 21 Tothill Street, London SW1

Department of Trade and Industry (Administrative Headquarters including Information Division), 1 Victoria Street, London SW1

Trade Associations and professional bodies

Public Relations Department of particular firms

Banking Information Service, 10 Lombard Street, London EC3

Economist Intelligence Unit, Subscriptions Department, 27 St James Place, London SW1

BOOKS AND PERIODICALS

Financial Times: Share prices and rates of exchange

Directory of Directors

Trade Directories of the World: list of trade directories

Directories and year book for individual professions and types of business, for example, *Retail Directory*, *Oil and Petroleum Year Book*, *Electrical and Electronics Trades Directory*

British Rate and Data (colloquially known as BRAD): monthly guide for advertisers. Mechanical data and information on rates for all British media trade journals and magazines

Kemp's Directory: firms in Great Britain, Ireland and overseas are classified by their type of business

Stock Exchange Official Yearbook

Building Societies Year Book

Insurance Blue Book and Guide

Guide to Key British Enterprises (Dun and Bradstreet Ltd): factual information about prominent British firms

British Middle Market Directory (Dun and Bradstreet Ltd): like the "Key" above but mainly private companies

Bankers Almanack and Year Book

Who Owns Whom (UK edition): information on British companies that are owned by American firms and information on the American firms that own them

Moodies Investment Digest (published annually by Moodies Services Ltd): financial information on more than 600 major British companies

Moodies Investment Handbook (published quarterly by Moodies Services Ltd): financial information on industrial trustee companies in Part I and on banks, insurance companies, property companies and others in Part II

Kelly's directories: for all important towns; streets are listed in alphabetical order with the occupiers of each house, flat or office; residents are listed alphabetically with their address; Kelly's London directories lists businesses only

Kelly's Manufacturers and Merchants Directory, Vol I, Great Britain and Ireland

Patents, Designs and Trade Marks (HMSO)

Trade and Industry (Department of Trade and Industry magazine)

International Business and Finance

ORGANISATIONS

Economist Intelligence Unit, Subscriptions Department, 27 St James Place, London SW1

Confederation of British Industry, 21 Tothill Street, London SW1

International Institute for Cotton, 17 Maddox Street, London W1

International Tin Council, 28 Haymarket, London SW1

International Wool Secretariat, 6 Carlton Gardens, London SW1

EEC Information Service, 23 Chesham Street, London SW1

DTI EFTA & Common Market Information Centre, 1 Victoria Street, London SW1

BOOKS

Kemps Directory

Bottin International: international business register

European Companies (CBD Research Ltd): a guide to sources of information on financial and other aspects of European companies
Janes Major Companies of Europe
Financial Times Yearbook: business information on 25 industrial countries
Bankers Almanack and Year Book
Who Owns Whom (Continental edition): international subsidiaries of American companies
Kelly's Manufacturers and Merchants Directory, Vol II, International
New Place Names of the World, Hebe Spaull, pub. Angus and Robertson
Organisations of the World (a description of major inter-governmental organisations of the world), Hebe Spaull, pub. Angus and Robertson
Yearbook of International Organisations: published annually

Economics

ORGANISATIONS

Department of Trade and Industry, 1 Victoria Street, London SW1
EEC Information Service, 23 Chesham Street, London SW1
Economist Intelligence Unit, Subscriptions Department, 27 St James Place, London SW1
Embassies and trade delegations

BOOKS

OECD Annual Economic Surveys (HMSO): articles and statistical tables on each of the 23 OECD countries
A Year Book of the Commonwealth (HMSO): production and trade statistics for the Commonwealth countries
Britain, An Official Handbook (HMSO): information about all aspects of Britain including industry and the economy
Annual Abstract of Statistics (HMSO)
Monthly Digest of Statistics (Department of Trade and Industry)

General and political information about countries and international organisations

ORGANISATIONS

United Nations London Information Centre, 14 Stratford Place, London W1
EEC Information Service, 23 Chesham Street, London SW1
Commonwealth Information Centre, Marlborough House, Pall Mall, London SW1
Embassies
Government departments

BOOKS

Britain (HMSO)
Hansard (official report of proceedings in Parliament)
Vacher's Parliamentary Companion: lists Members of the House of Commons and House of Lords, government ministers, staff of government and public offices

Dod's Parliamentary Companion: biographies of peers and members of Parliament, forms of address, constituencies, parliamentary terms, public offices
The Statesman's Year-Book
Europa Year Book, Vol I, *International Organisations and Europe*; Vol II, *Africa, America, Asia and Australasia*
A Year Book of the Commonwealth (HMSO)
UNESCO Statistical Yearbook
Acts of Parliament (HMSO)

Import and Export

ORGANISATIONS

EEC Information Service, 23 Chesham Street, London SW1
Department of Trade and Industry
Trade delegations
Confederation of British Industry, 21 Tothill Street, London SW1

BOOKS

Croner's Reference Book for Exporters
Croner's Reference Book for Importers
Hints for Businessmen (Department of Trade and Industry): Customs regulations in foreign countries
Exporters Yearbook: Export information and import regulations

Travel

ORGANISATIONS

Embassies and national tourist offices
Travel agencies
AA or RAC, for members only motoring in Britain or abroad
Airline offices
British Rail

BOOKS

Hints to Businessmen (Department of Trade and Industry): one for each country including information on climate, social and business customs, travel information, post and telephone. Free to exporters
AA Guide to Hotels and Restaurants in Great Britain and Ireland
AA Members' Handbook
RAC Guide and Handbook
RAC Continental Handbook and Guide to Western Europe
AA Continental Handbook
Atlas and Gazetteer
Road Maps
The ABC Railway Guide
The ABC World Airways Guide
The ABC Shipping Guide

Hotels and Restaurants in Britain: official guide of the British Tourist Authority

Bank and Public Holidays throughout the World (Morgan Guaranty Trust Company): published annually

Travellers Digest: a guide to six continents, published by BOAC

People

BOOKS

Debrett's Peerage, Baronetage, Knightage and Companionage

Burke's Landed Gentry

Burke's Peerage, Baronetage and Knightage

Kelly's Handbook: biographies, lists of peers, forms of address

Who's Who: information on prominent people who are living; also *Who Was Who* about prominent people who have died, and specialised *Who's Who,* such as *The International Who's Who*, *Who's Who in the USSR*, *Who's Who in Art* and *Who's Who in Education*

The Business Who's Who of British Chairmen, Chief Executives and Managing Directors (Leviathan)

Dictionary of National Biography: biographies of prominent people, past and present, of Britain, the Commonwealth and Colonial America

Chamber's Biographical Dictionary: prominent people from all over the world

The British Imperial Calendar and Civil Service List: members of royal households, public departments, Commonwealth representatives and others

Diplomatic Service List (HMSO): British representatives overseas and civil servants connected with diplomacy

The Army List, *The Navy List*, *The Air Force List* (HMSO): each volume gives a list of the officers, serving and retired in that service

The Medical Register: list of registered medical practitioners

The Dentists Register: list of registered dentists

The Law List, The Scottish Law Directory: legal directories

Kime's International Law Directory

Directory of Directors

Members of the Stock Exchange

Crockford's Clerical Directory

British Qualifications: degrees granted by British universities, professional qualifications and what they mean

Debrett's Correct Form: whom to contact about questions of protocol, forms of address

Shipping

BOOKS

Lloyds Register of Ships

Mercantile Navy List (HMSO)

Technical

ORGANISATIONS

Professional institutes, such as the Institution of Chemical Engineers and the Royal Institute of Chemistry, can suggest sources for information in their field. A complete list of professional bodies with their addresses can be found in *Whitaker's Almanack*

Specialist libraries: libraries with an emphasis on scientific and technical information can be found in many parts of the country. The reference librarian at the public library has information on specialist libraries in that area and on their availability to the public

BOOKS

Black's Medical Dictionary
Chambers's Technical Dictionary
Year Books and directories for technical industries, such as engineering

Miscellaneous

Oxford Companion to English Literature
Oxford Companion to Music
Dictionary of Art and Artists
Cruden's Concordance: index to the Bible
Willings Press Guide: list of all British periodicals and newspapers
Cassell's Directory of Publishing: directory of British and Commonwealth publishers
Books in Print: list of books available with their publisher and price; books listed in alphabetical order, authors and titles
The Writers' and Artists' Yearbook: lists all journals, magazines and other publications in Great Britain and some Commonwealth countries. Includes lists of publishers and literary agents and information of interest to writers, artists and composers.

FURTHER READING

British Sources of Reference and Information, edited by T. Besterman for the Association of Special Libraries and Information Bureaux (ASLIB).
Facts and How to Find them, W. Bagley.
Facts in Focus, compiled by the Central Statistical Office, Penguin Reference Books.
Guide to the Universal Decimal Classification, BS 1000C: 1963, British Standards Institution.
Recommendations for the Preparation of Indexes, BS 3700: 1964, British Standards Institution.
Library Use in Further Education, C. J. Parsons, Arnold 1973.

GROUP DISCUSSION

Divide the class into pairs. Each pair takes on a particular aspect of the life of the town/city—religious, industrial, commercial, voluntary service, arts, architecture, local government, eminent people past and present, old people's services, etc.—for research. Each pair produces a typed report with illustrations so that all contributions put together make a reference book of the town/city. Quotations may be included and sources of all information should be indicated.

EXERCISES

1 Explain the following:

trade journal
encyclopaedia
Yellow Pages classified directory
reference library
bibliography
statistics
gazetteer
protocol
contents page and index
Dewey Decimal Classification

2 To which books would you refer for the answers to the questions in the heading to this chapter?

3 You work for a firm in Manchester. Your boss is making a business trip: he is taking the train to London where he is staying in a hotel for two days, then he is flying to Paris and Frankfurt and back to London. He then wants to hire a car in London and drive back to Manchester through Towcester, but he does not know where Towcester is or what route to take.

Make a list of reference books and organisations that can help him make all his arrangements: travel, accommodation, car hire, driving. He also wants a list of organisations and books that will give him some information about firms in Paris and Frankfurt and their export regulations.

4 Why would you use the following periodicals and books?

Financial Times
Hints to Businessmen
Post Office Guide
Vacher's Parliamentary Companion
Debrett's Correct Form
Economist Intelligence Unit
Who's Who
Roget's Thesaurus

Use the following reference books to answer the questions:

5 *Usage and Abusage*

a Explain the following words clearly to bring out their meaning: complete, entire, whole.

b "Lightening" and "lighting". Do the words mean the same thing?

c What is "hyperbole"?

6 *Longmans English Larousse*

- a Who was Konrad Adenauer?
- b What is the population of Guyana?
- c When was Sir Harold Wilson born?
- d What is Leningrad and where is it?
- e "To circumambulate" means what?

7 *Modern English Usage*

- a When are "lunch" and "luncheon" used?
- b Give another word for "periphrasis".

8 *Deskbook of Correct English*

- a Which of these two sentences is better?
  - i The sooner that it is done the better.
  - ii The sooner it is done, the better.
- b When are these used: *; † ?
- c "However ill John felt he always went to work." Why is there no comma after "however"?
- d What other expressions could be used instead of "We are in receipt of . . ."?

9 *International Who's Who*

- a In what year was Dr K. A. Busia born?
- b Of what nationality is Stephan Korner?
- c Which University did Gideon Rafael attend?
- d Who is Anthony Favill Tuke and when was he born?
- e What are some of the publications of Antoni Zygmund?

10 *ABC of English Usage*

- a Explain the difference between "all together" and "altogether".
- b Use the following words in sentences to bring out their meanings: "credence" and "credentials".
- c Explain "moral" and "morale".

11 *Pears Cyclopaedia*

- a When was James Cook, the celebrated English navigator born?
- b Who was Hera?
- c When did the "Massacre of St Bartholomew" take place?
- d What is a "Ballade"?
- e Who invented "Basketball"?

12 *The Statesman's Year Book*

- a How many co-operative and credit unions are there in the Mackenzie District of Australia?

- b What was the population of the Central Clydeside conurbation in June, 1967?
- c Where is Colorado and when was it first settled?
- d How many teacher training Colleges are there in Peru?
- e What is the actual name of Pope Paul VI?

13 *Roget's Thesaurus of English Words and Phrases*

- a What is the meaning of disorder?
- b What part of speech is "oblivion"?
- c Give the different meanings of "advice"?
- d Find three words which have similar meanings to "epicure" and say in what contexts each would be used.
- e Give the different meanings of "semi-transparent".

14 *The Concise Oxford Dictionary*

- a Give the meanings of the following words: iodoform; monandry; pry; ultraist.
- b Explain the following abbreviations: AIB; NATSOPA; Wm; ASLIB.

15 *The Dictionary of Typewriting*

- a What is meant by "alignment" in typewriting?
- b What is the meaning of the term "catchword"?
- c Give the abbreviations of "temporary"; "Oxfordshire", "New Mexico", "Kilometer".
- d What is a "REAM"?
- e Explain the following Printers' Corrections: Caps; trs; #; NP.

16 *Whitaker's Almanack*

- a Who launched the 253,000 ton tanker "Esso Northumbria", the largest ship ever built in Britain?
- b What is the population of Manitoba?
- c What Acts regulate adoption of children in England and Wales?
- d What is the official town residence of the British Prime Minister?

17 *The Typist's Desk Book*

- a In typewriting what is meant by "combination signs and characters"? Give examples.
- b What are window or panel envelopes?
- c What is the meaning of: "cherchez la femme"?
- d How are these Roman Numerals read: VI; LI; CV; IV; XL.

18 *Titles and Forms of Address*

- a Explain the following abbreviations: AACCA; ADC; ARPS; FAO.
- b How should the Queen be addressed?

c How is an Archbishop addressed both in speech and writing?
d Who is a chancellor?
e Who is accorded the style of "Excellency" in the United Kingdom?

19 Your boss has been invited to join a Trade Mission to Gabon. The object of the mission is to promote trade between Gabon and your country. Your boss asks you to do some research and write up a brief for him on the economic, mercantile and cultural background of Gabon with particular reference to the products marketed by your company. Your company markets electrical equipment, including refrigerators and air-conditioners.

20 Your boss has been invited as Guest of Honour at the Annual Dinner of the Trade Association to which your company belongs. The Chairman has suggested that in his speech he might like to say something about trade prospects in the Caribbean. Consult the relevant reference books and write up brief notes which could form the basis of his speech.

12

Committee Procedure

"Most bosses require their secretaries to take minutes at one or two meetings throughout the year ... minute-taking is a difficult task and it seems that training institutions do not devote time to teaching this skill."

A. C. Pendlebury, op. cit.

There are two main types of meeting—informal and formal. The former may or may not have been officially notified—it may have been called verbally—and it may or may not be conducted in accordance with usual meeting procedures. If it has been called to discuss one particular item of business no agenda may have been prepared. An example of such a meeting is that called by a departmental manager to discuss with his supervisors the best methods of carrying out instructions given by the managing director. Sometimes a secretary is required to take notes at such a meeting. It is unlikely that minutes or a report will be required, but the departmental manager may like the main points discussed and any decisions taken to be typed out in note form.

The formal meeting has to be conducted according to certain rules, depending on the type of organisation involved, and either a report or minutes of the *proceedings*, i.e. business and discussions, must be produced. For the purpose of this chapter the title Secretary will refer to the secretary of a board or committee, while private secretary will refer to the person who, among other duties, takes notes at the meeting. Frequently a private secretary may act in both capacities.

ORGANISATION OF A MEETING

When a formal meeting is planned all the people who are to be present must be notified individually in writing a minimum period before the date set for the meeting. In the case of a General Meeting (Annual or Extraordinary/Special) of a public company, a notice must also appear in the press a minimum period before the meeting. Usually the Chairman and Secretary of the body concerned decide the most suitable date for the meeting. The Secretary draws up the agenda and submits it to the Chairman for approval. Thereafter all arrangements are in the hands of the Secretary, who in turn delegates most of them to his private secretary, or the Chairman's private secretary.

Assuming that the private secretary is asked to make overall arrangements for the meeting, she would proceed to deal with matters in a certain methodical order.

At the time when the decision to hold the meeting is taken

1 Ensure that the room to be used for the meeting is available at the time and on the date required, and reserve it. This is normally done verbally in the first instance, and then confirmed in writing. Frequently the reservation of conference/committee rooms is the responsibility of the Office Manager. General Meetings are often conducted in hotels or public buildings.

2 Duplicate the notice and agenda. Usually the two documents are merged into one. It is wise to produce sufficient extra copies of the agenda to give to members at the meeting since they often forget to bring the copy sent to them.

3 Before sending out the notice and agenda check (a) that the minutes of the previous meeting have been distributed—if not they should be sent out with the notice and agenda; and (b) whether there are any papers which should be circulated for study by the members before the meeting. Cards may have to be prepared and circulated to members for completion before the meeting to say whether or not they will attend the meeting and to appoint a proxy if necessary (see page 475).

4 If the meeting is a General Meeting, draft a notice for the press and send it direct to either a widely read national newspaper in the case of a company, or local newspaper in the case of an association, society or

club. In a large organisation the draft should be passed to the Advertising Department.

5 It may be necessary to have memoranda or other documents prepared by other people. Adequate notice must be given and a submission date should be stated in the request. (This date should be planned to allow time for editing and duplicating.) Material for discussion of a policy matter is usually presented in the form of a *memorandum*. Information about things which have happened is generally given in the form of a *report*. Both should be circulated before the meeting.

6 Notify the press if the meeting is public. This often takes the form of an invitation to the editors of appropriate newspapers.

7 Mark a folder in which to place papers or notes of items to be dealt with at the meeting.

8 Have name cards made to be placed on the table in the case of new committees or for meetings where the people may not know each other.

The day before the meeting

9 Check the accommodation and arrange for refreshments to be served at a suitable time.

10 Make sure a copy of the minutes of the previous meeting has been inserted into the *Minute Book* ready for the Chairman to sign. The Minute Book is a complete record of the business of the committee containing a signed copy of each set of minutes from the time the committee was first formed.

11 Sort papers (including correspondence) into the order in which they will be required at the meeting.

12 Flag the appropriate pages of your chief's personal file of minutes, i.e. if a previous paper or minute is referred to in the agenda.

13 Ensure that you have sufficient pencils, paper, spare copies of minutes, agendas and papers available for all members.

14 Have ready the *Attendance Book*, which the members attending the meeting will sign, Minute Book, files and reference books which may be needed.

The day of the meeting*

15 Check that the room is properly prepared—sufficient chairs, blotting pads, ashtrays, glasses and water. Place pencil and paper, and a spare copy of agenda etc. in each place. The Minute Book, files, etc. should be placed where the Secretary will sit; the Attendance Book, shorthand notebook and pencils where you will sit. Check the heating or air conditioning and adjust if necessary.

16 Inform the receptionist or commissionaire of the meeting and its venue so that those who are to attend can be directed accurately. A notice on the door or standing beside the door, indicating the meeting to be held

* Illustration of a correctly prepared Board Room is shown on p. 550.

in the room helps to assure visitors that they have come to the right place.

17 If it is possible for you to be in attendance in the meeting room about fifteen minutes before the starting time to greet members as they arrive, this is a courteous gesture.

18 A few minutes before the meeting check that your boss is ready.

During the meeting

19 Ensure that all those attending sign the Attendance Book.

20 Take notes of the main points of discussion, being careful to record motions and amendments verbatim.

21 Make a separate note of any specific actions which your own boss is asked to undertake.

After the meeting

22 As soon as possible draft the minutes. The Secretary may make alterations and ask for a redraft to show to the Chairman. Once approved by the Chairman the minutes should be duplicated and circulated to those who attended the meeting, and to anyone who should have a copy for information. A copy must be inserted in the Minute Book.

23 Bring to your boss's notice the points on which he has been asked to take action. In some cases you may be able to do the job yourself, for example, the circulation of a document.

DOCUMENTS

Notice of a meeting

People required to attend a meeting must be informed of the time, date and place. This is usually done by means of a formal notice. The notice may be combined with the agenda, or it may ask members to submit items for discussion, particularly in the case of technical committees.

The formal notice of an Annual General Meeting must be circulated to all members (of an association or society) or shareholders (of a company) and must also be published in the press a prescribed number of days before the date of the meeting.

Agenda

The agenda is a list of items to be discussed at a meeting. The agenda for the meeting of members of a committee which meets regularly always begins with Apologies for absence; Minutes of previous meeting; and Matters arising from the minutes. The items to be discussed follow. It is usual to have a final item 'Any other business' if members have not been asked to submit items for discussion. This allows them to bring matters of interest to the committee or matters which may have arisen since the agenda was circulated. It can also be useful to have 'Date of next meeting' as the final item on the agenda, particularly if the committee meets fairly regularly, so that members can note the date and keep it free.

The items on an agenda for an Annual General Meeting include those which must by law be disclosed to members of an organisation or shareholders of a company.

Chairman's agenda

A special agenda is prepared for the Chairman including details which will help him to conduct the meeting. Beside each item on the agenda are given details of action already taken, or the person who has been asked to investigate, etc. A wide space is left on the right-hand side of the paper so that the Chairman can make his own remarks.

Minutes

Minutes of a meeting (sometimes described as *Minutes of Resolution*) are a summary of the main points of discussion without detail. Motions and amendments must be recorded verbatim and the names of proposers and seconders must be given.

Minutes may be displayed in a number of ways. Each item of business must be shown separately with agreements and resolutions standing out clearly. The items will appear in the order in which they were discussed, i.e. in the same order as on the agenda.

An agreement may be a recommendation or suggestion (often concerning action which could be taken by someone or some body other than the committee) which is not enforceable. Alternatively it may cover action to be taken at a later date and is then referred to as 'agreement in principle'. For example it may be agreed in principle by the Advisory Committee for Recruitment of Technical Inspectors that technical inspectors are required for ten different trades, but for the time being only four trades should be covered pending further investigations into the other six trades.

A resolution is a decision taken after voting, and is binding upon the board or committee members.

Minutes may be produced with an "Action" column on the right-hand side. In this column are given the names of the people who are to undertake some particular job. This enables a member to pick out quickly what concerns him.

Minutes should always be numbered. Usually when a committee is formed the minutes are numbered from one and continue through, i.e. they do not start at one again for each meeting. It is helpful to add the year—658/72 means that this is minute number 658 at a meeting held in 1972. Sometimes minutes are numbered from one at the beginning of each year with the year being given. So the minutes of a meeting held in January, 1972 would start at 1/72 and in December may have reached, say 59/72. In January 1973 numbering would begin again from 1/73.

Reports

Reports of meetings are full records of the points raised and the discussion; they are sometimes referred to as *Minutes of Narration.* Often the names of the people who made specific statements are included.

A verbatim report is a word-for-word account of what was said during a meeting. Each speech is prefaced by the speaker's name. The most common examples of verbatim reporting are parliamentary meetings and law courts.

Examples of documents mentioned above are shown on pages 464 to 467.

Minute Book

A complete set of minutes, each document signed by the Chairman, must be kept in a Minute Book, as a record of the proceedings of the body. It is advisable to paste each sheet of the minutes on to a numbered page of a foolscap book to prevent extraction of any page later. It is useful to have an index at the end of the book under subject headings for quick reference. The heading of each minute will provide the appropriate subject heading for indexing.

NATIONAL ASSOCIATION OF TRADERS

P. O. Box 6891,
LAGOS.

To: All Members of the Advisory Committee
for Recruitment of Technical Inspectors

Notice of Meeting

A meeting of the Advisory Committee for Recruitment of Technical Inspectors is to be held at 2 p.m. on Wednesday, 10th May, 1972 in the Conference Room at Trading House, Government Road, Lagos.

The agenda and papers for the meeting will be circulated within the next few days.

John R. Bates
National General Secretary.

Notice of a meeting.

NATIONAL ASSOCIATION OF TRADERS

ADVISORY COMMITTEE FOR RECRUITMENT OF TECHNICAL INSPECTORS

Meeting at 2.00 p.m. on Wednesday,
10th May, 1972.

A G E N D A

1. Apologies for absence.
2. Minutes of previous meeting.
3. Matters arising from the minutes.
4. Trades for which inspectors are required.
5. Qualifications of inspectors.
6. Dates for advertisements, receipt of applications, selection test, invitation for interview, interviewing panels, appointment.
7. Any other business.

John R. Bates
National General Secretary.

Agenda.

NATIONAL ASSOCIATION OF TRADERS

ADVISORY COMMITTEE FOR RECRUITMENT OF TECHNICAL INSPECTORS

Meeting at 2.00 p.m. on Wednesday, 10th May, 1972

CHAIRMAN'S AGENDA

1.	Apologies		
2.	Minutes of previous meeting		
3.	Matters arising from the minutes	16/72 Mr. Nelson to report on his discussions with the Ministry of Education. 18/72 The Ministry of Labour has agreed to co-operate (see correspondence)	
4.	Trades for which inspectors are required	Ministry of Education suggest inspectors for groups of trades rather than individual trades.	
5.	Qualifications of inspectors	Mr. Nelson to report on his discussions with Ministry of Education. Ministry of Labour suggest City and Guilds Final Certificate (see correspondence)	
6.	Dates	Secretary suggests Advertisements:- 3.12.71 Receipt of applications:- 31.12.71 Selection test:- 10. 1.72 Invitation for interview:- 17. 1.72 Interviewing panels:- 24. 1.72 Offer of appointment:- 28. 1.72 Appointment effective:- 1. 3.72	
7.	Any other business		

Left
A Chairman's Agenda. The Chairman can make his own remarks in the wide space on the right-hand side of the paper.
Below
Minutes of meeting.

MINUTES OF THE MEETING OF THE ADVISORY COMMITTEE FOR RECRUITMENT OF TECHNICAL INSPECTORS HELD AT 2.00 P M ON WEDNESDAY 10TH MAY 1972 IN THE CONFERENCE ROOM AT TRADING HOUSE, GOVERNMENT ROAD, LAGOS.

Present: Mr P J Dunn Chairman
Mr C T Cooper
Mr F Edwards
Mr P Nelson
Mr S T Stanley
Mr E D Watts
Mr P S Wells

Apologies for absence were received from Mr T H Henley.

20/72 MINUTES OF PREVIOUS MEETING
The Minutes of the meeting held on 15th March 1972, having been circulated, were taken as read and unanimously approved.

21/72 MATTERS ARISING
16/72 Mr P Nelson reported that he had had discussions with senior officials of the Ministry of Education. Although willing to allow technical inspectors access to technical training institutions, there had at first been strong feeling against schools participating in the scheme. It had been pointed out that technical inspectors could assist schools to achieve realistic practical standards which would benefit those students who wished to enter industry direct. Eventually agreement had been reached that all schools and institutions under the Ministry's jurisdiction should participate in the scheme.

It was AGREED that the Permanent Secretary, Ministry of Education, should be asked to confirm his decision in writing.

18/72 The Secretary read a letter received from the Chief Labour Officer which stated that the Ministry of Labour would give full support to the scheme. A meeting to discuss methods of co-operation had been requested.

It was AGREED that the Chairman should meet the Chief Labour Officer to follow up the matter.

22/72 TRADES FOR WHICH INSPECTORS REQUIRED
A list of trades, attached as Appendix I, was handed to members. There was divergence of opinion as to whether inspectors should be recurited for each individual trade or for groups of trades, eg building, metal, fitting, etc. Mr Nelson reported that the Ministry of Education officials felt that as far as trade inspection in training institutions was concerned it would be uneconomic to have inspectors for individual trades. Mr Watts pointed out that inspectors working on the basis of trade groups could be much better deployed. He accordingly moved that

Technical Inspectors be recruited on the basis of their ability to deal with trades by groups.

After discussion the motion was seconded by Mr F Edwards and carried by a majority vote.

23/72 QUALIFICATIONS OF INSPECTORS
Mr Nelson reported that this question had been raised during his talks with the Ministry of Education officials...

The foregoing minutes could be produced with same heading but displayed as follows:

		ACTION BY
20/72	MINUTES OF PREVIOUS MEETING	
	The Minutes of the meeting held on 15th March 1972 having been circulated, were taken as read and unanimously approved.	
21/72	MATTERS ARISING	
	16/72 Mr P Nelson reported that he had had discussions with senior officials of the Ministry of Education. Although willing to allow technical inspectors access to technical training institutions, there had at first been strong feeling against schools participating in the scheme. It had been pointed out that technical inspectors could assist schools to achieve realistic practical standards which would benefit those students who wished to enter industry direct. Eventually agreement had been reached that all schools and institutions under the Ministry's jurisdiction should participate in the scheme.	Secretary
	It was AGREED that the Permanent Secretary, Ministry of Education, should be asked to confirm his decision in writing.	
	18/72 The Secretary read a letter received from the Chief Labour Officer which stated that the Ministry of Labour would give full support to the scheme. A meeting to discuss methods of co-operation had been requested.	
	It was AGREED that the Chairman should meet the Chief Labour Officer to follow up the matter.	Chairman
22/72	TRADES FOR WHICH INSPECTORS REQUIRED	
	A list of trades, attached as Appendix I, was handed to members. There was divergence of opinion as to whether inspectors should be recruited for each individual trade or for groups of trades, eg building, metal, fitting etc. Mr Nelson reported that the Ministry of Education officials felt that as far as trade inspection in training institutions was concerned it would be uneconomic to have inspectors for individual trades. Mr Watts pointed out that inspectors working on the basis of trade groups could be much better deployed. He accordingly moved that	
	Technical Inspectors be recruited on the basis of their ability to deal with trades by groups.	
	After discussion the motion was seconded by Mr F Edwards and carried by a majority vote.	
23/73	QUALIFICATIONS OF INSPECTORS	
	Mr Nelson reported that this question had been raised during his talks with the Ministry of Education officials......	

THE PETER WALL DECORATING CO LTD

NOTICE OF MEETING

20th April 1972

To: All Members of the Design Committee.

A meeting of the Design Committee will be held at 0900 hours in Conference Room 2 at Head Office on Tuesday 9th May 1972.

You are requested to submit items for the agenda to the Chief Designer by Friday 5th May 1972.

G D Painter

Assistant Chief Designer

To: Chief Designer Date: ....

From: ....

I request that the following items be included in the agenda for the meeting to be held on Tuesday 9th May 1972.

1. ....
2. ....
3. ....

Signed:.................

Notice of meeting requesting items for the Agenda.

THORPE LIGHTING COMPANY LIMITED

26th April 1972

To: Departmental Managers

A meeting of all Departmental Managers is to be held in the Chairman's Office at 9 30 a m on Thursday 11th May 1972 to discuss the 1972/3 budget.

A G E N D A

1. Maximum output potential.
2. Market Research Project results.
3. Sales staff.
4. Storage capacity
   i) for raw materials
   ii) for finished goods.
5. Capital requirements.

P D Lampe

Administrative Secretary

Combined Notice and Agenda.

1.

THORPE LIGHTING COMPANY LIMITED

REPORT OF MEETING OF DEPARTMENTAL MANAGERS HELD AT 9 30 A M ON THURSDAY 11TH MAY 1972 IN THE CHAIRMAN'S OFFICE.

INTRODUCTION

The General Manager explained that he had called the meeting of Departmental Managers because the sales figures for April had shown that sales as a whole were on a steep downward trend, and that certain individual products were at a standstill. The object of the meeting was to produce information which would enable the Board to revise their policies.

MAXIMUM OUTPUT POTENTIAL

The Works Manager produced a statement showing the maximum output potential of each of the manufacturing sections with overall production estimates covering various computations of products. He pointed out that the present tooling allowed only limited output of certain products. With existing space this could be changed only at the expense of decreasing the production of other lines.

MARKET RESEARCH PROJECT RESULTS

The Marketing Manager reported that the results of the Market Research Project were still coming in. Results so far received......

2.

BRAND CLOTHING SHOPS LIMITED

NOTICE IS HEREBY GIVEN that the Annual General Meeting of Brand Clothing Shops Limited will be held at the Company's Head Office, 14 Coate Street, Dresstown, at 11 30 a m on Wednesday 10th May 1972.

B D Shuman

Secretary

3.

ART PAINTING COMPANY LIMITED

MEETING OF THE BOARD TO BE HELD AT 2 P.M. ON MONDAY, 24TH APRIL, 1972.

A G E N D A

1. Apologies for absence.
2. Minutes of the meeting held on Monday, 27th March, 1972.
3. Matters arising from the minutes.
4. Proposal to experiment with new colour pigment.
   (Report of the Colour Standards Board attached - I).
5. Complaint from Universal Motors Ltd. (Letter attached - II).
6. Any other business.

P. G. ARTEY

Secretary

4.

BRAND CLOTHING SHOPS LIMITED

ANNUAL GENERAL MEETING

A G E N D A

1. Minutes of the Annual General Meeting held on 8th May 1971.
2. Matters Arising from the Minutes.
3. Chairman's Report for the year ended 31st March 1972.
4. Financial Accounts for the year ended 31st March 1972.
5. Election of two directors on the retirement of Mr J D Hanson and Mrs E T Waters. Mrs Waters is willing to stand for re-election.
6. Formation of a subsidiary company for the expansion of wholesale trade.

B D Shuman

Secretary

1—Report of meeting. 2—Notice of Annual General Meeting. 3—Agenda for Annual General Meeting. 4—Agenda for Board Meeting.

Supplementary Papers

There may be one or more documents which are either circulated before a meeting or presented to members at the meeting. The documents should be numbered and if prepared at the same time as the agenda the document numbers should be given as references on it. It can also be helpful if the various documents are produced in different colours.

A report, to which are attached a number of appendixes, should contain a list giving the number and subject of each appendix.

Committee Files

All papers relevant to any committee on which your boss serves—notices, agenda, minutes, reports, supplementary papers—should be filed together. If the papers are too voluminous separate files can be maintained, one for agendas and minutes, another for supplementary papers. References in agendas and/or minutes to previous minutes and/or supplementary papers should be indicated by 'flagging', i.e. affixing an index tab with a note of its significance to the appropriate sheet.

TYPES AND STRUCTURE OF COMMITTEES

All official bodies have rules or regulations, setting out the membership, *terms of reference,* i.e. the work to be done by the members, and the main procedures for meetings. The members may be stated by designation, or as representatives of official organisations. The method of their appointment is stated, e.g. by election, by the Head of State, etc. The rules sometimes include a clause allowing the co-option of one or more members. This means that the committee members themselves may by agreement appoint another person to join their ranks. Such a *co-opted* member will have voting rights.

The rules also state the number of members which shall form a quorum. This may be given in the form "half the total members of the committee" or it may be given as a specific number. Observers and ex-officio members cannot be counted for the purpose of forming a quorum. An *ex-officio member* is a person who attends a meeting by virtue of his official position. For example the Chief Education Officer or his representative might be an ex-officio member of a committee formed to make recommendations about the examination system. Such a member usually has no voting rights.

Official members of a committee are said to be present at a meeting; ex-officio members and observers are said to be in attendance. This must be clearly shown in the minutes.

An official body is usually 'incorporated' which means that it has legal existence under a charter or Act of Parliament. A private or public limited liability company is incorporated under the Companies Act. The Boards of public corporations are appointed under an Act of Parliament. The people appointed to serve on such bodies have included in their terms of reference the responsibility for making policy decisions. They may also have the right to appoint councils and/or committees to assist them in their work either in an advisory or functional capacity.

Commissions may be set up by parliamentary agreement to look into matters of national importance which need careful research. The Chairman and members are appointed by the minister responsible for the matter concerned, and are generally people of repute in public life, who will have authority and experience to make the necessary investigations.

Less important matters might be looked into by an *'Ad Hoc' Committee*, a group of people from within the organisation itself chosen to deal with this special matter. Once it has been dealt with the committee will be disbanded.

Committees usually have the right to delegate certain duties to *sub-committees* and indeed, this is often a way of getting work done more quickly. Co-opted members with specialised knowledge can be very useful for such work.

Committees which are not formed under any particular regulations, may be guided by Standing Orders drawn up by the members themselves, which set out the procedures for meetings in the same way as the rules for incorporated bodies.

The business of voluntary organisations is often run by a committee of people elected by the members of the organisation. The composition of the committee will be laid down in the organisation's charter but usually consists of a number of officers—Chairman, Honorary Secretary, Honorary Treasurer and Auditor (Honorary or professional) if money is handled by the organisation—and a certain number of members. Even when the organisation pays an employee (perhaps as an executive secretary) it is the committee and not the employee who is responsible for conducting the business of the organisation. The employee is responsible to the committee for doing what the committee directs.

All organisations that exist legally must hold an *Annual General Meeting*, i.e. a meeting of all the members including the committee. The officers of the committee must report how they have conducted the year's business and what the financial situation is. Company chairmen are also expected to outline future policy.

When a decision has to be taken which, according to regulations or law, needs the consent of members an *Extraordinary General Meeting* is called if the Annual General Meeting is not due. Usually the agenda for such a meeting includes only those items on which a decision is required.

General meetings, like committee meetings, are conducted by the Chairman, assisted by the Secretary.

COMPOSITION AND PROCEDURE OF A MEETING

A meeting is controlled by a *Chairman*. Before he 'declares the meeting open' (this should happen at the time appointed for the meeting) he must ensure that there is a *quorum* of members present. This is the minimum number of people who are needed to conduct the business of the committee as laid down in the Regulations (see page 468). If a quorum is not present the chairman may wait until sufficient members are in attendance and then open the meeting or he may *postpone* the meeting, i.e. put it off until another date.

If the Chairman is absent from the meeting the Vice-Chairman, if there is one, *'takes the chair'*, or the members nominate one of themselves to act as Chairman.

The meeting must be controlled by the person who takes the chair. He must guide the discussion, ensure that it is relevant to the items on the agenda, summarise discussion and put motions and amendments to the vote.

Unless it is agreed otherwise by members, he must take the items in the order in which they appear on the agenda. He should not allow independent discussion between small groups of members. Only one member may speak at a time, and he must ensure that every member has an opportunity to speak on each item. He is also responsible for conducting the meeting in accordance with the rules laid down. If a member draws his attention to any irregularity in the proceedings—this is known as a *point of order*—he should immediately give a decision. Voting should be controlled by the Chairman and if the votes for and against a motion are equal in number he usually has a *'casting' vote*, i.e. an extra vote, so that a definite decision is taken.

If the members at a meeting feel that the Chairman is not doing his job properly a motion of "no confidence" in the chair can be put to the vote and if passed, the Chairman would have to give way to another member, who would be elected to take his place.

The *Secretary* must be ready to advise the Chairman at any time during the meeting on points which may arise during discussion. He may also have to give guidance concerning the Regulations of the committee. He may be called upon to read the minutes of the previous meeting, though if these have been circulated to members it is more usual to 'take them as read', i.e. assume that members have already studied them. If the minutes are accepted by members as a true and accurate record of the proceedings he will pass the *Minute Book* to the Chairman who will sign them. If members do not accept the minutes as they stand but wish corrections or alterations to be made these must be agreed, after which it is moved that "subject to the amendments agreed, the minutes be adopted". Having been responsible for the preparation of papers for the meeting, the Secretary may be called upon to explain them in more detail. This he must do factually so that members can discuss the matter with understanding. It must be remembered that the members who attend a meeting are not always *au fait* with the details of the matters to be dealt with.

At an Annual General Meeting, and sometimes at ordinary committee meetings, there is an item on the agenda dealing with finance. An association or a voluntary organisation has a treasurer, whose duty it is to explain the financial statements in simple terms so that everyone can understand the situation. Companies must circulate to shareholders the Trading, and Profit and Loss Accounts and Balance Sheet for the year. Private organisations must circulate an Income and Expenditure Account and Balance Sheet. In both cases the accounts must have been audited. After explanation of any special points a vote is taken to accept or reject them.

Sometimes a *motion* is proposed and seconded, the proposer and seconder explaining their points of view and then it is discussed; or the seconder may be called upon to close the discussion. More usually, however, a matter is discussed and then a motion is proposed and seconded. An *amendment* may be proposed and this must be discussed and voted upon before the original motion. An amendment may be merely a slight addition to the original motion or it may completely change the intention of it. The members are then asked to *vote*, those in favour first, usually by a show of hands. The number in favour is counted and then the number against. If the majority, i.e. the greater number, are in favour of the motion, it is said to have been 'carried'. If the opposite is the case, the motion has been 'rejected'. If a lot of people are involved it may be necessary for members to *"go into division"*, i.e. those in favour separate from those against the motion for counting. This is done in the House of Commons and is known as Divisions, but is not usual in committees. Alternatively a *poll* may be taken, members signing a piece of paper headed "FOR" or "AGAINST". If the voting is to be secret for any reason a *ballot* is held, each person writing his vote on a slip of paper and 'posting' it in a sealed box.

After a resolution has been passed a member may wish to add something to it. Such an addition must be proposed, seconded and voted upon, and if agreed is known as a *rider*.

Frequently at meetings discussion becomes lengthy with members repeating points that have already been made. A member may move that the "question be now put" and if agreed the motion being discussed is put to the vote. When the Chairman puts a motion to the vote he is said to be "putting the question".

In certain cases a member who cannot be present at a meeting can appoint a *proxy* to vote on his behalf. The proxy is normally another official member of the committee. In the case of company general meetings when a shareholder may not be able to be present, he can give authority in writing, usually to the Chairman, to vote on his behalf. Two types of proxy form are illustrated on page 472. The first informs the Society that either one of two named people will vote on the member's behalf. The second shows a company form which a shareholder completes indicating how he wishes his proxy to vote on his behalf.

When a motion has been accepted either unanimously, i.e. by all present, or by a majority, a *resolution* has been made. Sometimes a motion may be upheld by some of the members, the rest abstaining. The motion is then said to have been carried 'nem. con.' (without opposition) or 'nem. dis.' (no one dissenting). This is binding upon the committee and cannot be revoked without a special resolution to that effect.

If for one reason or another no action can be taken on a matter, it is said to *"lie on the table"*. If the matter concerns an outside person or body, official notification should be given in writing by the Secretary that it was not possible for the Committee to take any action.

There are times when no agreement can be reached on a matter. In order not to delay the proceedings a motion may be carried "that the meeting proceed with the next business". This can also happen when it is generally

BRITISH SECRETARIES' SOCIETY

16 Queen Street, Bridgetown.

I,..of..in the

County of...................................a member of the British Secretaries'

Society hereby appoint..

or in his absence... both Members of

the Society, as my proxy to vote for me and on my behalf at the Annual General Meeting and the Extraordinary General Meeting to be held on 10th December, 1971, and at any adjournment thereof.

As witness my hand this............day of ....

Membership No..................Signature...

Please sign and return this form of proxy as early as possible.

JOSEPH SOAPE AND COMPANY LIMITED

FORM OF PROXY

218966/136

J. DUNCAN-SMITH, ESQ.
16 APPLE STREET
GRAPETOWN GRI 6ST

Please indicate how you wish your votes to be cast by inserting "X" in the appropriate spaces.

EXTRAORDINARY MEETING

RESOLUTION	FOR	AGAINST
No. 1		

(Signature)...

ANNUAL GENERAL MEETING

RESOLUTION	FOR	AGAINST
No. 1		
No. 2		
No. 3		
No. 4		

I/We being (a) Member(s) of Joseph Soape Company Limited, hereby appoint Edmund Soape (chairman) or failing him, Peter Barr (Deputy Chairman) or failing him, John St.John Soape (Joint Managing) or failing him, David Barr (Joint Managing Director)
or*..
of..
as my/our proxy to vote for me/our behalf in the manner indicated hereon at the Extraordinary and Annual General Meetings of the Company to be held on Tuesday, 13th June 1972 and at any adjournment thereof.

If you desire to appoint a proxy other than the above-named please delete their names and insert the name and address of your proxy, and initial alteration.

Dated this......................day of...............................1972   (Signature)...

agreed that the time is not right for a decision. The item will automatically come up again at the next meeting under "Matters Arising from the Minutes".

If specific or technical matters are likely to prove difficult or need lengthy discussion a special sub-committee, officially an 'ad hoc' committee, may be set up to deal with it. This may be composed of a few members of the main committee, or a member of the committee may be appointed chairman and asked to appoint his own members, particularly if technical business is involved. Such a sub-committee must report to the main body at the latter's direction.

It is possible that so many specialised matters are to be discussed that a committee is broken up into sub-committees, each one being given a specific subject or subjects, or aspects of a subject, to discuss. This is known as *"going into committee"*.

Sometimes the business of a meeting cannot be completed in the time allotted, or agreement cannot be reached. In this case if the members agree, the meeting may be *adjourned by consent*, and will be continued at a later date. If the date is not fixed the meeting is said to have been *adjourned sine die* (without date, i.e. indefinitely).

PREPARATION AND INDEXING OF MINUTES

Having taken shorthand notes of the main points of discussion during a meeting and having recorded verbatim all motions, agreements and resolutions, the private secretary must now produce draft minutes. She is well advised to do this as soon as possible while the matters raised at the meeting are still fresh in her mind.

The most important thing to remember is that minutes are a *summary* of the proceedings, and so should be brief, concise and clear. They must be factually accurate and unambiguous. It is not usual to include the names of the individuals who raised certain points unless the person concerned is representing an organisation and has made it clear that he is giving the view of that organisation.

A minute is primarily a record of a decision taken and may be termed a 'minute of decision' or a 'minute of resolution'. Usually some explanation is required, however brief, and this summary of the main points of discussion is known as a 'minute of narration'. The following is a minute of resolution.

> "It was resolved that all applications for the loan of books from the library must be accompanied by a fee of 50p refundable when the book is returned."

Such a resolution would certainly have been preceded by some explanation for its necessity. This would be recorded as follows.

> "The librarian stated that great difficulty was being experienced in obtaining the return of books borrowed by members. He suggested that a refundable fee might be charged which would help to cover the cost of replacing books irretrievably lost."

Speech is always recorded as reported speech using appropriate tenses. If the actual speech was in the past tense, the past perfect would be used in the minutes. For example: It was reported that the Department had objected. If the actual speech was in the present tense the past would be used. For example: It was reported that the Department objected. If the actual speech was in the future tense, the conditional would be used in reporting. For example: It was reported that the Department would object.

The draft minutes should be produced in either double or treble line spacing so that alterations can be made by the Secretary and/or the Chairman.

For methods of display and numbering of minutes refer to pages 465 and 466. It may be advisable to produce three copies so that each person concerned can have a copy to study.

When the draft minutes have been approved they are duplicated in final form. (Very occasionally an approved draft may be duplicated for distribution so that comments can be made by members who attended the meeting and others who may be concerned, before production in final form.)

GLOSSARY OF COMMITTEE TERMS

'Ad hoc' Committee	A group of people appointed to deal with a specific matter.
agenda	A list of items to be discussed at a meeting.
adjourned by consent	The unfinished business of a meeting will be discussed at another meeting by agreement of those present.
adjourned 'sine die'	The unfinished business of a meeting will be discussed at a further meeting for which a date is to be fixed later.
amendment	A change in a proposed motion.
Annual General Meeting	A meeting of all members of an organisation or shareholders of a company which must be held each year.
attendance book	The book in which each member present at a meeting signs his name.
ballot	Written vote with provision for preserving the secrecy of each individual's vote.
casting vote	An additional vote, usually held by the Chairman, to enable a decision to be taken in the case of an equal number of votes being given both for and against a motion.
Chairman	The person who controls the business of a meeting.
Chairman's agenda	The agenda prepared for use by the Chairman, containing notes about individual items and giving space for him to make his own notes.
Extraordinary General Meeting	A meeting of all members of an organisation or shareholders of a company to discuss some matter of importance for which the consent of all or the majority of members is necessary.
go into committee	Division of members at a meeting into groups, each group to undertake discussion of specified subjects.

go into division	Physical division of members for voting purposes.
lie on the table	A matter is said to "lie on the table" when no action can be taken on it.
majority	The greater number of members either for or against a motion.
memorandum	A document setting out information to enable the committee to make a policy decision.
minute book	A book containing a signed copy of every issue of minutes from the date of the first meeting of the committee.
minute of narration	A summary of all points raised in discussion before a decision is taken on a particular item of business.
minutes of resolution	A summary of all the resolutions passed; the resolutions, motions and amendments must be recorded verbatim; the names of proposers and seconders are usually given as well.
minutes	A summary of the proceedings of a meeting.
motion	A proposal that certain action be taken.
nem. con. (nemine contradicente)	The passing of a resolution without opposing votes but with some members abstaining.
nem. dis. (nemine dissentiente)	Sometimes used instead of 'nem. con.'.
notice	A notification to members of the time, date and place of a meeting.
point of order	A question from a committee member, or a suggestion that a certain procedure is irregular, or that a statement is inaccurate
poll	A count of votes, for and against a motion from lists of signatures.
postpone	Put off to a later date.
proceedings	The business discussed, main points of discussion, decisions and agreements taken at a meeting.
proposer	The person who recommends a particular decision to be taken by formally stating a motion.
proxy	A person authorised by a member to vote on his behalf.
quorum	The minimum number of members necessary for a meeting to be held.
report	(a) Full details of the business and discussion of a meeting.

	(b) Information presented to a committee of what has been done prior to the meeting.
resolution	Definitive decision made by a majority vote of members on a motion.
rider	An addition to a resolution.
seconder	A person who supports the proposer of a motion.
Secretary	The person responsible for all arrangements connected with a meeting and for advising the Chairman on procedures, etc.
sub-committee	A small number of people appointed by a main committee to undertake certain specified work on its behalf.
take the chair	Do the work of Chairman during a meeting.
terms of reference	Statement of the work to be done by a committee.
unanimously	With the agreement of all members present.
vote	Express, either verbally or in writing, whether one is 'for' or 'against' a motion.

FURTHER READING

So You're Going to a Meeting, W. Puckey, Maxwell, Love & Co Ltd.
Committees, how they work and how to work them, E. Anstey, George Allen and Unwin.
How to take Minutes, E. Martin and G. K. Bucknall, Pitmans.
Hours into Minutes, P. J. C. Perry, British Association for Commercial and Industrial Education.
Meetings, Hall, MacDonald & Evans.
Committee Procedure, Gilman, Methuen.

GROUP PROJECT

Divide the class into two groups. Each group is to be a committee. By discussion make plans to hold a meeting. All members of each group produce a notice of the meeting and agenda either separately or combined. Each group should appoint a Chairman and conduct a meeting. The members of the second group are to act as private secretaries, preparing the room and taking notes during the meeting. After the meetings have been held each group is to produce minutes of the meeting held by the other group.

EXERCISES

1 What is an Extraordinary General Meeting? When is such a meeting called?

2 What is meant by "Any Other Business" as an item on an agenda?

3 A motion may be passed in two ways. Explain them briefly.

4 You are personal secretary to the Company Secretary of a company manufacturing ladies' clothes. Your boss has to go abroad and asks you to cope with all the preparations for a Board meeting to be held the day after his return to the office. The main items for discussion at the meeting will be next year's budget; the opening of branches abroad including the appointment of overseas representatives; salary increases for design staff.

State what steps you would take up to the day of the meeting, producing any letters or documents needed.

5 As secretary to the senior official who organises the Staff Association it falls to you to produce the agenda for the committee meetings. You ask your junior to do this for you on one occasion and she produces the following:

AGENDA

1. Request for increase in salaries of junior clerical staff.
2. Provision of transport for married women workers.
3. Minutes of the previous meeting and matters arising.
4. Apologies.
5. Date of next meeting.
6. Any Other Business.

Comment on the agenda giving reasons for your comments.

6 Explain

(i) adjourned 'sine die'
(ii) go into committee
(iii) point of order
(iv) terms of reference
(v) vote.

7 What is the difference between

a a meeting that has been postponed and one that has been adjourned?
b a motion carried unanimously and a motion carried 'nem. con.'?
c a co-opted member and an ex-officio member of a committee?
d an agenda and a Chairman's agenda?
e a report of a meeting and minutes of a meeting?

8 What is a memorandum presented to a committee?

9 What books and documents should be available at a meeting?

10 You wish your junior to prepare a room for a meeting. She has never done this before. What instructions would you give her?

11 State five duties which are the responsibility of the person who takes the chair at a meeting.

12 Who is responsible for (a) drawing up an agenda for a meeting and (b) producing minutes of a meeting?

13 What is the purpose of the Attendance Book? Suggest reasons for its importance.

14 Your boss is Hon. Treasurer of the Works Sports Club. What will be his responsibility before and at the Annual General Meeting?

15 Complete the following sentences:

a When it is agreed that no action can be taken on a matter it ....

b All members agree that it is getting late and rest of the business should be left over until another time. The meeting is ....

c The Chairman decided that each item on the agenda should be discussed by a small group of members so they ....

d The member who proposed the motion subsequently changed his mind and proposed an ....

e The Chairman opened the meeting but immediately a member rose on a .... to say that he believed there were insufficient members to form a ....

16 Write a letter to the editor of a local newspaper inviting him to attend the Annual General Meeting of the Ladies' Dress Club of which your boss's wife is Chairman.

17 A meeting is due to be held at 3 p.m. Six members are needed to form a quorum but only five are present. What action may the Chairman take?

18 When taking notes at a meeting what steps will you take to ensure that you can prepare an accurate draft of the minutes for your boss?

19 You took your junior with you to a meeting to initiate her into taking notes at a meeting so that she will be able to stand in for you when you are on holiday. She produces draft minutes which include the following:

> "The motion was agreed to by the members but Mr Jones proposed an amendment which was carried. Members then voted—all in favour."

Comment and rewrite.

20 Your boss, who is Chairman of an important committee which meets regularly, complains that members bring up so many matters under "Any Other Business" that the meetings become very long. He asks if you can solve his problem. What suggestion or suggestions would you make?

13

Finance and Statistics

A secretary may never find herself working for a boss whose job is directly concerned with finance, but every boss—from middle management level up—must be concerned with costs and overheads in any organisation, and in a company or corporation profits are the *raison d'être*. Every boss's job is to get maximum productivity from those under him for minimum cost. This involves an understanding of accounting. His secretary also needs this basic understanding as well as the ability to keep simple day-to-day accounts herself.

Conventional handwritten book-keeping is not now practised in the bigger companies, though the principles of accounting are basically the principles of book-keeping adapted to quantitative output. A simple summary of book-keeping/accounting procedures is given below.

FINANCE RECORDS

An important principle in book-keeping is that every movement of goods or money must be supported by a *voucher*, that is a document appropriate to the transaction. Unless an entry in an accounts book can be cross-referenced with a voucher, no auditor will accept it as genuine. The accounts of all businesses and non-profit making organisations handling public money must be audited annually, and the audited accounts of public companies and corporations, and organisations using money donated by the public must be made available to the public.

Before a business is started there must be capital, including money; the latter is known as liquid capital. Money movements, either cash or cheques, are recorded in a *Cash Book*. Monies received are entered on the *debit* side (which is always the left-hand side) of a page, and monies paid out are entered on the credit side (which is always the right-hand side).

When money in the form of cash is received a *Receipt* should be issued, the duplicate, which is retained, being a voucher supporting the entry, although receipts are rarely issued in the United Kingdom for normal routine payments received by cheque or credit transfer. When payments are made the supporting voucher is the receipt issued by the creditor (the organisation to whom the payment is made). In order to know how much money is in hand or in the bank the Cash Book is *balanced*. The debit and credit sides are totalled separately; the smaller is subtracted from the larger and thus a balance is calculated. All accounts are balanced at regular intervals, although with any form of mechanisation this is done automatically. Normally there is a debit balance in the firm's books which represents the balance in hand, because debits in the Cash Account are items received and credits are items paid out.

Cash Account

		£			£
Capital		1000	Jan. 4	Purchases	400
Jan. 1	Sales	260	4	Rent	150
			6	Sundries	10
			8	Balance c/d	700
		1260			1260
Jan. 8	Balance b/d	700		Debit Balance	

Many businesses have to buy goods and raw materials either to re-sell, or to use in manufacturing. Such purchases are usually arranged 'on credit', i.e. the goods are supplied and the purchaser pays for them at an agreed later date. Goods purchased on credit are entered in a *Purchase Day Book*, the supporting voucher being the *Invoice*. If for any reason, some of the goods have to be returned to the supplier, a *Credit Note* is issued by him and this supports the purchaser's entry in the *Purchase Returns Book*. Similarly, when goods are sold on credit an entry is made in the *Sales Day Book* supported by a duplicate copy of the invoice, and returned goods are recorded in the *Sales Returns Book*, supported by the duplicate credit note. The day books are merely records of the movement of goods, not money.

In bigger businesses, day books are often not kept. The supporting documents are filed and used as day books, which saves a lot of time.

The books mentioned above are known as books of original entry. One more must be added—the *Journal.* This book is a record of any transaction which, because of its nature, cannot be entered in one of those already explained. For example, the purchase of office furniture cannot be entered in the Purchase Day Book because the articles are for the use of the company and will not be resold. If they are bought on credit they cannot be entered in the cash book until they are actually paid for. So a journal entry is made.

The books of original entry do not give a picture of the state of a debtor's (an organisation owing money) account, a creditor's account, or the organisation's own financial position. The Cash Book shows how much cash is in hand or in the bank; the day books show the amounts of goods purchased or sold on credit. So the real financial position is shown in three *Ledgers.*The Purchases Ledger contains a record of the accounts of all creditors. Each entry in the Purchases and Purchases Returns Books and appropriate entries from the credit side of the cash book are transferred or *posted* into the appropriate individual account in the Purchase Ledger. Each entry in the Sales and Sales Returns Books and appropriate entries from the debit side of the Cash Book are posted to the appropriate individual account in the Sales Ledger.

Ledger accounts have two sides, debit and credit, and the entries are made from the point of view of the person or company named in the account, that is, the *creditor* (in the case of the Purchases Ledger) or the *debtor* (in the case of the Sales Ledger). Thus, when money is paid to a creditor it is entered on the credit side of the cash book and posted to the debit side of the creditor's account in the Purchases Ledger because he is receiving the money. This is known as the *double entry* system of book-keeping.

The third ledger is the *General Ledger* which contains non-personal accounts. The monthly total of purchases are entered in the Purchases Account on the debit side (because the goods were received) thus completing the double entry with the individual creditors' accounts. The purchase of office furniture mentioned above is another example. Since this is not an item of selling stock there would be an Office Furniture Account in the General Ledger. Such items may be bought from several different companies but the business is concerned with the amount of money spent on office furniture as a whole, not with individual suppliers.

From the Balance Sheet it is possible to see whether a company is solvent or insolvent. It is solvent if its readily realisable assets are at least as much in value as its liabilities. A factory building is an asset but if it had to be realised, i.e. sold for cash, the business would not exist any more. Stock can be sold and it may be that a shortage of cash has temporarily arisen through the purchase of too much stock, the production of too many goods or a fall in sales. It is reasonable to suppose that the stock will be sold eventually so that debts can be paid.

If a company reaches the stage where the value of its assets are less than the value of its liabilities, i.e. if the whole business were wound up and everything sold all debts could not be paid, the business is highly insolvent. The organisation must then either seek more capital or go into liquidation. In such a case the business is placed in the hands of a *Receiver*, who supervises the winding up of the business. Each creditor will receive a portion of the amount owing to him.

The following examples show the basic documents and book-keeping entries involved in a simple purchase of raw materials.

Jones Weavers Limited send a purchase order to Silk Spinners Limited.

JONES WEAVERS LIMITED

Registered in England
No. 2374676

16 Leaden Street
Manchester MA6 7LB
Tel: 21735

Order 1268/73

Directors: N. French (Managing)
D. Webb
R. Szabado (Czech)

To: Silk Spinners Ltd.,
14 Web Lane,
Manchester M16 7JS

Date: 15th November, 1973.

PURCHASE ORDER

Please supply:

Qty.	*Item*		
1 gross White Cord	Silk (SB-A/W)	£1.25 per hank	Plus VAT
½ gross Blue Cord	Silk (SB-A/B)	£1.25 ,, ,,	Plus VAT
2 gross White String	Silk (SC-A/W)	£0.90 ,, ,,	Plus VAT

Terms: 25% Trade Discount
Delivery: Supplier's Van
Delivery Date: Not later than 30th November, 1973

Silk Spinners Limited are able to supply two of the items ordered from stock immediately. An invoice is raised and the goods are delivered.

Invoice No: Z 6891

SILK SPINNERS LIMITED
14 Web Lane, Manchester M16 7JS
VAT Reg No: 724 364637

Tel: 68719

Reg. no. 0003711
England

INVOICE

Date: 18th November 1973
Tax Point: 1st November 1973

Jones Weavers Ltd.,
16 Leaden Street,
Manchester, MA6 7LB

Your Order No: 1268/73

Terms: Nett
Type of Sale: Trade Sale

Ref.	Qty.	Unit	Item	Price	Cost	VAT Rate	VAT Amount
SB-A/W	1 gross	Hank	White Cord Silk	£1.25	£180.00	10%	£18.00
SB-A/B	½ gross	Hank	Blue Cord Silk	£1.25	£ 90.00	10%	£ 9.00
					270.00		27.00
			Less: 25% Trade Discount		67.50	10%	£ 6.75
					202.50	10%	£20.25
			Total VAT		20.25		
			Total Invoice		£222.75		

Delivery: Van

Order to be completed.

Note: In 1973 the VAT Rate was 10 per cent. The rate has since been varied. On most ordinary consumer goods it is currently 8 per cent (1977).

The remaining item of the order is delivered and another invoice is raised.

Invoice No. Z 6987

SILK SPINNERS LIMITED
14 Web Lane, Manchester M15 7JS
VAT Reg No. 724 364637

Tel: 68719

Reg. no. 0003711
England

INVOICE

Date: 25th November, 1973
Tax Point: 1st November 1973

Jones Weavers Ltd.,
16 Leaden Street,
Manchester, MA6 7LB

Terms: Nett
Type of Sale: Trade Sale

Your Order No: 1273/73

Ref.	Qty.	Unit	Item	Price	Cost	VAT Rate	VAT Amount
SC-C/W	2 gross	Hank	White string silk	£0.70	£201.60	10%	£20.16
			Less: 25% Trade Discount		50.40	10%	£ 5.04
					£151.20	10%	£15.12
			Total VAT		15.12		
			Total Invoice		£166.32		

A Delivery Note accompanies the goods and the invoice follows separately. The goods received should be checked against the Delivery Note, and when the invoice is received, the quantities charged should be checked against the Delivery Note and the prices against the original order.

The second delivery is not as ordered so Jones Weavers Limited return the goods. Silk Spinners Limited issue a credit note, which is usually prepared in red.

Credit Note No: 456

SILK SPINNERS LIMITED
14 Web Lane, Manchester M16 7JE
VAT Reg No. 364637

Tel: 68719

Reg. no. 0003711
England

CREDIT NOTE

Date: 26th November, 1973
Tax Point: 1st Nov 1973

Jones Weavers Ltd.,
16 Leaden Street
Manchester MA6 7LB

Type of sale: TRADE SALE

Goods as per invoice No. Z 6987 (Goods returned—not as Order)	£166.32

The day books of the two companies now look like this.

JONES WEAVERS LIMITED

PURCHASE DAY BOOK

1973		
Nov. 18	Silk Spinners Limited	£222.75
Nov. 25	Silk Spinners Limited	£166.32
		£389.07

PURCHASE RETURN BOOK

Note: This book is also referred to as the Returns Outwards Book.

1973		
Nov. 26	Silk Spinners Limited	£166.32

SILK SPINNERS LIMITED

SALES DAY BOOK

1973		
Nov. 18	Jones Weavers Limited	£222.75
Nov. 25	Jones Weavers Limited	£166.32
		£389.07

SALES RETURNS BOOK

Note: This book is also referred to as the Returns Inwards Book.

1973		
Nov. 26	Jones Weavers Limited	£166.32

In practice the Day Books would be totalled at the end of the week or month, but for the purposes of the example illustrated the new total has been shown immediately after the entry. At the end of the month each company posts the entries in the books of original entry to the Ledgers and balances.

Individual postings from the books of original entry are made daily to the personal accounts of creditors and debtors, so that at any point in time the personal accounts give an up-to-date picture. The total postings to the general ledger accounts (e.g. Purchases Account) would normally be done monthly.*

Silk Spinners now send a Statement of Account

SILK SPINNERS LIMITED
14 Web Lane, Manchester, M16 7JE
VAT Reg No. 364637

Reg. no. 0003711
England

STATEMENT OF ACCOUNT

In account with:
Jones Weavers Ltd.,
16 Leaden Street
Manchester MA6 7LB

30 November 1973

	Date	Debit	Credit	Balance
Inv. 26891	18.11.73	222.75		£222.75
Inv. 26987	25.11.73	166.32		£166.32
CN 456	26.11.73		166.32	£222.75
				Balance due

Jones Weavers Limited check the statement against the original documents and send a cheque (with the Statement) to Silk Spinners Limited for £222.75.

* See examples on pages 488 and 489.

Appropriate entries in the cash books of the companies are made. Note that the amounts for VAT are entered in a separate column.

JONES WEAVERS LIMITED

CASH BOOK

1973				1973			
				Dec. 4	Silk Spinners Ltd.	20.25	202.50

SILK SPINNERS LIMITED

CASH BOOK

1973				1973			
Dec. 5	Jones Weavers Ltd.	20.25	202.50				

Silk Spinners Limited return the receipted statement. The Cash Book entries are posted to the ledgers which now show nil balances.*

JONES WEAVERS LIMITED

PURCHASES LEDGER

1973				1973			
Dec. 4	Cash CB179	20.25	202.50	Nov. 30	Balance b/d	20.25	202.50†

SILK SPINNERS LIMITED

SALES LEDGER

Account of Jones Weavers Ltd.

1973				1973			
Nov. 30	Balance b/d	20.25	202.50	Dec. 5	Cash CB18	20.25	202.50

* At one time it was customary to prefix debit entries with "To" and credit entries with "By" and the practice has continued to a limited extent. However, as "to" and "by" are meaningless symbols they are best omitted entirely. Certainly no firm using any form of mechanised accounting is likely to use them.

† On November 30 Silk Spinners Ltd is *owed* (that is, is in credit) £202.50 by Jones Weavers Limited or, in other words, the account of Silk Spinners Ltd is in credit. (This is the only instance in book-keeping and accounts when the word "credit" is used in the layman's sense of meaning "money that stands to a person's credit".)

JONES WEAVERS LIMITED

PURCHASES LEDGER

Account of Silk Spinners Ltd.

1973				1973			
Nov. 26	Returns PR5	15.12	151.20	Nov. 18	Goods PB16	20.25	202.50
Nov. 30	Balance c/d	20.25	202.50	,, 25	Goods PB16	15.12	151.20
		35.37	353.70			35.37	353.70
				Nov. 30	Balance b/d	20.25	202.50*

GENERAL LEDGER

Purchases Account

1973							
Nov. 30	Purchases PB16	35.37	353.70				

Purchase Returns Account

1973				1973			
				Nov. 30	Returns PR5	15.12	151.20

SILK SPINNERS LIMITED

SALES LEDGER

Account of Jones Weavers Ltd.

1973				1973			
Nov. 18	Goods SB28	20.25	202.50	Nov. 26	Returns SR74	15.12	151.20
Nov. 25	Goods SB28	15.12	151.20	,, 30	Balance c/d	20.25	202.50
		35.37	353.70			35.37	353.70
Nov. 30	Balance b/d	20.25	202.50				

* Conversely, in the books of Silk Spinners Ltd, Jones Weavers Ltd are shown as owing £202.50.

GENERAL LEDGER

Sales Account

1973				1973			
				Nov. 30	Sales SB28	35.37	353.70

Sales Returns Account

1973							
Nov. 30	Returns SR74	15.12	151.20				

The ledgers show the financial state of individual accounts, which can be balanced at any time to see how much is owed to them or by them, the value of non-saleable goods bought, the amount spent on overheads, such as salaries, rent, electricity, telephones, etc. but this is not enough. An organisation carries on business for profit. To know its profit (or loss) a business has to produce Final Accounts, which are the accounts published annually. First a *Trading Account* is drawn up. This shows the value of stock on hand at the beginning of the period, to which is added the cost of goods purchased during the trading period and any expenditure involved in producing the goods, e.g. wages of the workers, rent for factory space, etc. On the other side of the account is the value of sales during the period plus the value of stock on hand at the end of the period. The excess of the value of sales and final stock over the value of production costs is known as gross profit. (A deficiency would mean a gross loss.)

TRADING ACCOUNT
for the year ended 31st December 1972.

	£	£		£	£
Stock at 1.1.72		125,000	Sales	1,789,000	
Purchases	987,500		Less Returns	46,700	1,742,300
Less Returns	101,700	885,800	Stock at 31.12.72		278,200
Production Expenses		121,000			
Gross Profit c/d		888,700			
		2,020,500			2,020,500

The gross profit is not the true profit of the business, because there are many other expenses that have to be met, which are concerned with the running of the business, though not with the production of the goods—salaries of office workers, for example. Office workers are essential but they are not concerned in any way with producing the goods. A *Profit and Loss Account* shows such expenditure. The resulting balance is the net profit or net loss.

PROFIT AND LOSS ACCOUNT
for the year ended 31st December 1972.

	£		£
Administration Expenses	126,650	Gross Profit b/d	888,700
Selling and Distribution Expenses	68,900		
Depreciation	12,000		
Sundry Expenses	2,500		
Interest on Loan	500		
Net Profit c/d	678,150		
	£888,700		£888,700

Now the organisation knows how much profit or loss it has made over a certain period—usually twelve months, though some big organisations prepare a trading account as often as every month—but it still does not know how much the business is worth. The next step is a *Balance Sheet*, which sets out the value of the assets and liabilities of an organisation. Assets are things owned by or amounts owed to the organisation; liabilities are amounts owed by the organisation. For example, a company may own a factory—this is an asset. The money to build the factory was made available by shareholders, so the amount of capital contributed by them is a liability, because if the company closed down the shareholders would have to be repaid.

BALANCE SHEET
as at 31st December, 1972.

	£	£		£	£
Issued Share Capital		300,000	Fixed Assets		
Loan		6,800	Buildings		175,000
			Equipment and Furniture		35,000
			Vans		19,750
					229,750
Current			Current Assets		
Creditors	76,000		Stock	278,200	
Taxation	200,000		Debtors	81,500	
Dividends owing	15,000	291,000	Cash	8,350	368,050
		597,800			597,800

The final accounts shown above are presented in the conventional book-keeping style. Many of the larger companies (and gradually more of the smaller ones) are representing these accounts in an abbreviated vertical form. The accounts shown above would appear as shown below. It should be noted that although the new style Profit Statement is gaining popularity the old style Balance Sheet is frequently still used.

PROFIT STATEMENT
for the year ended 31st December, 1972.

	£	£ 000
Sales less returns		1,742
less cost of goods sold:		
Stock 1.1.72	125	
Purchases less returns	886	
	1,011	
Less Stock 31.12	278	733
		1,009
Less Production Expenses		121
Gross Profit		888
less Trading expenses		
Administration	126	
Selling and Distributing	69	
Depreciation	12	
Interest on Loan	3	210
		£678

BALANCE SHEET
as at 31st December, 1972.

	£	£ 000
Assets Employed		
Fixed Assets		230
Net Current Assets		
Current Assets	368	
less Current Liabilities	291	77
		307
Capital Employed		
Share Capital		300
Loan		7
		307

Non-profit making organisations do not prepare Trading and Profit and Loss Accounts. An *Income and Expenditure Account* or *Revenue Account* is prepared. The example below shows the figures for the previous year as well as for the year just ended.

SOCIETY FOR THE ADVANCEMENT OF COMMERCE

REVENUE ACCOUNT for the year ended 30th June, 1971.

June 30/70 £		June 30/71 £
251	Development (Advertising and Publicity	362
2819	Administration	3891
421	Printing, Stationary, Postages and Telephone	536
1084	Circulation of Booklets, and services to members	989
257	Office Rent and Rates and Heating and Lighting	375
31	Audit Fee	65
83	Depreciation—Office Equipment	121
1266	Examination Expenses	2385
289	Staff Pension Fund	417
19	Corporation Tax	12
6520		9153
1172	Excess Income carried to Accumulated Fund	1235
£7692		£10,388

June 30/70 £		£	June 30/71 £
3182	Entrance, Transfer, Examination and Exemption Fees		4671
	Membership Subscriptions:		
	1968/69	58	
	1969/70	307	
	1970/71	5129	
4303			5494
207	Building Society Interest		223
£7692			£10,388

A balance sheet, showing the assets and liabilities of the organisation is produced in the same way as for a profit-making organisation.

MACHINES

In most business organisations of any size accounting work is carried out to a large extent by machines. Even in smaller organisations some simple machines are used.

Non-printing There are two main types of machine—non-printing and printing. Non-printing machines such as adding machines and comptometers are used for checking purposes. The operator presses the figure keys as required and the numbers are indicated on a panel. Simple adding machines of this type have what is known as a half-keyboard with keys from one to five. Larger numbers are produced by dividing them—six is produced by tapping three twice; seven by tapping three and four. Since the machine is simply reckoning and not printing this does not matter. Comptometers have the capacity to do all kinds of calculations including percentages, and in many organisations there is a large section of comptometer operators checking financial documents, etc.

Adding-listing The machines which print calculations start with the simple manual adding-listing machine, which can be used to add, subtract, sub-total and total, multiply by addition and insert numbers, e.g. account numbers, which are not to be included in the totalling. Such a machine is very easy to operate and an hour's practice is usually sufficient to gain proficiency in its use.

To operate the keyboard, the first, second and third fingers should be used. If the machine is electric the fourth finger is free to operate the control keys. There is a key for each figure from one to nine and for nought. Some

An NCR adding-listing machine.

machines also have keys for '00' and for '000' which saves depressing the nought keys several times for hundreds, thousands, etc.

The control keys vary slightly on different makes of machine but the signs are similar.

> represents a figure not included in the total
◇ represents a sub-total
* represents a total
— represents minus
× represents multiplication

The total key must be used before starting a new calculation to ensure that the machine is 'clear'.

On the simplest type of machine multiplication can be carried out by addition. 23 × 16 would be worked out as follows:

For the ten a nought is added to 23	230
23 is then listed 6 times	23
	23
	23
	23
	23
	23
Total	368

When multiplying, the control lever marked × is pushed into position after the figure keys have been tapped and then it is not necessary to tap the figure keys again until the required number of repeats have been printed, but the × lever must be returned to its non-working position before the last repeat is made.

Study the following extract from the 'tally roll' which is the roll of paper fitted to the back of the machine. It will be noted that there is a decimal point between the second and third figures from the right. This represents decimal money, the third figure from the right being the unit figure, but makes no difference to calculations for whole numbers. The first figure on the right becomes the unit figure in this case.

```
              *
7.4 8 5,9 6 <
      4,5 6
      1,2 3
      7,8 9
      7,5 3
      1,5 9
    2 2,8 0 ◇

      8,5 2   -
    1 4,2 8 *
```

Before the first figure, which represents an account number and is not included in the calculation, is an asterisk on its own; this indicates that the machine was first cleared by depressing the total key. The five figures after the account number are amounts to be added together. The figure 2280 is a sub-total and is printed in red if a two-coloured ribbon is used in the machine. The figure 852 is to be subtracted from the sub-total and a final total of 1428 is shown (also in red).

The chart on page 496 lists the main groups of machines available for calculating and data processing (routine procedures based on pre-determined facts) in ascending order of complexity. A secretary is not necessarily expected to operate such machines but she should be able to recognise them, know their possible uses and understand their function. For an explanation of the basic principles of the machines' operation see "Basic Business Studies—Office Practice" (Chapter 2).

(Left) The Burroughs C3000 electronic calculator. (Right) Burroughs F5000 Printing Accounting machine.

RECEIPTS AND PAYMENTS

Receiving money Whenever money is received a certain routine should be followed.

1 If receiving directly from a person, smile and say thank you.
2 Count the money if cash and say the amount.
3 If correct put away in till or cash box.
4 If not correct, count again and agree amount with the person who has paid it to you.
5 If change is needed, place the money aside* and count the change. Hand over the change either by counting into the person's hand, or by counting in your own hand and handing over. (Counting money into a person's hand is considered very discourteous in some countries.)
6 Place money in till or cash box.

* Aside (taking care that it cannot be snatched away).

Machine	Manual or electric	Input	Direct or indirect*	Output	Functions	Uses
1. Adding	Both	Key operation	D	(Non-printing)	Add, sub-total, total	Checking, totalling of figure columns for insertion of sub-totals and totals
2. Adding/ Listing	Both	Key operation	D	Tally roll	Add, subtract, multiply by addition, sub-total, total	List of cheques; columns of figures
3. Calculating	Both	Key operation	D	(Non-printing)	Add, subtract, multiply, divide, sub-total, total	Invoices, wages, stock records, etc.
4. Calculating	E	Key operation	D	Tally roll	As 3 plus combined use of the four arithmetic principles	Listing, conversion (e.g. foreign exchange) insurance premiums, percentages, square root discounts, interests, etc.
5. Accounting Keyboard	E	Key operation	D	Tally roll and/ or Forms	Calculate total, balance	Book-keeping including day book entries, analysis and ledger posting
6. Accounting Punched Card	E	Punched card	I	Forms (Continuous Stationery)	(a) Punch—punches a hole in a position to represent figure, which is a code for a piece of information (b) Verifying Punch—checks the accuracy of punching (c) Sorter—selects the cards according to information punched (d) Tabulator—prints information, calculates, prints results	As 3, 4 and 5, plus statistics and records of all kinds
7. Calculators (Electronic)	E	Punched card	I	Punched card	Read instructions from punched card, calculate and punch result (on same or another card)	Up-dating of information on punched cards
8. Calculators Desk computer	E	Key operation	D	Non-printing	Arithmetic and algebraic calculations, information storage	Solution of complex arithmetic and algebraic problems
9. Digital Computer (Electronic)	E	Punched card Punched tape Magnetic tape	I	Forms	Calculate, process data, i.e. vary calculations according to information fed in, print result, store information	As 6 plus forecasts (e.g. sales, stock requirements, capital, personnel, network analysis)

* M/E = Manual or electric
D/I = Direct or indirect, i.e. direct input is by manual operation of the machine, indirect is feeding in of data on card or tape.

7 Issue a receipt which should state the date, name of the person who has paid the money, amount of money received in words and figures. In some organisations the goods or service paid for is also shown on the receipt.
8 Sign the receipt and stamp with the organisation's official stamp.
9 Check the details written and then hand over the receipt with a smile.
10 If copies of the receipt have to be distributed tear them out of the book, removing carbon paper first, and place them in the 'Out' tray.
11 Replace the carbon sheets in the next set of forms ready for use.

Depending on the procedure for obtaining a receipt book, requisition for a new one in good time so that you have it available immediately the current one is finished.

If the payment is received in the form of a cheque, money order or other document, the date should be checked to make sure that the order is still valid. (The period of validity is usually six months but this should be checked for the various documents in different countries.) Check that the amount in words and in figures is identical and that the document has been signed. Any alterations should have a full signature beside or underneath them. If there is any discrepancy the document must on no account be altered but should be handed back for correction.

Paying money When paying money check the amount handed over and always check change. You will be responsible for any shortage so it is worth spending a few seconds checking. A receipt must be obtained for all monies paid out by the company, so if you are asked to take an invoice or statement and pay it, the document must be receipted immediately. Never hand over money without an official receipt being given. It does sometimes happen that a clerk will say the receipt book is finished and a temporary receipt will be given. This is wrong in principle and no-one can be forced to accept such a document.

In Government Departments there is, in most countries, an official regulation which states that an official receipt must be given for all monies paid by the public. Anyone accepting a temporary receipt—or no receipt at all—could never prove payment.

PETTY CASH

A secretary who is given responsibility for petty cash must keep a proper record.

There are two basic methods of keeping petty cash. The most usual in business is by the *Imprest* system. This means that a certain amount of money is allocated from which payments are to be made. At the end of a certain period, or when the amount is running low, reimbursement of the total amount spent is requested. At any time the amount of cash in hand plus the total of vouchers held for amounts paid out should equal the 'imprest'. An example of a petty cash record kept on a weekly imprest system is shown below.

On the following page the same record is shown with *analysis columns*. It will be seen that each payment is recorded twice, once in the credit total column and once in a column headed by the type of expenditure. This makes it easier to control expenditure as a glance is sufficient to show how much is being spent on each item.

Debit	Date	Item	V/N	Credit
20.00	13.11	To Balance b/d		
		By Bus fares	138	0.06
		,, Registered parcel post	139	0.38
		,, Window cleaning	140	1.50
	14.11	,, Wage envelopes	141	0.65
	16.11	,, Taxi fare to bank	142	0.30
		,, Bus fare from bank	143	0.05
	17.11	,, Cleaner	144	3.50
				6.44
6.44	20.11	To Cash		
		By Balance c/d		20.00
£26.44				£26.44
20.00	20.11	To Balance b/d		

Debit	Date	Item	V/N	Credit
14.11	13.11	To Balance b/d		
		By Cash Book	514	2.45
		,, Stationery	515	6.48
		,, Bus fares	516	0.14
	16.11	,, Refreshments	517	0.74
	17.11	,, Cleaner	518	3.50
		,, Balance	c/d	0.80
14.11				14.11
0.80	17.11	To Balance b/d		
10.00	20.11	,, Cash received		
	22.11	By First Aid kit	519	2.75
	23.11	,, Taxi fares	520	0.65
	24.11	,, Cleaner	521	3.50
		,, Balance	c/d	3.90
10.80				10.80
3.90	24.11	To Balance b/d		

Example of petty cash record by non-imprest system (see page 500).

Debit	Date	Item	V/N	Total	Fares	Post	Office Exs.	Staty.
20.00	13.11	To						
		By Bus fares	138	0.06	0.06			
		,, Registered parcel post	139	0.38		0.38		
		,, Window cleaning	140	1.50			1.50	
	14.11	,, Wage envelopes	141	0.65				0.65
	16.11	,, Taxi fare to bank	142	0.30	0.30			
		,, Bus fare from bank	143	0.05	0.05			
	17.11	,, Cleaner	144	3.50			3.50	
6.44	20.11	To Cash		6.44	0.41	0.38	5.00	0.65
		By Balance c/d		20.00				
£26.44				£26.44				
20.00	20.11	To Balance b/d						

The alternative method is to be given any amount of money whenever the cash is running low and the balance will consequently vary. An example of a petty cash record kept in this way over a period of two weeks is shown on page 498.

In the examples a voucher number is shown beside each payment. Usually a petty cash voucher form (see below) is completed by anyone requesting reimbursement from the petty cashier. It is approved by an authorising officer and the claimant also signs when receiving the money. Receipts are attached to the voucher—some items, such as taxi fares, cannot be covered by a receipt. The vouchers are numbered in order of payment and the number is entered in the appropriate column.

Alternatively the receipts themselves may be used as vouchers and numbered, and petty cash voucher forms are then used only to cover items for which no receipt is available.

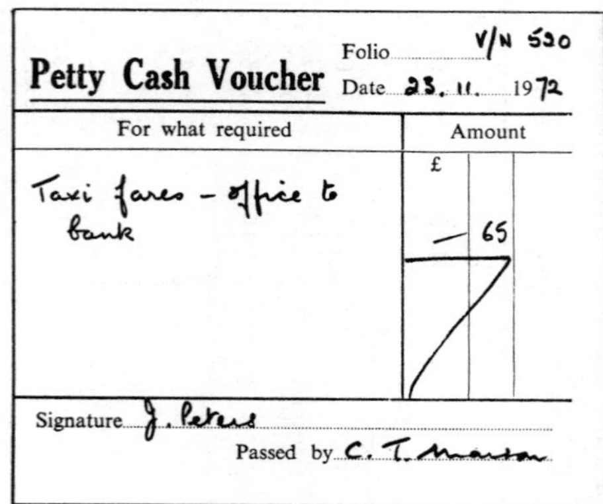

Petty Cash Voucher

Folio V/N 530

Date 23. 11. 1972

For what required	Amount £	
Taxi fares – office to bank	—	65

Signature J. Peters

Passed by C. T. Mason

BANKING

Bank accounts All business organisations need the services of a bank. Usually a firm banks with the nearest branch of the bank of its choice. In multiple organisations the same bank is used throughout, each branch of the organisation having an account or accounts with the nearest local branch of that bank.

Businesses are not usually concerned with *deposit accounts* or *savings accounts*, though voluntary organisations may be, if they have sums of money which will not be used for the time. Deposit and savings accounts are profitable as the money in them earns interest—the rate depends on the type of account. The bank may charge current account-holders a quarterly or half-yearly charge for the services provided by the bank; these charges are known as *bank charges* or *ledger fees.* In certain countries, Ghana for example, a current account attracts interest if a minimum credit balance stands for a whole calendar month.

When opening a current account it is usually necessary to give a reference. In the case of a multiple organisation this would be arranged by the Head Office. The person/s who will sign cheques on behalf of the company must give a *specimen signature* on a *Signature Card*. It is not usual for more than three people to be authorised to sign cheques and often either all cheques, or those above a certain amount, must be signed by two officials. This is to prevent fraud.

Paying-in An initial amount must be paid into the account before it can be used for working purposes. Whenever money is paid into an account a *paying-in slip* or *credit slip*, or a *Bank Giro Credit form* must be completed.

Businesses are usually given *paying-in books* which contain paying-in slips or credit slips in duplicate or triplicate. One copy of the slip is kept by the bank and the duplicate is retained in the book. If the forms are in triplicate, the duplicate is sent by the cashier to the appropriate section of the Accounts Department and the triplicate is retained in the book.

A completed paying-in slip is illustrated on page 502. It will be seen that the value of the various denominations of cash is shown—not the number of notes or coins. Some banks have separate paying-in slips for cash and for cheques. In some countries separate slips are used (1) for cheques drawn on banks in the town where the Head Office is situated and (2) for cheques drawn on banks in other towns. Details of the cheques being paid in are listed on the back of the paying-in slip.

When cash is paid into the bank it should be properly prepared. The notes should be faced and counted into hundreds. Each batch of a hundred should be banded. Coins must be sorted and bagged in certain quantities. Individual banks can be asked how the money should be counted but the following is a general guide for British banks:

50p coins	£10 bags
10p coins	£5 bags
5p coins	£5 bags
2p coins	£1 bags
1p and ½p coins (mixed)	50p bags
½p coins	25p bags

Paying-in slips, or credit slips, or paying-in books are used when a customer pays money into his account at the branch of the bank where his account is held. If a customer wishes to pay into his account at a time when he cannot reach his own branch, he can do so by completing a *Bank Giro Credit form*. The Bank Giro is a credit clearing system which enables money to be moved between the accounts of customers of all the banks in Great Britain. When a

DATE 10 Jan 1973		
CREDIT THE ACCOUNT OF E.F. Morgan		
Notes: over £1	10	—
Notes: £1	3	
50p	1	50
Silver (Ex. 6d.)		
Bronze		
1d. 3d. 6d.		
TOTAL CASH		
Postal Orders		
Cheques, etc.	73	31
TOTAL CREDIT £	87	81

BARCLAYS **CREDIT**

BARCLAYS BANK LIMITED

DATE 10 Jan 1973

Notes: over £1	10	—
Notes: £1	3	—
50p	1	50
Silver (Ex. 6d.)		
Bronze		
1d. 3d. 6d.		
TOTAL CASH		
Postal Orders		
Cheques, etc. (*Listed overleaf*)	73	31
£	87	81

ACCOUNT E.F. Morgan ACCOUNT NUMBER 09999999

Paid in by E.F. Morgan

C.S.2

Customers are advised that the Bank reserves the right at its discretion to postpone payment of cheques drawn against uncleared effects which may have been credited to the account.

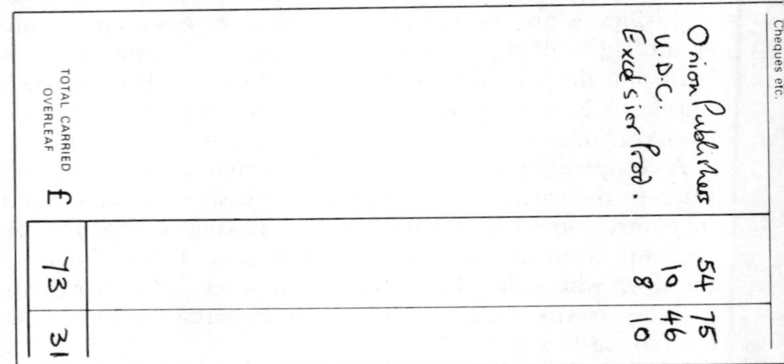

Cheques etc.		
Onion Publishers	54	75
U.D.C.	10	46
Excelsior Prod.	8	10
TOTAL CARRIED OVERLEAF £	73	31

When a bank customer pays money into his current account at the branch of the bank where his account is kept, he completes a paying-in slip. Each bank designs its own paying-in slips but they all contain the same information: the date, the name of the account-holder and the number of the account, the cash (listed in denominations) and the cheques being paid in. Details of the cheques being paid in are usually listed on the back of the paying-in slip. The person who is paying in the amount signs the form in the space provided. The cashier or teller stamps and initials the paying-in form and counterfoil, and then detaches the counterfoil and passes it back to the person who has signed the paying-in form. The counterfoil may be kept as a record of the transaction; it serves the same purpose as the duplicates in paying-in books.

BANK GIRO CREDIT ACKNOWLEDGMENT

Teller's Date Stamp and Initials

A/c. ....

at ....

£

Subject to verification of all items other than cash.

Form No. 765

bank giro credit

Date

To: Code No.

Teller's Date Stamp and Initials

Bank

Branch

Credit Account

Account No.

Paid in by

NOTES:		
Over £1		
£1		
50p		
Silver		
Bronze		
1d. 3d. 6d		
TOTAL CASH		
Cheques, Etc.		
TOTAL £		

A Bank Giro credit form with counterfoil.

customer completes a Bank Giro Credit form, the bank receiving the money and/or cheques will send the form to its head office who will pass them on to the customer's own branch where the amount will be credited to his account. This method of paying money into an account is known as *Credit Transfer 1*.

Statement of Account The sum of money standing in an account is known as the *credit balance*. A cheque book is used so that payments may be made from it by cheque. The procedure for making payments by cheque is explained in the section *Making payments* below. Only when special arrangements are made can payments be made from an account in which the credit balance is insufficient to meet the payment. This is known as *overdrawing*. If an account-holder writes a cheque for more than the balance in his account, his branch may refuse the cheque and it will be returned to the payee's branch marked 'R/D' (refer to drawer); the payee must then contact the account-holder who issued the cheque and try to get the money he is owed. Cheques marked 'R/D' are known as *dishonoured cheques* and are said 'to bounce'. It is illegal to bounce cheques.

At regular intervals the bank submits a *Statement of Account* which sets out all the transactions that have gone through the customer's account. *Debits* are sums deducted from the account which have been paid out, *credits* are sums paid into the account. The *balance* is the amount left in the account after each transaction. Statements are usually sent monthly to business organisations, though more frequent submissions can be arranged. The entries on the Statement must be checked against the duplicate or triplicate paying-in slips and cheque counterfoils. Most banks no longer send the used cheques, called *cancelled cheques*, with the statement unless an account-holder specifically instructs them to do so. They are, however, filed by the bank in case it is necessary to double check that a certain amount was drawn by a payee.

Making payments A *cheque* is *drawn* (written by the account-holder, who is the *drawer*, on the bank, the *drawee*) in favour of the *payee* (the person who will receive the money). Cheques are issued by the banks in book form with the name of the account-holder printed above the signature space ('personalised cheques'). A company or large organisation often has its name and address incorporated into a printed heading on its cheques. Cheques may be completed either in handwriting or by a machine. The details which must be inserted include the date, the name of the payee, the amount to be paid in words and figures and the signature of the account-holder or his representative/s (whose signatures appear on the bank's specimen signature card).

When writing a cheque it is important that no spaces are left. This is to prevent forged insertions being made. The payee's name should be written against the word 'Pay'. The amount should be written in words and any unused space should be filled in with a line. Figures should be written with a dash between the pounds and pence. If a mistake is made it can be deleted, not

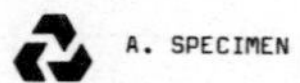

In account with
National Westminster Bank Limited
Anytown Branch
41 High Street Anytown Berks

Date	Detail	Debits	Credits	Balance when overdrawn marked DR
1972	BALANCE FORWARD			373.92
9FEB	78739	1.00		372.92
11FEB	CASH/CHEQUES		129.85	502.77
22FEB	CR. TRANSFER		29.15	531.92

BG Bank Giro Credit DV Dividend Account No 09999999 Statement No. 12
DD Direct Debit SO Standing Order

A bank statement. Against the date '9 FEB' is the number 78739 in the 'Detail' column; what does this number indicate? How are the abbreviations at the bottom of the statement used?

erased; the correction must then be signed in full. (See page 506 Amending a cheque.)

If cheques are handwritten by a clerk, a machine called a *cheque-signer* may be used to save the time of the senior official who is required to sign them. A plate containing the signature is used as a master. The machine has built-in safety devices, a locking system and a counter for checking the number of documents signed, for security. It can also be used for signing other documents such as share certificates.

For completing cheques entirely by machine a *cheque-writer* is used which inserts all the information. A cheque-writer is like a typewriter but it cuts the impression as well as printing it so that no alterations can be made.

In the illustration on page 505 the cheque has two vertical lines printed on it. These lines indicate that the cheque is a *crossed cheque*. If these lines are not printed they can be ruled in by hand. In Britain crossed cheques can be obtained from the banks, but in many countries this is not so. The crossing is a security measure to ensure that the cheque cannot be cashed by anyone over the counter at a bank. A crossed cheque must be paid into a bank account, or into the Post Office Giro or the National Savings Bank. If the payee endorses the crossed cheque it can be paid into someone else's account. Even if crossed cheques are lost or stolen, no one can cash them; therefore, only crossed

A crossed cheque and counterfoil.

cheques should be sent by post. In some European countries cheques are not crossed but a bank will not cash a cheque unless the person is known to them.

The two vertical lines across a cheque, with or without the words '& Co.' are classified as a *general crossing.* When '& Co.' is written between the lines it means that although the cheque cannot be cashed, it can be used to pay someone else. For example, Mr. A pays Mr. B the sum of £10 by cheque. Mr. B owes Mr. C the sum of £10 and decides to use Mr. A's cheque. By *endorsing* the cheque, that is signing his name on the back of it, Mr. B causes the cheque to become legal tender. Mr. C will then pay the cheque into his bank account. This process of endorsing and passing on can continue during the term of the cheque's validity (usually six months), but it is bad practice and is not encouraged by the banks. (This is also the meaning of 'or Order' printed on the cheque after the space for the payee's name.)

Other crossings such as 'A/c Payee only', 'Not Negotiable',* are known as *special crossings.* Special crossings may stipulate that the cheque must be paid into the account of the payee named. It is possible to go further and add the bank and branch. Another form of special crossing acts as a safeguard against fraud by stipulating the maximum amount payable; for example, the words 'Under £5' written between the lines of the crossing would prevent a cheque for £4 being altered to £40 or £400.

Whenever a cheque is written, it is important to fill in the corresponding *counterfoil.* It is a good rule to complete the counterfoil before writing the

*'The two remarks "account payee only" and "not negotiable" are added to cheques as additional safeguards, in case cheques fall into wrong hands. The phrases do not mean exactly what they seem to mean: "account payee only" sounds as if that cheque could only be paid into the named payee's account, and the words "not negotiable" seem to indicate that this cheque cannot be passed to anyone else. This is not the case. Both these cheques can in fact be paid into anyone's bank account, but the words "account payee only" will cause the collecting bank to look with extreme suspicion and exercise great care if the person paying in the cheque is not the named payee. The words "not negotiable" mean that if the cheque gets into the wrong hands anyone to whom it is given has no right to the money for which it stands.' Basic Business Studies Book 1, *Commerce, Swift, Stanwell and Warson*, Edward Arnold (Publishers) Ltd.

cheque to make sure that it is not overlooked. The counterfoil is an important record and should contain full details of the cheque including any special crossing.

Even the largest concerns need actual cash for paying wages and salaries, petty cash, etc. To obtain cash from a bank account a cheque has to be drawn. It must be an *open* cheque,* i.e. not crossed, and is made payable to "Cash". Some banks require "Cash" open cheques to be endorsed by the payee. When cashing large cheques there should be major security measures. At least two people should go to the bank together, preferably with a guard such as Securicor provide. (The same thing applies if large amounts of money are being taken to the bank for paying in.) Open "Cash" cheques must be cashed at the branch where the drawer has his account unless a special arrangement has been made at another branch. This is a safeguard for the bank and also for the drawer.

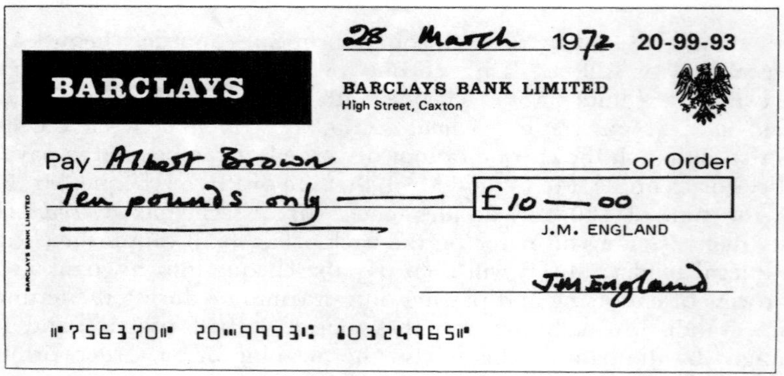

28 March 1972 20-99-93

BARCLAYS

BARCLAYS BANK LIMITED
High Street, Caxton

Pay Albert Brown or Order

Ten pounds only £10—00

J.M. ENGLAND

JM England

BARCLAYS BANK LIMITED

756370 20 9993 10324965

An open cheque. A crossed cheque cannot be cashed (unless it is 'uncrossed' and made out to 'Cash' or 'Self') but must be paid into a bank account or into the Post Office Giro or the National Savings Bank. If the payee endorses the crossed cheque it can be paid into someone else's account. An open cheque becomes a crossed cheque if the drawer puts two vertical lines on the cheque.

Amending a cheque After it has been completed, a cheque can be amended only by the drawer. He simply crosses out (erasing invalidates the cheque) the part he wants to change, writes the amendment next to it and initials or writes his signature in full under the alteration. This method may be used to change the date of a cheque presented more than six months after it was written. However, it is always safer to write out another cheque and destroy the original one. An amended cheque is illustrated on page 507.

Obtaining cash from the bank If a bank customer wants to draw money out of his current account, he can write a cheque to himself. This is called *cashing a cheque*. On the first line he writes 'cash' or 'self' instead of the name

*A crossed cheque can be "opened" if the drawer signs his name between the vertical lines, and an open cheque can be crossed if the drawer puts two vertical lines on the cheque.

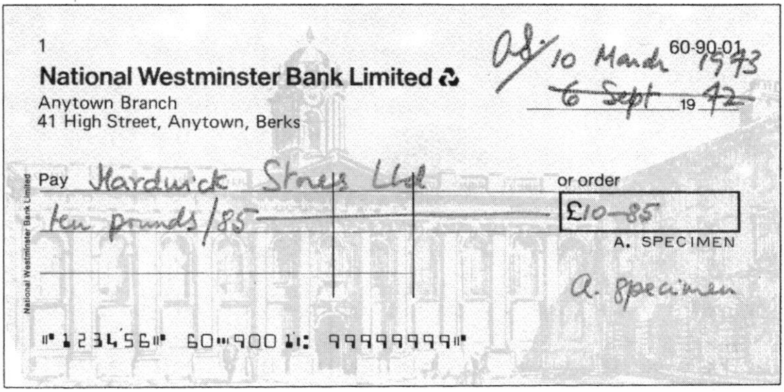

1

National Westminster Bank Limited

Anytown Branch
41 High Street, Anytown, Berks

60-90-01

A.S. 10 March 1973 ~~6 Sept~~ 19 ~~72~~

Pay Hardwick Stores Ltd or order

ten pounds/85 £10–85

A. SPECIMEN

A. Specimen

National Westminster Bank Limited

⑈123456⑈ 60⑉9001⑆ 99999999⑈

of a payee. The cheque must be endorsed (signed) on the back as well. He can cash cheques at his own bank branch or at another branch where he has previously made an arrangement.

If he needs cash during non-working hours certain banks provide a non-stop cash service by machine, known as the *24-hour cashcard*. With this card, a customer can go to a dispenser outside a bank and get £10 in cash any time of the day or night. Each customer has a code number which is not printed on the card but is indicated by a series of holes that can be 'read' by the machine in the dispenser. The customer puts his card in the dispenser and taps out his number on a set of buttons. If he has tapped the right number, £10 drops out in a plastic packet. The card disappears into the dispenser and it is sent back to the customer's bank where the £10 is deducted from his account. The code number is not printed on the card in case it is lost or stolen. Without the number, no one can use the card. If the wrong number is tapped out on the buttons, the dispenser will reject the card. The customer has three chances to tap out the correct number. After the third attempt, the machine keeps the card. A cashcard is illustrated on page 513.

Anyone who works away from his home town or journeys frequently to specific places may find it useful to have *cashing facilities* at another branch of his own bank. This means that he is able to cash cheques at the branch with which the arrangement has been made. The arrangement includes a maximum amount up to which cheques may be cashed in any one month (see also *Credit cards*, p. 511).

A *'bearer' cheque* is one which is payable to the person who presents the cheque for payment. When sending a messenger to cash a cheque the payee could be given as "bearer", but in Britain the drawer's endorsement is needed.

A cheque is valid for six months from the date on which it is drawn. Thereafter it is known as a *stale* cheque. You may hear people speak of a *post-dated* cheque. This is a cheque which is drawn on a certain date but the date inserted on the cheque is later. The banks object very strongly to the practice of post-dating cheques. Similarly a *blank cheque* should never be issued. A cheque which is completed in all particulars except the amount is a 'blank' cheque. The payee is left to insert the amount and the dangers are obvious.

If by any mischance a cheque is lost the fact must be reported to the bank immediately by telephone and confirmed in writing. This is known as *stopping a cheque*. The details on the counterfoil are given—cheque number, date, payee, amount—and the bank will then 'stop payment', that is no payment will be made from the drawer's account on which it has been drawn.

Credit transfer On page 501 we mentioned *Bank Giro*, the credit clearing system which enables money to be moved between the accounts of customers of all the banks in Great Britain. The method, known as *Credit Transfer 1*, enables an account-holder to complete a Bank Giro Credit form (see page 502) and pay in at any bank in the country, not necessarily the bank branch where his account is kept.

Credit Transfer 2 enables a customer to have any number of amounts transferred by issuing one cheque. Many firms use this method to pay their employees. All the payments are listed on a sheet showing the employees' branches and code numbers, and a credit slip is made out for each one. The firm writes one cheque for the total amount. The list of payments to be made, the slips and the cheque are sent or handed to the firm's own branch who then distributes the credits to the banks to which they are addressed.

The credit transfer system can also be used by a bank customer to instruct his branch to transfer money from his account to another account at any other bank. A non-customer, that is a person without a bank account, can also pay money through the Bank Giro credit transfer system; he hands in the amount of cash, completes a form and pays a small charge. There is no charge for the service so it is cheaper to use this method of payment than to obtain a postal order and mail it in a stamped envelope.

Traders' credits The system of traders' credits is available to anyone, whether or not he is an account-holder. An account-holder gives the bank a list of his creditors and the amount owed to each one. He writes out a cheque for the total amount. The bank debits his account for the sum on the cheque and makes credit transfers for the correct amount to each creditor's account. Someone without a bank account can give the bank cash for the total amount plus a service charge and the bank makes credit transfers to the creditors.

Some firms with a large number of bills to pay find it more economical to negotiate a fee for the bank to make their payments instead of employing staff to write out cheques and envelopes and paying for postage.

Direct Debit Another method of paying routine accounts is to give authority to the creditor to make a **direct debit**. This means that instead of the payer instructing his bank to pay the amount, the payee gives the instruction. When the amount of a regular payment is known a standing order can be arranged, but in the case of fluctuating amounts direct debit is useful to the creditor as

STANDING ORDER DIRECT DEBIT AUTHORITY

Name and address of Bank Branch: ....

....

....

I/We ....

....

authorise you with effect from .... and until further notice in writing to charge to my/our account with you, on or about the .... day of every month at the instance of the ABBEY NATIONAL BUILDING SOCIETY by direct debit the sum of £.............. (Amount in words .... pounds)

S.A.Y.E. ACCOUNT NUMBER .... Signature ....

Direct Debit Authority form.

it saves him checking to see if an account has been paid. It is also useful to the debtor because he does not have to check whether he has received and paid the account.

Standing Orders Many individuals and organisations have regular payments to make. These can be arranged as Standing Orders or Banker's Orders. The bank is instructed to pay a certain sum to a specific payee on a particular date each year, quarter or month. Payments are made automatically at the right time and then appear on the account-holder's Statement of Account. A customer can stop the standing order at any time.

If paying by Bankers' Order, please return this page intact to the RAC at the address shown overleaf

BANKERS' ORDER in favour of **THE ROYAL AUTOMOBILE CLUB**

NAME OF MEMBER'S BANK ....

BRANCH ADDRESS ....

Please pay **NOW** the sum of £ to NATIONAL WESTMINSTER BANK LTD., 1 St. James's Square, S.W.1.
Code No. 60-00-09 quoting A/c No. 13381989

and **ANNUALLY** thereafter on .... until further notice the sum of £
quoting A/c No. 13381997

Full Name ....
(BLOCK LETTERS)

To the Remitting Bank: Please quote the undermentioned reference on your CREDIT TRANSFER SLIP

Member's Signature ....
Member's Bank A/c No. ....
Date ....

__/ /____/____

A standing order form. Forms for standing orders are usually supplied by the firm or organisation to whom the money is to be paid. Instructions for standing orders may also be made by letter from the customer to his bank branch.

Clearing a cheque Clearing a cheque means passing it through the banking system so that the payee's account is credited and the drawer's account debited for the amount of the cheque. To explain the system of clearing a cheque we will use the example of a cheque drawn on the National Westminster Bank (where the drawer has his account) in favour of a payee with his account at Barclays Bank.

When the payee pays in the cheque at his branch, it is credited to his account. The cheque is sent together with all the other cheques paid in that day, to the Clearing Department at Barclays head office. (In addition to this system, each bank has its own branch clearing—cheques drawn on different branches of the same bank are settled between those branches—and some towns have local clearing, but finally all cheques are sent to the Clearing Department of the bank's head office.) The Clearing Department makes a list of all the cheques that come in that day and puts this record on microfilm. The cheque is then sent to the Clearing Department at the head office of National Westminster with all the other cheques drawn on the National Westminster. All the cheques are then sent back to the branches on which they are drawn (where they are filed, as explained on page 503), but the records are sent to the Clearing House, a building in Lombard Street in the City of London.

The Clearing House is the place where all the member banks, called Clearing Banks, meet to exchange records of cheques and to arrange the transfer of money to pay for these cheques. All the large British banks are Clearing Banks.

Because a payment by cheque is the transfer of money from the drawer's account to the payee's account, the bank on which the cheque is drawn, National Westminster, must transfer the amount of the cheque to the bank of the payee, Barclays. However, since millions of cheques are cleared every day, a separate transfer is not made for every individual cheque. Barclays adds up the total amount it is owed by National Westminster from cheques paid to Barclays and drawn on National Westminster that day. National Westminster adds up the total owed to it by Barclays from cheques paid into National Westminster and drawn on Barclays that day. For example, National Westminster may owe Barclays £1 million and Barclays may owe National Westminster £800,000. The difference between these totals for the day is the actual amount that is transferred, in this case £200,000, from National Westminster to Barclays. The transfer is made between the banks' accounts at the Bank of England.

Cheques drawn on different branches of the same bank are cleared within the branch clearing system of the bank. If the payee's branch and the drawer's branch are in the same locality outside London, the cheque may be cleared under local arrangements. All other cheques are sent to the Clearing Department at the banks' head offices in London to be cleared through the Clearing House.

Credit cards Credit cards are not really a method of payment because actual payment is made later, usually by cheque. There are many types of credit card; some are issued by banks to their customers, others can be obtained from credit card organisations either free, e.g. Barclaycard, or by giving good references and paying an annual subscription, e.g. Diners Club, American Express. Many

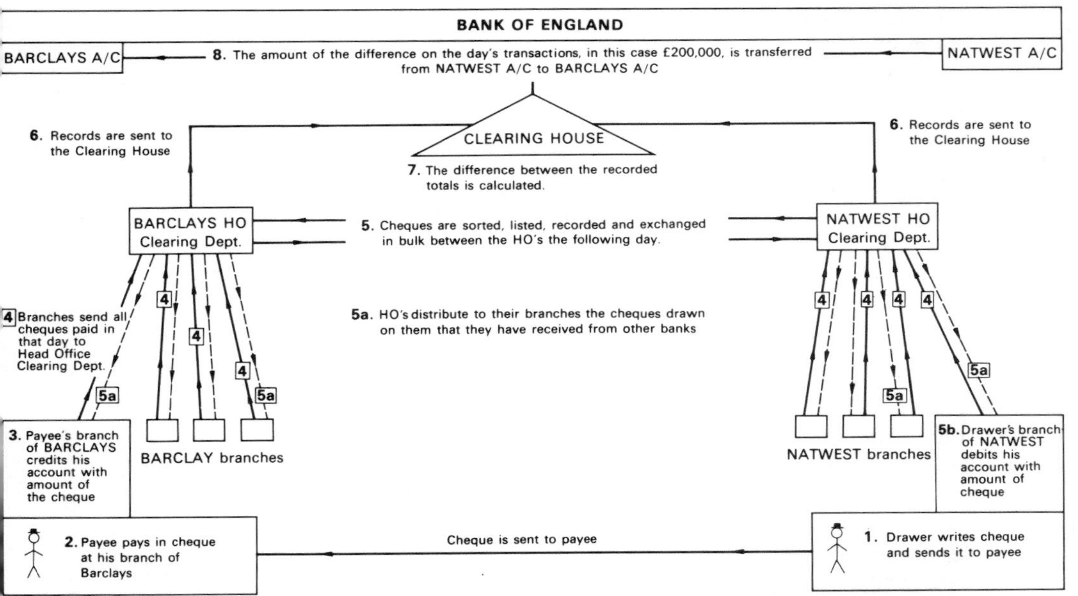

How a cheque is cleared. 1. The drawer writes a cheque and sends it to the payee. 2. The payee pays in the cheque at his branch of Barclays. 3. The payee's branch of Barclays credits his account with the amount of the cheque. 4. The branches send all cheques paid in that day to their Head Office Clearing Departments. 5. The clearing departments of the banks' head offices sort, list and record the cheques; the actual cheques are exchanged in bulk the following day. (5a. The Head Offices distribute to their branches the cheques drawn on them that they have received from other banks. 5b. The drawer's branch of NATWEST debits his account with amount of cheque.) 6. The clearing departments of the banks' head offices send the records to the Clearing House. 7. At the Clearing House the difference between the recorded totals is calculated to find out how much money one bank owes the other. 8. The amount of the difference on the day's transactions, in this case £200,000, is transferred from National Westminster Bank's account at the Bank of England to Barclays Bank's account at the Bank of England.

cards are issued by individual groups for specific purposes such as air travel, car hire, petrol, etc.

A firm which accepts credit cards invoices the appropriate company (Diners Club, Barclaycard, Access etc.) which pays the amount owed and in turn invoices the card user at the end of every month.

Barclaycard and Access allow holders an extended credit service whereby only a minimum of £6 or fifteen per cent of the total debt need be paid, the balance being carried forward at an interest charge of one and a half per cent. If a cash loan is required this can be obtained at any branch of the Barclays Group or the Bank of Scotland at an interest charge of two and a half per cent. Each cardholder has a credit limit which must not be exceeded by either credit spending, extended credit or loan.

Bank credit cards can be used for cashing cheques up to a certain amount at branches anywhere in the country, and in certain places in Europe.

Cheque cards In recent years the banks have introduced **cheque cards** to make it easier for customers to pay for goods. The cheque cards, which have a specimen signature, act as a form of identification for the customer. When a customer writes a cheque using his cheque card, the person receiving the cheque writes the number of the card on the back of the cheque. The bank guarantees to honour that cheque and pay the payee, even if the cheque would have bounced in normal circumstances. This guarantee is only on sums up to £50. With a cheque card a customer can cash cheques at any bank or buy goods and the bank cashing the cheque or the person selling the goods knows he will get his money providing the cheque has been drawn in accordance with the instructions issued with cheque cards.

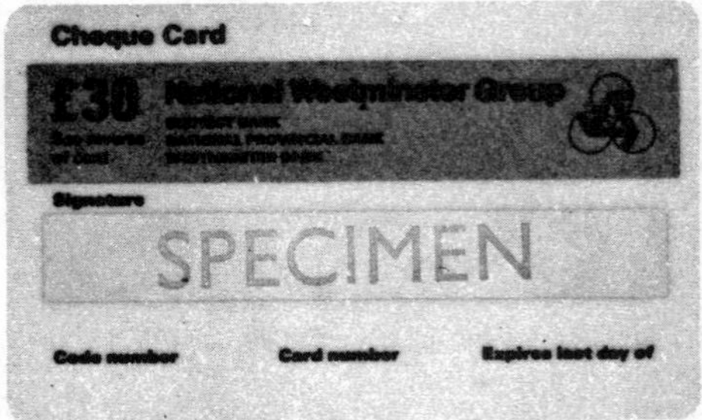

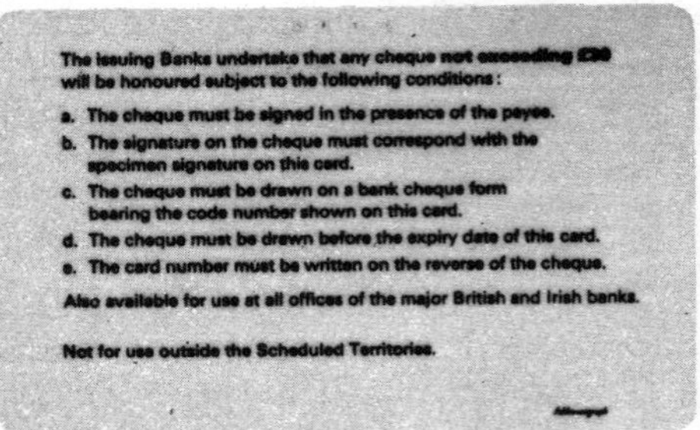

A cheque Card (front and back).

Barclaycard.

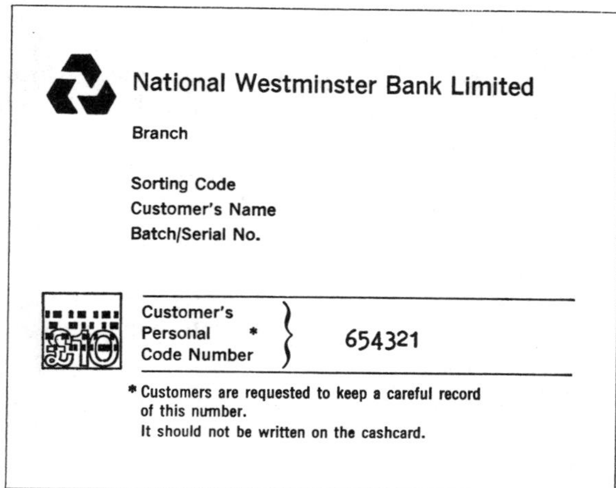

National Westminster Bank Limited

Branch

Sorting Code
Customer's Name
Batch/Serial No.

Customer's Personal * Code Number } 654321

* Customers are requested to keep a careful record of this number.
It should not be written on the cashcard.

24-hour cashcard and envelope.

Budget accounts As most people have large bills to pay at certain times of the year, the banks have a system called the *Budget Account* which, as its name suggests, helps customers to budget. The budget account-holder totals his expected annual expenditure on necessary items, such as electricity, clothes, rates and car licence. To this total is added a charge of operating the account. The final total is divided by 12 and each month this amount is transferred from the customer's account to the budget account.

The customer has a separate cheque book for his budget account and he can pay his bills when they arrive with the cheques as he would with a current account. The budget account-holder can make a payment that overdraws his account so long as that payment is not more than one-quarter of the annual total expenditure. No interest is charged on *budget account* overdrafts as this is covered by the service charge.

Bank Reconciliation Statement The balance shown on a Bank Statement seldom agrees with a firm's or an individual's own records; or, to put it another way, the final balance shown in the Bank Statement is rarely the current balance by the time the Statement is received. The reason for this is that the Bank Statement will not include records of transactions that have taken place since the last entry on it, which will of course have been made before the Statement was posted from the bank. During those few days some cheques may have been written which have not yet been debited; or some cheques may have been paid in but not yet credited; or some bank charges may have been debited which the account-holder has not included in his own calculations; or he may have forgotten to debit some standing orders.

To reconcile the two figures (the balance shown on the Bank Statement and the balance shown in his own records) an account-holder must prepare a *Bank Reconciliation Statement*, that is a statement which adjusts the balance shown in the Bank Statement to the current balance by entering those transactions which have taken place since the last entry on the Statement.

1 List the cheques outstanding, that is those which have not yet been presented for payment.
2 List credits outstanding, that is sums paid into the bank but not yet credited.
3 Enter as debits any banker's or standing orders or bank charges (ledger fees), and add any receipts such as salary credits received by the bank direct.

The importance of a Bank Reconciliation Statement can be understood when you think of the vast sums of money that could be outstanding to a Company's account at the bank.

Other banking facilities In addition to providing the various means for payment and for drawing cash which we have just described, banks provide many other facilities for their customers.

NIGHT SAFE A customer may make an arrangement with the bank which allows him to use the night safe. This is built into the outside wall of the bank. The bank gives the customer a pouch which has two keys; one key is held by the customer, the other is kept in the bank vault in a sealed envelope.

The customer fills in a paying-in slip or paying-in book in the usual way and puts it in the pouch with the money he wants to bank. Then he locks the pouch and puts it into the night safe. The next day, during normal banking hours, the customer goes to the bank and collects the pouch and the counterfoil of the paying-in slip or the paying-in book. This service is of great use to shopkeepers and other businessmen who are unable to pay-in during normal banking hours yet do not wish to keep large sums of money on their premises overnight.

LOANS AND OVERDRAFT FACILITIES Customers can borrow money from their banks and also overdraw—that is, draw money in excess of the balance in their current accounts—if they have previously obtained the permission of the bank manager.

TRAVELLER'S CHEQUES Banks sell traveller's cheques and foreign currency to customers who are going abroad either on holiday or on business. Sterling traveller's cheques are issued in denominations of £2, £5, £10, £20 and £50; traveller's cheques can also be bought in other currencies. It is important to make a note of the numbers on traveller's cheques as soon as they are bought in case they are lost or stolen. The list of numbers should, of course, be kept separately from the cheques. If traveller's cheques are mislaid, the issuing bank must be informed immediately so that 'cashing' by unauthorised persons can be stopped and reimbursement obtained.

OVERSEAS TRADE Banks assist their customers with references and exchange control formalities, and provide information on trade statistics, licensing regulations, foreign markets and economic conditions.

ADVICE AND INFORMATION Advice on insurance, income tax, investment, Trusts and Wills, is available from all the leading banks. A customer's bank will hold his Will and act as executor.

The Role of Banks in British Financial Institutions In this section we have concentrated on the methods of payment available through the banking services. The role of the banks and other financial institutions as suppliers of credit to finance commercial and industrial undertakings is described on pages 325 to 331 in Chapter 8, Business Background.

Overseas payments There are two principal methods of making payments to people or companies in countries abroad.
Bills of Exchange Bills of Exchange are used in the same way as cheques, except that a time for payment is set. Bills are normally payable 'at sight', i.e. within three days of presentation to a bank for payment, or at 30 days, 60 days, 90 days or 180 days. This means that the bills will be honoured at the stated number of days from date of issue and is a way of giving credit to customers. Sometimes the length of time is related to delivery date of the goods.
Documentary credit Documentary credit is a way of ensuring that the supplier and the customer can rely on receiving the money and the goods respectively. When goods are ordered the customer arranges for his bank to hold the required amount of money and is given a letter stating that this is being done. He sends a duplicate of the letter to the supplier, who, when he has despatched the goods, presents it (with the invoice and Bill of Lading) for payment.

Discount documents are used when customer and supplier have good business relations. The customer pays either at the time of ordering or shipment and is given a small discount by the supplier, who thus does not have to wait for payment.

THE POST OFFICE

The Post Office provides facilities for making payments in Britain and overseas through postal and money orders and the National Giro. Anyone can buy a postal or money order and anyone aged 15 or over or any business can open a National Giro account with the deposit of £1.

Making payments If you wish to send money through the post for small amounts, or to someone who does not have a bank account, or if you yourself do not have a bank account, a postal order can be bought at the post office.

Postal orders are available for amounts from 10p to £1 and for £2, £3, £4, £5, £6, £7, £8, £9 and £10. If you wish to send a postal order for a sum for which none is available, not more than two stamps may be stuck on the postal order to complete the required amount. For example, if you wished to send someone 19½p you would buy a 17½p postal order and stick on a 2p stamp.

When you buy a postal order you must pay a fee. This is the charge made for the issue of a postal order. The fee on a postal order of 10p to £1 in value is 8p, and on a postal order of £2 or more it is 10p.

To complete a postal order, fill in the name of the payee in the space provided and the office of payment. If you do not know the post office most convenient to the payee, fill in the name of the town or district where the payee lives. The order may then be cashed at any post office in the place named.

You should also complete the counterfoil which is provided on every postal order. When you have filled in the name of the payee, the date sent, the office of payment, etc., tear off the counterfoil and keep it with the correspondence covering the despatch of the postal order.

Postal orders may be 'crossed', like cheques. 'Crossed' postal orders may only be paid into a bank account.

An 'uncrossed' postal order may be cashed at a post office. Before payment is made the payee must sign his name in the space provided. This is a form of receipt.

INLAND TELEGRAPH MONEY ORDER An **inland telegraph money order** is used to send any sum of money (not exceeding £100) to a specified person by telegraph. Payment is made at the post office requested by the sender.

An application form, supplied by the post office, for the purchase of a money

Stamp of Office

REQUEST FOR INLAND MONEY ORDER | No.

FOR £ s. d. PLEASE FILL IN THIS FORM IN BLOCK CAPITAL LETTERS

PAYABLE TO | Mr., Mrs., or Miss | Christian Name (or Initials) or forename | Surname

PAYABLE AT ....POST OFFICE

NAME AND ADDRESS OF SENDER ....

PAYMENT THROUGH A BANK Do you wish the Order to be crossed for payment through a Bank?........................ (This is advisable if it will not inconvenience the Payee).

BY TELEGRAPH If you wish the Order to be telegraphed write "BY TELEGRAPH" across the front of this form and fill in, overleaf, the address and other particulars in the appropriate space.

P.T.O.

SENDER The name and address of the sender are required for official purposes.

PAYMENT Payment will be subject to the possession by the Postmaster of sufficient funds.

DEFERRED PAYMENT Payment of an ordinary Money Order may be deferred for any period not exceeding 10 days. No extra fee is charged and the Postmaster-General accepts no liability for the payment of an Order before the time specified has expired. If deferred payment is desired the Sender must fill in and sign the following request and INFORM THE ISSUING OFFICER so that instructions may be given to the Paying Office. Payment of a Telegraph Money Order may not be deferred.

I request that the Money Order relative to this application may not be paid until................days after the date of issue.

.... *Signature of Sender.*

FOR TELEGRAPH MONEY ORDERS ONLY.

If you wish the Order to be telegraphed write "BY TELEGRAPH" across the front of this form and fill in the particulars below. Telegraph Money Orders are made payable at the office nearest the recipient's address: but when the Telegraph Money Order is payable in Dublin, the name of the Post Office at which payment is required to be made should be stated in the appropriate space overleaf.

ADDRESS TO WHICH THIS TELEGRAPH ORDER IS TO BE SENT ....

PRIVATE MESSAGE (IF ANY) ....

The name (or name and address) of the Sender, if to be communicated to the Payee, must form part of the private message.

If the Payee is a woman the prefix "Mrs." or "Miss" should be given for inclusion in the telegram of advice.

If the Telegraph Order is to be called for at a Post Office the words "Post Office" should be entered in the address space and the Sender should inform the Payee where to apply for the Order.

P803B

2/63—McC & Co Ltd—51/7987

An Inland money order request form.

order must be completed. The words 'By Telegraph' must be written across the completed application form.

The charge for an inland telegraph money order is £3 plus:

1 a fixed charge of £1.40 plus Value Added Tax for the standard telegram of advice (£1.50 plus Value Added Tax for orders payable in the Irish Republic);
2 7p per word plus Value Added Tax for any private message sent with the order.

When you send a telegraph money order you will be given a certificate of issue.

OVERSEAS MONEY ORDERS may be used to send money to some foreign countries. The *Post Office Guide* gives full particulars of those countries to which money orders may be sent, and the maximum amount which may be transmitted. A special application form must be used. The issuing fee charged is higher than that on an inland money order. Money orders may also be sent by telegraph to some countries.

Applications to remit money orders to countries outside the Scheduled Territories (formerly known as the Sterling Area) must be made on form P810B, where the purpose of the remittance must be stated. The form is obtainable at any money order office, where it may be ascertained which countries are outside the Scheduled Territories. The Scheduled Territories are those countries, which, although they may have their own currencies for day-to-day purposes, use British currency as a common factor in overseas trading, to measure the value of goods and services bought and sold. About half the trade of the world is done in sterling.

THE NATIONAL GIRO The word Giro comes from the Greek *guros* meaning wheel and describes the circular way the Giro system passes money around from one person or firm to another. A form of the Giro system began in Austria in 1883 and since then it has spread throughout the Western hemisphere and is now operating in most European countries and in many parts of Africa and Asia.

The National Giro is the Post Office banking service which provides a fast and economic means of collecting money and making payments within the United Kingdom and to many other countries. The National Giro Centre at Bootle in Lancashire keeps records of all Giro accounts; it has large computers and the most modern accounting and data processing machines. Some Giro transactions may be carried out over the counter at post offices but the debiting and crediting of accounts is done at the National Giro Centre.

Types of account The National Giro offers two types of account: the private account for individuals and the business account for large organisations. Giro accounts like current accounts in banks are intended for making payments and no interest is paid on deposits. Application forms for Giro accounts are available at any post office.

Giro statement. Business account-holders receive a statement through the post from the National Giro Centre every day. The statement shows the state of the account on the day it is prepared: the opening balance; each debit to the account and the total debit; each credit and the total credit; the balance after the day's transactions. There is usually no charge for daily statements.

Private account-holders receive a statement every time money is credited to their accounts or after every ten debits, or every three months if there were no credits or fewer than ten debits during that period. These statements are free.

STATEMENT OF ACCOUNT
Number 58 627 3966 27FEB71

National Giro
Bootle
Lancs

CK 393433
Serial 9

Summary

previous balance	20FEB71	£52.17
total debits		49.88
total credits		32.53
current balance	27FEB71	£34.82

Transactions

		£
	DEBITS	
24FEB	S 2143211 BLDG SOC	19.35
26FEB	S 1769281 ANY UDC	4.00
27FEB	S 3173962 FPLY INS	5.00
27FEB	T 1031234 B GAS BD	11.50
27FEB	P 0016 OUTPAYMENT	10.00
	FEES	0.03
27FEB	CREDITS	
	D SELF	5.25
	T 4286237 PAY	27.28

THE VISITOR
GIRO EXHIBITION
ANYTOWN

A Automatic debit transfer
D Deposit
I Inpayment
P Payment
S Standing order
T Giro transfer
for further information see overleaf

A GIRO STATEMENT HELPS YOU TO KEEP A SIMPLE CHECK ON YOUR EXPENDITURE
YOU GET ONE EVERY TIME AN AMOUNT IS PAID INTO, OR WHENEVER 10 PAYMENTS
HAVE BEEN MADE FROM YOUR ACCOUNT

Stationery Each Giro account-holder has personalised forms for Giro transactions which he has to purchase unless he participates in a group scheme. Giro transfer forms, deposit forms and cheques are printed with the account-holder's name, address and account number. The account-holder is provided with envelopes, which are printed with the address of the National Giro Centre, giving free first-class postage. Since most forms have to be posted to the National Giro Centre, this saves the customer writing out an envelope and paying postage.

Account-holder paying money into his own account Account holders make deposits to their own accounts by paying money in at any of the 22,000 post offices in the United Kingdom or by sending bank cheques payable to them to the National Giro Centre. In both cases the account-holder fills in a personalised deposit form with the amount and gives it in or sends it with the deposit.

Account-holder paying another account-holder A person who has a Giro account uses a transfer to pay another Giro account holder. The person paying the money fills in his personalised transfer form with the amount of money to be transferred and the account number of the payee. A message for the payee can be written on the back of the transfer form. The completed form is sent in a postage-paid envelope to the National Giro Centre where the amount is debited from the account of the person making the transfer and credited to the account of the payee. The transfer form is sent to the payee with the statement showing the credit to his account.

Low balance charge The account-holder is not charged for making a transfer unless he has to pay a low balance charge. This charge of 4p is deducted from any account that has an opening balance of less than £30 on the day the account is debited.

Standing order If an account-holder wants to pay another account-holder a fixed sum of money at regular intervals he can arrange for a standing order. He fills in a standing order form giving the details of the amount to be paid, the dates of the payments, his account number and the account number of the payee. This form is sent to the National Giro Centre where his account is debited for the amount and the payee's account credited on the specified dates without further instructions. This service is free unless a low balance charge has to be applied on the day the debit is made.

Giro standing orders can only be made within the Giro system. A Giro account-holder cannot make out a standing order to someone who does not have a Giro account. Money cannot be transferred from a Giro account to a bank account except in one instance: a Giro account-holder can make one transfer a month from his Giro account to his own bank account.

Automatic debit transfers A Giro account-holder can pay varying amounts on fixed or variable dates to another account holder by an automatic debit transfer. For example, a Giro account-holder with a charge account at a department store may arrange to pay the store by automatic debit transfers, although the amounts vary and his visits to the store are irregular.

The account-holder signs an authorisation form and sends it to the store. The store sends the form to the National Giro Centre. After that the National Giro Centre will act at any time it is instructed by the store by making a transfer from the customer's account to the store's account for any amount specified by the store.

To safeguard the customer the store must agree that the National Giro Centre can reverse any transfer of money if the customer disputes the amount. In addition the store agrees to make up any loss to Giro through misuse of the automatic debit transfer system.

The customer receives a statement from Giro after every debit transfer is made. Both the statement and the transfer are free.

Person without a Giro account paying an account-holder. A person who does not have a Giro account can pay money to a Giro account-holder in two ways. If the person paying the money wants to pay in cash and if he knows the Giro account number of the payee, he can pay in the money at any post office using an Inpayment form for a small charge; or he can send a bank cheque to the payee who then sends the cheque to the National Giro Centre with a deposit form. A person without a Giro account should not send bank cheques directly to the National Giro Centre even if he knows the payee's account number.

When a Giro account-holder sends a bank cheque to the National Giro Centre there is a three day waiting period before the cheque is credited to his account so that the cheque can be cleared through the bank clearing system (see pages 509 to 510 for information on the bank clearing system).

Agent deposit service Some firms have branches, representatives or salesmen in different parts of the country who receive cash from customers. Under the agent deposit service all the salesmen of a firm can deposit money at their local post offices for credit to the firm's Giro account. If a firm uses this service the salesmen depositing money do not have to pay the usual inpayment charge. The firm's fee for the service is negotiated with the Post Office. If there are large sums of cash to be deposited, a post office van will pick up the money and take it to the post office for an extra fee.

Giro cheques The Giro cheque may be used like a bank cheque, although Giro account-holders can pay each other by transfer. All Giro cheques are open but the drawer should cross the cheque himself before he sends it or gives it to a person without a Giro account.

Girocheque 72–00–00

The Post Office
National Giro
Bootle Lancs GIR 0AA

19

2371

pay ________________ or order

amount ________________

£

<3>60 000 0001

at ________________ post office

signature/s

J B CARRINGTON
SPECIMEN ORDER ONLY
REFER TO
NATIONAL GIRO CENTRE
BOOTLE LANCS
GIR 0AA

Please leave the space below clear for use at the National Giro Centre

SPECIMEN ONLY

⑈72⑈ 2371⑆ 60000000⑈

Account-holder paying a person without a Giro account When a Giro account-holder uses the Giro system to pay someone without a Giro account, he writes out a personalised Giro cheque and crosses it. The payee can pay the Giro cheque into his bank account or endorse the cheque, that is sign it on the back, for someone else to pay into his bank or Giro account. A small charge is made to the Giro account-holder when a Giro cheque is debited to his account.

The Giro system cannot be used to settle a transaction if neither party is a Giro account-holder.

Withdrawing up to £30 by cashing a cheque Giro account-holders may withdraw up to £30 from their accounts by cashing one of their personalised open cheques at one of two post offices nominated for the purpose when they opened their accounts. The account-holder has a Giro card with a specimen of his signature which he presents with the cheque at the post office counter. The cheque is sent to the National Giro Centre where the account is debited for the amount on the cheque.

Giro Gold Card National Giro offers approved account-holders extended cheque cashing facilities which are similar to the cheque card available to bank customers. The Giro Gold Card enables an approved customer to cash cheques for amounts up to £50 on every other day at any post office in the United Kingdom.

No overdraft facilities Giro account-holders are not allowed overdraft facilities. If a Giro account-holder makes a transfer for an amount greater than his balance, the transfer is refused.

The rules about cashing cheques are designed to prevent accounts being overdrawn. Account-holders are allowed to cash cheques at only two nominated post offices so that the National Giro Centre can easily order cheques to be refused if the account-holder has no money in his account. As a further safeguard, account-holders may cash cheques on alternate days only. This allows the National Giro Centre time to inform the nominated post offices if the account-holder has emptied his account with the last cheque he has cashed.

If an account-holder overdraws his account by cashing a £19 cheque when he has a balance of only £17, for example, the National Giro Centre writes to the account-holder to warn him not to overdraw again. If the account-holder does overdraw again, his account is closed unless there are exceptional circumstances.

Authenticated cheques In certain circumstances listed below an account-holder must have a cheque authenticated by the National Giro Centre before he can cash it or send it to the payee. Authentication means that the amount on the cheque is debited to the drawer's account before the cheque is cashed by the drawer or given to the payee to cash. This is another safeguard to prevent overdrawing. The drawer is charged 10p for each authenticated cheque.

The circumstances where authentication is needed are:

1 When the account-holder wants to cash one of his own cheques for more than £30 (but less than £50) at one of the two nominated post offices.
2 When the account-holder wants to cash a cheque at a post office other than the two nominated ones.

3 When the account-holder wants to send or give the payee an open cheque that the payee can cash. If the open cheque is for more than £50, the drawer must nominate the post office where the cheque should be cashed.

Pre-authenticated cheques Business account-holders can arrange to have pre-authenticated Giro cheques. These are cheques that have already been authenticated and they may be cashed at any post office by the payee. Pre-authenticated cheques are used to pay employees working away from the firm's offices or to pay company pensions. This enables company pensions to be collected at the same time as state pensions.

International Giro Firms and individuals in Britain can make or receive payments through Giro to or from any other country operating a Giro system. These countries are Austria, Belgium, Denmark, Finland, France, Italy, Japan, Luxemburg, Netherlands, Norway, Spain, Sweden, Switzerland and West Germany. Outpayments can be made to any country in the world, subject to Exchange Control regulations.

MISCELLANEOUS SERVICES PROVIDED BY THE POST OFFICE

All post offices sell *National Insurance stamps* and the following pensions and allowances are paid at most post offices: widows' pensions, retirement pensions, war pensions, sickness benefit, supplementary pensions or allowances, maternity allowances, family allowances.

A *National Savings Bank Ordinary account* may be opened with 25p at any of the 21,000 savings bank post offices in the United Kingdom. Deposits earn interest at the rate of 5 per cent per annum.

An *Investment account* may be opened with an initial deposit of at least £1. The interest rate varies but is higher than the Ordinary account rate.

The National Savings Bank operates a service called *Save As You Earn* or *SAYE*. The saver signs an agreement to save a fixed amount (minimum £4, maximum £20) every month for five years. At the end of five years the saver is repaid the money he has saved in accordance with the revaluation of each payment in line with the Government Index of Retail Prices. Alternatively, the saver can leave his money in the Savings Bank for a further two years without making any more payments. At the end of that time he is repaid the re-adjusted value of his savings plus a bonus equal to two monthly payments. Anyone aged 16 or over can save through the SAYE service in one of three ways: (a) Through the Post Office—the saver can make cash payments each month at the post office or he can have the amount transferred to the National Savings Bank from his National Giro account every month. (b) Through a bank—a saver with a bank account can use a standing order to pay the monthly amount. (c) Through his employer—if the saver's employer participates in a SAYE service, the monthly amounts are deducted from the saver's wages or salary and paid directly to the

National Savings Bank. The SAYE contract forms are available from post offices, banks and participating employers.

Post offices also sell National Savings Stamps, National Savings Certificates, British Savings Bonds and Premium Savings Bonds.

British Savings Bonds are sold in units of £5. An interest rate of $8\frac{1}{2}$ per cent per annum is paid twice yearly on the current issue, and the Bonds are repayable at a premium, i.e. at more than purchase price at the end of five years.

Premium Savings Bonds may be bought in various denominations in £5 units, subject to a minimum of £5, but no person may own more than 2000. These Bonds earn no interest, but the owner of a Bond has the chance of winning a tax-free prize in monthly and weekly prize draws. No Bond is included in the draw until it has been held for three clear months.

The Post Office issues *broadcast receiving licences* and *dog licences*, and *renews motor licences.*

When a new vehicle is first licensed, the motor licence must be issued by the Driver and Vehicle Licensing Centre, Swansea. Motor vehicle licences can be renewed by personal application at the larger money order post offices during normal business hours (but not after 1 p.m. on Saturdays) from 14 days before the expiry of the licence to the 14th of the following month. You should make a note of the renewal date of your boss's motor licence, get a renewal form (R.F.1A) from the post office and prepare it ready for signature. You can get the motor licence renewed by taking the completed form to the post office together with the certificate of insurance, the current test certificate, the Vehicle

Note the *renewal date of your boss's motor licence* in your desk diary and prepare the necessary documents for his signature; car licences can be renewed at the larger money order post offices during normal business hours (but not after 1 p.m. on Saturdays) from 14 days before the expiry of the licence to the 14th of the following month.

Registration Document, the old licence and a cheque or cash covering the cost of the new licence. Licences are issued for four or twelve months. If there has been a change of colour or ownership since the previous licence was issued, the change should have been noted on the registration book by the local taxation authority. Forms (V.E.70) for notifying changes of ownership are obtained from any money order post office.

Application forms for Driving Licences are obtained from post offices, but the completed forms must be sent to the Driver and Vehicle Licensing Centre, Swansea. A *form of application for a Driving Test* is also obtainable from a post office. This form, when completed, must be sent to the Clerk of the Traffic Area where the test is taken. The names and addresses of the traffic areas are listed on the back of the application form.

PLANNING STATISTICS

Statistics are numerical facts collected on a systematic basis. Before collecting the facts it must be decided what purpose the statistics are intended to achieve and what facts are required for this purpose.

Statistics which give only part of a picture are not usually very effective. For example a table which states how many training courses of various kinds have been conducted in an organisation does not really say how much training has been done. To be of value the number of trainees and the number of hours of instruction should be included.

Consequently careful thought must be given to what information is needed before collection of the facts begins.

Statistical material is easiest to understand if it covers specific time periods, e.g. weeks, months, quarters, years. For comparative purposes the period must be identical for each set of figures. Comparison of the value of exports in May 1971 with those in August 1972 would mean nothing because there are factors dependent upon the time of the year which automatically make differences. However, if one wanted to see the trend in exports in recent times a comparison between the last few months would be worthwhile and would also show which particular commodities were increasing/decreasing.

Having decided what numerical facts are needed, collection begins. Statistics may be built up over a period of time as a result of reports being submitted at regular intervals, frequently on a form designed for the purpose.

PRESENTING STATISTICS

Having collected the facts the method of presentation has to be chosen. It will depend on the material to be presented and how it can be shown to best advantage, who is to see it, and what impact is required. There are five main methods of presentations: tables, graphs, charts, diagrams, control charts.

Tables Figures may be typed or printed in tabular columns with an explanatory column, i.e. a column which explains to what the figures refer, e.g. the name of a commodity or place. Presentation of the figures as they stand is not sufficient. There must also be a column showing the point of the statistics, i.e. the purpose, for example a percentage increase/decrease, or monthly/annual totals.

An example of a simple statistical table is shown below.

NUMBER OF TRAINEES

1st January to 30th June, 1972

Type of Course	Jan.	Feb.	Mar.	Apr.	May	June	Total
Reception	18	—	53	21	—	—	92
Telephone/Reception	24	—	42	—	21	—	87
Office Practice	—	—	18	19	—	—	37
Clerical Duties	10	—	—	16	—	—	26
Business Correspondence	—	15	—	—	10	11	36
Typists	—	24	—	—	24	—	48
Stenographers	—	—	21	—	—	—	21
Private Secretaries	—	—	—	—	—	22	22
	52	39	134	56	55	33	369

Graphs A graph is effective as the upward and downward lines enable the increases and decreases to be seen at a glance. Comparison is also easy to indicate in this way by having different types of lines for each subject. Here is an example of monthly sales figures for a period of one year shown on a graph.

Similar figures for a three-year period, using a different type of line for each year, make it easy to compare the difference at any specific time in each year and also to see the changing trend. Coloured

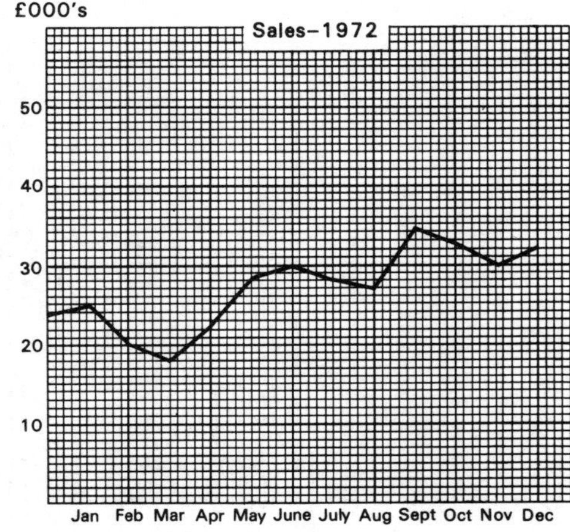

A line graph.

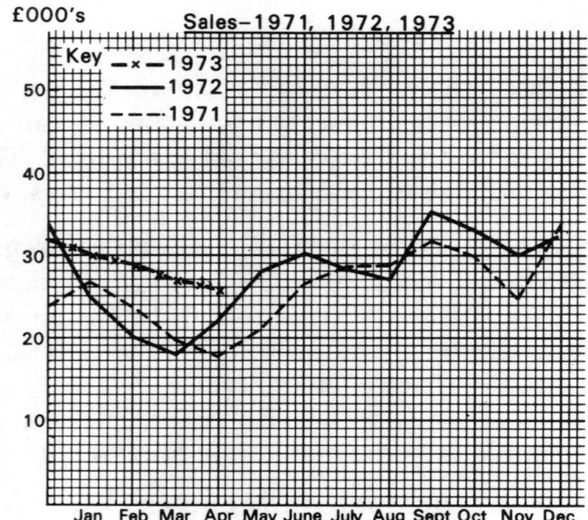

A multi-line graph.

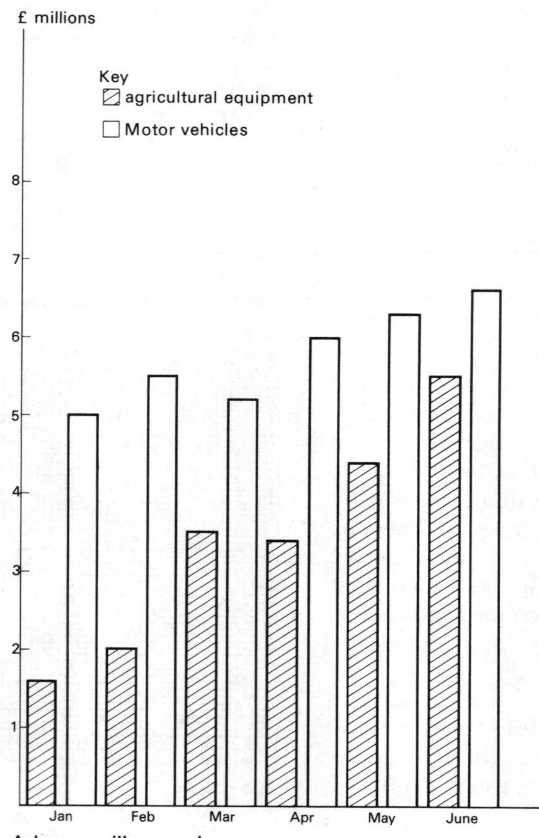

A bar or pillar graph.

lines could be used, a different colour for each year, instead of different types of line. This is sometimes known as a Z-graph.

Another form of graph is the *bar or pillar graph*, so called because columns are used to show the figure at each point. This form of graph is most useful for purposes of comparison. The pillar graph on page 526 shows that the value of agricultural equipment is increasing to the point where it has almost caught up with the value of motor vehicles exported, even though the latter has also increased to some degree.

Similar to the bar graph is a *histogram* which again uses blocks. The blocks are joined so that a continuous line is made.

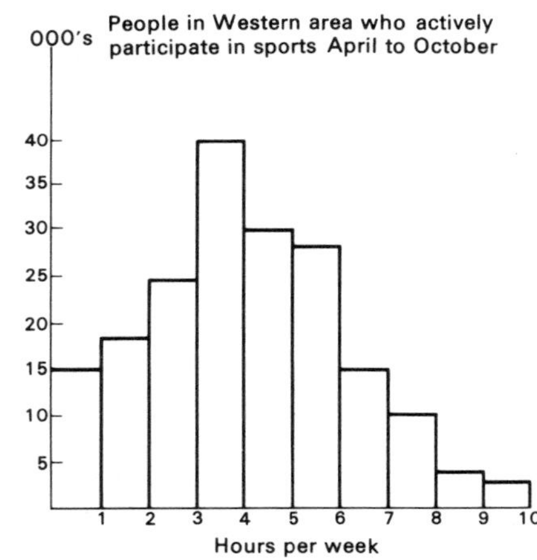

A histogram.

Charts To show the breakdown (or make-up) of statistics in relation to a total a *pie chart* can be drawn. The size of each wedge corresponds to the portion of the whole it represents. The pie chart below shows the percentage of schoolchildren in each of several different types of school.

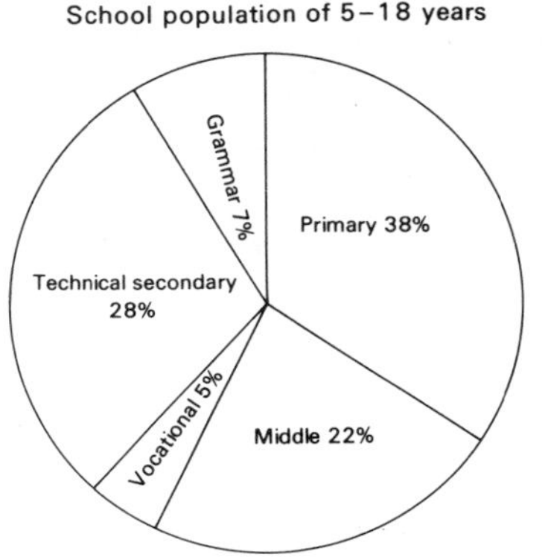

A pie chart.

Bar charts, also called *horizontal bar charts*, can be used to show comparison, e.g. the amount of income tax paid by different sectors of the community.

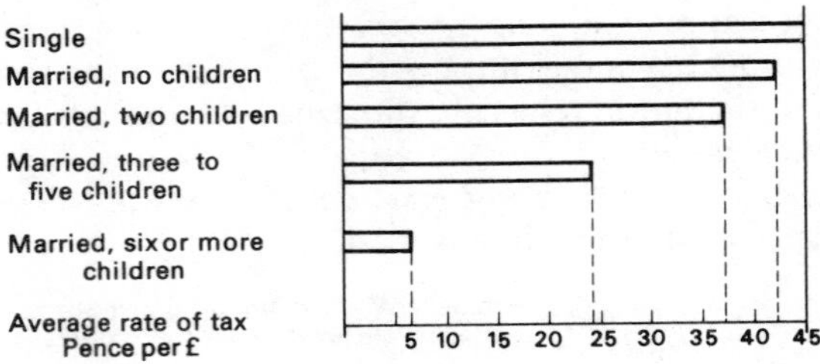

A bar chart is most often used to show time factor. The example below indicates the duration of sections of a job in sequence.

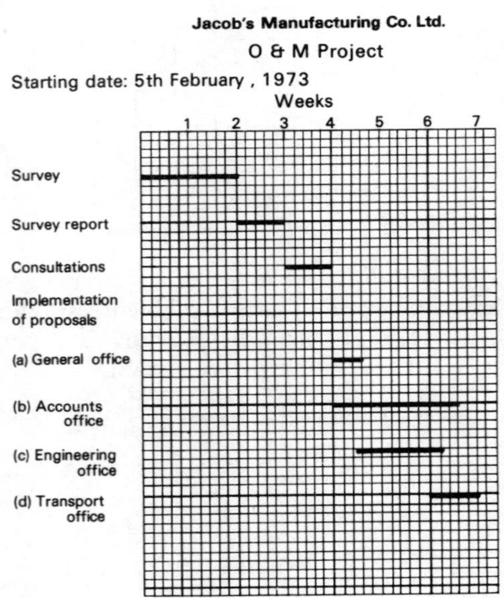

The *Gantt Chart* is a specialised type of bar chart, used to show comparison between work planned and work accomplished in relation to time schedules.

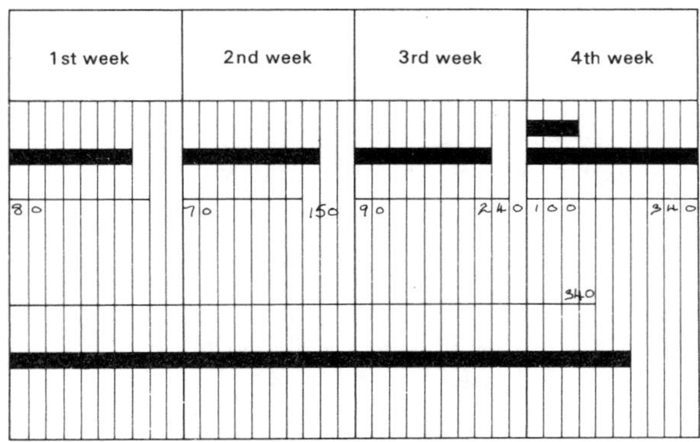

Gantt chart shows the scheduling of physical against budgeted production. The heavy line indicates work scheduled; the light line indicates work accomplished.

The typed chart below shows the assignment of staff to various jobs. A line of x's could be used instead of a straight line. It is easy to see whether any particular individual is free at a given time, or whether he is moderately or heavily loaded.

ASSIGNMENTS SECRETARIAL SECTION 1972

	April	May	June	July	Aug	Sept	Oct	Nov	Dec
Jenks	P. & T. 11—21	P. & T. 1—5 U.A.C. (2 hours p.w. English)	K.T.T.C. STC 22—25—16	U.T.C	Min. of Educ. 31—8 —25				
Lambert	P. & T. 11—21	P. & T. P. & T. 1—5 16—26	- - - - -	- - - -	- - - -	- - - -	- - - -	- - - -	- - - -
Peterson	Tel. 11–13	G.S.S. 3—31 U.T.C. 8—19 U.A.C. (4hrs. p.w. shorthand)	5—	Private Secretaries	—25				—1
Acock		Instructors 3—31	S.T.C. 5—16	S.T.C. 31—11					
Graft	Typists (O.P.) —28	Instructors 3—31	5—	Private Secretariess			U.T.C. (4 hrs. p.w. Bus. Corresp.)		
Pencroft	Typists (T. & E.) —28 U.A.C. (4 hrs. Typing and Office practice)	U.T.C. 8—19 Instructors 3—31	F.U.	Typists (English) 3—	—25	—22			
Anthony	Tel. 11–13	Instructors 3—31		Typists (Typing and O.P.) 3—		—22			

An attractive, simple and effective way of presenting information to a large audience is by a pictorial device known as a *pictogram.* A single figure represents a certain quantity; to increase the quantity more figures are shown—all figures must be the same size.

The pictogram below shows the number of house owners in different income groups.

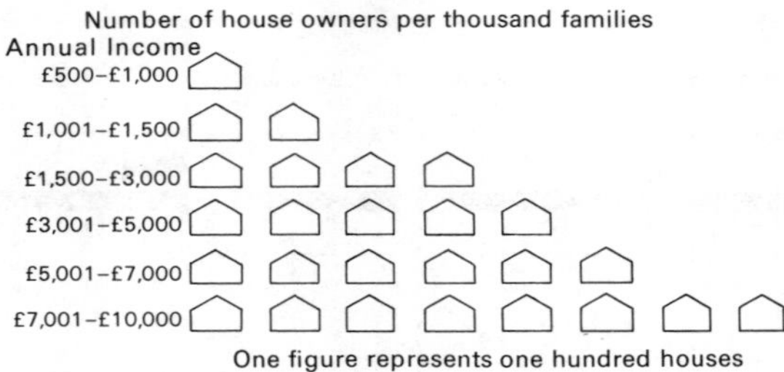

It should be noted that the amounts represented by figures in a pictogram are approximate only.

Diagrams There are many uses for diagrammatic illustration. Diagrams can be used to show the flow of documents, the layout of working areas, the sequential sections of a job, etc. A simple explanatory diagram is shown below.

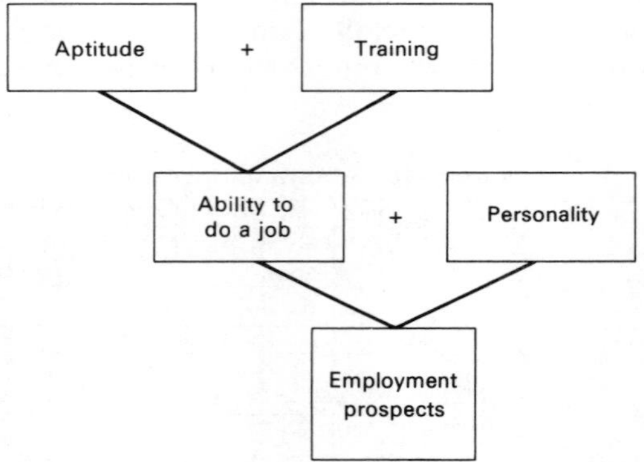

Control charts There are many kinds of charts and boards manufactured for different purposes to present information visually in the office. These aids are intended to give 'at a glance' information and can be kept right up to date by use of signals, flags, markers, etc. This enables a supervisor to keep the progress of jobs under constant surveyance and control. It is easy to see where changes can be made and what effect such changes will have on other aspects of the work. Loading of machines is an example.

Manufactured boards can be mounted singly on a wall, like a picture, or in groups on a pivot. A visual chart is illustrated on page 531.

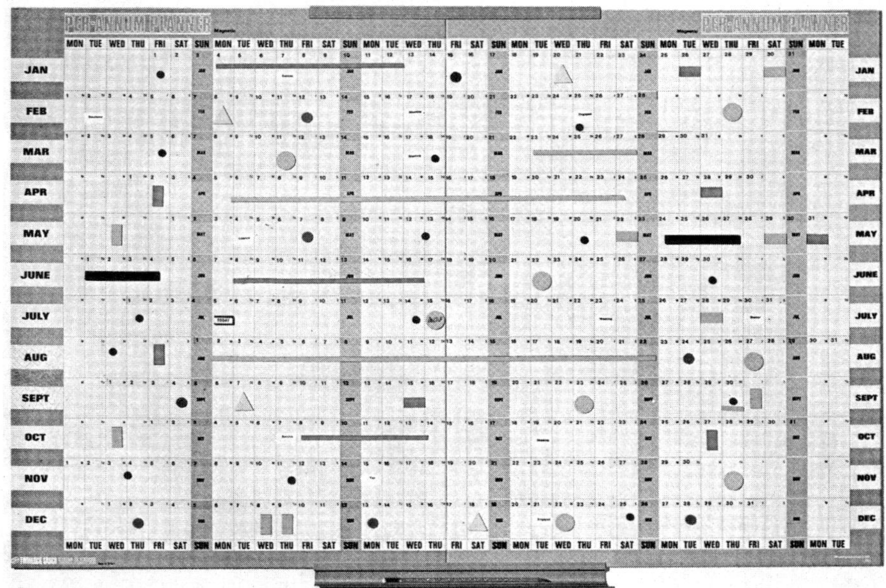

A visual planning chart allowing a day-by-day plan for a full year.

STOCK CONTROL

The purchasing and use of stock items must be carefully controlled. When supplies are ordered the Stores Receiving Officer is normally informed by a copy of the purchase order and/or the invoice. He may receive an advice note from the suppliers before the goods are despatched. A delivery, despatch or consignment note normally accompanies the goods. It is his job to inspect the consignment and make sure it is in good condition. He is responsible for opening the cases or packages and checking the contents. This may be done against the invoice, or it may be done by making an inventory which will be checked against the invoice in the accounts department. The latter method takes more time and can only be used for larger items. After checking a Goods Received Note is sent from the stores to the purchase accounts department so that the invoice can be certified for payment.

A careful record of each item must be kept. Usually a card is completed for each item—its name, reference number, size, colour. Four columns give details of the date of movement, number of articles received, number of articles issued, and the balance remaining. In the case of items for production the job number for which the issue was made may also be given. The cost of items received and issued may be included for certain types of goods and also depend on the accounting system used.

DUPLICATING PAPER Quarto/Pink		Ref. OS 16/3	Max/Min 60/20
Date	Receipt	Issue	Balance
1.8.72		10	25
3.8.72		6	19
14.8.72		5	14
26.8.72	40		64

Ideally no items should ever be 'out of stock'. To ensure this state of affairs it is essential that orders for new stock be placed a certain time in advance of requirements. Basically this means that the buyer must know what the average consumption of a particular item is at any given time (the consumption may vary from month to month, or with seasons) and the time required for delivery. He can then fix a 'minimum' level. This means that when the balance of a certain item comes down to the minimum level an order must be placed. For example, if the average consumption of bond quarto typewriting paper is fifty reams per month and the average time required for delivery is five weeks, this means that it would be wise to place an order when six weeks supply remains, i.e. seventy-five reams.

In the Finance section of this chapter it was mentioned that a company might be in difficulties for cash if it had too large stocks on hand. When a large variety of items is kept over-ordering of several thousand items can result in a serious situation. Therefore 'maximum' levels must also be set. These will depend on consumption and the duration of time for which supplies are to be ordered. Taking the typewriting paper example already mentioned, if it were considered that three months supply should be ordered that would be 150 reams. This would mean that normally an order for this quantity will be placed every three months, but the max/min levels (as they are called) enable the storekeeper to see at a glance whether average consumption is being maintained, falling off or increasing. If it is increasing an investigation might be needed to find the reason.

A secretary is responsible for ordering consumable office supplies for herself and her boss. In a large organisation this will be from the stores. She may also be responsible for supplying stationery to a department. Storage space is nearly always a problem in an office, so she does not want to have more stocks than necessary, but many organisations have specific weekly or monthly dates for ordering of supplies, so she must make sure that she has sufficient stock of every item for the period. The reason for specific requisition dates is to cut down the paper work involved and save the time of the storekeepers. It is useful to make a check list of all items of stationery and office supplies so that the requisition form can be completed from it without having to think of items which might be required. A physical check of the amount on hand is necessary in this case.

Where departmental supplies are under the secretary's control a record should be kept either on cards or in a stock book. Receipts and issues should be entered (with the date of movement) and a 'running balance' kept, i.e. a balance shown after each movement. Thus, it is possible to see at a glance what quantity of any item is on hand. A physical check of the stock against the record should be made at intervals.

Some organisations have a requisition form which is a list of all items available with space to insert the quantity required.

In a small office you may have to order from a stationery supplier. This should be done at regular intervals to avoid unnecessary paper work. Keep a check list and work out minimum levels so that it is easy to see when it is necessary to replenish each item. Monthly orders should be sufficient; less frequent ordering may be possible if reasonable storage facilities are available.

FROM: DEPARTMENT:

ROOM NO.

REQUISITION FOR STATIONERY & OFFICE SUNDRIES

Stationery Department Room M32. Hours of Opening:-

Mon, Tues, Thurs, Fri. 9.30a.m. - 12.30p.m /2 - 4.30p.m.

Weds. 9.30a.m. - 12.30p.m./Closed

QUANTITY	ITEMS

Please attach sample of any special stationery requirements.

SIGNED ....

DATE ....

ADM/10

Stationery can be a very large item of expenditure in an organisation. It is a commodity which lends itself to waste. An inspection of office wastepaper baskets any evening is a very revealing exercise from which it can easily be seen which people are skilled at their jobs. Secretarial staff are often among the worst offenders, throwing away dozens of sheets of typewriting paper, letterheads, duplicating paper, etc., every day. This can soon amount to reams. There is also the waste of time involved in producing work for scrap. These two factors play an important part in the cost of production, which is no less important in an office than it is in a factory. The good secretary sets an example in this, as in other things.

FURTHER READING

Basic Business Studies—Clerical Duties (Chapter 9), Norman E. Worrall, Edward Arnold (Publishers).

Modern Elementary Statistics (Chapter 2), John E. Freund, Prentice Hall.

GROUP DISCUSSION

Discuss—"Every employee in any organisation should be cost conscious." Why should this be so? What responsibility does each employee have for costs? How can every employee play his part in keeping costs to a minimum? Why are costs so important in relation to the financial position of an organisation?

EXERCISES

1 Explain briefly the uses of the Day Books, Cash Book and Journal.

2 What is meant by "balancing an account".

3 All entries made in books of original entry are posted to the ledger. What does this mean?

4 In what book of original entry would the following documents be recorded:

   a Credit note sent to a customer?
   b Invoice received from a supplier?
   c Cheque sent to a supplier?

5 Explain the term "final accounts".

6 What are

   a liabilities?
   b assets?
   c debtors?
   d creditors?
   e liquid capital?

7 State five calculations which can be made on an adding-listing machine.

8 What is meant by 'input' and 'output' in relation to accounting machines.

9 Say to what uses the following machines can be put:

a Non-printing calculating machines.
b Accounting punched card machines.
c Digital computer.

10 You are asked to train a junior clerk how to receive money and undertake the related procedures. Explain what instructions you will give.

11 The cheque shown below is handed to you by a customer. Comment.

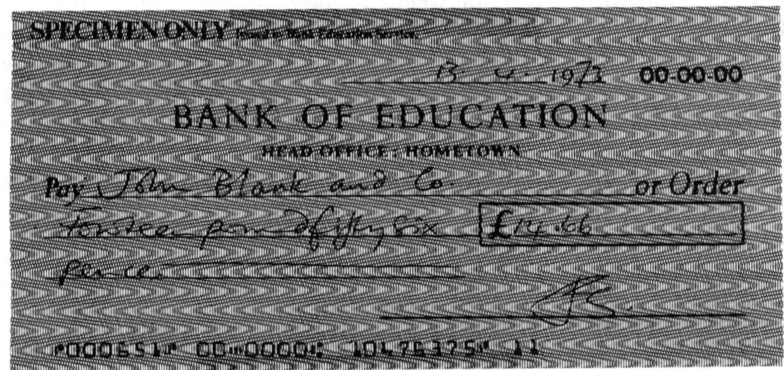

SPECIMEN ONLY

13-4-1973 00-00-00

BANK OF EDUCATION

HEAD OFFICE: HOMETOWN

Pay John Blank and Co or Order

Fourteen pounds fifty six pence £14.66

12 You go to a Government department to pay a sum of money. The cash clerk takes this money and then asks you to return tomorrow for the receipt as his book is finished. Say what action you will take and give reasons.

13 You are a secretary to the Chief Accountant who says he is dissatisfied with the present Petty Cash system used in the organisation. He asks you to write an instruction explaining how to keep an analysed Petty Cash Book using the imprest system.

14 The Chief Accountant complains about the amount of time spent in checking accounts to see if they have been paid. He asks you to draft a letter to be sent to customers explaining the direct debit system. He asks that you make clear the advantages to both the customer and the company.

15 What steps do companies take to prevent fraud in the issuing of cheques?

16 Briefly describe the following:

a an open cheque;
b an overdraft;
c cheque crossing;
d blank cheque;
e refer to drawer.

17 It is possible for anybody to use the National Giro Service for making payments. Explain how the system functions.

18 State the most suitable method of payment for each of the following:

a monthly hire purchase instalment;
b monthly account with a grocer;
c an individual payment of 40 pence for books to be supplied from another town;
d payment to a new overseas supplier;
e refund to a mail order customer.

19 When must traveller's cheques be signed and by whom?

20 Explain the difference between a line graph and a pillar graph. Illustrate your answer.

21 Type a chart headed "Leave Schedule 1973". There should be a vertical column for each month and a horizontal column for each member of staff. Below are the names of staff members (which should appear alphabetically on the chart) and the dates on which leave is to start. Indicate on the chart the leave period of four weeks for each person.

Mr. P. Addo	9th August
Mr. J. Zobli	3rd May
Miss S. Mensah	1st February
Miss P. Mensah	27th September
Mr. D. Frempong	4th January
Mr. T. Lartey	6th September
Mrs. S. T. Jibueler	31st May
Mr. N. T. Lartey	5th July
Miss G. Adjei	1st November
Mrs. T. Lamptey	6th December
Miss S. Donkoh	8th March
Mr. M. N. Sackey	4th October

Note: It is suggested that you use a diary or calendar to check when the leave periods will finish. Think how you will indicate the actual dates of starting and ending leave.

22 One of your duties is to be responsible for stationery for the department in which you work. You are to control receipts and issues. State what steps you will take to ensure that you are never out of stock of any item and that you can easily find out how much stock of any particular item you have on hand, and how you will ensure its security.

23 If possible use a printing adding-listing machine to work the exercise below:

(a) Indicate the Account Number of each company and add *across*, inserting the total at the end of each line. Clear the machine between each account.
(b) Add each of the six monthly columns vertically and insert totals.
(c) Check by adding the monthly totals across and the account totals vertically. The grand total should be the same in each case.

HALF-YEARLY SALES OF RECONDITIONED DRILLS

Account Number	Company	Jan.	Feb.	Mar.	Apr.	May	June	Total
194	Jacks Ltd.	87	56	50	100	46	39	......
259	Gibbs	133	36	30	20	6	13	......
298	Harvey	183	16	10	50	27	19	......
412	Premier	41	5	5	28	3	8	......
375	Rodgers	258	36	30	27	35	41	......
317	Adai Ltd.	63	6	6	3	7	11	......
379	Thompson	261	56	50	41	154	21	......

(d) Add the totals for January, February and March, and subtract from the grand total.
Answer ....

(e) Subtract the total of Harvey's account from the grand total.
Answer ....

(f) Multiply the grand total by four to get a two-year estimate.
Answer ....

24 Explain the following:

a Overseas Money Order
b Giro Inpayment form
c SAYE
d Premium Savings Bonds
e Telegraph Money Order.

25 From the following information produce a pie chart: The revenue of a manufacturing company is derived from a number of sources—

55% from sale of products to wholesalers
10% from direct retail sales
20% from chargeable services
15% from investments.

14

Human Relations

"As public relations representative, a secretary should first get to know her boss's personality. In effect, she should become his 'alter ego'. Then she can act on his behalf, when necessary."

John E. Kusik, Gregg Newsletter

As a private secretary your work is based to a very large extent on human relations. Nearly every task you perform involves you with people at some stage —your boss, your colleagues, junior staff, your boss's colleagues or the general public.

This aspect of your work requires very special personal qualities—tact, sympathy, tolerance, genuine liking for people and the desire to help them. Your relationship with people will be much easier if you understand the reaction of human beings to various situations which arise in the course of a normal business day. You must realise that people are individuals with their own characters, likes and dislikes, foibles and idiosyncracies, strengths and weaknesses.

APPEARANCE AND BEHAVIOUR

Human relations consist largely of impressions that one person makes upon another. When meeting people face to face this impression is created to some extent by a person's appearance. If you went into an office and met a secretary wearing a badly-stained dress, and looking untidy and as if she had paid no attention to her appearance, you would not form a favourable impression. If you analysed the reasons for this impression, apart from the natural one of distaste, you would probably find that your immediate reaction would be to think that a person who presented herself in such a way could not possibly be efficient. A natural corollary to this thought is that the company itself was not very efficient if it employed such people.

Grooming How should a secretary present herself? To look efficient does not mean wearing drab clothes and unattractive hair-styles. Simple clothes in appealing colours and contemporary fashion, a cared-for complexion, well-manicured hands, polished shoes in good repair—all these contribute to a groomed, attractive appearance.

Behaviour The position of secretary carries with it a great deal of responsibility and it is not only the appearance of the person holding the position but also her behaviour and comportment that will create an impression. To be dignified it is not necessary to be grim and cheerless. To be cheerful does not mean giggling and constantly talking.

You are often the representative of your boss and always a representative of your company. Your behaviour must therefore be above reproach. You have to know instinctively the correct way to behave in every situation and the right approach to every individual with whom you come into contact. The simple things, such as walking and sitting well, giving and receiving things graciously, add up to good behaviour.

RELATIONS WITH THE BOSS

His representative The relationship between a secretary and her boss is a unique one. You must get to know him very well indeed—the way he thinks, the way he acts, his reaction to people and situations, his likes and dislikes, particularly in small details, his relations with other people both inside and outside the company, his way of expressing himself both verbally and in writing, and the image he likes to present of himself. Although always a representative of the company, you are also the representative of your boss. You must think for him, speak for him, write for him, act for him. When a situation arises you must know what he would do and do it for him. Perhaps one of the highest accolades a secretary can be given is the remark from someone outside the company that he didn't know the boss was away, because queries, etc. had been handled as though he were there.

Personality Any person who is capable of being an efficient secretary is bound to have a strong personality of her own, but she must be adaptable and know how to establish a harmonious working relationship. To some degree a secretary needs to be schizophrenic, so that she can think with her boss's mind when it is necessary. With experience she will be able to develop her own judgment along the same lines as his.

Link and barrier The secretary plays the role of both link and barrier between her boss and those outside his office. However desirable the 'open door' policy might be, very few managers can adopt it, if they are to be productive. It is therefore the secretary's job to appraise people and situations and assess when to be a link and when to be a barrier. To be a barrier without giving offence needs tact and charm. Often you can deal with a query but either the enquirer has not thought to ask you, or feels he is sufficiently important to be dealt with by the top man. No-one must be made to feel 'brushed off'. Each person's business must be dealt with to his satisfaction, which means that your approach must be positive, and the action you take must give him confidence in your ability to help him.

Listening and criticising By virtue of his job a boss is often a lonely person. There may be only one person in the organisation with whom he can discuss his problems, not because he expects assistance in solving them, but simply as a means of clarifying points in his own mind. This person is likely to be you.

It goes without saying that *anything* he tells you must never under any circumstances be repeated. There is also the opposite side—some secretaries think it their duty to pass on to their bosses any information they get from other staff in the company. Nothing could be more damaging to your own or your boss's relations with other staff. If you hear a pleasing comment about a person or a policy or a decision which you think he would like to hear, it is quite in order to pass it on. If there is some point of discontent among the majority of the staff, it may be a good thing for the boss to know about it because he may wish to put such matters right. The utmost discretion must be used, and if there is the slightest possibility that harm might be done by 'talking out of turn' it is better to say nothing. Your boss may ask you what other staff think about a particular policy or proposal as he feels you are in more direct contact with them. You should in this case state what you have heard clearly and accurately. You should not include your own views unless asked to do so.

There are occasions when you may be able to criticise constructively. You may rarely feel like telling your boss he is wrong but you may be able to suggest improvements. This could apply, for example, in a case where you have met a person to whom the boss is writing and you feel that something he has dictated would upset the person. You may be able to suggest another way of saying the same thing which would not cause irritation.

There may be times when you are called upon to make excuses for your boss

—something he has not done, an appointment he has decided not to keep, a person he does not wish to see. He has reasons which justify his actions but he may leave to you the unpleasant part of making excuses. You must not mind telling a white lie sometimes. You may not think his reasons are adequate but it is not your job to criticise his decisions; your job is to justify them as far as you can.

His memory A busy man with major decisions to make and many problems to resolve relies on his secretary to see that he is in the right place at the right time, with the documents and files he needs. He also relies upon her to see that things such as driving licences and passport renewals are not overlooked. A busy person holding a post of considerable responsibility which makes heavy demands upon his memory and powers of concentration will also appreciate reminders about personal items such as details of holiday arrangements or private dinner invitations. If your boss comments casually about something he must remember to do in the future, make a note of it so that you can remind him in good time.

Liking and respect You cannot establish the right relationship with your boss unless you respect him as a person, as a professional and as a representative of the organisation. You must care about the interests of the firm you are both working for, the importance of your boss doing his work as well as he can and your role as part of the working partnership. It is important to like and respect the person with whom you are working, but guard against any emotional involvement which would make it difficult for you to assess situations objectively and maintain appropriate attitudes in front of other people. Nevertheless, a secretary is naturally an understanding person and when you have been working with your boss for some time you will almost certainly find yourself thinking of him in a more personal way. When he returns from a meeting looking somewhat drawn, he may appreciate the offer of a cup of tea or coffee. He may also appreciate your keeping a few household items in the office for emergencies, such as a first-aid kit, some aspirin and a needle and thread. If your boss has a car parked in a meter bay, note when the time expires so that the car can be moved—you could offer to move it yourself if you can drive. These isolated examples may seem trivial, but taken together and combined with all the minutiae of office life they contribute to the establishment of optimum working conditions by lessening the boss's memory-load and creating a harmonious working relationship.

Loyalty Because you work so closely with him, people may well ask about your boss, about his work, about policies, etc. You may hear criticism of him or his work. You should stop such a discussion before it begins. A polite but firm statement is usually all that is needed. 'Please remember that I work for Mr. Jones.' This applies also to other employees in the organisation.

RELATIONS WITHIN THE OFFICE AND COMPANY

There are three main groups of people within the company from the secretary's point of view—the seniors, who are your boss's colleagues; your own colleagues and other secretaries with whom you must work in close co-operation; and juniors, your own and other people's.

Handling people Each person is a human being and must be treated as such. Character and personality traits are often the result of a person's background of which other people know little or nothing. A person may be shy of making suggestions because in the past his opinions have been ignored. He should be encouraged to voice his thoughts because he may well be able to contribute substantially to the efficiency of the organisation. There are the people who 'know it all'. They can be difficult to deal with and need a firm approach, particularly when they have to be told that they are wrong. Being firm does not mean being discourteous. Perhaps the most difficult kind of person to have affable relations with is the man or woman who, for some reason, lacks confidence and feels insecure. Very often to cover this feeling (often called inferiority complex) such a person is domineering and has a blustering manner. If he can be made to feel that you are trying to be helpful and not critical he often responds to this approach as it boosts his morale and helps him to feel that you have confidence in him.

Dealing with seniors The boss's senior colleagues should be treated with respect. You are not your boss's private property, nor he yours, and the person who is willing to help others besides her immediate boss can become a kingpin of the organisation. You will need their help from time to time, especially when he is away.

Dealing with colleagues Every person working in an organisation is a member of a team. The aim of the company should be the aim of each individual working in it—to give the best possible service to the public. No one person is indispensable though some may be more valuable than others. Co-operation and good feeling amongst staff at all levels can speed up work flow and help to foster a good working atmosphere.

Dealing with juniors Because a person is a junior does not mean that he (or she) is inferior. Courtesy and consideration should be given to all from the chairman down to the most junior employee. Every senior needs the co-operation of juniors if he is to do his own job satisfactorily. The secretary is no exception. A word of praise for work well done, appreciation for extra help given, constructive criticism aimed at enabling the junior to improve his work, all pay dividends in increasing respect and willing co-operation. There must be discipline—unpunctuality, bad behaviour, slackness, should not be tolerated. A good example from a senior generally achieves the required result. If you are late arriving at the office you are not in a position to criticise a junior for unpunctuality.

There may be times when it is necessary to criticise someone working under you. This should not be done in front of other people. Try to find out first why the fault occurred—why was she late? why did she type this piece of work vertically instead of horizontally? why does she seem to object when given instructions? This approach often enables you to help the person concerned to solve a sub-conscious problem that has been worrying her even though she has not been able to pinpoint it in her own mind. Many people will respond to a genuine effort to help them overcome a difficulty.

Poor communication often creates a great many unnecessary problems between seniors and juniors. When giving an instruction state precisely and clearly what you want and make sure it is understood.

No-one can know a thing unless he has been taught and it is the job of the senior to find out what a junior knows already and fill in the gaps in his knowledge by training. Training on-the-job involves explanation, demonstration and supervised practice. It is a time-consuming operation but must be done if long-term benefit is to be achieved. An instruction to the new office boy to "staple these papers" is useless if the boy has never seen a stapling machine and doesn't know where staples should be placed. Even the simplest operation such as punching a document for filing must be taught if it is to be done correctly.

You will get the best out of people working for you if they know they can have confidence in you. This means being fair to everyone; supporting them when they are right; giving them more responsibility as they prove themselves ready to undertake it; helping them with work or private problems whenever possible; asking to be informed by the Personnel Department when anyone has an accident or is ill so that you can tell your boss and make enquiries on his behalf; keeping all employees informed of matters which affect them or their work; and respecting each one as an individual contributing his fair share to the effort of the team as a whole.

RELATIONS WITH THE OUTSIDE WORLD

Public relations Many people talk loosely about 'public relations'. Basically public relations means the efforts made by an organisation to bring itself into the eye and mind of the public. This involves creating an 'image' which is devised to attract the particular section or sections of the public with whom the organisation has, or wishes to have, dealings. It would be foolish for a company to promote an image of wealth and luxury if it wanted to sell cheap clothes to teenagers; such a company would want to project an up-to-date, youthful image in keeping with the mood of the times.

Many organisations have on their staff a *Public Relations Officer*. He must create and maintain the image, spread it and adapt it when necessary. The good public relations officer (PRO) knows every aspect of his own organisation—what it stands for, what its aims are, what it does and how it functions. It is his job to broadcast this image in the most appropriate ways, and selecting the most suitable media.

Secretary as public relations officer There are many ways in which good relations with the public can be developed—attractive advertisements and gimmicks of various kinds, such as free samples and cocktail parties, but the two best methods are to give good value for money, and efficient and courteous service.

You cannot influence the value for money aspect, except perhaps by passing on to your boss any comments you hear about your company's products or services, but efficient and courteous service are very much your affair. You are in daily contact with the public and it is your job to see that your relations with everybody are right.

Press facilities Senior officials of some organisations hold *press conferences* from time to time to announce major policy decisions. The editors of national newspapers and appropriate journals are invited to send reporters. News agencies such as Reuter and the Press Association would also be invited so that the information could be distributed both nationally and internationally. The usual procedure at a press conference is for a statement to be made and then for the reporters to ask questions. The statement is usually read but the answers to the questions will be "off the cuff". If you attend such a conference you should take down the questions and answers because, although officials are careful what they sat at a press conference, there is always the possibility of a speaker being misquoted or quoted out of context thus giving a wrong impression. A verbatim note of what was actually said would enable the speaker to correct such an error.

It is necessary for organisations to make announcements from time to time. Unless an announcement is made at a press conference, it is normally sent as a *press release* to newspapers and agencies for distribution. A press release may contain any information such as a Chairman's annual report and the financial accounts, information about a new product, or information about a trip abroad of a senior official, etc. Once information has been released to the press it is public property. It is necessary therefore to fix dates for press releases very carefully.

There are occasions when press reporters may make enquiries of you either about your boss or about a matter connected with the organisation. If there is a Public Relations Officer on the staff it is his job to handle the press and any editor or reporter should be referred to the Public Relations Department. If there is no such department, information should be given only if there is no intention of issuing a press release. In any case always find out exactly what is wanted and check with your boss before saying anything. The most innocent-sounding enquiry may have ulterior motives. If your boss gives you authority to deal with the matter it is advisable to give the information in writing so that there can be no excuse for misreporting. Check and double check any facts and figures you include. Even a minor error can create a major furore.

Remember that the press can be a two-edged weapon from the organisation's point of view. Fair and accurate reporting can be a valuable asset and the goodwill of editors is well worth cultivating. On the other hand an unkindly-disposed reporter can word a paragraph in such a way that the impression is bad even though the report is accurate. Your dealings with reporters need to be supported by charm and diplomacy.

Advertisements Usually advertisements are one of the responsibilities of the Public Relations Department. As well as reflecting the company's image an advertisement must always maximise the selling point of the product, service or job being advertised. The medium chosen for the advertisement must also be suitable. There is little point in advertising a £20,000 house in a magazine for teenagers.

The simplest form of advertisement is placed in the 'Classified Advertisements' section of a publication, or what is commonly called the 'small ads. column'. The charge for such insertions is by the line, with a certain number of words allowed for each line. The following advertisement would appear in the 'Situations Vacant' column of a newspaper or magazine.

> Shorthand-typist wanted for professional office. Good speeds and previous experience essential. Age 20–25. Salary not less than £30 p.w. Send C.V. to Box 6213.

When advertising vacant posts many organisations prefer to use a box number, as in the example above, rather than identify themselves. This means that an applicant sends his reply to the publication and quotes the box number on the envelope. The reply is then forwarded to the originator of the advertisement.

If a more conspicuous advertisement is required an insertion can be designed to use one or more inches of column depth, or be enclosed in a lined-frame and spread across two or three columns. In this case the charge is by 'column inch'. An advertisement which would cover three columns in width and three inches vertically would be charged as nine column inches.

> UNIVERSITY OF KENT
>
> SCHOOL OF LANGUAGE STUDIES
>
> *SCHOLARSHIP*
>
> Applications are invited for a scholarship, value £500 per annum tenable for two academic years starting in October, 1973.
> The Scholarship is open to men and women of British nationality between the ages of 25 and 35 who are graduates of approved universities or members of approved language institutions.
> The successful applicant will be expected to follow a full-time course of post-graduate studies leading to a master's degree.
> Write for full details and application forms to the Bursar, University of Kent, Canterbury. Completed applications must reach the Bursar not later than 30th June, 1973.

Some advertisements include a reference which should be quoted by customers. The same advertisement may appear in several publications with a different reference in each. This is to enable the public relations department to keep a record of the number of replies received as a result of each advertisement and to assess the effectiveness of each medium. The publications which produce few replies can be deleted from the list of those used, or be used less frequently, so ensuring that the advertising budget is used to maximum sales effectiveness.

Printed material Another aspect of public relations is the production of written material, often in the form of *brochures* or *catalogues*. In the first instance, the material must be collected—several people may be involved in producing written material, photographs, drawings, etc.—and typed in draft.

When the contents have been approved they must be prepared for the printer. Many organisations have their own printing department and it is the job of the public relations department to see that any material produced reflects the company's image in the best possible way. The draft should be produced on the typewriter and displayed as far as possible as it is to be printed. Different methods should be used to indicate different types of heading, e.g. spaced and closed letters (capital and small) with and without underscoring. When italics are required in the printing the word in the script should be underscored, not placed in inverted commas. Single inverted commas are used for words used in a special sense in the context. Double inverted commas should be used for trade names and titles of reports, books, documents, etc.

Always ask for a proof copy and check it most carefully with the original. Special attention should be given to names and figures. Corrections should be indicated with the conventional printer's correction signs which can be found in most secretarial reference books. If there are many corrections it is wise to ask for a second proof. A brochure published with a mistake in it would promote an unfavourable image.

Speeches Your boss may be invited to speak at a function from time to time. Making a bad speech can shatter a personal image, and that of the company too. A great deal of thought and time must be given to the preparation of a successful speech.

Some people write a speech out in full and read it at the function, but this is rarely effective. Other people prepare their speeches in full and then 'boil them down' to a few headings on postcards. Speeches which are not read are much more interesting to the listeners because they feel the speaker is talking to them. Your boss may ask you to comment on his speech when he prepares it. You should consider it from the point of view of the people who will listen to it. What will be their impression of your boss? Is he doing justice to himself, and to the organisation? Is there a clear theme running through the content? Is the language appropriate and clear and will it sound effective when spoken?

Speeches should be typed on good quality paper, one-side only, in one-and-a-half or double-line spacing. Speeches typed on A5 paper or as a series of headings on postcards fit conveniently into the pocket or handbag. The sheets or cards should be secured with a treasury tag to keep them in correct order and allow them to be turned over easily.

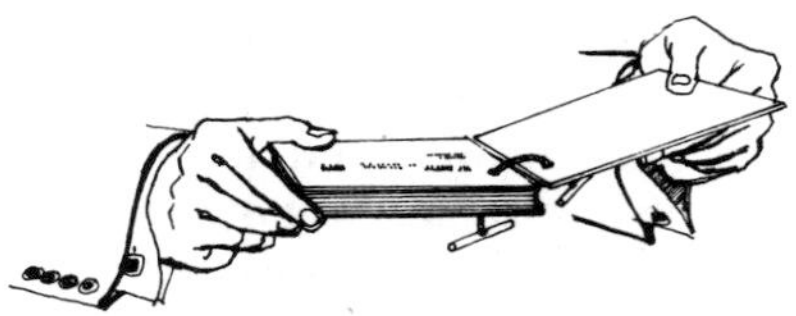

Conferences The planning and organisation necessary for conferences can also include *conventions*, *lectures*, *seminars*, *workshops*, and *in-company training courses*. As for every other major function a special file should be opened with a check list attached inside the front cover.

1 Plan the programme in consultation with the course director/lecturers/chairman.
2 Contact speakers/lecturers to confirm their availability and ask if any special equipment or facilities are required.
3 Reserve accommodation (a) for the business—a main room and several small syndicate rooms may be needed with appropriate furniture; (b) for the administration—the conference office should be near the main room; (c) for meals, including mid-morning and mid-afternoon refreshments; (d) for accommodation (i) for the lecturers and (ii) for the participants.
4 Cost the entire function—every item of expenditure must be covered so it is wise to include an overhead charge for such things as telephone calls, etc. and a small contingency charge for unexpected items.
5 Prepare programme for printing together with an application form if appropriate.
6 Prepare advertisements for newspapers/magazines/journals.
7 Arrange for translation facilities if necessary. This may have to be made available for all participants or for a few only. Put in hand arrangements for hiring equipment and engaging translators for the requisite languages.
8 Arrange for the hiring (if necessary) and transportation of equipment. This may include an overhead projector, cine film projector, filmstrip/slide projector, tape recorder with supply of tapes, spirit duplicator with supply of masters and running-off paper, photocopier with supply of negative and/or positive paper, films/filmstrips/slides, reference books, cartridge paper, felt markers, stop watches, chalkboard, chalk (white and coloured), bulldog clips, intercommunication between rooms, and external telephone if this is not already available. The electrical facilities available must be carefully checked to ensure that they are adequate and

to note what plugs and cable extensions will be necessary. Some hotels with good conference accommodation can provide almost all standatd equipment.

9 Make arrangements for the proceedings to be reported if required. The arrangements to be made will depend upon a number of factors:

a Are the speakers to be asked to supply a copy of their speeches either in advance or at the end of the session?

b Are verbatim records required of all the proceedings, i.e. lectures as well as questions, answers and any subsequent discussion?

c If summaries only are required, how long should they be?

d How soon should typed transcripts of the proceedings be available —by the following morning? within a month? or in time for the next edition of any professional publication connected with the conference or the sponsors of the function? How many copies of the transcripts will be needed?

e Are the proceedings to be simultaneously or consecutively interpreted? In how many languages are translated transcripts to be prepared and how soon will the transcripts be needed?

The answers to these questions will enable you to decide what reporting facilities you will need, e.g. tape-recorders, shorthand-writers, teams of verbatim reporters, teams of typists, numbers of typewriters and duplicators, additional clerical assistance.

10 Check that supplies are available for the participants and order if necessary. These may include name badges, folders, pads or sheets of paper (graph, ruled, plain, etc.), ball-point pens, pencils, rulers, handouts (i.e. printed materials), expense sheets.

11 List the equipment and supplies needed for the conference office, e.g. typewriter, ink and spirit duplicating machines with supplies, photocopier with supplies, stapling machine, perforator, guillotine, file covers, selection of stationery and forms, paper clips, pens, pencils, erasers, rulers.

12 Confirm transport for conveying equipment to the conference venue and for meeting participants and/or lecturers if necessary. At the same time order return transport.

13 Notify the press if appropriate.

14 Draw up a list of participants as applications are received; issue receipts for fees.

15 Despatch any documentation such as programme, working papers, etc. to participants.

16 Have place cards and name badges printed; obtain supplies and prepare a folder for each participant containing stationery and necessary documentation such as the programme, course director's instructions, introductory handout, list of delegates, etc.

17 Supervise transportation of equipment and supplies. Check functioning of equipment when installed. The conference rooms and office should

be prepared as reasonably far in advance as possible, but certainly the day before the starting date.

18 If sessions are to be chaired, make sure that the chairman for each session knows the name, title, company, and brief biographical details of the speaker he is introducing, and the title of the session and/or lecture.

19 Some preparatory stage-management ensures that the conference promotes a professional image, e.g. the platform should be attractively set out and well lighted, the table should be covered with a suitable cloth, drinking water and glasses should be provided and any screens or display boards should be well sited.

20 If the lecture is to be followed by questions, the possibility of an embarrassing silence is avoided if the first question is prepared in advance by briefing one of the delegates to "catch the chairman's eye"; similarly, the person who is to propose the vote of thanks should be arranged beforehand. A card giving details such as these should be handed to the chairman for the session so that he can conduct the proceedings smoothly.

21 Make a final check of meal and accommodation arrangements. Find out where cloakrooms are situated, where refreshments and meals are to be served, where drinks can be obtained before meals, so that participants can be told before business begins.

During the conference the secretary is expected to be available at all times to deal with emergencies as they arise. If the planning has been detailed and carefully checked these should occur very infrequently.

Participants often need help and advice, especially during the first day of a convention. Any difficulties that arise should be noted so that future planning can be improved to prevent their recurrence.

After the conference the secretary has follow-up duties. Equipment must be returned; unused supplies must be gathered up neatly for future use; letters of thanks should be drafted for the course director/chairman to send to guest speakers/lecturers; vouchers may have to be prepared to pay lecturers' fees; accounts must be checked as they are received and passed for payment if correct, or queried if incorrect.

Business entertaining You may be asked to attend a function either to assist generally or to act as hostess. In any case you must ensure that all arrangements are completed before the function begins whether you attend it or not. During the function you must make sure that all guests are being looked after by the waiters, that everyone has a drink, that food and cigarettes are being passed round, that records or tapes are changed if music is used. You should see that guests are introduced to each other and that people standing alone are brought into groups. If your boss has expressed a wish that certain people should meet each other you should help him to see that they do.

If you attend a function as a hostess you will greet the guests as they arrive and see them as they leave. You help them to find their places at table. It is your

A Board Room is sometimes used for Business functions. The Secretary is expected to organise light refreshments and may even be involved in discussing more elaborate menus with outside caterers.

particular job to look after the ladies. At a dinner given in a hotel you will take them to the powder room after the meal before meeting the men in the lounge for coffee. On no account should you parade your knowledge of the organisation and your boss's work; play your role with grace and tact.

Social functions Bringing people to meet the organisation is a useful way of creating good public relations. Various social functions are means of doing this but they must be impeccably arranged. Successful functions are the result of maximum attention to detail.

For each function open a file and inside the front cover attach a list of check points.

INFORMAL LUNCHEON OR DINNER FOR A SMALL NUMBER OF PEOPLE

1 List guests.
2 Invitations—people are usually invited to an informal luncheon by letter or telephone.
3 Reservation of table at hotel for provisional number of guests, to be confirmed later.
4 Menu and wines.
5 Place cards (if number of guests is more than six).
6 Confirmation of number of guests to the hotel.

FORMAL LUNCHEON, DINNER OR DINNER DANCE

1 Reserve room provisionally giving expected number of guests.
2 Approach speakers (if there are to be any) to check availability. If there is to be no speaker confirm that the Guest of Honour is available on the proposed date.
3 Alter the date of room reservation, if necessary, after agreement with guest speakers.
4 List of guests.
5 Draft invitation.
6 Printing of invitation cards.
7 Complete and despatch invitation cards.
8 Menu, wines, cigarettes and cigars.
9 Floral decoration. (Hotels often include this in the charges.)
10 Background music (recorded) if required—dinner only. Band or orchestra if required—dinner dance. Public address equipment for speakers.
11 Draft menu and programme of speeches and/or dances for printing. (Name of speakers with honours, degrees, etc. should be included.)
12 Printing of menus/programmes.
13 Table lay-out. (The principal guest is seated on the Chairman's right hand. A second speaker would be seated on the Chairman's left. Ladies present in a business capacity should be seated in accordance with their business status; wives should be seated beside men of their husband's status—but not beside their own husbands.)
14 Place cards.
15 Entertainment. (This may be required at a dinner or dinner dance.)
16 Notify press. Invitations to editors and/or reporters.
17 Master of Ceremonies (for dinner and dinner dance). This should be someone with personality, good voice and charm. The M.C. cannot cover up for bad organisation, but he can spoil good organisation. (It is possible to engage the services of professional masters of ceremonies for formal occasions.)
18 Arrange for V.I.P.'s to be met by car if arriving by train or plane, and at the door where the function is to be held; arrange return transport as required.

COCKTAIL PARTY

Nos. 1–7 as for dinner, etc.

8 Drinks—spirits, wines and soft—and ice.
9 Food (canapés).
10 Hiring of glasses and trays.
11 People to serve drinks and food (if the party is not held at a hotel).
12 Cigarettes and cigars.
13 Floral decoration (if any).

After almost every function there are details still to be attended to. The following are the most usual.

a Equipment to be collected, e.g. records, microphones, chairs.
b Return of hired equipment, e.g. glasses and trays, public address equipment.
c Accounts to be settled, e.g. hotel, flowers, band, hire of glasses.
d Letters of thanks to guest speakers and organisations which have given facilities of any kind.
e Filing of papers, etc. for future reference.

FURTHER READING

A Guide to Effective Office Supervision, The Institute of Administrative Management.
Personal Assistants and Senior Secretaries, Moore and Neal, The Industrial Society.
The Secretary's Role, Moore and Neal, The Industrial Society.

EXERCISES

1 a What do you understand by the term "human relations?"?
  b What human qualities, traits, characteristics, do you think help people to achieve good relations with their fellows?

2 Describe the appearance of a well-groomed secretary. You may suggest particular clothes and say why you think they are appropriate.

3 Suggest five actions on the part of a secretary which you think are examples of good behaviour, and five actions which would be considered bad behaviour.

4 You stayed very late at the office last night typing some documents needed by your boss for a meeting this morning. He glances through them and finds you have omitted a short paragraph on the last page. He makes a sarcastic comment in an unpleasant manner. How do you think you would react? Give reasons.

5 All your boss's visitors have to pass through your office. One senior executive invariably walks straight through without asking if your boss

is free. Your boss has mentioned to you that he likes to know who wishes to see him before you let him in. How would you deal with the situation?

6 One day when chatting with your boss you tell him, as a matter of interest, of a comment made to you by someone outside the organisation. There is a frozen silence before your boss asks you where you got the information. You don't know the person's name. Your boss tells you that the comment is a highly confidential matter known only to a few very senior officials of the organisation. What would be your reaction to (a) your boss? and (b) the person who told you?

7 Your boss grumbles to you that you remind him of unnecessary things, like appointments that are already written down in his diary, but not the things he is always forgetting, like collecting dry-cleaning, weekend engagements you don't know about, etc. What suggestions can you make to solve the problem?

8 Your boss asks you to do some shopping for him as his wife is busy preparing for a dinner party. This will mean that you will have to stay quite late at the office to complete work needed for the next day and you have a theatre date. This is not the first time this sort of thing has happened. How would you deal with the situation in such a way as to make your boss understand that you feel he is taking advantage of you, but without seeming unco-operative?

9 Your workload has become so great that your boss suggests you get a typist to help you. Explain the responsibilities you would have as her supervisor.

10 Your boss regularly arrives at the office late. His chief is usually early and often asks for your boss before starting his day's work. How would you deal with the chief's requests?

11 Your chief tells you he wants you to be responsible for the general running of the department including staff. How would you cover your responsibilities in relation to (a) Members of staff who were late (i) occasionally? (ii) frequently? (b) Poor cleaning by the firm contracted to do it? (c) Complaints from typists and stenographers that stationery supplies from the store were inadequate?

12 You have three assistants, a junior typist, a stenographer and a junior secretary. The junior secretary is constantly finding fault with the typist, whom you consider to be a good worker, willing and helpful with good potential for promotion. The stenographer has hinted that the typist may resign in the near future. Can you suggest reasons why the secretary behaves as she does and what action you would take to make sure you don't lose the services of the typist?

13 One of your boss's colleagues has a very discourteous manner to secretaries. He never greets them, never says 'please' or 'thank you' and treats each secretary as though she were there to take his orders at all times and attend to them before anything else. What attitude would you

adopt towards this executive? Would you consider it necessary to speak to your boss about it?

14 The private secretary of the organisation's managing director frequently telephones your boss and refuses to discuss any matter with you even when he is out or away. Consequently some matters are unnecessarily delayed. Is there a solution? If so, what could be done?

15 Consider any large organisation that is familiar to you (not one in which you have worked or are working) and say how you came to know about it. What is its 'image'?

17 Your boss (the Chairman of a cosmetic manufacturer) decides that he would like to employ a glamorous receptionist for the new ultra-modern reception hall at the factory. Write an advertisement for the post and suggest suitable media in which to insert it.

18 Below is a proof copy of a page for an "Office Manual" which is to be issued to all office staff in the organisation. Make an exact copy of it and then correct it using printers' correction signs.

Hear are a few tips for those of you who's job it is to lookafter

the office flies.

a Do your filing every day. Try to have a specific time each day alloted to this task. Then you wont get behind with an ever-growing pile of paper learing at you you from the filing tray.

b) Do not file copies of correspondents until the originals have been signed in case there are any alterations additions or retypes.

c - Be sure that the papers on each file are in strict chronological order, that is date order.

d With eny system of filing other than purely alphabetical keep a "Master"file. This is an Alphabeticle file - Lever Arch type is the most suitable- in which a copy of all the out-going letters and memoranda are filled. This is mot helpful where the contents of a letter)and hence the subject or number) cannot be remembered some time later

e papers to be destroyed should be burned, destroyed in a paper shredding m achine, or torn into smallpiexes.

19 Your boss has drafted the notes below for a speech. He asks you to condense it to paragraph headings and main points to go on an A5 card. He says you may display the material as you like, but the points must be easy to pick up.

"1 Vocational training which is job-aimed—enabling trainee to earn living or improve his present performance. Important because affects what is taught and how.

2 Basic precept of any institution training for employment—to train people only for jobs which exist. Occasionally for jobs which trained people will make available. Find out what employers need in numbers, categories, standards and knowledge. Sometimes

necessary to persuade employers to be more realistic in their demands, especially newly-trained people.

3 This is first stage in employer/instructor relationship—of utmost importance. When training beginners practical training needed—essential to complement classroom teaching with practical training given under working conditions. Then students must be placed in employment—employers are our customers.

4 After sales service required for vacuum cleaner—required also for products of training institutions. Further training particularly valuable as trainee is able to relate it to what he is doing. Rapid rate of development demands continual up-grading.

5 Students must be channelled into training for which employment opportunities exist. Can be difficult if basic qualifications unsuitable for training wanted by student. Good language knowledge necessary for secretarial skills. Wrong to think basic education unnecessary for those without academic ability. However, where strong desire for a particular kind of training exists satisfy it by training for lower levels. Clerical training does not have to be 'secretarial'. Digress to simpler shorthand systems. Alphabetical systems easier to learn and adequate speeds can be reached much more quickly than by symbol systems, but language difficulty still exists. Private commercial schools very suitable places for experiment as the girls tend to be not too well up in language and academic subjects.

6 There is a need for a National Vocational Training Institute responsible for co-ordinating all training activities and setting national standards, including all grades of secretarial staff, telephone operators, receptionists, etc. Training needed for people in employment both in short courses and on-the-job. Co-operation of employers, trade unions, training institutions essential."

20 Your chief, the Principal Secretary of the Ministry of Efficiency asks you to arrange a drinks party for all other Principal Secretaries and their Deputies in Government in three weeks' time. In addition he wants to invite the Heads of all public corporations and their deputies. He will give the party at a hotel. Open a file for the party arrangements. List all the information you will need to get and arrangements you will have to make in their correct order. Give dates for checking and follow-up. Draft an invitation for the printer.

21 The Minister of Productivity (the Hon. James Crayshaw, M.C.) was the guest speaker at a luncheon given by your boss (the Chairman) to eminent industrialists. You are asked to draft a letter of thanks to the Minister. (You may use imaginary details.)

15

Personnel

"Handling people really need not be so difficult—all you need is inexhaustible patience, unfailing insight, unshakable nervous stability, an unbreakable will, decisive judgment, infrangible physique, irrepressible spirits, plus unfeigned affection for all people—and an awful lot of experience."

How to win the business battle, Eric Webster, John Murray.

People are the most valuable asset of any business; although they are expensive to maintain, they make the firm into a successful enterprise if they are well cared for and wisely managed. Some staff are more valuable than others and more difficult to find and replace, but all employees have something to contribute—that is why they were engaged. Personnel management is an important aspect of general management and affects the efficiency and profitability of any organisation.

The concept of personnel management has developed in this century. During the nineteenth century only a few very enlightened employers took any interest in the welfare of their employees. The rest were mainly concerned with making their employees work as many hours as possible for the least money.

At the end of the last century an American, Frederick W. Taylor, experimented with ideas such as wage schemes and selection and placement, but these concepts were slow to reach Britain. However by 1914 British industry had several welfare officers, although their functions were limited.

One result of conscription during the First World War was a shortage of workers to fill the places of the men who had joined the armed forces, and scientific studies were carried out to discover how to make the best use of the available manpower—and womanpower. The studies revealed that after a certain number of hours of work, workers become tired and their rate of production decreases. Such an idea seems too obvious to mention today, but the recommendations of these studies, including the appointment of welfare officers in factories, were adopted by the Ministry of Munitions and a few progressive employers.

The economic depression between the world wars caused widespread unemployment and employers could afford to disregard the welfare of their employees. If an employee was displeased with his job, he could easily be dismissed and replaced by one of the unemployed who were eager for work. The economic crisis affected personnel managers too and many of the welfare officers who had been employed during the war were dismissed.

The Second World War brought an even greater need than the first for the best management of available workers. By the end of the war personnel departments with trained personnel officers had been established in most large firms. Their responsibilities had increased to include the welfare, health and safety of workers, industrial relations and the implementation of legislation for the protection of workers that had been passed during the war.

Personnel management today is considered to be a vital function of every firm, not just for specialists in personnel departments but for all employees who are responsible for subordinates. A position of authority, no matter how slight, means responsibility for the welfare of others, and requires a knowledge of the structure of the firm and the jobs in it, the wages policy, recruitment policy, the training of new and existing staff, industrial relations, the legal rights and duties of employees and employers, and a knowledge and understanding of authority and leadership. The policy which an organisation adopts towards these aspects of personnel management is known as its *personnel policy.*

STRUCTURE AND RECORDS

All firms have a structure. Large firms may be divided into departments, units or divisions with further sub-divisions into smaller units. Instructions are given by managers and supervisors and passed down the line of authority until they reach the person or people who must carry them out. All employees have a place in the structure either as a giver or receiver of orders or both. Some firms draw up charts to show how the organisation works (a typical example is shown on p. 311). If a firm is to be efficient it must have a well-defined chain of command, that is of authority and responsibility, which is understood and followed by all employees.

Authority relationships Authority does not simply mean giving orders. Authority or power implies responsibility—responsibility to subordinates to see that they are well treated, and responsibility to superiors to see that their orders are carried out.

LINE RELATIONSHIPS A supervisor or manager gives an order or instruction to his subordinate. The subordinate is required by his position to carry out that order. This is a line relationship, where a superior is in direct authority over a subordinate.

LATERAL RELATIONSHIPS Two employees are in a lateral relationship if their jobs are on a similar level, even if they are not of equal importance. One does not have authority over the other; for example, the personnel officer and the sales manager may have a lateral relationship. The sales manager and the personnel officer may both give their opinions in a meeting with the managing director, but the sales manager cannot give the personnel officer orders and the personnel officer has no authority over the sales manager.

FUNCTIONAL RELATIONSHIPS The personnel officer's function is dealing with employees and implementing the firm's personnel policy, whilst the sales manager's function is to market the firm's products. If the sales manager needs help in dealing with an employee, he will call in the specialist help of the personnel officer. Although the personnel officer has no line authority over the sales manager, he has the authority to put his specialist knowledge into practice. In this situation the sales manager and the personnel officer are in a functional relationship: the personnel officer has the authority to carry out his function concerning the employee in question, whilst being neither superior nor subordinate to the sales manager.

STAFF RELATIONSHIP Employees who assist and advise other employees are said to be in a staff relationship. When the sales manager receives an order from his superior to market a product he needs the advice of the advertising department. The advertising manager is, therefore, in a staff relationship with the sales manager. However, since the advice is being given by a specialist, the advertising manager, the question of authority may vary with the situation and a staff relationship may at times be a functional relationship.

Job analysis In order to define clearly the authority relationships in a firm, each person's responsibilities, authority and duties must be known and understood. Two or more people in a firm may think they have responsibility for the same work or they may believe they are responsible to one person while the management considers they are responsible to another. In an efficient firm the organisation structure in practice is the same as the structure established by the management.

Job analysis is the process of examining a job to identify the component parts and the circumstances in which it is performed. When these are studied and written down, each employee can see his place in the organisation structure, and management can rectify situations where responsibilities and duties overlap, or where no one is responsible for a certain task that must be performed.

Job analysis is done in three steps; the preparation of the job description, the job specification and the personnel specification. In addition to being used to define the structural organisation of a firm, job analysis is also the first step in producing a training programme; before a syllabus is drawn up for a specific job training course, the necessary skills and knowledge required must be scientifically studied and described.

JOB DESCRIPTION A job description is a broad statement of the purpose, scope, duties and responsibilities of a job (see page 560). There are various ways of preparing a job description. It can be written by the person in the job and then checked by his immediate superior; or the superior or the personnel officer can write the job description and then discuss it with the employee who is actually doing the job. The method chosen depends on the firm, but it is essential that the job description should be accurate as the rest of the process of job analysis is based on it. The form used in writing the job description depends on the emphasis required. Some firms may want to show the responsibility involved in the jobs and therefore decision-making may be the predominant feature; at other times or in lower level jobs, the duties and conditions of work may be emphasised.

JOB SPECIFICATION The job description is the first product of the process of job analysis. The job specification is a statement of the physical and mental requirements of the job: what the employee must do in the job; what knowledge and skills are used in doing it; what judgments are made and what factors must be taken into account when they are made.

PERSONNEL SPECIFICATION The personnel specification is the final result of job analysis. It is an interpretation of the job specification in terms of the sort of person who is suitable to do the job; the physical and mental characteristics necessary, the educational qualifications and special skills required, and the personal characteristics that are desirable such as the ability to get along well with others.

JOB DESCRIPTION	
TITLE	Senior secretary
DEPARTMENT	Personnel
HOURS OF WORK	9.30 am–5.30 pm, Monday to Friday
RESPONSIBLE TO	Personnel Officer
SUBORDINATES	Two junior secretaries, one clerk
JOB SUMMARY	To assist the Personnel Officer to carry out his function and supervise the clerical work of the department

DUTIES	LEVEL OF RESPONSIBILITY
1. Receive visitors to Personnel and ensure they complete any necessary forms	Complete
2. Deal with telephone calls	Partial
3. Make appointments for Personnel Officer	Partial
4. Compose routine memoranda	Complete
5. Take dictation and type highly confidential information	Complete
6. Take messages and deal with enquiries during absence of Personnel Officer	Partial
7. Direct and check work of clerical staff	Complete

Example of a Job Description for a senior secretary.

Job analysis records The records of job descriptions, job specifications and personnel specifications are kept with the personnel records. A study of the job descriptions enables management to see that all the duties are defined and allocated and that there is no overlapping. Job analysis records are also used in the selection and recruitment of employees, and for promotion, training, job evaluation and manpower planning.

RECRUITMENT AND SELECTION The process of finding and selecting a replacement for an employee is based on the information contained in the job description and personnel specification. In order to attract suitable applicants for a job, the duties and responsibilities must be clearly and accurately described.

PROMOTION If a vacancy is to be filled by promoting within the firm, the same factors must be considered as in recruiting a new employee: What does the job entail? What qualities are needed in the person who can perform the job?

TRAINING AND VOCATIONAL GUIDANCE Job analysis records provide the information necessary in setting realistic training objectives and preparing training programmes and drawing up specific syllabuses and schemes of work.

Some firms provide a vocational guidance service to their employees when selecting applicants for training programmes. From the personnel specification the training officer or personnel officer can judge whether the employee has the right qualities, aptitudes and abilities to benefit from a particular training course. If the training officer considers that the employee is unsuitable for the course for which he has applied, he may suggest a more appropriate training programme.

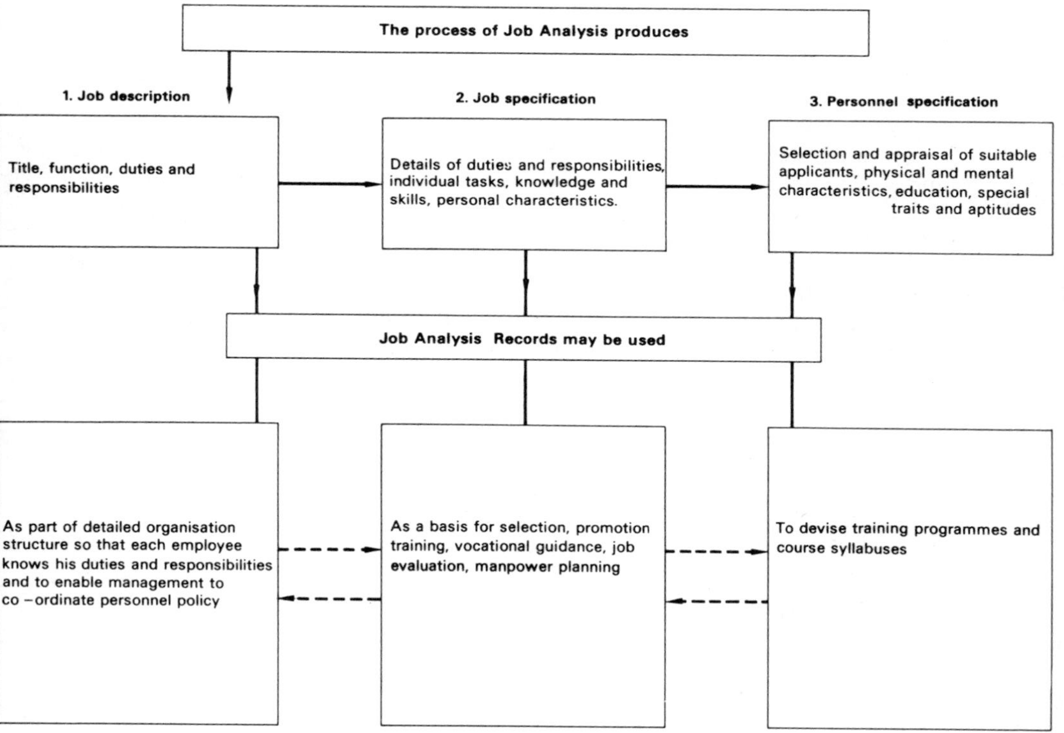

JOB EVALUATION Job evaluation is the process of deciding the relative worth to the firm of the jobs within it (see page 567). The value of a job cannot be appraised until the duties and responsibilities of the job have been defined; therefore the process of job evaluation starts with a study of the job analysis records.

MANPOWER PLANNING Manpower planning is a forecast of the number and type of employees who will be required by a firm in the future. Specialists in manpower planning consider the areas of work which are likely to expand and then study the quantity and quality of employees working in those areas;

from these studies they are able to propose recruitment and training programmes to fill future personnel requirements.

Personnel records In addition to job analysis records, personnel records are also kept for each employee. It is usual to have a file for each employee which contains information about his or her employment background, education, health, salary and other personal details. Personnel files are strictly confidential and access to them is normally limited to nominated staff in the personnel department who can pass on necessary items of information to supervisors or managers as required.

The information in each employee's file comes from various sources: the application form, records of attendance and accidents, medical history, reports on training, periodic assessments by supervisors on punctuality, performance and attitude, action taken concerning salary increases or promotion, and reports of disciplinary measures which may have been taken against the employee.

This information may subsequently be transferred on to a record card which can be neatly stored in a file drawer; personnel record cards should be well designed so that the information can be easily transferred as it is received from the various sources, and speedily located when needed.

Name:	Department:
Address:	Position:
Date of Birth: | M or F | Marital status:	Salary: Increases:
Examinations:	Date of appointment:
	Transfers or promotions:
Further education or specialist training	Training record: On the job: Off the job:
Employment record	Periods of sickness Month | Year | Numbers of days absent and reason
Medical history:	
National insurance number:	Date of leaving:
Referees given:	Reason:
Personnel record card. Ref. OPR/74	Western Alloys Limited

An example of a Personnel Record card. Note that the information on the left is about the employee's personal history; the information on the right is his employment record. This sort of simple, clear design makes the card easy to read and extract information from.

Employee record cards can be used to compile statistics about timekeeping, absenteeism, accidents, redundancy, etc. for the firm as a whole; this statistical information can be used by management to review the effectiveness of their personnel policy and plan any future changes.

Merit rating The personnel records contain the basic facts and figures about each employee and the job analysis records show the duties of each employee and the qualities he or she should have to carry out the job properly. In addition to this information, it is useful to know how well each job is being done and how each employee measures up to the standards given in the job description and personnel specification.

The personnel policy of many firms includes an *annual assessment* of the job performance of all employees. The assessment is usually carried out by the employee's immediate superior as he or she is in the best position to judge the employee's work. It is important for employees to understand the purpose of the assessment: it is their job performance that is being considered; it is not a judgment on them as people.

Assessing and rating employees on merit is a delicate operation. The assessor must not allow personal feelings to influence his judgment. He should not let his memory of a single mistake overshadow all the good work done by an employee, nor should he avoid giving bad ratings for fear that they may be interpreted as an adverse reflection on his ability to lead and train.

METHODS OF RATING EMPLOYEES The method of assessment adopted should avoid the dangers that can arise when employees rate each other's work. The method chosen should limit the assessment to such factors as work ability, dependability, time-keeping and leadership potential. It should also force the assessor to show that some employees are better than others.

In theory the method of *Rating Scales* should be the simplest and fairest to operate. The qualities to be rated are written as headings across the top of a sheet of paper. Each employee's name is written down the side and a rating is given under each heading. A disadvantage of this system is that the assessor can award average or good marks to all workers and avoid indicating those who are below or above the norm.

In the rating method known as *Rank Order* the assessor lists all the employees in his section in order of merit from best to worst. The merit of each worker is assessed on the basis of his overall job performance and his contribution to the organisation. Rank order forces the assessor to indicate the more valuable employees but it does not give him the opportunity to show how much better one employee may be, nor the aspects in which his work is superior to those of his colleagues.

The *Forced Choice* method of rating is intended to prevent personal feeling from influencing assessments. The assessor is presented with several groups of statements and he has to mark the statement in each group which best describes the employee. The statements must be written carefully so that it is difficult for the assessor to know or guess which is the "right" or most favourable statement and which is the "wrong" or least favourable statement. For example, one group of statements might be:

Indicate which of the following statements best describes the employee:	
1. Follows instructions carefully.	☐
2. Asks questions about instructions if they are not clear.	☐
3. Suggests new methods to supervisor.	☐

To get a clear all-round picture assessors may be asked to write descriptive essays about the work and abilities of each employee. The *Descriptive Essay* method of rating gives more information than other methods, but it is more time-consuming and assessors generally have to be trained in the techniques of writing clear, objective assessments.

None of these assessment methods is perfect and many firms have their own individual ways of rating the merits of their employees. The success of any method depends to a large extent on the attitude of the assessor and on his ability to make completely objective judgments.

POST APPRAISAL INTERVIEW After the assessment has been made some firms encourage the assessor to discuss the ratings with each employee in a private interview. The object of the interview is to be constructive. If the employee is doing well, the supervisor can compliment him on his performance; if his work is unsatisfactory, suggestions for improvement can be given.

If assessors are properly trained in rating and interviewing, the post appraisal interview can be helpful for both employee and firm by improving communication and work performance.

USES OF MERIT RATING If a firm's policy is to give salary increases on merit, the annual assessment is used as a guide (see page 563). It can also indicate those employees who have promotion potential and show up any faults in the organisation's promotion, recruitment and selection procedures by highlighting cases of employees who have been promoted beyond their capabilities or those who are incapable of carrying out the jobs for which they were engaged.

SALARIES AND WAGES

Every firm must pay its employees. This statement is obvious since one reason, frequently the main reason, why people work is to earn money. In addition to establishing wage scales a firm needs a policy to determine other matters related to the payment of salaries and wages, such as the frequency and amount of increments, and incentive schemes.

Salaries A salary is the amount of money an employee earns annually, for example £1,500 per annum. The salary is stated in the employee's contract of employment (see page 610) and it may be increased over a period of time. Once the annual salary is set it is not changed except in the two cases described below—by the addition of commission and bonuses. An employee receives his salary at fixed intervals, usually weekly or monthly.

COMMISSION Employees involved in selling are often paid on a commission basis. The employee may receive a low salary and the rest of his earnings come from commission. Commission is calculated as a percentage of the total selling price of all the goods sold by the employee or, in service industries such as hairdressing, as a percentage of the total takings derived from the employee's work. If an employee is engaged on the basis of "ten per cent commission", he is paid ten per cent of the selling price of the goods he sells. Commission is often paid at the same time as salary, although it may be paid at different intervals. In effect, if an employee is engaged on a commission basis his selling ability determines the amount of his total salary.

BONUSES Many firms pay salaried employees bonuses annually or at other intervals. The amount of the bonus is often a percentage of the salary; for example, a firm may give an annual bonus of three per cent of each employee's salary. The percentage set for the bonus usually depends on the profits made by the firm. If the firm has a profitable year, it may allocate part of the profits for the payment of bonuses and then calculate the individual distribution on a percentage basis.

FRINGE BENEFITS Fringe benefits are non-cash extras offered to salaried employees (some fringe benefits are referred to as *perks*, a slang abbreviation of *perquisite*). Luncheon vouchers are a common form of fringe benefit for office workers. Employees are given a voucher for each working day, usually at the same time as they receive their salaries. The value of the vouchers is printed on them, for example 15p, and they can be used to pay for meals or snacks or in part-payment at restaurants or cafés that participate in the

A specimen luncheon voucher.

luncheon voucher scheme. The employee does not pay tax on the amount of his luncheon vouchers up to a fixed amount and so they represent a considerable amount of money over the course of a year. Large firms may provide a canteen which serves subsidised low-priced lunches.

Salesmen and executives often receive a company car as a fringe benefit. As motoring costs are high, a car, petrol and repairs paid for by the company are an attractive addition to salary. Some firms also provide free or cheap transport for their employees. Many large companies offer their staff other fringe benefits such as pension schemes, staggered working hours, and life and health insurance schemes. Some of these benefits are taxable to some extent.

Wages Wages are paid weekly and are usually calculated on the work done during the week. An employee's wage is expressed as an amount for each hour, day or week worked, or for each item produced. Although the employee's rate remains constant over a period of a year or longer, the amount of work he does each week may vary and therefore his wages will not necessarily be the same each week. For example, if a man's rate is 50p per hour and he works 40 hours one week, his wages will be £20; if he is late one morning the following week, he may work only 38 hours and will therefore earn only £19 that week. If employees are represented by trade unions, the unions negotiate the rate of pay with the firm.

Most wage-earners are paid by *time rates*. The unit of time varies and may be per hour, per shift, per day, or per week. The weekly rate is calculated by multiplying the number of units of time worked by the amount of the rate.

Most workers on time rates are required to clock-in and clock-out. A Time Recorder Clock machine is placed near the entrance to the firm. When each employee arrives or departs he puts his time card into the machine and the time of arrival or departure is printed on it. This gives the firm a printed record of the exact number of hours or fraction of hours worked and removes the possibility of disputes.

When the time-rate is fixed the employer and the employee or the union representing him also agree upon a maximum amount of time to be worked at

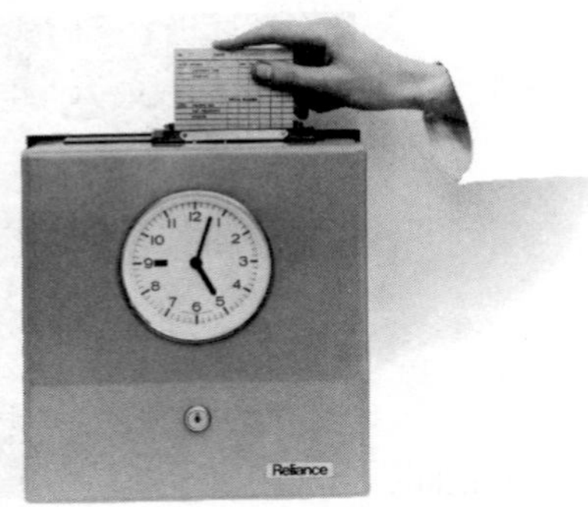

Time Recorder Clock.

that rate. Any time worked beyond that maximum is called 'overtime' and is paid at a higher rate. Overtime is quoted in the form of multiples of the basic rate; for example 'time and a half' means that one and a half times the basic rate will be paid, 'double time' means twice the basic rate. An employee may have more than one overtime rate. He may have one overtime rate for weekdays and a higher rate for Sundays and public holidays; or the overtime rate may increase after the employee has worked a certain number of hours' overtime paid at the lower rate.

Under the *piecework system* a rate is fixed for each item or piece the employee produces and at the end of the week an employee's wages are calculated by multiplying the number of pieces produced by the rate. For example, £30 for 30 pieces at £1 rate.

The *standard hour* method of payment is a combination of piecework and time rates. An employee's speed of work is studied to find out the average number of pieces he can produce in an hour, for example, three; and an hourly rate is negotiated for this average production, for example, 50p. The employee's rate is expressed as '50p per standard hour', but he is actually being paid 50p for producing three items.

Salaries and wages structures It is generally agreed that jobs requiring greater skills and ability and carrying more responsibility than others should be more highly paid. Of the three variables—skill, responsibility and ability or experience, responsibility is usually taken as the determining factor: the managing director of a manufacturing firm may not have the engineering skills of the craftsmen in his firm and he may have less experience than, say, the sales manager, but as he carries the greatest responsibility he is the most highly paid. Opinions differ on the relative importance of the other factors—skills and ability or experience.

It is relatively simple to accept that the managing director should be paid more than other employees; other questions which arise in establishing a salaries and wages structure are more difficult to answer; for example—Should the supervisor of the typing pool be paid more than the sales manager's personal assistant? Should the sales manager be paid the same as the personnel officer? Should the clerk in the personnel office be paid less than one of the typists in the typing pool? If there are to be differences in salaries, how great should these differences be? To settle questions like these, a firm needs an objective and reasoned approach to its salaries and wages structure.

JOB EVALUATION Job evaluation is the process of determining the relative worth of all the jobs in a firm; this means deciding the value of each job and listing all the jobs in order of value.

Note that the term is 'job evaluation'—'evaluation' means 'finding the value of'. This does not mean the value of the job to the employee or the merits of the person doing the job, but the value of the job to the firm. The tea-lady may be well-educated and efficient, but the evaluation of her job depends on the skills, experience and responsibility necessary to do it and the firm's estimation of its value.

Before an individual job can be evaluated a system of grades must be established. The lowest grade is for jobs that have the least value to the company and the value increases with the higher grades. A small firm with 20 employees may require only four grades, while a large firm employing thousands of people requires a much more complex system of grading to allow for the many different levels of responsibility. All jobs within the same grade have the same salary or wage range.

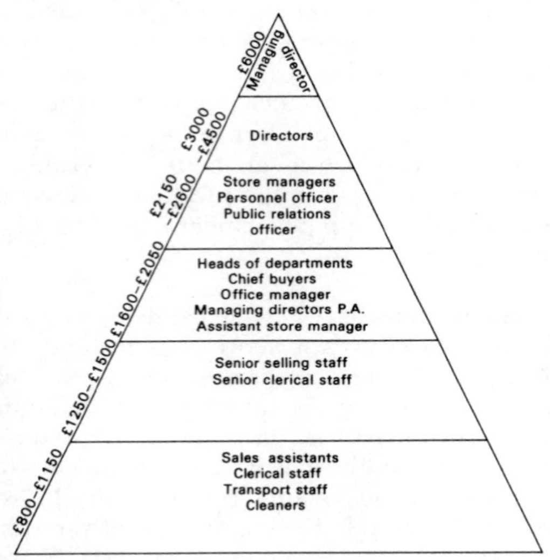

An example of Job Grades and Salary Scales.*

The first step in the evaluation of each job is job analysis (see page 558). The job description, job specification and personnel specification give the essential facts about the job—the level of responsibility, the skill and experience required. The job value and grade can be decided from these facts.

SETTING SALARIES AND WAGES Job evaluation puts jobs in grades of relative value to the firm. It is then necessary to set the salary or wage level for each grade. The pay for each grade should compare favourably with **the going rate** for the type of job or the firm will have difficulty in attracting and keeping good employees. If the salary scales are too high, however, the firm may find its operation is uneconomical. The going-rate for a job depends to a large extent on the employment situation (if there is a scarcity or surplus of a specific type of worker) and geographical location (salaries in south-east England and in London in particular tend to be higher than elsewhere in the United Kingdom).

* The reader is asked to make suitable allowance for inflation.

Large firms sometimes call on the specialist help of **management consultants** to help them to set realistic salary scales but such assistance is frequently too expensive for small and medium-sized firms.

Salary surveys can be used as a guide for setting salary scales for management and executive jobs. The salary survey, which can be purchased from specialist firms at regular intervals, lists a variety of jobs in different firms and the salaries paid for each job. These can only be a guide, as the title of a job gives very little indication of the range of responsibility, skills and experience required.

Another method which can be used as a guide for setting salaries and wages is to look at the pay offered in *advertisements* for jobs. It is necessary to consider more than one advertisement for each type of job and to take into account the type of firm offering the job and the differences between the advertised job and the job under consideration.

Salary scales should not be too rigid. It is usual to divide each grade into a number of steps to provide a salary range for each job within the grade. The steps provide a basis for giving increases or increments; they also enable a person with above-average qualifications to be given a higher starting salary. For example, a salary range might be from £900 to £1,200. An inexperienced person might start at £900, whilst a person with some experience might start at £1,000 or £1,050. As an employee gains experience his salary can be increased by steps (providing his work is satisfactory) until he reaches the maximum salary for the grade.

INCREMENTS It has become customary to give employees increases in salaries and wages at regular intervals, usually every year. Two arguments support this practice: firstly, the cost of living continues to rise and as goods cost more, employees need higher incomes; secondly, it is reasoned that experience in a job makes an employee more valuable and therefore worth a higher salary or wage.

Under a system of *fixed increments* every employee receives a rise at a certain interval, usually annually either on the anniversary of his joining the organisation or at the beginning of the calendar year. The amount of the increase may vary with the job but each employee knows beforehand what his increase will be. The advantage of this system is that it is simple to administer; on the other hand, it may not encourage employees to improve their work performance as they know the increases will be granted in any event. Employees with a better than average performance can only be rewarded by promotion to a higher grade.

In some firms the salaries of young employees, usually those under 21, are geared to their ages. Each employee receives a fixed rise in salary each birthday regardless of his job performance. There are arguments for and against this system. It can be argued that young employees should not be paid excessively in case they become irresponsible with money; and also, older employees may possibly resent high salaries being paid to young people. Opponents of wage scales tied to age say that if a young person is capable of doing a responsible job, he should be paid the going rate.

Merit increases, as the term suggests, are given only to those employees whose performance merits them. In many firms awards are decided after the annual assessment (see page 563).

Critics of this system say that it is difficult to administer and can lead to suspicions of unfairness and favouritism. They suggest that the only merit award should be promotion and employees on the same level should be paid on the same salary scale. However, it should be said in favour of the system that rewarding effort, if it is done fairly and consistently, encourages employees to improve their performances. Some firms use both systems: the fixed increment is given to all employees and merit increases are given in addition to those who deserve them.

Since inflation continues to increase the cost of living for all employees, some firms give a *cost of living increase* in addition to fixed or merit increments. The argument in favour of this scheme is that the usual increment may only just cover the rise in the cost of living, leaving the employee in relatively the same position as in the previous year. A special increase to cover a rise in the cost of living plus a merit or fixed increment gives an employee an actual rise in salary, or—in the language of economists—an increase in real wealth. It is probable that more firms will adopt the policy of giving cost of living increases since western economies seem unable to check their inflationary tendencies or control the ever-increasing rate of inflation.

As employees move up to the maximum within their grades, the payroll of the firm increases. If an employee earning the maximum in his grade is promoted or leaves or retires, the firm will effect what is known as *payroll saving* by replacing him with a person who is paid the minimum amount for the grade. Although payroll saving decreases the salary bill of a firm, it can mean that the best applicant is not hired if his experience would merit a salary on a middle or higher step of the grade. It is often the practice for a firm to apply payroll saving wherever possible and use the money saved to finance part or all of the annual increments. In this way employees receive higher salaries but the firm's total salaries and wages bill is not significantly increased.

INCENTIVE SCHEMES An incentive scheme is intended to encourage employees to work harder and stay with the firm. Incentive schemes for factory workers are linked to their wages so that the harder they work, the more they earn. The *basic incentive scheme* is the piecework system by which employees paid by piece-rates earn more if they increase their rate of production. However, the piecework system has not always proved to be successful in increasing production. More complicated schemes have been devised linked to total production rather than to the work of an individual, but because of the difficulties encountered in attempting to put them into practice, the value of these schemes has been doubted by some experts.

In highly automated factories and in production processes where the contribution of an individual employee is difficult to estimate, group and factory-wide incentive schemes have been set up. Similarly, as it is more difficult to measure office work (for example, the number of words taken in dictation or the number of pieces of paper filled) incentive schemes involving the whole firm have been devised. Like bonuses, these schemes are often linked to a firm's profits. A certain percentage of the profit is either distributed amongst the employees or used to buy shares in the company on behalf of the employees. This form of incentive is called *profit-sharing* and if it is done fairly it can significantly increase employees' interest in the firm's well-being.

Profit-sharing is an incentive scheme by which a certain percentage of a firm's profits is distributed amongst the employees or used to buy shares in the firm on the employees' behalf. If employees benefit from increased profits they will be more interested in the efficient running of the firm.

Employees can also be encouraged to improve their work-performance by *improving the working environment.* Although it may seem obvious that work can be done better in a well-heated and well-lit office, many firms still refuse to see the value of a pleasant environment. Proper cloakroom, toilet and canteen facilities also raise morale and improve work performance.

Well-designed offices and factories also encourage better work. If a typist has to move her chair every time anyone wants to pass behind her to get to the office copier, her work performance will suffer from frequent interruptions. If the files are stored a long way from a secretary's desk or if she has no fixed routine, the secretary may let papers accumulate instead of filing them regularly which could lead to the loss of important documents.

Incentives in the form of *fringe benefits*—such as good holidays, shorter hours, pension and insurance schemes, company cars, luncheon vouchers and free or cheap transport—are often offered to attract new recruits and keep existing employees.

Employees will work harder and have a better attitude towards a firm that treats them well. With this in mind, firms often provide sports and social facilities, loans and low-interest mortgages and legal and other advice. Probably the greatest incentive is a *good personnel policy* which makes every employee feel he is a valued member of the staff.

Deductions from salaries and wages When an employee joins a firm he agrees to a wage rate or yearly salary. The amount the employee earns each week or month is called *gross pay* but the employee does not receive the whole sum. Certain deductions are made from gross pay and the amount the employee actually receives after deductions is called *net pay*. There are two types of deductions made from gross pay: statutory and voluntary deductions. *Statutory deductions* are determined by law and the employer is required to subtract them from each employee's pay. *Voluntary deductions* are agreed by the employee and subtracted by the employer with the employee's consent.

INCOME TAX Income tax is a statutory deduction. Everyone who earns money is considered liable to pay income tax. Employees usually pay their income tax under the Pay As You Earn (PAYE) scheme by which an employee pays part of his yearly income tax every time he is paid. The exact amount to be paid each week is set out in printed tax tables supplied to each employer by the Inland Revenue.

The Inland Revenue allocates a *code number* to each employee in the PAYE scheme. To obtain your code number when you start work, you must complete a Claim for Allowances form which asks for information about your personal circumstances, such as the number of your dependents, your marital status and the amounts you may be paying for a mortgage or a life assurance policy. The form is returned to the Inland Revenue who assess your code number from the information you have given. To make sure your code number is updated when your circumstances change, you should complete a Claim for Allowances form every year.

Your code number determines the amount of your *tax free pay allowance*. A certain amount of the tax free pay is allowed each time you are paid and the

TABLE A–FREE PAY **WEEK 37** **Dec 14 to 20**

Code	Total free pay to date	Code	Total free pay to date	Code	Total free pay to date	Code	Total free pay to date	Code	Total free pay to date	Code	Total free pay to date	Code	Total free pay to date	Code	Total free pay to date
	£		£		£		£		£		£		£		£
0	NIL														
1	14·80	51	370·00	101	725·20	151	1082·25	201	1437·45	251	1792·65	301	2149·70	351	2504·90
2	22·20	52	377·40	102	732·60	152	1089·65	202	1444·85	252	1800·05	302	2155·25	352	2512·30
3	27·75	53	384·80	103	740·00	153	1095·20	203	1452·25	253	1807·45	303	2162·65	353	2519·70
4	35·15	54	392·20	104	747·40	154	1102·60	204	1459·65	254	1814·85	304	2170·05	354	2525·25
5	42·55	55	397·75	105	754·80	155	1110·00	205	1465·20	255	1822·25	305	2177·45	355	2532·65
6	49·95	56	405·15	106	762·20	156	1117·40	206	1472·60	256	1829·65	306	2184·85	356	2540·05
7	57·35	57	412·55	107	767·75	157	1124·80	207	1480·00	257	1835·20	307	2192·25	357	2547·45
8	64·75	58	419·95	108	775·15	158	1132·20	208	1487·40	258	1842·60	308	2199·65	358	2554·85
9	72·15	59	427·35	109	782·55	159	1137·75	209	1494·80	259	1850·00	309	2205·20	359	2562·25
10	77·70	60	434·75	110	789·95	160	1145·15	210	1502·20	260	1857·40	310	2212·60	360	2569·65
11	85·10	61	442·15	111	797·35	161	1152·55	211	1507·75	261	1864·80	311	2220·00		
12	92·50	62	447·70	112	804·75	162	1159·95	212	1515·15	262	1872·20	312	2227·40		

Table A.

rest of your gross pay is liable to income tax. In cases when tax free pay based on the code number is the same as or more than the gross pay earned up to that point in the tax year, no income tax is paid.

At the end of the tax year, which runs from 6 April of each year to 5 April of the next calendar year, the employer gives each employee a *P60 form* which states how much the employee has earned during the tax year and how much tax has been deducted. This important form should be kept in case you want to claim earnings-related social security benefits.

If you change jobs during the tax year, your employer will give you a *P45 form* which states how much you have earned, how much tax you have paid and your code number. When you go to your new firm, you must give the P45 form to the Salaries and Wages Department so that they have complete records for calculating your income tax deductions without delay.

NATIONAL INSURANCE National Insurance is also a statutory deduction. Under the Social Security Pensions Act 1975, every person over school-leaving age is liable to pay National Insurance contributions as an employed or self-employed person. Non-employed people can pay voluntary contributions if they wish.

Complete weeks of sickness or unemployment may mean that an employee can be credited with the contributions for that period. When contributions are credited, you do not have to pay them. You should apply to the local office of the Department of Health and Social Security in case of sickness, or the local Unemployment Benefit Office if you are unemployed. National Insurance contribution is normally due each week.

When you start work you must obtain a National Insurance number from the local Careers Office. You will receive an NI number card. The number shown on this card is recorded at the record office of the Department of Health and Social Security at Newcastle-upon-Tyne, and you should quote it when you make an enquiry or claim a benefit.

Under the Social Security Pensions Act 1975 there are two levels of contribution payable by employees and employers, depending on whether an employer is 'not-contracted-out' or is 'contracted-out'. Employees working for employers who are 'not-contracted-out' pay 6.5 per cent on their gross earnings from a lower limit (currently £15 per week) to an upper limit (currently £105 per week). The employer pays an amount equivalent to 10 per cent of the employee's gross earning within these same limits. Thus an employee earning £50 per week pays £3.25 and the employer pays £5.00, a total of £8.25 per week.

Employers who have 'contracted-out' operate an independent pension scheme approved by the Department of Health and Social Security. In this case employees pay 6.5 per cent on gross salary up to the lower limit and 4 per cent on the balance of earnings up to the upper limit. The employer pays 5.5 per cent on this balance. Thus on £50 a week gross earnings an employee would pay

6.5% on £15	£0.97½	
4% on £35	£1.40	£2.37½

The employer would pay

10% on £15	£1.50	
5.5% on £35	£1.92	£3.42
		£5.79½

(The halfpenny would be adjusted from week to week.)

No contributions are payable on earnings of less than £15 per week.

The employer completes a deduction card for each employee, using tables provided by the Department of Health and Social Security to calculate the amount due. He pays the employee's and his own contributions for National

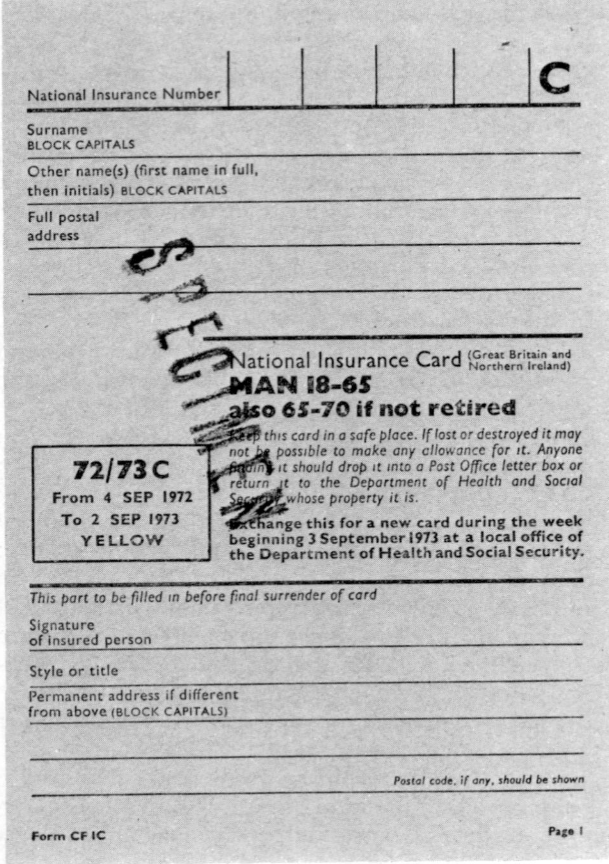

National Insurance Number | | | | | C

Surname
BLOCK CAPITALS

Other name(s) (first name in full, then initials) BLOCK CAPITALS

Full postal address

SPECIMEN

National Insurance Card (Great Britain and Northern Ireland)

MAN 18-65

also 65-70 if not retired

Keep this card in a safe place. If lost or destroyed it may not be possible to make any allowance for it. Anyone finding it should drop it into a Post Office letter box or return it to the Department of Health and Social Security whose property it is.

Exchange this for a new card during the week beginning 3 September 1973 at a local office of the Department of Health and Social Security.

72/73 C
From 4 SEP 1972
To 2 SEP 1973
YELLOW

This part to be filled in before final surrender of card

Signature of insured person

Style or title

Permanent address if different from above (BLOCK CAPITALS)

Postal code, if any, should be shown

Form CF IC

Page 1

A National Insurance card for a self-employed person or a non-employed person paying voluntary contributions.

Insurance together with income tax deductions monthly to HM Collector of Taxes, who then passes the National Insurance payments to the Department. The lower and upper limits on which National Insurance contributions have to be paid and the percentage rates of payment are to be revised from time to time. Up-to-date information can be obtained from the local Social Security office.

Self-employed and non-employed people wishing to pay voluntary contributions have to apply to the Department of Health and Social Security for approval to pay at the appropriate rates. They are issued with a National Insurance Card which they must stamp each week. National Insurance stamps can be purchased at post offices.

Regular National Insurance contributions mean that you are entitled to claim *benefits* for sickness, unemployment, injury at work, maternity and widowhood. Other benefits are a retirement pension and a payment to the next of kin on the death of the contributor. Your contributions also pay part of the cost of the National Health Service.

VOLUNTARY DEDUCTIONS Employees may agree to contribute towards fringe benefits provided by some firms, or the employees may have to contribute as a condition of employment. In the latter case the deductions cannot strictly be classified as 'voluntary' but they are not statutory in the sense of being required by written law or statute. These deductions can be for savings schemes, superannuation or pension schemes, insurance union dues, sports or social clubs. The employer subtracts voluntary deductions from gross pay at the same time as the statutory deductions are made.

ENGAGEMENT AND DISMISSAL OF STAFF

If you were asked to select a new typewriter or duplicator for your office, a straightforward plan of action would be to list the functions the machine would have to perform, and then to note the features required in the new machine. For example, the typewriter might be required to complete certain large documents, in which case you would need a machine with an extra long carriage. Then you could gather information about available machines from catalogues and brochures supplied by manufacturers or retailers. By putting together all the information and considering the amount of money you were permitted to spend and the price of the machines, you would be able to choose the machine that best suited your needs and budget.

Choosing a new employee is more complicated than selecting a machine, and much more important. People, unlike machines, are not labelled with printed descriptions of their capabilities and performance; nor do they have a money-back guarantee. If it is your responsibility to fill a vacancy, you have to discover each applicant's unique set of skills and personal qualities and decide if they equip him to do the job, to get on well with colleagues, supervisors and subordinates, and if he will derive satisfaction from working for your firm in that particular job. Having the right person in the right job is more valuable than any number of machines, whilst having the wrong person can cause work standards and employee morale to deteriorate. How can you ensure that you choose the right applicant?

The simple answer is that you cannot **ensure** that you choose the right applicant, but a well thought-out, realistic recruitment policy, carefully implemented, can help you to select the most suitable employees. Recruitment begins with making the vacancy known to suitable applicants and ends when the new recruit is introduced and settled into his new post.

Recruitment When a vacancy occurs the position can be filled in three ways:

1 By promoting an existing employee.
2 By engaging a new employee.
3 By allowing existing employees and outsiders to compete for the job.

Some firms have an established policy which lays down which method will be used whilst others allow the person responsible for recruitment to make his own decision. In both cases the person responsible for filling the vacancy should understand the advantages and disadvantages of each method.

PROMOTION In some firms where vacancies can be filled by promotion, there may be an established ladder of promotion whereby an employee automatically steps up to the next position when it becomes vacant. There are also cases where promotion is by seniority. This means the employee among those eligible for the job who has the longest service with the firm is automatically promoted. Neither of these systems takes into account the suitability of the employee for the job; they are based on the idea that experience fits an employee to take on more responsibility.

Where promotion is decided on merit, the senior secretary or supervisor may be authorised to select an employee who has shown he possesses the abilities and qualities for the job. Promotion by merit has advantages both for employees seeking promotion and for the supervisor filling a vacancy.

Employees with ability who work hard are rewarded by promotion to higher positions with more interesting work and more pay. This encourages them to stay with the firm and do a good job. As the employee has experience with the firm he knows where everything is and how the firm's systems operate. The induction and orientation period is shortened and less training is required. There is more information available about applicants who are already employed by the firm. Background details, records of attendance and other matters are on file in the Personnel Department. The supervisor may know the employee and be familiar with his personality and work.

There are also disadvantages. If a large number of employees are competing for a few promotions, some are bound to become frustrated if they are not promoted within a reasonable time. They may lose interest in their jobs and will probably look for a better position elsewhere. Sometimes a supervisor is wary of promoting a very able person to be his assistant in case the assistant proves to be more competent than the supervisor and eventually becomes a threat to the supervisor's own position.

Choosing one employee for promotion from several eligible candidates can cause resentment and lead to accusations of favouritism.

ENGAGING A NEW EMPLOYEE If the firm's policy allows it, there are times when it is preferable to engage a new employee. If the vacancy involves a skill that none of the applicants within the firm possesses, it may be cheaper and easier to recruit someone with the necessary skill rather than train an existing employee. New employees bring in new ideas. If everyone in the office is trained by the same supervisor or senior secretary, they are all likely to follow the same systems when they are promoted, even if these systems have become outmoded or need improving.

COMMUNICATION When you know the method by which you can fill a vacancy, the next step is to inform all possible applicants. In the case of promotion, unless you have one person in mind, you will want to inform all suitable candidates so that they can decide if they wish to apply. If there is a large number of eligible employees, you can post a job description and personnel specification on the firm's notice board or put an announcement in your company newspaper or house magazine. If these facilities are not available, you could write to all eligible applicants or to their supervisors asking them to inform their subordinates of the vacancies. If there are only a few possible candidates, you could tell them personally. It is bad policy just to let "word get around". Rumours lead to inaccuracies and weaken the authority of the supervisor. When employees have been informed of a vacancy and applied for it, the selection procedure can start.

Various methods are available for recruiting staff from outside. The method chosen depends on the job to be filled, the time available for recruitment and selection, and the firm's policy.

If you want to recruit someone without experience but with certain educational qualifications, you can make the vacancy known to *careers teachers at schools* and *appointments boards and officers at colleges and universities.* Some firms who regularly employ school, college or university leavers send a representative to the educational institutions to talk to students about the firm and the jobs available.

You can inform *Employment Offices* and *Job Centres* of a vacancy in your organisation. The vacancy may be treated in one of two ways.
1 Self-service, which means that anyone, whether employed or not, may select an advertised vacancy and arrange to be interviewed by the employer. 2 The officers at the Employment Office or Job Centre will interview people who are

seeking a job and suggest suitable vacancies to them. Employment Offices and Job Centres perform similar functions but Job Centres are more modern and tend to place more emphasis on self-service job selection. People under 18 years who are seeking their first job are interviewed at *Careers Offices*.

There is also a number of *Professional Executive Recruitment* offices throughout the country, some of which have divisions for the recruitment of executive secretaries. The employer pays a fee for the recruitment service when a person is engaged to fill the vacancy.

When vacancies occur some firms *display a notice* listing the available jobs outside their offices, factories or in the windows of their shops or restaurants. This costs the firm nothing but it does not ensure that all suitable candidates are informed of the vacancies.

An existing employee may recommend a relative or friend for a specific vacancy or as a possible future employee when a post becomes available. Many firms think very highly of the *recommendation system* as existing employees are unlikely to recommend someone who will do a poor job since it will reflect on them. A satisfied employee thus provides a firm with free advertising, and some companies offer bonuses to staff when an employee they recommend is engaged.

If a person wants to work for a particular firm, although no vacancies have been advertised he can make a *direct application* by writing to the personnel officer or staff manager, giving details of qualifications and experience, and inquiring about suitable jobs at present or in the future. If there is nothing immediately available, the applicant may be put on a waiting list and informed when a vacancy occurs. Some firms with good reputations can fill all vacancies on certain levels from direct applications.

Over the years it has become customary in some firms for the *trade unions* to nominate applicants for vacant positions. On the managerial level *professional associations* may include a VACANCIES column in their journals which are sent out to all members. Some professional associations also maintain a register of candidates for vacant posts.

In recent years increasing numbers of office staff, both temporary and permanent, have been recruited through *private employment agencies*. A firm has to pay an agency fee when they engage an applicant sent to them by the agency. In theory, agencies reduce the work involved in recruiting staff by screening applicants and sending for interview only those candidates who have suitable qualifications and experience.

Several *management consultant firms* also offer an employment agency service for manageraial staff. The consultant advertises the post without naming the client company, collects applications and interviews applicants. The consultant chooses the most suitable applicants who are put on a 'short-list'. A 'short-list' means what it says: it is a short list of names, only a few names. This saves time for the client firm as they do not have to read all the applications and interview unsuitable candidates—the short-listing is done for them and they only have to make the final decision.

All vacancies can be filled through *advertising*. Advertising can be expensive but it brings the vacancy to the attention of a large number of people. National and local newspapers have a 'Situations Vacant' section which is often sub-divided into classifications, such as General, Office Staff, Catering and Scientific. Specialised magazines and newspapers for particular trades, professions and types of industries usually carry job advertisements for their own field. Jobs can also be advertised on commercial television and radio; these media are expensive but they reach an extremely large audience.

If you have to place an advertisement for a job, you must carefully consider the medium for the advertisement and the wording. The medium carrying the advertisement can have an important influence on its success. If the wrong medium is chosen you will have wasted the firm's money and have few suitable applicants or perhaps none at all; but if your advertisement attracts several suitable candidates, the expense is justified.

National newspapers usually carry advertisements for jobs in London and other large cities. Local newspapers reach people living in the locality.

The attraction of the job depends to a great extent on the wording used in the advertisement. Obviously an advertisement for a secretary to a film producer would bring a large number of replies no matter how it was worded, but advertisements for less glamorous jobs should be carefully thought out.

That does not mean that you should make the job seem better or different than it is. The advertisement should be based on the job description and the personnel specification. If your firm's policy does not include job analysis, it is a good idea to analyse the vacancy you have to fill.

Once you have written an advertisement containing the important points of the job, you should then add such information as salary, hours of work, holidays and fringe benefits, such as luncheon vouchers. All these details help the readers to form a clear picture of the job. Make sure that the advertisement states the person to be written to or telephoned, and the firm's address and, if necessary, the telephone number. Once you have set out the necessary information there is no harm in adding a little sparkle to make your advertisement stand out from the rest—as long as you are not misleading. Remember, however, that the price of the advertisement is calculated on its length. Keep it brief, but do not leave out anything vital.

Selection The APPLICATIONS may be by letter, telephone or in person and all applicants should complete an application form at some stage.

The *letter of application**, including a curriculum vitae or personal history is your first introduction to the candidate. It should contain all the basic information about the applicant's age, qualifications, experience and other abilities. You can also get other clues about the applicant from the letter. Is it neat and businesslike with no errors in spelling or grammar? Is it a "three c's letter"—clear, complete and concise? Is it well organised? If the letter does not measure up to these standards, you should not disqualify the applicant. She may just be

* See Appendix A.

poor at writing letters of application but exceptionally good at her job. But unless her qualifications and experience are excellent, an untidy, confused letter is probably not worth following up.

Traditionally, the letter of application is handwritten with a handwritten or typed curriculum vitae or personal history. However, typed letters are perfectly permissible and may even be desired for applications for secretarial posts. The information on the curriculum vitae should be organised under headings and set out so that the facts can be read clearly.

If possible, you should reply to all letters of application, even if you are saying, "No, thank you." It is impolite and unfeeling to keep applicants ignorant of your decision regarding their application.

If your advertisement requested *telephone applications* or if you are using an employment agency which screens applicants and then tells the suitable candidates to telephone you, you must be prepared to receive the calls. The applicants will probably be nervous about talking about themselves on the telephone and it is up to you to help them through it by asking appropriate questions. Using the personnel specification as your guide, make a list of all the information you need to know and put it in a sensible order: name, age, education, diplomas, experience, special skills, such as shorthand and use of machines, speeds. Then write a brief outline of the duties and responsibilities of the job from the job description including any disadvantages of the job.

Your conversation should begin by finding out about the applicant. If she is unsuitable, you can tell her then without wasting both your time. Prepare a tactful phrase beforehand so that you do not get into an embarrassing situation on the phone.

Use a friendly tone and encourage the applicant to talk. After you have told her the details of the job, ask if she has any questions. If you are worried about your side of the conversation, have a practice run with a friend and note her comments on your approach. Keep a pencil or pen and paper handy so that you can make notes during the conversation. If the applicant is suitable and is still interested in the job, finish by arranging a time for an interview. Then when you have rung off note down your impressions and any areas you want to explore when she comes for the interview.

Sometimes an applicant will come to see you *in person* in the first instance, in which case you should have an application form or personal history form ready for her to complete. If you read this over quickly you can then proceed as in the interview below.

Every applicant has to complete an application form or personal history form at some point in the recruitment and selection procedure. Some firms send application forms to all suitable candidates after their letters have been received. The applicants fill them in and post them back to the firm where they are considered before candidates are chosen for interviews. Other firms ask applicants to complete the forms when they come for their interviews but before the actual interviews take place. Sometimes the form is completed only after the applicant has been engaged.

The application form asks for all the basic information that the applicant gives over the telephone or in her curriculum vitae, but in greater detail. It often also requests facts about medical history, hobbies and other skills, such as languages or driving. Some forms leave space for the applicant to write any extra notes about herself, and there may be additional blank spaces for the use of the recruitment officer or personnel department.

The form can serve two purposes: the information on it is the framework for the interview and if the applicant is successful it becomes part of the confidential personnel records. If it is to be used effectively, the application

INSTRUCTIONS Please answer each question clearly and completely. Type or print in black ink.	**LONGLY GLOBAL PRODUCTIONS** Application for employment as	Do not write in this space
Surname	Other names (Mr/Mrs/Miss)	

Education — Date of birth

NAME AND ADDRESS OF SCHOOL OR COLLEGE	FROM	TO	EXAMINATIONS PASSED OR CERTIFICATES OR DIPLOMAS	MAIN COURSE OF STUDY

Previous employment

NAME AND ADDRESS OF EMPLOYER	FROM	TO	POSITION

Knowledge of languages — MOTHER TONGUE

Other Languages	Very good	Good	Average	Poor

HOBBIES

References: List three persons not related to you, who are familiar with your character and qualifications

FULL NAME	FULL ADDRESS	BUSINESS OR OCCUPATION
1.		
2.		
3.		

I certify that the statements made by me in answer to the foregoing questions are true, complete and correct to the best of my knowledge and belief.

DATE ____________ SIGNATURE ____________

For use by Personnel Department only

MEDICAL REPORT		SCHOOL REPORT REFERENCES
DATE APPOINTED	DEPARTMENT	POSITION

An application form.

form must be designed so that it is clear and easy to read. Adequate space must be left for the applicant to write his answers and a logical order must be followed. Experience and qualifications details should come near the top of the form because these are amongst some of the first points the interviewer wants to discuss.

THE INTERVIEW Usually an applicant is not called for interview unless he has the basic qualifications, experience and skills to do the job. The purpose of the interview is to determine whether the applicant has the personal qualities necessary, such as the ability to organise and a sense of responsibility, and to gauge whether the applicant will fit in with other employees, including his immediate superior, and the firm. Both these things are difficult to judge in ideal circumstances, but the interview situation makes them even more complex because of the roles of the two people involved, the interviewer and the interviewee or applicant.

The applicant, anxious to make a good impression, tries to make himself appear as good as possible, while the interviewer, who wants to seem efficient, may be nervous about asking personal questions and sitting in judgment. Because the interviewer is human he may have emotional reactions that could affect his judgment: for example, if he discovers that he and the applicant went to the same school, or if he particularly dislikes the cut or colour of some item of the applicant's dress.

If you are interviewing applicants, you want the best person for the job and therefore you must try to overcome all these obstacles to making a clear, objective decision. Direct the conversation so that the applicant reveals something of her true self. You must take a positive attitude towards your role as interviewer: you are judging the person's fitness for the job so your questions should be directed towards that end; your decision, if it is negative, should only relate to the vacancy and should not be a vote of no-confidence in the applicant as a person. Finally, if you recognise that you have immediate emotional reactions for or against the applicant, you must try to ignore them. Also beware of "the halo effect" caused by one favourable quality which is so impressive that the applicant's possible shortcomings in other directions are ignored.

In order to decide on the applicant's suitability you must know:

1 What you are trying to find out about the applicant.
2 How to go about finding it out.

To settle the first point, you must turn to the job description and the personnel specification. Familiarise yourself with these so that during the interview you are not constantly reading them to check on some point or other, such as whether the job involves using the telephone. Your whole attention should be on what the applicant is saying—and not saying.

Besides the skills and qualities necessary for doing the job, you also have to find out whether the applicant will fit into the firm. You also have to learn about the applicant's temperament and manner, her reliability, ability to adjust and her potential for training and leadership.

Once the objectives of the interview are established, you must consider the second point, "How to find them out." As we have already mentioned, the applicant is on her best behaviour. To find out about the real person behind this "front" you must take the tension out of the interview situation. Most people are more willing to talk about themselves in a relaxed atmosphere.

Your opening remarks are most important and will set the tone for the rest of the interview. A friendly greeting and a pleasant smile make a good beginning. Then put the applicant at ease by asking a question on a lighter note. The application form she has filled in will provide a clue for this. Ask about a hobby, where she lives or a general question about her school or previous employer:

"I see you list making pottery as one of your hobbies. How did you become interested in this?"
"I see you live in Oakwood. What sort of a village is it?"
"I notice on your form that you transferred from an old school to a modern one. What differences did you find?"
"I see you worked for a year at the Tasty Biscuit Company. Did you get many samples?"

Once you have broken the ice, ask the applicant to summarise her schooling and working life. Although you have the basic facts on the application form, the details the applicant gives in conversation reveal a great deal about her personality. Keep a watch for inconsistencies, omissions or areas the candidate seems unwilling to discuss. When explored these show a lot about the real person. Ask about inconsistencies and omissions with sympathy and understanding and never be concerned or disapproving and never argue with the applicant. Unless you are neutral and impartial, the candidate will retreat.

Either during the summary or afterwards you can ask questions and make encouraging remarks. Questions, especially if they may be embarrassing or difficult, should be asked carefully. Try an indirect approach: instead of "Did you get on with your boss at Tasty Biscuits?" try, "Was there a pleasant working atmosphere at Tasty Biscuits?" Remarks, especially when the applicant is avoiding an issue or rambling, help the applicant to talk. Depending on the situation you might say:

"Do you mean that . . . ?"
"And then?"
"You thought you could find better opportunities for training elsewhere, did you?"
"That sounds very sensible."
"That must have been good experience."
"I see. In other words . . ."

Make sure you listen carefully so that you do not ask the applicant something she has just told you. More important, let the applicant see you are interested and listening. Look at her whilst she is speaking, do not stare out of the window or "doodle". Above all do not take copious notes. This can make the applicant feel she is being interrogated and she will watch what she says. It also interrupts the flow of conversation. You can make an occasional quick note, especially if it is after something good the applicant has said about herself, but try to remember the important points and write them down immediately the applicant leaves. Careful listening helps the interviewer "read between the lines" of what the applicant is saying and this gives a total impression which can be written down after the interview.

Ask a few personal—but not too personal—questions about the applicant's outside interests and home life. They may not be relevant to her ability to do the job but they give clues to her personality. Does she have any children, pets? Does she live at home, share a flat, have a bedsitter? Does she help with the gardening, housework? Where does she go on holiday? The answers are not as important as the general conversation they lead to. However, avoid references to anything really personal, such as boyfriends, politics, religion, home difficulties, or the way she spends her money.

Then it is your turn to talk about the firm, the job and the working conditions. Give the applicant a clear picture of the firm, by telling her a brief history and an outline of its products or services. Be clear about subjects like pay, holidays, sickness benefits, pension scheme, luncheon vouchers, canteen, hours and other company rules. Give details about the place of the job in the firm, its duties and responsibilities, any machines to be used, the type of office and the number of people in it, special duties such as making the tea, training given by the firm and prospects for promotion or transfer to another department.

When you have finished, ask if she has any questions. If you have been thorough, she may not have much to ask about, although she probably knows it is wise to ask about something. If her questions seem minor it may be more of a reflection on your thoroughness than her lack of interest. But watch for signs of enthusiasm about the job.

After she has asked about the firm, unless you have any further questions, you must bring the interview to a conclusion. Even if the applicant does not have a chance of getting the job, you must let her feel you will consider her application carefully without building up her hopes. A realistic and tactful way to end interviews, whether the applicant has a good chance or none at all is to follow a pattern something like this:

Thank the applicant for coming to talk to you.
Tell her you now have all the information you need about her.
Mention that there are, of course, other applicants and you must see each one before making any decision.
Make sure she understands what the next step is—that is, when you will let her know, in two days, a week, or whenever, and whether there will be a short-list and another interview with both you and your boss or whether you will write the final decision.
Finally, say "Goodbye" pleasantly, see her out of the office and make sure she can find her way out of the building.

ASSESSING THE APPLICANTS Even if you have an excellent memory, you should write your assessment of the applicant as soon as she leaves, while it is still fresh in your mind. In some firms a space is left on the application form for the interviewer to write his remarks. Otherwise the assessment can be written on a separate piece of paper and attached to the application form. The applicant's name should be written on the assessment in case it becomes separated from the other documents.

After all the applicants have been interviewed the difficult job of comparing them and selecting the one for the post must be tackled. One candidate may stand head and shoulders above the rest in all respects, but usually each candidate has some strong points and some weak ones. Therefore you need some standard of measurement. One method is to make a list of the abilities and experience required for the job and the personal qualities desirable in the person who will fill it, using the job description and personnel specification as a basis. Then write each quality as a heading across the top of a sheet of paper and each applicant's name down the side. Give each applicant a rating, perhaps out of 10, for each quality and write these under each heading. To show the importance of certain qualities, you could multiply the rating given by two. For example, if shorthand speed is more important than telephone manner, give a straight rating for telephone manner and double the rating for shorthand. Each candidate's total number of points indicates her total suitability. This should be considered as a guide rather than a final decision.

When you have finally chosen the successful candidate, let her know at once as she may be applying for other jobs. Write to the others as well so that they do not turn down other jobs in the hope of getting the one they applied for with your firm. Most organisations have standard letters to cover those situations; the successful applicant is sent a provisional letter of appointment saying that the appointment will be confirmed by a written contract of employment.

TESTS For some jobs tests are necessary. For example a shorthand or typewriting test is the best way to discover an applicant's speed and accuracy. The tests can be given before or after the interview. If the test is before the interview, the applicant can forget about it and concentrate on the conversation. If the test is given after the interview, the applicant will have a chance to relax and her work may suffer less from errors caused by nervousness.

Prepare a letter or another short piece of work for the test. Make sure you explain clearly what you want the applicant to do, and when you judge the result take into account that the applicant was nervous and may not have performed at her best.

Induction and orientation The successful candidate's first day at work is very important. First impressions have a strong effect on people and so it is wise to give the new employee a good start.

Some large firms have a planned induction and orientation programme which introduces the new employee to the firm and familiarises him with its organisation and procedures. In such a case the programme is probably carried out by the Personnel Department. In other firms it is the responsibility of the new employee's supervisor or senior to make the newcomer feel at home.

Before the new employee arrives, consider the points that should be covered in your induction and orientation programme. Try to remember what you wanted to know when you started at the firm. Make a list so that you can check that you have covered them all. Your list is bound to vary depending on your company and the employee's job but it should include the following:

1 Details about the company's history, products or services and its place in industry. These will have been mentioned in the interview but now that the new employee is part of the team, it is a good idea to refresh her memory and go into more detail. Many firms have a printed handbook giving this information which you can give to the newcomer.

2 The structure of the company. Who is the chairman or boss? What departments, subsidiaries, branches are there? What is the place of your department in the firm and what is the department's function?

3 Terms and conditions of employment. It does no harm to repeat details about holidays, sick pay and other matters even though you may have outlined them clearly in the interview. Are there any company sports clubs, social clubs or other voluntary benefits? Is there a staff association or staff union?

4 Company rules and regulations. Remind her about hours, lunch and tea breaks, personal telephone calls, medical certificates. Do employees have to clock in and out? Is there a timekeeping book to sign when she arrives in the morning? Is there a payment for overtime work?

5 Facilities. Where are the toilets? Is there a cloakroom, sick room, canteen? If so, where? If there is no canteen, suggest nearby cafés where employees have lunch.

6 Forms and cards. Are there any company forms to be completed? Tell her or show her where to take her National Insurance card and P45 tax form.

7 House style. What is the company's style for letters, memoranda, reports, minutes? How many carbon copies are usually taken? How is incoming and outgoing post handled? Is there an internal mail system?

8 Where things are and how to get them. How to get supplies of stationery, pens, pencils, carbon paper, envelopes, invoice forms, file cards or folders, typewriter ribbons and other necessary materials? What filing systems are used? What machines will she use? Where are they? How do they work? Whom should she tell when they break down?

9 Introductions. Introduce her to people with whom she will be working, including those she will have to contact in other departments. Ask a colleague to accompany her to lunch on the first day.

It is unlikely that the newcomer will remember everything you tell her as you will be mentioning a lot of names, departments, rooms, directions and rules. But as long as you have taken the trouble to tell her she will feel you have an interest in her welfare.

Encourage her to ask questions of you and other employees. You may not want to be bothered by what seem obvious questions, but it is preferable for her to learn the organisation's methods and rules from the beginning instead of making mistakes and getting into wrong habits.

DISMISSAL

It is preferable that whoever acts on behalf of an organisation regarding appointments should also act in matters of dismissal. In large organisations the power of dismissal normally rests with the head of the Personnel Department or the Staff Manager, and it is unlikely that the actual task of telling an employee he was being dismissed would be delegated to a secretary.

The topic is included here, however, because there are certain aspects of it which may be considered part of a senior secretary's general business knowledge; and in a very small firm the owner's secretary may well find herself put in the unenviable position of having to inform an employee of his/her dismissal, particularly if the person concerned is a junior clerk or typist who works directly under the secretary's supervision.

The Staff Manager is responsible for maintaining his organisation's good reputation for fairness and consistency in its personnel policy. His first duty is to make sure that the decision to terminate an employee's appointment has been made without bias or prejudice and that full consideration has been given to all those points of circumstance, personality and character which differ in each case; he must also talk personally to both the employee and the manager and any other supervisors who may be involved.

The second duty of the official responsible for terminating a contract of employment is to make sure that the organisation has complied with the employee's statutory rights under the Contract of Employment Act, the Redundancy Payments Act and the Employment Protection Act. (See pages 605 to 611). Generally speaking, a company will have a standard form for a letter of dismissal which ensures that correct procedure has been followed regarding stating grounds for dismissal, notice-periods, accrued holiday entitlement and the subsequent giving of references.

An employee cannot demand a reference from an employer, but employers are usually prepared to answer an enquiry in writing about an ex-employee and to give a testimonial if requested. Testimonials and references should be written impartially and be completely fair to both employees and future employers; the Staff Manager is the most suitable person to take responsibility for their wording as he can be more objective than the managers whose departments are affected by the dismissals.

No-one likes having to dismiss an employee and no matter how well justified the dismissal, staff morale will be affected by the incident; dismissal is a very severe blow not only to the victim, but it also causes other employees to feel unsettled and insecure, and the "hatchet-man" himself may experience an unwelcome feeling of antipathy and rejection.

Despite these unpleasant side effects, however, dismissals are sometimes necessary. A firm's interests are not well served by retaining the services of an incompetent employee; the employee's failure to perform his job satisfactorily endangers the jobs of others, damages the business and weakens the entire organisation.

Before a decision to dismiss an employee is taken, certain questions should be asked: Is the dismissal in the firm's best interests? Is the dismissal the result of a clash of personalities? Even if the employee is unsatisfactory in some aspects of his work, will his successor be any better? If the employee has shown some useful potential, could be given further training, or would it be better to start from the beginning with a new employee? Has the employee had reasonable warning? This latter point is important because under the Employment Protection Act, 1975 an employer can be accused of unfair dismissal if the employee has not been given an opportunity to fulfil the requirements of the job.

A vague complaint that his work is unsatisfactory is unlikely to bring about any improvement; but a straight personal talk giving the employee a specific description of his shortcomings, suggesting what he should do and setting a time limit, gives the employee "a last chance" to improve. Sometimes employees are unaware of their shortcomings and appreciate being told how they can improve their work and of facilities available for tuition and further study.

Sometimes a personal discussion will reveal that the employee is disappointed in the job, or is being asked to do work for which he was not employed and which he does not want to do. When this type of situation arises it may be better to transfer the person to another post more suited to his ability and more to his liking. Sometimes people react favourably to being given increased responsibility, a new job title, a position which increases their self-esteem or work from which they can derive genuine satisfaction.

If all possible steps have been taken to produce an improvement and the employee remains unsatisfactory, or is openly defiant, refuses to follow instructions, is insubordinate and an obvious source of trouble in the office, then the decision to dismiss him must be taken, and having been taken should be executed without delay.

Having ensured that the organisation has complied with the employee's statutory rights, select the right location for the interview. A glassed-in partitioned office is not the most suitable place; a secluded office where there is complete privacy will avoid any embarrassing scenes before the rest of the staff and will give the employee an opportunity to recover his composure before saying good-bye to his colleagues. Choose your words carefully: it is better to say, "It looks as though we've come to the end of the road," or, "I'm sorry I'm going to have to tell you to look for a job elsewhere," rather than "You're fired," or "You've got the sack;" after a tactful introduction, the employee may offer his resignation "for personal reasons" and this is less harmful to his self-respect and makes it easier when he applies for another job.

When the interview is over, arrange for the employee to be given his final salary cheque and the appropriate PAYE documents, wish him well and say goodbye. Then he can collect any personal belongings, say goodbye to his colleagues and leave. Most companies favour the practice of giving pay "in lieu of notice" rather than keeping on an employee under notice of dismissal or resignation.

INDUSTRIAL TRAINING

No business or organisation can operate at maximum efficiency if the staff are not trained to do their work properly. At one time training was considered necessary only for those jobs involving manual skills and this form of training was usually given in an apprenticeship scheme or as part of a course of study prior to full-time employment. Although apprenticeships and courses in skills such as shorthand and typewriting are still recognised methods of training, it is now accepted that training is necessary at all staff levels, up to and including senior management.

Industrial Training Act, 1964 The Industrial Training Act was formulated with three objectives:

1 To ensure that industry and commerce would have an adequate number of properly trained men and women at all levels.
2 To improve the quality and efficiency of industrial training.
3 To spread the cost of training more evenly amongst firms.

INDUSTRIAL TRAINING BOARDS In order to carry out these objectives, the Act gave the Secretary of State for Employment the power to establish industrial training boards for sections of industry and commerce. Each board is responsible for training in one area of work, such as air transport, hotels and catering, electrical, chemical, road transport and agriculture.

A training board consists of representatives of trade unions, employers, and education, and a government assessor. The board can set up specialist committees to make recommendations on aspects of its work. Decisions of the board are carried out by a staff of salaried officials who work at national, regional and local level.

The ITB's (Industrial Training Boards) are empowered to gather information from firms about their growth, their trade, their plans for expansion and their future manpower needs. On the basis of this information combined with advice from specialist committees on minimum standards of training for each type of work, the boards can ensure that there are adequate courses and facilities for training sufficient staff at all levels. Firms can use the facilities and courses provided by education authorities or they can devise their own training programmes within the firm, but company training schemes must be submitted to the ITB's for approval. The ITB's test trainees during or at the end of the training programmes to make sure that the programmes are being properly conducted and that the training conforms with the boards' own standards.

LEVIES AND GRANTS Some firms object to the cost of training. If a firm runs its own training schemes, specialists are needed to devise and conduct the training programmes. One or more rooms may be required for teaching and demonstration. The trainees who are attending courses are, of course, unable to do their normal jobs so extra employees may have to be employed to cover the trainees' work. If firms send employees to technical colleges or other training institutions, the firms have to pay the course fees and the cost of textbooks and materials; they also have to make arrangements for the trainees' work to be done whilst they are away.

The Industrial Training Act reflects the government's attitude towards industrial training: that although training is expensive, it pays in the long run because staff become more skilled and efficient in their jobs. However, the Act recognises that some firms have more resources to spend on training than others.

The levy and grant system of the Act was devised to provide a financial incentive to firms to provide training; it also spreads the cost of training over all firms in each type of work.

Under the levy and grant system, every employer covered by the Act must pay a levy to the appropriate ITB. The levy is a fixed percentage of the firm's payroll, so firms with a large number of employees pay higher sums than small firms with fewer employees. The boards use part of the money collected by levies to finance their operations—paying running costs and staff salaries. The remainder of the money is used to pay grants to firms whose training programmes are approved or who send employees on approved courses of training elsewhere. Firms having generous staff training programmes may receive back all the money paid as levies in the form of grants; in some cases the grants are greater than the levies.

OFF-THE-JOB TRAINING Polytechnics, colleges of further education and other educational establishments offer both *day and evening courses.* Trainees can be released from work to attend special training courses often given at local colleges of further education. Some *day release* and *part-time day courses* require attendance at evening classes as well.

There are also approved *correspondence courses.* The lessons are posted to the trainee who does the work in his own home and posts it back to the correspondence college for checking. Firms pay the course fees and any additional expenses incurred by the trainees.

Training at a higher level for technical skills, supervisors and management may require attendance of several days, weeks or months away from work. These *block-release courses* are usually given at universities or other centres where the trainees are in residence. Such supervisory and management courses include group discussions, case studies, projects and special techniques such as business games and role-playing where the trainees act out the parts of employees and employers or supervisors in business situations.

Sandwich courses consist of alternate periods of study in a university or further education establishment and of industrial, commercial or professional experience. They provide a balanced programme of academic and practical training.

ON-THE-JOB TRAINING On-the-job (or in-firm, in-service, in-plant, or on-site) training is given to all levels of staff. A supervisor is responsible for training

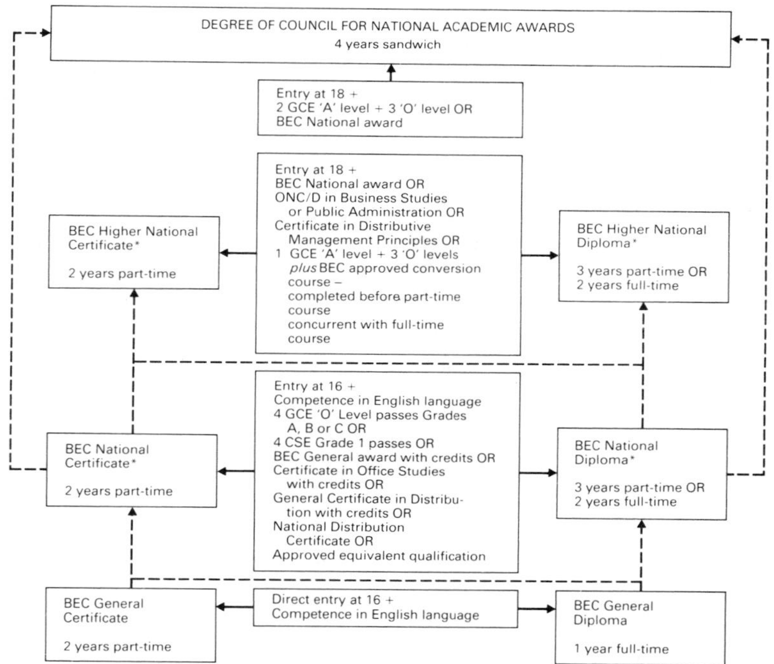

Chart to show the range of courses that leads to national qualifications in business studies awarded by the Business Education Council (BEC) and the Council for National Academic Awards (CNAA).

his subordinates to apply their skills. Many large firms appoint training officers who are responsible for organising special training programmes within the firm as well as selecting appropriate courses for off-the-job training.

On-the-job training may consist of demonstrations, lectures and group discussions or it may employ the latest *audio-visual teaching equipment* such as models of machinery, films, film strips, slides, film loops, tape-recorders, tape-casettes or closed-circuit television.

Programmed learning allows the trainee to teach himself in simple steps. It can be done using a book or using a teaching machine operated mechanically or electrically which passes the visual material through a viewing window. The information to be taught is divided into a series of frames. Each frame teaches one unit of learning or learning step; the trainee masters the information in one frame before moving on to the next. After several frames, or after each frame, there is a question which tests whether the trainee has understood the information on the previous frame. The trainee checks his answer by looking at the next frame; if his answer is correct he can continue to work through the programme, if his answer is incorrect he must go back and work through the preceding steps again.

Other teaching techniques used in on-the-job training include *in-tray exercises* and *algorithms*. In an in-tray exercise the trainee is presented with a number of situations, items or documents of the type normally met in the job; he then has to decide in which order he would deal with the documents or cases and the appropriate action to be taken.

An *algorithm* is a chart which leads the trainee step by step through a logical sequence of questions and answers to a desired conclusion. The procedure is reduced to a series of simple yes/no decisions and the sequence of the questions teaches the trainee how to order his thoughts when he is confronted with an actual situation.

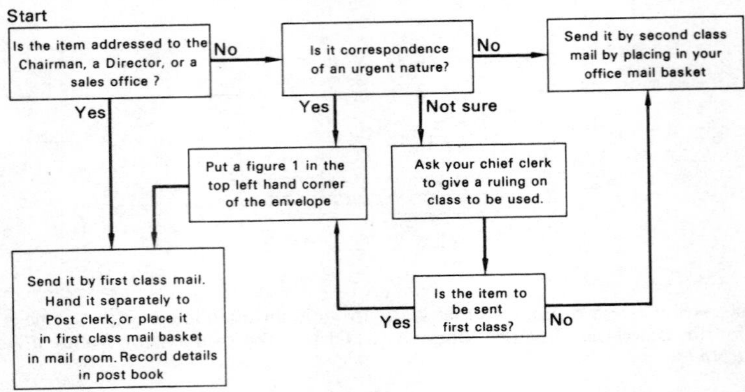

Example of an algorithm to teach 'Company use of the two-class mail system' from Booklet No. 8, *The Training of Clerks*, Engineering Industry Training Board, page 18.

Retraining With the rapid advances in technology, workers in technical jobs may find that every few years they require special training to work with a new product or a different process. To keep pace with new developments workers in many fields need specialised courses either on- or off-the-job at regular intervals.

Just as many factory workers lost their jobs when processes became automated, now office staff are finding that new business methods and the increasing use of computers are making their jobs obsolete. The government has a retraining programme which can teach new skills to some employees who have lost their jobs to machines, but employees themselves should think about the possibility of taking additional training at some time in their careers to adapt to new ideas and conditions.

Staff at management and supervisory levels in industry, commerce and the professions also have a personal responsibility to keep abreast of new developments in their areas of specialisation; this may even involve taking courses of study in preparation for newly established examinations.

INDUSTRIAL RELATIONS

Trade Union Structure There are approximately 150 trade unions in Britain. Of these only a handful are very large and well-known, such as the largest, the Transport and General Workers Union (TGWU). A small number of the rest have more than 200,000 members but the majority of trade unions are fairly small with 40,000–100,000 members. However, unions, like many large firms, have seen advantages in mergers and some unions have joined together to increase their membership and strength; the result of these mergers has been to decrease the actual number of unions although the number of union members is on the increase.

TYPES OF UNION Trade unions can be divided into four broad groups according to the kind of workers they represent. *Craft unions* were the first to be

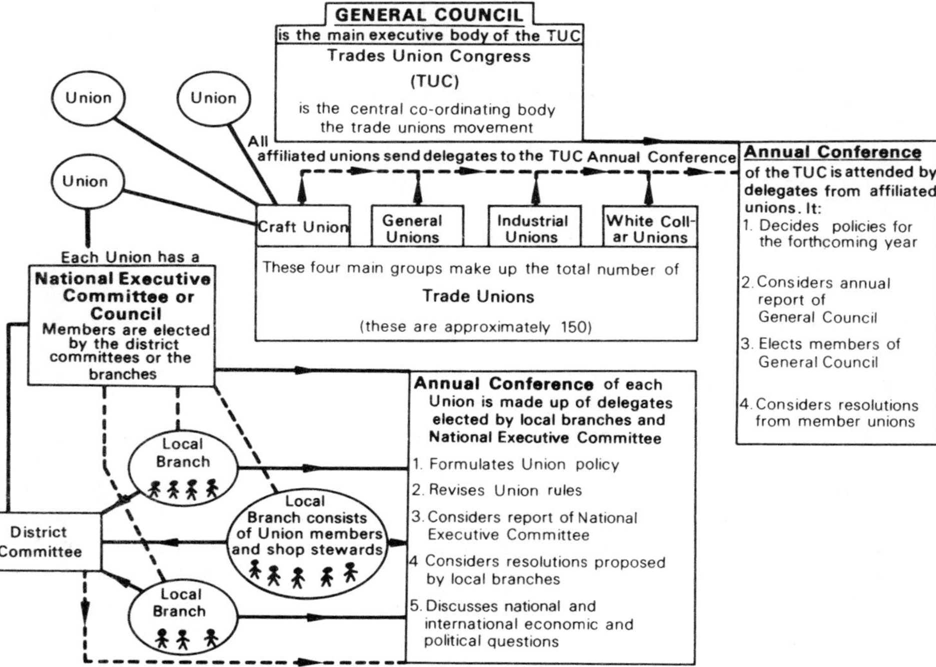

Diagram to illustrate the framework of trade union structure in Great Britain.

formed in the nineteenth century. They are based on apprenticeship systems and each craft union represents members who have a particular skill or craft, for example, the Plumbing Trades Union. *General unions* developed during the nineteenth century when unskilled and semiskilled workers were employed in factories. Membership is based on the job a person does, rather than on any skill he has acquired. Unlike craft unions, members do not have to have had an apprenticeship or training before they can join. The most famous general union is the Transport and General Workers Union. Each *industrial union* represents workers in a particular industry rather than workers with a certain skill or type of job; examples are the National Union of Mineworkers and the National Union of Railwaymen. The term "white collar" as in "white collar worker" or "white collar job" or *white collar unions* originally referred to jobs for which the employee was required to wear a suit with a collar and tie, in other words, clerical, managerial or professional workers. This distinguished those employees from manual workers and those doing jobs for which dress was unimportant and overalls or "dirty" clothes could be worn.

In recent years white collar workers have felt that they were not gaining the benefits of higher pay and better conditions achieved for manual workers by their unions. White collar unions representing clerical and administrative staff in offices, and technicians and supervisors in industry, have been growing in strength and number. A few professional people, including doctors and teachers, have formed unions because it was felt they were needed. Two large white collar unions are the National Association of Local Government Officers (NALGO) and the Association of Scientific, Technical and Managerial Staff (ASTMS).

Unions have organisation structures like large firms, starting with the shop steward in a factory and going up to the top officials who are responsible for the union's activities throughout the country. The major difference between trade union organisation structure and company organisation structure is that most officials of the union have been elected to their offices by the members and in theory at least the members run the union through the elected officials who are their representatives.

SHOP STEWARD The shop steward is elected by the members of the union in one place of work. In some unions the election is subject to confirmation by union officers. In very large firms there may be more than one shop steward for each union, with a chief shop steward or convenor. In such cases the convenor and sometimes the shop stewards as well may have office facilities supplied by the firm, including secretarial help and the use of a telephone.

The shop steward is both a union official and the representative of the other union members in the firm. The shop steward's responsibilities vary depending upon the union and the circumstances of the firm. In general as an official of the union, the shop steward should promote its interests, communicate between the shop floor and the next level, the union branch, and in some cases collect union membership subscriptions. As the representative of the other union members in the firm he may represent individual members or all the firm's union members when there is a grievance against the management; he may speak for the members during collective negotiations; he may check that the firm's management is keeping to the terms of its agreement with the members and with the union.

UNION BRANCH Every union member belongs to a local branch of the union which is determined by where he lives or where he works. The branch collects subscriptions either directly from members or through shop stewards and distributes union benefits, such as strike pay. Delegates to local organisations where the union is represented are appointed by the branch. In some unions voting for the national executive or other officials is at branch level. At their branch meetings, union members formulate resolutions for the national executive committee which go through the district committee. In most cases the branch has no authority to deal with local disputes between union members and their employers.

Branches of all unions in a town or local area appoint representatives to the trades council which acts as a spokesman for the local union members in dealing with local government.

DISTRICT COMMITTEE The district committee is a divisional area or regional committee or council that covers a number of local branches. It is made up of delegates elected by local branches and usually has a full-time paid district secretary who attends the committee's meetings.

The chief responsibilities of the district committee are overseeing branch functions and negotiations with employers and sorting out and discussing resolutions from local branches for submission to the annual conference. Generally the district committee has no power to authorise strike action.

NATIONAL EXECUTIVE COMMITTEE OR COUNCIL The executive committee or council performs the main executive functions of the union and is responsible for the day-to-day decisions and running of the union organisation. It is usually housed in permanent headquarters and a proportion of the committee members are full-time officials who are paid a salary by the union, such as the union's president, vice-president, general secretary and treasurer. Sometimes all the members of the committee are salaried and full-time, although there are usually some part-time members who continue to work in industry. Committee members are elected for terms ranging from one to five years; however, committee members usually serve for longer periods as there are frequent re-elections.

Besides supervising the administration of the union and co-ordinating its activities, the national executive committee also controls union funds, has the responsibility for national negotiations of wages and conditions and considers the effect on union members of national government policies and the state of the economy. The national committee must approve strike action.

ANNUAL CONFERENCE As its name suggests, the annual conference meets once a year. It is made up of delegates elected by the local branches and the national executive committee. The conference formulates union policy and revises union rules. The national committee presents its report on its work over the previous year and the delegates discuss, debate and criticise the report. Resolutions prepared by local branches are debated and national and international economic and political questions are discussed.

TRADES UNION CONGRESS (TUC) The Trades Union Congress was first convened in 1868. It is the central co-ordinating body of the trade union movement and aims to promote the interests of its affiliated unions which number about 130 including most of the large unions. It also acts as the spokesman for trade union opinion nationally, for example, in discussions with government and other organisations.

The TUC annual conference or congress is a meeting of delegates from affiliated unions. Congress debates and decides general policies for the next year, considers the annual report of the general council and elects the members of the general council.

The general council of the TUC is the permanent executive body of congress. It consists of 36 members representing the 19 trade groups of affiliated unions and special interest groups, such as women trade unionists. The general secretary is the only full-time member of the general council. Other members are usually general secretaries or presidents of unions affiliated to the TUC.

The work of the general council includes the co-ordination of industrial action by affiliated unions and working for common action on general questions of wages and hours. It prepares statements on TUC policy and deals with policies, relations and disputes between its affiliated unions. As the central body of trade unionism, the general council studies industrial and economic changes and considers new government legislation that may affect its members.

Most of the general council's work is carried out through committees which are appointed annually. Each council member serves on several committees and outside experts may be asked to join certain committees. Main committees include finance and general purposes, economic and education.

Employers' Organisations Although firms within the same type of industry may be competitors, they also have many common interests. They are concerned about technical progress, the expansion of the economy in general and their industry in particular, and the regulation of wages, terms of employment and training. In many sections of industry and commerce, firms have joined together to form employers' organisations to promote their common interests. Each member firm contributes towards the running costs of the organisation and receives the benefits of its services, such as specialist assistance with settling industrial disputes, which the smaller member firms probably could not afford on their own.

EMPLOYERS' ASSOCIATIONS An employers' association is formed by firms in the same type of industry, although in countries where the number of employers is relatively small one national association is formed by all firms regardless of their business function. The association negotiates with trade unions representing employees of member firms. It also looks into matters such as wages and salaries, recruitment, training, safety and the conditions of employment within the industry concerned. Some associations represent employers throughout the country while others are based on a region. The regional associations belong to national federations of employers' associations for particular industries.

TRADE ASSOCIATIONS A trade association represents the commercial and trading interests of the member firms and gives attention to such matters as pricing policies and technical innovations. In some industries one organisation acts as both an employers' association and a trade association.

CONFEDERATION OF BRITISH INDUSTRIES (CBI) The CBI was formed in 1965 when three bodies of employers' organisations amalgamated. It is mainly concerned with firms in manufacturing industries but membership is open to any employers or employers' organisations; CBI members include individual firms, public corporations, national employers' associations, federations of regional employers' associations and trade associations.

The CBI is governed by a council composed of 400 elected representatives of its members. The head of the council is called the President. The CBI has a full-time staff headed by the Director-General. Like the TUC, the CBI acts as a national spokesman; it does not take part directly in negotiations with trade unions but it can make recommendations to members about negotiations. Committees can be set up to make studies of various aspects of industry and employment for the CBI and other bodies; a committee was set up to study redundancy payments for the Department of Employment in preparation for the Redundancy Payments Act, 1965. The CBI can also speak for employers as a whole in discussions with government.

Collective bargaining When an executive joins a firm, he negotiates his pay and conditions of employment with the management and the resulting terms are written into his contract of employment. In a firm employing a large number of workers doing the same or similar jobs, instead of negotiating a contract with each individual employee, the firm bargains with the trade union collectively representing the workers. The result of collective bargaining is a contract of employment for all the workers concerned, called a *collective agreement*. Collective bargaining can be carried out at different levels:

1. *Nationally*. A craft union representing skilled workers who are employed in several different types of industry may make a national collective agreement on wages and conditions with all the employers concerned on behalf of all its members. 2. *Industry level*. A union may carry out collective bargaining with

an employers' association representing all the firms in one type of industry. To increase its bargaining strength, the union may join with other unions in the same industry in a federation of unions to negotiate with the employers' association. Collective bargaining at industry level may also be carried out through a **joint industrial council** or a **wages council**. A joint industrial council is composed of equal numbers of representatives of management and trade unions. A wages council can be set up in industries where there is inadequate collective bargaining. It is made up of representatives of management and unions in equal numbers and three independent members appointed by the Secretary of State for Employment. Its decisions can be made legally binding on the firms within the industry concerned. 3. *District level.* Since wages and conditions vary in different parts of the country owing to differences in the cost of living and other factors, the district committee of a trade union may negotiate on behalf of its members in that district with one or more employers or employers' associations. 4. *Company level.* Large firms, such as the Ford Motor Company, negotiate with trade unions for a collective agreement covering workers in their factories. 5. *Factory level.* A firm can have collective bargaining with one or more unions representing the firm's employees. The collective agreement will apply only to that particular firm. 6. *Shop floor level.* There is a trend in many firms towards negotiating directly with the shop steward about the wages and conditions of employment of the union members he represents. Collective bargaining at this level is faster, more flexible and enables the firm and the shop steward to take local conditions into consideration. In this type of bargaining the power and responsibility of the shop steward are increased.

Industrial action If employers and unions cannot reach an agreement in their collective bargaining, either side can take industrial action to put pressure on the other side to come to terms. Industrial action taken by a union is not official unless it has been sanctioned by the national executive committee.

Unofficial industrial action is most common at shop floor level where the employees of a firm or a particular section of them disapproves of the management's action, for example in introducing new machinery which may make them redundant. Unofficial industrial action, usually organised by one or more shop stewards, can be made official by the national executive committee of the union.

WORK-TO-RULE In many cases it has been shown that a work-to-rule is a very effective means of industrial action. A work-to-rule is just what it says: working strictly according to the rules of the firm or industry. Most employees always work according to the rules of their firm or, at least, according to the spirit of the rules. In a work-to-rule the letter of a firm's regulations are followed and the participants in the industrial action take extra time to follow every detail in their handbook of rules.

Although the business of a firm is not halted by a work-to-rule, it can be impeded to such an extent that the income of the firm suffers. A work-to-rule is often the industrial action chosen by employees in public service industries where a more severe form of action, such as a strike, would completely disrupt the country. However, in a situation such as a work-to-rule by electricity workers the effects can only be considered by the public as disruptive.

STRIKE A strike is a stoppage of work by a group of employees. If a key group in a firm goes on strike, even though they are few in number, they may bring the business of the firm to a standstill and thus cause large numbers of other workers, not directly involved in the strike, to be temporarily unemployed. Strikers usually picket their firm; this means they stand outside the entrance, often holding placards. It is a fundamental trade union practice that a member of a union will not cross an official picket line even if it is composed of members of other unions.

LOCK-OUT The lock-out is the employer's version of the strike. A firm may literally lock out the workers from a factory or office by refusing to open the premises, or the employers may suspend work for a period. A lock-out is intended to put pressure on employees by depriving them of their livelihood, but in a welfare state such as Great Britain where unemployment and social security benefits are available, the lock-out is less effective than it was in the early days of the trade union movement.

Employment Protection Act, 1975 The Employment Protection Act, 1975 was designed to give employees greater certainty, improved security and increased benefits in their employment, and the number of employees protected by the law was extended by including all people who work for 16 hours a week or more and those working at least 8 hours a week who have 5 years' service. The main provisions of the Act cover collective bargaining, the establishment of the Advisory, Conciliation and Arbitration Service (ACAS), the Central Arbitration Committee (CAC) and the Employment Appeal Tribunal, which hears appeals from the decisions of industrial tribunals, as statutory bodies, the appointment of a Certification Officer responsible for certifying the independence of trade unions, recognition by employers of independent trade unions for collective bargaining, disclosure of information, wages councils, and terms and conditions of employment.

ADVISORY, CONCILIATION AND ARBITRATION SERVICE (ACAS) offers industrial advice, provides a conciliation service in cases of dispute between unions and employers and may arrange for arbitration by CAC where conciliation fails. Matters concerning the recognition of trade unions, minimum terms, equal pay, disclosure of information are among those which are the concern of the CAC and ACAS. ACAS also has responsibility for publishing Codes of Practice relevant to certain provisions of the Act.

CODES OF PRACTICE The Employment Protection Act charges ACAS with the responsibility for publishing Codes of Practice relating to various provisions of the Act. Though not of itself a legal document, a Code of Practice may be used by industrial tribunals and the Central Arbitration Committee when its contents are relevant to any matter being investigated.

The first code was published in June 1977 entitled "Code of Practice 1 Disciplinary practice and procedures in employment". It is a guide to the proper conduct of employers in connection with the establishment of disciplinary rules and their implementation.

Disclosure of Information. For the purpose of collective bargaining unions may ask the employer for information which may help them in their negotiations for wage increases and other improved conditions of service. There are limits set to the information which must be disclosed. For example, an employer should not disclose information against the interest of national security, information which has been received in confidence or information which is about an individual.

The type of information which should be disclosed is set out in "Code of Practice 2 Disclosure of information to trade unions for collective bargaining purposes" published by ACAS in August 1977. Examples of the type of information to be provided include details of pay and benefits, conditions of service, manpower, performance and financial information.

A union which considers that relevant information has been withheld can complain to the Central Arbitration Committee. If the Committee upholds the complaint it can make a declaration to that effect. The Committee is empowered to take further action if the employer still refuses to disclose the required information.

Terms and conditions of employment. The Employment Protection Act extends the rights of employees assured under other employment legislation. The most important of these additional rights are explained briefly below.

1 Guarantee payments for a limited period for employees who lose pay because of short-time working or lay-offs, unless there is no work as a result of industrial action by other employees of the same or an associated employer.
2 Normal wage payments up to a maximum period of 26 weeks for employees suspended on medical grounds.
3 Security of employment during pregnancy unless a woman is unable to continue her job by virtue of her pregnancy, in which case she must be offered alternative employment if possible.
4 Payment of a proportion of normal wages for a woman during the first six weeks of absence to have a baby. A maternity pay fund has been established to which all employers contribute. Employers who make maternity payments can claim a refund from the fund.
5 A woman is entitled to return to her job or a suitable alternative job at any time up to 29 weeks after having her baby, provided she has worked for the same employer for two years, has worked up to eleven weeks

before the birth and has indicated her intention to her employer to return to work before stopping work to have the baby.

6 An official of a recognised, independent trade union is entitled to reasonable paid time off to carry out his official duties connected with industrial relations where they concern his employer, and for approved training related to those duties.

7 Employees who are members of a recognised, independent trade union are entitled to reasonable time off in working hours to take part in the union's activities (other than industrial action). ACAS have published a Code of Practice giving guidance on what constitutes "reasonable time off" and which elements of such time off must be paid for by the employer.

8 Employers must consult the appropriate trade union/s when planning redundancies—see the Redundancy Payments Act 1965.

9 Employees are entitled to longer notice of dismissal than previously—see Contracts of Employment Act, 1972.

10 Employees have the right to join an independent trade union of their own choice, or one of the specified unions in a closed shop agreement and may not be penalised by their employers for so doing.

11 Employees have the right not to join a trade union, even if a closed shop agreement has been negotiated between union and employer, if they have genuine religious objections to doing so.

12 An employer and a union may negotiate a closed shop agreement and employees refusing to join the union concerned may be dismissed.

The Department of Employment has published a series of twelve booklets covering various aspects of the Employment Protection Act. Information on specific points can be obtained from the Department or from any of the regional offices of ACAS.

UNFAIR DISMISSAL Under the Trade Union and Labour Relations Act, 1974 and the Employment Protection Act, 1975 the employee is strongly protected against unfair dismissal. Dismissal for membership of or activities in a trade union, participation in industrial action, on the grounds of sex, on the grounds of race, colour or creed or for minor acts of misconduct would all constitute unfair dismissal.

An employer may dismiss an employee in certain circumstances but he must act fairly and reasonably in so doing. Fair reasons for dismissal are normally considered to be one or more of

1 incompetence, i.e. the employee cannot or does not do his job adequately;
2 misconduct,
3 redundancy.

The provisions against unfair dismissal are intended to create good management practice where this does not already exist by ensuring that employees are given an opportunity to correct their faults and are given adequate warning as to what action will be taken if they do not perform satisfactorily. In this respect the ACAS Code on Discipline is particularly important.

Sex Discrimination Act 1975 Under this Act discrimination on the grounds of sex is unlawful in employment, training and related matters including discrimination against married people. Individuals who feel that an employer has discriminated against them have the right of direct access to the civil courts and industrial tribunals. The Act established the Equal Opportunities Commission to help enforce legislation and to promote equality of opportunity between the sexes generally.

Employers must now give equal opportunities to women and men when recruiting personnel, unless there are genuine occupational reasons why only a female or only a male person is acceptable for a particular job. Advertisements for vacant posts must normally state clearly that both men and women are eligible to apply for the post. Men and women must be employed under the same terms and conditions of service, including benefits, facilities and services, e.g. pension schemes. See Equal Pay Act, 1970. Women must be given the same training, transfer and promotion opportunities as men and employers may not now take into consideration the fact that a woman is married when considering her for recruitment, training, etc. Married women are now given greater protection and benefits under the Employment Protection Act, 1975 (see page 599).

The Trade Union and Labour Relations Acts, 1974 and 1976 The Trade Union and Labour Relations Act, 1974 repealed the Industrial Relations Act, 1971, but re-enacted certain provisions of that Act relating to codes of practice, unfair dismissal, jurisdiction and procedure of industrial tribunals and the role of conciliation officers. The Acts mainly concern the legal status of trade unions and employers' associations and give wider scope for the growth of trade union membership and collective bargaining, and strengthen the rights of employees to belong to a trade union and to play a full part in trade union activities without risk of losing employment or other sanctions.

INSTITUTIONS One of the major features of the Trade Union and Labour Relations Act, 1974 was the abolition of the National Industrial Relations Court. Disputes relating to unfair dismissal, trade union membership or any other matter covered by the Act, are dealt with by an industrial tribunal. An appeal against a decision of a tribunal is now taken to the Employment Appeal Tribunal established by the Employment Protection Act, 1975 or to the High Court or the Court of Sessions in Scotland on a point of law.

The *Industrial Tribunals* were created in 1965 initially to deal with matters arising from other acts such as the Industry Training Act, the Redundancy Payments Act and the Contracts of Employment Act. The Industrial Relations Act, now repealed, extended the jurisdiction of the industrial tribunals to enable them to deal with such matters as complaints about unfair dismissal, a power which is retained under the new Act of 1974. An industrial tribunal consists of a legally qualified chairman with two other members who have knowledge or experience of industry or commerce. Tribunals sit in different areas as they are required. Employers or employees may represent themselves at a tribunal hearing or have legal or other representation, such as an employers' association or a trade union.

The Trade Union and Labour Relations Act, 1974 re-enacts the provision for the appointment of *conciliation officers* whose role it is to promote voluntary settlements of complaints of unfair dismissal and infringement of workers' trade union rights but these are now officers of the Advisory, Conciliation and Arbitration Service (ACAS).

Certification of Trade Unions. A new process of legal identity for trade unions was created under TULRA. Any organisation which exists to help determine the wages and conditions of its members may apply to the newly created Certification Officer who, if he is satisfied that the body is free of employer domination or influence, will issue a certificate that the body is an "independent trade union". Only such bodies can claim the various legal rights under the various Acts, e.g. the right to claim the disclosure of information from employers; to seek legal support for recognition; the right to time off for union activities and other significant legal rights.

CODE OF PRACTICE The Code of Practice formulated by the Secretary of State for Employment under the Industrial Relations Act, 1971 came into effect on 28 February 1972 and remains in force under the new Act. It is intended to serve as a handbook for employers, trade unions and individual workers. The Code's provisions are set out under the following headings: responsibilities of all parties; employment policies including recruitment and selection, training, payment systems and working conditions; communication and consultation; collective bargaining; employee representation; grievance and disputes procedures; disciplinary procedures. The Code is not legally binding but the industrial tribunals take into account whether its provisions have been observed by the parties in a proceeding. The Employment Protection Act 1975 gives authority and responsibility to ACAS to prepare for Parliamentary approval other specific codes of practice. By the beginning of 1978 three important codes—on Disciplinary procedures, Disclosure of Information and Time Off for Trade Union activities had been issued and the provisions of these codes are now taken into account in Tribunal cases.

THE EMPLOYEE'S RIGHTS The Trade Union and Labour Relations Act gives employees certain basic rights in relation to Trade Unions.

1 The right to belong and take part in union activities.
2 The right to time off for specified union activities.
3 The right to complain to a tribunal if he is dismissed for union activities or penalised by his employer.

If a union member is denied membership of a union he may have his case considered by a special TUC Appeal Committee. Conversely, if a trade union has reached a Union Membership Agreement (a closed shop) with an employer a non-member may be dismissed if he is covered by the conditions of that agreement and has no religious objection to joining a union.

A Union Membership Agreement means that an employer agrees with one or more trade unions that all employees of a specified category or categories shall be members of the appropriate union. Only employees with a conscientious objection to a trade union membership may be exempted from this regulation.

There are many variations of a closed shop agreement. In its most rigid form a prospective employee has not only to be a member of a trade union but is also selected for employment by the union concerned. However, the majority of closed shop agreements tend to be more flexible. For example, existing employees may be exempt, or employees of certain specialised trades only may be subject to the closed shop agreement. In some cases the union will agree that employees who do not wish to join the union may pay the equivalent of the union membership subscription to an approved charity.

Disclosure of Information. Employers must disclose information to recognised, independent trade unions with whom they negotiate if the union would be hindered in negotiation without the information. More details are given in the Code of Practice issued by ACAS under the Employment Protection Act, 1975.

Legally Enforceable Agreements. The Act assumes that any written collective agreement reached after the Act came into force is not intended to be legally enforceable unless it contains a statement to the contrary.

TRADE UNION RECOGNITION One of the most important objectives which the Employment Protection Act gives to independent trade unions is to seek legal support if it can show that an employer has failed to 'recognise' the union, i.e. that it refuses to carry out collective bargaining on various issues with a union having membership amongst employees. In order to activate this part of the Act (Section 11) the union applies to ACAS who, if it believes it appropriate, will carry out an enquiry or survey into employees' views about union membership and recognition. ACAS will attempt to reach a conciliated settlement between the employer and the union(s) involved. If not successful it may then issue a recommendation if it believes that the membership or potential membership is sufficient to justify recognition. Such a recommendation can ultimately be given full legal support by the Central Arbitration Committee, another of the bodies created by the Employment Protection Act. The CAC also considers two other important types of issue raised by independent trade unions—employers' failure to disclose information or complaints that employers are not meeting agreed area or industry agreed rates of pay.

FREEDOM OF THE PRESS The main provision of the Trade Union and Labour Relations (Amendment) Act, 1976 is the provision for a charter to safeguard the freedom of the press in the face of closed shop agreements for all employees of newspapers. The Act allows employers of journalists, editors and representatives of journalists' unions to draft a charter for presentation to Parliament. If the parties cannot agree on the contents of the document the Secretary of State is responsible for preparing a draft for consideration by Parliament.

INDUSTRIAL PARTICIPATION The basis of good industrial relations is consultation at all levels between all the parties concerned in a decision. It is considered by some people that this indirect participation in the affairs of an organisation is inadequate and that employees should participate directly in policy-making. The debate on employee participation has been long and heated and there are many proposals for increased employee responsibility in the running of businesses. Probably the only matter on which everyone agrees is that people should be involved when decisions which affect them are to be made, e.g. removing a factory from one place to another or making employees redundant. In fact the Employment Protection Act now requires advance warning of redundancy to be given to trade unions.

The major question about employee participation is whether it shall develop voluntarily by discussion and agreement between employers and unions or whether it shall be enforced by legislation. Participation in various forms is already practised in many organisations and it may be said that generally speaking there is little enthusiasm for enforcement by legislation.

A Commission was set up by the Government in December 1975 to make recommendations for future legislation. The *Bullock Report* was published by the Commission in January 1977 giving two sets of recommendations. These were the recommendations of the majority of the members of the Commission. These provide for the Boards of companies to consist of equal representation of shareholders and employees with joint election of co-opted independent members. Employee representatives would be selected through the trade union machinery at the company. Initially only companies of 2000 or more employees would be subject to the legislation.

The second set of recommendations was made by a minority of the members of the Commission who objected to the terms of reference as being too rigid because they pre-supposed legislation instead of allowing the Commission to recommend other methods of developing employee participation. The minority recommendations follow the European model and provide for a two-tier structure of boards consisting of a Supervisory Board to comprise one-third employee representatives, one-third shareholder representatives and one-third independent members, and a Management Board which would be responsible or the day-to-day running of the business. The minority recommendations are more specific than the majority recommendations as to the eligibility of employees to act as representatives and the powers of the Boards.

At the time of writing there is little indication as to whether the Government will attempt to legislate on the lines of the majority recommendations or whether further investigations will be made. There is, however, progress in the public sector where the board of the Post Office has been reconstituted to include employee (trade union) members and five independent members, including two specifically representing consumer interests. It is likely that further such changes will be made in other nationalised industries. It is also possible that progress will be encouraged in another form of participation—that of profit-sharing.

The effect of industrial relations upon the national economy has been amply demonstrated within recent years and the subject of industrial relations is one which no well-informed person can afford to neglect; our personal lives and standard of living and also our work in whatever fields we are employed are affected by employer–employee relations. A change of government may cause industrial legislation to be amended if certain provisions cannot be enforced, or if it fails in some way to achieve its objectives. To keep abreast of changes and developments in this sphere, it is important to read a newspaper which has a good Industrial News section.

COMMON LAW RIGHTS AND DUTIES

Under Common Law an employee (servant) is entitled to a safe place of work, safe access to that place, safe tools with which to perform his tasks and safe work fellows. He is under an obligation to give his employer (master) regular attendance according to agreed hours, performance of his work to the best of his ability, and loyalty, e.g. he should not reveal the trade secrets of his master.

These Common Law rights and duties cannot be affected by Statute and are frequently fallen back upon when statutory protection proves insufficient.

STATUTORY RIGHTS AND DUTIES

With the increasing importance and complexity of industry and commerce in modern society, governments have felt it necessary to regulate many areas of business through legislation, especially those areas which affect the rights of employees. During the nineteenth century several Acts of Parliament were passed to protect employees from exploitation and to safeguard their rights, although many of the Acts concerned conditions of work which good employers would have granted voluntarily. As well as safeguarding employees' rights, it is also recognised in legislation that employers have rights which may need protecting. However, since employers by virtue of their position have inherent advantages over employees, the emphasis in most legislation is on the duties of the employer and the protection of employees' rights, although employees' duties and employers' rights are also taken into consideration.

The Offices, Shops and Railway Premises Act, 1963 In 1833 the Factories Act provided for some regulation of the working conditions of young people in the textile industry. Although very limited in its coverage of workers, this Act marked the beginning of State concern for the welfare of employees.

Its most far-reaching provision was the setting up of the Factory Inspectorate which to this day supervises the implementation of government regulations regarding working conditions.

The Offices, Shops and Railway Premises Act of 1963 extended government regulation to an additional eight million workers for whom it set out minimum standards of working conditions for health, safety and convenience.

Under the Act, employers of office or shop staff had to register with their local authorities and obtain a fire certificate where more than twenty people were employed, or more than ten were working above the ground floor.

The main provisions for health, safety and convenience cover a number of points:

1 All floors, stairs, passages and other areas used by employees must be cleaned by washing or sweeping at least once a week.

2 In general rooms and workrooms, lighting must be adequate for safety and to avoid strain.

3 In rooms not open to the public, the temperature must reach 60°F (16° Centigrade) within one hour of work starting and a thermometer must be on view for employees. In shops or offices where an outside door is continually open, special means must be provided for employees to warm themselves.

4 Ventilation must be adequate for health.

5 Forty square feet of floor space must be allowed per person in a normal room or 400 cubic feet if the ceiling is under ten feet high.

6 A certain number of lavatories and basins with running hot water and towels according to the number of workers on the premises must be provided, with separate facilities for men and women.

7 Fresh drinking water must be available for employees.

8 All workers who sit while working must have suitably designed chairs including foot rests if their feet are off the ground. If workers normally stand, at least one chair for every three employees must be provided and whenever possible they should be allowed to sit down.

9 Cloakroom facilities must be provided for clothes, such as overcoats, that are not worn during working hours.

10 A suitable room must be provided if food is eaten on the premises.

11 Stairs must have an outside railing, be safe and not slippery. Guards must be provided for dangerous machinery unless it is supervised by an experienced person.

12 First-aid boxes must be provided and a qualified person available to give first-aid where more than 150 people are employed. The person qualified to give first-aid should be made known to employees.

13 After inspection by the fire authorities, a certificate must be displayed stating the number of people who may safely be employed on the premises. The firm must have fire-fighting appliances, fire escapes, alarms and drills.

The Health and Safety at Work Act 1974(HASAWA) sets out employers' responsibilities concerning the health, safety and welfare of all employees, particularly including the provision and maintenance of safe machinery and equipment, the provisions of necessary instruction, training and supervision, and the provision of a safe and healthy working environment. Every firm must prepare a written statement of its health and welfare policies and provide details of the organisation and arrangements for carrying out this policy. The document must be brought to the notice of employees and should state the arrangements that are being made, the name of the boss, the particular arrangements which are being made for such hazards as fire-fighting, and the relationships with the local inspectorate. The document should also give information on the employee's role in the new arrangements including details of joint consultation.

The Act also states that every employee has a duty while at work to take reasonable care for the health and safety of himself and others.

Under the provisions of the Act, the *Health and Safety Commission* was established on 1 October 1974, and the *Health and Safety Executive* on 1 January 1975. The Health and Safety Commission is reponsible for the development and implementation of national policy on health and safety at work. The Commission is appointed by the Secretary of State for Employment; it carries out his directions and keeps him informed of its work. The Commission has powers to approve and issue codes of practice. The Health and Safety Executive is directly responsible to the Commission, and together with the Inspectorate will advise industry and Government and enforce the law. The *Inspectorate* unifies all previous specialist inspectorates, such as those for factories, mines, quarries and explosives. It is responsible for enforcing the requirements of the Act.

The penalty for any person not complying with the regulations or requirements of the Act is a fine not exceeding £400 and/or a term of imprisonment not exceeding two years. Further reading: "The Employer's Guide to Health, Safety and Welfare at Work", by Ewan Mitchell published by Better Books Ltd.

The Employment Medical Advisory Service which was set up by the Employment Medical Advisory Service Act 1972 (EMAS) will continued to function, but the 1972 EMAS Act will be absorbed into the new Health and Safety at Work Act. The Employment Medical Advisory Service is now part of the Health and Safety Executive and gives advice and information on medical problems connected with employment. The Service employs medical advisers who have the right to enter factory premises in the course of their duties; they may also carry out a medical examination of any employee whose health may be in danger because of his work, subject to the consent of the employee.

Redundancy Payments Act, 1965 This Act requires all employers to pay a lump sum compensation payment, called a *redundancy payment*, to all employees who are dismissed because they are redundant and who are not included in the list of exceptions below. Redundancy can be caused by a number of reasons, including a slump in the economy of the country and the decline of the business of a particular firm or the merger of two firms. If an employee is no longer required by his firm because the firm has no work for him to do, the employee is considered to be redundant.

EXCEPTIONS TO REDUNDANCY Certain employees are not eligible for redundancy payments even if they have been dismissed because they are redundant.

1 Employees with less than 104 weeks (two years) of continuous employment with the employer.
2 Employees who work less than 16 hours a week or 8 hours where the employee has five years' continuous service with the same employer.
3 Male employees who are made redundant after their 65th birthday or female employees made redundant after their 60th birthday.
4 Employees with fixed-term contracts for two years or more who have agreed to forego a redundancy payment at the end of their contract.
5 Certain classes of employees, such as registered dock workers employed on dock work.
6 Employees who are husbands or wives of employers or domestic servants who are close relatives of their employer.

ALTERNATIVE WORK If the employer offers the redundant employee alternative suitable work, and in doing so fulfils the conditions set down in the Act, the employee is not entitled to a redundancy payment unless he has reasonable grounds for refusing the offer. Reasonable grounds could be that the employee had arranged to sell his house and move to another area after the notice of redundancy was given but before the employer offered him suitable alternative work. If the alternative work offered is with a separate company, the employer is still obliged to make redundancy payments. Any disputes about this or other requirements of the Act should be referred to the Advisory, Conciliation and Arbitration Service. If the dispute cannot be settled at this level it must be referred to an industrial tribunal.

LAY-OFFS AND SHORT-TIME If an employer has no work for some of his employees but expects to give them work in the near future, he can lay them off. This means that the employee is temporarily unemployed, although he is still officially employed by his employer. If the employer does not have enough work to keep his employees fully employed and they work at an hourly rate, he can put them on short-time. That means that the employees work less than half the number of normal hours each week and therefore earn only half the normal amount of pay.

Under certain conditions, an employee who has been laid off or put on short-time for a substantial period can claim a redundancy payment if there is no reasonable prospect of normal work being resumed. However, the employee cannot receive his redundancy payment until after he has terminated his employment with his firm.

OTHER REDUNDANCY SITUATIONS If an employer sells his premises to another employer who wants to carry on a completely different type of business, the former employer is liable to make redundancy payments to his employees even if some of them get jobs with the new employer. Apprentices are not entitled to redundancy payments if they are not engaged by their employer at the end of the contract of apprenticeship, unless the employer usually offers apprentices employment, but cannot do so because he is making workers redundant. However, if the apprentice is made redundant before his apprenticeship agreement ends, the employer may be obliged to make a redundancy payment.

CONSULTATION Under the Employment Protection Act, 1975 employers are obliged to consult independent, recognised trade unions when redundancies are planned, even if only one employee is to be dismissed. Where between 10 and 99 employees are to lose their jobs over a period of 30 days or less, consultation must begin at least 60 days before the first dismissal takes effect. If 100 or more employees are to be dismissed over a period of 90 days or less at least 90 days must be allowed for consultation. If the employer fails to comply with these requirements a complaint by a union or an employee to an industrial tribunal may result in the employer losing a portion of his rebate from the Redundancy Payments Fund (see below) and/or a fine of up to £400.

TIME OFF Also under the Employment Protection Act, 1975 the employee under notice of redundancy must be allowed reasonable time off to look for another job or to make arrangements for training for future employment. The amount of time considered 'reasonable' depends on individual circumstances.

CALCULATING THE AMOUNT OF REDUNDANCY PAYMENT The amount of the redundancy payment is calculated on the number of years, i.e. 52-week periods, of continuous service. Employment before the employee's 18th birthday does not count. Payments for each complete year of service vary from ½ week's pay to 1½ weeks' pay.

INCOME TAX Employers must give each redundant employee a written statement explaining how the redundancy payment was calculated. Failure to do so without a reasonable excuse could lead to a fine on the employer. Employees are not normally required to pay income tax on a redundancy payment required under the Act.

REDUNDANCY PAYMENTS FUND Employers make a weekly contribution of a specified amount for each employee to the Redundancy Fund. An employer who makes a redundancy payment as required by the Act may claim a rebate from the fund of fifty per cent of the cost of the payments.

If an employer who should make redundancy payments is bankrupt, the Department of Employment will make the payments to redundant employees from the fund and claim repayment from the employers with his other creditors. If there is a dispute about the redundancy payment which is taken to the industrial tribunal, the tribunal may order the employer to pay. If the employer still refuses to do so, the Department of Employment will pay the employee from the fund and take proceedings against the employer to recover the money.

A redundancy payment cannot be claimed later than six months after the termination of employment and the rebate must be claimed from the fund within six months of the date of the redundancy payment.

Wages Councils Act, 1959 The Secretary of State for Employment may establish a Wages Council for a particular section of workers if he feels there is no adequate machinery for regulating their pay. A joint application for a Wages Council may also be made by workers' and employers' organisations.

The wages council considers matters regarding the industrial conditions of employers and workers under its jurisdiction when these are referred to the council by the Secretary of State or another government department.

Under the Employment Protection Act, 1975 the powers of Wages Councils have been extended. They can now fix, instead of merely recommend, *all* terms and conditions of service and also fix the date from which the new minimum pay and terms of employment shall operate. Employers are required to give their employees the terms and conditions laid down by the Council. Failure to do so can result in court action and a fine if convicted.

Wages Councils consist of three independent members and an equal number of workers' and employers' representatives. Councils may now be converted into statutory joint industrial councils without independent members, a procedure aimed to establish voluntary bargaining.

Equal Pay Act, 1970 The Equal Pay Act, 1970, which came into force on 29 December 1975 is aimed at eliminating discrimination between men and women in their pay and conditions of employment. Women are employed on work of the same or a broadly similar nature to that of men or who have a job which is different to a man's job but which has an equal value in a job evaluation scheme are legally entitled to the same pay and conditions of employment after the Act comes into force. The comparison between men's jobs and women's jobs must be within the same firm.

DISPUTES If an employer and a woman employee disagree about her rights, the question can be referred to an industrial tribunal. The Secretary of State may refer a case to a tribunal if he sees the woman has a claim but he feels it is not reasonable to expect her to go to the tribunal herself. A claim can be made to a tribunal up to six months after the woman has left a firm as well as during the time she is employed there. The claim can be for pay in arrears or damages for non-cash benefits her employer should have given her for a period up to two years before the date of the claim. However, she may not claim for any arrears for time before 29 December 1975.

TERMS AND CONDITIONS As the Act covers all terms and conditions of employment, a woman has the right to equal treatment under the Act with men doing the same or broadly similar work; she is therefore entitled to the same contract of employment with the following exceptions:

1 The terms and conditions of employment of women workers must comply with the law regulating the employment of women. For example, a man's contract of employment may give him the right to work a certain number of hours of overtime. If the law prohibited women from working that number of hours, the woman could not claim an equal provision in her contract of employment.
2 Women must be given special terms and conditions in regard to the birth or expected birth of a child (see Employment Protection Act, 1975).
3 Equal treatment is not required in terms of employment relating to retirement, marriage or death of an employee.
4 The general provisions of the Act do not apply to women in the police force or the armed forces.

PROVISION FOR MEN Finally, the Act makes it clear that equal treatment of men and women applies to both groups. Women have the right to equal treatment with men and where women receive better pay and conditions than men—if such cases exist—men are entitled to equal treatment with women.

Contracts of Employment Act, 1972 The Contracts of Employment Act, 1972 re-enacted the Contracts of Employment Act, 1963 with amendments. The later act has subsequently been amended by the Trade Union and Labour Relations Act, 1974, the Employment Protection Act, 1975 and the Social Security Pensions Act, 1975. The main provisions of the Act are:

1 Employers and employees have rights to minimum periods of notice to terminate employment.
2 Employers must give their employees written particulars of their main terms of employment.
3 Employers must inform employees in writing about certain rights of employees under the Industrial Relations Act, 1971.

PERIODS OF NOTICE Under the Act and associated legislation all employees have the right to stated minimum periods of notice except for certain groups, such as Crown servants and some employees with fixed term contracts. The minimum notice the employer must give the employee is as follows:

4 weeks or more continuous service: at least one week's notice
2 years or more continuous service: at least two weeks' notice
1 additional week's notice for each further complete year of continuous employment up to twelve weeks' notice if the employee has been employed by him continuously for twelve years or more.

After four weeks of continuous service the employee is required to give his employer one week's notice. This period does not increase with length of service. However, an individual's contract with his employer may state longer periods of notice on both sides than is required under the Act. If an employee's contract states shorter periods of notice, these are automatically altered by the Act to the legal minimum periods.

The employer or employee may voluntarily give up his own rights to notice or the employee may accept pay in lieu of notice. For example, an employee with ten years of service would be given six weeks' notice by his employer; if the employee would prefer to leave before his notice expires, say after two weeks, the Act does not prevent him from making such an arrangement with his employer. Alternatively, if the employer offers the employee six weeks' pay in lieu of the six weeks' notice, the Act allows the employee to accept the money instead of working out the period of notice.

The employer or the employee may terminate a contract of employment without notice if the behaviour of the other party justifies this. Any dispute about the period of notice given or about termination without notice must be settled by a civil action for damages in the courts.

TERMS OF EMPLOYMENT It is the duty of all employers to give employees a written statement of the main terms of employment not later than thirteen weeks after employment has begun. The Act establishes that the statement must contain the following:

1 The names of the employer and employee and the date when employment began.
2 The scale or rate of pay or the method of calculating pay including piecework rates or overtime pay.
3 The intervals—weekly, monthly or some other period—when the employee is paid.
4 Terms and conditions relating to hours of work.
5 Entitlement to holidays including public holidays and terms or holiday pay in sufficient detail for the employee to calculate precisely his entitlement to holidays or, on termination of his employment, his holiday pay.
6 Terms and conditions relating to incapacity for work due to sickness or injury, including any provisions for sick pay.
7 Company pensions and pension schemes.
8 Period of notice the employer must give the employee and the employee must give the employer, even if the notice periods are the minimum laid down in the Act; if the contract is for a fixed term, the date the contract expires.

EMPLOYEES' RIGHTS The written statement must also set out the individual's statutory rights under the Trade Union and Labour Relations Act and Employment Protection Act to trade union membership and activities and explain procedures to be taken if the employee has a grievance, as follows:

1 Employee's right to belong to a recognised, independent trade union of his choice.
2 Employee's right not to belong to any particular union or organisation.
3 Employee's right to take part within working hours in activities of a registered trade union, including seeking and holding office.
4 The effect of an employee's rights of any closed shop agreement which applies to him.*
5 Name or title of person to whom the employee can apply if he has a grievance about his employment and the method of application.
6 The courses of action in a grievance procedure which are available to an employee.

Recent government legislation effecting employees' rights

Employees' rights

Offices, Shops and Railway premises Act 1963
Lays down minimum standards for health, safety and convenience, e.g. adequate lighting, seating, temperature, ventilation, working space, lavatories, cloakroom facilities, fire-escapes, drinking water, room where food can be eaten.

Trade Union and Labour Relations Acts, 1974 and 1976
Repeals the Industrial Relations Act, 1975 but re-enacts certain provisions of that Act. Establishes the status and regulations of trade unions and employers' associations.

Industrial Training Act 1964
Although the Act does not give employees the right to demand training, it implies that employers have a duty to provide some form of staff training.

Employment Protection Act 1975
Provides greater certainty and security of employment to a greater number of employees and increased benefits to certain categories of employees. Establishes the Advisory Conciliation and Arbitration Service and the Central Arbitration Committee.

Equal Pay Act 1970
Aims at ending discrimination between men and women in their pay and conditions of employment.

Health and Safety at Work Act, 1974
Sets out the employers' responsibilities concerning the health, safety and welfare of all employees.

Contracts of Employment Act 1972
Makes provision for employers' and employees' rights to minimum periods of notice to terminate employment, employees' rights to written particulars of their main terms of employment.

Redundancy Payments Act 1965
Establishes employees' rights to redundancy payments, the methods of calculating the amounts of the payments and the employee's position regarding offer of alternative work.

Wages councils Act 1969
Makes provision for the establishment of a Wages Council for any section of workers who have no adequate machinery for negotiating their pay and conditions of service.

Employees also have rights under Common Law. These rights cannot be affected by Statute and are frequently fallen back upon when statutory protection proves insufficient. The body of Common Law affecting employees' rights is known as The Law of Master and Servant.

* The expression *closed shop agreement* is explained in the section on the Trade Union and Labour Relations Acts, 1974 and 1976.

Instead of setting out all this information in each employee's contract of employment, the employer may in the contract refer the employee to a document which is reasonably accessible to him, for example, a collective agreement, works handbook or firm's notice about such matters as pension schemes. If the terms of employment change, the employer must inform the employee by a written statement or by keeping any reference documents up to date.

INDUSTRIAL TRIBUNALS An employee who has not received a written statement of terms and conditions after thirteen weeks of continuous service may refer the matter to an industrial tribunal. Any dispute about particulars in a contract that are covered by provisions in the Act may be referred to a tribunal by the employer or the employee.

THE OFFICE SUPERVISOR

The office supervisor, whether she is in charge of one junior secretary or a whole typing pool, has authority and responsibility as the leader of a working group. Some people are born leaders and in any grouping of their friends or associates they will be conspicuous for their reliability, decisiveness and ability to judge and direct the thoughts of others. Being a natural leader, however, does not necessarily fit a person to supervise a working group. Both natural leaders and people born without those qualities can learn the skills of leadership required by the office supervisor.

Authority and responsibility The office supervisor has authority over her subordinates and responsibility for their work and welfare. The more subordinates she has under her control, the greater will be her authority and responsibility; but the principles and practice of good supervision remain constant regardless of the number of subordinates.

To the management of the firm, the office supervisor is one of the employees, a person to whom they can give orders which they expect to be carried out. But to her subordinates, the supervisor is the first link in the chain of management. She is in direct authority over them and stands between them and higher management.

Authority in the office means being in a position to give instructions to other employees which they will carry out. With this authority goes responsibility. The supervisor is responsible for seeing that her instructions are carried out, and carried out properly. She must make sure that management policies are explained and understood, and she is responsible for the discipline and job satisfaction of those under her control and also for their training. Carrying out the authority and responsibility vested in a supervisor is a management function and the supervisor, if she is going to do a good job, must see herself as part of management and not as a subordinate who has been given a more responsible job, even if she has only recently been promoted.

DELEGATION In exercising authority effectively, the supervisor may have to delegate some of the decision-making to her subordinates. This is not avoiding responsibility or giving away power, but a sign that the supervisor has trained her subordinates to a level where they can take some decisions on their own without her guidance. The supervisor is bound to be away from the office at some time because of illness or holidays and she would have failed as a good supervisor if the department could not run smoothly for a short time during her absence.

It is not always easy to decide which decisions can be delegated. In the first place it is unwise for the supervisor to insist on approving every minor decision. Employees find more satisfaction in their jobs if they feel they are trusted to carry out their duties. No one likes to have a supervisor who is always watching them too closely. For example, if a senior secretary gives her junior a parcel to be wrapped and posted to Kenya, she could refer the junior to the Post Office Guide but she should not expect the junior to keep on coming back to her to check every detail of the procedure. If the junior cannot do the task on her own, it means that she is unsuited for the job or improperly trained. In either case, it is the supervisor's fault for selecting the wrong person or neglecting her training.

The question of delegating authority in more important matters depends to a great extent on the circumstances. Before deciding to delegate or not to delegate, the supervisor must consider her subordinates' abilities and their potential for decision-making, the level of their training and the skills and knowledge necessary to make decisions on the matter in question.

However, before she can delegate some of her authority, the supervisor must first have gained the respect of her subordinates as their leader and she must have established that she is a suitable person to hold a position of authority and responsibility.

Leadership of a Working Group Making someone a supervisor does not automatically give her the respect and liking of her subordinates. She must earn these things herself. If she fails to do so, the working group will no longer look to her for leadership and the natural leaders amongst her subordinates will take over direction of the group's thinking. Such a situation is the beginning of a breakdown of co-operation between the group and the management represented by the supervisor. Job performance suffers, and as the group's work is the supervisor's responsibility, the management can lose confidence in the supervisor's abilities.

The effective supervisor is conscious of the dangers of poor leadership and tries to develop the skills that will make her the accepted leader of her working group. She knows that her first objective must be to win the respect of her subordinates by showing that she is qualified, knowledgeable and competent to hold her position; having gained respect for her professional ability, her next objective should be to win the affection of the working group because, in general, people work better for supervisors whom they like and respect and admire.

KNOWLEDGE OF THE ORGANISATION As a part of management, the supervisor should know and understand the firm's objectives, policies, operations, methods and products. This is especially important with personnel policy. Employees tend to turn in the first instance to their immediate supervisor whom they know well rather than to a personnel officer who may be almost a stranger.

No supervisor can be expected to know everything about a firm but if she does not know the answer to a question she should know how to find the answer or where to direct the employee to find the answer. This entails a thorough knowledge of the structure of the firm and the working of each department.

PLANNING AND ORGANISING WORK To organise her department or section and plan the flow of work through it, the supervisor must understand the jobs done by subordinates and the methods used. If there are machines in the department, the supervisor must know how they work. The supervisor would look foolish, for example, if she instructed an assistant to duplicate a report in two colours if the duplicator could not produce multi-colour work.

Planning an even flow of work requires organisation and a knowledge of the capabilities of subordinates. Ideally all subordinates should be kept equally busy without overloading any of them. Resentment can build up if one person has too much work while another has very little or nothing to do. It is equally important that the supervisor does not promise her superiors more work than her group can produce within a given period of time. Rushing through too much work too quickly lowers the standard of performance, and causes subordinates to lose confidence in the organising ability of the supervisor.

CHECKING WORK As the supervisor is responsible to her own superiors for the work done by her subordinates, she must ensure that standards of quantity and quality are maintained. If the amount of work being produced by subordinates is less than they are capable of, the supervisor should investigate, find the cause and correct it: Does one person need further training to carry out her tasks? Are the methods used slowing down the flow of work? Could the methods be improved? Is closer supervision necessary in the form of deputies to the supervisor who can be responsible for the work of smaller groups within the group as a whole? Are there problems of discipline or friction amongst the subordinates?

Checking the accuracy of work done by subordinates is necessary, but the supervisor should not forget that employees are human. If it becomes known that the supervisor accepts inaccurate work, the assistants will lower their standards. Checking at once also saves more work in the future: if papers are wrongly filed, it will be necessary to search through all the files at a later date; if invoices are sent to the wrong firms, new invoices will have to be sent out; if letters containing errors are passed and submitted for signature, they will be returned with instructions for retyping. At the same time the supervisor must be reasonable about her standards. If a rough draft has a thumb print in the corner or a poor erasure, it should not automatically be sent back to the typist for retyping as a final form will have to be typed in any case.

TRAINING OF SUBORDINATES It is the supervisor's responsibility to train new members of staff, train existing staff in areas where they are deficient and prepare assistants with potential for promotion to higher positions. A new member of staff may have all the necessary skills to do the job but she will not be familiar with the firm and its methods. The supervisor should begin with a programme of induction and orientation (see page 585) to tell the newcomer how the firm works and where everything is located. The methods in the department or section must also be explained as they may be completely different from those in her last firm. Explaining methods properly requires a good deal of thinking and planning. They will probably seem obvious to the supervisor who has worked with the firm for a long time, but they may be bewildering to a newcomer.

New employees as well as existing ones may need training in the skills involved in their jobs. The first step is identifying the training needs of the subordinate: Does she need to learn typewriting? Improve her typewriting? Learn more about PAYE and how to make deductions from salaries and wages? Learn how to use the new office copying machine? Once the training needs are established, a training programme that teaches each task separately must be designed.

The ability to teach a task or skill does not altogether depend upon the amount of knowledge possessed by the teacher. Some of the world's most brilliant men and women who are experts in their subjects are unable to pass on their knowledge to others. The secret of teaching is the ability to break down the task or skill into a series of simple steps or sub-skills, and then to prepare a step-by-step learning programme that explains each stage clearly and thus enables the student to master each step before moving on to the next. The preparation of such a training programme takes time but it makes the teaching process much simpler and enables the trainee to learn more quickly.

The method of training depends on the firm's policy. Some firms have their own training officer who arranges outside courses or special courses and equipment for on-the-job training (see page 590). In other firms training is left to each supervisor who has to teach the necessary skills mainly by explanation and demonstration.

Employees who show potential for promotion should be given training in supervision and in taking authority and responsibility. The supervisor's responsibility in this matter may be merely to tell management of those subordinates who have potential, or the supervisor may simply write her assessment in the annual merit rating and leave higher management to pick out the potential future supervisors. If the supervisor is expected to prepare a subordinate for a supervisory post, she could delegate some of her authority to the subordinate and have regular discussions about the way the subordinate is exercising her new authority.

EMPLOYEE RELATIONS As the office supervisor is in charge of people and not machines, probably the most important aspect of her leadership is personal relations with her subordinates. Fifty years ago this problem would not have arisen as the supervisor gave the orders and anyone who disagreed with her either left or was dismissed.

Changing attitudes in employee–employer relations mean that the supervisor has to take great care to adopt the correct position of balance between friendship on the one hand and authority on the other. If the supervisor puts herself in an exalted position and is inconsiderate or distant, her assistants will not respect her leadership and may resent her authority. If she is too friendly with one or more assistants, they may accuse her of favouritism or ignore her authority or discipline. Therefore her general attitude must be polite, kind, and interested without being too 'chummy'—and a sense of humour at the right time is always a help.

Praise. A good supervisor knows that praise given when deserved is a strong incentive to improve work performance. However, it must be genuine praise to be effective; if the supervisor tells all her assistants every week that they are doing a grand job, no-one will take this seriously. On the other hand, if the supervisor never praises her subordinates when it is deserved, they will feel that their efforts are not being noticed and perhaps are not worth the trouble.

If an employee deserves special praise she should be told privately so that other employees do not feel it is an implied criticism of their work. It will also relieve the subordinate of any embarrassment she may feel when her work is praised in front of her colleagues.

Time-off. At some time or another all subordinates will need to take some time off to go to the dentist, the hospital, the optician or for sickness, bereavement or other emergencies. The company may have rules regarding the amount of time-off permitted for these occasions, or it may be left to the supervisor to use her own judgment. The supervisor must take each case on its merits and try to be fair to all. Some subordinates may try to take advantage of a supervisor's sympathetic nature but this can usually be avoided if the supervisor knows her subordinates as people and not just as employees.

Discipline. Disciplinary action must be taken when it is necessary. Although a supervisor may find it unpleasant to reprimand a subordinate for being late, for example, she must do so otherwise it would be unfair to other employees who have attended punctually. As long as the working group recognises that the supervisor is fair in dealing with rule-breakers, they will respect her attempts to make the section or department conform with the firm's policies and regulations.

For disciplinary measures to be effective, the supervisor must ensure that "the punishment fits the crime". One breach of company rules can be dealt with immediately by "a word to the wise" given in private, whilst other matters may require more serious action; for example, regularly being late, leaving early, frequently taking too long for lunch, making too many personal telephone calls, disturbing colleagues who are trying to work by constantly chatting, disappearing on visits to other departments, frequent absenteeism without acceptable reasons, refusing to carry out instructions.

The supervisor holds the ultimate weapon, viz. recommending dismissal, but this should not be used unless it is obvious that the employee will not or cannot conform to the rules of the firm. If the employee does not respond to the first brief warning, the supervisor should arrange for an interview with the offender. The supervisor must be firm but sympathetic as the subordinate may have reasons for her actions which the supervisor can help her to sort out. However, it must be made clear, without making threats, that the supervisor cannot permit rules to be broken continuously.

If the interview fails to bring results, sterner measures can be taken. These depend on the personnel policy of the firm. Sometimes a memorandum is officially sent to the offender warning her that if she continues to break company rules, her position in the firm may have to be reconsidered—in other words, she will be dismissed. A copy of the memorandum may be placed in the employee's personnel record file or attached to her record card, and possibly removed at a later stage if she improves her behaviour. Other measures may involve financial penalties. The supervisor may ask for a bonus or a salary increase to be withheld until the subordinate stops breaking the firm's rules.

If the rule-breaking persists and the supervisor has taken all the actions that her conscience and the law could demand, then she has no choice but to recommend the dismissal of the offender. Ignoring continuous rule-breaking would cause a breakdown of discipline amongst other employees.

The employee should be told of her dismissal in a private interview. The supervisor should be straightforward and businesslike to avoid any display of anger or an emotional scene. The reason for dismissal should be clearly stated and it should be pointed out that the supervisor has made repeated attempts to improve the situation, and the employee has refused to respond. The interview should be brief as neither party will want to make the situation worse. The supervisor should avoid future embarrassment by telling the employee whether she would consider giving her a reference for a future job.

FURTHER READING

J. M. Fraser, *Introduction to Personnel Management*, Thomas Nelson & Sons Ltd.

M. R. Williams, *Supervisory Management in the Office*, William Heinemann Ltd in association with the Institute of Supervisory Management.

TUC Structure and Development (1970), Trades Union Congress.

CBI Spokesman for British Industry and Commerce, Confederation of British Industry.

Explanatory booklets about new legislation in the employment field, free from the Department of Employment.
Acts and government reports, HMSO.
Glossary of Training Terms, HMSO.
Industrial Relations Training, HMSO.
Clerical Work Measurement, HMSO.

GROUP DISCUSSION

"People are the most valuable asset of any organisation or firm." Discuss this statement and the importance of economic and political factors in the development of current personnel management practices and legislation affecting conditions of employment, labour relations, and employees' rights and duties.

EXERCISES

1 Write brief notes on the following terms and expressions:

commission	contract of employment
personnel policy	fringe benefits
to clock-in	job evaluation
salary survey	fixed increments
merit increases	payroll saving
incentive schemes	net pay
code number	piecework system

2 Describe the structure of a typical firm or any organisation with which you are well acquainted. Indicate the direction and type of authority relationships.

3 Describe the documents produced by job analysis and indicate the ways in which a firm might use job analysis records.

4 What is merit rating? Describe four merit rating methods and indicate their respective advantages and disadvantages.

5 Describe the payment of wages by (a) time-rates, (b) piecework, and discuss the advantages and disadvantages of each system.

6 Distinguish between statutory and voluntary deductions from salaries and wages. What compulsory deductions would be made from the salaries of (a) a 17-year-old girl who is earning £15 a week and is unmarried, (b) a married man, aged 35, who has three children aged between four and twelve, and who earns £40 a week.

7 Write notes on the following:

P60 form	tax free pay allowance
short-listing	contracted-out employees
role-playing	promotion by seniority
block release courses	curriculum vitae
sandwich courses	on-the-job training
in-tray exercises	algorithms

8 A vacancy can be filled by:

a promoting an existing employee, or
b engaging a new employee, or
c allowing existing employees and outsiders to compete for the job.

Discuss the relative merits of these three recruitment methods.

9 List and discuss the merits of the various ways of informing possible applicants of a job vacancy.

10 What points would you bear in mind if you were interviewing applicants for a vacancy? What methods could you use to assess the applicants and ensure that you made the most suitable appointment.

11 A new shorthand-typist has been engaged to work in your department. As secretary to the head of the department you have been asked by the Personnel Officer to introduce the newcomer and make her feel at home. List the points that should be included in your induction and orientation programme.

12 What were the main provisions of the Industrial Training Act 1964? Describe the achievements of any industrial training board with which you are familiar.

13 Study the algorithm on page 592 which enables a clerk to decide whether a letter should be sent by first class or second class mail. Design an algorithm to enable:

a your assistant to decide whether a parcel should be sent by express post or British Rail Red Star service;
b a typist to decide whether eight copies of a document should be obtained by (i) photocopying, (ii) carbon-copying, (iii) spirit duplicating;
c Your boss to decide whether he should (i) ask you to take a letter in shorthand, (ii) ask you to reply in your own words, (iii) record his dictation on a dictating machine, (iv) draft the reply himself in longhand;
d a decision to be reached in any set of circumstances you consider suitable for solving by this method.

14 Write brief notes on the following:

TUC Annual Conference	employers' associations
CBI	collective bargaining
work-to-rule	lock-out
disclosure of information	Code of Practice
agency shop agreement	sole bargaining rights
unfair industrial practices	redundancy payments
lay-offs and short-time	Equal Pay Act, 1970

15 Describe the structure of the trade union movement in Great Britain, or in the country where you are studying, or in the country where you expect to work, or in your home country.

Part IV Application

16

Secretarial Work Planning

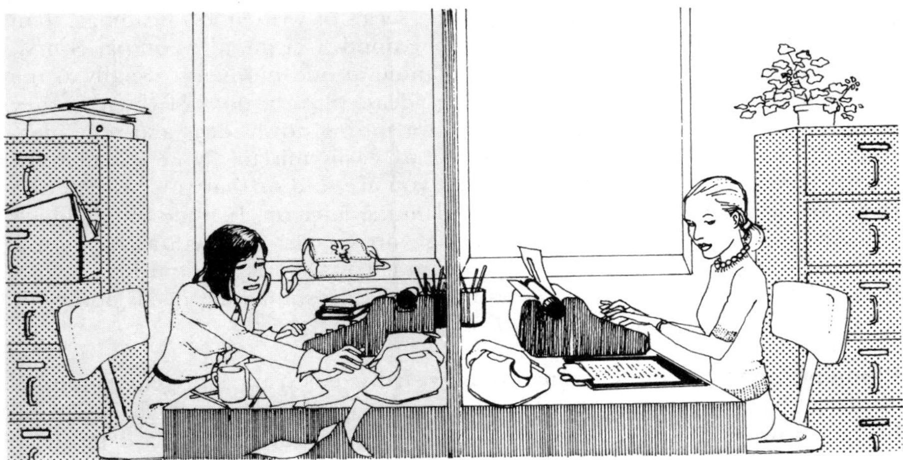

"Before you organise others, organise yourself." *How to win the business battle*, Eric Webster

John Murray

The object of the preceding chapters was to help you to understand the work of your organisation, your boss's role in it, and your own role in the boss/secretary partnership. You have learned how to apply your skills and knowledge to the wide variety of situations which may arise in the course of your work, and which depend to a large extent upon the type of organisation for which you work and your boss's particular job and personality. These situations can be classified as 'routine'; but unexpected situations can also arise. How will you manage to cope with the unexpected, the unscheduled tasks as well as manage to get through the mass of routine work? The answer is: by organising your work methodically and by careful planning.

OUTLINE PLANNING

In most organisations there are certain times of the year when 'next year's' course is charted and this will affect your own planning. However, 'planning time' usually means time for *detailed* planning and this can be done only if the outline plan already exists. Outline plans are usually self-producing to a considerable extent in that a job being done now may give rise to other jobs which will have to be done in the future. The preparation of an outline plan should be going on all the time by the simple process of writing down every expected future job.

It cannot be stressed too strongly that planning is a written exercise. However good your memory you may forget something, and in any case there is no point in using your memory to remember details which can just as well be noted on a piece of paper. Detailed planning is a breakdown of major items and it is easier to divide something tangible, like a series of written job headings, than something nebulous, like a few ideas in the mind. Get the ideas on paper first. Since thoughts and ideas come into the mind at odd moments, usually as the end product of an association of other ideas, make a note of them as they occur. Always have a notebook to hand for jotting down ideas and reminders —do not use odd scraps of paper which are easily mislaid. Note any items of information relating to future work that you are told or that you hear so that they can be inserted into your formal planning later on. Include things which you know have to be done, even though no specific instructions have been given. If you start planning a job in good time you will ease the burden on your boss. It is your responsibility to remind him that something needs doing—it is not for him to remind you.

Planning units Planning units can be visualised as years, half-years, months, weeks and days. The largest unit contains the outline plan, which has to be broken down into smaller units which become increasingly more detailed as each individual section and sub-section is considered as a planning unit.

Your boss has just had his revaccination. This will have to be renewed in three years' time. Note it immediately in the appropriate month of the year-plan sheet for three years ahead. Later, when the detailed planning is done, it will be noted in the appropriate week of the month-plan sheet, depending on your boss's workload and other commitments. Finally, it will be allocated to a particular day, again depending on workload and the availability of an appointment. It is important to look ahead all the time so that items can be dealt with at the most suitable time.

A good time to plan the year unit is when each quarter is planned. In this way, the outline year plan is regularly modified and brought up-to-date. Planning the next quarter is best done about the middle of the last month of a quarter. Next month is usually planned during the last week of the current month; next week should be planned on Thursday or Friday of the previous week; and tomorrow should be planned the night before.

Outline planning and detailed planning are inseparable. From the chart on page 625 it can be seen that the detailed planning for each unit is carried out concurrently with the outline planning for the following unit. Thus planning can be pictured as a cone, the finest degree of detail being at the point, i.e. the

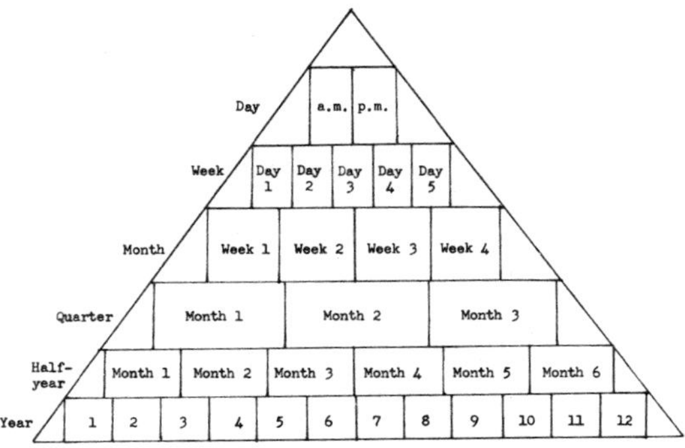

smallest unit of time—the day; and the bare outline at the largest unit of time, which may be a year or more.

Unit content The content of each unit will depend to some extent on the organisation in which you work, and your boss's job. As secretary to a chief accountant your work plan may be different in some areas from the work plan of a colleague who is secretary to the chief engineer. It is unlikely that the outline plan will be very different—this is dictated by the organisation as a whole, and similar items will be included in both. The plans will differ in detail according to the type of work and the length of time taken to carry out different aspects of the same job. For example it may take longer to produce the accounts for a Board meeting than to produce an engineering report—or vice versa. Details of planning for personal aspects of the job—dealing with things personal to your boss—will obviously be individual to him.

Mechanics of planning Keep a supply of prepared sheets ready for use. A year plan divided into months is shown below. A brief or A3 size sheet is best for this. Foolscap or A4 size sheets are suitable for the month plan divided into weeks, and the weekly plan divided into days—though this last may be done in a desk diary. Specimen forms are illustrated on page 626.

These are your 'note sheets'. Keep them handy so that you can insert notes in the appropriate places as soon as you get the information.

1974

JANUARY	FEBRUARY	MARCH	APRIL
MAY	JUNE	JULY	AUGUST
SEPTEMBER	OCTOBER	NOVEMBER	DECEMBER

A year-plan sheet.

1974
JANUARY

Week beginning 31.12.73	
7.1.74	
14.1.74	
21.1.74	
28.1.74	

A month-plan sheet.

Week beginning: ....

MONDAY
TUESDAY
WEDNESDAY
THURSDAY
FRIDAY

A weekly plan sheet.

DETAILED PLANNING

Routine work The backbone of your plan will be routine work which has to be done at precise intervals. Do not omit these routine jobs from your written plan just because they are routine. It is possible to forget them when planning the non-routine work, the special jobs.

When the details of each unit are planned it is important to avoid overloading. The monthly unit content should be spread over the four weeks; the weekly unit content should be spread over the five days. The amount of non-routine work which can be allocated to a particular unit depends on the amount of essential routine work that has to be done at that time.

A schedule of the routine work which will appear in many secretaries' work plans is shown below.

Day	*Week*	*Month*
Office Housekeeping. Opening and distribution of mail. Correspondence. Discussion with boss. Telephone calls. Press cuttings. Filing. Appointments list. Next day's work plan.	Reports including Statistics. Petty Cash. Postage Book. Wages. Circulate publications. Stationery requisition. Refreshments. Replace old magazines in reception area. Regular meetings including preparation and distribution of agenda and minutes. Next week's work plan.	Regular meetings. Reports including Statistics. Salaries. Payment of accounts. Circulate publications. Regular visits. Next month's work plan.

Quarter	*Half Year*	*Year*
Board meetings. Regular visits. Reports including statistics. Next quarter's work plan.	Staff Reports. Regular visits. Laundering of cushion. covers, curtains, etc. "Spring clean" files. including stencils. Next half year's work plan.	Christmas Cards, Calendars and Gifts. Boss's licences, vaccination/inoculation certificates. Income Tax Returns. National Insurance Returns. Training Board Payment and Grants. Recommendations for increments and promotions. Renewal of publications subscriptions. Regular visits. Next year's work plan.

Example of a schedule of routine work.

Non-routine work Non-routine work is constantly arising, some of it urgent, some of it with adequate time for preparation, and some of it 'to be done some time'. All should be included in the overall planning and any job without a specific deadline should be given a time schedule, otherwise it will get pushed away until it becomes urgent. This is a danger with jobs for which there is plenty of time. Because they are not urgent they get pushed aside for others which 'seem' more urgent, but probably are not.

PLANNING THE DAY

Having worked out the day's schedule you must then 'plan the day'. First establish priorities—jobs which *must* be done; jobs which should be done; jobs which could be done.

Your day's work plan might look something like this.

Jobs which must be done

Routine:

Office housekeeping. This includes cleaning the typewriter; preparing your own desk; preparing your boss's desk—dusting if necessary, inserting clean blotting paper in the pad, sharpening pencils, note pad, changing date on calendar, filling desk lighter; checking that the reception area and cloakrooms are clean and attractive; checking that the cleaners have done their work properly; watering plants; arranging ashtrays on conference table.

Listen for instructions on the dictation machine.

Check follow up/bring forward files/cards/diary.

Open and distribute mail. The secretary may have to do this for the whole organisation if it is a small one.

Deal with routine correspondence.

Take dictation.

Discuss with boss any points/queries/problems.

Obtain information required for letters, etc.

Transcribe notes.

Filing.

Appointments list.

Non-routine:

Take notes at a meeting.

Receive visitors and deal with telephone calls.

Research.

Remind boss about dental check-up.

Remind boss to start work on quarterly Production Report.

Jobs which should be done

Prepare draft minutes of meeting.

Buy adaptor for photocopier.

Order duplicating supplies for production of house magazine.

Jobs which could be done

Revise circulation slip for next printing.

Time allocation The time factor is vital in planning. It is frustrating if you constantly underestimate the amount of time needed for each job, particularly when there is a deadline. When allocating time for a job with a deadline, always allow extra for the unforeseen interruptions. It should be possible to make an accurate estimate of the time you will need to do a routine job and a fairly accurate estimate for a non-routine job. If you find this difficult, practise until you can do it easily. Study a job that comes to you; think of what is involved. Estimate how long it will take and make a note of the time. Note the time when you begin and check the time you finish. See how much variation there was between your estimated time and the actual time taken. You will be surprised how quickly you can improve the accuracy of your estimating.

MAKING THE PLAN WORK

When settling down to your day's work, you may be tempted to 'get the bits and pieces out of the way first', so that you can cope with a big job knowing that everything else has been dealt with. If the 'bits and pieces' are simple routine jobs or urgent matters, they should be dealt with first, but if a lot of unimportant jobs are done the big job is all too often not done at all, either because insufficient time is left to deal with it properly and/or you are too tired to give it the concentration it needs. You may be tempted to put off in this way jobs which you dislike. If they are tackled early in the day when you are fresh in mind and can think clearly and logically, you despatch them with little effort—and wonder afterwards why you made so much fuss in your mind about doing them.

Working tidily It takes less time to work tidily than to work untidily. When you are selecting top copy and carbons before feeding the pack into the typewriter, it takes much longer to find the right size and weight of paper if the stationery drawer is not neatly arranged in separate sections; and the file or letter tossed aside and forgotten means several minutes hunting through the filing cabinet before you realise that it is not there.

The following 'aids to tidiness' are worth remembering:

1 Keep stationery either in a rack or in a drawer fitted with dividers.
2 Use four filing trays—for incoming mail, outgoing mail, work in hand and papers released for filing.
3 Keep reference books on a shelf close at hand with bookends to support them.
4 Have a locking drawer allocated for petty cash and postage books and other such records.
5 Keep a memo. pad and pencil by the telephone.
6 Keep 'office sundries' (paper clips, etc.) in the top right-hand desk drawer.
7 Have a special place on the desk for stapling machine, perforator, rubber stamp stand, etc. and put each article back in its right place after use.

Planning flexibility No plan can ever be 'firm'. A plan is a *guide* and should be treated as such. When travelling to a strange place by road you plan your route beforehand, but deviations may be made and delays may occur for many reasons such as a puncture, a road closed for repairs, bad weather. The day's work is like a journey—it is interrupted and changed for any one of a vast number of reasons. It is this very uncertainty that makes planning such an essential exercise. The only way to be sure of having time to cope with unexpected occurrences is by having a flexible plan and by including in it some allowance for contingencies.

There are quite a number of routine secretarial jobs which cannot possibly be planned—such things as receiving visitors, receiving and making telephone calls, research, special errands—for which time must be allowed. Work peaks occur in every office—some can be foreseen, others cannot. Sickness of staff cannot be anticipated and absences often occur at the most inconvenient time. A good plan can be adapted to cope with any emergency—but a plan has to have been made before it can be adapted.

PLANNING REVISION

If, in spite of careful planning, you find that you cannot cope with your workload, you must ask some questions to see if time can be saved by any means.

Look at each job on your schedule and ask:

a Why is it done?
b Is there a better way to do it? Could it be done by a simpler method, or by machine?
c Can it be done by someone else?
d Is it done at the right time? Is it left until the last moment? If it is a big job, is it done at the quietest time of the day? Is it the sort of job that can best be done when the boss is away?

e Is it done at the time of optimum productive effort? (Everyone has peak production times during the day.)

f Does it fit in with the boss's schedule to the best advantage?

If you find it difficult to give answers you could either discuss the questions with your boss or with someone from the O & M department if there is one in your organisation.

If the answers indicate that there is nothing wrong with your planning and that the workload is in fact too heavy for one person to carry, the solution might be either to employ a junior to work with you, or to offload some of the routine work to the secretarial pool, if this can be arranged. It is important to find a solution because no secretary can give of her best if she is regularly overworked, nor will she be able to continue playing her full role in the boss/secretary partnership if she is constantly working under pressure.

GROUP DISCUSSION

Divide into groups and discuss how planning can assist each individual to use time to maximum advantage in his daily life.

EXERCISES

1 Below is a list of jobs which have to be done on a Tuesday. Divide them into priorities.

Prepare new stationery requisition form for departmental use for printing.
Correspondence.
Prepare an agenda to be distributed on Thursday.
Filing.
Run off ten copies from an old stencil for a meeting on Friday.
Enquire about supply of new curtains for conference room needed in two/three months.
Make reservations for boss's visit to the north next week.
Weekly stationery requisition.
Complain to cleaning contractors about standard of work.

2 You are secretary to a Personnel Director. On page 632 is a 1974/75 year unit divided into months. Break down the content of each month and allocate into weekly units, adding normal routine jobs. (Use a calendar to find the "week beginning" dates.) Board Meetings are held on the last Wednesday of the month in which they occur. House Bulletins are published during the last week of the half year.

3 Choose eight of the most heavily loaded weekly units prepared for Exercise 2 and break them down into daily units, adding normal routine jobs.

1974 APRIL	MAY	JUNE	JULY
Board meeting Revision of house rules.	Retired staff outing.	Appointment of junior typist. Publication of House Bulletin.	Board meeting. Subscription renewals. Recruitment of school leavers.
AUGUST	**SEPTEMBER**	**OCTOBER**	**NOVEMBER**
Boss's wedding anniversary (17th).	Christmas Card list. Boss's insurance renewals. Preparation of new careers brochures.	Post Overseas Christmas cards. Board meeting. Staff dance. Boss's passport renewal. Publication of 1975 training programme.	Staff annual reports.
DECEMBER	**1975 JANUARY**	**FEBRUARY**	**MARCH**
Post home Christmas cards. Staff increments. Publication of House Bulletin.	Staff party. Board meeting.	Boss's winter holiday	Boss's driving licence renewal. Redecorate offices; new curtains.

4 During next week you have the following work to do in addition to routine daily and weekly tasks.

- a Type the minutes of a meeting held last Friday morning, first in draft and then duplicated.
- b Prepare the agenda for the following Friday's meeting of Heads of Department.
- c Circulate agenda and minutes.
- d Make the various arrangements necessary for next Friday's meeting.
- e Collect invitation cards from the printer, complete them with guests' names, and distribute.
- f Collect your chief's passport from the German Embassy where it has been left for a visa.
- g Make appointments for your chief to see his bank manager on Thursday, go to the doctor for inoculation on Wednesday.
- h Make all necessary arrangements for your chief to visit a town 150 miles away on Tuesday of the week after next, returning to the home town the next day.

Draw up your week's work programme allocating the various jobs to be done to appropriate days. Remember that some jobs include a considerable number of details. which must be dealt with in their proper order. In your programme include also the routine weekly jobs, but *not* routine daily jobs.

17

Making the Most of Your Job

"For the secretary who is not satisfied, who knows she has talents and energies and concerns not being utilized, let her take heart and believe she has a role to play in management, as has been proved by those who have made the grade."

The Secretary with an Eye on Management, article by Mary E. Dunn, Director of the Centre for Secretarial Studies, University of Strathclyde, in *Memo*, 10 November 1972.

Well-qualified secretaries sometimes express disappointment in their first jobs; a complaint not infrequently heard is that whereas they have been trained to undertake a wide variety of tasks and to shoulder a fair amount of responsibility, their bosses are unaware of the breadth and content of their training, are reluctant to delegate work, and treat their secretaries as little more than personal shorthand-typists and office housekeepers.

There is no doubt that these complaints are often justified. They are also indicative of a marked change of attitude towards their work which has been developing amongst secretaries within recent years: formerly the ambition of most secretaries was to obtain a well-paid secretarial post at management level, and having reached the top, they tended to enjoy their positions and seek no further advancement. Nowadays fewer and fewer secretaries regard a top secretarial post as the height of their ambition; and more and more look upon a secretarial job as the first step in a career structure which they hope will eventually lead to an executive or management position—for although they have no intention of spending their days tied to a typewriter, they recognise that the ability to type is still the key which opens many doors and that even today the secretarial door is woman's simplest entrée to the business world.

Several causes may be cited for this change of attitude. Firstly, more women are graduating from universities than ever before and increasing numbers of them, having rejected academic careers, find it easier to get jobs in industry or commerce if they have first taken intensive post-graduate secretarial courses. Whilst graduate secretaries accept that they will not be able to take senior positions as soon as they have completed their training and realise that employers may prefer a girl who has 'A' levels and several years' experience to a graduate with secretarial qualifications and no experience, they are nevertheless intelligent women whose education has trained them to think critically, to assess situations and to take decisions; it is therefore not surprising that they regard their first jobs as unavoidable and possibly tedious stages through which they must pass whilst they are acquiring an introduction to business life and preparing themselves for more responsible work later on.

Secondly, secretarial examinations have become more complex. Examination successes in shorthand, typewriting and in a subject such as Secretarial Duties, Secretarial or Office Practice were formerly the aim of most secretarial courses. Nowadays such courses may include one or more foreign languages, including shorthand dictation and transcription in selected languages, as well as a study of the Business World, Economics, Law, Management Appreciation, Computers and Office Administration. As secretarial certificate and diploma examination syllabuses have stipulated a more intensive study of a wider range of subjects than ever before it is hardly surprising if the holders of these certificates and diplomas are unsatisfied with jobs that ask little more from them than the basic skills, plus a pleasing appearance, common sense and a good memory.

The theme developed in *Secretary—An Enquiry into the Female Ghetto** may be mentioned as a third factor which has contributed to the changing attitude of

**Secretary—An Enquiry into the Female Ghetto*, Mary Kathleen Benét, Sidgwick & Jackson.

secretaries towards their work; a paragraph from the Conclusion is of relevance to our discussion:

> "The secretarial era can be looked on as the time when men taught women about the business world. At first they said, 'This is ours—you keep out'. But when the knocking on the door became too insistent, and it was obvious that there was more than enough work inside to go round, they began to say, 'OK—you'll have to do the typing and keep your mouths shut, but you can stay'. To make it work, they had to divulge the secret of how it all operated—a secretary can't file the papers if the file is locked. Now they have a corps of fully-trained women on their hands, who are beginning to demand admittance to the executive suite. They can't now say, 'That wasn't part of the bargain'; some of them, at least, are now going to have to move over.
>
> "Secretarial work has served its purpose in the long task of reintegrating women into the modern world. It has given them a look behind the boardroom doors, it has taken them out of the house, and it has given them the beginnings of financial power."

SECRETARIAL CAREER STRUCTURES

Some typical secretarial career development patterns are illustrated in the diagram on pages 638–9. Having "arrived", having achieved her ambition to be an executive secretary at management level or personal assistant/secretary to a professional man or woman, the top secretary has several courses open to her.

Not every secretary has managerial ambitions and there will always be many women who wish to play a supportive role. These women, probably the majority, enjoy being at the top of the secretarial profession; they seek no further advancement and may stay in the same job through successive changes of bosses; they will probably leave eventually, either to get work nearer their homes or to have more time to devote to their families.

A smaller group whose ambitions are not fulfilled see their only advancement in working for a succession of increasingly important men; in other words, their jobs can only become more important (in the sense of commanding a higher salary, more authority, more responsibility, better working conditions) by virtue of the increasing importance of their bosses; some achieve this by leap-frogging up the secretarial ladder from one organisation to another, others by making themselves so indispensable that as their bosses are promoted to higher positions they take their secretaries with them—sometimes to new companies, new industries, or even to new countries.

An even smaller group use their positions to train as understudies, so that when the boss is promoted they are able to take over his job. Others, given encouragement and an opportunity to prove themselves, may leave the organisation and use their experience to get an executive post in a similar organisation.

GETTING THE MOST OUT OF YOUR JOB

It is often said that the majority of women in management today started their careers as secretaries or shorthand typists. There are few who would question this assertion, nor dispute the opinion that *until recently* the proportion of secretaries who succeeded in obtaining management positions was very small indeed, probably less than one per cent. It is certainly true to say that the move from being a secretary to being an executive or a manager is neither simple nor customary.

Here are some suggestions which may help you to develop your job or prepare yourself for a position in management if this is your ultimate ambition.

1. *Job development.* Even if your job seems a bit slight at first, there will be ways in which it can be built up into something you take a pride in doing. Your predecessor may not have been particularly resourceful or dependable and it will take some time for your boss to realise that he can delegate work to you and that you are completely reliable.

2. *Initiative.* Having made sure that you are efficiently fulfilling your main secretarial functions by providing the basic skills and doing all you can to contribute to the smooth-running of the office by taking responsibility for as much routine work as possible, try your hand at some of the non-routine work. For example, if your boss has to produce a quarterly report, try to produce a draft for him; there will undoubtedly be a file of copies of previous reports which you have typed, so you know the layout and his style of writing and it is reasonable to assume that you already know or have access to the facts to be included in the next report; it is equally true that very few people actually enjoy writing reports—your boss will probably be more than pleased to hand over the drafting of reports to you so that all he has to do is to read them through and make minor alterations before final typing.

3. *Potential.* As well as using your initiative by doing things without being told, demonstrate your potential by showing that you are capable of taking over more and more tasks. It is more than likely that the boss will delegate an increasing amount of work to you and you will soon find yourself making decisions instead of following instructions—and when you start to make decisions, you will have taken your first executive action.

4. *Study your boss's specialisation.* It is necessary to acquire certain qualifications before entering such professions as the law, medicine and architecture. You cannot hope to become, say, a chartered accountant by working as secretary to an accountant. Nevertheless, a study of your boss's subject and particularly a knowledge of its specialised terminology will enable you to work more intelligently and thus derive more enjoyment and satisfaction from your position. As administrative work begins to occupy the greater part of your working day, you may have a junior secretary to whom you can dictate some of the routine work. By this time you will have become a personal assistant and will be ready to move into a full-time executive post.

5. *Select a suitable sphere.* If you are determined upon a management career,

select a sphere of work such as advertising, public relations, travel, or a branch of commerce such as importing and exporting which does not demand a long period of formal education leading up to qualifying examinations. Then make the most of the unique learning position in which you find yourself. Learn as much as you can about your boss's work; if he is dictating a letter about something which you do not understand, ask him to explain it to you when he has finished dictating—most bosses welcome intelligent questions from their secretaries and are only too pleased to have an opportunity to explain the technical details of their work. Try to understand the objectives of your boss's job and carefully observe the strategy he uses to achieve them. Note the processes by which important policy decisions are made. In short, take advantage of your position which enables you to stand on the sidelines next to the centre of power; you can watch management in action more closely than the young male executive who is receiving a more formal training in managerial skills. An intelligent woman, with aptitude and ability, will soon be able to establish what her boss's job is all about; her immediate aim must be to become his *alter ego*, her ultimate should be to prepare herself to do his job. This "big jump" to the other side of the desk (rather like the understudy who waits for her big chance when the star of the show suddenly falls ill) is often a question of luck, of being in the right place at the right time—but the girl with an eye on a managerial post will start preparing for it as soon as she has decided that she has found the ladder she wants to climb.*

6. *Study the art of leadership.* There are many books on the art of leadership and as with so many other subjects, from cookery to callisthenics, if you can read you are half-way to mastering them; the other half is a matter of practice. Qualities of leadership are an essential part of management so when you have studied some books on leadership and general management, practise the attitudes of a good manager so that they become part of your natural manner.

It seems that there will always be a demand for efficient secretaries, so having studied this book and acquired your basic skills you will be ready to think about where you want to start your business career. Attitudes towards secretarial work are slowly changing and secretaries themselves are anxious to improve their status in the business world; associations such as the Institute of Qualified Private Secretaries and the Executive Secretaries Association hold meetings at which experienced secretaries meet together to discuss their work and pass on the benefits of their experience to younger women. Details of these and other associations are given in Appendix J, page 685.

It has been said that the slavery of women in domestic service has been transformed into the equally exploited slavery of secretarial service. This need not be the case; it depends upon your attitude towards your work and the professional manner in which you do it. Remember that the job is very much what you make it; show your employer that you are intelligent and reliable and he will give you the recognition and responsibility you deserve—if he is unwilling to do so,

* See *The Secretary Game—Two ways to play*, Stanwell and Morton, Edward Arnold (Publishers) Ltd.

SOME SECRETARIAL
CAREER STRUCTURES
COLLEGE
Successfully completing a
Secretarial Course
First job Shorthand-typist/
Junior Secretary
First or second job
Secretary at middle
management level
Second, third or fourth job
Executive Secretary at top
management level or PA/Secretary
to Professional man/woman
What next?
Remains in same job, gets married,
may eventually leave
Improves status by being promoted
with boss or by working for succession
of increasingly important people

then the best course may be to look around for another post where your ability will be more fully appreciated and utilised.

Remember to regard your secretarial work as an important preparatory stage. Apart from doing your own job, you are in an invaluable position to learn how your boss does his job, to watch the variety of jobs done by other people and to appreciate how all these work together to carry out the main purpose of the organisation. It is not beyond the capabilities of any woman who starts with a good secretarial training to get to the top in whatever business career she selects as her own specific field of interest.

APPENDIX A

Job Applications and Resignations

APPLYING FOR POSTS AND INTERVIEWS

The various methods by which firms and organisations recruit staff were discussed in Chapter 15, Personnel, under such headings as advertising, selection and interviewing. The information was included in the main text of the book because it forms part of a business person's general knowledge; it was also included as a source of reference material to guide any secretary who was asked to assist in the process of staff recruitment. At some time or other, however, everyone applies for a job and in this appendix we are looking at the recruitment process from the point of view of the applicant.

Finding out about jobs Getting your first job is a big step. Previously you may have had holiday or Saturday jobs but these were only for a limited time. Your first permanent full-time job is more important. It will occupy you for eight or nine hours a day, five days a week for an indefinite period. This is a large proportion of your time so it is worth some thought, effort and hard work to make sure you get the right job.

Finding out about jobs.

RECOMMENDATIONS Perhaps a friend or one of your relatives works in a firm which appeals to you. If so, you can get first-hand information about the place and your friend or relative can tell you if they hear about a vacancy on the staff, as many firms first notify their own employees when a post is available. If there are no vacancies, your acquaintance can enquire at the personnel department and ask whether the firm is interested in engaging more secretarial staff.

A friend cannot get you a job, but she can give you a helping hand by mentioning you to the staff manager or personnel officer. A personal recommendation, especially from a good member of staff, can be of great assistance. You will then have to carry on yourself by writing or telephoning or going to see the official concerned; in the same way, your lecturers at college may have heard of vacancies from employers in the area, or your college may have its own employment bureau or careers officer.

NEWSPAPER ADVERTISEMENTS Secretarial jobs are usually advertised in newspapers under "Office Vacancies". When you find an advertisement that interests you, be sure to read the details carefully. For example, if it says, "Must have a current driving licence" there is no point in applying if you do not hold a current licence. If the firm wants someone with five years' experience, they will not be interested in anyone applying for a first job. The advertisement will invite interested applicants either to write or to telephone. Although you may feel hesitant about discussing yourself with a future employer on the telephone, you must do what the advertisement asks. Writing letters of application and telephoning for jobs are discussed on page 643.

AGENCIES In recent years there has been a boom in employment agencies for office staff. One advantage in using an agency is that it makes a preliminary selection of suitable jobs and thus saves the time of both employers and applicants. When you go to an agency, they will take down personal details; they may also ask you to do a shorthand and typewriting test. If you pass the test, the agency will put you on their register at the appropriate grade, e.g. 100 words per minute shorthand/50 words per minute typewriting. They may have jobs available immediately or they may ask you to wait until they contact you. The agency fees are paid by the employers, not by the applicants. Using an agency saves the effort of writing letters.

DIRECT APPLICATION Certain large organisations, such as the Civil Service, the BBC and big industrial concerns, can be approached directly for jobs. They will often put applicants on a waiting list if they do not have jobs available immediately and will contact applicants when suitable vacancies arise. There is no reason why you should not enquire about possible vacancies if you know of a firm where you would like to work.

Letters of application If you are answering an advertisement or applying directly, your letter of application is your representative, your spokesman, so it is worthwhile taking the trouble to produce a letter which creates an excellent impression. There are a few rules for writing letters of application:

1. Be brief but include all necessary information and do not sell yourself short. If you won a college prize for typewriting, include this information in your letter. If you have spent the last two holidays doing typing and filing for a local firm, let your prospective employer know. Compose your letter of application carefully so that you do not remember something you forgot to include just as the letter slips through the slot in the post box.

2 Make sure your letter is correctly worded and contains no spelling or punctuation errors. The aim of the letter is to secure an interview, so you must show you can produce a perfect letter. No boss would trust a secretary to compose her own letters or write or sign letters on his behalf, if she could not spell and write correctly.

3 Letters from applicants for secretarial posts may be typed, unless the advertisement specifically says "Apply in own handwriting". Even though it is handwritten, it is a business letter and should be attractively and properly displayed.

SECRETARY

REQUIRED FOR management consultants. Age 19 plus. College leaver considered. As duties will include attendance at conferences, applicants must have a pleasant adaptable personality and good telephone manner. Accurate shorthand and typing essential. Good salary plus luncheon vouchers and 4 weeks' holiday.

Mr. John D. Taylor, Workwell Management Consultants, High Street, Newtown.

64 Oak Street
Newtown, NT4 6MH

27 May 1973

John D Taylor Esq
Workwell Management Consultants
High Street
NEWTOWN
NT4 7MH

Dear Mr Taylor

I should like to apply for the position of secretary advertised in this morning's "Newtown Gazette".

I shall be leaving Newtown Secretarial College on 10 June. My studies included a course in Commerce which discussed management in business and industry. I found this part of the course most interesting and I should very much like to work in the field of management consultancy. I enclose a curriculum vitae.

I am available for an interview any afternoon.

Yours faithfully

Mary Smith
Mary Smith

Enc.

Letters of application.

CURRICULUM VITAE

Name: Mary Smith Date of birth: 7.2.1954
Address: 64 Oak Street, Newtown, NT4 6MH Age: 19

EDUCATION:

1965-1972 Newtown Secondary School
1972-1973 Newtown Secretarial College

QUALIFICATIONS:

1972 - General Certificate of Education 'O' Level - English, French and Arithmetic

1973 - Royal Society of Arts, Stage II Typewriting
Royal Society of Arts, 100 w.p.m. Shorthand

London Chamber of Commerce, Private Secretary's Certificate examination) result awaited.

REFERENCES:

1. C V Woodward Esq
14 Meadow Close
Newtown, NT4 2MH

2. Mrs B A Sopp MA
3 Orwell Street
Newtown, NT4 8MH

Curriculum vitae.

Your letter should be accompanied by a Curriculum Vitae or Personal History Sheet which lists details of your age, education, qualifications and experience. It should be typed and the information should be arranged under headings. Remember to put your name and address at the top of the sheet in case it becomes separated from your letter. A typical advertisement from a newspaper and a specimen letter of application and curriculum vitae are shown on p. 642. It is convenient to start the letter by referring to the post advertised. The second paragraph could say why you are interested and suited for the post; perhaps you have had a similar holiday job and enjoyed it, or perhaps the firm publishes a fashion magazine and you design your own clothes and are interested in the fashion world. Mention that you are enclosing a curriculum vitae and end by saying when you are available for interview.

A letter of direct application is very similar to a letter in reply to an advertisement, but a direct application should say why you are writing to that particular firm. You should express an interest in the firm and be prepared to talk about your interest if you are asked to attend for an interview.

Applying by telephone Some employers who like to hire staff quickly ask for replies by telephone. This method has two advantages: there is no need to write a letter of application and you usually know immediately if you are being invited for an interview.

Before you telephone write out a curriculum vitae so that you will have all the facts about yourself clearly set out in front of you. If you are using a coin box have several coins ready in case the conversation is prolonged. Make sure you ask for the right person. Give your name clearly, state which job you are applying for and where you saw it advertised. The employer will probably then help you by asking questions. If not, tell him the facts on your curriculum vitae fairly slowly so that he can make notes. Once you have started to talk about yourself, you will probably feel more relaxed. Another advantage of a telephone application is that it gives you the opportunity to ask questions about the vacancy so that if you are asked to go for an interview, you are fairly sure in your own mind that you will accept the post if it is offered to you.

Application forms A firm may reply to your letter of application by sending a form for you to complete. The questions on the form are usually straightforward, but watch for instructions in small print, such as "Use block capitals".

Some forms have a blank space at the end with the caption: "If there is anything else you would like to say about yourself, please use this space". It is a good idea to look through the form before you begin to complete it to see if you should keep some items of information in reserve to add in such a space.

Complete the form as neatly as you can, preferably on the typewriter. Draft your answers in pencil on a spare sheet of paper first so that you will have no occasion to erase or change your mind about some item of information.

The form may ask for the names of referees to whom the firm can refer for information about you. Always ask a person's permission before you give his or her name as a referee and make sure you can spell the person's name correctly and know the full initials, degrees or qualifications, position and address. You will probably need at least two referees, so it is a good idea to approach people and get their permission before you start job-hunting.

Additional Space for Applicant

For Official Use

Signature of Interviewer .... Date ....

Cat. No. 6046 AS/1

CONFIDENTIAL

BBC REFERENCE ....

BBC

BRITISH BROADCASTING CORPORATION

This application form will provide us with information concerning your qualifications/experience. Would you, therefore, in your own interest, complete it accurately and legibly and return it to:

Appointments Department, BBC, Broadcasting House, London W1A 1AA.

TO BE COMPLETED IN BLOCK LETTERS

Surname (Mr/Mrs/Miss) .... **Christian or Forenames** ....

Home or Permanent Address .... Present Address (if different) ....

Since what Date? .... Telephone: Private ....

Date of Birth .... Age .... Business ....

State Kind of Post Wanted .... Salary Expected £ .... p.a.

Present Shorthand Speed .... Present Typing Speed (manual) .... (electric) ....

SCHOOLS (name, type), **UNIVERSITY, COLLEGES, INSTITUTES**	From	To

Certificates, Degrees, etc. obtained/awaiting results ....

Other Qualifications (including examinations to be taken) ....

LANGUAGES (if any)

State in the appropriate column whether your proficiency is Excellent, Very Good, Good, Fair or Nil:

Name of Language	Speaking	Translating		Writing	Shorthand (speed)	Typing (speed)
		Into English	From English			

SUMMARY OF CAREER

Starting with your last or present employer, it should include particulars of employment.
Periods of no occupation or freelance work should be described as such:

Name and Address of Employers	Employer's Profession or Business	Period of Employment		Position, Duties & Salary
		From	To	

N.B. Any additional papers should be attached at the back of this form and any further particulars about yourself or your career may be given on pages 3 and 4.

PERSONAL REFEREES (Please complete in BLOCK LETTERS)

Whilst the BBC prefers to take up references with Employers, School and/or College rather than with Personal Referees, particulars of two Personal Referees (i.e. not a relative, or Bank Manager) to whom immediate reference may be made should be given in this space:

1. Name .... Occupation ....
   Address ....
2. Name .... Occupation ....
   Address ....

Please say whether reference may be made **now** to:

a Your **present** employers Yes/No* **b** Your **previous** employers Yes/No*

* Delete as Applicable

MEDICAL HISTORY

Is your health good? ....

Are you willing to be examined by the BBC Doctor if considered necessary? ....

Have you or any of your family suffered from Tuberculosis? ....

Have you suffered from: (State Yes or No):–

Rheumatic or Scarlet Fever .... Malaria, Dysentery or Typhoid Fever ....

Diabetes .... Diphtheria ....

Heart Trouble .... Pleurisy, Pneumonia or Chest Trouble ....

Gastric or Duodenal Ulcer .... Kidney Trouble ....

Nervous Trouble .... Fits or Fainting ....

Dermatitis .... Eye or Ear Trouble ....

Dates of above, or details of any other serious illness, injury or operation, or of any physical defect or disability:

How many days' absence have you had due to illness in the last two years? ....

Have you Registered under the Disabled Persons (Employment) Act 1944? ....

PERSONAL INFORMATION

Have you previously applied for employment with the BBC (give dates)? .... Have you ever been employed by the BBC (give dates)? ....

Where in the United Kingdom do you wish to work? ....

If offered an employment, how soon would you be free? ....

Present Nationality .... Nationality at Birth ....

Place of Birth ....

Full name at birth of: 1. Father .... 2. Mother* .... 3. Husband or Wife* .... *Maiden Name — Nationality at birth: 1. .... 2. .... 3. ....

Date of arrival in the United Kingdom (if born or previously resident abroad) ....

Last Address abroad (if longer duration than 6 months) ....

Alien's Registration No. (if applicable) .... If applicant or parents are naturalised state number, date & name in which certificate was granted ....

Additional Space for Applicant
(If necessary continue overleaf)

Signature of Applicant .... Date ....

Example of complex application form.

The interview So far your efforts have been aimed at getting to the interview. The important thing is to be ready for the encounter. Getting through an interview well is a skill which can be acquired with the right preparations.

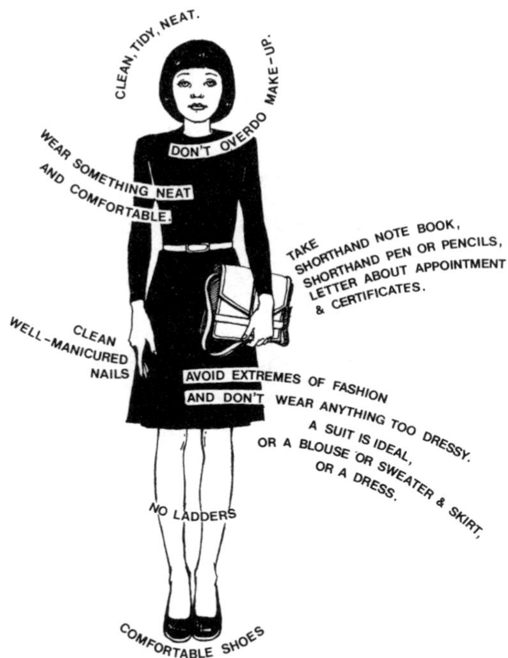

Getting ready for the interview.

GETTING THERE Make sure you know where the office is and the best way of getting there. If you have the opportunity, it is helpful to make a test run of the journey so that you know the time it takes and the look of the building. If the person interviewing you has an unusual name, ring the switchboard the day before and ask how his name is pronounced.

ON THE DAY Leave in plenty of time, allowing for heavy traffic or any other problem. If you have to wait when you get there, spend your time studying the room or looking at any magazines which will tell you something about the firm or the industry.

When you are shown into the office of the person who is to interview you, follow his lead. Shake hands if he offers his; take a seat when you are invited to; try to strike a happy medium between appearing either over-confident or extremely nervous. Most people are nervous at the beginning of interviews, but if you concentrate on the questions you are being asked and listen intelligently and answer the questions as fully as you can,

INTERVIEW CHECKLIST

Conditions of employment

Hours of work

Salary, paid weekly or monthly

Increments - granted on merit or length of service

Holidays

Lunch and tea breaks

Luncheon vouchers and fringe benefits

Canteen

Pension scheme

Welfare and medical services

Social or sports club

Promotion and career prospects

Work and the office environment

Electric or manual typewriter

Who is your immediate boss?

Dictation - shorthand and/or audio

Other duties - filing, mail handling, copy-typing

Reception and/or switchboard duties

Figure work

Use of office machinery

Large office shared with others or own room

you will find yourself relaxing and the interview will become more like a friendly conversation.

If you do not know the answer to a question, say so; you will not be expected to know everything and your honesty will be appreciated. Towards the end of the interview, you will probably be asked if you have any questions; make sure you ask at least one question even if you have been told everything. The check list on p. 646 includes most of the information you should learn from an interview so that you can decide whether you will accept the job if it is offered to you.

You may be asked to do a test, even if you have already done one for the agency. Your interviewer will be impressed by your fore-thought and efficiency if you have taken your shorthand notebook, your shorthand pen and pencils and your typewriting eraser with you. In both your shorthand and typewriting tests accuracy is more important than speed. If it is your first job, an employer will know that your speed will increase as you gain confidence and experience.

In a few cases an employer will offer the job on the spot if he has decided the applicant is the right person. If you are sure you want the job, accept it. If you have any doubts at all, ask for a day or two to think it over. An employer will understand that you may want to discuss the matter with your parents and more experienced friends.

Usually an employer will say that he will let you know. This is not to be taken as a sign that you have not got the job. It probably means that he wants an opportunity to compare all the applicants before he chooses. Employing a secretary is important and he will want to make sure that he selects the right person.

If you feel at the interview that you do not want that job, keep this decision to yourself. You will have the opportunity to refuse if the job is eventually offered to you and, in any case, upon reflection, you may change your mind.

When the employer indicates that the interview is over, be sure to thank him for seeing you. Shake hands if he offers his hand and do not suddenly start chattering to him at the door as he may have other applicants waiting. Say goodbye with a smile and close the door behind you. The final impression is as important as the first one.

If you receive a letter in a few days offering you the job, all your preparations and efforts will have been worthwhile. Reply immediately with a neat, businesslike letter. Repeat the terms of employment that are mentioned in the offer of employment if you are accepting the job. If you have decided that you do not want the job, thank the employer for offering it to you and decline it politely; it is not necessary to explain why.

If the long-awaited letter says you have not been successful, do not be too disappointed. The employer may be doing you a favour by saving you from an unsuitable job. He may have judged from his experience that you would not have been happy there. In any event, the interview was good experience and the next time you will have more confidence.

RESIGNING

The importance of knowing how to apply for a job is obvious; the importance of knowing how to leave correctly and graciously is perhaps not so obvious, but we all change our jobs at one time or another and when you get a new job you will need to know how to resign from your present one.

NOTICE The amount of notice you must give your present employer is written into your Contract of Employment (see Contracts of Employment, 1963, page 612), so read it carefully before telling your new employer when you can start work. The Contracts of Employment Act, 1963, requires an employee to give one week's notice after thirteen weeks of continuous employment, but an individual contract may stipulate a longer period. If your contract specifies "a calendar month's notice" and if notice has to be handed in at the end of a month, this could mean that you would have to wait nearly eight weeks before you could leave.

HOLIDAY ARRANGEMENTS You may have accepted your new post on the basis of "existing holiday arrangements honoured", which means that your new employer is going to permit you to take a holiday previously arranged even if you will not have earned any leave by the time you planned to start your holiday. If you have earned a holiday entitlement with your present firm, you may wish to take your holiday before you hand in your notice; or you may be able to receive pay in lieu. Here again you must consult your Contract of Employment which will contain full details of your entitlement to holidays and holiday pay.

PENSION FUND If you have been with a firm for some time and have contributed to a pension fund, you may be able to transfer your benefits to the pension fund of your new firm, or your contributions may be paid back to you together with any interest they have earned.

INSURANCE CARDS AND INCOME TAX FORMS When you are given your final pay by your present employer, you must also collect your National Insurance card and your P45 form which states how much pay you have earned, how much tax you have paid and your code number. Your new employer will need both these documents.

LETTER OF RESIGNATION It is, of course, a matter of common courtesy for you to go personally to the head of your department or your immediate superior and tell him that you are leaving; but you must also hand in your official notice in writing. Your letter of resignation must state that you are giving your employer the notice to which he is entitled in your Contract of Employment (or any other period which you may have agreed is the most convenient for you both in the circumstances), the date from which the notice will start and the date on which you propose to leave. If you want to leave earlier than your contract allows, you should ask permission in your letter of resignation, and state your reasons. Few employers are unreasonable about such requests particularly if you ask politely and if your reasons are justifiable.

It is polite in any case to mention your reasons for leaving when you give in your written notice; even if you are leaving in difficult circumstances there is nothing to be gained by being brusque and ungracious—and always bear in mind that it may be necessary to refer back to your employment at some future date, and it will help the person who has to deal with the matter if your reasons for leaving are "on file in writing" in your letter of resignation.

In the final paragraph of your letter you could add that you have enjoyed working with the organisation and thank them for the experience you have gained or any new skills you have learnt or knowledge you have acquired. It may well be that what you have learnt whilst working for the firm has helped you to get your new job.

TESTIMONIALS AND REFERENCES A testimonial is an open letter addressed 'TO WHOM IT MAY CONCERN' written by your employer testifying to your employment. It may state only the period of your employment but it is customary for a testimonial to include favourable remarks concerning your work, attitude, character, punctuality and attendance. Few employers refuse a request for a testimonial. On the other hand, a reference, in this instance, is a personal communication from your present or past employer to your prospective employer; as it is not meant to be read by the person to whom it refers, a reference can include more confidential information than a testimonial. If you think you may wish to give your present employer's name as a referee at some future date, you could ask his permission before you leave the firm.

HANDING-OVER NOTES The person who is appointed to the job you are leaving will appreciate it if you write out some handing-over notes for her. These could include such details as: how your boss likes his incoming mail dealt with, when he likes to give dictation, how he likes you to screen his phone calls, when he likes his letters presented for signature, how and when he likes his tea and coffee, a list of any specialised terms or vocabulary (spelling and meaning), a list of any routine jobs such as weekly or monthly statistical reports, and any of his personal foibles, eccentricities or "pet hates".

YOUR LAST DAY In many offices there is an informal farewell ceremony when a member of staff leaves, perhaps a round of drinks, a presentation and a few speeches. If this is the custom in your organisation, be prepared for it and plan some remarks to express your thanks and appreciation. In any case make a point of going round to your colleagues to say goodbye to them; finally say goodbye to the head of the firm or department or your immediate superior and wish him and the organisation every success in the future.

APPENDIX B

Business Terms

TRADING

A/C., account current
ad val., ad valorem
A/R., all risks (marine)
A/S., account sales

B/E., bill of exchange
B/L., bill of lading
B/P., bills payable
B/R., bills receivable

C. & F., cost and freight
carr. fwd., carriage forward
carr. pd., carriage paid
C.B.D., cash before delivery
c.i.f., cost, insurance, freight
c.i.f. & c., cost, insurance, freight and commission
c.i.f. & e., cost, insurance, freight and exchange
c.i.f.i., cost, insurance, freight and interest
cld., cleared
C/R., carrier's risk
c/s., case(s)
C.W.O., cash with order

D/a., days after acceptance; documents against acceptance
D/D., delivered at docks
debs., debentures
D/N., debit note
D/O., delivery order
D/P., documents against payment
D/W., dock warrant

E. & O.E., errors and omissions excepted
E.O.M., end of month following date of sale
Exd., examined
Ex.Int., not including interest

f.a.s., free alongside ship
F/D., free docks
f.f.a., free from alongside
f.o., free overside
f.o.b., free on board
f.o.c., free of charge(s)
f.o.d., free of damage
f.o.r., free on rail
f.o.s., free on steamer
f.o.t., free on truck
f.o.w., free on wagon
Frt., freight
Fwd., forward

G/A., general average
g.r.t., gross registered tonnage

H.M.C., Her Majesty's Customs

I.B.R.D., International Bank for Reconstruction and Development (World Bank)
I.C.A., International Co-operative Administration
I.M.F., International Monetary Fund
ins., insurance
int., interest
in trans., in transit
inv., invoice

J/A., joint account

Lt., long ton

mdse., merchandise
M.I.P., marine insurance policy
M.P., months after payment
M.S., months after sight
M.T., mail transfer

N.E., no effects
N.F., no funds
N/O., no orders
n.o.p., not otherwise provided
n.s., not specified

O/a., on account
O/d., on demand
O/o., order of
O.R., owner's risk

P.A., private account
pcs., pieces
pd., paid
p.f., pro forma
pkgs., packages
P.L., partial loss
pm., premium

R.I., reinsurance

S/a., without date
S.D.B.L., sight draft bill of lading
shipt., shipment
S/N., shipping note
S.O., seller's option
S.T. or **S.tn.**, short ton
Stg., sterling

T.L.O., total loss only
T.T., telegraphic transfer

U/w., underwriters

W.B., way bill
W/M., weight or measurement
W.O.G., with other goods
W/R., warehouse receipt
W/W., warehouse warrant

BANKING

A/c or **acct.**, account
A/C, current account, account giving no interest: money can be withdrawn on demand
At Sight, payable on demand

Bank rate, rate charged by Bank of England for discounting bills
B/D., bank draft
Bk., bank, book
B.N., bank note
B.o., branch office
B.S., balance sheet, statement of assets and liabilities

C/A., capital account
Cert A.I.B., Certificated Associate, Institute of Bankers
Cheque, a written order to a banker to pay a named sum to a named person
Clearing House, where banks exchange money for cheques drawn on one another
C/O, cash order
Credit transfer, method of settling debts with bank as intermediary, by paying amounts straight into creditor's bank (useful to people with no bank account)
Cum div., with dividend

D/A, deposit account, account giving interest, money can be withdrawn only after notice
Devalue, reduce the exchange rate of currency
D/P, documents against payment
Drawer, person who draws cheque upon another; the person who writes the cheque.

Endorse, to sign document, especially cheque, on the back
Ex div., without dividend

Fiduciary Issue, issue of banknotes without gold backing
Floaters, Government bonds etc. as securities
Funding, changing short-term to long-term debt

Gilt-edged Securities, securities of the highest class which are easy to cash
Giro system, one run by Post Office and one run by clearing banks for the payment of money by e.g. cheques
Gold Reserve, amount of gold coin and bullion held by the Bank of England or by another country

Hard Currency, any strong currency used as a medium of exchange, e.g. US dollars
H.O., head office

I.M.F., International Monetary Fund
Industrial Bankers, specialists in financing hire-purchase transactions
IOU, I owe you, memorandum of a debt
Issuing House, financial institution concerned with new issues of stocks and shares

J/A, joint account

£, pound
L/C, Letter of credit, authorising a person to draw money in another place, up to a sum specified by the person's bank
Ledger, principal book of accounts, made up at regular intervals
Legal tender, money which creditor is bound to accept in payment
Liquid Asset, quickly converted into cash
Liquidity Ratio, ratio of a banker's liquid assets to liabilities—traditionally kept at over 30 per cent in Britain
Lombard Street, a term often used when referring to the London money market

M/C., marginal credit.
M.D., memorandum of deposit
m/d, months after date
Mint, place where money is coined

N/A, no advice, non-acceptance
N/E, **n/f**, no effects, no funds, written by banker on a dishonoured cheque
Negotiable Instruments, documents which are transferred carrying legal rights to the final holder, such as a bank note or a bill of exchange
Not Negotiable, words on a cheque *warning* that a thief *may* not get a good title
N.P., Notary Public, usually a solicitor, authorised to attest contracts etc. and protest bills of exchange
n.s., not sufficient funds, written by banker on a dishonoured cheque

o/d, on demand
Orders not to pay, written by banker on a dishonoured cheque

Overdraft, authorised drawing from current account in excess of balance
Overdraw, accidental drawing from current account when the balance is nil

P.A., private account
Paper money, all engagements to pay issued by banks or Government Departments and circulated in place of coin, such as money orders and bank notes
Payee, person or firm to whom a cheque or bill of exchange is made payable
Paying-in slip, paper showing amount paid into a person's account in cash or cheques
P/N, promissory note, signed, written document promising to pay a certain sum to a specified person at a certain time

Realisation Account, especially opened account when a firm is being wound up or sold
Refer to drawer, written by banker on a dishonoured cheque

Securities, document giving the holder the right to property which is not in his possession, such as mortgages, insurance policies, bills of lading, bonds, stocks or shares
Sight Bill, bill of exchange payable when presented
Sovereign, British gold coin of £1 face value
Special deposit, certain amount of Joint Stock Banks' money which must be put into Bank of England during a Credit Squeeze
Statement, document issued to customer showing the state of his current account
Sterling Area, countries which trade in currencies based on the British monetary system now referred to as Scheduled Territories
Stop a cheque, drawer instructs bank in writing not to cash cheque when it is presented

Teller, bank cashier
T.M.O., telegraph money order
Token money, coins of less metallic value than the sum written on them
Travellers' Cheques, written orders drawn upon bank in Britain, paid for in this country, and cashable overseas
Treasury, British Government Department managing public revenue
Treasury Bill, issued by the Treasury to raise money for short periods and sold to the highest bidder

Usance, customary period allowed for payment of bills of exchange between two countries

Wall Street, the address of the New York Stock Exchange

INSURANCE

Accident, an unexpected mishap
Act of God, an event which no human foresight can prevent, e.g. earthquake, but *not* frost damage which can be prevented if precautions are taken
Agent, a person who acts on behalf of another, called the principal
Annuity, annual payment for a specified time or until death
Assignment, transfer of right or property; document making such a transfer
Assurance (or **Insurance**), see Insurance
Assured (or **Insured**), see Insured
Assurer (or **Insurer**), see Insurer

Bond, an undertaking by somebody to pay a sum of money or to do or not do a certain thing
Broker, an intermediary who advises his clients and arranges their insurance
Brokerage, see Commission

Commission, an agent's or broker's remuneration. It is also called brokerage
Cover, a synonym for insure or insurance, or the scope of any insurance, e.g. The cover includes fire
Cover Note, a temporary document proving that cover exists until the issue of the stamped policy

Days of Grace, the period during which the policy is kept in force pending payment of a premium (usually 15 days for monthly premiums and one month for premiums payable quarterly, half-yearly or annually)

Endorsement, amendment or addition to policy, certificate or cover note; the endorsement is attached to the original document

Endowment Assurance, a policy with the sum assured payable on a fixed future date, or at death if the person assured dies before the end of the term. It can be with or without profits

Ex gratia, a payment made voluntarily, where no legal liability exists

Fidelity Bond, policy guaranteeing fidelity of employees, especially those handling large amounts of money

Good faith, see Utmost good faith

Indemnity, compensation for loss or injury

Insurable interest, a person taking out insurance must have a pecuniary interest in the person or thing insured

Insurance, a contract whereby the insurer undertakes to indemnify another person or to pay that person a sum of money if and when a specified event, such as death, happens

Insured, the policyholder or other person who is indemnified under a policy of insurance

Lloyd's, a Corporation which does no underwriting but provides facilities for its underwriting members who deal with marine and other classes of insurance

Loss, the amount for which the insurer is liable when a claim is made under a policy; event which results in a claim under a policy

Mortgagee, a person who lends money on the security of property

Mortgagor, an owner who borrows money on the security of his property

Premium, the money paid by the insured person to the insurers for the cover to be provided; payable annually, half-yearly, quarterly, monthly or weekly

Proposal form, the form on which a proposal is made to an insurer

Proprietary Office, an Insurance company with shareholders

Risk, the subject of insurance, either a person or thing; a hazard the insurer covers, but not an inevitable happening

Salvage, reward or compensation paid to a person who saves goods at sea from shipwreck or other loss

Subrogation, the right of the insurer to keep an amount up to the claim paid of any money received from others responsible or partly responsible for the loss

Surrender, cancellation of an insurance before the normal time

Surrender value, the sum payable to the insured when a life policy is surrendered

Tariff, a scale of rates adopted in common by a number of companies

Tort, a civil wrong causing injury to a person or his property; the injured party can claim reparation for his loss; not a crime

Underwriter, name given to an insurer who underwrites a risk by accepting liability for a loss

Underwriting, accepting liability for any loss to the person or property insured from an insured hazard

Utmost good faith, the insurer accepts information he is given about the subject of the insurance in good faith; if the information is untrue the insurer may repudiate claims under the policy

With Profits (Participating) Policy, the policy-holder is entitled to share in the profits of the company. Bonuses, which are payable with the sum assured, are usually declared at intervals of one to five years

NOTE For secretaries who are engaged in specialist work, such as the law, medicine or technology, it is recommended that specialised dictionaries are obtained.

APPENDIX C

Abbreviations and Initials in Common Use

It is becoming increasingly common to print and type abbreviations without full stops, particularly in the case of acronyms such as NATO and UNESCO

a, ampere
A.1, first class
A/A, articles of association
A.A., Automobile Association; Associate in Arts; Associate in Accounting
A.B., able-bodied seaman
A.B.A., Amateur Boxing Association
abbr., **abbrev.**, abbreviation
abr., abridge; abridgment
A.C., Alpine Club; alternating current
a/c., account; account current
A.C.A., Associate of the Institute of Chartered Accountants
A.C.G.I., Associate of City and Guilds Institute
A.C.I.S., Associate of the Chartered Institute of Secretaries
A.D., *anno domini*, in the year of our Lord
A.D.C., *aide-de-camp*
ad fin., *ad finem*, at, to the end
A.E.C., Atomic Energy Commission; Association of Education Committees
ad lib., *ad libitum*, at pleasure
ad loc., *ad locum*, at this place
Adm., Admiral; Admiralty; administrator
ad val., *ad valorem*, according to the value
advt., advertisement
A.E.R.E., Atomic Energy Research Establishment
A.E.U., Amalgamated Engineering Union
A.F.A., Amateur Football Association
A.F.C., Air Force Cross
A.F.M., Air Force Medal
A.-G., Attorney-General
Ag., *argentum*, silver
agric., agricultur(e) -al
A.G.S.M., Associate of the Guildhall School of Music
agt., agent; agreement
A.I., artificial insemination
A.I.C., Associate of the Institute of Chemistry of Great Britain and Ireland
A.I.C.E., Associate of the Institution of Civil Engineers
A.I.Mech.E., Associate of the Institution of Mechanical Engineers
A.L.C.M., Associate of the London College of Music
Ald., Alderman
a.m., *ante meridiem*, before noon
A.M.I.Chem.E., Associate Member of the Institution of Chemical Engineers
A.M.I.E.E., Associate Member of the Institution of Electrical Engineers
A.M.I.Mech.E., Associate Member of the Institution of Mechanical Engineers
amt., amount
anon., anonymous
A.O.D., Ancient Order of Druids; Army Ordnance Department
A.P., Associated Press
ap., *apud*, according to
app., appendix; appointed; apprentice
A.R.A., Associate of the Royal Academy
A.R.A.M., Associate of the Royal Academy of Music
A.R.C.A., Associate of the Royal College of Art

A.R.B.A., Associate of the Royal Society of British Artists
archit., architecture
A.R.C.M., Associate of the Royal College of Music
A.R.I.B.A., Associate of the Royal Institute of British Architects
A.R.I.C., Associate of the Royal Institute of Chemistry
A.S.A., Amateur Swimming Association; Atomic Scientists' Association

B.A., Bachelor of Arts; British Airways
B.A.C.I.E., British Association for Commercial and Industrial Education
B.A.O.R., British Army of the Rhine
B.B., Boys' Brigade; double black (lead pencils)
B.B.C., British Broadcasting Corporation
B.C., Before Christ; British Columbia
B.Ch., *Baccalaureus Chiurgiae*, Bachelor of Surgery
B.D., Bachelor of Divinity
B.E.A., British European Airways
B.E.M., British Empire Medal
B.I.F., British Industries Fair
B.I.M., British Institute of Management
B.I.R., Board of Inland Revenue
B.L., Bachelor of Laws; Bachelor of Letters; British Legion
B.M., Bachelor of Medicine; British Museum
B.M.A., British Medical Association
B.M.J., British Medical Journal
B.O.A.C., British Overseas Airways Corporation
B.R., British Rail
B.S., Bachelor of Science; Bachelor of Surgery; British Standard; balance sheet; bill of sale
B.Sc., Bachelor of Science
B.S.I., British Standards Institution
B.S.T., British Summer Time
Bt., Baronet
B.T., Board of Trade; Board of Treasury
B.T.U., British thermal unit
B.U.P., British United Press

C., centigrade
cat., catalogue
C.B.E., Commander of the Order of the British Empire
C.C., County Council
C.E., Civil Engineer
cf., compare
chq., cheque
C.I.D., Criminal Investigation department
cm, centimetre
CN, credit note; circular note
C.N.D., Campaign for Nuclear Disarmament
Co., Company; county
c/o, care of
C.O.D., cash on delivery
C. of E., Church of England
C.o.I.D., Council of Industrial Design
Co-op., Co-operative Society
C.R.O., Criminal Records Office
C.U., Cambridge University
cwt., hundredweight

d.b., Day Book
D.B.E., Dame Commander of the Order of the British Empire
d.c., direct current
D.C.L., Doctor of Civil Law
D.D., Doctor of Divinity
D/D, demand draft
def., deferred
deg., degree
dept., department
D.E.S., Department of Education and Science
dft., draft
dis., discount
dist., district
div., division
D.Lit(t)., Doctor of Literature (Letters)
D.M., Doctor of Medicine; Doctor of Music
do., ditto
doz., dozen
Dr., debtor; doctor; director
dr., drachma; dram
D.S.C., Distinguished Service Cross
D.S(c)., Doctor of Science
D.V., God willing (*deo volente*)

Ed., edition; editor
e.e., errors excepted
E.F.T.A., European Free Trade Association
e.g., for example
e. & o.e., errors and omissions excepted
Esq., Esquire
etc., and so forth (*et cetera*)
E.T.U., Electrical Trades Union

ex., examined; out of; without

F., Fahrenheit
F.A., Football Association; Faculty of Actuaries
F.B.A., Fellow of the British Academy
F.C.A., Fellow of the Institute of Chartered Accountants
F.C.I.S., Fellow of the Chartered Institute of Secretaries
F.C.P., Fellow of the College of Preceptors
F.M., Field Marshal
F.O., firm offer; Flying Officer; Field Officer; Foreign Office
F.P.A., Family Planning Association; Foreign Press Association
F.R.A.M., Fellow of the Royal Academy of Music
F.R.A.S., Fellow of the Royal Astronomical Society
F.R.C.M., Fellow of the Royal College of Music
F.R.C.P., Fellow of the Royal College of Physicians
F.R.C.S., Fellow of the Royal College of Surgeons
F.R.G.S., Fellow of the Royal Geographical Society
F.R.I.B.A., Fellow of the Royal Institute of British Architects
F.R.I.C.S., Fellow of the Royal Institution of Chartered Surveyors
F.R.S., Fellow of the Royal Society
F.R.S.M., Fellow of the Royal Society of Medicine
ft., feet; foot
F.Z.S., Fellow of the Zoological Society

g., gauge; gramme
gal., gallon(s)
G.B., Great Britain
Gen., General
G.H.Q., General Headquarters
G.L.C., Greater London Council
G.M.C., General Medical Council
G.M.T., Greenwich Mean Time
G.N.P., Gross National Product
G.P., general practitioner
G.P.O., General Post Office
gr., grain; grammar
gr wt., gross weight
gym., gymnasium; gymnastics

H.E., His Eminence; His Excellency
H.H., His (Her) Highness; His Holiness
H.M.I., His (Her) Majesty's Inspector
H.M.S.O., His (Her) Majesty's Stationery Office
H.P., high pressure; hire purchase; House Physician
H.Q., Headquarters
H.T., high tension
H.W.M., High Water Mark

i/c., in charge
I.C.I., Imperial Chemical Industries
I.L.E.A., Inner London Education Authority
i.e., that is (*id est*)
I.L.O., International Labour Office
I.L.P., Independent Labour Party
in., inch; inches
Inc., Incorporated
init., in the beginning (*in initio*)
I.N.R.I., *Jesus Nazarenus, Rex Judaeorum* (Jesus of Nazareth, King of the Jews)
I.O.M., Isle of Man
I.R.A., Irish Republican Army
I.R.O., Inland Revenue Office
I.S.O., International Organisation for Standardisation
iss., issue
I.T.B., Industrial Training Board
I.W. or **I.o.W.**, Isle of Wight

J.A., Judge Advocate
J.P., Justice of the Peace
jr., junior
junc., junction

K.B., King's Bench; Knight Bachelor; Knight of the Order of the Bath
K.B.E., Knight Commander of the Order of the British Empire
K.C., King's College; King's Council; Knight(s) of Columbus
K.C.B., Knight Commander of the Order of the Bath
K.C.M.G., Knight Commander St. Michael and St. George
K.C.V.O., Knight Commander of the Royal Victorian Order
K.G., Knight of the Order of the Garter
kg, kilogramme
km, kilometre
k.-o., knock-out
K.T., Knight of the Thistle
kw, kilowatt

L, Latin; learner (on motor vehicle)
Lab., Labour; Labrador
L.A.C., Leading Aircraftman; London Athletic Club
lb, pound (weight)
L.C., Lord Chancellor; Lord Chamberlain
L.C.J., Lord Chief Justice
L.C.P., Licentiate of the College of Preceptors
L.D.S., Licentiate of Dental Surgery
Litt.D., Doctor of Letters
LL.B., Bachelor of Laws
LL.D., Doctor of Laws
LL.M., Master of Laws
L.R.A.M., Licentiate of the Royal Academy of Music
L.R.C.P., Licentiate of the Royal College of Physicians
L.R.C.S., Licentiate of the Royal College of Surgeons
L.R.C.V.S., Licentiate of the Royal College of Veterinary Surgeons
L.T.A., Lawn Tennis Association; London Teachers Association
Ltd., Limited
L.T.E., London Transport Executive
L.W.M., Low Water Mark

m, metre
M.A., Master of Arts
M.B., Bachelor of Medicine
M.B.E., Member of the Order of the British Empire
M.C., Military Cross; Master of Ceremonies
M.C.C., Marylebone Cricket Club
M.Ch., Master of Surgery
M.C.P., Member of the College of Preceptors
M.D., Doctor of Medicine
M.D.S., Master in Dental Surgery
M.E., Mining Engineer; Middle English
memo, memorandum
M.F.H., Master of Foxhounds
M.I.C.E., Member of the Institution of Civil Engineers
M.I.C.R., Magnetic ink character recognition
M.I.E.E., Member of the Institution of Electrical Engineers
M.I.Mech.E., Member of the Institution of Mechanical Engineers
min, minute
M.J.I., Member of the Institute of Journalists
M.M., Military Medal
M.O., Medical Officer; money order
M.O.H., Medical Officer of Health
M.P., Member of Parliament
M.P.S., Member of the Pharmaceutical Society
M.R., Master of the Rolls
M.R.C., Medical Research Council
M.R.C.P., Member of the Royal College of Physicians
M.R.C.S., Member of the Royal College of Surgeons
M.R.C.V.S., Member of the Royal College of Veterinary Surgeons
ms(s), Manuscript(s)
M.Sc., Master of Science
M.S.I.A., Member of the Society of Industrial Artists
Mus.B., Bachelor of Music
M.V.O., Member of the Victorian Order

N.A., North America
N.A.L.G.O., National Association of Local Government Officers
N.A.T.O., North Atlantic Treaty Organisation
N.B., *nota bene* (note well)
N.C.V., no commercial value
N.F.U., National Farmers Union
nom., nominal
N.O.O., not on original
N.P., Notary Public
N.P.L., National Physical Laboratory
N.S., Nova Scotia; Newspaper Society
N.S.P.C.C., National Society for the Prevention of Cruelty to Children
N.T., New Testament
nt.wt., net weight
N.U.J., National Union of Journalists
N.U.R., National Union of Railwaymen
N.U.T., National Union of Teachers
N.Y., New York
N.Z., New Zealand

O.B.E., Order of the British Empire
O.C.R., Optical Character Recognition
O.E., Old English
O.H.M.S., On His (Her) Majesty's Service
O.K., all correct (slang abbreviation)
O.M., Order of Merit
O.R., Official Receiver; other ranks
O.T., Old Testament
O.U., Oxford University
Oxon., of Oxford
oz, ounce, ounces

p., per; page
p.a., by the year (*per annum*)
par., paragraph; parallel
P.C., Privy Council; police constable; post-card
p.c.b., Petty Cash Book

Per pro. or **p.p.**, on behalf of
P.E.R.T., Programme Evaluation and Review Technique
Pf., pfennig (German coin)
Ph.D., Doctor of Philosophy
P.L., profit and loss
P.L.A., Port of London Authority
p.m., after mid-day (*post meridiem*)
P.M.G., Postmaster-General
P.O., Petty Officer; Post Office; postal order
pp., pages; see per pro above
pr., pair
P.R.A., President of the Royal Academy
pro and con, for and against
pro tem., for the time being
P.R.S., President of the Royal Society
P.S., postscript; Privy Seal
pt., pint; point
P.T.A., Parent-Teacher Association
P.T.O., please turn over

Q.C., Queen's Counsel
Q.E.D., which was to be demonstrated (*quod erat demonstrandum*)
Q.M.G., Quartermaster General
Q.M.S., Quartermaster Sergeant
qr., quarter; quire
Q.S., Quarter-Sessions; Queen's Scholar
q.v., which see (*quod vide*)

R.A., Royal Academy; Royal Artillery; Rear-Admiral
R.A.C., Royal Armoured Corps; Royal Automobile Club
R.A.D.A., Royal Academy of Dramatic Art
R.A.F., Royal Air Force
R.A.M., Royal Academy of Music
R.A.M.C., Royal Army Medical Corps
R.A.O.C., Royal Army Ordnance Corps
R.A.S., Royal Astronomical Society; Royal Asiatic Society
R.B., Rifle Brigade
R.B.A., Royal Society of British Artists
R.C., Red Cross; Roman Catholic
R.C.P., Royal College of Physicians
R.C.S., Royal College of Surgeons
R.D., Royal Dragoons; Rural Dean
R.D.C., Rural District Council
re, with reference to
R.E., Right Excellent; Royal Engineers; Royal Exchange
ref., reference
regd., registered
R.G.S., Royal Geographical Society
R.H.S., Royal Humane Society; Royal Horticultural Society
R.I.B.A., Royal Institute of British Architects
R.I.P., rest in peace (*requiescat in pace*)
R.L.S.S., Royal Life Saving Society
Rly., Railway
R.M., Royal Mail; Royal Marines; Resident Magistrate
R.M.A., Royal Marine Artillery; Royal Military Academy (Sandhurst)
R.M.S., Royal Mail Service; Royal Mail Steamer; Royal Microscopical Society
R.N., Royal Navy
R.N.R., Royal Naval Reserve
R.N.V.R., Royal Naval Volunteer Reserve
R.P.M., revolutions per minute
R.S., Royal Society
R.S.A., Royal Scottish Academy; Royal Society of Arts
R.S.P.A., Royal Society for the Prevention of Cruelty to Animals
R.S.V.P., reply please (*répondez, s'il vous plaît*)
R.T.C., Royal Tank Corps
Rt. Rev., Right Reverend
R.T.S.A., Retail Trading Standards Association
R.F.U., Rugby Football Union
R.V., Revised Version (bible); Rifle Volunteers
R.Y.S., Royal Yacht Squadron

S.A., South Africa; South America; Salvation Army; subject to approval
S.C.F., Save the Children Fund
S.C.J., Supreme Court of Judicature
s.d., indefinitely (*sine die*)
S.D.F., Social Democratic Federation
S.E., Stock Exchange
S.E.A.T.O., South East Asia Treaty Organisation
S.G., Solicitor-General
S.I. units, Système International d'Unités (International System of Metric Units)
S.M., Short Metre; Senior Magistrate
S.O., Sub-Office
Soc., Society
S.P.C.K., Society for Promoting Christian Knowledge

S.P.G., Society for the Propagation of the Gospel in Foreign Parts
s./s., same size
S.S., Secretary of State; Straits Settlements; Sunday School; steamship
St., Saint; street
st, stone (weight)
stk., stock
supt., superintendent
S.W.G., standard wire gauge

T.A., Territorial Army
T.B., Trial Balance; tuberculosis
T.G.W.U., Transport and General Workers Union
T.N.T., trinitrotoluene (dynamite)
T.O., Telegraph Office; turn over
Treas., Treasurer; Treasury
T.R.H., Their Royal Highnesses
T.T., telegraphic transfers; tuberculin tested (milk)
T.U.C., Trades Union Congress

U.C., University College
U.D.C., Urban District Council; Union of Democratic Control
U.F.C., United Free Church of Scotland
U.K., United Kingdom
Ult., last (*ultimo*)
U.N., United Nations
U.N.A., United Nations Association of Great Britain and Northern Ireland
U.N.I.C.E.F., United Nations Children's Fund
U.N.O., United Nations Organisation
U.S.A., United States of America
U.S.S.R., Union of Soviet Socialist Republics

v., versus; volt
V.A., Vice-Admiral
V. & A., Order of Victoria and Albert
V.A.D., Voluntary Aid Detachment
V.A.T., Value Added Tax
V.C., Vice-Consul; Victoria Cross
V.D., Volunteer Decoration
V.H.F., very high frequency
via, by way of
viz., namely (*videlicet*)
vol., volume; volunteer
V.P., Vice-President
V.S., Veterinary Surgeon
V.T.R., Video Tape Recording (Systems)

W.A., Western Australia; West Africa
W.D., War Department; Works Department
W.E.A., Workers' Educational Association
whf., wharf
W.H.O., World Health Organisation
Whse., warehouse
W.I., West Indies; Women's Institute
wk., week
W.O., War Office; Warrant Officer
W.S., Writer to the Signet

x.c., ex coupon
x.d., ex dividend
x.in., ex interest

Y.B., Year Book
yd., yard
Y.H.A., Youth Hostels Association
Y.M.C.A., Young Men's Christian Association
Y.W.C.A., Young Women's Christian Association

Z.G., Zoological Garden

APPENDIX D

Foreign Words and Phrases in Common Use

ab absurdo (L), from absurdity
ab initio (L), from the beginning
à bon marché (F), cheap; a bargain
ab origine (L), from the origin
ad extremum (L), at last; to the extremity
ad hoc (L), for this (special) purpose
ad infinitum (L), to infinity; without limit or end
ad interim (L), for the meanwhile
ad libitum (L), (abb. *ad lib.*), at pleasure
ad nauseam (L), to produce a feeling of disgust
ad referendum (L), to be further considered
ad rem (L), to the thing; to the point; to the purpose
ad valorem (L), (abbr. *ad val.*), according to the value
a fortiori (L), with stronger reason
aide-de-camp (F), (pl. **aides-**) (abbr. A.D.C.), a help; associate; officer attendant on a general
à la (F), in the style of
à la carte (F), selected from the bill of fare
à la française (F), in the French manner
à la lettre (F), word for word; literally
à la mode (F), according to fashion
al fresco (It), in the open air
alma mater (L), foster mother—generally applied to a university
alter ego (L), another self
amour-propre (F), vanity; self-esteem
anno domini (L), in the year of our Lord
ante meridiem (L), (abbr. *a.m.*), before noon
à peu près (F), nearly
a posteriori (L), from the effect to the cause
a priori (L), from the cause to the effect
aqua (L), water
à quoi bon? (F), what's the good?
arrière-pensée (F), mental reservation; afterthought
au courant (F), acquainted with, conversant
au fait (F), expert; well instructed in
au naturel (F), in the natural state
au pair (F), board and lodging without payment, in exchange for some work
au revoir (F), till we meet again; goodbye
à votre santé (F), to your health

beau monde (F), the world of fashion
bête noire (F), pet aversion
bientôt (F), soon
billet doux (F), love letter
bona fide (L), in good faith
bonhomie (F), good nature
bonjour (F), good day; hello
bon mot (F) (pl. **bons mots**), a witticism
bon ton (F), the height of fashion
bon vivant (F), one who lives well
bon voyage (F), a good voyage or journey!
bourgeois (F) (fem. **bourgeoise**; pl. **bourgeoisie**), one of the middle class

carte blanche (F), full powers
cause célèbre (F), a famous case
caveat emptor (L), let the buyer beware
chacun à son goût (F), everyone to his taste
chargé d'affaires (F), person entrusted with

state affairs at a foreign court
chef-d'œuvre (F), a masterpiece
cherchez la femme (F), look for the woman in the case
chez moi (F), at (my) home
circa (L), about
coiffeur (F), hairdresser
coiffure (F), hair style
comme ci, comme ça (F), so-so
comme il faut (F), in good taste
communiqué (F), an official communication
compos mentis (L), of sound mind
compte rendu (F), an account rendered, a report
condominium (L), joint rule or sovereignty
confrère (F), a colleague
coram (L), in the presence of
cordon bleu (F), (lit. blue ribbon), a first-class cook
corps diplomatique (F), the diplomatic body
corpus delicti (L), the whole body or nature of the offence
coup d'état (F), a sudden stroke of policy or violence in state affairs
coup de grâce (F), a finishing stroke
crème de la crème (F), the very best; the cream
cui bono? (L), whom does it benefit?
cul-de-sac (F), a street or lane with no outlet
cum grano salis (L), with a grain of salt

d'accord (F), agreed
d'aujourd'hui en huit (F), this day week
de facto (L), in fact; in reality
dégagé (F), free; unrestrained
de jure (L), by right in law
de novo (L), afresh
de profundis (L), from the depths
dérangé (F), disturbed; unwell
de règle (F), customary
de rigueur (F), compulsory; indispensible
desideratum (L), a thing desired; much wanted
détente (F), a relaxing; relief from diplomatic tension
de trop (F), something too much
dies non (L), a day when legal proceedings cannot be taken
Dieu et mon droit (F), God and my right (motto of English sovereigns)
distrait (F), absent-minded
double entente (F), a double meaning
dramatis personae (L), characters of the drama

élan (F), vigour, impetuosity
emeritus (L), title of honour, e.g. professor emeritus; retired from duty but retaining honorary rank
émigré (F), emigrant
en bloc (F), in the lump
en famille (F), among the family; unceremoniously
enfant terrible (F) (lit. an awful child), an embarrassing or uncontrollable person
en masse (F), in a body
en passant (F), in passing, by the way
en rapport (F), in touch; well versed in a subject
en route (F), on the way
entourage (F), surroundings, staff attendants
entrepôt (F), a warehouse
ergo (L), therefore
erratum (L) (pl. errata), error, mistake—in printing or writing
esprit de corps (F), corporate feeling
et cetera (L) (abbr. etc.), and so forth; and the rest
et sequentia (L) (abbr. *et seq.*) and what follows
ex cathedra (L), with authority, from the chair
excelsior (L), higher
exeunt omnes (L), all retire, leave
ex officio (L), by virtue of office
ex parte (L), on one side only
ex post facto (L), restrospective
extra muros (L), beyond the walls

façon de parler (F), manner of speaking
factotum (L), a do-all; general agent, servant or deputy
fait accompli (F), an accomplished fact, something already done
faute de mieux (F), for want of something better
faux pas (F), a false step, a blunder
fiat (L), let it be done; a peremptory order
flagrante delicto (L), in the very act; in the commission of a crime; red-handed

force majeure (F), superior force; the right of the stronger
garçon (F), boy, waiter
gauche (F), left, clumsy
gendarme (F), policeman
gendarmerie (F), police force
genre (F), kind, type
genus (L) (pl. **genera**), type; kind
gourmand (F), glutton
gourmet (F), connoisseur of food and wine
goût (F), taste

habeas corpus (L) (abbr. hab. corp.) (lit. you may have the body), writ to deliver a person from imprisonment
habitué (F), a frequent visitor of a place
hara-kiri (Jap), suicide
hoi polloi (Gk), the multitude
honi soit qui mal y pense (F), evil be to him who evil thinks
hors de combat (F), out of condition to fight
hôtel de ville (F), town hall

ibidem (L), in the same place
ich dien (G), I serve (motto of the Prince of Wales)
idée fixe (F), a fixed idea
idem (L), the same, or as mentioned before
id est (L), (abbr. *i.e.*) that is
impasse (F), an insurmountable difficulty
in camera (L), in private
in extenso (L), in full (without abridgement)
infra dignitatem (L) (abbr. *infra dig.*), beneath one's dignity
in perpetuum (L), for ever
in re (L), in the matter of
in situ (L), in position
inter alia (L), among other things
interim (L), in the mean time
in toto (L), entirely
in vino veritas (L), truth comes out under the influence of wine
ipse dixit (L), dogmatic assertion
ipso facto (L), by the fact itself, obvious from the facts of the case

jus gentium (L), the law of nations

laissez-faire (F), to let things alone to take their own course; a policy of non-interference
lapsus linguae (L), slip of the tongue
lèse-majesté (F), insulting the throne; treason
libretto (It), words of a musical work. Writer —librettist
loco citato (L), (abbr. *loc. cit.*), at the place or passage quoted
locum tenens (L), a deputy or substitute
locus standi (L), right to appear before a court

maestro (It), master, composer
magnum opus (L), a great work
maître d'hôtel (F), restaurant manager
mala fide (L), in bad faith
mal de mer (F), sea sickness
mariage de convenance (F), a prudent marriage
ménage (F), household, housekeeping
mille (F), a thousand
minutiae (L), the smallest details
mirabile dictu (L), wonderful to be told
mise en scène (F), manner in which a drama is put on stage; scenic effects
modus operandi (L), manner of working
modus vivendi (L), method of living
multum in parvo (L), much in little
mutatis mutandis (L), necessary changes being made

né, née (F), born
nemine contradicente (L) (abbr. *nem. con.*) without opposition
nemine dissentiente (L) (abbr. *nem. diss.*), without dissent
noblesse oblige (F), noble persons should act nobly
nom de guerre (F), an assumed name
nom de plume (F), pen-name
nonchalance (F), carelessness; indifference
non compos mentis (L), not of sound mind
non sequitur (L) (abbr. *non seq.*), it does not follow logically
nota bene (L) (abbr. N.B.), mark well
nulli secundus (L), second to none

obiter dictum (L) (pl. **obiter dicta**), a thing said by the way
opus (L), a work
opus citatum (L) (abbr. *op. cit.*), the work cited
outré (F), extravagant

par excellence (F), eminently
pari passu (L), side by side

parvenu (F), one newly risen in position or wealth
passe-partout (F), a master key
pension (F), boarding house
per annum (L), by the year
per capita (L), by the head; individually
per diem (L), by the day
per procurationem (L) (abbr. *per pro.*), on behalf of
per se (L), by itself
persona grata (L), a favoured person
persona non grata (L), a person out of favour
piazza (It), public open square
pièce de résistance (F), the principal dish
pied-à-terre (F), a temporary lodging or resting place
piquant (F), pointed; pungent
pis aller (F), the last resort
a poco a poco (It), little by little
post mortem (L), after death; an examination of a corpse
poste restante (F), place at the Post Office where letters can be addressed to remain until called for
post meridiem (L), (abbr. *p.m.*), after noon
précis (F), a summary
prima donna (It) (pl. **prime donne**) leading lady, operatic singer
prima facie (L), at first sight
primus inter pares (L), first among his equals
pro bono publico (L), for the public good
pro et con (L), for and against
pro forma (L), for the sake of form, a formality
pro rata (L), in proportion
pro tempore (L) (abbr. *pro tem.*), for the time being

quasi (L), as if
quid pro quo (L), one thing for another; tit for tat
quod erat demonstrandum (L) (abbr. Q.E.D.), which was to be proved
quod vide (L), (abbr. q.v.), which see

raison d'être (F), reason for existence
rapprochement (F), reconciliation
reductio ad absurdum (L), reducing an argument to an absurdity
répondez, s'il vous plaît (F) (abbr. R.S.V.P.), reply, if you please
résumé (F), a summary

sang-froid (F), cold blood; indifference; apathy
sans souci (F), without care, free and easy
savant (F), a man of learning
savoir faire (F), ability; skill; wits
sine die (L), without appointing a day; adjournment for an indefinite period
sine qua non (L), an indisputable condition
soi-disant (F), self-styled; would-be
soirée (F), an evening party
sotto voce (It), in an undertone
status quo (L), as things stand or stood
stet (L), let it stand
sub judice (L), under consideration by the courts
sub poena (L), under a penalty
sub rosa (L), secretly
supra (L), above

table d'hôte (F), (pl. **tables d'hôte**), ordinary
tant mieux (F), so much the better
tant pis (P), so much the worse
tempus fugit (L), time flies
terra firma (L), solid earth
terra incognita (L), an unknown country
tête-à-tête (F), face to face; a private conversation

ubique (L), everywhere
ultra vires (L), in excess of legal rights
una voce (L), with one voice; unanimously

verbatim et literatim (L), word for word, and letter for letter
via media (L), a middle course
vice versa (L), the reverse
videlicet (L) (abbr. viz.), namely
visa (F), an endorsement on a passport
vis-à-vis (F), opposite; face to face
viva voce (L), by or with the voice; orally
volte-face (F), about-turn: change of attitude
vox populi (L), the voice of the people; public opinion

wagon-lit (F), sleeping car

APPENDIX E

Forms of Address The following lists include formal and informal styles of address for persons of rank and title. More comprehensive information is given in *Debrett's Correct Form*, and *Titles and Forms of Address*, published by Adam and Charles Black.

It used to be the custom within the body of a formal letter to use special words instead of the word *you* when referring to the person addressed. For example, instead of writing "We should be glad to send you" it was considered correct to write "We should be glad to send your Grace" when addressing a Duchess. Nowadays, however, in accordance with the general trend towards less formality, this practice is not so commonly used and it is acceptable in almost all cases to use the word 'you'.

TITLE	ADDRESS	FORMAL		INFORMAL	
		Opening	Closing	Opening	Closing
Peers, Baronets and Knights					
Duke	His Grace the Duke of . . .	My Lord Duke *or* Sir	Yours faithfully	Dear Duke *or* Dear Duke of . . .	Yours sincerely
Duchess	Her Grace the Duchess of . . .	Madam	Yours faithfully	Dear Duchess *or* Dear Duchess of . . .	Yours sincerely
Marquess	The Most Hon. the Marquess of . . .	My Lord Marquess *or* Sir	Yours faithfully	Dear Lord . . .	Yours sincerely
Marchioness	The Most Hon. the Marchioness of . . .	Madam	Yours faithfully	Dear Lady . . .	Yours sincerely
Earl	The Right Hon. the Earl (of) . . .	My Lord *or* Sir	Yours faithfully	Dear Lord . . .	Yours sincerely
Countess	The Right Hon. the Countess of . . .	Madam	Yours faithfully	Dear Lady . . .	Yours sincerely
Viscount	The Right Hon. the Viscount . . .	My Lord *or* Sir	Yours faithfully	Dear Lord . . .	Yours sincerely
Viscountess	The Right Hon. the Viscountess . . .	Madam	Yours faithfully	Dear Lady . . .	Yours sincerely
Baron	The Right Hon. the Lord . . .	My Lord *or* Sir	Yours faithfully	Dear Lord . . .	Yours sincerely
Baroness	The Right Hon. the Lady . . .	Madam	Yours faithfully	Dear Lady . . .	Yours sincerely
Baronet	Sir . . . ., Bt.	Sir	Yours faithfully	Dear Sir . . .	Yours sincerely
Baronet's Wife	Lady . . .	Madam	Yours faithfully	Dear Lady . . .	Yours sincerely
Knight	Sir . . . . . . (add appropriate letters, e.g. G.C.V.O., if a Knight of a British Order of Chivalry)	Sir	Yours faithfully	Dear Sir . . .	Yours sincerely

TITLE	ADDRESS	FORMAL		INFORMAL	
		Opening	Closing	Opening	Closing
The Law					
The Lord Chancellor	The Right Hon. the Lord High Chancellor	My Lord	Yours faithfully	Dear Lord . . .	Yours sincerely
The Lord Chief Justice	The Right Hon. the Lord Chief Justice of England	My Lord	Yours faithfully	Dear Lord . . .	Yours sincerely
The Solicitor-General	The Right Hon. Sir . . . . . ., Solicitor-General, Q.C.	Sir	Yours faithfully	Dear Sir . . .	Yours sincerely
Judge of the High Court of Justice in England, Chancery and other Divisions	The Hon. Mr. Justice . . . *or* The Hon. Sir . . .	My Lord *or* Sir	Yours faithfully	Dear Mr. . . . *or* Dear Sir . . .	Yours sincerely
Judge of the Court of Session in Scotland	The Hon. Lord . . .	My Lord	Yours faithfully	Dear Lord . . .	Yours sincerely
Civic Dignitaries					
Lord Mayor	* The Right Hon. the Lord Mayor of . . . *or* The Lord Mayor of . . .	My Lord *or* Sir	Yours faithfully	Dear Lord . . .	Yours sincerely
Mayor	Of a city: The Right Worshipful the Mayor of . . . Of a borough: To the Worshipful the Mayor of . . .	Sir (*or* Madam)	Yours faithfully	Dear Mr. Mayor (Madam Mayor) *or* Dear Mr. . . . (Miss *or* Mrs. . . .)	Yours sincerely
Diplomatic Service					
British Ambassador abroad	His Excellency Her Britannic Majesty's Ambassador Extraordinary and Plenipotentiary to . . .	Sir	Yours faithfully	Dear . . .	Yours sincerely
Foreign Ambassador to the Court of St James†	His Excellency the Ambassador Extraordinary and Plenipotentiary of . . .	Sir	Yours faithfully	—	—

* The Lord Mayors of London, York, Belfast, Dublin, Cardiff, Sydney, Melbourne, Adelaide, Perth (Western Australia), Brisbane and Hobart are the only Lord Mayors who are addressed as "Right Hon."
† to Britain

TITLE	ADDRESS	FORMAL		INFORMAL	
		Opening	Closing	Opening	Closing
British Consul abroad	. . . . . . Esq., Consul of Her Britannic Majesty at . . .	Sir	Yours faithfully	Dear	Yours sincerely
United Nations					
Secretary-General	His Excellency, ..., Secretary General of the United Nations	Excellency	Yours faithfully	Dear Mr. Secretary-General *or* Dear	Yours sincerely
Ambassador to the United Nations	His Excellency, ..., Representative of . . . to the United Nations	Excellency	Yours faithfully	Dear Mr. Ambassador	Yours sincerely
Medical Profession					
Surgeon	. . . . . ., Esq (plus any letters, e.g. FRCS)	Dear Sir	Yours faithfully	Dear Mr. . . .	Yours sincerely
General Practitioner	Dr. . . . . . . *or* . . . . . . Esq., MD (or other letters)	Dear Sir	Yours faithfully	Dear Dr. . . .	Yours sincerely
The Church					
Archbishop	His Grace the Lord Archbishop of . . .	Dear Sir	Yours faithfully	Dear Archbishop *or* Dear Archbishop of . . .	Yours sincerely
Cardinal	His Eminence Cardinal . . . (Archbishop of . . .)	My Lord Cardinal *or* My Lord	Yours faithfully	Dear Cardinal *or* Dear Cardinal . . .	Yours sincerely
Bishop	The Right Rev. the Lord Bishop of . . .	My Lord Bishop	Yours faithfully	Dear Bishop *or* Dear Bishop of . . .	Yours sincerely
Rector, Vicar, Curate, Minister or Priest	The Rev.	Reverend Sir	Yours faithfully	Dear Mr. . . . (Dear Father for a Roman Catholic priest)	Yours sincerely

Foreign letterheads The secretary frequently finds herself replying to letters from overseas firms and correspondents and it is not always obvious which figures refer to the date, the reference number, the postal code, the telephone and Telex numbers and so on. Below you will find illustrations of French, German and American letterheads which should help you to compile the correct address for the reply.

SOCIÉTÉ ANONYME AU CAPITAL DE 500.000 F.

TÉL. 742-39-15

8, rue Saint-Augustin - PARIS - 2e

ADR. TÉL. STENOGRAND-PARIS
R. C. Seine 55 B 14.250
Chèques Postaux Paris 580-76

FRENCH

Name:	Sténotype Grandjean	*Tel. no.:*	742-39-15
Address:	8 rue Saint-Augustin	*Telegraphic address:*	STENOGRAND-PARIS
	PARIS 2e	*Commercial registration:*	R. C. Seine 55 B 14.250
		Bank Giro:	Paris 580-76

Limited company; paid-up capital Fr.500,000: Société anonyme au capital de 500.000 F.

Public Relations
Herbert L. Stoolman
(603) 964—9140

AMERICAN

Camden County
Name: Mr. Herbert L. Stoolman
Public Relations
Address and ZIP Code:
Court House,
Camden County,
New Jersey 08101

Tel.: Camden (609) 964-9140

Not incorporated.

GROSSVERSANDHAUS QUELLE GUSTAV SCHICKEDANZ KG
FUERTH/BAYERN (WESTERN GERMANY)

Großversandhaus Quelle Export 8510 Fürth/Bay. 500 (Western Germany)

EXPORT

8510 FÜRTH/BAY. 500

Ihre Zeichen | Ihre Nachricht vom | (bei Antwort bitte angeben) Unsere Zeichen | Tag

GERMAN

Name: Grossversandhaus Quelle, Export
Gustav Schickedanz KG
Address and postcode:
8510 Fuerth/Bayern 500
Western Germany

Limited company: KG

Your ref.: Ihre Zeichen
Your communication of: Ihre Nachricht vom
Our ref.: Unsere Zeichen
Date: Tag

The following chart lists the words used for street, road, postal box, bank giro and so on in the more common overseas countries.

LANGUAGE	Road, Street, Avenue etc.	P.O. Box	Telephone	Company Limited	Company Registration	Your reference Our reference	Postcode	Date	Bank, giro and postal-cheque
French	rue, avenue, boulevard, place, chaussée	Boîte Postale	téléphone Tél.	S.A. (Société Anonyme), S.A.R.L. (Société à responsabilité limitée)	R.C.B. (Registre du commerce)	—	follows name of town	—	Banque, C.CH.POST, C.C.P.
German	Strasse, -allee, -damm, -gang, -gasse, -platz, -weg	Postfach	Telefon Fernsprecher	G.m.b.H. (Gesellschaft mit beschränkter Haftung)	—	Ihre Zeichen Unsere Zeichen	number precedes place name. East Germany 'X' precedes number, Austria 'A' precedes number, Switzerland 'CH' precedes number	Tag	Postscheckkonto, Bankkonten, Girokonto
Italian	galleria, piazza, strada, via, viale	Casella Postale	Telefono	S.p.A. (Società per azione), S.R.L. (Società a Responsabilità Limitata)	iscrizione c. commercio, c.c.i.	Rif.	number precedes town	—	C.C.P., C.C., Credito Italiano
Spanish	avenida, avda, calle, via	apartado postal	téléfono	S.A. (Sociedad anonima)	—	Referencia	number follows name of town	—	No. de Giro
Dutch	-weg, straat, -plein	Postbus	Tel.	n.v. (Naamloze Vennootschap) B.V. (Besloten Vennootschap)	—	—	—	—	Postgiro, Bank Rekening
Swedish	-gatan, -vägen	Box, Fack	Tel.	AB. (Aktiebolag in front of the name)	—	—	number precedes town	—	Postgiro
Norwegian	-gate, vei, -plass	P.O. Boks	Telf.	AB. Aksjeselskap (in front of or after name)	—	Vår (our) Deres (your)	(N-) followed by number then town	—	Bankgiro
Danish	-gade, vej	P.O. Box	Tlf.	A/S (Aktreselskab)	—	—	DK followed by number then town	—	Postgiro
Portuguese	avenida, largo, praça, rua	Caixa Postal	tel.	Cia. Ltda.	—	—	—	—	Vale do crreio
American	As in England	As in England	As in England	Inc. (Incorporated)	—	—	Number follows state name or abbreviation of it	—	—

APPENDIX F

PUBLIC HOLIDAYS

If your boss wanted to make a business trip to New York in December, he would not plan to arrive there on December 25 as he would know that all firms close then for Christmas. This would be obvious to anyone in Britain as Christmas is a public holiday throughout the Western world. However, many countries celebrate different religious holidays and each country has its own national holidays. Travelling abroad on a business trip without finding out about that country's holidays might mean wasted days if a person arrived in America on George Washington's birthday or in Israel on Independence Day or in France on Bastille Day.

When your boss gives you his travel plans and asks you to make plane and hotel reservations you should always check that the countries he is visiting are not having public holidays when he is there. The major national and religious holidays celebrated in many countries of the world are listed in the following pages.

Some firms also close early on the day before a holiday or open late on the day following. In addition, some holidays that fall on a Sunday, for example, may mean that Monday is also a non-working day. The dates of some religious and national holidays vary each year and some countries may have a public holiday for a special purpose, such as on the day of an election. Although this list is as comprehensive as possible, it is essential to double check with the embassy or high commission or the consulate of the country your boss is planning to visit. They can give complete information on the dates of public holidays in their countries.

FURTHER REFERENCE

Travellers Guide, published by BOAC.

Bank and Public Holidays throughout the World, published by Morgan Guaranty Trust Company.

STATUTORY HOLIDAYS

Argentina 1 Jan; Holy Thurs; Good Fri; 1, 25 May; 20 June; 10 July; 17 Aug; 8, 25 Dec.

Australia 1 Jan; first Mon after 26 Jan (Australia Day); Easter; 25 April (Anzac Day); Labour Day (varies from state to state); Queen's official birthday (June); 25, 26 Dec; various state holidays.

Austria 1, 6 Jan; Easter Mon; 1 May (Labour Day); Ascension Day; Whit Mon; Corpus Christi; Assumption; 26 Oct (National Day); All Saints Day; Immaculate Conception; 25, 26 Dec.

Bahamas	1 Jan; Good Fri; Easter Mon; Whit Mon; Labour Day (June); 10 July (Independence Day); Emancipation Day (Aug); 12 Oct (Discovery Day); 25, 26 Dec.
Belgium	1 Jan; Easter; 28 April; 1 May; Ascension Day; Whit Mon; 21 July; Assumption Day; 1 Nov; 25 Dec.
Bermuda	1 Jan; Good Fri; 24 May (Commonwealth Day) Queen's birthday; two inter-island cricket Cup Match days in August; Armistice Day; 25, 26 Dec.
Brazil	1, 20, 25 Jan; 6, 7, 8, 17 Feb; 19, 23, 24 Mar; 21 April; 1, 4, 25 May; 24 Jun; 16 July; 7, 8 Sept; 2, 15 Nov; 8, 25 Dec.
Burma	4 Jan; 2, 27 Mar; 1, 17 April; 1 May; 19 July; 2 Oct; 27 Nov; 25 Dec; other variable holidays.
Canada	1 Jan; Easter; 22 May; 1 July; 4 Sept; 9 Oct; 11 Nov; 25, 26 Dec.
Chile	1 Jan; Easter; 1, 21 May; 18, 19 Sept; 12 Oct; 1 Nov; 8, 25 Dec.
China	1 Jan; Spring Festival or Chinese New Year (3 days in Jan or Feb); 1 May (Labour Day); 2, 3 Oct (National Days).
Cyprus	First weekday in Jan; Epiphany Day; 20 Feb; 25 Mar; Good Fri; Easter Sat and Mon (Greek Orthodox); 28 Oct; 11 Nov; 25, 26 Dec.
Czechoslovakia	1 Jan; Easter Mon; 1 May (Labour Day); 8, 9 May (National Day); 25, 26 Dec.
Denmark	1 Jan; Maundy Thurs; Easter; fourth Fri after Easter; 4 May; Ascension Day; Whit Mon; 5 June; 25, 26 Dec.
Ecuador	1 Jan; Mon & Tues before Lent (carnival); Easter eve; Good Fri; 1, 24 May; 30 Jun; 24 July; 10 Aug; 9, 12 Oct; 2, 3 Nov; 6, 25, 30 Dec.
Egyptian Arab Republic	1 Jan; 8 Mar; 1 May; 23 July; 1, 4, 5 Sept; 6, 24 Oct; 11, 12 Nov; 2 Dec; various Coptic and Moslem holidays.
Ethiopia	Christmas (Jan); 20 Feb; 2 Mar; Easter; 1 May; 11, 12, 27 Sept; 11 Nov. (Ethiopia has its own calendar and time system.)
Finland	1 Jan; Easter; 1 May; Midsummer's Eve (June); 6, 25, 26 Dec.
France	1 Jan; Easter; 1, 3, 4, 13, 15 May; 13, 14, 15 July; 14, 15 Aug; 31 Oct; All Saints' Day; 11 Nov; 25 Dec.
Gambia	1 Jan; 18 Feb; Good Fri; Easter Mon; 15 Aug; 25 Dec; various Moslem holidays.
Germany	1 Jan; Easter; 1, 15 May; Day of Prayer and Repentance (Nov); 25 Dec.
Ghana	1, 13 Jan; 6 Mar; Easter; 1 July; 25, 26 Dec.
Greece	1, 6 Jan; 25 Mar; Lent Mon; Easter; Whit Mon; 15 Aug; 28 Oct; Christmas.
India	1, 26 Jan; 1 May; 30 June; 15 Aug; 2 Oct; 25 Dec; numerous Hindu feast days.
Iran	Half-day Thurs; Fri; numerous Moslem holidays.

Iraq	Half-day Thurs; Fri; Moslem holidays.
Israel	Jewish holidays and 11 May (Independence Day).
Italy	1 Jan; Easter Mon; 25 Apr; 1 May; 14, 15 Aug; 1 Nov; 8, 25, 26 Dec; patron saints' days in all cities.
Jamaica	1 Jan; Ash Wed; Good Fri; Easter Mon; 23 May; Independence Day (first Mon in Aug); 16 Oct; 25, 26 Dec.
Japan	1, 2, 3, 16 Jan; 11 Feb; 21 Mar (variable); 29 April; 3, 5 May; 15, 23 Sept (variable); 10 Oct; 3, 23 Nov.
Kenya	1 Jan; Easter; 1 May; 1 Jun; 5–7 Sept; 20 Oct; 12, 25, 26 Dec.
Lebanon	1 Jan; 9, 18 Feb; Easter; 1 May; 15 Aug; 2 Sept; 10, 22 Nov; 1, 9, 25 Dec; numerous Moslem holidays.
Malaysia	1 Jan; Easter; 1 May; various Malay, Chinese and Indian festivals.
Mexico	1 Jan; 5 Feb; 21 Mar; Easter; 1, 5 May; 1 Sept; 12 Oct; 2, 20 Nov; 25, 31 Dec.
Netherlands	1 Jan; Easter; Ascension Day; Whit Mon; 1 May (Queen's birthday); 25, 26 Dec.
New Zealand	1, 2 Jan; Good Fri; Easter Mon; 25 April (Anzac Day); Queen's birthday (June); Labour Day (Oct); 25, 26 Dec.
Nigeria	1 Jan; 21 Feb; Good Fri; Easter Mon; 5, 6, 29 Sept; 13 Nov; 25, 26 Dec; various Moslem holidays.
Norway	1 Jan; Maundy Thurs; Good Fri; Easter Sat ($\frac{1}{2}$ day); Easter Mon; 1 May; Ascension Day; 17 May; Whit Mon; 25, 26 Dec.
Pakistan	23 Mar; 1 May; 1 July; 14 Aug; 6, 11 Sept; 25, 31 Dec; certain Moslem festivals.
Peru	1 Jan; 23, 24 Mar; 1 May; 24, 29, 30 June; 28, 29 July; 30 Aug; 9 Oct; 1 Nov; 8, 25 Dec.
Poland	1 Jan; Easter Mon; 1 May (Labour Day); Corpus Christi; 22 July (National Day); All Saints' Day; 25, 26 Dec.
Portugal	1 Jan; 7 Feb; 23, 24 Mar; 25 April; 1, 25 May; 10, 13 24 Jun; 15 Aug; 5 Oct; 1 Nov; 1, 8, 25 Dec.
Sierra Leone	1 Jan; Good Fri; Easter Mon; 19 April; 25, 26 Dec; various Moslem festivals.
Singapore	1 Jan; 7, 8 Feb; 1, 21 May; 9 Aug; 25 Dec; various Malay, Chinese and Indian feast days.
Spain	1, 6 Jan; Maundy Thurs; Good Fri; Ascension Day; Corpus Christi; 24 June; 18, 25 July; 15 Aug; 12 Oct; 1 Nov; 8, 25, 26 Dec.
Sudan	1 Jan; 3 Mar; 25 May; 12 Oct; 25 Dec; various Christian, Moslem and Eastern holidays.
Sweden	1, 6 Jan; 24, 25, 27 Mar; 4, 15 May; 23, 24 June; 4 Nov; 25, 26 Dec.
Switzerland	1 Jan; Easter Mon; 1 May; Ascension Day; Whit Mon; 1 Aug; 25, 26 Dec.

Taiwan	Chinese New Year (late Jan or early Feb); Spring Festival; local festivals.
Tanzania	12 Jan; 5 Feb; Easter; 26 April; 1 May; 7 July; 9, 25 Dec; various Moslem holidays.
Trinidad and Tobago	1 Jan; Good Fri; Easter Mon; Whit Mon; Corpus Christi; 19 June; first Mon in Aug; 31 Aug (Independence Day); 25 September; 25, 26 Dec.
Turkey	23 April; 1, 19, 27 May; 30 Aug; 29, 30 Oct; various Moslem holidays.
Uganda	20 Feb; Easter; 9 Oct; 25, 26 Dec.
U.S.A.	1 Jan; 13, 20 Feb; 30 May; 4 July; first Mon in Sept; 9 Oct; 11 Nov; last Thurs in Nov (Thanksgiving); 25 Dec.
U.S.S.R.	1 Jan; 8 Mar (Woman's Day); 1 & 2 May (International Labour Days); 9 May (Victory Day); 7 Oct; 7 & 8 Nov (Anniversary of the October Revolution).
Venezuela	1 Jan; 24 June; 5, 24 July; 12 Oct; various Christian holidays.
Yugoslavia	1 & 2 Jan; 1 & 2 May; 4 July (Fighters Day); 29 & 30 Nov (Day of the Republic); various holidays in each republic.

APPENDIX G

Abbreviations: (BK) Bankers' rate
(T) Tourist rate
(F) Free rate
(A) Approximate rate, no direct quotation available.
(Bas) Basic rate
(ex/c) exchange certificate rate
(com) commercial rate
(P) Based on U.S. dollar parities and going sterling-dollar rate.
(n/c) non-commercial rate

PRINCIPAL COUNTRIES OF THE WORLD—capitals, airports, currencies, distances, time-zones, religions, languages

COUNTRY	CAPITAL	MAIN AIRPORT/S	CURRENCY		RATE*	MILES FROM LONDON	HOURS + OR − GMT	PREDOMINANT RELIGIONS	LANGUAGES	
			Unit	Divisions					Main	Understood
Argentina	Buenos Aires	Ezeiza	Peso	Centavos	990.06	6,919	−4	Roman Catholic	Spanish	English
Australia	Canberra	All main cities	A. dollar	Shillings	1.615	10,575	+8 to 10	Protestant, Roman Catholic and Anglican	English	—
Austria	Vienna	Schwechat	Schilling	Gröschen	29.05	791	+1	Roman Catholic	German	English, French
Bahamas	Nassau	Nassau International	B. pound	Shillings	1.8175	4,335	−5	Church of England	English	—
Belgium	Brussels	Brussels, Antwerp	Franc	Cents	63.95	217	GMT	Roman Catholic	Flemish and French	English
Bermuda	Hamilton	Kindley Field	Dollar	Cents	1.8175	3,430	−4	Church of England	English	—
Brazil	Brazilia	Galeao, Rio de Janeiro	Cruzeiro	Centavos	28.26	5,750	−3	Roman Catholic	Portuguese	English
Burma	Rangoon	Mingaladon	Kyat	Pyas	12.76	5,585	+6½	Buddhism	Burmese	English
Canada	Ottawa	All main cities	Dollar	Cents	2.0145	3,547	−5	Protestant, Roman Catholic and Anglican	English and French	—
Chile	Santiago	Los Cerrillos	Escudo	Cestesimos	(BK) 46.28	7,244	−4	Roman Catholic	Spanish	English
Chinese People's Republic	Peking	Peking	Yuan	Chiao	3.2717	5,000	+8	Confucianism, Buddhism and Taoism	Chinese (of Peking)	Dialects
Cyprus	Nicosia	Nicosia Int.	Pound	Mils	0.726	2,009	+2	Greek Orthodox	Greek, Turkish	English
Czechoslovakia	Prague	Prague	Koruna	Haler	(com) 9.80 (n/c) 19.50 (T) 17.06	649	+1	Roman Catholic	Czech, Slovak	—
Denmark	Copenhagen	Copenhagen	Krone	Øre	11.11¼	608	+1	Protestant	Danish	English
Ecuador	Quito	Mariscal Sucre	Sucre	Centavos	(O) 45.39 (F) 48.00	5,713	−5	Roman Catholic	Spanish	English
Egyptian Arab Republic	Cairo	Cairo Int.	Pound	Piastres	(O) 0.676 (T) 1.21	2,194	+2	Moslem	Arabic	English, French

* [illegible] rates may fluctuate daily. The ones given here were quoted on 22 Nov. 1977. Rates of exchange should be checked before making a journey. A full list is published in

COUNTRY	CAPITAL	MAIN AIRPORT/S	CURRENCY		RATE*	MILES FROM LONDON	HOURS + OR − GMT	PREDOMINANT RELIGIONS	LANGUAGES	
			Unit	Divisions					Main	Understood
Ethiopia	Addis Ababa	Bolé	Dollar	Cents	(P) 3.76653	3,647	+3	Coptic Christian	Amharic	English, French
Finland	Helsinki	Helsinki	Markka	Pennia	7.625	1,149	+2	Lutheran	Finnish	Swedish, English
France	Paris	Orly	Franc	Centimes	8.81¾	227	GMT	Roman Catholic	French	English, German
Gambia	Bathurst	Yumdum	Dalasi	—	4	2,785	GMT	Moslem	English	—
Germany	Bonn	All main cities	D-Mark	Pfennige	4.07	407	+1	Protestant (north) Roman Catholic (south)	German	English, French
Ghana	Accra	Accra	Cedi	Cents	2.0825 (sg)	3,169	GMT	Christian and Moslem	English	—
Greece	Athens	Central, Athens	Drachma	—	65.866	1,501	+2	Greek Orthodox	Greek	French
India	New Delhi	All main cities	Rupee	Paise	15.6715 (sg)	4,183	+5½	Hinduism	Hindi	English
Iran	Tehran	Mehrabad	Rial	—	(A) 1.9	2,860	+3½	Moslem	Farsi	English, French
Iraq	Baghdad	Baghdad West	Dinar	Fils	0.5392	2,554	+3	Moslem	Arabic	English
Israel	Jerusalem	Lod (Lydda)	Israeli £	Agorot	27.750	2,230	+2	Jewish	Hebrew	English
Italy	Rome	Leonardo da Vinci	Lira	—	1,594½	908	+1	Roman Catholic	Italian	English, French
Jamaica	Kingston	Palisadoes	Dollar	Cents	2.271875	4,671	−5	Protestant	English	—
Japan	Tokyo	Tokyo Int.	Yen	—	445½	5,959	+9	Buddhism and Shintoism	Japanese	English
Kenya	Nairobi	Nairobi	Kenya shilling	Cents	14.9238	4,250	+3	Moslem and Christian	Swahili	English
Lebanon	Beirut	Beirut Int.	Pound	Piastres	5.57973	2,163	+2	Moslem and Christian	Arabic	English, French
Malaysia	Kuala Lumpur	Kuala Lumpur	Ringgit	Cents	4.34	6,567	+7½	Moslem	Malay	English
Mexico	Mexico City	Mexico Central	Peso	Centavos	41.37	5,534	−6	Roman Catholic	Spanish	English
Netherlands	The Hague	Schiphol	Guilder	Cents	4.39	231	GMT	Protestant and Roman Catholic	Dutch	English
New Zealand	Wellington	All main cities	NZ dollar	—	1.82845	11,394	+12	Anglican	English	—
Nigeria	Lagos	Kano	Naira	Kobo	1.182580 (sg)	3,109	+1	Moslem (north) Christian (south)	Many local dialects	English
Norway	Oslo	Oslo, Bergen, Trondheim	Kroner	Öre	9.91	723	+1	Lutheran	Norwegian	English
Pakistan	Karachi	Karachi Civil	Rupee	Paisa	18.06 (sg)	3,938	+5	Moslem	Urdu	English

Peru	Lima	Callao Int.	Sol	Cents	(ex/c)(A)80.90 (F)(A)100.91	6,307	−5	Roman Catholic	Spanish	English
Poland	Warsaw	Warsaw	Zloty	Groszy	(Cm)34.32 (T)59	913	+1	Roman Catholic	Polish	German, English
Portugal	Lisbon	Potela de Sacavém	Escudos	Centavos	73.90	972	GMT	Roman Catholic	Portuguese	English
Sierra Leone	Freetown	Freetown (Lungi)	Leone	Cents	2.0	3,047	GMT	Moslem and Christian	English	—
Singapore	Singapore City	Paya Lebar	Dollar	Cents	$4.33\frac{1}{4}$	6,758	$+7\frac{1}{2}$	Moslem	Malay, English	Chinese
Spain	Madrid	Barajas, Madrid	Peseta	Centimos	150.60	774	GMT	Roman Catholic	Spanish	English
Sudan	Khartoum	Khartoum Civil	Pound	Piastres	(A)0.6328535	3,073	+2	Moslem	Arabic	English
Sweden	Stockholm	Stockholm	Kronor	Öre	$8.71\frac{1}{4}$	889	+1	Lutheran	Swedish	English, German
Switzerland	Bern	Zürich, Kloten, Geneva, Cointrin	Franc	Centimes	$3.99\frac{3}{4}$	469	+1	Roman Catholic and Protestant	French, German, Italian	English
Taiwan (Formosa)	Taipei	Taipei	new Taiwan dollar	—	(P)69.065	6,000	+8	Confucianism	Chinese	—
Tanzania	Dar-es-Salaam	Dar-es-Salaam	Tan. shilling	Cents	14.915	4,664	+3	Moslem and Christian	Swahili	English
Trinidad	Port-of-Spain	Piarco	W.I. dollar	Cents	4.362	4,408	−4	Moslem, Christian and Hindu	English	—
Turkey	Istanbul	Yesilkoy	Lira	Kuru	33.55	1,562	+2	Moslem	Turkish	French, German
Uganda	Kampala	Entebbe	Ug. shilling	Cents	14.725	4,036	+3	Moslem and Christian	English	Swahili
U.S.A.	Washington	All main cities	Dollar	Cents	1.8175	3,442	−5	Protestant, Roman Catholic and Jewish	English	—
U.S.S.R.	Moscow	All main cities	Rouble	Kopek	1.28	1,558	+3–4	Russian Orthodox	Russian	National languages
Venezuela	Caracas	Maiquetia	Bolivar	Centimos	7.84	4,641	$-4\frac{1}{2}$	Roman Catholic	Spanish	—
Yugoslavia	Belgrade	Belgrade	Dinar	Para	33.1042	1,043	+1	Eastern Orthodox, Roman Catholic	Serbo-Croat, Macedonian, Slovene	—

* Foreign exchange rates may fluctuate daily. The ones given here were quoted on 22 Nov. 1977. Rates of exchange should be checked before making a journey. A full list is published in the *Financial Times* each Tuesday under the heading *World Value of the Pound*.

APPENDIX H

METRICATION

British industry and commerce have been in the process of adopting the metric system for some years. Some manufacturing industries have already adopted the metric system. Most changes in the retail trade will be completed by 1980 with the exception of weighed-out foods, which are likely to be sold in Imperial weights to some extent until the early 1980s. Petrol will also not be sold in metric quantities until the early 1980s.

The Metrication Board is responsible for making the metric system of units widely known. The responsibility for authorising the units to be used in the United Kingdom rests with the Department of Prices and Consumer Protection. The British Standards Institution is responsible for defining the application and use of metric units in industry.

The metric system was founded during the French Revolution and gained rapid acceptance in Europe during the nineteenth century; it has now been adopted for general use by most countries, the notable exceptions being the United Kingdom, some Commonwealth countries and the United States of America.

The Metre Convention, an international treaty signed by seventeen countries including the USA in 1875 and by the UK in 1884, established and defined the values of units to be used. The Convention set up a number of permanent bodies of which the CGPM (Conférence Général des Poids et Mesures—General Conference of Weights and Measures) is the most important. Its members are appointed by the governments of the participating countries. A senior scientist from the National Physical Laboratory is the United Kingdom representative on the CGPM.

Two other international organisations are concerned with metric units, the International Organisation of Legal Metrology and the International Organisation for Standardisation (ISO—Internationale Système Organisation).

The work of these bodies has culminated in the establishment of the International System of Units (Système International d'Unités), known by the abbreviation SI in most languages, and formally adopted in 1960.

ISO is responsible for the development of international industrial and commercial standards in almost every field of technology. It is supported by 55 nations including the United Kingdom and the United States of America. The members of ISO are the national standards organisations. Their main task is to work out technical agreements which are published as ISO Recommendations. The United Kingdom member of ISO is the British Standards Institution.

The International System of Units

The International System of Units

The International System (SI) is built up from three kinds of units: base units; derived units; and supplementary units.

A. Base Units

There are at present six base units:

Physical Quantity	*Unit*	*Symbol*
length	metre	m
mass	kilogramme	kg
time	second	s
electric current	ampere	A
thermodynamic temperature	kelvin	K
luminous intensity	candela	cd

A seventh base unit, the mole (symbol: mol), for amount of substance, has been recommended by the International Committee on Weights and Measures for adoption at the next CGPM General Conference in October 1971.

B. Derived Units

These units, used for measuring other physical quantities, are derived from the base units by multiplication or division, without the introduction of numerical factors other than unity. Some examples are:

Physical Quantity	*Derived Unit*	*Symbol*
area	square metre	m^2
volume	cubic metre	m^3
speed	metre per second	m/s
acceleration	metre per second squared	m/s^2
density	kilogramme per cubic metre	kg/m^3

Some of the derived units have special names and symbols, for example:

6

Physical Quantity	*Derived Unit*	*Definition*	*Symbol*
force	newton	$kg\ m/s^2$	N
work, energy, quantity of heat	joule	$N\ m = kg\ m^2/s^2$	J
power	watt	$J/s = kg\ m^2/s^3$	W
electric potential, potential difference, tension, electromotive force	volt	$W/A = kg\ m^2/s^3\ A$	V
electric charge	coulomb	A s	C
electric capacitance	farad	$A\ s/V = A^2\ s^4/kg\ m^2$	F
electric resistance	ohm	$V/A = kg\ m^2/s^3\ A^2$	Ω
frequency	hertz	1/s	Hz

For pressure and stress, the derived unit is the newton per square metre. The special name, pascal, and symbol Pa ($N/m^2 = kg/m\ s^2$), have been recommended for the derived unit of pressure and stress by the International Committee on Weights and Measures, but they have not yet been adopted by CGPM. Another unit for pressure, the bar ($10^5\ N/m^2$) is used in some countries, including the United Kingdom. The millibar is used generally for the measurement of atmospheric pressure.

C. Supplementary Units

There are in addition to the base units and the derived units two supplementary units.

Physical Quantity	*Unit*	*Symbol*
plane angle	radian	rad
solid angle	steradian	sr

D. Prefixes

An essential feature of SI is the systematic use of prefixes to designate decimal multiples and decimal fractions of the base units and the derived units. The most commonly used of these SI prefixes are:

Prefix	*Factor*	*Symbol*
mega	One million times (10^6)	M
kilo	One thousand times (10^3)	k
hecto	One hundred times (10^2)	h
deca	Ten times (10)	da
deci	One tenth of (10^{-1})	d
centi	One hundredth of (10^{-2})	c
milli	One thousandth of (10^{-3})	m
micro	One millionth of (10^{-6})	μ

7

Some units so formed have long-established special names, such as:

Physical Quantity	*Special Name*	*Definition*	*Symbol*
length	micron	10^{-6} m	μm
area	hectare	$hm^2 = 10^4\ m^2$	ha
volume	litre	$dm^3 = 10^{-3}\ m^3$	l
mass	tonne	$Mg = 10^3$ kg	t
pressure	millibar	$10^2\ N/m^2$	mbar

The litre is at present defined in the United Kingdom law on the basis of the 1901 CGPM definition and is therefore strictly equivalent to 1·000028 dm^3. The need to amend the present definition to accord with SI is under consideration.

E. Some Non-SI Units

Some units, not belonging to the International System, are well established internationally and will remain in use along with SI units. Among these are:

Physical Quantity	*Unit*	*Symbo*
plane angle	degree	..°
time ·	minute	min
	hour	h
	day	d
	month	–
	year	–
length	international nautical mile (1 852 m)	n mile
speed	kilometre per hour	km/h
	knot (international nautical mile per hour)	kn
energy	kilowatt hour	kW h
temperature	degree Celsius	°C

8

Some everyday units

The units which have been chosen for everyday use include a few which are not strictly part of SI but which are nevertheless established internationally. The table overleaf sets out some everyday units and relates them to SI base units.

Some Everyday Units

Physical Quantity	SI Base Units	Everyday Unit	Symbol	Definition
length	metre	millimetre	mm	one thousandth of a metre (10^{-3} m)
		centimetre	cm	one hundredth of a metre (10^{-2} m)
		metre	m	
		kilometre	km	one thousand metres (10^{3} m)
		international nautical mile	n mile	1 852 metres
area		square metre	m^2	
		hectare	ha	ten thousand square metres (10^{4} m^2)
volume and capacity*		cubic centimetre	cm^3	one millionth of a cubic metre (10^{-6} m^3)
		cubic metre	m^3	
		millilitre	ml	one millionth of a cubic metre or one thousandth of a litre (10^{-6} m^3 or cm^3)
		litre	l	one thousandth of a cubic metre (10^{-3} m^3) or 1 cubic decimetre (dm^3)
weight†	kilogramme	gramme	g	one thousandth of a kilogramme (10^{-3} kg)
		kilogramme	kg	
		tonne	tonne	one thousand kilogrammes (10^{3} kg or Mg)
time	second	second	s	
		minute	min	
		hour	h	
		day	d	
		month	–	
		year	–	

10

Physical Quantity	SI Base Units	Everyday Unit	Symbol	Definition
speed	metre second	metre per second	m/s	
		kilometre per hour	km/h	
		International knot	kn	International nautical mile per hour or 1 852 metres in 3 600 seconds or 0·514444 m/s
electric current	ampere	ampere	A	
power	kilogramme metre second	watt	W	kg m^2/s^3
		kilowatt	kW	one thousand watts (10^{3} W)
energy‡		kilowatt hour	kW h	
		megajoule	MJ	one million joules (10^{6} J)
electric potential difference	kilogramme metre second ampere	volt	V	W/A
electric resistance		ohm	Ω	V/A
frequency	second	hertz	Hz	1/s
temperature	kelvin	degree Celsius§	°C	°C=K

Notes to Table

*Although the cubic centimetre and the millilitre are identical and interchangeable, it is common practice to use the cubic centimetre and the cubic metre for measuring the volume of solids, but the millilitre and the litre for measuring the volume of liquids and the capacity of containers for liquids. The accepted abbreviation for litre is 'l' which can be confused in typescript with the figure 'one'. It may therefore be advisable not to abbreviate 'litre'.

†Strictly the gramme, kilogramme and tonne are units of mass. For most people and for ordinary trading purposes the word weight has the same meaning as mass. The SI symbol for

Notes continued overleaf

11

'tonne' is 't' but, to avoid confusion with the commonly used abbreviation 't' for the imperial ton, it is advisable for the present not to abbreviate 'tonne'.

‡ The strict SI unit of energy is the joule (J=kg m^2/s^2). The kilowatt hour is equal to 3·6 MJ. The joule is already used extensively in scientific work and will be increasingly used in technology. The joule will become an everyday unit when, as already recommended, it becomes established in dietetics in place of the calorie (4·1868 J).

§ The degree Celsius is a unit of temperature interval identical with the kelvin. When a temperature is expressed as so many degrees Celsius the corresponding thermodynamic temperature is obtained by adding 273·15 kelvins. Thus a statement that water freezes at 0°C means that water freezes at 273·15 K. The degree Celsius is at present known in Britain as the degree Centigrade. The term 'Centigrade' is, however, used in some other countries to denote fractions of a right angle, and, to avoid confusion, it has been agreed internationally that, for the measurement of temperature, the name 'degree Centigrade' shall be replaced by 'degree Celsius'.

12

Notes

1 In many countries the comma (,) is employed where in the UK a decimal ('full') point is used, either on the line or slightly above it. In the UK a comma is often used to separate the digits of large numbers into groups of three, e.g. 1,456,789. To avoid confusion in international documents the digits of large numbers are often separated by small gaps into groups of three starting from the decimal point e.g. 1 456 789. Greater detail can be found in BS 1957 : 1953 "The presentation of numerical values".

2 The spellings of the units of length (*metre*) and mass (*kilogramme*) have been adopted in the UK as they are the same as those used by the CGPM. In North America the spellings are *meter* and *kilogram.*

3 One advantage of SI is that it is simple and consistent. The names of multiples and submultiples of the base units are formed by the use of prefixes which have the same form and meaning irrespective of the unit to which they are applied, e.g.

1 kilometre (km) = 1000 metres
1 millimetre (mm) = 0.001 metre

Here are the names of the prefixes with some examples:

Prefix	*Symbol*		*Factor by which the unit is multiplied*	*Example*
tera	T	10^{12} =	1 000 000 000 000	
giga	G	10^{9} =	1 000 000 000	gigahertz (GHz)
mega	M	10^{6} =	1 000 000	megawatt (MW)
kilo	k	10^{3} =	1 000	kilometre (km)
hecto*	h	10^{2} =	100	
deca*	da	10^{1} =	10	
deci*	d	10^{-1} =	0·1	
centi*	c	10^{-2} =	0·01	
milli	m	10^{-3} =	0·001	milligramme (mg)
micro	μ	10^{-6} =	0·000 001	microsecond (μs)
nano	n	10^{-9} =	0·000 000 001	nanometre (nm)
pico	p	10^{-12} =	0·000 000 000 001	picofarad (pF)
femto	f	10^{-15} =	0·000 000 000 000 001	
atto	a	10^{-18} =	0·000 000 000 000 000 001	

4 Rules for writing and typing in SI are being produced by leading national organisations.* We are at present in a period of transition but there would appear to be general agreement on the following recommendations:

(a) As the comma is used in some countries as a decimal point, commas should not be used to mark thousands.

(b) Numbers up to four figures can be blocked, e.g.

1752 0.1752 10.1752

(c) Numbers of five figures or more may be blocked in threes, e.g.

123 456.0 0.123 456

(d) The decimal point may be central when handwritten or when a typewriter has a central point key, but otherwise will be typed on the line, using a full stop, e.g.

12·34 12.34

(e) No full stops are put after the symbols except at the end of a sentence, and none between them, e.g.

mm not mm. and not m.m.

(f) Symbols are the same in the singular as in the plural except for *tonne* and *litre* which become *tonnes* and *litres*.

(g) For quantities less than one, always place a zero in front of the decimal point, e.g.

0.123 0.0123

* *Handbook for the typing services, 2—metrication for typists*, Central Electricity Generating Board, 1971. *Writing and typing metric units*, The Gas Council, 1971.

Metrication in Business Equipment*

1. In a number of manufacturing areas whilst it will not be difficult to adopt metric terminology (i.e. quote sizes, weights, etc. in metric units) it will not be possible for some years to redesign products on a metric basis (that is, designs based on metric units as opposed to simply quoting the equivalent metric units for imperial based designs).

2. Data Processing Equipment: The most common media onto which data is encoded for processing are paper tape, magnetic tape and punched cards. These will not be changed by metrication; they have internationally inch-based dimensions.

3. Continuous Stationery for computer print-out is inch-based and will remain so, i.e. 8 in and 12 in form depths and 0.5 in sprocket spacing. Continuous stationery printers will continue to use 10 characters and 6 lines to the inch.

4. Computer printout: There has recently been international agreement that character sets for optical character recognition (OCR) and magnetic ink character recognition (MICR) will be standardised at 10 characters to the inch.

5. Most British reprographic machines (spirit, stencil and offset-litho duplicators) are capable of using paper sizes up to 14 in × 9 in. They can, therefore, accommodate A4 without adjustment.

6. Printing: There is no international standardisation for typographic measurement. The ISO A paper sizes offer little choice for paper sizes for booklets etc. and present feeling is that the British Standards Institute will recommend the retention of some crown sizes together with A4 and A5. (Further information—various booklets on metrication and the printing industry have been produced by the British Federation of Master Printers).

7. Typewriters: The standard carriage width of 11 in easily accommodates A4. Longer carriage machines, 18 in wide and over, will be suitable for papers up to A3 lengthways (16.54 in). The use of six lines to the inch for vertical spacing and 10 or 12 characters to the inch horizontally (see BS 2481) has been internationally accepted for all office machines and computer printout.

8. Paper substance: Paper weight (formerly called 'substance' now to be called 'grammage') will be measured in grammes per square metre (g/m^2) instead of pounds per ream.

9. Paper and envelope sizes are listed in Chapter 2.

10. Filing equipment, cabinets, folders, files and record cards: The majority of filing cabinets and folders etc. are foolscap and can therefore accommodate the A4 size without difficulty.

* *Metrication in Business Equipment*, a **beta** 'Guide to Users' publication. Business Equipment Trade Association.

APPENDIX I

Weights, Measures and Clothing Sizes

WEIGHTS AND MEASURES

Linear Measure

1 inch = 2.54 centimetres
12 inches = 1 foot = 0.3048 metre
3 feet = 1 yard = 0.9144 metre
$5\frac{1}{2}$ yards or $16\frac{1}{2}$ feet = 1 rod (or pole or perch) = 5.029 metres
40 rods = 1 furlong = 201.17 metres
8 furlongs or 1,760 yards or 5,280 feet = 1 (statute) mile = 1,609.3 metres
3 miles = 1 (land) league = 4.83 kilometres

Square Measure

1 square inch = 6.452 square centimetres
144 square inches = 1 square foot = 929 square centimetres
9 square feet = 1 square yard = 0.8361 square metre
$30\frac{1}{4}$ square yards = 1 square rod (or square pole or square perch) = 25.29 square metres
160 square rods or 4,840 square yards or 43,560 square feet = 1 acre = 0.4047 hectare
640 acres = 1 square mile = 259 hectares or 2.59 square kilometres

Cubic Measure

1 cubic inch = 16.387 cubic centimetres
1,728 cubic inches = 1 cubic foot = 0.0283 cubic metre
27 cubic feet = 1 cubic yard = 0.7646 cubic metre (in units for cordwood, etc.)
16 cubic feet = 1 cord foot
8 cord feet = 1 cord = 3.625 cubic metres

Nautical Measure

6 feet = 1 fathom = 1.829 metres
100 fathoms = 1 cable's length (ordinary) (In the US Navy 120 fathoms or 720 feet = 1 cable's length; in the British Navy, 608 feet = 1 cable's length.)
10 cables' lengths = 1 nautical mile (6,076.10333 feet, by international agreement in 1954) = 1.852 kilometres
1 nautical mile (Also called geographical, sea, or air mile, and, in Great Britain, Admiralty mile.) = 1.1508 statute miles (the length of a minute of longitude at the equator)
3 nautical miles = 1 marine league (3.45 statute miles) = 5.56 kilometres
60 nautical miles = 1 degree of a great circle of the earth

Dry Measure

1 pint = 33.60 cubic inches = 0.5505 litre
2 pints = 1 quart = 67.20 cubic inches = 1.1012 litres
8 quarts = 1 peck = 537.61 cubic inches = 8.8096 litres
4 pecks = 1 bushel = 2,150.42 cubic inches = 35.2383 litres
1 British dry quart = 1.032 US dry quarts.

According to United States government standards, the following are the weights avoirdupois for single bushels of the specified grains: for wheat, 60 pounds; for barley, 48 pounds; for oats, 32 pounds; for rye, 56 pounds; for corn, 56 pounds. Some States have specifications varying from these.

Liquid Measure

1 gill = 4 fluid ounces (see next table) = 7.219 cubic inches = 0.1183 litre
4 gills = 1 pint = 28.875 cubic inches = 0.4732 litre
2 pints = 1 quart = 57.75 cubic inches = 0.9463 litre
4 quarts = 1 gallon = 231 cubic inches = 3.7853 litres

The British imperial gallon (4 imperial quarts) = 277.42 cubic inches = 4.546 litres. The barrel in Great Britain equals 36 imperial gallons, in the United States, usually 31½ gallons.

Apothecaries' Fluid Measure

1 minim = 0.0038 cubic inch = 0.0616 millilitre
60 minims = 1 fluid dram = 0.2256 cubic inch = 3.6966 millilitres
8 fluid drams = 1 fluid ounce = 1.8047 cubic inches = 0.0296 litre
16 fluid ounces = 1 pint = 28.875 cubic inches = 0.4732 litre
See table immediately preceding for quart and gallon equivalents. The British pint = 20 fluid ounces.

Circular (or Angular) Measure

60 seconds (″) = 1 minute (′)
60 minutes = 1 degree (°)
90 degrees = 1 quadrant or 1 right angle
4 quadrants or 360 degrees = 1 circle

Avoirdupois Weight

(The grain, equal to 0.0648 gramme, is the same in all three tables of weight)
1 dram or 27.34 grains = 1.772 grammes
16 drams or 437.5 grains = 1 ounce = 28.3495 grammes
16 ounces or 7,000 grains = 1 pound = 453.59 grammes
100 pounds = 1 hundredweight = 45.36 kilogrammes
2,000 pounds = 1 ton = 907.18 kilogrammes

In Great Britain, 14 pounds (6.35 kilogrammes) = 1 stone, 112 pounds (50.80 kilogrammes) = 1 hundredweight, and 2,240 pounds (1,016.05 kilogrammes) = 1 long ton.

Troy Weight

(The grain, equal to 0.0648 gram, is the same in all three tables of weight)
3.086 grains = 1 carat = 200 milligrammes
24 grains = 1 pennyweight = 1.5552 grammes
20 pennyweights or 480 grains = 1 ounce = 31.1035 grammes
12 ounces or 5,760 grains = 1 pound = 373.24 grammes

Apothecaries' Weight

(The grain, equal to 0.0648 gramme, is the same in all three tables of weight)
20 grains = 1 scruple = 1.296 grammes
3 scruples = 1 dram = 3.888 grammes
8 drams or 480 grains = 1 ounce = 31.1035 grammes
12 ounces or 5,760 grains = 1 pound = 373.24 grammes

THE METRIC SYSTEM

Linear Measure

10 millimetres = 1 centimetre = 0.3937 inch
10 centimetres = 1 decimetre = 3.937 inches
10 decimetres = 1 metre = 39.37 inches or 3.28 feet
10 metres = 1 decametre = 393.7 inches
10 decametres = 1 hectometre = 328 feet 1 inch
10 hectometres = 1 kilometre = 0.621 mile
10 kilometres = 1 myriametre = 6.21 miles

Square Measure

100 square millimetres = 1 square centimetre = 0.15499 square inch
100 square centimetres = 1 square decimetre = 15.499 square inches
100 square decimetres = 1 square metre = 1,549.9 square inches or 1.196 square yards
100 square metres = 1 square decametre = 119.6 square yards

100 square decametres = 1 square hectometre = 2.471 acres
100 square hectometres = 1 square kilometre = 0.386 square mile

Land Measure

1 square metre = 1 centiare = 1,549.9 square inches
100 centiares = 1 are = 119.6 square yards
100 ares = 1 hectare = 2.471 acres
100 hectares = 1 square kilometre = 0.386 square mile

Volume Measure

1,000 cubic millimetre = 1 cubic centimetre = 0.06102 cubic inch
1,000 cubic centimetres = 1 cubic decimetre = 61.02 cubic inches
1,000 cubic decimetres = 1 cubic metre = 35.314 cubic feet (the unit is called a *stere* in measuring firewood)

Capacity Measure

10 millilitres = 1 centilitre = 0.338 fluid ounce
10 centilitres = 1 decilitre = 3.38 fluid ounces
10 decilitres = 1 litre = 1.0567 liquid quarts or 0.9081 dry quart
10 litres = 1 decalitre = 2.64 gallons or 0.284 bushel
10 decalitres = 1 hectolitre = 26.418 gallons or 2.838 bushels
10 hectolitres = 1 kilolitre = 264.18 gallons or 35.315 cubic feet

Weights

10 milligrammes = 1 centigramme = 0.1543 grain
10 centigrammes = 1 decigramme = 1.5432 grains
10 decigrammes = 1 gramme = 15.432 grains
10 grammes = 1 decagramme = 0.3527 ounce
10 decagrammes = 1 hectogramme = 3.5274 ounces
10 hectogrammes = 1 kilogramme = 2.2046 pounds
10 kilogrammes = 1 myriagramme = 22.046 pounds
10 myriagrammes = 1 quintal = 220.46 pounds
10 quintals = 1 metric ton = 2,204.6 pounds

APPENDIX J

SECRETARIAL ORGANISATIONS

THE INSTITUTE OF QUALIFIED PRIVATE SECRETARIES was formed in 1957 following the establishment of the Private Secretary's Diploma examination by the Commercial Education Department of the London Chamber of Commerce and Industry. The basic aim of the Institute is to establish the status of the *qualified* private secretary.

To be eligible for membership a secretary must have attained the Private Secretary's Diploma. Associate membership is open to younger secretaries who have passed the Private Secretary's Certificate examination. Graduates of the Office Management Department of the University of Strathclyde and other courses of similar standing are eligible initially for associate membership with automatic transfer to full membership after two years.

Student membership is available to students who are studying for the Private Secretary's Certificate and Diploma examinations. The student membership period is from October each year to June of the following year when the examinations are held. During this period the Institute issues study notes and reading material. Regional branches organise one-day seminars at which lectures give guidance for the forthcoming examinations.

The Institute has approximately 2000 members, and branches in Reading and District, North Thames, South Thames, Wessex, East Midlands, West Midlands, Leicester and Country, Essex, South Yorkshire and Northamptonshire and District. The Institute holds regular meetings and publishes a quarterly journal and a newsletter four or five times a year.

Further information from: Miss R. Betts (Secretary), Institute of Qualified Private Secretaries, 126 Farnham Road, Slough, Bucks.

THE EXECUTIVE SECRETARIES ASSOCIATION was formed in 1970 to 'increase the professional standing of the truly executive secretary who forms a vital part of a director's or senior executive's administrative function'.

The Association has several hundred members; its main aims are to improve the secretary's status in terms of professional qualifications, and to get improved salary scales which will reflect the level of responsibility undertaken by secretaries.

The Association is particularly interested in forming action groups to improve the promotion opportunities of the senior secretary who, even after several years' experience, is frequently overlooked when selection takes place.

Meetings of the Association are held bi-monthly in London and at branches in Staffordshire, Merseyside, Cheshire and Avon.

Further information from: Miss S. J. Vick (President), Executive Secretaries Association, 45 Milford Close, Abbey Wood, London SE2 0DS.

THE ASSOCIATION OF PERSONAL ASSISTANTS AND SECRETARIES LIMITED was formed to enhance the professionalism of those engaged in PA and secretarial work.

The objectives of the Association are:

1 to establish the status of the qualified Personal Assistant and Secretary;

2 to provide members with information on salary rates, job opportunities at home and abroad, and careers in different types of businesses and industries;
3 to offer members advice on professional matters;
4 to promote an interchange of views and opinion between members.

The grades of membership are: Associate (students undertaking a course of study for a private secretary's diploma, or people who have completed this course within the last three years); Member (people who have successfully completed a secretarial course, and have at least three years' secretarial experience); Fellow (people whose qualifications and experience are outstanding, and who have at least five years' senior secretarial experience).

A Newsletter containing articles of interest and correspondence columns is published quarterly. The Association is represented in a number of overseas countries.

Further information from: Mrs Pat Schumacher, F.A.P.A.S., The Association of Personal Assistants and Secretaries Limited, 14 Victoria Terrace, Royal Leamington Spa, Warwickshire.

THE EUROPEAN ASSOCIATION OF PROFESSIONAL SECRETARIES was formed in 1974 with headquarters in Paris. The aims of the Association are:

1 to be the recognised voice of the secretarial profession in Europe;
2 to create an image throughout Europe of the top secretary as an essential element of the management team;
3 to form a nucleus of highly qualified European Secretaries, able to advise on secretarial development in their own companies;
4 to provide useful European contacts for business information.

Full membership is open to executive secretaries who have at least three years' experience at this level. An executive secretary is defined as a person who has sufficient knowledge of her chief's activities and the area in which he or she works to be able to have a considerable amount of work delegated to her. She is able to take decisions, give instructions and represent her chief on business occasions.

The Association has national branches in Austria, Belgium, Denmark, Finland, France, Germany, Ireland, The Netherlands, Norway, Sweden, Switzerland and the United Kingdom.

The Association holds an annual conference which is hosted by a different national branch each year in its own country. Business and social meetings are held nationally during the year.

Further information from: Mrs Gwen Cowan, National Secretary, European Association of Professional Secretaries, c/o The Chairman's Office, British Railways Board, 222 Marylebone Road, London NW1 6JJ.

Acknowledgments

The authors are indebted to the Royal Society of Arts Manufactures and Commerce, and to the London Chamber of Commerce and Industry for permission to use questions from past examination papers and to the following firms for their help and guidance: Speedwriting International, The Palantype Organisation, Caribonum Sales Ltd, Kores Manufacturing Co Ltd and the United Africa Co of Ghana Ltd.

We would also like to thank the following for their permission to reproduce copyright photographs and material:

Accounting and Computer Systems Ltd (215); Addressograph-Multigraph Ltd (219 bottom, 220 top); Adler Office and Electronic Machines Ltd (50 top); Ambidex (264); Barnaby's Picture Library (550); BACIE: from *A Guide to Job Analysis* by T. H. Boydell (£0.75 to members, £1.50 to non-members) (560); BEA (292); Better Typing Attachments Ltd (51); British Rail (169); British Stationery and Office Equipment Ass. (84, 85, 86, 87, 228, 229); Business Books, from *Modern Filing Methods and Equipment* by Continolo (260); Caribonum Ltd (58 top and bottom, 195); C. W. Cave and Co Ltd (280); Thomas Collorator Ltd (222); Comtalk Communications Ltd (128 right); Copyholders Ltd (61, 63); Data Efficiency Ltd (276, 296, 297); A. B. Dick Ltd (205, 199, 100); Elliott Business Machines Ltd (156 bottom right, 157); Expandex Ltd (247, 251 top right); Financial Times (295); Friden (213 left); Gestetner Ltd (181, 185, 188, 203); Hermes Paillard Ltd (47 bottom, 50 bottom, 52 top); Honeywell Information Systems Ltd (318); Controller of Her Majesty's Stationery Office from *Methods in Miniature* (273); IBM (UK) Ltd (34 top, 48, 49 top, 213 right, 217, 219 top, 288 top); Imperial Typewriter Co Ltd (46, 49); International Computers Ltd (285); International Photon Ltd (220 bottom); Noeline Kelly (32, 40, 60, 242, 293, 565); Kodak (293); Lewis Security Systems Ltd (389 left); London Express News and Feature Services (235); 3 M (208, 274); Master Addresser Ltd (156 bottom left); National City Ltd (328); Nig Banda Ltd (191, 192, 193, 194, 210); Ofrex Ltd (252 right); Ozalid Ltd (211); The Palantype Organisation Ltd (28); Paramount Ltd (281); Philips (25, 34 bottom, 35, 36); Pitman Publishing (283); Pitney-Bowes Ltd (154, 155, 156 top, 159); Plessey (130 bottom); Post Office (119 bottom, 123, 132 left, 135, 137, 138, 139, 167, 168, 284, 417, 427, 429); Prentice Hall Inc, from Joseph Limassie: *Essentials of Management* 2nd Ed. © 1971 (342); Pye TMC Ltd (119 top); Rank Xerox Ltd (130 top, 177, 202, 204, 272 left); The Reliance Telephone Co Ltd (128 left, 129 left); Rex Rotory (184); Robophone (Holdings) Ltd (134 left and right, 389 right); Rotaprint Ltd (198); SCM UK Ltd (47 top); Shannon (246, 248); Shipton Group (129 right, 131, 140); Sperry Rand Ltd (248, 251 bottom, 252, 253, 257, 258, 271, 272 right, 260); Thomas Collator Ltd (187, 222, 225 bottom); Triumph

Business Systems (South Wales) Ltd (249); Typit (52 bottom); Ultronic Data Systems Ltd (214); Unwin Brothers Ltd for *Typewriter Composition* by Alistair McIntosh (89); Wiggins Teape Ltd (73); Peter Williams (Dictation Systems) Ltd (37, 38); Frank Wilson (Filing) Ltd (250, 251 top left)

Cover: Photograph of Ryman head office, courtesy of Ryman Ltd, photographer—Noeline Kelly.

Index